Core Java®

Volume I—Fundamentals

Tenth Edition

Core Java®

Volume I—Fundamentals

Tenth Edition

Cay S. Horstmann

PRENTICE
HALL

Boston • Columbus • Indianapolis • New York • San Francisco • Amsterdam • Cape Town
Dubai • London • Madrid • Milan • Munich • Paris • Montreal • Toronto • Delhi • Mexico City
Sao Paulo • Sidney • Hong Kong • Seoul • Singapore • Taipei • Tokyo

For information about buying this title in bulk quantities, or for special sales opportunities (which may include electronic versions; custom cover designs; and content particular to your business, training goals, marketing focus, or branding interests), please contact our corporate sales department at corpsales@pearsoned.com or (800) 382-3419.

For government sales inquiries, please contact governmentsales@pearsoned.com.

For questions about sales outside the United States, please contact international@pearsoned.com.

Visit us on the Web: informit.com/ph

Library of Congress Cataloging-in-Publication Data
Names: Horstmann, Cay S., 1959- author.
Title: Core Java / Cay S. Horstmann.
Description: Tenth edition. | New York : Prentice Hall, [2016] | Includes
    index.
Identifiers: LCCN 2015038763 | ISBN 9780134177304 (volume 1 : pbk. : alk.
    paper) | ISBN 0134177304 (volume 1 : pbk. : alk. paper)
Subjects: LCSH: Java (Computer program language)
Classification: LCC QA76.73.J38 H6753 2016 | DDC 005.13/3—dc23
LC record available at http://lccn.loc.gov/2015038763

ISBN-13: 978-0-13-417730-4
ISBN-10: 0-13-417730-4

Text printed in the United States on recycled paper at RR Donnelley in Crawfordsville, Indiana.
First printing, December 2015

Contents

Preface

To the Reader

In late 1995, the Java programming language burst onto the Internet scene and gained instant celebrity status. The promise of Java technology was that it would become the *universal glue* that connects users with information wherever it comes from—web servers, databases, information providers, or any other imaginable source. Indeed, Java is in a unique position to fulfill this promise. It is an extremely solidly engineered language that has gained wide acceptance. Its built-in security and safety features are reassuring both to programmers and to the users of Java programs. Java has built-in support for advanced programming tasks, such as network programming, database connectivity, and concurrency.

Since 1995, nine major revisions of the Java Development Kit have been released. Over the course of the last 20 years, the Application Programming Interface (API) has grown from about 200 to over 4,000 classes. The API now spans such diverse areas as user interface construction, database management, internationalization, security, and XML processing.

The book you have in your hands is the first volume of the tenth edition of *Core Java®*. Each edition closely followed a release of the Java Development Kit, and each time, we rewrote the book to take advantage of the newest Java features. This edition has been updated to reflect the features of Java Standard Edition (SE) 8.

As with the previous editions of this book, *we still target serious programmers who want to put Java to work on real projects.* We think of you, our reader, as a programmer with a solid background in a programming language other than Java, and we assume that you don't like books filled with toy examples (such as toasters, zoo animals, or "nervous text"). You won't find any of these in our book. Our goal is to enable you to fully understand the Java language and library, not to give you an illusion of understanding.

In this book you will find lots of sample code demonstrating almost every language and library feature that we discuss. We keep the sample programs purposefully simple to focus on the major points, but, for the most part, they aren't fake and they don't cut corners. They should make good starting points for your own code.

We assume you are willing, even eager, to learn about all the advanced features that Java puts at your disposal. For example, we give you a detailed treatment of

- Object-oriented programming
- Reflection and proxies
- Interfaces and inner classes
- Exception handling
- Generic programming
- The collections framework
- The event listener model
- Graphical user interface design with the Swing UI toolkit
- Concurrency

With the explosive growth of the Java class library, a one-volume treatment of all the features of Java that serious programmers need to know is no longer possible. Hence, we decided to break up the book into two volumes. The first volume, which you hold in your hands, concentrates on the fundamental concepts of the Java language, along with the basics of user-interface programming. The second volume, *Core Java®, Volume II—Advanced Features*, goes further into the enterprise features and advanced user-interface programming. It includes detailed discussions of

- The Stream API
- File processing and regular expressions
- Databases
- XML processing
- Annotations
- Internationalization
- Network programming
- Advanced GUI components
- Advanced graphics
- Native methods

When writing a book, errors and inaccuracies are inevitable. We'd very much like to know about them. But, of course, we'd prefer to learn about each of them only once. We have put up a list of frequently asked questions, bug fixes, and workarounds on a web page at http://horstmann.com/corejava. Strategically placed at the end of the errata page (to encourage you to read through it first) is a form you can use to report bugs and suggest improvements. Please don't be disappointed if we don't answer every query or don't get back to you immediately. We do read all e-mail and appreciate your input to make future editions of this book clearer and more informative.

A Tour of This Book

Chapter 1 gives an overview of the capabilities of Java that set it apart from other programming languages. We explain what the designers of the language set out to do and to what extent they succeeded. Then, we give a short history of how Java came into being and how it has evolved.

In **Chapter 2**, we tell you how to download and install the JDK and the program examples for this book. Then we guide you through compiling and running three typical Java programs—a console application, a graphical application, and an applet—using the plain JDK, a Java-enabled text editor, and a Java IDE.

Chapter 3 starts the discussion of the Java language. In this chapter, we cover the basics: variables, loops, and simple functions. If you are a C or C++ programmer, this is smooth sailing because the syntax for these language features is essentially the same as in C. If you come from a non-C background such as Visual Basic, you will want to read this chapter carefully.

Object-oriented programming (OOP) is now in the mainstream of programming practice, and Java is an object-oriented programming language. **Chapter 4** introduces encapsulation, the first of two fundamental building blocks of object orientation, and the Java language mechanism to implement it—that is, classes and methods. In addition to the rules of the Java language, we also give advice on sound OOP design. Finally, we cover the marvelous javadoc tool that formats your code comments as a set of hyperlinked web pages. If you are familiar with C++, you can browse through this chapter quickly. Programmers coming from a non-object-oriented background should expect to spend some time mastering the OOP concepts before going further with Java.

Classes and encapsulation are only one part of the OOP story, and **Chapter 5** introduces the other—namely, *inheritance*. Inheritance lets you take an existing class and modify it according to your needs. This is a fundamental technique for programming in Java. The inheritance mechanism in Java is quite similar to that in C++. Once again, C++ programmers can focus on the differences between the languages.

Chapter 6 shows you how to use Java's notion of an *interface*. Interfaces let you go beyond the simple inheritance model of Chapter 5. Mastering interfaces allows you to have full access to the power of Java's completely object-oriented approach to programming. After we cover interfaces, we move on to *lambda expressions*, a concise way for expressing a block of code that can be executed at a later point in time. We then cover a useful technical feature of Java called *inner classes*.

Chapter 7 discusses *exception handling*—Java's robust mechanism to deal with the fact that bad things can happen to good programs. Exceptions give you an efficient way of separating the normal processing code from the error handling. Of course, even after hardening your program by handling all exceptional conditions, it still might fail to work as expected. In the final part of this chapter, we give you a number of useful debugging tips.

Chapter 8 gives an overview of generic programming. Generic programming makes your programs easier to read and safer. We show you how to use strong typing and remove unsightly and unsafe casts, and how to deal with the complexities that arise from the need to stay compatible with older versions of Java.

The topic of **Chapter 9** is the collections framework of the Java platform. Whenever you want to collect multiple objects and retrieve them later, you should use a collection that is best suited for your circumstances, instead of just tossing the elements into an array. This chapter shows you how to take advantage of the standard collections that are prebuilt for your use.

Chapter 10 starts the coverage of GUI programming. We show how you can make windows, how to paint on them, how to draw with geometric shapes, how to format text in multiple fonts, and how to display images.

Chapter 11 is a detailed discussion of the event model of the AWT, the *abstract window toolkit*. You'll see how to write code that responds to events, such as mouse clicks or key presses. Along the way you'll see how to handle basic GUI elements such as buttons and panels.

Chapter 12 discusses the Swing GUI toolkit in great detail. The Swing toolkit allows you to build cross-platform graphical user interfaces. You'll learn all about the various kinds of buttons, text components, borders, sliders, list boxes, menus, and dialog boxes. However, some of the more advanced components are discussed in Volume II.

Chapter 13 shows you how to deploy your programs, either as applications or applets. We describe how to package programs in JAR files, and how to deliver applications over the Internet with the Java Web Start and applet mechanisms. We also explain how Java programs can store and retrieve configuration information once they have been deployed.

Chapter 14 finishes the book with a discussion of concurrency, which enables you to program tasks to be done in parallel. This is an important and exciting application of Java technology in an era where most processors have multiple cores that you want to keep busy.

The **Appendix** lists the reserved words of the Java language.

Conventions

As is common in many computer books, we use `monospace type` to represent computer code.

 NOTE: Notes are tagged with "note" icons that look like this.

 TIP: Tips are tagged with "tip" icons that look like this.

 CAUTION: When there is danger ahead, we warn you with a "caution" icon.

 C++ NOTE: There are many C++ notes that explain the differences between Java and C++. You can skip over them if you don't have a background in C++ or if you consider your experience with that language a bad dream of which you'd rather not be reminded.

Java comes with a large programming library, or Application Programming Interface (API). When using an API call for the first time, we add a short summary description at the end of the section. These descriptions are a bit more informal but, we hope, also a little more informative than those in the official online API documentation. The names of interfaces are in italics, just like in the official documentation. The number after a class, interface, or method name is the JDK version in which the feature was introduced, as shown in the following example:

`Application Programming Interface 1.2`

Programs whose source code is on the book's companion web site are presented as listings, for instance:

Listing 1.1 InputTest/InputTest.java

Sample Code

The web site for this book at http://horstmann.com/corejava contains all sample code from the book, in compressed form. You can expand the file either with one of the familiar unzipping programs or simply with the jar utility that is part of the Java Development Kit. See Chapter 2 for more information on installing the Java Development Kit and the sample code.

Acknowledgments

Writing a book is always a monumental effort, and rewriting it doesn't seem to be much easier, especially with the continuous change in Java technology. Making a book a reality takes many dedicated people, and it is my great pleasure to acknowledge the contributions of the entire Core Java team.

A large number of individuals at Prentice Hall provided valuable assistance but managed to stay behind the scenes. I'd like them all to know how much I appreciate their efforts. As always, my warm thanks go to my editor, Greg Doench, for steering the book through the writing and production process, and for allowing me to be blissfully unaware of the existence of all those folks behind the scenes. I am very grateful to Julie Nahil for production support, and to Dmitry Kirsanov and Alina Kirsanova for copyediting and typesetting the manuscript. My thanks also to my coauthor of earlier editions, Gary Cornell, who has since moved on to other ventures.

Thanks to the many readers of earlier editions who reported embarrassing errors and made lots of thoughtful suggestions for improvement. I am particularly grateful to the excellent reviewing team who went over the manuscript with an amazing eye for detail and saved me from many embarrassing errors.

Reviewers of this and earlier editions include Chuck Allison (Utah Valley University), Lance Andersen (Oracle), Paul Anderson (Anderson Software Group), Alec Beaton (IBM), Cliff Berg, Andrew Binstock (Oracle), Joshua Bloch, David Brown, Corky Cartwright, Frank Cohen (PushToTest), Chris Crane (devXsolution), Dr. Nicholas J. De Lillo (Manhattan College), Rakesh Dhoopar (Oracle), David Geary (Clarity Training), Jim Gish (Oracle), Brian Goetz (Oracle), Angela Gordon, Dan Gordon (Electric Cloud), Rob Gordon, John Gray (University of Hartford), Cameron Gregory (olabs.com), Marty Hall (coreservlets.com, Inc.), Vincent Hardy (Adobe Systems), Dan Harkey (San Jose State University), William Higgins (IBM), Vladimir Ivanovic (PointBase), Jerry Jackson (CA Technologies), Tim Kimmet (Walmart), Chris Laffra, Charlie Lai (Apple), Angelika Langer, Doug Langston, Hang Lau (McGill University), Mark Lawrence, Doug Lea (SUNY Oswego), Gregory Longshore, Bob Lynch (Lynch Associates), Philip Milne (consultant), Mark Morrissey (The Oregon Graduate Institute), Mahesh Neelakanta (Florida Atlantic University), Hao Pham, Paul Philion, Blake Ragsdell, Stuart Reges (University of Arizona), Rich Rosen (Interactive Data Corporation), Peter Sanders (ESSI University, Nice, France), Dr. Paul Sanghera (San Jose State University and

Brooks College), Paul Sevinc (Teamup AG), Devang Shah (Sun Microsystems), Yoshiki Shibata, Bradley A. Smith, Steven Stelting (Oracle), Christopher Taylor, Luke Taylor (Valtech), George Thiruvathukal, Kim Topley (StreamingEdge), Janet Traub, Paul Tyma (consultant), Peter van der Linden, Christian Ullenboom, Burt Walsh, Dan Xu (Oracle), and John Zavgren (Oracle).

Cay Horstmann
Biel/Bienne, Switzerland
November 2015

CHAPTER **1**

An Introduction to Java

In this chapter

The first release of Java in 1996 generated an incredible amount of excitement, not just in the computer press, but in mainstream media such as the *New York Times*, the *Washington Post*, and *BusinessWeek*. Java has the distinction of being the first and only programming language that had a ten-minute story on National Public Radio. A $100,000,000 venture capital fund was set up solely for products using a *specific* computer language. I hope you will enjoy the brief history of Java that you will find in this chapter.

1.1 Java as a Programming Platform

In the first edition of this book, my coauthor Gary Cornell and I had this to write about Java:

"As a computer language, Java's hype is overdone: Java is certainly a *good* programming language. There is no doubt that it is one of the better languages available to serious programmers. We think it could *potentially* have been a great programming language, but it is probably too late for that. Once a language is out in the field, the ugly reality of compatibility with existing code sets in."

Our editor got a lot of flack for this paragraph from someone very high up at Sun Microsystems, the company that originally developed Java. The Java language has a lot of nice features that we will examine in detail later in this chapter. It has its share of warts, and some of the newer additions to the language are not as elegant as the original features because of the ugly reality of compatibility.

But, as we already said in the first edition, Java was never just a language. There are lots of programming languages out there, but few of them make much of a splash. Java is a whole *platform*, with a huge library, containing lots of reusable code, and an execution environment that provides services such as security, portability across operating systems, and automatic garbage collection.

As a programmer, you will want a language with a pleasant syntax and comprehensible semantics (i.e., not C++). Java fits the bill, as do dozens of other fine languages. Some languages give you portability, garbage collection, and the like, but they don't have much of a library, forcing you to roll your own if you want fancy graphics or networking or database access. Well, Java has everything—a good language, a high-quality execution environment, and a vast library. That combination is what makes Java an irresistible proposition to so many programmers.

1.2 The Java "White Paper" Buzzwords

The authors of Java wrote an influential white paper that explains their design goals and accomplishments. They also published a shorter overview that is organized along the following 11 buzzwords:

1. Simple
2. Object-Oriented
3. Distributed
4. Robust
5. Secure
6. Architecture-Neutral
7. Portable
8. Interpreted
9. High-Performance

10. Multithreaded

11. Dynamic

In this section, you will find a summary, with excerpts from the white paper, of what the Java designers say about each buzzword, together with a commentary based on my experiences with the current version of Java.

 NOTE: The white paper can be found at www.oracle.com/technetwork/java/langenv-140151.html. You can retrieve the overview with the 11 buzzwords at http://horstmann.com/corejava/java-an-overview/7Gosling.pdf.

1.2.1 Simple

We wanted to build a system that could be programmed easily without a lot of esoteric training and which leveraged today's standard practice. So even though we found that C++ was unsuitable, we designed Java as closely to C++ as possible in order to make the system more comprehensible. Java omits many rarely used, poorly understood, confusing features of C++ that, in our experience, bring more grief than benefit.

The syntax for Java is, indeed, a cleaned-up version of C++ syntax. There is no need for header files, pointer arithmetic (or even a pointer syntax), structures, unions, operator overloading, virtual base classes, and so on. (See the C++ notes interspersed throughout the text for more on the differences between Java and C++.) The designers did not, however, attempt to fix all of the clumsy features of C++. For example, the syntax of the switch statement is unchanged in Java. If you know C++, you will find the transition to the Java syntax easy.

At the time that Java was released, C++ was actually not the most commonly used programming language. Many developers used Visual Basic and its drag-and-drop programming environment. These developers did not find Java simple. It took several years for Java development environments to catch up. Nowadays, Java development environments are far ahead of those for most other programming languages.

Another aspect of being simple is being small. One of the goals of Java is to enable the construction of software that can run stand-alone on small machines. The size of the basic interpreter and class support is about 40K; the basic standard libraries and thread support (essentially a self-contained microkernel) add another 175K.

This was a great achievement at the time. Of course, the library has since grown to huge proportions. There is now a separate Java Micro Edition with a smaller library, suitable for embedded devices.

1.2.2 Object-Oriented

Simply stated, object-oriented design is a programming technique that focuses on the data (= objects) and on the interfaces to that object. To make an analogy with carpentry, an "object-oriented" carpenter would be mostly concerned with the chair he is building, and secondarily with the tools used to make it; a "non-object-oriented" carpenter would think primarily of his tools. The object-oriented facilities of Java are essentially those of C++.

Object orientation was pretty well established when Java was developed. The object-oriented features of Java are comparable to those of C++. The major difference between Java and C++ lies in multiple inheritance, which Java has replaced with the simpler concept of interfaces. Java has a richer capacity for runtime introspection than C++ (which is discussed in Chapter 5).

1.2.3 Distributed

Java has an extensive library of routines for coping with TCP/IP protocols like HTTP and FTP. Java applications can open and access objects across the Net via URLs with the same ease as when accessing a local file system.

Nowadays, one takes this for granted, but in 1995, connecting to a web server from a C++ or Visual Basic program was a major undertaking.

1.2.4 Robust

Java is intended for writing programs that must be reliable in a variety of ways. Java puts a lot of emphasis on early checking for possible problems, later dynamic (runtime) checking, and eliminating situations that are error-prone. . . The single biggest difference between Java and C/C++ is that Java has a pointer model that eliminates the possibility of overwriting memory and corrupting data.

The Java compiler detects many problems that in other languages would show up only at runtime. As for the second point, anyone who has spent hours chasing memory corruption caused by a pointer bug will be very happy with this aspect of Java.

1.2.5 Secure

Java is intended to be used in networked/distributed environments. Toward that end, a lot of emphasis has been placed on security. Java enables the construction of virus-free, tamper-free systems.

From the beginning, Java was designed to make certain kinds of attacks impossible, among them:

- Overrunning the runtime stack—a common attack of worms and viruses
- Corrupting memory outside its own process space
- Reading or writing files without permission

Originally, the Java attitude towards downloaded code was "Bring it on!" Untrusted code was executed in a sandbox environment where it could not impact the host system. Users were assured that nothing bad could happen because Java code, no matter where it came from, was incapable of escaping from the sandbox.

However, the security model of Java is complex. Not long after the first version of the Java Development Kit was shipped, a group of security experts at Princeton University found subtle bugs that allowed untrusted code to attack the host system.

Initially, security bugs were fixed quickly. Unfortunately, over time, hackers got quite good at spotting subtle flaws in the implementation of the security architecture. Sun, and then Oracle, had a tough time keeping up with bug fixes.

After a number of high-profile attacks, browser vendors and Oracle became increasingly cautious. Java browser plug-ins no longer trust remote code unless it is digitally signed and users have agreed to its execution.

 NOTE: Even though in hindsight, the Java security model was not as successful as originally envisioned, Java was well ahead of its time. A competing code delivery mechanism from Microsoft relied on digital signatures alone for security. Clearly this was not sufficient—as any user of Microsoft's own products can confirm, programs from well-known vendors do crash and create damage.

1.2.6 Architecture-Neutral

The compiler generates an architecture-neutral object file format—the compiled code is executable on many processors, given the presence of the Java runtime system. The Java compiler does this by generating bytecode instructions which have nothing to do with a particular computer architecture. Rather, they are designed to be both easy to interpret on any machine and easily translated into native machine code on the fly.

Generating code for a "virtual machine" was not a new idea at the time. Programming languages such as Lisp, Smalltalk, and Pascal had employed this technique for many years.

Of course, interpreting virtual machine instructions is slower than running machine instructions at full speed. However, virtual machines have the option of translating the most frequently executed bytecode sequences into machine code—a process called just-in-time compilation.

Java's virtual machine has another advantage. It increases security because it can check the behavior of instruction sequences.

1.2.7 Portable

Unlike C and C++, there are no "implementation-dependent" aspects of the specification. The sizes of the primitive data types are specified, as is the behavior of arithmetic on them.

For example, an `int` in Java is always a 32-bit integer. In C/C++, int can mean a 16-bit integer, a 32-bit integer, or any other size that the compiler vendor likes. The only restriction is that the `int` type must have at least as many bytes as a `short int` and cannot have more bytes than a `long int`. Having a fixed size for number types eliminates a major porting headache. Binary data is stored and transmitted in a fixed format, eliminating confusion about byte ordering. Strings are saved in a standard Unicode format.

The libraries that are a part of the system define portable interfaces. For example, there is an abstract `Window` class and implementations of it for UNIX, Windows, and the Macintosh.

The example of a `Window` class was perhaps poorly chosen. As anyone who has ever tried knows, it is an effort of heroic proportions to implement a user interface that looks good on Windows, the Macintosh, and ten flavors of UNIX. Java 1.0 made the heroic effort, delivering a simple toolkit that provided common user interface elements on a number of platforms. Unfortunately, the result was a library that, with a lot of work, could give barely acceptable results on different systems. That initial user interface toolkit has since been replaced, and replaced again, and portability across platforms remains an issue.

However, for everything that isn't related to user interfaces, the Java libraries do a great job of letting you work in a platform-independent manner. You can work with files, regular expressions, XML, dates and times, databases, network connections, threads, and so on, without worrying about the underlying operating system. Not only are your programs portable, but the Java APIs are often of higher quality than the native ones.

1.2.8 Interpreted

The Java interpreter can execute Java bytecodes directly on any machine to which the interpreter has been ported. Since linking is a more incremental and lightweight process, the development process can be much more rapid and exploratory.

This seems a real stretch. Anyone who has used Lisp, Smalltalk, Visual Basic, Python, R, or Scala knows what a "rapid and exploratory" development process is. You try out something, and you instantly see the result. Java development environments are not focused on that experience.

1.2.9 High–Performance

While the performance of interpreted bytecodes is usually more than adequate, there are situations where higher performance is required. The bytecodes can be translated on the fly (at runtime) into machine code for the particular CPU the application is running on.

In the early years of Java, many users disagreed with the statement that the performance was "more than adequate." Today, however, the just-in-time compilers have become so good that they are competitive with traditional compilers and, in some cases, even outperform them because they have more information available. For example, a just-in-time compiler can monitor which code is executed frequently and optimize just that code for speed. A more sophisticated optimization is the elimination (or "inlining") of function calls. The just-in-time compiler knows which classes have been loaded. It can use inlining when, based upon the currently loaded collection of classes, a particular function is never overridden, and it can undo that optimization later if necessary.

1.2.10 Multithreaded

[The] benefits of multithreading are better interactive responsiveness and real-time behavior.

Nowadays, we care about concurrency because Moore's law is coming to an end. Instead of faster processors, we just get more of them, and we have to keep them busy. Yet when you look at most programming languages, they show a shocking disregard for this problem.

Java was well ahead of its time. It was the first mainstream language to support concurrent programming. As you can see from the white paper, its motivation was a little different. At the time, multicore processors were exotic, but web programming had just started, and processors spent a lot of time waiting for a response from the server. Concurrent programming was needed to make sure the user interface didn't freeze.

Concurrent programming is never easy, but Java has done a very good job making it manageable.

1.2.11 Dynamic

In a number of ways, Java is a more dynamic language than C or C++. It was de-signed to adapt to an evolving environment. Libraries can freely add new methods and instance variables without any effect on their clients. In Java, finding out runtime type information is straightforward.

This is an important feature in the situations where code needs to be added to a running program. A prime example is code that is downloaded from the Internet to run in a browser. In C or C++, this is indeed a major challenge, but the Java designers were well aware of dynamic languages that made it easy to evolve a running program. Their achievement was to bring this feature to a mainstream programming language.

 NOTE: Shortly after the initial success of Java, Microsoft released a product called J++ with a programming language and virtual machine that were almost identical to Java. At this point, Microsoft is no longer supporting J++ and has instead introduced another language called C# that also has many similarities with Java but runs on a different virtual machine. This book does not cover J++ or C#.

1.3 Java Applets and the Internet

The idea here is simple: Users will download Java bytecodes from the Internet and run them on their own machines. Java programs that work on web pages are called *applets*. To use an applet, you only need a Java-enabled web browser, which will execute the bytecodes for you. You need not install any software. You get the latest version of the program whenever you visit the web page containing the applet. Most importantly, thanks to the security of the virtual machine, you never need to worry about attacks from hostile code.

Inserting an applet into a web page works much like embedding an image. The applet becomes a part of the page, and the text flows around the space used for the applet. The point is, this image is *alive*. It reacts to user commands, changes its appearance, and exchanges data between the computer presenting the applet and the computer serving it.

Figure 1.1 shows a good example of a dynamic web page that carries out sophisticated calculations. The Jmol applet displays molecular structures. By using the mouse, you can rotate and zoom each molecule to better understand its structure. This kind of direct manipulation is not achievable with static web pages, but applets make it possible. (You can find this applet at `http://jmol.sourceforge.net`.)

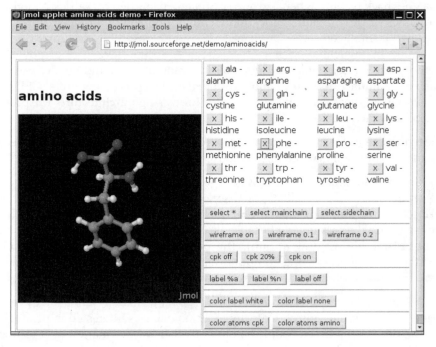

Figure 1.1 The Jmol applet

When applets first appeared, they created a huge amount of excitement. Many people believe that the lure of applets was responsible for the astonishing popularity of Java. However, the initial excitement soon turned into frustration. Various versions of the Netscape and Internet Explorer browsers ran different versions of Java, some of which were seriously outdated. This sorry situation made it increasingly difficult to develop applets that took advantage of the most current Java version. Instead, Adobe's Flash technology became popular for achieving dynamic effects in the browser. Later, when Java was dogged by serious security issues, browsers and the Java browser plug-in became increasingly restrictive. Nowadays, it requires skill and dedication to get applets to work in your browser. For example, if you visit the Jmol web site, you will likely encounter a message exhorting you to configure your browser for allowing applets to run.

1.4 A Short History of Java

This section gives a short history of Java's evolution. It is based on various published sources (most importantly an interview with Java's creators in the July 1995 issue of *SunWorld*'s online magazine).

Java goes back to 1991, when a group of Sun engineers, led by Patrick Naughton and James Gosling (a Sun Fellow and an all-around computer wizard), wanted to design a small computer language that could be used for consumer devices like cable TV switchboxes. Since these devices do not have a lot of power or memory, the language had to be small and generate very tight code. Also, as different manufacturers may choose different central processing units (CPUs), it was important that the language not be tied to any single architecture. The project was code-named "Green."

The requirements for small, tight, and platform-neutral code led the team to design a portable language that generated intermediate code for a virtual machine.

The Sun people came from a UNIX background, so they based their language on C++ rather than Lisp, Smalltalk, or Pascal. But, as Gosling says in the interview, "All along, the language was a tool, not the end." Gosling decided to call his language "Oak" (presumably because he liked the look of an oak tree that was right outside his window at Sun). The people at Sun later realized that Oak was the name of an existing computer language, so they changed the name to Java. This turned out to be an inspired choice.

In 1992, the Green project delivered its first product, called "*7." It was an extremely intelligent remote control. Unfortunately, no one was interested in producing this at Sun, and the Green people had to find other ways to market their technology. However, none of the standard consumer electronics companies were interested either. The group then bid on a project to design a cable TV box that could deal with emerging cable services such as video-on-demand. They did not get the contract. (Amusingly, the company that did was led by the same Jim Clark who started Netscape—a company that did much to make Java successful.)

The Green project (with a new name of "First Person, Inc.") spent all of 1993 and half of 1994 looking for people to buy its technology. No one was found. (Patrick Naughton, one of the founders of the group and the person who ended up doing most of the marketing, claims to have accumulated 300,000 air miles in trying to sell the technology.) First Person was dissolved in 1994.

While all of this was going on at Sun, the World Wide Web part of the Internet was growing bigger and bigger. The key to the World Wide Web was the browser translating hypertext pages to the screen. In 1994, most people were using Mosaic, a noncommercial web browser that came out of the supercomputing center at the University of Illinois in 1993. (Mosaic was partially written by Marc Andreessen as an undergraduate student on a work-study project, for $6.85 an hour. He moved on to fame and fortune as one of the cofounders and the chief of technology at Netscape.)

In the *SunWorld* interview, Gosling says that in mid-1994, the language developers realized that "We could build a real cool browser. It was one of the few things in the client/server mainstream that needed some of the weird things we'd done: architecture-neutral, real-time, reliable, secure—issues that weren't terribly important in the workstation world. So we built a browser."

The actual browser was built by Patrick Naughton and Jonathan Payne and evolved into the HotJava browser, which was designed to show off the power of Java. The builders made the browser capable of executing Java code inside web pages. This "proof of technology" was shown at SunWorld '95 on May 23, 1995, and inspired the Java craze that continues today.

Sun released the first version of Java in early 1996. People quickly realized that Java 1.0 was not going to cut it for serious application development. Sure, you could use Java 1.0 to make a nervous text applet that moved text randomly around in a canvas. But you couldn't even *print* in Java 1.0. To be blunt, Java 1.0 was not ready for prime time. Its successor, version 1.1, filled in the most obvious gaps, greatly improved the reflection capability, and added a new event model for GUI programming. It was still rather limited, though.

The big news of the 1998 JavaOne conference was the upcoming release of Java 1.2, which replaced the early toylike GUI and graphics toolkits with sophisticated scalable versions and came a lot closer to the promise of "Write Once, Run Anywhere"™ than its predecessors. Three days after (!) its release in December 1998, Sun's marketing department changed the name to the catchy *Java 2 Standard Edition Software Development Kit Version 1.2*.

Besides the Standard Edition, two other editions were introduced: the Micro Edition for embedded devices such as cell phones, and the Enterprise Edition for server-side processing. This book focuses on the Standard Edition.

Versions 1.3 and 1.4 of the Standard Edition were incremental improvements over the initial Java 2 release, with an ever-growing standard library, increased performance, and, of course, quite a few bug fixes. During this time, much of the initial hype about Java applets and client-side applications abated, but Java became the platform of choice for server-side applications.

Version 5.0 was the first release since version 1.1 that updated the Java *language* in significant ways. (This version was originally numbered 1.5, but the version number jumped to 5.0 at the 2004 JavaOne conference.) After many years of research, generic types (roughly comparable to C++ templates) have been added—the challenge was to add this feature without requiring changes in the virtual machine. Several other useful language features were inspired by C#: a "for each" loop, autoboxing, and annotations.

Version 6 (without the .0 suffix) was released at the end of 2006. Again, there were no language changes but additional performance improvements and library enhancements.

As datacenters increasingly relied on commodity hardware instead of specialized servers, Sun Microsystems fell on hard times and was purchased by Oracle in 2009. Development of Java stalled for a long time. In 2011, Oracle released a new version with simple enhancements as Java 7.

In 2014, the release of Java 8 followed, with the most significant changes to the Java language in almost two decades. Java 8 embraces a "functional" style of programming that makes it easy to express computations that can be executed concurrently. All programming languages must evolve to stay relevant, and Java has shown a remarkable capacity to do so.

Table 1.1 shows the evolution of the Java language and library. As you can see, the size of the application programming interface (API) has grown tremendously.

Table 1.1 Evolution of the Java Language

Version	Year	New Language Features	Number of Classes and Interfaces
1.0	1996	The language itself	211
1.1	1997	Inner classes	477
1.2	1998	The strictfp modifier	1,524
1.3	2000	None	1,840
1.4	2002	Assertions	2,723
5.0	2004	Generic classes, "for each" loop, varargs, autoboxing, metadata, enumerations, static import	3,279
6	2006	None	3,793
7	2011	Switch with strings, diamond operator, binary literals, exception handling enhancements	4,024
8	2014	Lambda expressions, interfaces with default methods, stream and date/time libraries	4,240

1.5 Common Misconceptions about Java

This chapter closes with a commented list of some common misconceptions about Java.

Java is an extension of HTML.

Java is a programming language; HTML is a way to describe the structure of a web page. They have nothing in common except that there are HTML extensions for placing Java applets on a web page.

I use XML, so I don't need Java.

Java is a programming language; XML is a way to describe data. You can process XML data with any programming language, but the Java API contains excellent support for XML processing. In addition, many important XML tools are implemented in Java. See Volume II for more information.

Java is an easy programming language to learn.

No programming language as powerful as Java is easy. You always have to distinguish between how easy it is to write toy programs and how hard it is to do serious work. Also, consider that only seven chapters in this book discuss the Java language. The remaining chapters of both volumes show how to put the language to work, using the Java *libraries*. The Java libraries contain thousands of classes and interfaces and tens of thousands of functions. Luckily, you do not need to know every one of them, but you do need to know surprisingly many to use Java for anything realistic.

Java will become a universal programming language for all platforms.

This is possible in theory. But in practice, there are domains where other languages are entrenched. Objective C and its successor, Swift, are not going to be replaced on iOS devices. Anything that happens in a browser is controlled by JavaScript. Windows programs are written in C++ or C#. Java has the edge in server-side programming and in cross-platform client applications.

Java is just another programming language.

Java is a nice programming language; most programmers prefer it to C, C++, or C#. But there have been hundreds of nice programming languages that never gained widespread popularity, whereas languages with obvious flaws, such as C++ and Visual Basic, have been wildly successful.

Why? The success of a programming language is determined far more by the utility of the *support system* surrounding it than by the elegance of its syntax. Are there useful, convenient, and standard libraries for the features that you need to implement? Are there tool vendors that build great programming and debugging environments? Do the language and the toolset integrate with the rest of the computing infrastructure? Java is successful because its libraries let you easily do things such as networking, web applications, and concurrency. The fact that Java reduces pointer errors is a bonus, so programmers seem to be more productive with Java—but these factors are not the source of its success.

Java is proprietary, and it should therefore be avoided.

When Java was first created, Sun gave free licenses to distributors and end users. Although Sun had ultimate control over Java, they involved many other companies in the development of language revisions and the design of new libraries. Source code for the virtual machine and the libraries has always been freely available, but only for inspection, not for modification and redistribution. Java was "closed source, but playing nice."

This situation changed dramatically in 2007, when Sun announced that future versions of Java would be available under the General Public License (GPL), the same open source license that is used by Linux. Oracle has committed to keeping Java open source. There is only one fly in the ointment—patents. Everyone is given a patent grant to use and modify Java, subject to the GPL, but only on desktop and server platforms. If you want to use Java in embedded systems, you need a different license and will likely need to pay royalties. However, these patents will expire within the next decade, and at that point Java will be entirely free.

Java is interpreted, so it is too slow for serious applications.

In the early days of Java, the language was interpreted. Nowadays, the Java virtual machine uses a just-in-time compiler. The "hot spots" of your code will run just as fast in Java as they would in C++, and in some cases even faster.

People used to complain that Java desktop applications are slow. However, today's computers are much faster than they were when these complaints started. A slow Java program will still run quite a bit better today than those blazingly fast C++ programs did a few years ago.

All Java programs run inside a web page.

All Java *applets* run inside a web browser. That is the definition of an applet—a Java program running inside a browser. But most Java programs are stand-alone applications that run outside of a web browser. In fact, many Java programs run on web servers and produce the code for web pages.

Java programs are a major security risk.

In the early days of Java, there were some well-publicized reports of failures in the Java security system. Researchers viewed it as a challenge to find chinks in the Java armor and to defy the strength and sophistication of the applet security model. The technical failures that they found have all been quickly corrected. Later, there were more serious exploits, to which Sun, and later Oracle, responded too slowly. Browser manufacturers reacted, and perhaps overreacted, by deactivating Java by default. To keep this in perspective, consider the literally millions of virus attacks in Windows executable files and Word macros that cause real grief but surprisingly little criticism of the weaknesses of the attacked platform.

Some system administrators have even deactivated Java in company browsers, while continuing to permit their users to download executable files and Word documents which pose a far greater risk. Even 20 years after its creation, Java is far safer than any other commonly available execution platform.

JavaScript is a simpler version of Java.

JavaScript, a scripting language that can be used inside web pages, was invented by Netscape and originally called LiveScript. JavaScript has a syntax that is reminiscent of Java, and the languages' names sound similar, but otherwise they are unrelated. A subset of JavaScript is standardized as ECMA-262. JavaScript is more tightly integrated with browsers than Java applets are. In particular, a JavaScript program can modify the document that is being displayed, whereas an applet can only control the appearance of a limited area.

With Java, I can replace my desktop computer with a cheap "Internet appliance."

When Java was first released, some people bet big that this was going to happen. Companies produced prototypes of Java-powered network computers, but users were not ready to give up a powerful and convenient desktop for a limited machine with no local storage. Nowadays, of course, the world has changed, and for a large majority of end users, the platform that matters is a mobile phone or tablet. The majority of these devices are controlled by the Android platform, which is a derivative of Java. Learning Java programming will help you with Android programming as well.

CHAPTER 2

The Java Programming Environment

In this chapter

In this chapter, you will learn how to install the Java Development Kit (JDK) and how to compile and run various types of programs: console programs, graphical applications, and applets. You can run the JDK tools by typing commands in a terminal window. However, many programmers prefer the comfort of an integrated development environment. You will learn how to use a freely available development environment to compile and run Java programs. Although easier to learn, integrated development environments can be resource-hungry and tedious to use for small programs. Once you have mastered the techniques in this chapter and picked your development tools, you are ready to move on to Chapter 3, where you will begin exploring the Java programming language.

2.1 Installing the Java Development Kit

The most complete and up-to-date versions of the Java Development Kit (JDK) are available from Oracle for Linux, Mac OS X, Solaris, and Windows. Versions in various states of development exist for many other platforms, but those versions are licensed and distributed by the vendors of those platforms.

2.1.1 Downloading the JDK

To download the Java Development Kit, visit the web site at www.oracle.com/ technetwork/java/javase/downloads and be prepared to decipher an amazing amount of jargon before you can get the software you need. See Table 2.1 for a summary.

You already saw the abbreviation JDK for Java Development Kit. Somewhat confusingly, versions 1.2 through 1.4 of the kit were known as the Java SDK (Software Development Kit). You will still find occasional references to the old term. There is also a Java Runtime Environment (JRE) that contains the virtual machine but not the compiler. That is not what you want as a developer. It is intended for end users who have no need for the compiler.

Next, you'll see the term Java SE everywhere. That is the Java Standard Edition, in contrast to Java EE (Enterprise Edition) and Java ME (Micro Edition).

You might run into the term Java 2 that was coined in 1998 when the marketing folks at Sun felt that a fractional version number increment did not properly communicate the momentous advances of JDK 1.2. However, because they had that insight only after the release, they decided to keep the version number 1.2 for the *development kit*. Subsequent releases were numbered 1.3, 1.4, and 5.0. The *platform*, however, was renamed from Java to Java 2. Thus, we had Java 2 Standard Edition Software Development Kit Version 5.0, or J2SE SDK 5.0.

Fortunately, in 2006, the numbering was simplified. The next version of the Java Standard Edition was called Java SE 6, followed by Java SE 7 and Java SE 8. However, the "internal" version numbers are 1.6.0, 1.7.0, and 1.8.0.

When Oracle makes a minor version change to fix urgent issues, it refers to the change as an update. For example, Java SE 8u31 is the 31st update of Java SE 8, and it has the internal version number 1.8.0_31. An update does not need to be installed over a prior version—it contains the most current version of the whole JDK. Also, not all updates are released to the public, so don't panic if update 31 isn't followed by update 32.

Table 2.1 Java Jargon

Name	Acronym	Explanation
Java Development Kit	JDK	The software for programmers who want to write Java programs
Java Runtime Environment	JRE	The software for consumers who want to run Java programs
Server JRE	—	The software for running Java programs on servers
Standard Edition	SE	The Java platform for use on desktops and simple server applications
Enterprise Edition	EE	The Java platform for complex server applications
Micro Edition	ME	The Java platform for use on cell phones and other small devices
Java FX	—	An alternate toolkit for graphical user interfaces that is included in Oracle's Java SE distribution
OpenJDK	—	A free and open source implementation of Java SE. It does not include browser integration or JavaFX.
Java 2	J2	An outdated term that described Java versions from 1998 until 2006
Software Development Kit	SDK	An outdated term that described the JDK from 1998 until 2006
Update	u	Oracle's term for a bug fix release
NetBeans	—	Oracle's integrated development environment

With Windows or Linux, you need to choose between the x86 (32-bit) and x64 (64-bit) versions. Pick the one that matches the architecture of your operating system.

With Linux, you have a choice between an RPM file and a .tar.gz file. We recommend the latter—you can simply uncompress it anywhere you like.

Now you know how to pick the right JDK. To summarize:

- You want the JDK (Java SE Development Kit), not the JRE.
- Windows or Linux: Choose x86 for 32 bit, x64 for 64 bit.
- Linux: Pick the .tar.gz version.

Accept the license agreement and download the file.

 NOTE: Oracle offers a bundle that contains both the Java Development Kit and the NetBeans integrated development environment. I suggest that you stay away from all bundles and install only the Java Development Kit at this time. If you later decide to use NetBeans, simply download it from http://netbeans.org.

2.1.2 Setting up the JDK

After downloading the JDK, you need to install it and figure out where it was installed—you'll need that information later.

- Under Windows, launch the setup program. You will be asked where to install the JDK. It is best not to accept a default location with spaces in the path name, such as c:\Program Files\Java\jdk1.8.0_version. Just take out the Program Files part of the path name.
- On the Mac, run the installer. It installs the software into /Library/Java/ JavaVirtualMachines/jdk1.8.0_version.jdk/Contents/Home. Locate it with the Finder.
- On Linux, simply uncompress the .tar.gz file to a location of your choice, such as your home directory or /opt. Or, if you installed from the RPM file, double-check that it is installed in /usr/java/jdk1.8.0_version.

In this book, the installation directory is denoted as jdk. For example, when referring to the jdk/bin directory, I mean the directory with a name such as /opt/jdk1.8.0_31/bin or c:\Java\jdk1.8.0_31\bin.

When you install the JDK on Windows or Linux, you need to carry out one additional step: Add the jdk/bin directory to the executable path—the list of directories that the operating system traverses to locate executable files.

- On Linux, add a line such as the following to the end of your ~/.bashrc or ~/.bash_profile file:

  ```
  export PATH=jdk/bin:$PATH
  ```

  Be sure to use the correct path to the JDK, such as /opt/jdk1.8.0_31.
- Under Windows, start the Control Panel, select System and Security, select System, then select Advanced System Settings (see Figure 2.1). In the System Properties dialog, click the Advanced tab, then click the Environment button.

Scroll through the System Variables list until you find a variable named Path. Click the Edit button (see Figure 2.2). Add the *jdk\bin* directory to the beginning of the path, using a semicolon to separate the new entry, like this:

jdk\bin;other stuff

Be careful to replace *jdk* with the actual path to your Java installation, such as c:\Java\jdk1.8.0_31. If you ignored the advice to drop the Program Files directory, enclose the entire path segment in double quotes: "c:\Program Files\Java\ jdk1.8.0_31\bin";*other stuff*.

Save your settings. Any new console windows that you start will have the correct path.

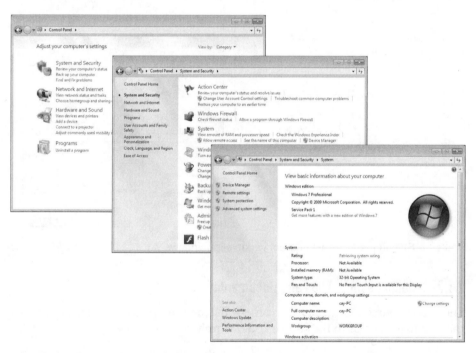

Figure 2.1 Setting system properties in Windows 7

Here is how you test whether you did it right: Start a terminal window. Type the line

```
javac -version
```

and press the Enter key. You should get a display such as this one:

```
javac 1.8.0_31
```

If instead you get a message such as "javac: command not found" or "The name specified is not recognized as an internal or external command, operable program or batch file", then you need to go back and double-check your installation.

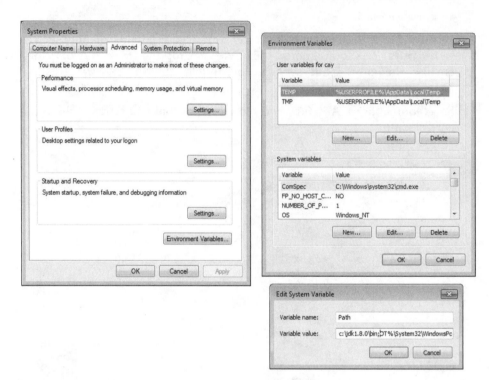

Figure 2.2 Setting the `Path` environment variable in Windows 7

2.1.3 Installing Source Files and Documentation

The library source files are delivered in the JDK as a compressed file `src.zip`. Unpack that file to get access to the source code. Simply do the following:

1. Make sure the JDK is installed and that the *jdk/bin* directory is on the executable path.

2. Make a directory `javasrc` in your home directory. If you like, you can do this from a terminal window.

   ```
   mkdir javasrc
   ```

3. Inside the *jdk* directory, locate the file src.zip.

4. Unzip the src.zip file into the javasrc directory. In a terminal window, you can execute the commands

```
cd javasrc
jar xvf jdk/src.zip
cd ..
```

 TIP: The src.zip file contains the source code for all public libraries. To obtain even more source (for the compiler, the virtual machine, the native methods, and the private helper classes), go to http://jdk8.java.net.

The documentation is contained in a compressed file that is separate from the JDK. You can download the documentation from www.oracle.com/technetwork/java/javase/downloads. Simply follow these steps:

1. Download the documentation zip file. It is called jdk-*version*-docs-all.zip, where *version* is something like 8u31.

2. Unzip the file and rename the doc directory into something more descriptive, like javadoc. If you like, you can do this from the command line:

```
jar xvf Downloads/jdk-version-docs-all.zip
mv doc javadoc
```

where *version* is the appropriate version number.

3. In your browser, navigate to javadoc/api/index.html and add this page to your bookmarks.

You should also install the *Core Java* program examples. You can download them from http://horstmann.com/corejava. The programs are packaged into a zip file corejava.zip. Just unzip them into your home directory. They will be located in a directory corejava. If you like, you can do this from the command line:

```
jar xvf Downloads/corejava.zip
```

2.2 Using the Command-Line Tools

If your programming experience comes from using a development environment such as Microsoft Visual Studio, you are accustomed to a system with a built-in text editor, menus to compile and launch a program, and a debugger. The JDK contains nothing even remotely similar. You do *everything* by typing in commands in a terminal window. This sounds cumbersome, but it is nevertheless an essential skill. When you first install Java, you will want to troubleshoot your installation before you install a development environment. Moreover, by executing the basic steps yourself, you gain a better understanding of what a development environment does behind your back.

However, after you have mastered the basic steps of compiling and running Java programs, you will want to use a professional development environment. You will see how to do that in the following section.

Let's get started the hard way: compiling and launching a Java program from the command line.

1. Open a terminal window.
2. Go to the `corejava/v1ch02/Welcome` directory. (The `corejava` directory is the directory into which you installed the source code for the book examples, as explained in Section 2.1.3, "Installing Source Files and Documentation," on p. 22.)
3. Enter the following commands:

```
javac Welcome.java
java Welcome
```

You should see the output shown in Figure 2.3 in the terminal window.

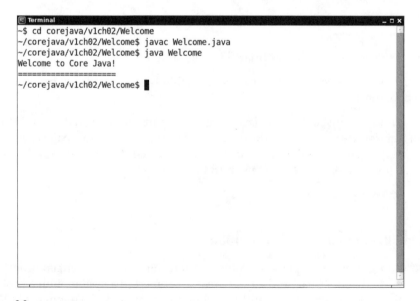

Figure 2.3 Compiling and running `Welcome.java`

Congratulations! You have just compiled and run your first Java program.

What happened? The `javac` program is the Java compiler. It compiles the file `Welcome.java` into the file `Welcome.class`. The `java` program launches the Java virtual machine. It executes the bytecodes that the compiler placed in the class file.

The `Welcome` program is extremely simple. It merely prints a message to the console. You may enjoy looking inside the program, shown in Listing 2.1. You will see how it works in the next chapter.

Listing 2.1 `Welcome/Welcome.java`

```
 1  /**
 2   * This program displays a greeting for the reader.
 3   * @version 1.30 2014-02-27
 4   * @author Cay Horstmann
 5   */
 6  public class Welcome
 7  {
 8     public static void main(String[] args)
 9     {
10        String greeting = "Welcome to Core Java!";
11        System.out.println(greeting);
12        for (int i = 0; i < greeting.length(); i++)
13           System.out.print("=");
14        System.out.println();
15     }
16  }
```

In the age of visual development environments, many programmers are unfamiliar with running programs in a terminal window. Any number of things can go wrong, leading to frustrating results.

Pay attention to the following points:

- If you type in the program by hand, make sure you correctly enter the upper-case and lowercase letters. In particular, the class name is `Welcome` and not `welcome` or `WELCOME`.

- The compiler requires a *file name* (`Welcome.java`). When you run the program, you specify a *class name* (`Welcome`) without a `.java` or `.class` extension.

- If you get a message such as "Bad command or file name" or "javac: command not found", then go back and double-check your installation, in particular the executable path setting.

- If javac reports that it cannot find the file Welcome.java, then you should check whether that file is present in the directory.

  Under Linux, check that you used the correct capitalization for Welcome.java.

  Under Windows, use the dir command, *not* the graphical Explorer tool. Some text editors (in particular Notepad) insist on adding an extension .txt to every file's name. If you use Notepad to edit Welcome.java, it will actually save it as Welcome.java.txt. Under the default Windows settings, Explorer conspires with Notepad and hides the .txt extension because it belongs to a "known file type." In that case, you need to rename the file, using the ren command, or save it again, placing quotes around the file name: "Welcome.java".

- If you launch your program and get an error message complaining about a java.lang.NoClassDefFoundError, then carefully check the name of the offending class.

  If you get a complaint about welcome (with a lowercase w), then you should reissue the java Welcome command with an uppercase W. As always, case matters in Java.

  If you get a complaint about Welcome/java, it means you accidentally typed java Welcome.java. Reissue the command as java Welcome.

- If you typed java Welcome and the virtual machine can't find the Welcome class, check if someone has set the CLASSPATH environment variable on your system. It is not a good idea to set this variable globally, but some poorly written software installers in Windows do just that. Follow the same procedure as for setting the PATH environment variable, but this time, remove the setting.

 TIP: The excellent tutorial at http://docs.oracle.com/javase/tutorial/getStarted/cupojava goes into much greater detail about the "gotchas" that beginners can run into.

2.3 Using an Integrated Development Environment

In the preceding section, you saw how to compile and run a Java program from the command line. That is a useful skill, but for most day-to-day work, you should use an integrated development environment. These environments have become so powerful and convenient that it simply doesn't make much sense to labor on without them. Excellent choices are the freely available Eclipse, NetBeans, and IntelliJ IDEA programs. In this chapter, you will learn how to get started with Eclipse. Of course, if you prefer a different development environment, you can certainly use it with this book.

In this section, you will see how to compile a program with Eclipse, an integrated development environment that is freely available from http://eclipse.org/downloads. Versions exist for Linux, Mac OS X, Solaris, and Windows. When you visit the download site, pick the "Eclipse IDE for Java Developers". Choose between the 32- or 64-bit versions, matching your operating system.

Simply unzip Eclipse to a location of your choice, and execute the eclipse program inside the zip file.

Here are the steps to write a program with Eclipse.

1.   After starting Eclipse, select File → New → Project from the menu.

2.   Select "Java Project" from the wizard dialog (see Figure 2.4).

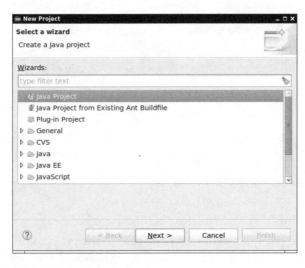

Figure 2.4 The New Project dialog in Eclipse

3. Click the Next button. *Uncheck* the "Use default location" checkbox. Click on Browse and navigate to the corejava/v1ch02/Welcome directory (see Figure 2.5).

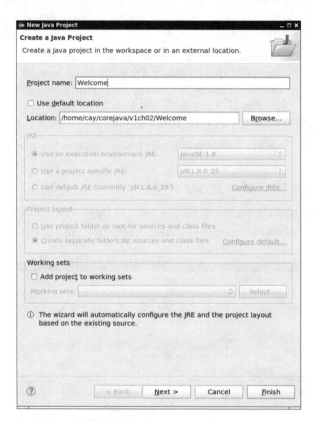

Figure 2.5 Configuring a project in Eclipse

4. Click the Finish button. The project is now created.
5. Click on the triangles in the left pane next to the project until you locate the file Welcome.java, and double-click on it. You should now see a pane with the program code (see Figure 2.6).

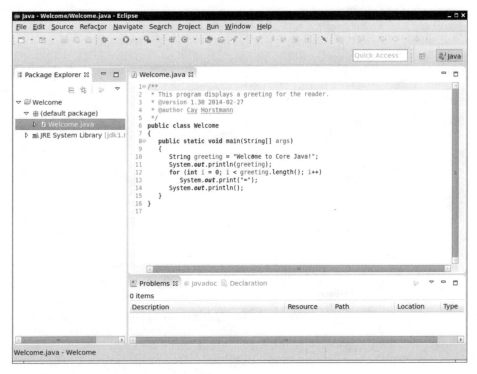

Figure 2.6 Editing a source file with Eclipse

6. With the right mouse button, click on the project name (Welcome) in the left pane. Select Run → Run As → Java Application. The program output is displayed in the console pane.

Presumably, this program does not have typos or bugs. (It was only a few lines of code, after all.) Let us suppose, for the sake of argument, that your code occasionally contains a typo (perhaps even a syntax error). Try it out—ruin your file, for example, by changing the capitalization of String as follows:

```
string greeting = "Welcome to Core Java!";
```

Note the wiggly line under string. In the tabs below the source code, click on Problems and expand the triangles until you see an error message that complains about an unknown string type (see Figure 2.7). Click on the error message. The cursor moves to the matching line in the edit pane, where you can correct your error. This feature allows you to fix your errors quickly.

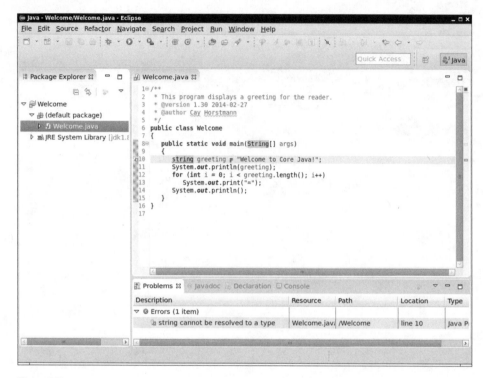

Figure 2.7 Error messages in Eclipse

 TIP: Often, an Eclipse error report is accompanied by a lightbulb icon. Click on the lightbulb to get a list of suggested fixes.

2.4 Running a Graphical Application

The `Welcome` program was not terribly exciting. Next, try out a graphical application. This program is a simple image file viewer that loads and displays an image. Again, let us first compile and run it from the command line.

1. Open a terminal window.

2. Change to the directory `corejava/v1ch02/ImageViewer`.

3. Enter the following:

    ```
    javac ImageViewer.java
    java ImageViewer
    ```

A new program window pops up with the ImageViewer application (see Figure 2.8).

Figure 2.8 Running the ImageViewer application

Now, select File → Open and look for an image file to open. (There are a couple of sample files in the same directory.) To close the program, click on the Close box in the title bar or select File → Exit from the menu.

Have a quick look at the source code (Listing 2.2). The program is substantially longer than the first program, but it is not too complex if you consider how much code it would take in C or C++ to write a similar application. You'll learn how to write graphical programs like this in Chapters 10 through 12.

Listing 2.2 ImageViewer/ImageViewer.java

```java
1  import java.awt.*;
2  import java.io.*;
3  import javax.swing.*;
4
5  /**
6   * A program for viewing images.
7   * @version 1.30 2014-02-27
```

(Continues)

Listing 2.2 *(Continued)*

```
 8    * @author Cay Horstmann
 9    */
10   public class ImageViewer
11   {
12      public static void main(String[] args)
13      {
14         EventQueue.invokeLater(() -> {
15            JFrame frame = new ImageViewerFrame();
16            frame.setTitle("ImageViewer");
17            frame.setDefaultCloseOperation(JFrame.EXIT_ON_CLOSE);
18            frame.setVisible(true);
19         });
20      }
21   }
22
23   /**
24    * A frame with a label to show an image.
25    */
26   class ImageViewerFrame extends JFrame
27   {
28      private JLabel label;
29      private JFileChooser chooser;
30      private static final int DEFAULT_WIDTH = 300;
31      private static final int DEFAULT_HEIGHT = 400;
32
33      public ImageViewerFrame()
34      {
35         setSize(DEFAULT_WIDTH, DEFAULT_HEIGHT);
36
37         // use a label to display the images
38         label = new JLabel();
39         add(label);
40
41         // set up the file chooser
42         chooser = new JFileChooser();
43         chooser.setCurrentDirectory(new File("."));
44
45         // set up the menu bar
46         JMenuBar menuBar = new JMenuBar();
47         setJMenuBar(menuBar);
48
49         JMenu menu = new JMenu("File");
50         menuBar.add(menu);
51
52         JMenuItem openItem = new JMenuItem("Open");
53         menu.add(openItem);
```

```
54      openItem.addActionListener(event -> {
55          // show file chooser dialog
56              int result = chooser.showOpenDialog(null);
57
58              // if file selected, set it as icon of the label
59              if (result == JFileChooser.APPROVE_OPTION)
60              {
61                  String name = chooser.getSelectedFile().getPath();
62                  label.setIcon(new ImageIcon(name));
63              }
64          });
65
66          JMenuItem exitItem = new JMenuItem("Exit");
67          menu.add(exitItem);
68          exitItem.addActionListener(event -> System.exit(0));
69      }
70  }
```

2.5 Building and Running Applets

The first two programs presented in this book are Java *applications*—stand-alone programs like any native programs. On the other hand, as mentioned in the previous chapter, most of the early hype about Java came from its ability to run *applets* inside a web browser.

If you are interested in experiencing a "blast from the past," follow along to see how to build and run an applet and how to display it in a web browser; if you aren't interested, by all means, skip this example and move on to Chapter 3.

Open a terminal window and go to the directory corejava/v1ch02/RoadApplet, then enter the following commands:

```
javac RoadApplet.java
jar cvfm RoadApplet.jar RoadApplet.mf *.class
appletviewer RoadApplet.html
```

Figure 2.9 shows what you see in the applet viewer window. This applet visualizes how traffic jams can be caused by drivers who randomly slow down. In 1996, applets were a great tool for creating such visualizations.

The first command is the now-familiar command to invoke the Java compiler. This compiles the RoadApplet.java source into the bytecode file RoadApplet.class.

This time, however, you do not run the java program. First, you bundle the class files into a "JAR file," using the jar utility. Then you invoke the appletviewer program, a tool included with the JDK that lets you quickly test an applet. You need to give this program an HTML file name, rather than the name of a Java class file. The contents of the RoadApplet.html file are shown at the end of this section in Listing 2.3.

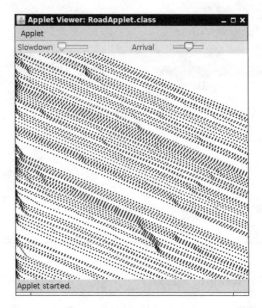

Figure 2.9 The RoadApplet as viewed by the applet viewer

If you are familiar with HTML, you will notice standard HTML markup and the `applet` tag, telling the applet viewer to load the applet whose code is stored in `RoadApplet.jar`. The applet viewer ignores all HTML tags except for the `applet` tag.

Of course, applets are meant to be viewed in a browser. Unfortunately, nowadays, many browsers do not have Java support, or make it difficult to enable it. Your best bet is to use Firefox.

If you use Windows or Mac OS X, Firefox should automatically pick up the Java installation on your computer. Under Linux, you need to enable the plug-in with the following commands:

```
mkdir -p ~/.mozilla/plugins
cd ~/.mozilla/plugins
ln -s jdk/jre/lib/amd64/libnpjp2.so
```

To double-check, type `about:plugins` into the address bar and look for the Java Plug-in. Make sure it uses the Java SE 8 version of the plug-in—look for a MIME type of `application/x-java-applet;version=1.8`.

Next, turn your browser to `http://horstmann.com/applets/RoadApplet/RoadApplet.html`, agree to all the scary security prompts, and make sure the applet appears.

Unfortunately, that is not enough to test the applet that you just compiled. The applet on the `horstmann.com` server is digitally signed. I had to expend some effort, getting a certificate issuer that is trusted by the Java virtual machine to trust me and sell me a certificate, which I used to sign the JAR file. The browser plug-in will no longer run untrusted applets. This is a big change from the past, when a simple applet that draws pixels on the screen would have been confined to the "sandbox" and would work without being signed. Sadly, not even Oracle has faith in the security of the sandbox any more.

To overcome this problem, you can temporarily configure Java to trust applets from the local file system. First, open the Java control panel.

- In Windows, look inside the Programs section of the control panel.
- On a Mac, open System Preferences.
- On Linux, run `jcontrol`.

Then click the Security tab and the Edit Site List button. Click Add and type in `file:///`. Click OK, accept another security prompt, and click OK again (see Figure 2.10).

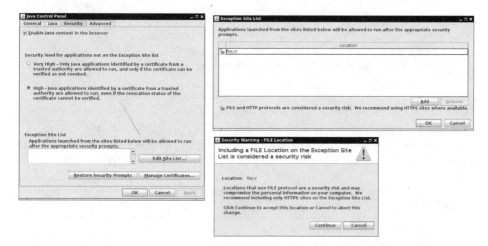

Figure 2.10 Configuring Java to trust local applets

Now you should be able to load the file `corejava/v1ch02/RoadApplet/RoadApplet.html` into your browser and have the applet appear, together with the surrounding text. It will look something like Figure 2.11.

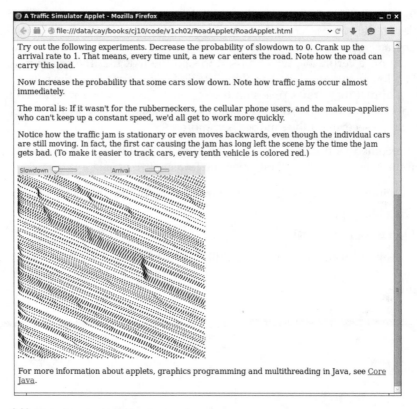

Figure 2.11 Running the RoadApplet in a browser

The code for the applet class is shown in Listing 2.4. At this point, do not give it more than a glance. We will come back to writing applets in Chapter 13.

Listing 2.3 RoadApplet/RoadApplet.html

```
 1  <html xmlns="http://www.w3.org/1999/xhtml">
 2    <head><title>A Traffic Simulator Applet</title></head>
 3    <body>
 4      <h1>Traffic Simulator Applet</h1>
 5
 6      <p>I wrote this traffic simulation, following the article &quot;Und nun die
 7      Stauvorhersage&quot; of the German Magazine <i>Die Zeit</i>, June 7,
 8      1996. The article describes the work of Professor Michael Schreckenberger
 9      of the University of Duisburg and unnamed collaborators at the University
10      of Cologne and Los Alamos National Laboratory. These researchers model
11      traffic flow according to simple rules, such as the following: </p>
```

```
12   <ul>
13       <li>A freeway is modeled as a sequence of grid points. </li>
14       <li>Every car occupies one grid point. Each grid point occupies at most
15       one car. </li>
16       <li>A car can have a speed of 0 - 5 grid points per time interval. </li>
17       <li>A car with speed of less than 5 increases its speed by one unit in
18       each time interval, until it reaches the maximum speed. </li>
19       <li>If a car's distance to the car in front is <i>d</i> grid points, its
20       speed is reduced to <i>d</i>-1 if necessary to avoid crashing into it.
21       </li>
22       <li>With a certain probability, in each time interval some cars slow down
23       one unit for no good reason whatsoever. </li>
24   </ul>
25
26   <p>This applet models these rules. Each line shows an image of the same
27   stretch of road. Each square denotes one car. The first scrollbar lets you
28   adjust the probability that some cars slow down. If the slider is all the
29   way to the left, no car slows down. If it is all the way to the right,
30   every car slows down one unit. A typical setting is that 10% - 20% of the
31   cars slow down. The second slider controls the arrival rate of the cars.
32   When it is all the way to the left, no new cars enter the freeway. If it
33   is all the way to the right, a new car enters the freeway every time
34   interval, provided the freeway entrance is not blocked. </p>
35
36   <p>Try out the following experiments. Decrease the probability of slowdown
37   to 0. Crank up the arrival rate to 1. That means, every time unit, a new
38   car enters the road. Note how the road can carry this load. </p>
39
40   <p>Now increase the probability that some cars slow down. Note how traffic
41   jams occur almost immediately. </p>
42
43   <p>The moral is: If it wasn't for the rubberneckers, the cellular phone
44   users, and the makeup-appliers who can't keep up a constant speed, we'd all
45   get to work more quickly. </p>
46
47   <p>Notice how the traffic jam is stationary or even moves backwards, even
48   though the individual cars are still moving. In fact, the first car
49   causing the jam has long left the scene by the time the jam gets bad.
50   (To make it easier to track cars, every tenth vehicle is colored red.) </p>
51
52   <p><applet code="RoadApplet.class" archive="RoadApplet.jar"
53           width="400" height="400" alt="Traffic jam visualization">
54   </applet></p>
55
56   <p>For more information about applets, graphics programming and
57   multithreading in Java, see
58   <a href="http://horstmann.com/corejava">Core Java</a>. </p>
59   </body>
60 </html>
```

Listing 2.4　RoadApplet/RoadApplet.java

```java
 1  import java.awt.*;
 2  import java.applet.*;
 3  import javax.swing.*;
 4
 5  public class RoadApplet extends JApplet
 6  {
 7     private RoadComponent roadComponent;
 8     private JSlider slowdown;
 9     private JSlider arrival;
10
11     public void init()
12     {
13        EventQueue.invokeLater(() ->
14           {
15              roadComponent = new RoadComponent();
16              slowdown = new JSlider(0, 100, 10);
17              arrival = new JSlider(0, 100, 50);
18
19              JPanel p = new JPanel();
20              p.setLayout(new GridLayout(1, 6));
21              p.add(new JLabel("Slowdown"));
22              p.add(slowdown);
23              p.add(new JLabel(""));
24              p.add(new JLabel("Arrival"));
25              p.add(arrival);
26              p.add(new JLabel(""));
27              setLayout(new BorderLayout());
28              add(p, BorderLayout.NORTH);
29              add(roadComponent, BorderLayout.CENTER);
30           });
31     }
32
33     public void start()
34     {
35        new Thread(() ->
36           {
37              for (;;)
38              {
39                 roadComponent.update(
40                    0.01 * slowdown.getValue(),
41                    0.01 * arrival.getValue());
42                 try { Thread.sleep(50); } catch(InterruptedException e) {}
43              }
44           }).start();
45     }
46  }
```

In this chapter, you learned about the mechanics of compiling and running Java programs. You are now ready to move on to Chapter 3 where you will start learning the Java language.

CHAPTER

3

CHAPTER

Fundamental Programming Structures in Java

In this chapter

At this point, we are assuming that you successfully installed the JDK and were able to run the sample programs that we showed you in Chapter 2. It's time to start programming. This chapter shows you how the basic programming concepts such as data types, branches, and loops are implemented in Java.

Unfortunately, in Java you can't easily write a program that uses a GUI—you need to learn a fair amount of machinery to put up windows, add text boxes and buttons that respond to them, and so on. Introducing the techniques needed to write GUI-based Java programs would take us too far away from our goal of covering the basic programming concepts, so the sample programs in this chapter are "toy" programs designed to illustrate a concept. All these examples simply use a terminal window for input and output.

Finally, if you are an experienced C++ programmer, you can get away with just skimming this chapter: Concentrate on the C/C++ notes that are interspersed throughout the text. Programmers coming from another background, such as Visual Basic, will find most of the concepts familiar, but the syntax is very different—you should read this chapter very carefully.

3.1 A Simple Java Program

Let's look more closely at one of the simplest Java programs you can have—one that simply prints a message to console:

```
public class FirstSample
{
   public static void main(String[] args)
   {
      System.out.println("We will not use 'Hello, World!'");
   }
}
```

It is worth spending all the time you need to become comfortable with the framework of this sample; the pieces will recur in all applications. First and foremost, *Java is case sensitive*. If you made any mistakes in capitalization (such as typing Main instead of main), the program will not run.

Now let's look at this source code line by line. The keyword public is called an *access modifier*; these modifiers control the level of access other parts of a program have to this code. We have more to say about access modifiers in Chapter 5. The keyword class reminds you that everything in a Java program lives inside a class. Although we will spend a lot more time on classes in the next chapter, for now think of a class as a container for the program logic that defines the behavior of an application. As mentioned in Chapter 1, classes are the building blocks with which all Java applications and applets are built. *Everything* in a Java program must be inside a class.

Following the keyword class is the name of the class. The rules for class names in Java are quite generous. Names must begin with a letter, and after that, they can have any combination of letters and digits. The length is essentially unlimited. You cannot use a Java reserved word (such as public or class) for a class name. (See Appendix A for a list of reserved words.)

The standard naming convention (which we follow in the name FirstSample) is that class names are nouns that start with an uppercase letter. If a name consists of multiple words, use an initial uppercase letter in each of the words. (This use of uppercase letters in the middle of a word is sometimes called "camel case" or, self-referentially, "CamelCase".)

You need to make the file name for the source code the same as the name of the public class, with the extension .java appended. Thus, you must store this code in a file called FirstSample.java. (Again, case is important—don't use firstsample.java.)

If you have named the file correctly and not made any typos in the source code, then when you compile this source code, you end up with a file containing the bytecodes for this class. The Java compiler automatically names the bytecode file FirstSample.class and stores it in the same directory as the source file. Finally, launch the program by issuing the following command:

```
java FirstSample
```

(Remember to leave off the .class extension.) When the program executes, it simply displays the string We will not use 'Hello, World!' on the console.

When you use

```
java ClassName
```

to run a compiled program, the Java virtual machine always starts execution with the code in the main method in the class you indicate. (The term "method" is Java-speak for a function.) Thus, you *must* have a main method in the source file for your class for your code to execute. You can, of course, add your own methods to a class and call them from the main method. (We cover writing your own methods in the next chapter.)

 NOTE: According to the Java Language Specification, the main method must be declared public. (The Java Language Specification is the official document that describes the Java language. You can view or download it from http://docs.oracle.com/javase/specs.)

However, several versions of the Java launcher were willing to execute Java programs even when the `main` method was not `public`. A programmer filed a bug report. To see it, visit `http://bugs.java.com/bugdatabase/index.jsp` and enter the bug identification number 4252539. That bug was marked as "closed, will not be fixed." A Sun engineer added an explanation that the Java Virtual Machine Specification (at `http://docs.oracle.com/javase/specs/jvms/se8/html`) does not mandate that `main` is `public` and that "fixing it will cause potential troubles." Fortunately, sanity finally prevailed. The Java launcher in Java SE 1.4 and beyond enforces that the `main` method is `public`.

There are a couple of interesting aspects about this story. On the one hand, it is frustrating to have quality assurance engineers, who are often overworked and not always experts in the fine points of Java, make questionable decisions about bug reports. On the other hand, it is remarkable that Sun made the bug reports and their resolutions available for anyone to scrutinize, long before Java was open source. At one point, Sun even let programmers vote for their most despised bugs and used the vote counts to decide which of them would get fixed in the next JDK release.

Notice the braces { } in the source code. In Java, as in C/C++, braces delineate the parts (usually called *blocks*) in your program. In Java, the code for any method must be started by an opening brace { and ended by a closing brace }.

Brace styles have inspired an inordinate amount of useless controversy. We follow a style that lines up matching braces. As whitespace is irrelevant to the Java compiler, you can use whatever brace style you like. We will have more to say about the use of braces when we talk about the various kinds of loops.

For now, don't worry about the keywords `static void`—just think of them as part of what you need to get a Java program to compile. By the end of Chapter 4, you will understand this incantation completely. The point to remember for now is that every Java application must have a `main` method that is declared in the following way:

```
public class ClassName
{
   public static void main(String[] args)
   {
      program statements
   }
}
```

C++ NOTE: As a C++ programmer, you know what a class is. Java classes are similar to C++ classes, but there are a few differences that can trap you. For example, in Java *all* functions are methods of some class. (The standard terminology refers to them as methods, not member functions.) Thus, in Java you must have a shell class for the `main` method. You may also be familiar with the idea of *static member functions* in C++. These are member functions defined inside a class that do not operate on objects. The `main` method in Java is always static. Finally, as in C/C++, the `void` keyword indicates that this method does not return a value. Unlike C/C++, the `main` method does not return an "exit code" to the operating system. If the `main` method exits normally, the Java program has the exit code `0`, indicating successful completion. To terminate the program with a different exit code, use the `System.exit` method.

Next, turn your attention to this fragment:

```
{
    System.out.println("We will not use 'Hello, World!'");
}
```

Braces mark the beginning and end of the *body* of the method. This method has only one statement in it. As with most programming languages, you can think of Java statements as sentences of the language. In Java, every statement must end with a semicolon. In particular, carriage returns do not mark the end of a statement, so statements can span multiple lines if need be.

The body of the `main` method contains a statement that outputs a single line of text to the console.

Here, we are using the `System.out` object and calling its `println` method. Notice the periods used to invoke a method. Java uses the general syntax

object.method(*parameters*)

as its equivalent of a function call.

In this case, we are calling the `println` method and passing it a string parameter. The method displays the string parameter on the console. It then terminates the output line, so that each call to `println` displays its output on a new line. Notice that Java, like C/C++, uses double quotes to delimit strings. (You can find more information about strings later in this chapter.)

Methods in Java, like functions in any programming language, can use zero, one, or more *parameters* (some programmers call them *arguments*). Even if a method takes no parameters, you must still use empty parentheses. For example, a variant of the `println` method with no parameters just prints a blank line. You invoke it with the call

```
System.out.println();
```

 NOTE: `System.out` also has a `print` method that doesn't add a newline character to the output. For example, `System.out.print("Hello")` prints `Hello` without a newline. The next output appears immediately after the letter `o`.

3.2 Comments

Comments in Java, as in most programming languages, do not show up in the executable program. Thus, you can add as many comments as needed without fear of bloating the code. Java has three ways of marking comments. The most common form is a `//`. Use this for a comment that runs from the `//` to the end of the line.

```
System.out.println("We will not use 'Hello, World!'"); // is this too cute?
```

When longer comments are needed, you can mark each line with a `//`, or you can use the `/*` and `*/` comment delimiters that let you block off a longer comment.

Finally, a third kind of comment can be used to generate documentation automatically. This comment uses a `/**` to start and a `*/` to end. You can see this type of comment in Listing 3.1. For more on this type of comment and on automatic documentation generation, see Chapter 4.

Listing 3.1 `FirstSample/FirstSample.java`

```java
1  /**
2   * This is the first sample program in Core Java Chapter 3
3   * @version 1.01 1997-03-22
4   * @author Gary Cornell
5   */
6  public class FirstSample
7  {
8     public static void main(String[] args)
9     {
10       System.out.println("We will not use 'Hello, World!'");
11    }
12 }
```

CAUTION: /* */ comments do not nest in Java. That is, you might not be able to deactivate code simply by surrounding it with /* and */ because the code you want to deactivate might itself contain a */ delimiter.

3.3 Data Types

Java is a *strongly typed language*. This means that every variable must have a declared type. There are eight *primitive types* in Java. Four of them are integer types; two are floating-point number types; one is the character type char, used for code units in the Unicode encoding scheme (see Section 3.3.3, "The char Type," on p. 50); and one is a boolean type for truth values.

 NOTE: Java has an arbitrary-precision arithmetic package. However, "big numbers," as they are called, are Java *objects* and not a new Java type. You will see how to use them later in this chapter.

3.3.1 Integer Types

The integer types are for numbers without fractional parts. Negative values are allowed. Java provides the four integer types shown in Table 3.1.

Table 3.1 Java Integer Types

Type	Storage Requirement	Range (Inclusive)
int	4 bytes	−2,147,483,648 to 2,147,483, 647 (just over 2 billion)
short	2 bytes	−32,768 to 32,767
long	8 bytes	−9,223,372,036,854,775,808 to 9,223,372,036,854,775,807
byte	1 byte	−128 to 127

In most situations, the int type is the most practical. If you want to represent the number of inhabitants of our planet, you'll need to resort to a long. The byte and short types are mainly intended for specialized applications, such as low-level file handling, or for large arrays when storage space is at a premium.

Under Java, the ranges of the integer types do not depend on the machine on which you will be running the Java code. This alleviates a major pain for the programmer who wants to move software from one platform to another, or even between operating systems on the same platform. In contrast, C and C++ programs use the most efficient integer type for each processor. As a result, a C program that runs well on a 32-bit processor may exhibit integer overflow on a 16-bit system. Since Java programs must run with the same results on all machines, the ranges for the various types are fixed.

Long integer numbers have a suffix L or l (for example, 4000000000L). Hexadecimal numbers have a prefix 0x or 0X (for example, 0xCAFE). Octal numbers have a prefix 0 (for example, 010 is 8)—naturally, this can be confusing, so we recommend against the use of octal constants.

Starting with Java SE 7, you can write numbers in binary, with a prefix 0b or 0B. For example, 0b1001 is 9. Also starting with Java SE 7, you can add underscores to number literals, such as 1_000_000 (or 0b1111_0100_0010_0100_0000) to denote one million. The underscores are for human eyes only. The Java compiler simply removes them.

 C++ NOTE: In C and C++, the sizes of types such as int and long depend on the target platform. On a 16-bit processor such as the 8086, integers are 2 bytes, but on a 32-bit processor like a Pentium or SPARC they are 4-byte quantities. Similarly, long values are 4-byte on 32-bit processors and 8-byte on 64-bit processors. These differences make it challenging to write cross-platform programs. In Java, the sizes of all numeric types are platform independent.

Note that Java does not have any unsigned versions of the int, long, short, or byte types.

3.3.2 Floating-Point Types

The floating-point types denote numbers with fractional parts. The two floating-point types are shown in Table 3.2.

Table 3.2 Floating-Point Types

Type	Storage Requirement	Range
float	4 bytes	Approximately ±3.40282347E+38F (6–7 significant decimal digits)
double	8 bytes	Approximately ±1.79769313486231570E+308 (15 significant decimal digits)

The name double refers to the fact that these numbers have twice the precision of the float type. (Some people call these *double-precision* numbers.) The limited precision of float (6–7 significant digits) is simply not sufficient for many situations. Use float values only when you work with a library that requires them, or when you need to store a very large number of them.

Numbers of type float have a suffix F or f (for example, 3.14F). Floating-point numbers without an F suffix (such as 3.14) are always considered to be of type double. You can optionally supply the D or d suffix (for example, 3.14D).

NOTE: You can specify floating-point literals in hexadecimal. For example, 0.125 = 2^{-3} can be written as 0x1.0p-3. In hexadecimal notation, you use a p, not an e, to denote the exponent. (An e is a hexadecimal digit.) Note that the mantissa is written in hexadecimal and the exponent in decimal. The base of the exponent is 2, not 10.

All floating-point computations follow the IEEE 754 specification. In particular, there are three special floating-point values to denote overflows and errors:

* Positive infinity
* Negative infinity
* NaN (not a number)

For example, the result of dividing a positive number by 0 is positive infinity. Computing 0/0 or the square root of a negative number yields NaN.

NOTE: The constants Double.POSITIVE_INFINITY, Double.NEGATIVE_INFINITY, and Double.NaN (as well as corresponding Float constants) represent these special values, but they are rarely used in practice. In particular, you cannot test

```
if (x == Double.NaN) // is never true
```

to check whether a particular result equals Double.NaN. All "not a number" values are considered distinct. However, you can use the Double.isNaN method:

```
if (Double.isNaN(x)) // check whether x is "not a number"
```

CAUTION: Floating-point numbers are *not* suitable for financial calculations in which roundoff errors cannot be tolerated. For example, the command System.out.println(2.0 - 1.1) prints 0.8999999999999999, not 0.9 as you would expect. Such roundoff errors are caused by the fact that floating-point numbers are represented in the binary number system. There is no precise binary representation of the fraction 1/10, just as there is no accurate representation of the fraction 1/3 in the decimal system. If you need precise numerical computations without roundoff errors, use the BigDecimal class, which is introduced later in this chapter.

3.3.3 The char Type

The char type was originally intended to describe individual characters. However, this is no longer the case. Nowadays, some Unicode characters can be described with one char value, and other Unicode characters require two char values. Read the next section for the gory details.

Literal values of type char are enclosed in single quotes. For example, 'A' is a character constant with value 65. It is different from "A", a string containing a single character. Values of type char can be expressed as hexadecimal values that run from \u0000 to \uFFFF. For example, \u2122 is the trademark symbol (™) and \u03C0 is the Greek letter pi (π).

Besides the \u escape sequences, there are several escape sequences for special characters, as shown in Table 3.3. You can use these escape sequences inside quoted character literals and strings, such as '\u2122' or "Hello\n". The \u escape sequence (but none of the other escape sequences) can even be used *outside* quoted character constants and strings. For example,

```
public static void main(String\u005B\u005D args)
```

is perfectly legal—\u005B and \u005D are the encodings for [and].

Table 3.3 Escape Sequences for Special Characters

Escape sequence	Name	Unicode Value
\b	Backspace	\u0008
\t	Tab	\u0009
\n	Linefeed	\u000a
\r	Carriage return	\u000d
\"	Double quote	\u0022
\'	Single quote	\u0027
\\	Backslash	\u005c

CAUTION: Unicode escape sequences are processed before the code is parsed. For example, "\u0022+\u0022" is *not* a string consisting of a plus sign surrounded by quotation marks (U+0022). Instead, the \u0022 are converted into " before parsing, yielding ""+"", or an empty string.

Even more insidiously, you must beware of \u inside comments. The comment

```
// \u00A0 is a newline
```

yields a syntax error since \u00A0 is replaced with a newline when the program is read. Similarly, a comment

```
// Look inside c:\users
```

yields a syntax error because the \u is not followed by four hex digits.

3.3.4 Unicode and the char Type

To fully understand the char type, you have to know about the Unicode encoding scheme. Unicode was invented to overcome the limitations of traditional character encoding schemes. Before Unicode, there were many different standards: ASCII in the United States, ISO 8859-1 for Western European languages, KOI-8 for Russian, GB18030 and BIG-5 for Chinese, and so on. This caused two problems. A particular code value corresponds to different letters in the different encoding schemes. Moreover, the encodings for languages with large character sets have variable length: Some common characters are encoded as single bytes, others require two or more bytes.

Unicode was designed to solve these problems. When the unification effort started in the 1980s, a fixed 2-byte code was more than sufficient to encode all characters used in all languages in the world, with room to spare for future expansion—or so everyone thought at the time. In 1991, Unicode 1.0 was released, using slightly less than half of the available 65,536 code values. Java was designed from the ground up to use 16-bit Unicode characters, which was a major advance over other programming languages that used 8-bit characters.

Unfortunately, over time, the inevitable happened. Unicode grew beyond 65,536 characters, primarily due to the addition of a very large set of ideographs used for Chinese, Japanese, and Korean. Now, the 16-bit char type is insufficient to describe all Unicode characters.

We need a bit of terminology to explain how this problem is resolved in Java, beginning with Java SE 5.0. A *code point* is a code value that is associated with a character in an encoding scheme. In the Unicode standard, code points are written in hexadecimal and prefixed with U+, such as U+0041 for the code point of the Latin letter A. Unicode has code points that are grouped into 17 *code planes*. The first code plane, called the *basic multilingual plane*, consists of the "classic" Unicode characters with code points U+0000 to U+FFFF. Sixteen additional planes, with code points U+10000 to U+10FFFF, hold the *supplementary characters*.

The UTF-16 encoding represents all Unicode code points in a variable-length code. The characters in the basic multilingual plane are represented as 16-bit values, called *code units*. The supplementary characters are encoded as consecutive pairs of code units. Each of the values in such an encoding pair falls into a range of 2048 unused values of the basic multilingual plane, called the *surrogates area* (U+D800 to U+DBFF for the first code unit, U+DC00 to U+DFFF for the second code unit). This is rather clever, because you can immediately tell whether a code unit encodes a single character or it is the first or second part of a supplementary character. For example, ⊙ (the mathematical symbol for the set of octonions, http://math.ucr.edu/home/baez/octonions) has code point U+1D546 and is encoded by the two code units U+D835 and U+DD46. (See http://en.wikipedia.org/wiki/UTF-16 for a description of the encoding algorithm.)

In Java, the char type describes a *code unit* in the UTF-16 encoding.

Our strong recommendation is not to use the char type in your programs unless you are actually manipulating UTF-16 code units. You are almost always better off treating strings (which we will discuss in Section 3.6, "Strings," on p. 65) as abstract data types.

3.3.5 The boolean Type

The boolean type has two values, false and true. It is used for evaluating logical conditions. You cannot convert between integers and boolean values.

 C++ NOTE: In C++, numbers and even pointers can be used in place of boolean values. The value 0 is equivalent to the bool value false, and a nonzero value is equivalent to true. This is *not* the case in Java. Thus, Java programmers are shielded from accidents such as

```
if (x = 0) // oops... meant x == 0
```

In C++, this test compiles and runs, always evaluating to false. In Java, the test does not compile because the integer expression x = 0 cannot be converted to a boolean value.

3.4 Variables

In Java, every variable has a *type*. You declare a variable by placing the type first, followed by the name of the variable. Here are some examples:

```
double salary;
int vacationDays;
long earthPopulation;
boolean done;
```

Notice the semicolon at the end of each declaration. The semicolon is necessary because a declaration is a complete Java statement.

A variable name must begin with a letter and must be a sequence of letters or digits. Note that the terms "letter" and "digit" are much broader in Java than in most languages. A letter is defined as 'A'-'Z', 'a'-'z', '_', '$', or *any* Unicode character that denotes a letter in a language. For example, German users can use umlauts such as 'ä' in variable names; Greek speakers could use a π. Similarly, digits are '0'-'9' and *any* Unicode characters that denote a digit in a language. Symbols like '+' or '©' cannot be used inside variable names, nor can spaces. *All* characters in the name of a variable are significant and *case is also significant.* The length of a variable name is essentially unlimited.

 TIP: If you are really curious as to what Unicode characters are "letters" as far as Java is concerned, you can use the isJavaIdentifierStart and isJavaIdentifierPart methods in the Character class to check.

 TIP: Even though $ is a valid Java letter, you should not use it in your own code. It is intended for names that are generated by the Java compiler and other tools.

You also cannot use a Java reserved word as a variable name. (See Appendix A for a list of reserved words.)

You can declare multiple variables on a single line:

```
int i, j; // both are integers
```

However, we don't recommend this style. If you declare each variable separately, your programs are easier to read.

 NOTE: As you saw, names are case sensitive, for example, `hireday` and `hireDay` are two separate names. In general, you should not have two names that only differ in their letter case. However, sometimes it is difficult to come up with a good name for a variable. Many programmers then give the variable the same name as the type, for example

```
Box box; // "Box" is the type and "box" is the variable name
```

Other programmers prefer to use an "a" prefix for the variable:

```
Box aBox;
```

3.4.1 Initializing Variables

After you declare a variable, you must explicitly initialize it by means of an assignment statement—you can never use the value of an uninitialized variable. For example, the Java compiler flags the following sequence of statements as an error:

```
int vacationDays;
System.out.println(vacationDays); // ERROR--variable not initialized
```

You assign to a previously declared variable by using the variable name on the left, an equal sign (=), and then some Java expression with an appropriate value on the right.

```
int vacationDays;
vacationDays = 12;
```

You can both declare and initialize a variable on the same line. For example:

```
int vacationDays = 12;
```

Finally, in Java you can put declarations anywhere in your code. For example, the following is valid code in Java:

```
double salary = 65000.0;
System.out.println(salary);
int vacationDays = 12; // OK to declare a variable here
```

In Java, it is considered good style to declare variables as closely as possible to the point where they are first used.

C++ NOTE: C and C++ distinguish between the *declaration* and *definition* of a variable. For example,

```
int i = 10;
```

is a definition, whereas

```
extern int i;
```

is a declaration. In Java, no declarations are separate from definitions.

3.4.2 Constants

In Java, you use the keyword `final` to denote a constant. For example:

```
public class Constants
{
   public static void main(String[] args)
   {
      final double CM_PER_INCH = 2.54;
      double paperWidth = 8.5;
      double paperHeight = 11;
      System.out.println("Paper size in centimeters: "
         + paperWidth * CM_PER_INCH + " by " + paperHeight * CM_PER_INCH);
   }
}
```

The keyword `final` indicates that you can assign to the variable once, and then its value is set once and for all. It is customary to name constants in all uppercase.

It is probably more common in Java to create a constant so it's available to multiple methods inside a single class. These are usually called *class constants*. Set up a class constant with the keywords `static final`. Here is an example of using a class constant:

```
public class Constants2
{
   public static final double CM_PER_INCH = 2.54;

   public static void main(String[] args)
   {
      double paperWidth = 8.5;
      double paperHeight = 11;
      System.out.println("Paper size in centimeters: "
         + paperWidth * CM_PER_INCH + " by " + paperHeight * CM_PER_INCH);
   }
}
```

Note that the definition of the class constant appears *outside* the main method. Thus, the constant can also be used in other methods of the same class. Furthermore, if the constant is declared, as in our example, public, methods of other classes can also use it—in our example, as Constants2.CM_PER_INCH.

C++ NOTE: const is a reserved Java keyword, but it is not currently used for anything. You must use final for a constant.

3.5 Operators

The usual arithmetic operators +, -, *, / are used in Java for addition, subtraction, multiplication, and division. The / operator denotes integer division if both arguments are integers, and floating-point division otherwise. Integer remainder (sometimes called *modulus*) is denoted by %. For example, 15 / 2 is 7, 15 % 2 is 1, and 15.0 / 2 is 7.5.

Note that integer division by 0 raises an exception, whereas floating-point division by 0 yields an infinite or NaN result.

NOTE: One of the stated goals of the Java programming language is portability. A computation should yield the same results no matter which virtual machine executes it. For arithmetic computations with floating-point numbers, it is surprisingly difficult to achieve this portability. The double type uses 64 bits to store a numeric value, but some processors use 80-bit floating-point registers. These registers yield added precision in intermediate steps of a computation. For example, consider the following computation:

```
double w = x * y / z;
```

Many Intel processors compute x * y, leave the result in an 80-bit register, then divide by z, and finally truncate the result back to 64 bits. That can yield a more accurate result, and it can avoid exponent overflow. But the result may be *different* from a computation that uses 64 bits throughout. For that reason, the initial specification of the Java virtual machine mandated that all intermediate computations must be truncated. The numeric community hated it. Not only can the truncated computations cause overflow, they are actually *slower* than the more precise computations because the truncation operations take time. For that reason, the Java programming language was updated to recognize the conflicting demands for optimum performance and perfect reproducibility. By default, virtual machine designers are now permitted to use extended precision for intermediate computations. However, methods tagged with the strictfp keyword must use strict floating-point operations that yield reproducible results.

For example, you can tag `main` as

```
public static strictfp void main(String[] args)
```

Then all instructions inside the `main` method will use strict floating-point computations. If you tag a class as `strictfp`, then all of its methods must use strict floating-point computations.

The gory details are very much tied to the behavior of the Intel processors. In the default mode, intermediate results are allowed to use an extended exponent, but not an extended mantissa. (The Intel chips support truncation of the mantissa without loss of performance.) Therefore, the only difference between the default and strict modes is that strict computations may overflow when default computations don't.

If your eyes glazed over when reading this note, don't worry. Floating-point overflow isn't a problem that one encounters for most common programs. We don't use the `strictfp` keyword in this book.

3.5.1 Mathematical Functions and Constants

The `Math` class contains an assortment of mathematical functions that you may occasionally need, depending on the kind of programming that you do.

To take the square root of a number, use the `sqrt` method:

```
double x = 4;
double y = Math.sqrt(x);
System.out.println(y); // prints 2.0
```

 NOTE: There is a subtle difference between the `println` method and the `sqrt` method. The `println` method operates on the `System.out` object. But the `sqrt` method in the `Math` class does not operate on any object. Such a method is called a *static* method. You can learn more about static methods in Chapter 4.

The Java programming language has no operator for raising a quantity to a power: You must use the `pow` method in the `Math` class. The statement

```
double y = Math.pow(x, a);
```

sets y to be x raised to the power a (x^a). The `pow` method's parameters are both of type `double`, and it returns a `double` as well.

The `floorMod` method aims to solve a long-standing problem with integer remainders. Consider the expression n % 2. Everyone knows that this is 0 if n is even and 1 if n is odd. Except, of course, when n is negative. Then it is -1. Why? When the first computers were built, someone had to make rules for how integer division and remainder should work for negative operands. Mathematicians had known the optimal (or "Euclidean") rule for a few hundred years: always leave the remainder ≥ 0. But, rather than open a math textbook, those pioneers came up with rules that seemed reasonable but are actually inconvenient.

Consider this problem. You compute the position of the hour hand of a clock. An adjustment is applied, and you want to normalize to a number between 0 and 11. That is easy: (position + adjustment) % 12. But what if the adjustment is negative? Then you might get a negative number. So you have to introduce a branch, or use ((position + adjustment) % 12 + 12) % 12. Either way, it is a hassle.

The floorMod method makes it easier: floorMod(position + adjustment, 12) always yields a value between 0 and 11. (Unfortunately, floorMod gives negative results for negative divisors, but that situation doesn't often occur in practice.)

The Math class supplies the usual trigonometric functions:

```
Math.sin
Math.cos
Math.tan
Math.atan
Math.atan2
```

and the exponential function with its inverse, the natural logarithm, as well as the decimal logarithm:

```
Math.exp
Math.log
Math.log10
```

Finally, two constants denote the closest possible approximations to the mathematical constants π and e:

```
Math.PI
Math.E
```

TIP: You can avoid the Math prefix for the mathematical methods and constants by adding the following line to the top of your source file:

```
import static java.lang.Math.*;
```

For example:

```
System.out.println("The square root of \u03C0 is " + sqrt(PI));
```

We discuss static imports in Chapter 4.

NOTE: The methods in the `Math` class use the routines in the computer's floating-point unit for fastest performance. If completely predictable results are more important than performance, use the `StrictMath` class instead. It implements the algorithms from the "Freely Distributable Math Library" `fdlibm`, guaranteeing identical results on all platforms. See `www.netlib.org/fdlibm` for the source code of these algorithms. (Whenever `fdlibm` provides more than one definition for a function, the `StrictMath` class follows the IEEE 754 version whose name starts with an "e".)

3.5.2 Conversions between Numeric Types

It is often necessary to convert from one numeric type to another. Figure 3.1 shows the legal conversions.

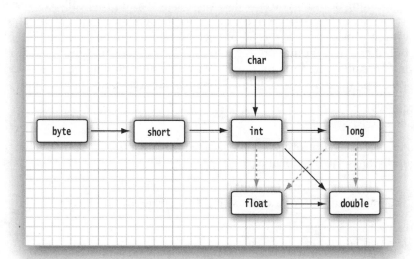

Figure 3.1 Legal conversions between numeric types

The six solid arrows in Figure 3.1 denote conversions without information loss. The three dotted arrows denote conversions that may lose precision. For example, a large integer such as 123456789 has more digits than the float type can represent. When the integer is converted to a float, the resulting value has the correct magnitude but loses some precision.

```
int n = 123456789;
float f = n; // f is 1.23456792E8
```

When two values are combined with a binary operator (such as n + f where n is an integer and f is a floating-point value), both operands are converted to a common type before the operation is carried out.

- If either of the operands is of type double, the other one will be converted to a double.

- Otherwise, if either of the operands is of type float, the other one will be converted to a float.

- Otherwise, if either of the operands is of type long, the other one will be converted to a long.

- Otherwise, both operands will be converted to an int.

3.5.3 Casts

In the preceding section, you saw that int values are automatically converted to double values when necessary. On the other hand, there are obviously times when you want to consider a double as an integer. Numeric conversions are possible in Java, but of course information may be lost. Conversions in which loss of information is possible are done by means of *casts*. The syntax for casting is to give the target type in parentheses, followed by the variable name. For example:

```
double x = 9.997;
int nx = (int) x;
```

Now, the variable nx has the value 9 because casting a floating-point value to an integer discards the fractional part.

If you want to *round* a floating-point number to the *nearest* integer (which in most cases is a more useful operation), use the Math.round method:

```
double x = 9.997;
int nx = (int) Math.round(x);
```

Now the variable nx has the value 10. You still need to use the cast (int) when you call round. The reason is that the return value of the round method is a long, and a long can only be assigned to an int with an explicit cast because there is the possibility of information loss.

 CAUTION: If you try to cast a number of one type to another that is out of range for the target type, the result will be a truncated number that has a different value. For example, (byte) 300 is actually 44.

C++ NOTE: You cannot cast between `boolean` values and any numeric type. This convention prevents common errors. In the rare case when you want to convert a `boolean` value to a number, you can use a conditional expression such as `b ? 1 : 0`.

3.5.4 Combining Assignment with Operators

There is a convenient shortcut for using binary operators in an assignment. For example,

```
x += 4;
```

is equivalent to

```
x = x + 4;
```

(In general, place the operator to the left of the = sign, such as *= or %=.)

NOTE: If the operator yields a value whose type is different than that of the left-hand side, then it is coerced to fit. For example, if x is an `int`, then the statement

```
x += 3.5;
```

is valid, setting x to `(int)(x + 3.5)`.

3.5.5 Increment and Decrement Operators

Programmers, of course, know that one of the most common operations with a numeric variable is to add or subtract 1. Java, following in the footsteps of C and C++, has both increment and decrement operators: `n++` adds 1 to the current value of the variable n, and `n--` subtracts 1 from it. For example, the code

```
int n = 12;
n++;
```

changes n to 13. Since these operators change the value of a variable, they cannot be applied to numbers themselves. For example, `4++` is not a legal statement.

There are two forms of these operators; you've just seen the postfix form of the operator that is placed after the operand. There is also a prefix form, `++n`. Both change the value of the variable by 1. The difference between the two appears only when they are used inside expressions. The prefix form does the addition first; the postfix form evaluates to the old value of the variable.

```
int m = 7;
int n = 7;
```

```
int a = 2 * ++m; // now a is 16, m is 8
int b = 2 * n++; // now b is 14, n is 8
```

We recommend against using ++ inside expressions because this often leads to confusing code and annoying bugs.

3.5.6 Relational and boolean Operators

Java has the full complement of relational operators. To test for equality, use a double equal sign, ==. For example, the value of

```
3 == 7
```

is false.

Use a != for inequality. For example, the value of

```
3 != 7
```

is true.

Finally, you have the usual < (less than), > (greater than), <= (less than or equal), and >= (greater than or equal) operators.

Java, following C++, uses && for the logical "and" operator and || for the logical "or" operator. As you can easily remember from the != operator, the exclamation point ! is the logical negation operator. The && and || operators are evaluated in "short circuit" fashion: The second argument is not evaluated if the first argument already determines the value. If you combine two expressions with the && operator,

   expression$_1$ **&&** *expression*$_2$

and the truth value of the first expression has been determined to be false, then it is impossible for the result to be true. Thus, the value for the second expression is *not* calculated. This behavior can be exploited to avoid errors. For example, in the expression

```
x != 0 && 1 / x > x + y // no division by 0
```

the second part is never evaluated if x equals zero. Thus, 1 / x is not computed if x is zero, and no divide-by-zero error can occur.

Similarly, the value of *expression*$_1$ || *expression*$_2$ is automatically true if the first expression is true, without evaluating the second expression.

Finally, Java supports the ternary ?: operator that is occasionally useful. The expression

   condition ? *expression*$_1$: *expression*$_2$

evaluates to the first expression if the condition is true, to the second expression otherwise. For example,

```
x < y ? x : y
```

gives the smaller of x and y.

3.5.7 Bitwise Operators

When working with any of the integer types, you have operators that can work directly with the bits that make up the integers. This means that you can use masking techniques to get at individual bits in a number. The bitwise operators are

```
& ("and")    | ("or")    ^ ("xor")    ~ ("not")
```

These operators work on bit patterns. For example, if n is an integer variable, then

```
int fourthBitFromRight = (n & 0b1000) / 0b1000;
```

gives you a 1 if the fourth bit from the right in the binary representation of n is 1, and 0 otherwise. Using & with the appropriate power of 2 lets you mask out all but a single bit.

NOTE: When applied to boolean values, the & and | operators yield a boolean value. These operators are similar to the && and || operators, except that the & and | operators are not evaluated in "short circuit" fashion—that is, both arguments are evaluated before the result is computed.

There are also >> and << operators which shift a bit pattern to the right or left. These operators are convenient when you need to build up bit patterns to do bit masking:

```
int fourthBitFromRight = (n & (1 << 3)) >> 3;
```

Finally, a >>> operator fills the top bits with zero, unlike >> which extends the sign bit into the top bits. There is no <<< operator.

CAUTION: The right-hand argument of the shift operators is reduced modulo 32 (unless the left-hand argument is a long, in which case the right-hand argument is reduced modulo 64). For example, the value of 1 << 35 is the same as 1 << 3 or 8.

C++ NOTE: In C/C++, there is no guarantee as to whether >> performs an arithmetic shift (extending the sign bit) or a logical shift (filling in with zeroes). Implementors are free to choose whichever is more efficient. That means the C/C++ >> operator may yield implementation-dependent results for negative numbers. Java removes that uncertainty.

3.5.8 Parentheses and Operator Hierarchy

Table 3.4 shows the precedence of operators. If no parentheses are used, operations are performed in the hierarchical order indicated. Operators on the same level are processed from left to right, except for those that are right-associative, as indicated in the table. For example, && has a higher precedence than ||, so the expression

    a && b || c

means

    (a && b) || c

Table 3.4 Operator Precedence

Operators	Associativity
[] . () (method call)	Left to right
! ~ ++ -- + (unary) - (unary) () (cast) new	Right to left
* / %	Left to right
+ -	Left to right
<< >> >>>	Left to right
< <= > >= instanceof	Left to right
== !=	Left to right
&	Left to right
^	Left to right
|	Left to right
&&	Left to right
||	Left to right
?:	Right to left
= += -= *= /= %= &= |= ^= <<= >>= >>>=	Right to left

Since += associates right to left, the expression

```
a += b += c
```

means

```
a += (b += c)
```

That is, the value of b += c (which is the value of b after the addition) is added to a.

 C++ NOTE: Unlike C or C++, Java does not have a comma operator. However, you can use a *comma-separated list of expressions* in the first and third slot of a for statement.

3.5.9 Enumerated Types

Sometimes, a variable should only hold a restricted set of values. For example, you may sell clothes or pizza in four sizes: small, medium, large, and extra large. Of course, you could encode these sizes as integers 1, 2, 3, 4 or characters S, M, L, and X. But that is an error-prone setup. It is too easy for a variable to hold a wrong value (such as 0 or m).

You can define your own *enumerated type* whenever such a situation arises. An enumerated type has a finite number of named values. For example:

```
enum Size { SMALL, MEDIUM, LARGE, EXTRA_LARGE };
```

Now you can declare variables of this type:

```
Size s = Size.MEDIUM;
```

A variable of type Size can hold only one of the values listed in the type declaration, or the special value null that indicates that the variable is not set to any value at all.

We discuss enumerated types in greater detail in Chapter 5.

3.6 Strings

Conceptually, Java strings are sequences of Unicode characters. For example, the string "Java\u2122" consists of the five Unicode characters J, a, v, a, and ™. Java does not have a built-in string type. Instead, the standard Java library contains a pre-defined class called, naturally enough, String. Each quoted string is an instance of the String class:

```
String e = ""; // an empty string
String greeting = "Hello";
```

3.6.1 Substrings

You can extract a substring from a larger string with the substring method of the String class. For example,

```
String greeting = "Hello";
String s = greeting.substring(0, 3);
```

creates a string consisting of the characters "Hel".

The second parameter of substring is the first position that you *do not* want to copy. In our case, we want to copy positions 0, 1, and 2 (from position 0 to position 2 inclusive). As substring counts it, this means from position 0 inclusive to position 3 *exclusive*.

There is one advantage to the way substring works: Computing the length of the substring is easy. The string s.substring(a, b) always has length b − a. For example, the substring "Hel" has length 3 − 0 = 3.

3.6.2 Concatenation

Java, like most programming languages, allows you to use + to join (concatenate) two strings.

```
String expletive = "Expletive";
String PG13 = "deleted";
String message = expletive + PG13;
```

The preceding code sets the variable message to the string "Expletivedeleted". (Note the lack of a space between the words: The + operator joins two strings in the order received, *exactly* as they are given.)

When you concatenate a string with a value that is not a string, the latter is converted to a string. (As you will see in Chapter 5, every Java object can be converted to a string.) For example,

```
int age = 13;
String rating = "PG" + age;
```

sets rating to the string "PG13".

This feature is commonly used in output statements. For example,

```
System.out.println("The answer is " + answer);
```

is perfectly acceptable and prints what you would expect (and with the correct spacing because of the space after the word is).

If you need to put multiple strings together, separated by a delimiter, use the static join method:

```
String all = String.join(" / ", "S", "M", "L", "XL");
    // all is the string "S / M / L / XL"
```

3.6.3 Strings Are Immutable

The String class gives no methods that let you *change* a character in an existing string. If you want to turn greeting into "Help!", you cannot directly change the last positions of greeting into 'p' and '!'. If you are a C programmer, this will make you feel pretty helpless. How are we going to modify the string? In Java, it is quite easy: Concatenate the substring that you want to keep with the characters that you want to replace.

```
greeting = greeting.substring(0, 3) + "p!";
```

This declaration changes the current value of the greeting variable to "Help!".

Since you cannot change the individual characters in a Java string, the documentation refers to the objects of the String class as *immutable*. Just as the number 3 is always 3, the string "Hello" will always contain the code-unit sequence for the characters H, e, l, l, o. You cannot change these values. Yet you can, as you just saw, change the contents of the string *variable* greeting and make it refer to a different string, just as you can make a numeric variable currently holding the value 3 hold the value 4.

Isn't that a lot less efficient? It would seem simpler to change the code units than to build up a whole new string from scratch. Well, yes and no. Indeed, it isn't efficient to generate a new string that holds the concatenation of "Hel" and "p!". But immutable strings have one great advantage: The compiler can arrange that strings are *shared*.

To understand how this works, think of the various strings as sitting in a common pool. String variables then point to locations in the pool. If you copy a string variable, both the original and the copy share the same characters.

Overall, the designers of Java decided that the efficiency of sharing outweighs the inefficiency of string editing by extracting substrings and concatenating. Look at your own programs; we suspect that most of the time, you don't change strings—you just compare them. (There is one common exception—assembling strings from individual characters or from shorter strings that come from the keyboard or a file. For these situations, Java provides a separate class that we describe in Section 3.6.9, "Building Strings," on p. 77.)

C++ NOTE: C programmers are generally bewildered when they see Java strings for the first time because they think of strings as arrays of characters:

```
char greeting[] = "Hello";
```

That is a wrong analogy: A Java string is roughly analogous to a `char*` pointer,

```
char* greeting = "Hello";
```

When you replace `greeting` with another string, the Java code does roughly the following:

```
char* temp = malloc(6);
strncpy(temp, greeting, 3);
strncpy(temp + 3, "p!", 3);
greeting = temp;
```

Sure, now `greeting` points to the string `"Help!"`. And even the most hardened C programmer must admit that the Java syntax is more pleasant than a sequence of `strncpy` calls. But what if we make another assignment to `greeting`?

```
greeting = "Howdy";
```

Don't we have a memory leak? After all, the original string was allocated on the heap. Fortunately, Java does automatic garbage collection. If a block of memory is no longer needed, it will eventually be recycled.

If you are a C++ programmer and use the `string` class defined by ANSI C++, you will be much more comfortable with the Java `String` type. C++ `string` objects also perform automatic allocation and deallocation of memory. The memory management is performed explicitly by constructors, assignment operators, and destructors. However, C++ strings are mutable—you can modify individual characters in a string.

3.6.4 Testing Strings for Equality

To test whether two strings are equal, use the `equals` method. The expression

```
s.equals(t)
```

returns `true` if the strings `s` and `t` are equal, `false` otherwise. Note that `s` and `t` can be string variables or string literals. For example, the expression

```
"Hello".equals(greeting)
```

is perfectly legal. To test whether two strings are identical except for the upper/lowercase letter distinction, use the `equalsIgnoreCase` method.

```
"Hello".equalsIgnoreCase("hello")
```

Do *not* use the == operator to test whether two strings are equal! It only determines whether or not the strings are stored in the same location. Sure, if strings are in the same location, they must be equal. But it is entirely possible to store multiple copies of identical strings in different places.

```
String greeting = "Hello"; //initialize greeting to a string
if (greeting == "Hello") . . .
    // probably true
if (greeting.substring(0, 3) == "Hel") . . .
    // probably false
```

If the virtual machine always arranges for equal strings to be shared, then you could use the == operator for testing equality. But only string *literals* are shared, not strings that are the result of operations like + or substring. Therefore, *never* use == to compare strings lest you end up with a program with the worst kind of bug—an intermittent one that seems to occur randomly.

 C++ NOTE: If you are used to the C++ string class, you have to be particularly careful about equality testing. The C++ string class does overload the == operator to test for equality of the string contents. It is perhaps unfortunate that Java goes out of its way to give strings the same "look and feel" as numeric values but then makes strings behave like pointers for equality testing. The language designers could have redefined == for strings, just as they made a special arrangement for +. Oh well, every language has its share of inconsistencies.

C programmers never use == to compare strings but use strcmp instead. The Java method compareTo is the exact analog to strcmp. You can use

```
if (greeting.compareTo("Hello") == 0) . . .
```

but it seems clearer to use equals instead.

3.6.5 Empty and Null Strings

The empty string "" is a string of length 0. You can test whether a string is empty by calling

```
if (str.length() == 0)
```

or

```
if (str.equals(""))
```

An empty string is a Java object which holds the string length (namely 0) and an empty contents. However, a String variable can also hold a special value, called null, that indicates that no object is currently associated with the variable. (See

Chapter 4 for more information about `null`.) To test whether a string is `null`, use the condition

```
if (str == null)
```

Sometimes, you need to test that a string is neither `null` nor empty. Then use the condition

```
if (str != null && str.length() != 0)
```

You need to test that `str` is not `null` first. As you will see in Chapter 4, it is an error to invoke a method on a `null` value.

3.6.6 Code Points and Code Units

Java strings are implemented as sequences of `char` values. As we discussed in Section 3.3.3, "The `char` Type," on p. 50, the `char` data type is a code unit for representing Unicode code points in the UTF-16 encoding. The most commonly used Unicode characters can be represented with a single code unit. The supplementary characters require a pair of code units.

The `length` method yields the number of code units required for a given string in the UTF-16 encoding. For example:

```
String greeting = "Hello";
int n = greeting.length(); // is 5.
```

To get the true length—that is, the number of code points—call

```
int cpCount = greeting.codePointCount(0, greeting.length());
```

The call `s.charAt(n)` returns the code unit at position `n`, where `n` is between `0` and `s.length()` - 1. For example:

```
char first = greeting.charAt(0); // first is 'H'
char last = greeting.charAt(4); // last is 'o'
```

To get at the `i`th code point, use the statements

```
int index = greeting.offsetByCodePoints(0, i);
int cp = greeting.codePointAt(index);
```

 NOTE: Like C and C++, Java counts code units and code points in strings starting with `0`.

Why are we making a fuss about code units? Consider the sentence

𝕆 is the set of octonions

The character 𝕆 (U+1D546) requires two code units in the UTF-16 encoding. Calling

```
char ch = sentence.charAt(1)
```

doesn't return a space but the second code unit of 𝕆. To avoid this problem, you should not use the `char` type. It is too low-level.

If your code traverses a string, and you want to look at each code point in turn, you can use these statements:

```
int cp = sentence.codePointAt(i);
if (Character.isSupplementaryCodePoint(cp)) i += 2;
else i++;
```

You can move backwards with the following statements:

```
i--;
if (Character.isSurrogate(sentence.charAt(i))) i--;
int cp = sentence.codePointAt(i);
```

Obviously, that is quite painful. An easier way is to use the `codePoints` method that yields a "stream" of `int` values, one for each code point. (We will discuss streams in Chapter 2 of Volume II.) You can just turn it into an array (see Section 3.10, "Arrays," on p. 111) and traverse that.

```
int[] codePoints = str.codePoints().toArray();
```

Conversely, to turn an array of code points to a string, use a *constructor*. (We discuss constructors and the `new` operator in detail in Chapter 4.)

```
String str = new String(codePoints, 0, codePoints.length);
```

3.6.7 The String API

The `String` class in Java contains more than 50 methods. A surprisingly large number of them are sufficiently useful so that we can imagine using them frequently. The following API note summarizes the ones we found most useful.

 NOTE: These API notes, found throughout the book, will help you understand the Java Application Programming Interface (API). Each API note starts with the name of a class, such as `java.lang.String` (the significance of the so-called *package* name `java.lang` is explained in Chapter 4). The class name is followed by the names, explanations, and parameter descriptions of one or more methods.

We typically do not list all methods of a particular class but select those that are most commonly used and describe them in a concise form. For a full listing, consult the online documentation (see Section 3.6.8, "Reading the Online API Documentation," on p. 74).

We also list the version number in which a particular class was introduced. If a method has been added later, it has a separate version number.

`java.lang.String` 1.0

- `char charAt(int index)`

  returns the code unit at the specified location. You probably don't want to call this method unless you are interested in low-level code units.

- `int codePointAt(int index)` 5.0

  returns the code point that starts at the specified location.

- `int offsetByCodePoints(int startIndex, int cpCount)` 5.0

  returns the index of the code point that is `cpCount` code points away from the code point at `startIndex`.

- `int compareTo(String other)`

  returns a negative value if the string comes before `other` in dictionary order, a positive value if the string comes after `other` in dictionary order, or 0 if the strings are equal.

- `IntStream codePoints()` 8

  returns the code points of this string as a stream. Call `toArray` to put them in an array.

- `new String(int[] codePoints, int offset, int count)` 5.0

  constructs a string with the `count` code points in the array starting at `offset`.

- `boolean equals(Object other)`

  returns `true` if the string equals `other`.

- `boolean equalsIgnoreCase(String other)`

  returns `true` if the string equals `other`, except for upper/lowercase distinction.

- `boolean startsWith(String prefix)`
- `boolean endsWith(String suffix)`

  returns `true` if the string starts or ends with `suffix`.

(Continues)

---

java.lang.String 1.0 *(Continued)*

- `int indexOf(String str)`
- `int indexOf(String str, int fromIndex)`
- `int indexOf(int cp)`
- `int indexOf(int cp, int fromIndex)`

returns the start of the first substring equal to the string `str` or the code point `cp`, starting at index 0 or at `fromIndex`, or -1 if `str` does not occur in this string.

- `int lastIndexOf(String str)`
- `int lastIndexOf(String str, int fromIndex)`
- `int lastindexOf(int cp)`
- `int lastindexOf(int cp, int fromIndex)`

returns the start of the last substring equal to the string `str` or the code point `cp`, starting at the end of the string or at `fromIndex`.

- `int length()`

returns the number of code units of the string.

- `int codePointCount(int startIndex, int endIndex)` 5.0

returns the number of code points between `startIndex` and `endIndex` - 1.

- `String replace(CharSequence oldString, CharSequence newString)`

returns a new string that is obtained by replacing all substrings matching `oldString` in the string with the string `newString`. You can supply `String` or `StringBuilder` objects for the `CharSequence` parameters.

- `String substring(int beginIndex)`
- `String substring(int beginIndex, int endIndex)`

returns a new string consisting of all code units from `beginIndex` until the end of the string or until `endIndex` - 1.

- `String toLowerCase()`

  `String toUpperCase()`

returns a new string containing all characters in the original string, with uppercase characters converted to lowercase, or lowercase characters converted to uppercase.

- `String trim()`

returns a new string by eliminating all leading and trailing whitespace in the original string.

- `String join(CharSequence delimiter, CharSequence... elements)` 8

Returns a new string joining all elements with the given delimiter.

NOTE: In the API notes, there are a few parameters of type `CharSequence`. This is an *interface* type to which all strings belong. You will learn about interface types in Chapter 6. For now, you just need to know that you can pass arguments of type `String` whenever you see a `CharSequence` parameter.

3.6.8 Reading the Online API Documentation

As you just saw, the `String` class has lots of methods. Furthermore, there are thousands of classes in the standard libraries, with many more methods. It is plainly impossible to remember all useful classes and methods. Therefore, it is essential that you become familiar with the online API documentation that lets you look up all classes and methods in the standard library. The API documentation is part of the JDK. It is in HTML format. Point your web browser to the `docs/api/index.html` subdirectory of your JDK installation (Figure 3.2).

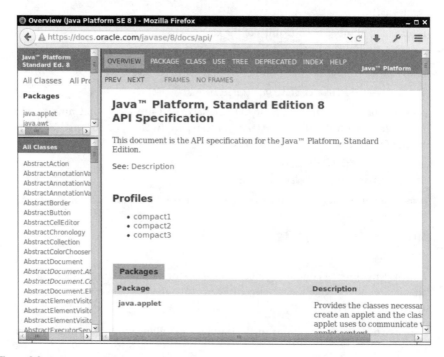

Figure 3.2 The three panes of the API documentation

The screen is organized into three frames. A small frame on the top left shows all available packages. Below it, a larger frame lists all classes. Click on a class name, and the API documentation for the class is displayed in the large frame to the right (see Figure 3.3). For example, to get more information on the methods of the String class, scroll the second frame until you see the String link, then click on it.

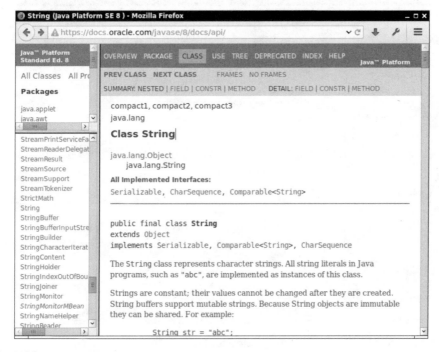

Figure 3.3 Class description for the String class

Then scroll the frame on the right until you reach a summary of all methods, sorted in alphabetical order (see Figure 3.4). Click on any method name for a detailed description of that method (see Figure 3.5). For example, if you click on the compareToIgnoreCase link, you'll get the description of the `compareToIgnoreCase` method.

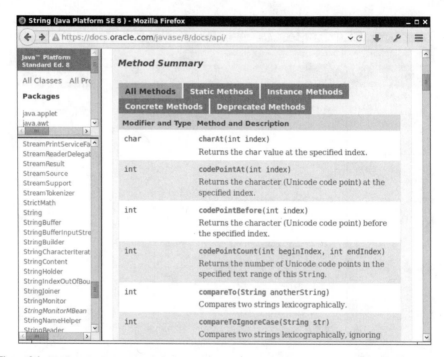

Figure 3.4 Method summary of the `String` class

 TIP: Bookmark the `docs/api/index.html` page in your browser right now.

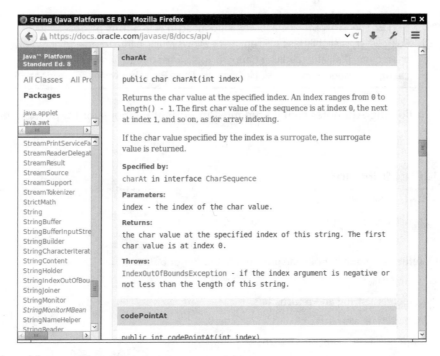

Figure 3.5 Detailed description of a `String` method

3.6.9 Building Strings

Occasionally, you need to build up strings from shorter strings, such as keystrokes or words from a file. It would be inefficient to use string concatenation for this purpose. Every time you concatenate strings, a new `String` object is constructed. This is time consuming and wastes memory. Using the `StringBuilder` class avoids this problem.

Follow these steps if you need to build a string from many small pieces. First, construct an empty string builder:

```
StringBuilder builder = new StringBuilder();
```

Each time you need to add another part, call the `append` method.

```
builder.append(ch); // appends a single character
builder.append(str); // appends a string
```

When you are done building the string, call the `toString` method. You will get a `String` object with the character sequence contained in the builder.

```
String completedString = builder.toString();
```

NOTE: The StringBuilder class was introduced in JDK 5.0. Its predecessor, StringBuffer, is slightly less efficient, but it allows multiple threads to add or remove characters. If all string editing happens in a single thread (which is usually the case), you should use StringBuilder instead. The APIs of both classes are identical.

The following API notes contain the most important methods for the StringBuilder class.

---

java.lang.StringBuilder 5.0

- StringBuilder()

  constructs an empty string builder.
- int length()

  returns the number of code units of the builder or buffer.
- StringBuilder append(String str)

  appends a string and returns this.
- StringBuilder append(char c)

  appends a code unit and returns this.
- StringBuilder appendCodePoint(int cp)

  appends a code point, converting it into one or two code units, and returns this.
- void setCharAt(int i, char c)

  sets the ith code unit to c.
- StringBuilder insert(int offset, String str)

  inserts a string at position offset and returns this.
- StringBuilder insert(int offset, char c)

  inserts a code unit at position offset and returns this.
- StringBuilder delete(int startIndex, int endIndex)

  deletes the code units with offsets startIndex to endIndex - 1 and returns this.
- String toString()

  returns a string with the same data as the builder or buffer contents.

3.7 Input and Output

To make our example programs more interesting, we want to accept input and properly format the program output. Of course, modern programs use a GUI for collecting user input. However, programming such an interface requires more tools and techniques than we have at our disposal at this time. Our first order of business is to become more familiar with the Java programming language, so we make do with the humble console for input and output for now. GUI programming is covered in Chapters 10 through 12.

3.7.1 Reading Input

You saw that it is easy to print output to the "standard output stream" (that is, the console window) just by calling System.out.println. Reading from the "standard input stream" System.in isn't quite as simple. To read console input, you first construct a Scanner that is attached to System.in:

```
Scanner in = new Scanner(System.in);
```

(We discuss constructors and the new operator in detail in Chapter 4.)

Now you can use the various methods of the Scanner class to read input. For example, the nextLine method reads a line of input.

```
System.out.print("What is your name? ");
String name = in.nextLine();
```

Here, we use the nextLine method because the input might contain spaces. To read a single word (delimited by whitespace), call

```
String firstName = in.next();
```

To read an integer, use the nextInt method.

```
System.out.print("How old are you? ");
int age = in.nextInt();
```

Similarly, the nextDouble method reads the next floating-point number.

The program in Listing 3.2 asks for the user's name and age and then prints a message like

```
Hello, Cay. Next year, you'll be 57
```

Finally, note the line

```
import java.util.*;
```

at the beginning of the program. The Scanner class is defined in the java.util package. Whenever you use a class that is not defined in the basic java.lang package, you need to use an import directive. We look at packages and import directives in more detail in Chapter 4.

Listing 3.2 InputTest/InputTest.java

```java
 1 import java.util.*;
 2
 3 /**
 4  * This program demonstrates console input.
 5  * @version 1.10 2004-02-10
 6  * @author Cay Horstmann
 7  */
 8 public class InputTest
 9 {
10    public static void main(String[] args)
11    {
12       Scanner in = new Scanner(System.in);
13
14       // get first input
15       System.out.print("What is your name? ");
16       String name = in.nextLine();
17
18       // get second input
19       System.out.print("How old are you? ");
20       int age = in.nextInt();
21
22       // display output on console
23       System.out.println("Hello, " + name + ". Next year, you'll be " + (age + 1));
24    }
25 }
```

 NOTE: The Scanner class is not suitable for reading a password from a console since the input is plainly visible to anyone. Java SE 6 introduces a Console class specifically for this purpose. To read a password, use the following code:

```java
Console cons = System.console();
String username = cons.readLine("User name: ");
char[] passwd = cons.readPassword("Password: ");
```

For security reasons, the password is returned in an array of characters rather than a string. After you are done processing the password, you should immediately overwrite the array elements with a filler value. (Array processing is discussed in Section 3.10, "Arrays," on p. 111.)

Input processing with a Console object is not as convenient as with a Scanner. You must read the input a line at a time. There are no methods for reading individual words or numbers.

---

java.util.Scanner 5.0

- Scanner(InputStream in)

  constructs a Scanner object from the given input stream.
- String nextLine()

  reads the next line of input.
- String next()

  reads the next word of input (delimited by whitespace).
- int nextInt()
- double nextDouble()

  reads and converts the next character sequence that represents an integer or floating-point number.
- boolean hasNext()

  tests whether there is another word in the input.
- boolean hasNextInt()
- boolean hasNextDouble()

  tests whether the next character sequence represents an integer or floating-point number.

---

java.lang.System 1.0

- static Console console() 6

  returns a Console object for interacting with the user through a console window if such an interaction is possible, null otherwise. A Console object is available for any program that is launched in a console window. Otherwise, the availability is system dependent.

---

java.io.Console 6

- static char[] readPassword(String prompt, Object... args)
- static String readLine(String prompt, Object... args)

  displays the prompt and reads the user input until the end of the input line. The args parameters can be used to supply formatting arguments, as described in the next section.

3.7.2 Formatting Output

You can print a number x to the console with the statement `System.out.print(x)`. That command will print x with the maximum number of nonzero digits for that type. For example,

```
double x = 10000.0 / 3.0;
System.out.print(x);
```

prints

```
3333.3333333333335
```

That is a problem if you want to display, for example, dollars and cents.

In early versions of Java, formatting numbers was a bit of a hassle. Fortunately, Java SE 5.0 brought back the venerable `printf` method from the C library. For example, the call

```
System.out.printf("%8.2f", x);
```

prints x with a *field width* of 8 characters and a *precision* of 2 characters. That is, the printout contains a leading space and the seven characters

```
3333.33
```

You can supply multiple parameters to `printf`. For example:

```
System.out.printf("Hello, %s. Next year, you'll be %d", name, age);
```

Each of the *format specifiers* that start with a % character is replaced with the corresponding argument. The *conversion character* that ends a format specifier indicates the type of the value to be formatted: f is a floating-point number, s a string, and d a decimal integer. Table 3.5 shows all conversion characters.

Table 3.5 Conversions for `printf`

Conversion Character	Type	Example
d	Decimal integer	159
x	Hexadecimal integer	9f
o	Octal integer	237
f	Fixed-point floating-point	15.9

(Continues)

Table 3.5 *(Continued)*

Conversion Character	Type	Example
e	Exponential floating-point	1.59e+01
g	General floating-point (the shorter of e and f)	—
a	Hexadecimal floating-point	0x1.fccdp3
s	String	Hello
c	Character	H
b	boolean	true
h	Hash code	42628b2
t*x* or T*x*	Date and time (T forces uppercase)	Obsolete, use the java.time classes instead—see Chapter 6 of Volume II
%	The percent symbol	%
n	The platform-dependent line separator	—

In addition, you can specify *flags* that control the appearance of the formatted output. Table 3.6 shows all flags. For example, the comma flag adds group separators. That is,

```
System.out.printf("%,.2f", 10000.0 / 3.0);
```

prints

```
3,333.33
```

You can use multiple flags, for example "%,(.2f" to use group separators and enclose negative numbers in parentheses.

 NOTE: You can use the s conversion to format arbitrary objects. If an arbitrary object implements the Formattable interface, the object's formatTo method is invoked. Otherwise, the toString method is invoked to turn the object into a string. We discuss the toString method in Chapter 5 and interfaces in Chapter 6.

You can use the static String.format method to create a formatted string without printing it:

```
String message = String.format("Hello, %s. Next year, you'll be %d", name, age);
```

Table 3.6 Flags for `printf`

Flag	Purpose	Example
+	Prints sign for positive and negative numbers.	+3333.33
space	Adds a space before positive numbers.	| 3333.33|
0	Adds leading zeroes.	003333.33
-	Left-justifies field.	|3333.33 |
(	Encloses negative numbers in parentheses.	(3333.33)
,	Adds group separators.	3,333.33
# (for f format)	Always includes a decimal point.	3,333.
# (for x or o format)	Adds 0x or 0 prefix.	0xcafe
$	Specifies the index of the argument to be formatted; for example, `%1$d %1$x` prints the first argument in decimal and hexadecimal.	159 9F
<	Formats the same value as the previous specification; for example, `%d %<x` prints the same number in decimal and hexadecimal.	159 9F

In the interest of completeness, we briefly discuss the date and time formatting options of the `printf` method. For new code, you should use the methods of the `java.time` package described in Chapter 6 of Volume II. But you may encounter the `Date` class and the associated formatting options in legacy code. The format consists of two letters, starting with `t` and ending in one of the letters of Table 3.7; for example,

```
System.out.printf("%tc", new Date());
```

prints the current date and time in the format

```
Mon Feb 09 18:05:19 PST 2015
```

As you can see in Table 3.7, some of the formats yield only a part of a given date—for example, just the day or just the month. It would be a bit silly if you had to supply the date multiple times to format each part. For that reason, a format string can indicate the *index* of the argument to be formatted. The index must immediately follow the %, and it must be terminated by a $. For example,

```
System.out.printf("%1$s %2$tB %2$te, %2$tY", "Due date:", new Date());
```

prints

```
Due date: February 9, 2015
```

Alternatively, you can use the < flag. It indicates that the same argument as in the preceding format specification should be used again. That is, the statement

```
System.out.printf("%s %tB %<te, %<tY", "Due date:", new Date());
```

yields the same output as the preceding statement.

Table 3.7 Date and Time Conversion Characters

Conversion Character	Type	Example
c	Complete date and time	Mon Feb 09 18:05:19 PST 2015
F	ISO 8601 date	2015-02-09
D	U.S. formatted date (month/day/year)	02/09/2015
T	24-hour time	18:05:19
r	12-hour time	06:05:19 pm
R	24-hour time, no seconds	18:05
Y	Four-digit year (with leading zeroes)	2015
y	Last two digits of the year (with leading zeroes)	15
C	First two digits of the year (with leading zeroes)	20
B	Full month name	February
b or h	Abbreviated month name	Feb
m	Two-digit month (with leading zeroes)	02
d	Two-digit day (with leading zeroes)	09
e	Two-digit day (without leading zeroes)	9
A	Full weekday name	Monday
a	Abbreviated weekday name	Mon
j	Three-digit day of year (with leading zeroes), between 001 and 366	069
H	Two-digit hour (with leading zeroes), between 00 and 23	18

(Continues)

Table 3.7 *(Continued)*

Conversion Character	Type	Example
k	Two-digit hour (without leading zeroes), between 0 and 23	18
I	Two-digit hour (with leading zeroes), between 01 and 12	06
l	Two-digit hour (without leading zeroes), between 1 and 12	6
M	Two-digit minutes (with leading zeroes)	05
S	Two-digit seconds (with leading zeroes)	19
L	Three-digit milliseconds (with leading zeroes)	047
N	Nine-digit nanoseconds (with leading zeroes)	047000000
p	Morning or afternoon marker	pm
z	RFC 822 numeric offset from GMT	-0800
Z	Time zone	PST
s	Seconds since 1970–01–01 00:00:00 GMT	1078884319
Q	Milliseconds since 1970–01–01 00:00:00 GMT	1078884319047

 CAUTION: Argument index values start with 1, not with 0: %1$... formats the first argument. This avoids confusion with the 0 flag.

You have now seen all features of the printf method. Figure 3.6 shows a syntax diagram for format specifiers.

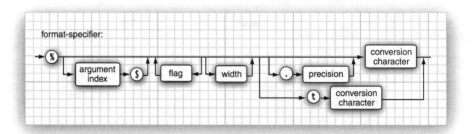

Figure 3.6 Format specifier syntax

NOTE: The formatting of numbers and dates is *locale specific*. For example, in Germany, the group separator is a period, not a comma, and Monday is formatted as Montag. Chapter 7 of Volume II shows how to control the international behavior of your applications.

3.7.3 File Input and Output

To read from a file, construct a `Scanner` object like this:

```
Scanner in = new Scanner(Paths.get("myfile.txt"), "UTF-8");
```

If the file name contains backslashes, remember to escape each of them with an additional backslash: `"c:\\mydirectory\\myfile.txt"`.

 NOTE: Here, we specify the UTF-8 character encoding, which is common (but not universal) for files on the Internet. You need to know the character encoding when you read a text file—see Volume II, Chapter 2 for more information. If you omit the character encoding, then the "default encoding" of the computer running the Java program is used. That is not a good idea—the program might act differently depending on where it is run.

Now you can read from the file, using any of the `Scanner` methods that we already described.

To write to a file, construct a `PrintWriter` object. In the constructor, supply the file name and the character encoding:

```
PrintWriter out = new PrintWriter("myfile.txt", "UTF-8");
```

If the file does not exist, it is created. You can use the `print`, `println`, and `printf` commands as you did when printing to `System.out`.

 CAUTION: You can construct a `Scanner` with a string parameter, but the scanner interprets the string as data, not a file name. For example, if you call

```
Scanner in = new Scanner("myfile.txt"); // ERROR?
```

then the scanner will see ten characters of data: `'m'`, `'y'`, `'f'`, and so on. That is probably not what was intended in this case.

NOTE: When you specify a relative file name, such as `"myfile.txt"`, `"mydirectory/myfile.txt"`, or `"../myfile.txt"`, the file is located relative to the directory in which the Java virtual machine was started. If you launched your program from a command shell, by executing

```
java MyProg
```

then the starting directory is the current directory of the command shell. However, if you use an integrated development environment, it controls the starting directory. You can find the directory location with this call:

```
String dir = System.getProperty("user.dir");
```

If you run into grief with locating files, consider using absolute path names such as `"c:\\mydirectory\\myfile.txt"` or `"/home/me/mydirectory/myfile.txt"`.

As you just saw, you can access files just as easily as you can use `System.in` and `System.out`. There is just one catch: If you construct a `Scanner` with a file that does not exist or a `PrintWriter` with a file name that cannot be created, an exception occurs. The Java compiler considers these exceptions to be more serious than a "divide by zero" exception, for example. In Chapter 7, you will learn various ways of handling exceptions. For now, you should simply tell the compiler that you are aware of the possibility of an "input/output" exception. You do this by tagging the `main` method with a `throws` clause, like this:

```
public static void main(String[] args) throws IOException
{
   Scanner in = new Scanner(Paths.get("myfile.txt"), "UTF-8");
   . . .
}
```

You have now seen how to read and write files that contain textual data. For more advanced topics, such as dealing with different character encodings, processing binary data, reading directories, and writing zip files, turn to Chapter 2 of Volume II.

NOTE: When you launch a program from a command shell, you can use the redirection syntax of your shell and attach any file to `System.in` and `System.out`:

```
java MyProg < myfile.txt > output.txt
```

Then, you need not worry about handling the `IOException`.

---

java.util.Scanner 5.0

- `Scanner(Path p, String encoding)`

  constructs a `Scanner` that reads data from the given path, using the given character encoding.

- `Scanner(String data)`

  constructs a `Scanner` that reads data from the given string.

---

java.io.PrintWriter 1.1

- `PrintWriter(String fileName)`

  constructs a `PrintWriter` that writes data to the file with the given file name.

---

java.nio.file.Paths 7

- `static Path get(String pathname)`

  constructs a `Path` from the given path name.

3.8 Control Flow

Java, like any programming language, supports both conditional statements and loops to determine control flow. We will start with the conditional statements, then move on to loops, to end with the somewhat cumbersome `switch` statement that you can use to test for many values of a single expression.

C++ NOTE: The Java control flow constructs are identical to those in C and C++, with a few exceptions. There is no `goto`, but there is a "labeled" version of `break` that you can use to break out of a nested loop (where, in C, you perhaps would have used a `goto`). Finally, there is a variant of the `for` loop that has no analog in C or C++. It is similar to the `foreach` loop in C#.

3.8.1 Block Scope

Before learning about control structures, you need to know more about *blocks*.

A block or compound statement consists of a number of Java statements, surrounded by a pair of braces. Blocks define the scope of your variables. A block can be *nested* inside another block. Here is a block that is nested inside the block of the main method:

```java
public static void main(String[] args)
{
   int n;
   . . .
   {
      int k;
      . . .
   } // k is only defined up to here
}
```

You may not declare identically named variables in two nested blocks. For example, the following is an error and will not compile:

```java
public static void main(String[] args)
{
   int n;
   . . .
   {
      int k;
      int n; // Error--can't redefine n in inner block
      . . .
   }
}
```

 C++ NOTE: In C++, it is possible to redefine a variable inside a nested block. The inner definition then shadows the outer one. This can be a source of programming errors; hence, Java does not allow it.

3.8.2 Conditional Statements

The conditional statement in Java has the form

    if (*condition*) *statement*

The condition must be surrounded by parentheses.

In Java, as in most programming languages, you will often want to execute multiple statements when a single condition is true. In this case, use a *block statement* that takes the form

```
{
   statement₁
   statement₂
   . . .
}
```

For example:

```
if (yourSales >= target)
{
   performance = "Satisfactory";
   bonus = 100;
}
```

In this code all the statements surrounded by the braces will be executed when yourSales is greater than or equal to target (see Figure 3.7).

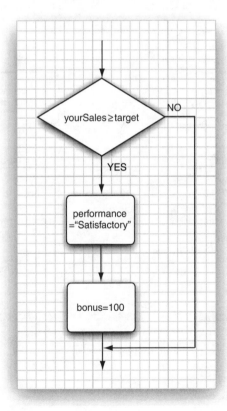

Figure 3.7 Flowchart for the if statement

NOTE: A block (sometimes called a *compound statement*) enables you to have more than one (simple) statement in any Java programming structure that otherwise allows for a single (simple) statement.

The more general conditional in Java looks like this (see Figure 3.8):

if *(condition)* *statement₁* else *statement₂*

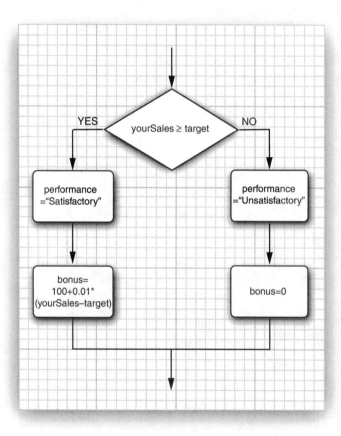

Figure 3.8 Flowchart for the if/else statement

For example:

```
if (yourSales >= target)
{
   performance = "Satisfactory";
   bonus = 100 + 0.01 * (yourSales - target);
}
else
{
   performance = "Unsatisfactory";
   bonus = 0;
}
```

The else part is always optional. An else groups with the closest if. Thus, in the statement

```
if (x <= 0) if (x == 0) sign = 0; else sign = -1;
```

the else belongs to the second if. Of course, it is a good idea to use braces to clarify this code:

```
if (x <= 0) { if (x == 0) sign = 0; else sign = -1; }
```

Repeated if . . . else if . . . alternatives are common (see Figure 3.9). For example:

```
if (yourSales >= 2 * target)
{
   performance = "Excellent";
   bonus = 1000;
}
else if (yourSales >= 1.5 * target)
{
   performance = "Fine";
   bonus = 500;
}
else if (yourSales >= target)
{
   performance = "Satisfactory";
   bonus = 100;
}
else
{
   System.out.println("You're fired");
}
```

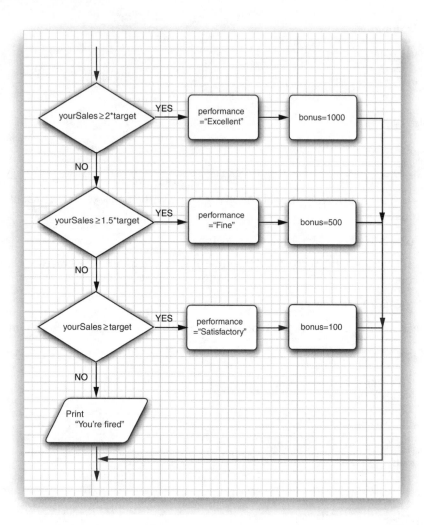

Figure 3.9 Flowchart for the if/else if (multiple branches)

3.8.3 Loops

The while loop executes a statement (which may be a block statement) while a condition is true. The general form is

    while (condition) statement

The while loop will never execute if the condition is false at the outset (see Figure 3.10).

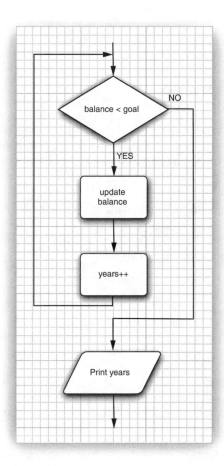

Figure 3.10 Flowchart for the while statement

The program in Listing 3.3 determines how long it will take to save a specific amount of money for your well-earned retirement, assuming you deposit the same amount of money per year and the money earns a specified interest rate.

In the example, we are incrementing a counter and updating the amount currently accumulated in the body of the loop until the total exceeds the targeted amount.

```
while (balance < goal)
{
   balance += payment;
   double interest = balance * interestRate / 100;
   balance += interest;
   years++;
}
System.out.println(years + " years.");
```

(Don't rely on this program to plan for your retirement. We left out a few niceties such as inflation and your life expectancy.)

A while loop tests at the top. Therefore, the code in the block might never be executed. If you want to make sure a block is executed at least once, you need to move the test to the bottom, using the do/while loop. Its syntax looks like this:

```
do statement while (condition);
```

This loop executes the statement (which is typically a block) and only then tests the condition. If it's true, it repeats the statement and retests the condition, and so on. The code in Listing 3.4 computes the new balance in your retirement account and then asks if you are ready to retire:

```
do
{
   balance += payment;
   double interest = balance * interestRate / 100;
   balance += interest;
   year++;
   // print current balance
   . . .
   // ask if ready to retire and get input
   . . .
}
while (input.equals("N"));
```

As long as the user answers "N", the loop is repeated (see Figure 3.11). This program is a good example of a loop that needs to be entered at least once, because the user needs to see the balance before deciding whether it is sufficient for retirement.

Listing 3.3 Retirement/Retirement.java

```java
1  import java.util.*;
2
3  /**
4   * This program demonstrates a <code>while</code> loop.
5   * @version 1.20 2004-02-10
6   * @author Cay Horstmann
7   */
8  public class Retirement
9  {
10     public static void main(String[] args)
11     {
12        // read inputs
13        Scanner in = new Scanner(System.in);
14
15        System.out.print("How much money do you need to retire? ");
16        double goal = in.nextDouble();
17
18        System.out.print("How much money will you contribute every year? ");
19        double payment = in.nextDouble();
20
21        System.out.print("Interest rate in %: ");
22        double interestRate = in.nextDouble();
23
24        double balance = 0;
25        int years = 0;
26
27        // update account balance while goal isn't reached
28        while (balance < goal)
29        {
30           // add this year's payment and interest
31           balance += payment;
32           double interest = balance * interestRate / 100;
33           balance += interest;
34           years++;
35        }
36
37        System.out.println("You can retire in " + years + " years.");
38     }
39  }
```

Listing 3.4 Retirement2/Retirement2.java

```java
1  import java.util.*;
2
3  /**
4   * This program demonstrates a <code>do/while</code> loop.
5   * @version 1.20 2004-02-10
6   * @author Cay Horstmann
7   */
8  public class Retirement2
9  {
10     public static void main(String[] args)
11     {
12        Scanner in = new Scanner(System.in);
13
14        System.out.print("How much money will you contribute every year? ");
15        double payment = in.nextDouble();
16
17        System.out.print("Interest rate in %: ");
18        double interestRate = in.nextDouble();
19
20        double balance = 0;
21        int year = 0;
22
23        String input;
24
25        // update account balance while user isn't ready to retire
26        do
27        {
28           // add this year's payment and interest
29           balance += payment;
30           double interest = balance * interestRate / 100;
31           balance += interest;
32
33           year++;
34
35           // print current balance
36           System.out.printf("After year %d, your balance is %,.2f%n", year, balance);
37
38           // ask if ready to retire and get input
39           System.out.print("Ready to retire? (Y/N) ");
40           input = in.next();
41        }
42        while (input.equals("N"));
43     }
44  }
```

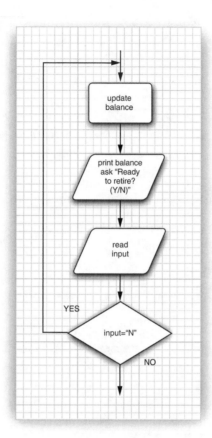

Figure 3.11 Flowchart for the `do/while` statement

3.8.4 Determinate Loops

The `for` loop is a general construct to support iteration controlled by a counter or similar variable that is updated after every iteration. As Figure 3.12 shows, the following loop prints the numbers from 1 to 10 on the screen.

```
for (int i = 1; i <= 10; i++)
   System.out.println(i);
```

The first slot of the `for` statement usually holds the counter initialization. The second slot gives the condition that will be tested before each new pass through the loop, and the third slot specifies how to update the counter.

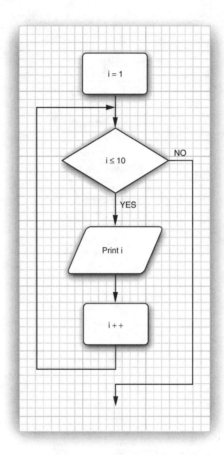

Figure 3.12 Flowchart for the `for` statement

Although Java, like C++, allows almost any expression in the various slots of a `for` loop, it is an unwritten rule of good taste that the three slots should only initialize, test, and update the same counter variable. One can write very obscure loops by disregarding this rule.

Even within the bounds of good taste, much is possible. For example, you can have loops that count down:

```
for (int i = 10; i > 0; i--)
   System.out.println("Counting down . . . " + i);
System.out.println("Blastoff!");
```

CAUTION: Be careful about testing for equality of floating-point numbers in loops. A for loop like this one

```
for (double x = 0; x != 10; x += 0.1) . . .
```

might never end. Because of roundoff errors, the final value might not be reached exactly. In this example, x jumps from `9.99999999999998` to `10.09999999999998` because there is no exact binary representation for 0.1.

When you declare a variable in the first slot of the for statement, the scope of that variable extends until the end of the body of the for loop.

```
for (int i = 1; i <= 10; i++)
{
    . . .
}
// i no longer defined here
```

In particular, if you define a variable inside a for statement, you cannot use its value outside the loop. Therefore, if you wish to use the final value of a loop counter outside the for loop, be sure to declare it outside the loop header.

```
int i;
for (i = 1; i <= 10; i++)
{
    . . .
}
// i is still defined here
```

On the other hand, you can define variables with the same name in separate for loops:

```
for (int i = 1; i <= 10; i++)
{
    . . .
}
. . .
for (int i = 11; i <= 20; i++) // OK to define another variable named i
{
    . . .
}
```

A for loop is merely a convenient shortcut for a while loop. For example,

```
for (int i = 10; i > 0; i--)
    System.out.println("Counting down . . . " + i);
```

can be rewritten as

```
int i = 10;
while (i > 0)
{
   System.out.println("Counting down . . . " + i);
   i--;
}
```

Listing 3.5 shows a typical example of a for loop.

The program computes the odds of winning a lottery. For example, if you must pick six numbers from the numbers 1 to 50 to win, then there are (50 × 49 × 48 × 47 × 46 × 45)/(1 × 2 × 3 × 4 × 5 × 6) possible outcomes, so your chance is 1 in 15,890,700. Good luck!

In general, if you pick k numbers out of n, there are

$$\frac{n \times (n-1) \times (n-2) \times \cdots \times (n-k+1)}{1 \times 2 \times 3 \times 4 \times \cdots \times k}$$

possible outcomes. The following for loop computes this value:

```
int lotteryOdds = 1;
for (int i = 1; i <= k; i++)
   lotteryOdds = lotteryOdds * (n - i + 1) / i;
```

 NOTE: See Section 3.10.1, "The 'for each' Loop," on p. 113 for a description of the "generalized for loop" (also called "for each" loop) that was added to the Java language in Java SE 5.0.

Listing 3.5 LotteryOdds/LotteryOdds.java

```
 1  import java.util.*;
 2
 3  /**
 4   * This program demonstrates a <code>for</code> loop.
 5   * @version 1.20 2004-02-10
 6   * @author Cay Horstmann
 7   */
 8  public class LotteryOdds
 9  {
10     public static void main(String[] args)
11     {
12        Scanner in = new Scanner(System.in);
13
14        System.out.print("How many numbers do you need to draw? ");
15        int k = in.nextInt();
16
```

```
17      System.out.print("What is the highest number you can draw? ");
18      int n = in.nextInt();
19
20      /*
21       * compute binomial coefficient n*(n-1)*(n-2)*...*(n-k+1)/(1*2*3*...*k)
22       */
23
24      int lotteryOdds = 1;
25      for (int i = 1; i <= k; i++)
26         lotteryOdds = lotteryOdds * (n - i + 1) / i;
27
28      System.out.println("Your odds are 1 in " + lotteryOdds + ". Good luck!");
29   }
30 }
```

3.8.5 Multiple Selections—The switch Statement

The if/else construct can be cumbersome when you have to deal with multiple selections with many alternatives. Java has a switch statement that is exactly like the switch statement in C and C++, warts and all.

For example, if you set up a menu system with four alternatives like that in Figure 3.13, you could use code that looks like this:

```
Scanner in = new Scanner(System.in);
System.out.print("Select an option (1, 2, 3, 4) ");
int choice = in.nextInt();
switch (choice)
{
   case 1:
      . . .
      break;
   case 2:
      . . .
      break;
   case 3:
      . . .
      break;
   case 4:
      . . .
      break;
   default:
      // bad input
      . . .
      break;
}
```

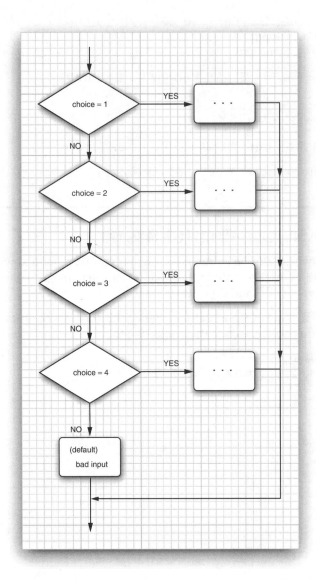

Figure 3.13 Flowchart for the `switch` statement

Execution starts at the `case` label that matches the value on which the selection is performed and continues until the next `break` or the end of the switch. If none of the case labels match, then the `default` clause is executed, if it is present.

CAUTION: It is possible for multiple alternatives to be triggered. If you forget to add a break at the end of an alternative, execution falls through to the next alternative! This behavior is plainly dangerous and a common cause for errors. For that reason, we never use the switch statement in our programs.

If you like the switch statement better than we do, consider compiling your code with the -Xlint:fallthrough option, like this:

```
javac -Xlint:fallthrough Test.java
```

Then the compiler will issue a warning whenever an alternative does not end with a break statement.

If you actually want to use the fallthrough behavior, tag the surrounding method with the annotation @SuppressWarnings("fallthrough"). Then no warnings will be generated for that method. (An annotation is a mechanism for supplying information to the compiler or a tool that processes Java source or class files. We discuss annotations in detail in Chapter 8 of Volume II.)

A case label can be

- A constant expression of type char, byte, short, or int
- An enumerated constant
- Starting with Java SE 7, a string literal

For example,

```
String input = . . .;
switch (input.toLowerCase())
{
   case "yes": // OK since Java SE 7
      . . .
      break;
   . . .
}
```

When you use the switch statement with enumerated constants, you need not supply the name of the enumeration in each label—it is deduced from the switch value. For example:

```
Size sz = . . .;
switch (sz)
{
   case SMALL: // no need to use Size.SMALL
      . . .
      break;
   . . .
}
```

3.8.6 Statements That Break Control Flow

Although the designers of Java kept goto as a reserved word, they decided not to include it in the language. In general, goto statements are considered poor style. Some programmers feel the anti-goto forces have gone too far (see, for example, the famous article of Donald Knuth called "Structured Programming with goto statements"). They argue that unrestricted use of goto is error-prone but that an occasional jump *out of a loop* is beneficial. The Java designers agreed and even added a new statement, the labeled break, to support this programming style.

Let us first look at the unlabeled break statement. The same break statement that you use to exit a switch can also be used to break out of a loop. For example:

```
while (years <= 100)
{
   balance += payment;
   double interest = balance * interestRate / 100;
   balance += interest;
   if (balance >= goal) break;
   years++;
}
```

Now the loop is exited if either years > 100 occurs at the top of the loop or balance >= goal occurs in the middle of the loop. Of course, you could have computed the same value for years without a break, like this:

```
while (years <= 100 && balance < goal)
{
   balance += payment;
   double interest = balance * interestRate / 100;
   balance += interest;
   if (balance < goal)
      years++;
}
```

But note that the test balance < goal is repeated twice in this version. To avoid this repeated test, some programmers prefer the break statement.

Unlike C++, Java also offers a *labeled break* statement that lets you break out of multiple nested loops. Occasionally something weird happens inside a deeply nested loop. In that case, you may want to break completely out of all the nested loops. It is inconvenient to program that simply by adding extra conditions to the various loop tests.

Here's an example that shows the break statement at work. Notice that the label must precede the outermost loop out of which you want to break. It also must be followed by a colon.

```
Scanner in = new Scanner(System.in);
int n;
read_data:
while (. . .) // this loop statement is tagged with the label
{
   . . .
   for (. . .) // this inner loop is not labeled
   {
      System.out.print("Enter a number >= 0: ");
      n = in.nextInt();
      if (n < 0) // should never happen-can't go on
         break read_data;
         // break out of read_data loop
      . . .
   }
}
// this statement is executed immediately after the labeled break
if (n < 0) // check for bad situation
{
   // deal with bad situation
}
else
{
   // carry out normal processing
}
```

If there is a bad input, the labeled break moves past the end of the labeled block. As with any use of the break statement, you then need to test whether the loop exited normally or as a result of a break.

 NOTE: Curiously, you can apply a label to any statement, even an if statement or a block statement, like this:

```
label:
   {
      . . .
      if (condition) break label; // exits block
      . . .
   }
   // jumps here when the break statement executes
```

Thus, if you are lusting after a goto and if you can place a block that ends just before the place to which you want to jump, you can use a break statement! Naturally, we don't recommend this approach. Note, however, that you can only jump *out of* a block, never *into* a block.

Finally, there is a continue statement that, like the break statement, breaks the regular flow of control. The continue statement transfers control to the header of the innermost enclosing loop. Here is an example:

```
Scanner in = new Scanner(System.in);
while (sum < goal)
{
   System.out.print("Enter a number: ");
   n = in.nextInt();
   if (n < 0) continue;
   sum += n; // not executed if n < 0
}
```

If n < 0, then the continue statement jumps immediately to the loop header, skipping the remainder of the current iteration.

If the continue statement is used in a for loop, it jumps to the "update" part of the for loop. For example:

```
for (count = 1; count <= 100; count++)
{
   System.out.print("Enter a number, -1 to quit: ");
   n = in.nextInt();
   if (n < 0) continue;
   sum += n; // not executed if n < 0
}
```

If n < 0, then the continue statement jumps to the count++ statement.

There is also a labeled form of the continue statement that jumps to the header of the loop with the matching label.

 TIP: Many programmers find the break and continue statements confusing. These statements are entirely optional—you can always express the same logic without them. In this book, we never use break or continue.

3.9 Big Numbers

If the precision of the basic integer and floating-point types is not sufficient, you can turn to a couple of handy classes in the java.math package: BigInteger and BigDecimal. These are classes for manipulating numbers with an arbitrarily long sequence of digits. The BigInteger class implements arbitrary-precision integer arithmetic, and BigDecimal does the same for floating-point numbers.

Use the static valueOf method to turn an ordinary number into a big number:

```
BigInteger a = BigInteger.valueOf(100);
```

Unfortunately, you cannot use the familiar mathematical operators such as + and * to combine big numbers. Instead, you must use methods such as add and multiply in the big number classes.

```
BigInteger c = a.add(b); // c = a + b
BigInteger d = c.multiply(b.add(BigInteger.valueOf(2))); // d = c * (b + 2)
```

 C++ NOTE: Unlike C++, Java has no programmable operator overloading. There was no way for the programmers of the BigInteger class to redefine the + and * operators to give the add and multiply operations of the BigInteger classes. The language designers did overload the + operator to denote concatenation of strings. They chose not to overload other operators, and they did not give Java programmers the opportunity to overload operators in their own classes.

Listing 3.6 shows a modification of the lottery odds program of Listing 3.5, updated to work with big numbers. For example, if you are invited to participate in a lottery in which you need to pick 60 numbers out of a possible 490 numbers, you can use this program to tell you your odds of winning. They are 1 in 716395843461995557415116222540092933411717612789263493493351013459481104668848. Good luck!

The program in Listing 3.5 computed the statement

```
lotteryOdds = lotteryOdds * (n - i + 1) / i;
```

When big numbers are used, the equivalent statement becomes

```
lotteryOdds = lotteryOdds.multiply(BigInteger.valueOf(n - i + 1)).divide(BigInteger.valueOf(i));
```

Listing 3.6 BigIntegerTest/BigIntegerTest.java

```
1  import java.math.*;
2  import java.util.*;
3
4  /**
5   * This program uses big numbers to compute the odds of winning the grand prize in a lottery.
6   * @version 1.20 2004-02-10
7   * @author Cay Horstmann
8   */
9  public class BigIntegerTest
10 {
11    public static void main(String[] args)
12    {
13       Scanner in = new Scanner(System.in);
14
```

(Continues)

Listing 3.6 *(Continued)*

```
15        System.out.print("How many numbers do you need to draw? ");
16        int k = in.nextInt();
17
18        System.out.print("What is the highest number you can draw? ");
19        int n = in.nextInt();
20
21        /*
22         * compute binomial coefficient n*(n-1)*(n-2)*...*(n-k+1)/(1*2*3*...*k)
23         */
24
25        BigInteger lotteryOdds = BigInteger.valueOf(1);
26
27        for (int i = 1; i <= k; i++)
28           lotteryOdds = lotteryOdds.multiply(BigInteger.valueOf(n - i + 1)).divide(
29                 BigInteger.valueOf(i));
30
31        System.out.println("Your odds are 1 in " + lotteryOdds + ". Good luck!");
32     }
33  }
```

---

java.math.BigInteger 1.1

- BigInteger add(BigInteger other)
- BigInteger subtract(BigInteger other)
- BigInteger multiply(BigInteger other)
- BigInteger divide(BigInteger other)
- BigInteger mod(BigInteger other)

  returns the sum, difference, product, quotient, and remainder of this big integer and other.

- int compareTo(BigInteger other)

  returns 0 if this big integer equals other, a negative result if this big integer is less than other, and a positive result otherwise.

- static BigInteger valueOf(long x)

  returns a big integer whose value equals x.

---

java.math.BigDecimal 1.1

- BigDecimal add(BigDecimal other)
- BigDecimal subtract(BigDecimal other)
- BigDecimal multiply(BigDecimal other)
- BigDecimal divide(BigDecimal other, RoundingMode mode) 5.0

  returns the sum, difference, product, or quotient of this big decimal and other. To compute the quotient, you must supply a *rounding mode*. The mode RoundingMode.HALF_UP is the rounding mode that you learned in school: round down the digits 0 to 4, round up the digits 5 to 9. It is appropriate for routine calculations. See the API documentation for other rounding modes.

- int compareTo(BigDecimal other)

  returns 0 if this big decimal equals other, a negative result if this big decimal is less than other, and a positive result otherwise.

- static BigDecimal valueOf(long x)
- static BigDecimal valueOf(long x, int scale)

  returns a big decimal whose value equals x or $x / 10^{scale}$.

3.10 Arrays

An array is a data structure that stores a collection of values of the same type. You access each individual value through an integer *index*. For example, if a is an array of integers, then a[i] is the ith integer in the array.

Declare an array variable by specifying the array type—which is the element type followed by []—and the array variable name. For example, here is the declaration of an array a of integers:

```
int[] a;
```

However, this statement only declares the variable a. It does not yet initialize a with an actual array. Use the new operator to create the array.

```
int[] a = new int[100];
```

This statement declares and initializes an array of 100 integers.

The array length need not be a constant: new int[n] creates an array of length n.

NOTE: You can define an array variable either as

```
int[] a;
```

or as

```
int a[];
```

Most Java programmers prefer the former style because it neatly separates the type int[] (integer array) from the variable name.

The array elements are *numbered from 0 to 99* (and not 1 to 100). Once the array is created, you can fill the elements in an array, for example, by using a loop:

```
int[] a = new int[100];
for (int i = 0; i < 100; i++)
   a[i] = i; // fills the array with numbers 0 to 99
```

When you create an array of numbers, all elements are initialized with zero. Arrays of boolean are initialized with false. Arrays of objects are initialized with the special value null, which indicates that they do not (yet) hold any objects. This can be surprising for beginners. For example,

```
String[] names = new String[10];
```

creates an array of ten strings, all of which are null. If you want the array to hold empty strings, you must supply them:

```
for (int i = 0; i < 10; i++) names[i] = "";
```

CAUTION: If you construct an array with 100 elements and then try to access the element a[100] (or any other index outside the range from 0 to 99), your program will terminate with an "array index out of bounds" exception.

To find the number of elements of an array, use *array*.length. For example:

```
for (int i = 0; i < a.length; i++)
   System.out.println(a[i]);
```

Once you create an array, you cannot change its size (although you can, of course, change an individual array element). If you frequently need to expand the size of an array while your program is running, you should use a different data structure called an *array list*. (See Chapter 5 for more on array lists.)

3.10.1 The "for each" Loop

Java has a powerful looping construct that allows you to loop through each element in an array (or any other collection of elements) without having to fuss with index values.

The *enhanced* for loop

```
for (variable : collection) statement
```

sets the given variable to each element of the collection and then executes the statement (which, of course, may be a block). The *collection* expression must be an array or an object of a class that implements the Iterable interface, such as ArrayList. We discuss array lists in Chapter 5 and the Iterable interface in Chapter 9.

For example,

```
for (int element : a)
    System.out.println(element);
```

prints each element of the array a on a separate line.

You should read this loop as "for each element in a". The designers of the Java language considered using keywords, such as foreach and in. But this loop was a late addition to the Java language, and in the end nobody wanted to break the old code that already contained methods or variables with these names (such as System.in).

Of course, you could achieve the same effect with a traditional for loop:

```
for (int i = 0; i < a.length; i++)
    System.out.println(a[i]);
```

However, the "for each" loop is more concise and less error-prone, as you don't have to worry about those pesky start and end index values.

 NOTE: The loop variable of the "for each" loop traverses the *elements* of the array, not the index values.

The "for each" loop is a pleasant improvement over the traditional loop if you need to process all elements in a collection. However, there are still plenty of opportunities to use the traditional for loop. For example, you might not want to traverse the entire collection, or you may need the index value inside the loop.

TIP: There is an even easier way to print all values of an array, using the `toString` method of the `Arrays` class. The call `Arrays.toString(a)` returns a string containing the array elements, enclosed in brackets and separated by commas, such as `"[2, 3, 5, 7, 11, 13]"`. To print the array, simply call

```
System.out.println(Arrays.toString(a));
```

3.10.2 Array Initializers and Anonymous Arrays

Java has a shortcut for creating an array object and supplying initial values at the same time. Here's an example of the syntax at work:

```
int[] smallPrimes = { 2, 3, 5, 7, 11, 13 };
```

Notice that you do not call `new` when you use this syntax.

You can even initialize an *anonymous array*:

```
new int[] { 17, 19, 23, 29, 31, 37 }
```

This expression allocates a new array and fills it with the values inside the braces. It counts the number of initial values and sets the array size accordingly. You can use this syntax to reinitialize an array without creating a new variable. For example,

```
smallPrimes = new int[] { 17, 19, 23, 29, 31, 37 };
```

is shorthand for

```
int[] anonymous = { 17, 19, 23, 29, 31, 37 };
smallPrimes = anonymous;
```

 NOTE: It is legal to have arrays of length 0. Such an array can be useful if you write a method that computes an array result and the result happens to be empty. Construct an array of length 0 as

```
new elementType[0]
```

Note that an array of length 0 is not the same as `null`.

3.10.3 Array Copying

You can copy one array variable into another, but then *both variables refer to the same array*:

```
int[] luckyNumbers = smallPrimes;
luckyNumbers[5] = 12; // now smallPrimes[5] is also 12
```

Figure 3.14 shows the result. If you actually want to copy all values of one array into a new array, you use the copyOf method in the Arrays class:

```
int[] copiedLuckyNumbers = Arrays.copyOf(luckyNumbers, luckyNumbers.length);
```

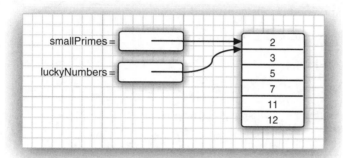

Figure 3.14 Copying an array variable

The second parameter is the length of the new array. A common use of this method is to increase the size of an array:

```
luckyNumbers = Arrays.copyOf(luckyNumbers, 2 * luckyNumbers.length);
```

The additional elements are filled with 0 if the array contains numbers, false if the array contains boolean values. Conversely, if the length is less than the length of the original array, only the initial values are copied.

 C++ NOTE: A Java array is quite different from a C++ array on the stack. It is, however, essentially the same as a pointer to an array allocated on the *heap*. That is,

```
int[] a = new int[100]; // Java
```

is not the same as

```
int a[100]; // C++
```

but rather

```
int* a = new int[100]; // C++
```

In Java, the [] operator is predefined to perform *bounds checking*. Furthermore, there is no pointer arithmetic—you can't increment a to point to the next element in the array.

3.10.4 Command-Line Parameters

You have already seen one example of a Java array repeated quite a few times. Every Java program has a `main` method with a `String[] args` parameter. This parameter indicates that the `main` method receives an array of strings—namely, the arguments specified on the command line.

For example, consider this program:

```
public class Message
{
   public static void main(String[] args)
   {
      if (args.length == 0 || args[0].equals("-h"))
         System.out.print("Hello,");
      else if (args[0].equals("-g"))
         System.out.print("Goodbye,");
      // print the other command-line arguments
      for (int i = 1; i < args.length; i++)
         System.out.print(" " + args[i]);
      System.out.println("!");
   }
}
```

If the program is called as

```
java Message -g cruel world
```

then the `args` array has the following contents:

```
args[0]: "-g"
args[1]: "cruel"
args[2]: "world"
```

The program prints the message

```
Goodbye, cruel world!
```

 C++ NOTE: In the `main` method of a Java program, the name of the program is not stored in the `args` array. For example, when you start up a program as

```
java Message -h world
```

from the command line, then `args[0]` will be "-h" and not "Message" or "java".

3.10.5 Array Sorting

To sort an array of numbers, you can use one of the sort methods in the Arrays class:

```
int[] a = new int[10000];
   . . .
Arrays.sort(a)
```

This method uses a tuned version of the QuickSort algorithm that is claimed to be very efficient on most data sets. The Arrays class provides several other convenience methods for arrays that are included in the API notes at the end of this section.

The program in Listing 3.7 puts arrays to work. This program draws a random combination of numbers for a lottery game. For example, if you play a "choose 6 numbers from 49" lottery, the program might print this:

```
Bet the following combination. It'll make you rich!
   4
   7
   8
   19
   30
   44
```

To select such a random set of numbers, we first fill an array numbers with the values 1, 2, . . ., n:

```
int[] numbers = new int[n];
for (int i = 0; i < numbers.length; i++)
   numbers[i] = i + 1;
```

A second array holds the numbers to be drawn:

```
int[] result = new int[k];
```

Now we draw k numbers. The Math.random method returns a random floating-point number that is between 0 (inclusive) and 1 (exclusive). By multiplying the result with n, we obtain a random number between 0 and n - 1.

```
int r = (int) (Math.random() * n);
```

We set the ith result to be the number at that index. Initially, that is just r + 1, but as you'll see presently, the contents of the numbers array are changed after each draw.

```
result[i] = numbers[r];
```

Now we must be sure never to draw that number again—all lottery numbers must be distinct. Therefore, we overwrite numbers[r] with the *last* number in the array and reduce n by 1.

```
numbers[r] = numbers[n - 1];
n--;
```

The point is that in each draw we pick an *index*, not the actual value. The index points into an array that contains the values that have not yet been drawn.

After drawing k lottery numbers, we sort the result array for a more pleasing output:

```
Arrays.sort(result);
for (int r : result)
    System.out.println(r);
```

Listing 3.7 LotteryDrawing/LotteryDrawing.java

```
1  import java.util.*;
2
3  /**
4   * This program demonstrates array manipulation.
5   * @version 1.20 2004-02-10
6   * @author Cay Horstmann
7   */
8  public class LotteryDrawing
9  {
10     public static void main(String[] args)
11     {
12        Scanner in = new Scanner(System.in);
13
14        System.out.print("How many numbers do you need to draw? ");
15        int k = in.nextInt();
16
17        System.out.print("What is the highest number you can draw? ");
18        int n = in.nextInt();
19
20        // fill an array with numbers 1 2 3 . . . n
21        int[] numbers = new int[n];
22        for (int i = 0; i < numbers.length; i++)
23           numbers[i] = i + 1;
24
25        // draw k numbers and put them into a second array
26        int[] result = new int[k];
27        for (int i = 0; i < result.length; i++)
28        {
29           // make a random index between 0 and n - 1
30           int r = (int) (Math.random() * n);
31
```

```
32          // pick the element at the random location
33          result[i] = numbers[r];
34
35          // move the last element into the random location
36          numbers[r] = numbers[n - 1];
37          n--;
38       }
39
40       // print the sorted array
41       Arrays.sort(result);
42       System.out.println("Bet the following combination. It'll make you rich!");
43       for (int r : result)
44          System.out.println(r);
45    }
46 }
```

---

java.util.Arrays 1.2

- static String toString(*type*[] a) 5.0

  returns a string with the elements of a, enclosed in brackets and delimited by commas.

  Parameters: a   An array of type int, long, short, char, byte, boolean, float, or double.

- static *type*[] copyOf(*type*[] a, int length) 6
- static *type*[] copyOfRange(*type*[] a, int start, int end) 6

  returns an array of the same type as a, of length either length or end - start, filled with the values of a.

  Parameters: a   An array of type int, long, short, char, byte, boolean, float, or double.

  start   The starting index (inclusive).

  end   The ending index (exclusive). May be larger than a.length, in which case the result is padded with 0 or false values.

  length   The length of the copy. If length is larger than a.length, the result is padded with 0 or false values. Otherwise, only the initial length values are copied.

- static void sort(*type*[] a)

  sorts the array, using a tuned QuickSort algorithm.

  Parameters: a   An array of type int, long, short, char, byte, float, or double.

(Continues)

`java.util.Arrays` 1.2 *(Continued)*

- `static int binarySearch(type[] a, type v)`
- `static int binarySearch(type[] a, int start, int end, type v)` 6

  Uses the binary search algorithm to search for the value v. If it is found, its index is returned. Otherwise, a negative value r is returned; -r - 1 is the spot at which v should be inserted to keep a sorted.

Parameters:	a	a *sorted* array of type `int`, `long`, `short`, `char`, `byte`, `float`, or `double`.
	start	The starting index (inclusive).
	end	The ending index (exclusive).
	v	A value of the same type as the elements of a.

- `static void fill(type[] a, type v)`

  Sets all elements of the array to v.

Parameters:	a	An array of type `int`, `long`, `short`, `char`, `byte`, `boolean`, `float`, or `double`.
	v	A value of the same type as the elements of a.

- `static boolean equals(type[] a, type[] b)`

  Returns `true` if the arrays have the same length and if the elements in corresponding indexes match.

Parameters:	a, b	Arrays of type `int`, `long`, `short`, `char`, `byte`, `boolean`, `float`, or `double`.

3.10.6 Multidimensional Arrays

Multidimensional arrays use more than one index to access array elements. They are used for tables and other more complex arrangements. You can safely skip this section until you have a need for this storage mechanism.

Suppose you want to make a table of numbers that shows how much an investment of $10,000 will grow under different interest rate scenarios in which interest is paid annually and reinvested (Table 3.8).

You can store this information in a two-dimensional array (matrix), which we call `balances`.

Declaring a two-dimensional array in Java is simple enough. For example:

```
double[][] balances;
```

Table 3.8 Growth of an Investment at Different Interest Rates

10%	11%	12%	13%	14%	15%
10,000.00	10,000.00	10,000.00	10,000.00	10,000.00	10,000.00
11,000.00	11,100.00	11,200.00	11,300.00	11,400.00	11,500.00
12,100.00	12,321.00	12,544.00	12,769.00	12,996.00	13,225.00
13,310.00	13,676.31	14,049.28	14,428.97	14,815.44	15,208.75
14,641.00	15,180.70	15,735.19	16,304.74	16,889.60	17,490.06
16,105.10	16,850.58	17,623.42	18,424.35	19,254.15	20,113.57
17,715.61	18,704.15	19,738.23	20,819.52	21,949.73	23,130.61
19,487.17	20,761.60	22,106.81	23,526.05	25,022.69	26,600.20
21,435.89	23,045.38	24,759.63	26,584.44	28,525.86	30,590.23
23,579.48	25,580.37	27,730.79	30,040.42	32,519.49	35,178.76

You cannot use the array until you initialize it. In this case, you can do the initialization as follows:

```
balances = new double[NYEARS][NRATES];
```

In other cases, if you know the array elements, you can use a shorthand notation for initializing a multidimensional array without a call to new. For example:

```
int[][] magicSquare =
   {
      {16, 3, 2, 13},
      {5, 10, 11, 8},
      {9, 6, 7, 12},
      {4, 15, 14, 1}
   };
```

Once the array is initialized, you can access individual elements by supplying two pairs of brackets—for example, balances[i][j].

The example program stores a one-dimensional array interest of interest rates and a two-dimensional array balances of account balances, one for each year and interest rate. We initialize the first row of the array with the initial balance:

```
for (int j = 0; j < balances[0].length; j++)
   balances[0][j] = 10000;
```

Then we compute the other rows, as follows:

```
for (int i = 1; i < balances.length; i++)
{
   for (int j = 0; j < balances[i].length; j++)
   {
      double oldBalance = balances[i - 1][j];
      double interest = . . .;
      balances[i][j] = oldBalance + interest;
   }
}
```

Listing 3.8 shows the full program.

 NOTE: A "for each" loop does not automatically loop through all elements in a two-dimensional array. Instead, it loops through the rows, which are themselves one-dimensional arrays. To visit all elements of a two-dimensional array a, nest two loops, like this:

```
for (double[] row : a)
   for (double value : row)
      do something with value
```

 TIP: To print out a quick-and-dirty list of the elements of a two-dimensional array, call

```
System.out.println(Arrays.deepToString(a));
```

The output is formatted like this:

```
[[16, 3, 2, 13], [5, 10, 11, 8], [9, 6, 7, 12], [4, 15, 14, 1]]
```

Listing 3.8 CompoundInterest/CompoundInterest.java

```
1  /**
2   * This program shows how to store tabular data in a 2D array.
3   * @version 1.40 2004-02-10
4   * @author Cay Horstmann
5   */
6  public class CompoundInterest
7  {
8     public static void main(String[] args)
9     {
10       final double STARTRATE = 10;
11       final int NRATES = 6;
```

```
12          final int NYEARS = 10;
13
14          // set interest rates to 10 . . . 15%
15          double[] interestRate = new double[NRATES];
16          for (int j = 0; j < interestRate.length; j++)
17             interestRate[j] = (STARTRATE + j) / 100.0;
18
19          double[][] balances = new double[NYEARS][NRATES];
20
21          // set initial balances to 10000
22          for (int j = 0; j < balances[0].length; j++)
23             balances[0][j] = 10000;
24
25          // compute interest for future years
26          for (int i = 1; i < balances.length; i++)
27          {
28             for (int j = 0; j < balances[i].length; j++)
29             {
30                // get last year's balances from previous row
31                double oldBalance = balances[i - 1][j];
32
33                // compute interest
34                double interest = oldBalance * interestRate[j];
35
36                // compute this year's balances
37                balances[i][j] = oldBalance + interest;
38             }
39          }
40
41          // print one row of interest rates
42          for (int j = 0; j < interestRate.length; j++)
43             System.out.printf("%9.0f%%", 100 * interestRate[j]);
44
45          System.out.println();
46
47          // print balance table
48          for (double[] row : balances)
49          {
50             // print table row
51             for (double b : row)
52                System.out.printf("%10.2f", b);
53
54             System.out.println();
55          }
56       }
57    }
```

3.10.7 Ragged Arrays

So far, what you have seen is not too different from other programming languages. But there is actually something subtle going on behind the scenes that you can sometimes turn to your advantage: Java has *no* multidimensional arrays at all, only one-dimensional arrays. Multidimensional arrays are faked as "arrays of arrays."

For example, the balances array in the preceding example is actually an array that contains ten elements, each of which is an array of six floating-point numbers (Figure 3.15).

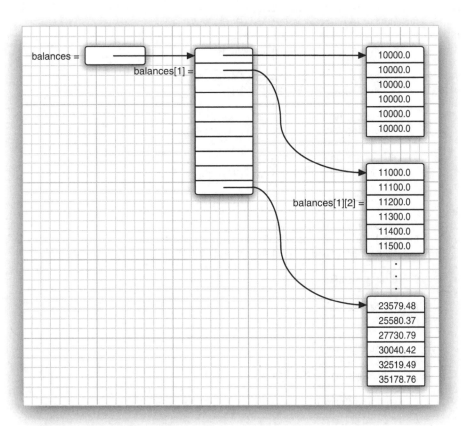

Figure 3.15 A two-dimensional array

The expression `balances[i]` refers to the `i`th subarray—that is, the `i`th row of the table. It is itself an array, and `balances[i][j]` refers to the `j`th element of that array.

Since rows of arrays are individually accessible, you can actually swap them!

```
double[] temp = balances[i];
balances[i] = balances[i + 1];
balances[i + 1] = temp;
```

It is also easy to make "ragged" arrays—that is, arrays in which different rows have different lengths. Here is the standard example. Let us make an array in which the element at row `i` and column `j` equals the number of possible outcomes of a "choose `j` numbers from `i` numbers" lottery.

```
1
1  1
1  2  1
1  3  3  1
1  4  6  4  1
1  5  10 10  5 1
1  6  15 20 15 6 1
```

As `j` can never be larger than `i`, the matrix is triangular. The `i`th row has `i + 1` elements. (We allow choosing 0 elements; there is one way to make such a choice.) To build this ragged array, first allocate the array holding the rows.

```
int[][] odds = new int[NMAX + 1][];
```

Next, allocate the rows.

```
for (int n = 0; n <= NMAX; n++)
   odds[n] = new int[n + 1];
```

Now that the array is allocated, we can access the elements in the normal way, provided we do not overstep the bounds.

```
for (int n = 0; n < odds.length; n++)
   for (int k = 0; k < odds[n].length; k++)
   {
      // compute lotteryOdds
      . . .
      odds[n][k] = lotteryOdds;
   }
```

Listing 3.9 gives the complete program.

C++ NOTE: In C++, the Java declaration

```
double[][] balances = new double[10][6]; // Java
```

is not the same as

```
double balances[10][6]; // C++
```

or even

```
double (*balances)[6] = new double[10][6]; // C++
```

Instead, an array of ten pointers is allocated:

```
double** balances = new double*[10]; // C++
```

Then, each element in the pointer array is filled with an array of six numbers:

```
for (i = 0; i < 10; i++)
    balances[i] = new double[6];
```

Mercifully, this loop is automatic when you ask for a `new double[10][6]`. When you want ragged arrays, you allocate the row arrays separately.

Listing 3.9 LotteryArray/LotteryArray.java

```
1  /**
2   * This program demonstrates a triangular array.
3   * @version 1.20 2004-02-10
4   * @author Cay Horstmann
5   */
6  public class LotteryArray
7  {
8     public static void main(String[] args)
9     {
10        final int NMAX = 10;
11
12        // allocate triangular array
13        int[][] odds = new int[NMAX + 1][];
14        for (int n = 0; n <= NMAX; n++)
15           odds[n] = new int[n + 1];
16
17        // fill triangular array
18        for (int n = 0; n < odds.length; n++)
19           for (int k = 0; k < odds[n].length; k++)
20           {
21              /*
22               * compute binomial coefficient n*(n-1)*(n-2)*...*(n-k+1)/(1*2*3*...*k)
23               */
```

```
24          int lotteryOdds = 1;
25          for (int i = 1; i <= k; i++)
26             lotteryOdds = lotteryOdds * (n - i + 1) / i;
27
28          odds[n][k] = lotteryOdds;
29       }
30
31    // print triangular array
32    for (int[] row : odds)
33    {
34       for (int odd : row)
35          System.out.printf("%4d", odd);
36       System.out.println();
37    }
38  }
39 }
```

You have now seen the fundamental programming structures of the Java language. The next chapter covers object-oriented programming in Java.

Objects and Classes

In this chapter

In this chapter, we

- Introduce you to object-oriented programming;
- Show you how you can create objects that belong to classes from the standard Java library; and
- Show you how to write your own classes.

If you do not have a background in object-oriented programming, you will want to read this chapter carefully. Object-oriented programming requires a different way of thinking than procedural languages. The transition is not always easy, but you do need some familiarity with object concepts to go further with Java.

For experienced C++ programmers, this chapter, like the previous chapter, presents familiar information; however, there are enough differences between the two languages that you should read the later sections of this chapter carefully. You'll find the C++ notes helpful for making the transition.

4.1 Introduction to Object-Oriented Programming

Object-oriented programming, or OOP for short, is the dominant programming paradigm these days, having replaced the "structured" or procedural programming techniques that were developed in the 1970s. Since Java is object oriented, you have to be familiar with OOP to become productive with Java.

An object-oriented program is made of objects. Each object has a specific functionality, exposed to its users, and a hidden implementation. Many objects in your programs will be taken "off-the-shelf" from a library; others will be custom designed. Whether you build an object or buy it might depend on your budget or on time. But, basically, as long as an object satisfies your specifications, you don't care how the functionality is implemented.

Traditional structured programming consists of designing a set of procedures (or *algorithms*) to solve a problem. Once the procedures are determined, the traditional next step was to find appropriate ways to store the data. This is why the designer of the Pascal language, Niklaus Wirth, called his famous book on programming *Algorithms + Data Structures = Programs* (Prentice Hall, 1975). Notice that in Wirth's title, algorithms come first, and data structures come second. This reflects the way programmers worked at that time. First, they decided on the procedures for manipulating the data; then, they decided what structure to impose on the data to make the manipulations easier. OOP reverses the order: puts the data first, then looks at the algorithms to operate on the data.

For small problems, the breakdown into procedures works very well. But objects are more appropriate for larger problems. Consider a simple web browser. It might require 2,000 procedures for its implementation, all of which manipulate a set of global data. In the object-oriented style, there might be 100 classes with an average of 20 methods per class (see Figure 4.1). This structure is much easier for a programmer to grasp. It is also much easier to find bugs in. Suppose the data of a particular object is in an incorrect state. It is far easier to search for the culprit among the 20 methods that had access to that data item than among 2,000 procedures.

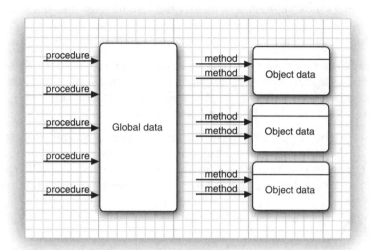

Figure 4.1 Procedural vs. OO programming

4.1.1 Classes

A *class* is the template or blueprint from which objects are made. Think about classes as cookie cutters. Objects are the cookies themselves. When you *construct* an object from a class, you are said to have created an *instance* of the class.

As you have seen, all code that you write in Java is inside a class. The standard Java library supplies several thousand classes for such diverse purposes as user interface design, dates and calendars, and network programming. Nonetheless, in Java you still have to create your own classes to describe the objects of your application's problem domain.

Encapsulation (sometimes called *information hiding*) is a key concept in working with objects. Formally, encapsulation is simply combining data and behavior in one package and hiding the implementation details from the users of the object. The bits of data in an object are called its *instance fields*, and the procedures that operate on the data are called its *methods*. A specific object that is an instance of a class will have specific values of its instance fields. The set of those values is the current *state* of the object. Whenever you invoke a method on an object, its state may change.

The key to making encapsulation work is to have methods *never* directly access instance fields in a class other than their own. Programs should interact with object data *only* through the object's methods. Encapsulation is the way to give an object its "black box" behavior, which is the key to reuse and reliability. This means a class may totally change how it stores its data, but as long as it continues to use the same methods to manipulate the data, no other object will know or care.

When you start writing your own classes in Java, another tenet of OOP will make this easier: Classes can be built by *extending* other classes. Java, in fact, comes with a "cosmic superclass" called `Object`. All other classes extend this class. You will learn more about the `Object` class in the next chapter.

When you extend an existing class, the new class has all the properties and methods of the class that you extend. You then supply new methods and data fields that apply to your new class only. The concept of extending a class to obtain another class is called *inheritance*. See the next chapter for details on inheritance.

4.1.2 Objects

To work with OOP, you should be able to identify three key characteristics of objects:

- The object's *behavior*—what can you do with this object, or what methods can you apply to it?
- The object's *state*—how does the object react when you invoke those methods?
- The object's *identity*—how is the object distinguished from others that may have the same behavior and state?

All objects that are instances of the same class share a family resemblance by supporting the same *behavior*. The behavior of an object is defined by the methods that you can call.

Next, each object stores information about what it currently looks like. This is the object's *state*. An object's state may change over time, but not spontaneously. A change in the state of an object must be a consequence of method calls. (If an object's state changed without a method call on that object, someone broke encapsulation.)

However, the state of an object does not completely describe it, because each object has a distinct *identity*. For example, in an order processing system, two orders are distinct even if they request identical items. Notice that the individual objects that are instances of a class *always* differ in their identity and *usually* differ in their state.

These key characteristics can influence each other. For example, the state of an object can influence its behavior. (If an order is "shipped" or "paid," it may reject a method call that asks it to add or remove items. Conversely, if an order is "empty"—that is, no items have yet been ordered—it should not allow itself to be shipped.)

4.1.3 Identifying Classes

In a traditional procedural program, you start the process at the top, with the `main` function. When designing an object-oriented system, there is no "top," and new-comers to OOP often wonder where to begin. The answer is: Identify your classes and then add methods to each class.

A simple rule of thumb in identifying classes is to look for nouns in the problem analysis. Methods, on the other hand, correspond to verbs.

For example, in an order-processing system, some of the nouns are

- Item
- Order
- Shipping address
- Payment
- Account

These nouns may lead to the classes `Item`, `Order`, and so on.

Next, look for verbs. Items are *added* to orders. Orders are *shipped* or *canceled*. Payments are *applied* to orders. With each verb, such as "add," "ship," "cancel," or "apply," you identify the object that has the major responsibility for carrying it out. For example, when a new item is added to an order, the order object should be the one in charge because it knows how it stores and sorts items. That is, `add` should be a method of the `Order` class that takes an `Item` object as a parameter.

Of course, the "noun and verb" is but a rule of thumb; only experience can help you decide which nouns and verbs are the important ones when building your classes.

4.1.4 Relationships between Classes

The most common relationships between classes are

- *Dependence* ("uses–a")
- *Aggregation* ("has–a")
- *Inheritance* ("is–a")

The *dependence*, or "uses–a" relationship, is the most obvious and also the most general. For example, the Order class uses the Account class because Order objects need to access Account objects to check for credit status. But the Item class does not depend on the Account class, because Item objects never need to worry about customer accounts. Thus, a class depends on another class if its methods use or manipulate objects of that class.

Try to minimize the number of classes that depend on each other. The point is, if a class A is unaware of the existence of a class B, it is also unconcerned about any changes to B. (And this means that changes to B do not introduce bugs into A.) In software engineering terminology, you want to minimize the *coupling* between classes.

The *aggregation*, or "has–a" relationship, is easy to understand because it is concrete; for example, an Order object contains Item objects. Containment means that objects of class A contain objects of class B.

 NOTE: Some methodologists view the concept of aggregation with disdain and prefer to use a more general "association" relationship. From the point of view of modeling, that is understandable. But for programmers, the "has–a" relationship makes a lot of sense. We like to use aggregation for another reason as well: The standard notation for associations is less clear. See Table 4.1.

The *inheritance*, or "is–a" relationship, expresses a relationship between a more special and a more general class. For example, a RushOrder class inherits from an Order class. The specialized RushOrder class has special methods for priority handling and a different method for computing shipping charges, but its other methods, such as adding items and billing, are inherited from the Order class. In general, if class A extends class B, class A inherits methods from class B but has more capabilities. (We describe inheritance more fully in the next chapter, in which we discuss this important notion at some length.)

Many programmers use the UML (Unified Modeling Language) notation to draw *class diagrams* that describe the relationships between classes. You can see an example of such a diagram in Figure 4.2. You draw classes as rectangles, and relationships as arrows with various adornments. Table 4.1 shows the most common UML arrow styles.

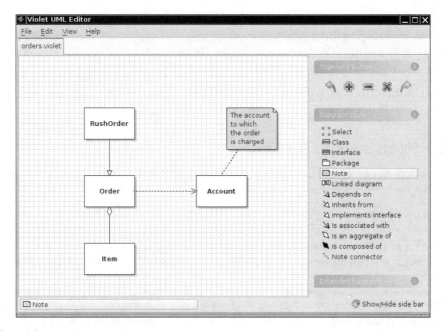

Figure 4.2 A class diagram

Table 4.1 UML notation for class relationships

Relationship	UML Connector
Inheritance	——————▷
Interface implementation	– – – – – – –▷
Dependency	– – – – – – –→
Aggregation	◇———————
Association	———————
Directed association	——————→

4.2 Using Predefined Classes

You can't do anything in Java without classes, and you have already seen several classes at work. However, not all of these show off the typical features of object orientation. Take, for example, the Math class. You have seen that you can use methods of the Math class, such as Math.random, without needing to know how they are implemented—all you need to know is the name and parameters (if any).

That's the point of encapsulation, and it will certainly be true of all classes. But the Math class *only* encapsulates functionality; it neither needs nor hides data. Since there is no data, you do not need to worry about making objects and initializing their instance fields—there aren't any!

In the next section, we will look at a more typical class, the Date class. You will see how to construct objects and call methods of this class.

4.2.1 Objects and Object Variables

To work with objects, you first construct them and specify their initial state. Then you apply methods to the objects.

In the Java programming language, you use *constructors* to construct new instances. A constructor is a special method whose purpose is to construct and initialize objects. Let us look at an example. The standard Java library contains a Date class. Its objects describe points in time, such as "December 31, 1999, 23:59:59 GMT".

 NOTE: You may be wondering: Why use a class to represent dates rather than (as in some languages) a built-in type? For example, Visual Basic has a built-in date type, and programmers can specify dates in the format #6/1/1995#. On the surface, this sounds convenient—programmers can simply use the built-in date type without worrying about classes. But actually, how suitable is the Visual Basic design? In some locales, dates are specified as month/day/year, in others as day/month/year. Are the language designers really equipped to foresee these kinds of issues? If they do a poor job, the language becomes an unpleasant muddle, but unhappy programmers are powerless to do anything about it. With classes, the design task is offloaded to a library designer. If the class is not perfect, other programmers can easily write their own classes to enhance or replace the system classes. (To prove the point: The Java date library started out a bit muddled, and it has been redesigned twice.)

Constructors always have the same name as the class name. Thus, the constructor for the Date class is called Date. To construct a Date object, combine the constructor with the new operator, as follows:

```
new Date()
```

This expression constructs a new object. The object is initialized to the current date and time.

If you like, you can pass the object to a method:

```
System.out.println(new Date());
```

Alternatively, you can apply a method to the object that you just constructed. One of the methods of the Date class is the toString method. That method yields a string representation of the date. Here is how you would apply the toString method to a newly constructed Date object:

```
String s = new Date().toString();
```

In these two examples, the constructed object is used only once. Usually, you will want to hang on to the objects that you construct so that you can keep using them. Simply store the object in a variable:

```
Date birthday = new Date();
```

Figure 4.3 shows the object variable birthday that refers to the newly constructed object.

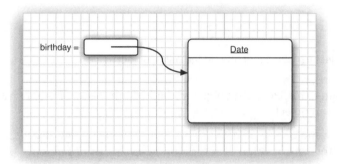

Figure 4.3 Creating a new object

There is an important difference between objects and object variables. For example, the statement

```
Date deadline; // deadline doesn't refer to any object
```

defines an object variable, deadline, that can refer to objects of type Date. It is important to realize that the variable deadline *is not an object* and, in fact, does not even refer to an object yet. You cannot use any Date methods on this variable at this time. The statement

```
s = deadline.toString(); // not yet
```

would cause a compile-time error.

You must first initialize the deadline variable. You have two choices. Of course, you can initialize the variable with a newly constructed object:

```
deadline = new Date();
```

Or you can set the variable to refer to an existing object:

```
deadline = birthday;
```

Now both variables refer to the *same* object (see Figure 4.4).

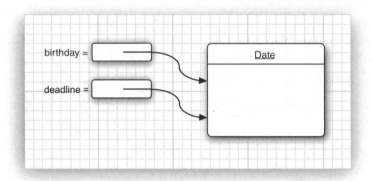

Figure 4.4 Object variables that refer to the same object

It is important to realize that an object variable doesn't actually contain an object. It only *refers* to an object.

In Java, the value of any object variable is a reference to an object that is stored elsewhere. The return value of the new operator is also a reference. A statement such as

```
Date deadline = new Date();
```

has two parts. The expression new Date() makes an object of type Date, and its value is a reference to that newly created object. That reference is then stored in the deadline variable.

You can explicitly set an object variable to null to indicate that it currently refers to no object.

```
deadline = null;
. . .
if (deadline != null)
   System.out.println(deadline);
```

If you apply a method to a variable that holds null, a runtime error occurs.

```
birthday = null;
String s = birthday.toString(); // runtime error!
```

Local variables are not automatically initialized to null. You must initialize them, either by calling new or by setting them to null.

C++ NOTE: Many people mistakenly believe that Java object variables behave like C++ references. But in C++ there are no null references, and references cannot be assigned. You should think of Java object variables as analogous to *object pointers* in C++. For example,

```
Date birthday; // Java
```

is really the same as

```
Date* birthday; // C++
```

Once you make this association, everything falls into place. Of course, a `Date*` pointer isn't initialized until you initialize it with a call to `new`. The syntax is almost the same in C++ and Java.

```
Date* birthday = new Date(); // C++
```

If you copy one variable to another, then both variables refer to the same date—they are pointers to the same object. The equivalent of the Java `null` reference is the C++ `NULL` pointer.

All Java objects live on the heap. When an object contains another object variable, it contains just a pointer to yet another heap object.

In C++, pointers make you nervous because they are so error-prone. It is easy to create bad pointers or to mess up memory management. In Java, these problems simply go away. If you use an uninitialized pointer, the runtime system will reliably generate a runtime error instead of producing random results. You don't have to worry about memory management, because the garbage collector takes care of it.

C++ makes quite an effort, with its support for copy constructors and assignment operators, to allow the implementation of objects that copy themselves automatically. For example, a copy of a linked list is a new linked list with the same contents but with an independent set of links. This makes it possible to design classes with the same copy behavior as the built-in types. In Java, you must use the `clone` method to get a complete copy of an object.

4.2.2 The `LocalDate` Class of the Java Library

In the preceding examples, we used the `Date` class that is a part of the standard Java library. An instance of the `Date` class has a state, namely *a particular point in time*.

Although you don't need to know this when you use the `Date` class, the time is represented by the number of milliseconds (positive or negative) from a fixed point, the so-called *epoch*, which is 00:00:00 UTC, January 1, 1970. UTC is the

Coordinated Universal Time, the scientific time standard which is, for practical purposes, the same as the more familiar GMT, or Greenwich Mean Time.

But as it turns out, the Date class is not very useful for manipulating the kind of calendar information that humans use for dates, such as "December 31, 1999". This particular description of a day follows the Gregorian calendar, which is the calendar used in most countries of the world. The same point in time would be described quite differently in the Chinese or Hebrew lunar calendars, not to mention the calendar used by your customers from Mars.

 NOTE: Throughout human history, civilizations grappled with the design of calendars to attach names to dates and bring order to the solar and lunar cycles. For a fascinating explanation of calendars around the world, from the French Revolutionary calendar to the Mayan long count, see *Calendrical Calculations* by Nachum Dershowitz and Edward M. Reingold (Cambridge University Press, 3rd ed., 2007).

The library designers decided to separate the concerns of keeping time and attaching names to points in time. Therefore, the standard Java library contains two separate classes: the Date class, which represents a point in time, and the LocalDate class, which expresses days in the familiar calendar notation. Java SE 8 introduced quite a few other classes for manipulating various aspects of date and time—see Chapter 6 of Volume II.

Separating time measurement from calendars is good object-oriented design. In general, it is a good idea to use separate classes to express different concepts.

You do not use a constructor to construct objects of the LocalDate class. Instead, use static *factory methods* that call constructors on your behalf. The expression

```
LocalDate.now()
```

constructs a new object that represents the date at which the object was constructed.

You can construct an object for a specific date by supplying year, month, and day:

```
LocalDate.of(1999, 12, 31)
```

Of course, you will usually want to store the constructed object in an object variable:

```
LocalDate newYearsEve = LocalDate.of(1999, 12, 31);
```

Once you have a LocalDate object, you can find out the year, month, and day with the methods getYear, getMonthValue, and getDayOfMonth:

```
int year = newYearsEve.getYear(); // 1999
int month = newYearsEve.getMonthValue(); // 12
int day = newYearsEve.getDayOfMonth(); // 31
```

This may seem pointless because they are the very same values that you just used to construct the object. But sometimes, you have a date that has been computed, and then you will want to invoke those methods to find out more about it. For example, the plusDays method yields a new LocalDate that is a given number of days away from the object to which you apply it:

```
LocalDate aThousandDaysLater = newYearsEve.plusDays(1000);
year = aThousandDaysLater.getYear(); // 2002
month = aThousandDaysLater.getMonthValue(); // 09
day = aThousandDaysLater.getDayOfMonth(); // 26
```

The LocalDate class has encapsulated instance fields to maintain the date to which it is set. Without looking at the source code, it is impossible to know the representation that the class uses internally. But, of course, the point of encapsulation is that this doesn't matter. What matters are the methods that a class exposes.

 NOTE: Actually, the Date class also has methods to get the day, month, and year, called getDay, getMonth, and getYear, but these methods are *deprecated*. A method is deprecated when a library designer realizes that the method should have never been introduced in the first place.

These methods were a part of the Date class before the library designers realized that it makes more sense to supply separate classes to deal with calendars. When an earlier set of calendar classes was introduced in Java 1.1, the Date methods were tagged as deprecated. You can still use them in your programs, but you will get unsightly compiler warnings if you do. It is a good idea to stay away from using deprecated methods because they may be removed in a future version of the library.

4.2.3 Mutator and Accessor Methods

Have another look at the plusDays method call that you saw in the preceding section:

```
LocalDate aThousandDaysLater = newYearsEve.plusDays(1000);
```

What happens to newYearsEve after the call? Has it been changed to be a thousand days later? As it turns out, it has not. The plusDays method yields a new LocalDate object, which is then assigned to the aThousandDaysLater variable. The original object remains unchanged. We say that the plusDays method does not *mutate* the object on which it is invoked. (This is similar to the toUpperCase method of the String class that you saw in Chapter 3. When you call toUpperCase on a string, that string stays the same, and a new string with uppercase characters is returned.)

An earlier version of the Java library had a different class for dealing with calendars, called GregorianCalendar. Here is how you add a thousand days to a date represented by that class:

```
GregorianCalendar someDay = new GregorianCalendar(1999, 11, 31);
    // Odd feature of that class: month numbers go from 0 to 11
someDay.add(Calendar.DAY_OF_MONTH, 1000);
```

Unlike the LocalDate.plusDays method, the GregorianCalendar.add method is a *mutator method*. After invoking it, the state of the someDay object has changed. Here is how you can find out the new state:

```
year = someDay.get(Calendar.YEAR); // 2002
month = someDay.get(Calendar.MONTH) + 1; // 09
day = someDay.get(Calendar.DAY_OF_MONTH); // 26
```

That's why we called the variable someDay and not newYearsEve—it no longer is new year's eve after calling the mutator method.

In contrast, methods that only access objects without modifying them are sometimes called *accessor methods*. For example, LocalDate.getYear and GregorianCalendar.get are accessor methods.

 C++ NOTE: In C++, the const suffix denotes accessor methods. A method that is not declared as const is assumed to be a mutator. However, in the Java programming language, no special syntax distinguishes accessors from mutators.

We finish this section with a program that puts the LocalDate class to work. The program displays a calendar for the current month, like this:

```
Mon Tue Wed Thu Fri Sat Sun
                          1
  2   3   4   5   6   7   8
  9  10  11  12  13  14  15
 16  17  18  19  20  21  22
 23  24  25  26* 27  28  29
 30
```

The current day is marked with an asterisk (*). As you can see, the program needs to know how to compute the length of a month and the weekday of a given day.

Let us go through the key steps of the program. First, we construct an object that is initialized with the current date.

```
LocalDate date = LocalDate.now();
```

We capture the current month and day.

```
int month = date.getMonthValue();
int today = date.getDayOfMonth();
```

Then we set date to the first of the month and get the weekday of that date.

```
date = date.minusDays(today - 1); // Set to start of month
DayOfWeek weekday = date.getDayOfWeek();
int value = weekday.getValue(); // 1 = Monday, ... 7 = Sunday
```

The variable weekday is set to an object of type DayOfWeek. We call the getValue method of that object to get a numerical value for the weekday. This yields an integer that follows the international convention where the weekend comes at the end of the week, returning 11 for Monday, 2 for Tuesday, and so on. Sunday has value 7.

Note that the first line of the calendar is indented, so that the first day of the month falls on the appropriate weekday. Here is the code to print the header and the indentation for the first line:

```
System.out.println("Mon Tue Wed Thu Fri Sat Sun");
for (int i = 1; i < value; i++)
   System.out.print("    ");
```

Now, we are ready to print the body of the calendar. We enter a loop in which date traverses the days of the month.

In each iteration, we print the date value. If date is today, the date is marked with an *. Then, we advance date to the next day. If we reach the beginning of each new week, we print a new line:

```
while (date.getMonthValue() == month)
{
   System.out.printf("%3d", date.getDayOfMonth());
   if (date.getDayOfMonth() == today)
      System.out.print("*");
   else
      System.out.print(" ");
   date = date.plusDays(1);
   if (date.getDayOfWeek().getValue() == 1) System.out.println();
}
```

When do we stop? We don't know whether the month has 31, 30, 29, or 28 days. Instead, we keep iterating while date is still in the current month.

Listing 4.1 shows the complete program.

As you can see, the LocalDate class makes it possible to write a calendar program that takes care of complexities such as weekdays and the varying month lengths. You don't need to know *how* the LocalDate class computes months and weekdays. You just use the *interface* of the class—the methods such as plusDays and getDayOfWeek.

The point of this example program is to show you how you can use the interface of a class to carry out fairly sophisticated tasks without having to know the implementation details.

Listing 4.1 CalendarTest/CalendarTest.java

```java
 1  import java.time.*;
 2
 3  /**
 4   * @version 1.5 2015-05-08
 5   * @author Cay Horstmann
 6   */
 7
 8  public class CalendarTest
 9  {
10     public static void main(String[] args)
11     {
12        LocalDate date = LocalDate.now();
13        int month = date.getMonthValue();
14        int today = date.getDayOfMonth();
15
16        date = date.minusDays(today - 1); // Set to start of month
17        DayOfWeek weekday = date.getDayOfWeek();
18        int value = weekday.getValue(); // 1 = Monday, ... 7 = Sunday
19
20        System.out.println("Mon Tue Wed Thu Fri Sat Sun");
21        for (int i = 1; i < value; i++)
22           System.out.print("    ");
23        while (date.getMonthValue() == month)
24        {
25           System.out.printf("%3d", date.getDayOfMonth());
26           if (date.getDayOfMonth() == today)
27              System.out.print("*");
28           else
29              System.out.print(" ");
30           date = date.plusDays(1);
31           if (date.getDayOfWeek().getValue() == 1) System.out.println();
32        }
33        if (date.getDayOfWeek().getValue() != 1) System.out.println();
34     }
35  }
```

---

java.time.LocalDate 8

- static LocalTime now()

  constructs an object that represents the current date.
- static LocalTime of(int year, int month, int day)

  constructs an object that represents the given date.
- int getYear()
- int getMonthValue()
- int getDayOfMonth()

  get the year, month, and day of this date.
- DayOfWeek getDayOfWeek

  Gets the weekday of this date as an instance of the DayOfWeek class. Call getValue to get a weekday between 1 (Monday) and 7 (Sunday).
- LocalDate plusDays(int n)
- LocalDate minusDays(int n)

  Yields the date that is n days after or before this date.

4.3 Defining Your Own Classes

In Chapter 3, you started writing simple classes. However, all those classes had just a single main method. Now the time has come to show you how to write the kind of "workhorse classes" that are needed for more sophisticated applications. These classes typically do not have a main method. Instead, they have their own instance fields and methods. To build a complete program, you combine several classes, one of which has a main method.

4.3.1 An Employee Class

The simplest form for a class definition in Java is

```
class ClassName
{
    field₁
    field₂
    . . .
    constructor₁
    constructor₂
    . . .
```

```
    method₁
    method₂
    . . .
}
```

Consider the following, very simplified, version of an `Employee` class that might be used by a business in writing a payroll system.

```
class Employee
{
   // instance fields
   private String name;
   private double salary;
   private LocalDate hireDay;

   // constructor
   public Employee(String n, double s, int year, int month, int day)
   {
      name = n;
      salary = s;
      hireDay = LocalDate.of(year, month, day);
   }

   // a method
   public String getName()
   {
      return name;
   }

   // more methods
   . . .
}
```

We break down the implementation of this class, in some detail, in the sections that follow. First, though, Listing 4.2 is a program that shows the `Employee` class in action.

In the program, we construct an `Employee` array and fill it with three employee objects:

```
Employee[] staff = new Employee[3];

staff[0] = new Employee("Carl Cracker", . . .);
staff[1] = new Employee("Harry Hacker", . . .);
staff[2] = new Employee("Tony Tester", . . .);
```

Next, we use the `raiseSalary` method of the `Employee` class to raise each employee's salary by 5%:

```
for (Employee e : staff)
   e.raiseSalary(5);
```

Finally, we print out information about each employee, by calling the getName, getSalary, and getHireDay methods:

```
for (Employee e : staff)
    System.out.println("name=" + e.getName()
        + ",salary=" + e.getSalary()
        + ",hireDay=" + e.getHireDay());
```

Note that the example program consists of *two* classes: the Employee class and a class EmployeeTest with the public access specifier. The main method with the instructions that we just described is contained in the EmployeeTest class.

The name of the source file is EmployeeTest.java because the name of the file must match the name of the public class. You can only have one public class in a source file, but you can have any number of nonpublic classes.

Next, when you compile this source code, the compiler creates two class files in the directory: EmployeeTest.class and Employee.class.

You then start the program by giving the bytecode interpreter the name of the class that contains the main method of your program:

```
java EmployeeTest
```

The bytecode interpreter starts running the code in the main method in the EmployeeTest class. This code in turn constructs three new Employee objects and shows you their state.

Listing 4.2 EmployeeTest/EmployeeTest.java

```
1  import java.time.*;
2
3  /**
4   * This program tests the Employee class.
5   * @version 1.12 2015-05-08
6   * @author Cay Horstmann
7   */
8  public class EmployeeTest
9  {
10     public static void main(String[] args)
11     {
12         // fill the staff array with three Employee objects
13         Employee[] staff = new Employee[3];
14
15         staff[0] = new Employee("Carl Cracker", 75000, 1987, 12, 15);
16         staff[1] = new Employee("Harry Hacker", 50000, 1989, 10, 1);
17         staff[2] = new Employee("Tony Tester", 40000, 1990, 3, 15);
18
```

(Continues)

Listing 4.2 *(Continued)*

```
19        // raise everyone's salary by 5%
20        for (Employee e : staff)
21           e.raiseSalary(5);
22
23        // print out information about all Employee objects
24        for (Employee e : staff)
25           System.out.println("name=" + e.getName() + ",salary=" + e.getSalary() + ",hireDay="
26              + e.getHireDay());
27     }
28  }
29
30  class Employee
31  {
32     private String name;
33     private double salary;
34     private LocalDate hireDay;
35
36     public Employee(String n, double s, int year, int month, int day)
37     {
38        name = n;
39        salary = s;
40        hireDay = LocalDate.of(year, month, day);
41     }
42
43     public String getName()
44     {
45        return name;
46     }
47
48     public double getSalary()
49     {
50        return salary;
51     }
52
53     public LocalDate getHireDay()
54     {
55        return hireDay;
56     }
57
58     public void raiseSalary(double byPercent)
59     {
60        double raise = salary * byPercent / 100;
61        salary += raise;
62     }
63  }
```

4.3.2 Use of Multiple Source Files

The program in Listing 4.2 has two classes in a single source file. Many programmers prefer to put each class into its own source file. For example, you can place the Employee class into a file Employee.java and the EmployeeTest class into EmployeeTest.java.

If you like this arrangement, you have two choices for compiling the program. You can invoke the Java compiler with a wildcard:

```
javac Employee*.java
```

Then, all source files matching the wildcard will be compiled into class files. Or, you can simply type

```
javac EmployeeTest.java
```

You may find it surprising that the second choice works even though the Employee.java file is never explicitly compiled. However, when the Java compiler sees the Employee class being used inside EmployeeTest.java, it will look for a file named Employee.class. If it does not find that file, it automatically searches for Employee.java and compiles it. Moreover, if the timestamp of the version of Employee.java that it finds is newer than that of the existing Employee.class file, the Java compiler will *automatically* recompile the file.

 NOTE: If you are familiar with the make facility of UNIX (or one of its Windows cousins, such as nmake), then you can think of the Java compiler as having the make functionality already built in.

4.3.3 Dissecting the Employee Class

In the sections that follow, we will dissect the Employee class. Let's start with the methods in this class. As you can see by examining the source code, this class has one constructor and four methods:

```
public Employee(String n, double s, int year, int month, int day)
public String getName()
public double getSalary()
public LocalDate getHireDay()
public void raiseSalary(double byPercent)
```

All methods of this class are tagged as public. The keyword public means that any method in any class can call the method. (The four possible access levels are covered in this and the next chapter.)

Next, notice the three instance fields that will hold the data manipulated inside an instance of the Employee class.

```
private String name;
private double salary;
private LocalDate hireDay;
```

The `private` keyword makes sure that the *only* methods that can access these instance fields are the methods of the `Employee` class itself. No outside method can read or write to these fields.

 NOTE: You could use the `public` keyword with your instance fields, but it would be a very bad idea. Having `public` data fields would allow any part of the program to read and modify the instance fields, completely ruining encapsulation. Any method of any class can modify public fields—and, in our experience, some code *will* take advantage of that access privilege when you least expect it. We strongly recommend to make all your instance fields `private`.

Finally, notice that two of the instance fields are themselves objects: The `name` and `hireDay` fields are references to `String` and `LocalDate` objects. This is quite usual: Classes will often contain instance fields of class type.

4.3.4 First Steps with Constructors

Let's look at the constructor listed in our `Employee` class.

```
public Employee(String n, double s, int year, int month, int day)
{
   name = n;
   salary = s;
   LocalDate hireDay = LocalDate.of(year, month, day);
}
```

As you can see, the name of the constructor is the same as the name of the class. This constructor runs when you construct objects of the `Employee` class—giving the instance fields the initial state you want them to have.

For example, when you create an instance of the `Employee` class with code like this:

```
new Employee("James Bond", 100000, 1950, 1, 1)
```

you have set the instance fields as follows:

```
name = "James Bond";
salary = 100000;
hireDay = LocalDate.of(1950, 1, 1); // January 1, 1950
```

There is an important difference between constructors and other methods. A constructor can only be called in conjunction with the `new` operator. You can't apply a constructor to an existing object to reset the instance fields. For example,

```
james.Employee("James Bond", 250000, 1950, 1, 1) // ERROR
```

is a compile-time error.

We will have more to say about constructors later in this chapter. For now, keep the following in mind:

- A constructor has the same name as the class.
- A class can have more than one constructor.
- A constructor can take zero, one, or more parameters.
- A constructor has no return value.
- A constructor is always called with the `new` operator.

 C++ NOTE: Constructors work the same way in Java as they do in C++. Keep in mind, however, that all Java objects are constructed on the heap and that a constructor must be combined with `new`. It is a common error of C++ programmers to forget the `new` operator:

```
Employee number007("James Bond", 100000, 1950, 1, 1);
    // C++, not Java
```

That works in C++ but not in Java.

 CAUTION: Be careful not to introduce local variables with the same names as the instance fields. For example, the following constructor will not set the salary:

```
public Employee(String n, double s, . . .)
{
   String name = n; // Error
   double salary = s; // Error
   . . .
}
```

The constructor declares *local* variables `name` and `salary`. These variables are only accessible inside the constructor. They *shadow* the instance fields with the same name. Some programmers accidentally write this kind of code when they type faster than they think, because their fingers are used to adding the data type. This is a nasty error that can be hard to track down. You just have to be careful in all of your methods to not use variable names that equal the names of instance fields.

4.3.5 Implicit and Explicit Parameters

Methods operate on objects and access their instance fields. For example, the method

```
public void raiseSalary(double byPercent)
{
   double raise = salary * byPercent / 100;
   salary += raise;
}
```

sets a new value for the salary instance field in the object on which this method is invoked. Consider the call

```
number007.raiseSalary(5);
```

The effect is to increase the value of the number007.salary field by 5%. More specifically, the call executes the following instructions:

```
double raise = number007.salary * 5 / 100;
number007.salary += raise;
```

The raiseSalary method has two parameters. The first parameter, called the *implicit* parameter, is the object of type Employee that appears before the method name. The second parameter, the number inside the parentheses after the method name, is an *explicit* parameter. (Some people call the implicit parameter the *target* or *receiver* of the method call.)

As you can see, the explicit parameters are explicitly listed in the method declaration, for example, double byPercent. The implicit parameter does not appear in the method declaration.

In every method, the keyword this refers to the implicit parameter. If you like, you can write the raiseSalary method as follows:

```
public void raiseSalary(double byPercent)
{
   double raise = this.salary * byPercent / 100;
   this.salary += raise;
}
```

Some programmers prefer that style because it clearly distinguishes between instance fields and local variables.

C++ NOTE: In C++, you generally define methods outside the class:

```
void Employee::raiseSalary(double byPercent) // C++, not Java
{
    . . .
}
```

If you define a method inside a class, then it is, automatically, an inline method.

```
class Employee
{
    . . .
    int getName() { return name; } // inline in C++
}
```

In Java, all methods are defined inside the class itself. This does not make them inline. Finding opportunities for inline replacement is the job of the Java virtual machine. The just-in-time compiler watches for calls to methods that are short, commonly called, and not overridden, and optimizes them away.

4.3.6 Benefits of Encapsulation

Finally, let's look more closely at the rather simple getName, getSalary, and getHireDay methods.

```
public String getName()
{
    return name;
}

public double getSalary()
{
    return salary;
}

public LocalDate getHireDay()
{
    return hireDay;
}
```

These are obvious examples of accessor methods. As they simply return the values of instance fields, they are sometimes called *field accessors*.

Wouldn't it be easier to make the name, salary, and hireDay fields public, instead of having separate accessor methods?

However, the name field is a read-only field. Once you set it in the constructor, there is no method to change it. Thus, we have a guarantee that the name field will never be corrupted.

The salary field is not read-only, but it can only be changed by the raiseSalary method. In particular, should the value ever turn out wrong, only that method needs to be debugged. Had the salary field been public, the culprit for messing up the value could have been anywhere.

Sometimes, it happens that you want to get and set the value of an instance field. Then you need to supply *three* items:

- A private data field;
- A public field accessor method; and
- A public field mutator method.

This is a lot more tedious than supplying a single public data field, but there are considerable benefits.

First, you can change the internal implementation without affecting any code other than the methods of the class. For example, if the storage of the name is changed to

```
String firstName;
String lastName;
```

then the getName method can be changed to return

```
firstName + " " + lastName
```

This change is completely invisible to the remainder of the program.

Of course, the accessor and mutator methods may need to do a lot of work and convert between the old and the new data representation. That leads us to our second benefit: Mutator methods can perform error checking, whereas code that simply assigns to a field may not go into the trouble. For example, a setSalary method might check that the salary is never less than 0.

 CAUTION: Be careful not to write accessor methods that return references to mutable objects. In a previous edition of this book, we violated that rule in our Employee class in which the getHireDay method returned an object of class Date:

```
class Employee
{
    private Date hireDay;
    . . .
    public Date getHireDay()
    {
        return hireDay; // Bad
    }
    . . .
}
```

Unlike the LocalDate class, which has no mutator methods, the Date class has a mutator method, setTime, where you can set the number of milliseconds.

The fact that Date objects are mutable breaks encapsulation! Consider the following rogue code:

```
Employee harry = . . .;
Date d = harry.getHireDay();
double tenYearsInMilliSeconds = 10 * 365.25 * 24 * 60 * 60 * 1000;
d.setTime(d.getTime() - (long) tenYearsInMilliSeconds);
// let's give Harry ten years of added seniority
```

The reason is subtle. Both d and harry.hireDay refer to the same object (see Figure 4.5). Applying mutator methods to d automatically changes the private state of the employee object!

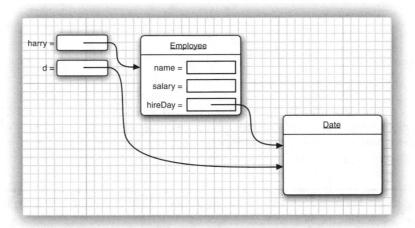

Figure 4.5 Returning a reference to a mutable data field

If you need to return a reference to a mutable object, you should *clone* it first. A clone is an exact copy of an object stored in a new location. We discuss cloning in detail in Chapter 6. Here is the corrected code:

```
class Employee
{
   . . .
   public Date getHireDay()
   {
      return (Date) hireDay.clone(); // Ok
   }
   . . .
}
```

> As a rule of thumb, always use `clone` whenever you need to return a copy of a mutable field.

4.3.7 Class-Based Access Privileges

You know that a method can access the private data of the object on which it is invoked. What many people find surprising is that a method can access the private data of *all objects of its class*. For example, consider a method `equals` that compares two employees.

```
class Employee
{
   . . .
   public boolean equals(Employee other)
   {
      return name.equals(other.name);
   }
}
```

A typical call is

```
if (harry.equals(boss)) . . .
```

This method accesses the private fields of `harry`, which is not surprising. It also accesses the private fields of `boss`. This is legal because `boss` is an object of type `Employee`, and a method of the `Employee` class is permitted to access the private fields of *any* object of type `Employee`.

C++ NOTE: C++ has the same rule. A method can access the private features of any object of its class, not just of the implicit parameter.

4.3.8 Private Methods

When implementing a class, we make all data fields private because public data are dangerous. But what about the methods? While most methods are public, private methods are useful in certain circumstances. Sometimes, you may wish to break up the code for a computation into separate helper methods. Typically, these helper methods should not be part of the public interface—they may be too close to the current implementation or require a special protocol or calling order. Such methods are best implemented as `private`.

To implement a private method in Java, simply change the `public` keyword to `private`.

By making a method private, you are under no obligation to keep it available if you change your implementation. The method may well be *harder* to implement or *unnecessary* if the data representation changes; this is irrelevant. The point is that as long as the method is private, the designers of the class can be assured that it is never used outside the other class, so they can simply drop it. If a method is public, you cannot simply drop it because other code might rely on it.

4.3.9 Final Instance Fields

You can define an instance field as `final`. Such a field must be initialized when the object is constructed. That is, you must guarantee that the field value has been set after the end of every constructor. Afterwards, the field may not be modified again. For example, the `name` field of the `Employee` class may be declared as `final` because it never changes after the object is constructed—there is no `setName` method.

```
class Employee
{
   private final String name;
   . . .
}
```

The `final` modifier is particularly useful for fields whose type is primitive or an *immutable class*. (A class is immutable if none of its methods ever mutate its objects. For example, the `String` class is immutable.)

For mutable classes, the `final` modifier can be confusing. For example, consider a field

```
private final StringBuilder evaluations;
```

that is initialized in the `Employee` constructor as

```
evaluations = new StringBuilder();
```

The `final` keyword merely means that the object reference stored in the `evaluations` variable will never again refer to a different `StringBuilder` object. But the object can be mutated:

```
public void giveGoldStar()
{
   evaluations.append(LocalDate.now() + ": Gold star!\n");
}
```

4.4 Static Fields and Methods

In all sample programs that you have seen, the main method is tagged with the static modifier. We are now ready to discuss the meaning of this modifier.

4.4.1 Static Fields

If you define a field as static, then there is only one such field per class. In contrast, each object has its own copy of all instance fields. For example, let's suppose we want to assign a unique identification number to each employee. We add an instance field id and a static field nextId to the Employee class:

```
class Employee
{
   private static int nextId = 1;

   private int id;
   . . .
}
```

Every employee object now has its own id field, but there is only one nextId field that is shared among all instances of the class. Let's put it another way. If there are 1,000 objects of the Employee class, then there are 1,000 instance fields id, one for each object. But there is a single static field nextId. Even if there are no employee objects, the static field nextId is present. It belongs to the class, not to any individual object.

 NOTE: In some object-oriented programming languages, static fields are called *class fields*. The term "static" is a meaningless holdover from C++.

Let's implement a simple method:

```
public void setId()
{
   id = nextId;
   nextId++;
}
```

Suppose you set the employee identification number for harry:

```
harry.setId();
```

Then, the id field of harry is set to the current value of the static field nextId, and the value of the static field is incremented:

```
harry.id = Employee.nextId;
Employee.nextId++;
```

4.4.2 Static Constants

Static variables are quite rare. However, static constants are more common. For example, the Math class defines a static constant:

```
public class Math
{
    . . .
    public static final double PI = 3.14159265358979323846;
    . . .
}
```

You can access this constant in your programs as Math.PI.

If the keyword static had been omitted, then PI would have been an instance field of the Math class. That is, you would need an object of this class to access PI, and every Math object would have its own copy of PI.

Another static constant that you have used many times is System.out. It is declared in the System class as follows:

```
public class System
{
    . . .
    public static final PrintStream out = . . .;
    . . .
}
```

As we mentioned several times, it is never a good idea to have public fields, because everyone can modify them. However, public constants (that is, final fields) are fine. Since out has been declared as final, you cannot reassign another print stream to it:

```
System.out = new PrintStream(. . .); // Error--out is final
```

 NOTE: If you look at the System class, you will notice a method setOut that sets System.out to a different stream. You may wonder how that method can change the value of a final variable. However, the setOut method is a *native* method, not implemented in the Java programming language. Native methods can bypass the access control mechanisms of the Java language. This is a very unusual workaround that you should not emulate in your programs.

4.4.3 Static Methods

Static methods are methods that do not operate on objects. For example, the `pow` method of the `Math` class is a static method. The expression

```
Math.pow(x, a)
```

computes the power x^a. It does not use any `Math` object to carry out its task. In other words, it has no implicit parameter.

You can think of static methods as methods that don't have a `this` parameter. (In a nonstatic method, the `this` parameter refers to the implicit parameter of the method—see Section 4.3.5, "Implicit and Explicit Parameters," on p. 152.)

A static method of the `Employee` class cannot access the `id` instance field because it does not operate on an object. However, a static method can access a static field. Here is an example of such a static method:

```
public static int getNextId()
{
   return nextId; // returns static field
}
```

To call this method, you supply the name of the class:

```
int n = Employee.getNextId();
```

Could you have omitted the keyword `static` for this method? Yes, but then you would need to have an object reference of type `Employee` to invoke the method.

 NOTE: It is legal to use an object to call a static method. For example, if `harry` is an `Employee` object, then you can call `harry.getNextId()` instead of `Employee.getNextId()`. However, we find that notation confusing. The `getNextId` method doesn't look at `harry` at all to compute the result. We recommend that you use class names, not objects, to invoke static methods.

Use static methods in two situations:

- When a method doesn't need to access the object state because all needed parameters are supplied as explicit parameters (example: `Math.pow`).
- When a method only needs to access static fields of the class (example: `Employee.getNextId`).

C++ NOTE: Static fields and methods have the same functionality in Java and C++. However, the syntax is slightly different. In C++, you use the :: operator to access a static field or method outside its scope, such as Math::PI.

The term "static" has a curious history. At first, the keyword static was introduced in C to denote local variables that don't go away when a block is exited. In that context, the term "static" makes sense: The variable stays around and is still there when the block is entered again. Then static got a second meaning in C, to denote global variables and functions that cannot be accessed from other files. The keyword static was simply reused, to avoid introducing a new keyword. Finally, C++ reused the keyword for a third, unrelated, interpretation—to denote variables and functions that belong to a class but not to any particular object of the class. That is the same meaning the keyword has in Java.

4.4.4 Factory Methods

Here is another common use for static methods. Classes such as LocalDate and NumberFormat use static *factory methods* that construct objects. You have already seen the factory methods LocalDate.now and LocalDate.of. Here is how the NumberFormat class yields formatter objects for various styles:

```
NumberFormat currencyFormatter = NumberFormat.getCurrencyInstance();
NumberFormat percentFormatter = NumberFormat.getPercentInstance();
double x = 0.1;
System.out.println(currencyFormatter.format(x)); // prints $0.10
System.out.println(percentFormatter.format(x)); // prints 10%
```

Why doesn't the NumberFormat class use a constructor instead? There are two reasons:

- You can't give names to constructors. The constructor name is always the same as the class name. But we want two different names to get the currency instance and the percent instance.

- When you use a constructor, you can't vary the type of the constructed object. But the factory methods actually return objects of the class DecimalFormat, a subclass that inherits from NumberFormat. (See Chapter 5 for more on inheritance.)

4.4.5 The main Method

Note that you can call static methods without having any objects. For example, you never construct any objects of the Math class to call Math.pow.

For the same reason, the main method is a static method.

```
public class Application
{
   public static void main(String[] args)
   {
      // construct objects here
      . . .
   }
}
```

The `main` method does not operate on any objects. In fact, when a program starts, there aren't any objects yet. The static `main` method executes, and constructs the objects that the program needs.

 TIP: Every class can have a `main` method. That is a handy trick for unit testing of classes. For example, you can add a `main` method to the `Employee` class:

```
class Employee
{
   public Employee(String n, double s, int year, int month, int day)
   {
      name = n;
      salary = s;
      LocalDate hireDay = LocalDate.now(year, month, day);
   }
   . . .
   public static void main(String[] args) // unit test
   {
      Employee e = new Employee("Romeo", 50000, 2003, 3, 31);
      e.raiseSalary(10);
      System.out.println(e.getName() + " " + e.getSalary());
   }
   . . .
}
```

If you want to test the `Employee` class in isolation, simply execute

```
java Employee
```

If the `Employee` class is a part of a larger application, you start the application with

```
java Application
```

and the `main` method of the `Employee` class is never executed.

The program in Listing 4.3 contains a simple version of the `Employee` class with a static field `nextId` and a static method `getNextId`. We fill an array with three `Employee` objects and then print the employee information. Finally, we print the next available identification number, to demonstrate the static method.

Note that the Employee class also has a static main method for unit testing. Try running both

    java Employee

and

    java StaticTest

to execute both main methods.

Listing 4.3 StaticTest/StaticTest.java

```
1  /**
2   * This program demonstrates static methods.
3   * @version 1.01 2004-02-19
4   * @author Cay Horstmann
5   */
6  public class StaticTest
7  {
8     public static void main(String[] args)
9     {
10       // fill the staff array with three Employee objects
11       Employee[] staff = new Employee[3];
12
13       staff[0] = new Employee("Tom", 40000);
14       staff[1] = new Employee("Dick", 60000);
15       staff[2] = new Employee("Harry", 65000);
16
17       // print out information about all Employee objects
18       for (Employee e : staff)
19       {
20          e.setId();
21          System.out.println("name=" + e.getName() + ",id=" + e.getId() + ",salary="
22             + e.getSalary());
23       }
24
25       int n = Employee.getNextId(); // calls static method
26       System.out.println("Next available id=" + n);
27    }
28 }
29
30 class Employee
31 {
32    private static int nextId = 1;
33
34    private String name;
35    private double salary;
```

(Continues)

Listing 4.3 *(Continued)*

```
36     private int id;
37
38     public Employee(String n, double s)
39     {
40        name = n;
41        salary = s;
42        id = 0;
43     }
44
45     public String getName()
46     {
47        return name;
48     }
49
50     public double getSalary()
51     {
52        return salary;
53     }
54
55     public int getId()
56     {
57        return id;
58     }
59
60     public void setId()
61     {
62        id = nextId; // set id to next available id
63        nextId++;
64     }
65
66     public static int getNextId()
67     {
68        return nextId; // returns static field
69     }
70
71     public static void main(String[] args) // unit test
72     {
73        Employee e = new Employee("Harry", 50000);
74        System.out.println(e.getName() + " " + e.getSalary());
75     }
76  }
```

4.5 Method Parameters

Let us review the computer science terms that describe how parameters can be passed to a method (or a function) in a programming language. The term *call by value* means that the method gets just the value that the caller provides. In contrast, *call by reference* means that the method gets the *location* of the variable that the caller provides. Thus, a method can *modify* the value stored in a variable passed by reference but not in one passed by value. These "call by . . ." terms are standard computer science terminology describing the behavior of method parameters in various programming languages, not just Java. (There is also a *call by name* that is mainly of historical interest, being employed in the Algol programming language, one of the oldest high-level languages.)

The Java programming language *always* uses call by value. That means that the method gets a copy of all parameter values. In particular, the method cannot modify the contents of any parameter variables passed to it.

For example, consider the following call:

```
double percent = 10;
harry.raiseSalary(percent);
```

No matter how the method is implemented, we know that after the method call, the value of percent is still 10.

Let us look a little more closely at this situation. Suppose a method tried to triple the value of a method parameter:

```
public static void tripleValue(double x) // doesn't work
{
    x = 3 * x;
}
```

Let's call this method:

```
double percent = 10;
tripleValue(percent);
```

However, this does not work. After the method call, the value of percent is still 10. Here is what happens:

1. x is initialized with a copy of the value of percent (that is, 10).

2. x is tripled—it is now 30. But percent is still 10 (see Figure 4.6).

3. The method ends, and the parameter variable x is no longer in use.

There are, however, two kinds of method parameters:

*   Primitive types (numbers, boolean values)
*   Object references

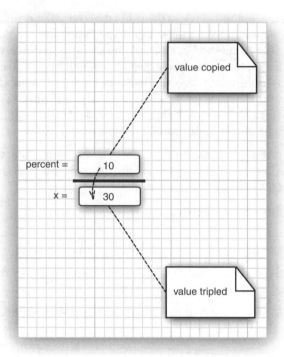

Figure 4.6 Modifying a numeric parameter has no lasting effect.

You have seen that it is impossible for a method to change a primitive type parameter. The situation is different for object parameters. You can easily implement a method that triples the salary of an employee:

```
public static void tripleSalary(Employee x) // works
{
    x.raiseSalary(200);
}
```

When you call

```
harry = new Employee(. . .);
tripleSalary(harry);
```

then the following happens:

1. x is initialized with a copy of the value of harry, that is, an object reference.
2. The raiseSalary method is applied to that object reference. The Employee object to which both x and harry refer gets its salary raised by 200 percent.

3. The method ends, and the parameter variable x is no longer in use. Of course, the object variable harry continues to refer to the object whose salary was tripled (see Figure 4.7).

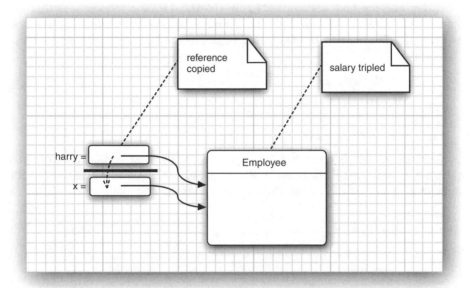

Figure 4.7 Modifying an object parameter has a lasting effect.

As you have seen, it is easily possible—and in fact very common—to implement methods that change the state of an object parameter. The reason is simple. The method gets a copy of the object reference, and both the original and the copy refer to the same object.

Many programming languages (in particular, C++ and Pascal) have two mechanisms for parameter passing: call by value and call by reference. Some programmers (and unfortunately even some book authors) claim that Java uses call by reference for objects. That is false. As this is such a common misunderstanding, it is worth examining a counterexample in detail.

Let's try to write a method that swaps two employee objects:

```
public static void swap(Employee x, Employee y) // doesn't work
{
   Employee temp = x;
   x = y;
   y = temp;
}
```

If Java used call by reference for objects, this method would work:

```
Employee a = new Employee("Alice", . . .);
Employee b = new Employee("Bob", . . .);
swap(a, b);
// does a now refer to Bob, b to Alice?
```

However, the method does not actually change the object references that are stored in the variables a and b. The x and y parameters of the swap method are initialized with *copies* of these references. The method then proceeds to swap these copies.

```
// x refers to Alice, y to Bob
Employee temp = x;
x = y;
y = temp;
// now x refers to Bob, y to Alice
```

But ultimately, this is a wasted effort. When the method ends, the parameter variables x and y are abandoned. The original variables a and b still refer to the same objects as they did before the method call (see Figure 4.8).

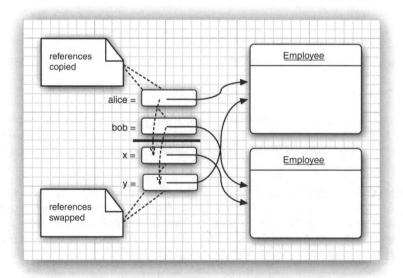

Figure 4.8 Swapping object parameters has no lasting effect.

This demonstrates that the Java programming language does not use call by reference for objects. Instead, *object references are passed by value.*

Here is a summary of what you can and cannot do with method parameters in Java:

- A method cannot modify a parameter of a primitive type (that is, numbers or `boolean` values).
- A method can change the *state* of an object parameter.
- A method cannot make an object parameter refer to a new object.

The program in Listing 4.4 demonstrates these facts. The program first tries to triple the value of a number parameter and does not succeed:

```
Testing tripleValue:
Before: percent=10.0
End of method: x=30.0
After: percent=10.0
```

It then successfully triples the salary of an employee:

```
Testing tripleSalary:
Before: salary=50000.0
End of method: salary=150000.0
After: salary=150000.0
```

After the method, the state of the object to which `harry` refers has changed. This is possible because the method modified the state through a copy of the object reference.

Finally, the program demonstrates the failure of the `swap` method:

```
Testing swap:
Before: a=Alice
Before: b=Bob
End of method: x=Bob
End of method: y=Alice
After: a=Alice
After: b=Bob
```

As you can see, the parameter variables `x` and `y` are swapped, but the variables `a` and `b` are not affected.

 C++ NOTE: C++ has both call by value and call by reference. You tag reference parameters with &. For example, you can easily implement methods `void tripleValue(double& x)` or `void swap(Employee& x, Employee& y)` that modify their reference parameters.

Listing 4.4 ParamTest/ParamTest.java

```
1  /**
2   * This program demonstrates parameter passing in Java.
3   * @version 1.00 2000-01-27
4   * @author Cay Horstmann
5   */
6  public class ParamTest
7  {
8     public static void main(String[] args)
9     {
10        /*
11         * Test 1: Methods can't modify numeric parameters
12         */
13        System.out.println("Testing tripleValue:");
14        double percent = 10;
15        System.out.println("Before: percent=" + percent);
16        tripleValue(percent);
17        System.out.println("After: percent=" + percent);
18
19        /*
20         * Test 2: Methods can change the state of object parameters
21         */
22        System.out.println("\nTesting tripleSalary:");
23        Employee harry = new Employee("Harry", 50000);
24        System.out.println("Before: salary=" + harry.getSalary());
25        tripleSalary(harry);
26        System.out.println("After: salary=" + harry.getSalary());
27
28        /*
29         * Test 3: Methods can't attach new objects to object parameters
30         */
31        System.out.println("\nTesting swap:");
32        Employee a = new Employee("Alice", 70000);
33        Employee b = new Employee("Bob", 60000);
34        System.out.println("Before: a=" + a.getName());
35        System.out.println("Before: b=" + b.getName());
36        swap(a, b);
37        System.out.println("After: a=" + a.getName());
38        System.out.println("After: b=" + b.getName());
39     }
40
41     public static void tripleValue(double x) // doesn't work
42     {
43        x = 3 * x;
44        System.out.println("End of method: x=" + x);
45     }
46
```

```
47    public static void tripleSalary(Employee x) // works
48    {
49        x.raiseSalary(200);
50        System.out.println("End of method: salary=" + x.getSalary());
51    }
52
53    public static void swap(Employee x, Employee y)
54    {
55        Employee temp = x;
56        x = y;
57        y = temp;
58        System.out.println("End of method: x=" + x.getName());
59        System.out.println("End of method: y=" + y.getName());
60    }
61 }
62
63 class Employee // simplified Employee class
64 {
65    private String name;
66    private double salary;
67
68    public Employee(String n, double s)
69    {
70        name = n;
71        salary = s;
72    }
73
74    public String getName()
75    {
76        return name;
77    }
78
79    public double getSalary()
80    {
81        return salary;
82    }
83
84    public void raiseSalary(double byPercent)
85    {
86        double raise = salary * byPercent / 100;
87        salary += raise;
88    }
89 }
```

4.6 Object Construction

You have seen how to write simple constructors that define the initial state of
your objects. However, since object construction is so important, Java offers quite

a variety of mechanisms for writing constructors. We go over these mechanisms in the sections that follow.

4.6.1 Overloading

Some classes have more than one constructor. For example, you can construct an empty `StringBuilder` object as

```
StringBuilder messages = new StringBuilder();
```

Alternatively, you can specify an initial string:

```
StringBuilder todoList = new StringBuilder("To do:\n");
```

This capability is called *overloading*. Overloading occurs if several methods have the same name (in this case, the `StringBuilder` constructor method) but different parameters. The compiler must sort out which method to call. It picks the correct method by matching the parameter types in the headers of the various methods with the types of the values used in the specific method call. A compile-time error occurs if the compiler cannot match the parameters, either because there is no match at all or because there there is not one that is better than all others. (The process of finding a match is called *overloading resolution*.)

 NOTE: Java allows you to overload any method—not just constructor methods. Thus, to completely describe a method, you need to specify its name together with its parameter types. This is called the *signature* of the method. For example, the `String` class has four public methods called `indexOf`. They have signatures

```
indexOf(int)
indexOf(int, int)
indexOf(String)
indexOf(String, int)
```

The return type is not part of the method signature. That is, you cannot have two methods with the same names and parameter types but different return types.

4.6.2 Default Field Initialization

If you don't set a field explicitly in a constructor, it is automatically set to a default value: numbers to `0`, `boolean` values to `false`, and object references to `null`. Some people consider it poor programming practice to rely on the defaults. Certainly, it makes it harder for someone to understand your code if fields are being initialized invisibly.

 NOTE: This is an important difference between fields and local variables. You must always explicitly initialize local variables in a method. But in a class, if you don't initialize a field, it is automatically initialized to a default (0, `false`, or `null`).

For example, consider the `Employee` class. Suppose you don't specify how to initialize some of the fields in a constructor. By default, the `salary` field would be initialized with 0 and the `name` and `hireDay` fields would be initialized with `null`.

However, that would not be a good idea. If anyone called the `getName` or `getHireDay` method, they would get a `null` reference that they probably don't expect:

```
LocalDate h = harry.getHireDay();
int year = h.getYear(); // throws exception if h is null
```

4.6.3 The Constructor with No Arguments

Many classes contain a constructor with no arguments that creates an object whose state is set to an appropriate default. For example, here is a constructor with no arguments for the `Employee` class:

```
public Employee()
{
    name = "";
    salary = 0;
    hireDay = LocalDate.now();
}
```

If you write a class with no constructors whatsoever, then a no-argument constructor is provided for you. This constructor sets *all* the instance fields to their default values. So, all numeric data contained in the instance fields would be 0, all `boolean` values would be `false`, and all object variables would be set to `null`.

If a class supplies at least one constructor but does not supply a no-argument constructor, it is illegal to construct objects without supplying arguments. For example, our original `Employee` class in Listing 4.2 provided a single constructor:

```
Employee(String name, double salary, int y, int m, int d)
```

With that class, it was not legal to construct default employees. That is, the call

```
e = new Employee();
```

would have been an error.

CAUTION: Please keep in mind that you get a free no-argument constructor *only* when your class has no other constructors. If you write your class with even a single constructor of your own and you want the users of your class to have the ability to create an instance by a call to

```
new ClassName()
```

then you must provide a no-argument constructor. Of course, if you are happy with the default values for all fields, you can simply supply

```
public ClassName()
{
}
```

4.6.4 Explicit Field Initialization

By overloading the constructor methods in a class, you can build many ways to set the initial state of the instance fields of your classes. It is always a good idea to make sure that, regardless of the constructor call, every instance field is set to something meaningful.

You can simply assign a value to any field in the class definition. For example:

```
class Employee
{
   private String name = "";
   . . .
}
```

This assignment is carried out before the constructor executes. This syntax is particularly useful if all constructors of a class need to set a particular instance field to the same value.

The initialization value doesn't have to be a constant value. Here is an example in which a field is initialized with a method call. Consider an Employee class where each employee has an id field. You can initialize it as follows:

```
class Employee
{
   private static int nextId;
   private int id = assignId();
   . . .
   private static int assignId()
   {
      int r = nextId;
      nextId++;
```

```
    return r;
  }
    . . .
}
```

 C++ NOTE: In C++, you cannot directly initialize instance fields of a class. All fields must be set in a constructor. However, C++ has a special initializer list syntax, such as

```
Employee::Employee(String n, double s, int y, int m, int d) // C++
: name(n),
  salary(s),
  hireDay(y, m, d)
{
}
```

C++ uses this special syntax to call field constructors. In Java, there is no need for that because objects have no subobjects, only pointers to other objects.

4.6.5 Parameter Names

When you write very trivial constructors (and you'll write a lot of them), it can be somewhat frustrating to come up with parameter names.

We have generally opted for single-letter parameter names:

```
public Employee(String n, double s)
{
  name = n;
  salary = s;
}
```

However, the drawback is that you need to read the code to tell what the n and s parameters mean.

Some programmers prefix each parameter with an "a":

```
public Employee(String aName, double aSalary)
{
  name = aName;
  salary = aSalary;
}
```

That is quite neat. Any reader can immediately figure out the meaning of the parameters.

Another commonly used trick relies on the fact that parameter variables *shadow* instance fields with the same name. For example, if you call a parameter salary, then `salary` refers to the parameter, not the instance field. But you can still access the instance field as `this.salary`. Recall that `this` denotes the implicit parameter, that is, the object being constructed. Here is an example:

```
public Employee(String name, double salary)
{
   this.name = name;
   this.salary = salary;
}
```

 C++ NOTE: In C++, it is common to prefix instance fields with an underscore or a fixed letter. (The letters m and x are common choices.) For example, the salary field might be called _salary, mSalary, or xSalary. Java programmers don't usually do that.

4.6.6 Calling Another Constructor

The keyword `this` refers to the implicit parameter of a method. However, this keyword has a second meaning.

If *the first statement of a constructor* has the form `this(. . .)`, then the constructor calls another constructor of the same class. Here is a typical example:

```
public Employee(double s)
{
   // calls Employee(String, double)
   this("Employee #" + nextId, s);
   nextId++;
}
```

When you call `new Employee(60000)`, the `Employee(double)` constructor calls the `Employee(String, double)` constructor.

Using the `this` keyword in this manner is useful—you only need to write common construction code once.

 C++ NOTE: The this reference in Java is identical to the this pointer in C++. However, in C++ it is not possible for one constructor to call another. If you want to factor out common initialization code in C++, you must write a separate method.

4.6.7 Initialization Blocks

You have already seen two ways to initialize a data field:

- By setting a value in a constructor
- By assigning a value in the declaration

There is a third mechanism in Java, called an *initialization block*. Class declarations can contain arbitrary blocks of code. These blocks are executed whenever an object of that class is constructed. For example:

```java
class Employee
{
   private static int nextId;

   private int id;
   private String name;
   private double salary;

   // object initialization block
   {
      id = nextId;
      nextId++;
   }

   public Employee(String n, double s)
   {
      name = n;
      salary = s;
   }

   public Employee()
   {
      name = "";
      salary = 0;
   }

   . . .
}
```

In this example, the id field is initialized in the object initialization block, no matter which constructor is used to construct an object. The initialization block runs first, and then the body of the constructor is executed.

This mechanism is never necessary and is not common. It is usually more straightforward to place the initialization code inside a constructor.

NOTE: It is legal to set fields in initialization blocks even if they are only defined later in the class. However, to avoid circular definitions, it is not legal to read from fields that are only initialized later. The exact rules are spelled out in section 8.3.2.3 of the Java Language Specification (`http://docs.oracle.com/javase/specs`). The rules are complex enough to baffle the compiler implementors—early versions of Java implemented them with subtle errors. Therefore, we suggest that you always place initialization blocks after the field definitions.

With so many ways of initializing data fields, it can be quite confusing to give all possible pathways for the construction process. Here is what happens in detail when a constructor is called:

1. All data fields are initialized to their default values (`0`, `false`, or `null`).
2. All field initializers and initialization blocks are executed, in the order in which they occur in the class declaration.
3. If the first line of the constructor calls a second constructor, then the body of the second constructor is executed.
4. The body of the constructor is executed.

Naturally, it is always a good idea to organize your initialization code so that another programmer could easily understand it without having to be a language lawyer. For example, it would be quite strange and somewhat error-prone to have a class whose constructors depend on the order in which the data fields are declared.

To initialize a static field, either supply an initial value or use a static initialization block. You have already seen the first mechanism:

```
private static int nextId = 1;
```

If the static fields of your class require complex initialization code, use a static initialization block.

Place the code inside a block and tag it with the keyword `static`. Here is an example. We want the employee ID numbers to start at a random integer less than 10,000.

```
// static initialization block
static
{
    Random generator = new Random();
    nextId = generator.nextInt(10000);
}
```

Static initialization occurs when the class is first loaded. Like instance fields, static fields are `0`, `false`, or `null` unless you explicitly set them to another value.

All static field initializers and static initialization blocks are executed in the order in which they occur in the class declaration.

 NOTE: Amazingly enough, up to JDK 6, it was possible to write a "Hello, World" program in Java without ever writing a `main` method.

```
public class Hello
{
   static
   {
      System.out.println("Hello, World");
   }
}
```

When you invoked the class with `java Hello`, the class was loaded, the static initialization block printed "Hello, World", and only then was a message displayed that `main` is not defined. Since Java SE 7, the `java` program first checks that there is a `main` method.

The program in Listing 4.5 shows many of the features that we discussed in this section:

- Overloaded constructors
- A call to another constructor with `this(...)`
- A no-argument constructor
- An object initialization block
- A static initialization block
- An instance field initialization

Listing 4.5 ConstructorTest/ConstructorTest.java

```
1  import java.util.*;
2
3  /**
4   * This program demonstrates object construction.
5   * @version 1.01 2004-02-19
6   * @author Cay Horstmann
7   */
8  public class ConstructorTest
9  {
10    public static void main(String[] args)
11    {
```

(Continues)

Listing 4.5 *(Continued)*

```
12        // fill the staff array with three Employee objects
13        Employee[] staff = new Employee[3];
14
15        staff[0] = new Employee("Harry", 40000);
16        staff[1] = new Employee(60000);
17        staff[2] = new Employee();
18
19        // print out information about all Employee objects
20        for (Employee e : staff)
21           System.out.println("name=" + e.getName() + ",id=" + e.getId() + ",salary="
22                 + e.getSalary());
23     }
24 }
25
26 class Employee
27 {
28    private static int nextId;
29
30    private int id;
31    private String name = ""; // instance field initialization
32    private double salary;
33
34    // static initialization block
35    static
36    {
37       Random generator = new Random();
38       // set nextId to a random number between 0 and 9999
39       nextId = generator.nextInt(10000);
40    }
41
42    // object initialization block
43    {
44       id = nextId;
45       nextId++;
46    }
47
48    // three overloaded constructors
49    public Employee(String n, double s)
50    {
51       name = n;
52       salary = s;
53    }
54
55    public Employee(double s)
56    {
57       // calls the Employee(String, double) constructor
58       this("Employee #" + nextId, s);
59    }
```

```
60
61    // the default constructor
62    public Employee()
63    {
64       // name initialized to ""--see above
65       // salary not explicitly set--initialized to 0
66       // id initialized in initialization block
67    }
68
69    public String getName()
70    {
71       return name;
72    }
73
74    public double getSalary()
75    {
76       return salary;
77    }
78
79    public int getId()
80    {
81       return id;
82    }
83 }
```

---

java.util.Random 1.0

- Random()

  constructs a new random number generator.

- int nextInt(int n) 1.2

  returns a random number between 0 and $n - 1$.

4.6.8 Object Destruction and the finalize Method

Some object-oriented programming languages, notably C++, have explicit destructor methods for any cleanup code that may be needed when an object is no longer used. The most common activity in a destructor is reclaiming the memory set aside for objects. Since Java does automatic garbage collection, manual memory reclamation is not needed, so Java does not support destructors.

Of course, some objects utilize a resource other than memory, such as a file or a handle to another object that uses system resources. In this case, it is important that the resource be reclaimed and recycled when it is no longer needed.

You can add a `finalize` method to any class. The `finalize` method will be called before the garbage collector sweeps away the object. In practice, *do not rely on the* `finalize` *method* for recycling any resources that are in short supply—you simply cannot know when this method will be called.

 NOTE: The method call `System.runFinalizersOnExit(true)` guarantees that finalizer methods are called before Java shuts down. However, this method is inherently unsafe and has been deprecated. An alternative is to add "shutdown hooks" with the method `Runtime.addShutdownHook`—see the API documentation for details.

If a resource needs to be closed as soon as you have finished using it, you need to manage it manually. Supply a `close` method that does the necessary cleanup, and call it when you are done with the object. In Section 7.2.5, "The Try-with-Resources Statement," on p. 376, you will see how you can ensure that this method is called automatically.

4.7 Packages

Java allows you to group classes in a collection called a *package*. Packages are convenient for organizing your work and for separating your work from code libraries provided by others.

The standard Java library is distributed over a number of packages, including `java.lang`, `java.util`, `java.net`, and so on. The standard Java packages are examples of hierarchical packages. Just as you have nested subdirectories on your hard disk, you can organize packages by using levels of nesting. All standard Java packages are inside the `java` and `javax` package hierarchies.

The main reason for using packages is to guarantee the uniqueness of class names. Suppose two programmers come up with the bright idea of supplying an `Employee` class. As long as both of them place their class into different packages, there is no conflict. In fact, to absolutely guarantee a unique package name, use an Internet domain name (which is known to be unique) written in reverse. You then use subpackages for different projects. For example, consider the domain `horstmann.com`. When written in reverse order, it turns into the package `com.horstmann`. That package can then be further subdivided into subpackages such as `com.horstmann.corejava`.

From the point of view of the compiler, there is absolutely no relationship between nested packages. For example, the packages `java.util` and `java.util.jar` have nothing to do with each other. Each is its own independent collection of classes.

4.7.1 Class Importation

A class can use all classes from its own package and all *public* classes from other packages.

You can access the public classes in another package in two ways. The first is simply to add the full package name in front of *every* class name. For example:

```
java.time.LocalDate today = java.time.LocalDate.now();
```

That is obviously tedious. A simpler, and more common, approach is to use the `import` statement. The point of the `import` statement is to give you a shorthand to refer to the classes in the package. Once you use `import`, you no longer have to give the classes their full names.

You can import a specific class or the whole package. You place `import` statements at the top of your source files (but below any `package` statements). For example, you can import all classes in the `java.util` package with the statement

```
import java.util.*;
```

Then you can use

```
LocalDate today = LocalDate.now();
```

without a package prefix. You can also import a specific class inside a package:

```
import java.time.LocalDate;
```

The `java.time.*` syntax is less tedious. It has no negative effect on code size. However, if you import classes explicitly, the reader of your code knows exactly which classes you use.

 TIP: In Eclipse, you can select the menu option Source → Organize Imports. Package statements such as `import java.util.*;` are automatically expanded into a list of specific imports such as

```
import java.util.ArrayList;
import java.util.Date;
```

This is an extremely convenient feature.

However, note that you can only use the `*` notation to import a single package. You cannot use `import java.*` or `import java.*.*` to import all packages with the `java` prefix.

Most of the time, you just import the packages that you need, without worrying too much about them. The only time that you need to pay attention to packages is when you have a name conflict. For example, both the `java.util` and `java.sql` packages have a `Date` class. Suppose you write a program that imports both packages.

```
import java.util.*;
import java.sql.*;
```

If you now use the `Date` class, you get a compile-time error:

```
Date today; // Error--java.util.Date or java.sql.Date?
```

The compiler cannot figure out which `Date` class you want. You can solve this problem by adding a specific `import` statement:

```
import java.util.*;
import java.sql.*;
import java.util.Date;
```

What if you really need both `Date` classes? Then you need to use the full package name with every class name.

```
java.util.Date deadline = new java.util.Date();
java.sql.Date today = new java.sql.Date(...);
```

Locating classes in packages is an activity of the *compiler*. The bytecodes in class files always use full package names to refer to other classes.

 C++ NOTE: C++ programmers sometimes confuse `import` with `#include`. The two have nothing in common. In C++, you must use `#include` to include the declarations of external features because the C++ compiler does not look inside any files except the one that it is compiling and its explicitly included header files. The Java compiler will happily look inside other files provided you tell it where to look.

In Java, you can entirely avoid the `import` mechanism by explicitly naming all classes, such as `java.util.Date`. In C++, you cannot avoid the `#include` directives.

The only benefit of the `import` statement is convenience. You can refer to a class by a name shorter than the full package name. For example, after an `import java.util.*` (or `import java.util.Date`) statement, you can refer to the `java.util.Date` class simply as `Date`.

In C++, the construction analogous to the package mechanism is the namespace feature. Think of the `package` and `import` statements in Java as the analogs of the `namespace` and `using` directives in C++.

4.7.2 Static Imports

A form of the `import` statement permits the importing of static methods and fields, not just classes.

For example, if you add the directive

```
import static java.lang.System.*;
```

to the top of your source file, then you can use the static methods and fields of the `System` class without the class name prefix:

```
out.println("Goodbye, World!"); // i.e., System.out
exit(0); // i.e., System.exit
```

You can also import a specific method or field:

```
import static java.lang.System.out;
```

In practice, it seems doubtful that many programmers will want to abbreviate `System.out` or `System.exit`. The resulting code seems less clear. On the other hand,

```
sqrt(pow(x, 2) + pow(y, 2))
```

seems much clearer than

```
Math.sqrt(Math.pow(x, 2) + Math.pow(y, 2))
```

4.7.3 Addition of a Class into a Package

To place classes inside a package, you must put the name of the package at the top of your source file, *before* the code that defines the classes in the package. For example, the file `Employee.java` in Listing 4.7 starts out like this:

```
package com.horstmann.corejava;

public class Employee
{
   . . .
}
```

If you don't put a `package` statement in the source file, then the classes in that source file belong to the *default package*. The default package has no package name. Up to now, all our example classes were located in the default package.

Place source files into a subdirectory that matches the full package name. For example, all source files in the `com.horstmann.corejava` package should be in a subdirectory `com/horstmann/corejava` (`com\horstmann\corejava` on Windows). The compiler places the class files into the same directory structure.

The program in Listings 4.6 and 4.7 is distributed over two packages: The `PackageTest` class belongs to the default package, and the `Employee` class belongs to the `com.horstmann.corejava` package. Therefore, the `Employee.java` file must be in a subdirectory `com/horstmann/corejava`. In other words, the directory structure is as follows:

```
. (base directory)
    ├── PackageTest.java
    ├── PackageTest.class
    └── com/
            └── horstmann/
                    └── corejava/
                            ├── Employee.java
                            └── Employee.class
```

To compile this program, simply change to the base directory and run the command

```
javac PackageTest.java
```

The compiler automatically finds the file `com/horstmann/corejava/Employee.java` and compiles it.

Let's look at a more realistic example, in which we don't use the default package but have classes distributed over several packages (`com.horstmann.corejava` and `com.mycompany`).

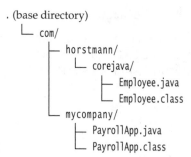

```
. (base directory)
    └── com/
            ├── horstmann/
            │       └── corejava/
            │               ├── Employee.java
            │               └── Employee.class
            └── mycompany/
                    ├── PayrollApp.java
                    └── PayrollApp.class
```

In this situation, you still must compile and run classes from the *base* directory—that is, the directory containing the `com` directory:

```
javac com/mycompany/PayrollApp.java
java com.mycompany.PayrollApp
```

Note again that the compiler operates on *files* (with file separators and an extension .java), whereas the Java interpreter loads a *class* (with dot separators).

TIP: Starting with the next chapter, we will use packages for the source code. That way, you can make an IDE project for each chapter instead of each section.

 CAUTION: The compiler does *not* check the directory structure when it compiles source files. For example, suppose you have a source file that starts with the directive

```
package com.mycompany;
```

You can compile the file even if it is not contained in a subdirectory com/mycompany. The source file will compile without errors *if it doesn't depend on other packages*. However, the resulting program will not run unless you first move all class files to the right place. The *virtual machine* won't find the classes if the packages don't match the directories.

Listing 4.6 PackageTest/PackageTest.java

```java
1  import com.horstmann.corejava.*;
2  // the Employee class is defined in that package
3
4  import static java.lang.System.*;
5
6  /**
7   * This program demonstrates the use of packages.
8   * @version 1.11 2004-02-19
9   * @author Cay Horstmann
10  */
11 public class PackageTest
12 {
13    public static void main(String[] args)
14    {
15       // because of the import statement, we don't have to use
16       // com.horstmann.corejava.Employee here
17       Employee harry = new Employee("Harry Hacker", 50000, 1989, 10, 1);
18
19       harry.raiseSalary(5);
20
21       // because of the static import statement, we don't have to use System.out here
22       out.println("name=" + harry.getName() + ",salary=" + harry.getSalary());
23    }
24 }
```

Listing 4.7 PackageTest/com/horstmann/corejava/Employee.java

```
1  package com.horstmann.corejava;
2
3  // the classes in this file are part of this package
4
5  import java.time.*;
6
7  // import statements come after the package statement
8
9  /**
10  * @version 1.11 2015-05-08
11  * @author Cay Horstmann
12  */
13  public class Employee
14  {
15     private String name;
16     private double salary;
17     private LocalDate hireDay;
18
19     public Employee(String name, double salary, int year, int month, int day)
20     {
21        this.name = name;
22        this.salary = salary;
23        hireDay = LocalDate.of(year, month, day);
24     }
25
26     public String getName()
27     {
28        return name;
29     }
30
31     public double getSalary()
32     {
33        return salary;
34     }
35
36     public LocalDate getHireDay()
37     {
38        return hireDay;
39     }
40
41     public void raiseSalary(double byPercent)
42     {
43        double raise = salary * byPercent / 100;
44        salary += raise;
45     }
46  }
```

4.7.4 Package Scope

You have already encountered the access modifiers `public` and `private`. Features tagged as `public` can be used by any class. Private features can be used only by the class that defines them. If you don't specify either `public` or `private`, the feature (that is, the class, method, or variable) can be accessed by all methods in the same *package*.

Consider the program in Listing 4.2. The `Employee` class was not defined as a public class. Therefore, only the other classes (such as `EmployeeTest`) in the same package—the default package in this case—can access it. For classes, this is a reasonable default. However, for variables, this was an unfortunate choice. Variables must explicitly be marked `private`, or they will default to being package visible. This, of course, breaks encapsulation. The problem is that it is awfully easy to forget to type the `private` keyword. Here is an example from the `Window` class in the `java.awt` package, which is part of the source code supplied with the JDK:

```java
public class Window extends Container
{
   String warningString;
   . . .
}
```

Note that the `warningString` variable is not `private`! That means the methods of all classes in the `java.awt` package can access this variable and set it to whatever they like (such as `"Trust me!"`). Actually, the only methods that access this variable are in the `Window` class, so it would have been entirely appropriate to make the variable private. We suspect that the programmer typed the code in a hurry and simply forgot the `private` modifier. (We won't mention the programmer's name to protect the guilty—you can look into the source file yourself.)

 NOTE: Amazingly enough, this problem has never been fixed, even though we have pointed it out in nine editions of this book—apparently the library implementors don't read *Core Java*. Not only that—new fields have been added to the class over time, and about half of them aren't private either.

Is this really a problem? It depends. By default, packages are not closed entities. That is, anyone can add more classes to a package. Of course, hostile or clueless programmers can then add code that modifies variables with package visibility. For example, in early versions of Java, it was an easy matter to smuggle another class into the `java.awt` package. Simply start out the class with

```java
package java.awt;
```

Then, place the resulting class file inside a subdirectory java/awt somewhere on the class path, and you have gained access to the internals of the java.awt package. Through this subterfuge, it was possible to set the warning string (see Figure 4.9).

Figure 4.9 Changing the warning string in an applet window

Starting with version 1.2, the JDK implementors rigged the class loader to explicitly disallow loading of user-defined classes whose package name starts with "java.". Of course, your own classes won't benefit from that protection. Instead, you can use another mechanism, *package sealing*, to address the issue of promiscuous package access. If you seal a package, no further classes can be added to it. You will see in Chapter 9 how you can produce a JAR file that contains sealed packages.

4.8 The Class Path

As you have seen, classes are stored in subdirectories of the file system. The path to the class must match the package name.

Class files can also be stored in a JAR (Java archive) file. A JAR file contains multiple class files and subdirectories in a compressed format, saving space and improving performance. When you use a third-party library in your programs, you will usually be given one or more JAR files to include. The JDK also supplies a number of JAR files, such as the file *jre*/lib/rt.jar that contains thousands of library classes. You will see in Chapter 9 how to create your own JAR files.

TIP: JAR files use the ZIP format to organize files and subdirectories. You can use any ZIP utility to peek inside `rt.jar` and other JAR files.

To share classes among programs, you need to do the following:

1. Place your class files inside a directory, for example, `/home/user/classdir`. Note that this directory is the *base* directory for the package tree. If you add the class `com.horstmann.corejava.Employee`, then the `Employee.class` file must be located in the subdirectory `/home/user/classdir/com/horstmann/corejava`.

2. Place any JAR files inside a directory, for example, `/home/user/archives`.

3. Set the *class path*. The class path is the collection of all locations that can contain class files.

In UNIX, the elements on the class path are separated by colons:

```
/home/user/classdir:.:/home/user/archives/archive.jar
```

In Windows, they are separated by semicolons:

```
c:\classdir;.;c:\archives\archive.jar
```

In both cases, the period denotes the current directory.

This class path contains

- The base directory `/home/user/classdir` or `c:\classdir`;
- The current directory (`.`); and
- The JAR file `/home/user/archives/archive.jar` or `c:\archives\archive.jar`.

Starting with Java SE 6, you can specify a wildcard for a JAR file directory, like this:

```
/home/user/classdir:.:/home/user/archives/'*'
```

or

```
c:\classdir;.;c:\archives\*
```

In UNIX, the `*` must be escaped to prevent shell expansion.

All JAR files (but not .class files) in the `archives` directory are included in this class path.

The runtime library files (`rt.jar` and the other JAR files in the `jre/lib` and `jre/lib/ext` directories) are always searched for classes; don't include them explicitly in the class path.

CAUTION: The `javac` compiler always looks for files in the current directory, but the `java` virtual machine launcher only looks into the current directory if the "." directory is on the class path. If you have no class path set, this is not a problem—the default class path consists of the "." directory. But if you have set the class path and forgot to include the "." directory, your programs will compile without error, but they won't run.

The class path lists all directories and archive files that are *starting points* for locating classes. Let's consider our sample class path:

```
/home/user/classdir:.:/home/user/archives/archive.jar
```

Suppose the virtual machine searches for the class file of the `com.horstmann.corejava.Employee` class. It first looks in the system class files that are stored in archives in the `jre/lib` and `jre/lib/ext` directories. It won't find the class file there, so it turns to the class path. It then looks for the following files:

- `/home/user/classdir/com/horstmann/corejava/Employee.class`
- `com/horstmann/corejava/Employee.class` starting from the current directory
- `com/horstmann/corejava/Employee.class` inside `/home/user/archives/archive.jar`

The compiler has a harder time locating files than does the virtual machine. If you refer to a class without specifying its package, the compiler first needs to find out the package that contains the class. It consults all `import` directives as possible sources for the class. For example, suppose the source file contains directives

```
import java.util.*;
import com.horstmann.corejava.*;
```

and the source code refers to a class `Employee`. The compiler then tries to find `java.lang.Employee` (because the `java.lang` package is always imported by default), `java.util.Employee`, `com.horstmann.corejava.Employee`, and `Employee` in the current package. It searches for *each* of these classes in all of the locations of the class path. It is a compile-time error if more than one class is found. (Classes must be unique, so the order of the `import` statements doesn't matter.)

The compiler goes one step further. It looks at the *source files* to see if the source is newer than the class file. If so, the source file is recompiled automatically. Recall that you can import only public classes from other packages. A source file can only contain one public class, and the names of the file and the public class must match. Therefore, the compiler can easily locate source files for public classes. However, you can import nonpublic classes from the current package. These classes may be defined in source files with different names. If you import a class from the current package, the compiler searches *all* source files of the current package to see which one defines the class.

4.8.1 Setting the Class Path

It is best to specify the class path with the -classpath (or -cp) option:

```
java -classpath /home/user/classdir:.:/home/user/archives/archive.jar MyProg
```

or

```
java -classpath c:\classdir;.;c:\archives\archive.jar MyProg
```

The entire command must be typed onto a single line. It is a good idea to place such a long command line into a shell script or a batch file.

Using the -classpath option is the preferred approach for setting the class path. An alternate approach is the CLASSPATH environment variable. The details depend on your shell. With the Bourne Again shell (bash), use the command

```
export CLASSPATH=/home/user/classdir:.:/home/user/archives/archive.jar
```

With the Windows shell, use

```
set CLASSPATH=c:\classdir;.;c:\archives\archive.jar
```

The class path is set until the shell exits.

CAUTION: Some people recommend to set the CLASSPATH environment variable permanently. This is generally a bad idea. People forget the global setting, and are surprised when their classes are not loaded properly. A particularly reprehensible example is Apple's QuickTime installer in Windows. For several years, it globally set CLASSPATH to point to a JAR file it needed, but did not include the current directory in the classpath. As a result, countless Java programmers were driven to distraction when their programs compiled but failed to run.

CAUTION: Some people recommend to bypass the class path altogether, by dropping all JAR files into the jre/lib/ext directory. That is truly bad advice, for two reasons. Archives that manually load other classes do not work correctly when they are placed in the extension directory. (See Volume II, Chapter 9 for more information on class loaders.) Moreover, programmers have a tendency to forget about the files they placed there months ago. Then, they scratch their heads when the class loader seems to ignore their carefully crafted class path because it is actually loading long-forgotten classes from the extension directory.

4.9 Documentation Comments

The JDK contains a very useful tool, called javadoc, that generates HTML documentation from your source files. In fact, the online API documentation that we described in Chapter 3 is simply the result of running javadoc on the source code of the standard Java library.

If you add comments that start with the special delimiter /** to your source code, you too can easily produce professional-looking documentation. This is a very nice approach because it lets you keep your code and documentation in one place. If you put your documentation into a separate file, then, as you probably know, the code and comments tend to diverge over time. When documentation comments are in the same file as the source code, it is an easy matter to update both and run javadoc again.

4.9.1 Comment Insertion

The javadoc utility extracts information for the following items:

- Packages
- Public classes and interfaces
- Public and protected fields
- Public and protected constructors and methods

Protected features are introduced in Chapter 5, interfaces in Chapter 6.

You can (and should) supply a comment for each of these features. Each comment is placed immediately *above* the feature it describes. A comment starts with a /** and ends with a */.

Each /** . . . */ documentation comment contains *free-form text* followed by *tags*. A tag starts with an @, such as @author or @param.

The *first sentence* of the free-form text should be a *summary statement*. The javadoc utility automatically generates summary pages that extract these sentences.

In the free-form text, you can use HTML modifiers such as . . . for emphasis, . . . for strong emphasis, and even <img . . .> to include an image. You should, however, stay away from headings <h1> or rules <hr> because they can interfere with the formatting of the document. To type monospaced code, use {@code ... } instead of <code>...</code>—then you don't have to worry about escaping < characters inside the code.

NOTE: If your comments contain links to other files such as images (for example, diagrams or images of user interface components), place those files into a subdirectory of the directory containing the source file, named `doc-files`. The `javadoc` utility will copy the `doc-files` directories and their contents from the source directory to the documentation directory. You need to use the `doc-files` directory in your link, for example `<img src="doc-files/uml.png" alt="UML diagram"/>`.

4.9.2 Class Comments

The class comment must be placed *after* any `import` statements, directly before the class definition.

Here is an example of a class comment:

```
/**
 * A {@code Card} object represents a playing card, such
 * as "Queen of Hearts". A card has a suit (Diamond, Heart,
 * Spade or Club) and a value (1 = Ace, 2 . . . 10, 11 = Jack,
 * 12 = Queen, 13 = King)
 */
public class Card
{
    . . .
}
```

NOTE: There is no need to add an * in front of every line. For example, the following comment is equally valid:

```
/**
    A <code>Card</code> object represents a playing card, such
    as "Queen of Hearts". A card has a suit (Diamond, Heart,
    Spade or Club) and a value (1 = Ace, 2 . . . 10, 11 = Jack,
    12 = Queen, 13 = King).
*/
```

However, most IDEs supply the asterisks automatically and rearrange them when the line breaks change.

4.9.3 Method Comments

Each method comment must immediately precede the method that it describes. In addition to the general-purpose tags, you can use the following tags:

- @param *variable description*

  This tag adds an entry to the "parameters" section of the current method. The description can span multiple lines and can use HTML tags. All @param tags for one method must be kept together.

- @return *description*

  This tag adds a "returns" section to the current method. The description can span multiple lines and can use HTML tags.

- @throws *class description*

  This tag adds a note that this method may throw an exception. Exceptions are the topic of Chapter 10.

Here is an example of a method comment:

```
/**
 * Raises the salary of an employee.
 * @param byPercent the percentage by which to raise the salary (e.g. 10 means 10%)
 * @return the amount of the raise
 */
public double raiseSalary(double byPercent)
{
   double raise = salary * byPercent / 100;
   salary += raise;
   return raise;
}
```

4.9.4 Field Comments

You only need to document public fields—generally that means static constants. For example:

```
/**
 * The "Hearts" card suit
 */
public static final int HEARTS = 1;
```

4.9.5 General Comments

The following tags can be used in class documentation comments:

- @author *name*

  This tag makes an "author" entry. You can have multiple @author tags, one for each author.

- @version *text*

  This tag makes a "version" entry. The text can be any description of the current version.

The following tags can be used in all documentation comments:

- @since *text*

  This tag makes a "since" entry. The text can be any description of the version that introduced this feature. For example, @since version 1.7.1.

- @deprecated *text*

  This tag adds a comment that the class, method, or variable should no longer be used. The *text* should suggest a replacement. For example:

  ```
  @deprecated Use <code>setVisible(true)</code> instead
  ```

You can use hyperlinks to other relevant parts of the javadoc documentation, or to external documents, with the @see and @link tags.

- @see *reference*

  This tag adds a hyperlink in the "see also" section. It can be used with both classes and methods. Here, *reference* can be one of the following:

  ```
  package.class#feature label
  <a href="...">label</a>
  "text"
  ```

  The first case is the most useful. You supply the name of a class, method, or variable, and javadoc inserts a hyperlink to the documentation. For example,

  ```
  @see com.horstmann.corejava.Employee#raiseSalary(double)
  ```

  makes a link to the raiseSalary(double) method in the com.horstmann.corejava.Employee class. You can omit the name of the package, or both the package and class names. Then, the feature will be located in the current package or class.

  Note that you must use a #, not a period, to separate the class from the method or variable name. The Java compiler itself is highly skilled in guessing the various meanings of the period character as separator between packages, subpackages, classes, inner classes, and methods and variables. But the javadoc utility isn't quite as clever, so you have to help it along.

  If the @see tag is followed by a < character, then you need to specify a hyperlink. You can link to any URL you like. For example:

  ```
  @see <a href="www.horstmann.com/corejava.html">The Core Java home page</a>
  ```

In each of these cases, you can specify an optional *label* that will appear as the link anchor. If you omit the label, the user will see the target code name or URL as the anchor.

If the `@see` tag is followed by a " character, then the text is displayed in the "see also" section. For example:

```
@see "Core Java 2 volume 2"
```

You can add multiple `@see` tags for one feature, but you must keep them all together.

- If you like, you can place hyperlinks to other classes or methods anywhere in any of your documentation comments. Insert a special tag of the form

  ```
  {@link package.class#feature label}
  ```

  anywhere in a comment. The feature description follows the same rules as for the `@see` tag.

4.9.6 Package and Overview Comments

Place the class, method, and variable comments directly into the Java source files, delimited by /** . . . */ documentation comments. However, to generate *package* comments, you need to add a separate file in each package directory. You have two choices:

1. Supply an HTML file named `package.html`. All text between the tags `<body>...</body>` is extracted.
2. Supply a Java file named `package-info.java`. The file must contain an initial Javadoc comment, delimited with /** and */, followed by a `package` statement. It should contain no further code or comments.

You can also supply an overview comment for all source files. Place it in a file called `overview.html`, located in the parent directory that contains all the source files. All text between the tags `<body>...</body>` is extracted. This comment is displayed when the user selects "Overview" from the navigation bar.

4.9.7 Comment Extraction

Here, *docDirectory* is the name of the directory where you want the HTML files to go. Follow these steps:

1. Change to the directory that contains the source files you want to document. If you have nested packages to document, such as `com.horstmann.corejava`, you must be working in the directory that contains the subdirectory `com`. (This is the directory that contains the `overview.html` file, if you supplied one.)

2. Run the command

   ```
   javadoc -d docDirectory nameOfPackage
   ```

   for a single package. Or, run

   ```
   javadoc -d docDirectory nameOfPackage₁ nameOfPackage₂...
   ```

   to document multiple packages. If your files are in the default package, run instead

   ```
   javadoc -d docDirectory *.java
   ```

If you omit the `-d docDirectory` option, the HTML files are extracted to the current directory. That can get messy, and we don't recommend it.

The `javadoc` program can be fine-tuned by numerous command-line options. For example, you can use the `-author` and `-version` options to include the `@author` and `@version` tags in the documentation. (By default, they are omitted.) Another useful option is `-link`, to include hyperlinks to standard classes. For example, if you use the command

```
javadoc -link http://docs.oracle.com/javase/8/docs/api *.java
```

all standard library classes are automatically linked to the documentation on the Oracle web site.

If you use the `-linksource` option, each source file is converted to HTML (without color coding, but with line numbers), and each class and method name turns into a hyperlink to the source.

For additional options, we refer you to the online documentation of the `javadoc` utility at `http://docs.oracle.com/javase/8/ docs/technotes/guides/javadoc/`.

 NOTE: If you need further customization—for example, to produce documentation in a format other than HTML—you can supply your own *doclet* to generate the output in any form you desire. Clearly, this is a specialized need; for details on doclets, we refer you to the online documentation at `http://docs.oracle.com/javase/8/docs/technotes/guides/javadoc/doclet/overview.html`.

4.10 Class Design Hints

Without trying to be comprehensive or tedious, we want to end this chapter with some hints that will make your classes more acceptable in well-mannered OOP circles.

1. *Always keep data private.*

    This is first and foremost; doing anything else violates encapsulation. You may need to write an accessor or mutator method occasionally, but you are still better off keeping the instance fields private. Bitter experience shows that the data representation may change, but how this data are used will change much less frequently. When data are kept private, changes in their representation will not affect the user of the class, and bugs are easier to detect.

2. *Always initialize data.*

    Java won't initialize local variables for you, but it will initialize instance fields of objects. Don't rely on the defaults, but initialize all variables explicitly, either by supplying a default or by setting defaults in all constructors.

3. *Don't use too many basic types in a class.*

    The idea is to replace multiple *related* uses of basic types with other classes. This keeps your classes easier to understand and to change. For example, replace the following instance fields in a Customer class:

    ```
    private String street;
    private String city;
    private String state;
    private int zip;
    ```

    with a new class called Address. This way, you can easily cope with changes to addresses, such as the need to deal with international addresses.

4. *Not all fields need individual field accessors and mutators.*

    You may need to get and set an employee's salary. You certainly won't need to change the hiring date once the object is constructed. And, quite often, objects have instance fields that you don't want others to get or set, such as an array of state abbreviations in an Address class.

5. *Break up classes that have too many responsibilities.*

    This hint is, of course, vague: "too many" is obviously in the eye of the beholder. However, if there is an obvious way to break one complicated class into two classes that are conceptually simpler, seize the opportunity. (On the other hand, don't go overboard; ten classes, each with only one method, are usually an overkill.)

Here is an example of a bad design:

```
public class CardDeck // bad design
{
    private int[] value;
    private int[] suit;

    public CardDeck() { . . . }
    public void shuffle() { . . . }
    public int getTopValue() { . . . }
    public int getTopSuit() { . . . }
    public void draw() { . . . }
}
```

This class really implements two separate concepts: a *deck of cards*, with its shuffle and draw methods, and a *card*, with the methods to inspect its value and suit. It makes sense to introduce a Card class that represents an individual card. Now you have two classes, each with its own responsibilities:

```
public class CardDeck
{
    private Card[] cards;

    public CardDeck() { . . . }
    public void shuffle() { . . . }
    public Card getTop() { . . . }
    public void draw() { . . . }
}

public class Card
{
    private int value;
    private int suit;

    public Card(int aValue, int aSuit) { . . . }
    public int getValue() { . . . }
    public int getSuit() { . . . }
}
```

6. *Make the names of your classes and methods reflect their responsibilities.*

Just as variables should have meaningful names that reflect what they represent, so should classes. (The standard library certainly contains some dubious examples, such as the Date class that describes time.)

A good convention is that a class name should be a noun (Order), or a noun preceded by an adjective (RushOrder) or a gerund (an "-ing" word, like

BillingAddress). As for methods, follow the standard convention that accessor methods begin with a lowercase get (getSalary) and mutator methods use a lowercase set (setSalary).

7. *Prefer immutable classes*

The LocalDate class, and other classes from the java.time package, are im-mutable—no method can modify the state of an object. Instead of mutating objects, methods such as plusDays return new objects with the modified state.

The problem with mutation is that it can happen concurrently when multiple threads try to update an object at the same time. The results are unpredictable. When classes are immutable, it is safe to share their objects among multiple threads.

Therefore, it is a good idea to make classes immutable when you can. This is particularly easy with classes that represent values, such as a string or a point in time. Computations can simply yield new values instead of updating existing ones.

Of course, not all classes should be immutable. It would be strange to have the raiseSalary method return a new Employee object when an employee gets a raise.

In this chapter, we covered the fundamentals of objects and classes that make Java an "object-based" language. In order to be truly object oriented, a program-ming language must also support inheritance and polymorphism. The Java support for these features is the topic of the next chapter.

Inheritance

Chapter 4 introduced you to classes and objects. In this chapter, you will learn about *inheritance*, another fundamental concept of object-oriented programming. The idea behind inheritance is that you can create new classes that are built on existing classes. When you inherit from an existing class, you reuse (or inherit) its methods, and you can add new methods and fields to adapt your new class to new situations. This technique is essential in Java programming.

This chapter also covers *reflection*, the ability to find out more about classes and their properties in a running program. Reflection is a powerful feature, but it is undeniably complex. Since reflection is of greater interest to tool builders than to application programmers, you can probably glance over that part of the chapter upon first reading and come back to it later.

5.1 Classes, Superclasses, and Subclasses

Let's return to the Employee class that we discussed in the previous chapter. Suppose (alas) you work for a company where managers are treated differently from other employees. Managers are, of course, just like employees in many respects. Both employees and managers are paid a salary. However, while employees are expected to complete their assigned tasks in return for receiving their salary, managers get *bonuses* if they actually achieve what they are supposed to do. This is the kind of situation that cries out for inheritance. Why? Well, you need to define a new class, Manager, and add functionality. But you can retain some of what you have already programmed in the Employee class, and *all* the fields of the original class can be preserved. More abstractly, there is an obvious "is–a" relationship between Manager and Employee. Every manager *is an* employee: This "is–a" relationship is the hallmark of inheritance.

 NOTE: In this chapter, we use the classic example of employees and managers, but we must ask you to take this example with a grain of salt. In the real world, an employee can become a manager, so you would want to model being a manager as a role of an employee, not a subclass. In our example, however, we assume the corporate world is populated by two kinds of people: those who are forever employees, and those who have always been managers.

5.1.1 Defining Subclasses

Here is how you define a Manager class that inherits from the Employee class. Use the Java keyword extends to denote inheritance.

```
public class Manager extends Employee
{
    added methods and fields
}
```

 C++ NOTE: Inheritance is similar in Java and C++. Java uses the extends keyword instead of the : token. All inheritance in Java is public inheritance; there is no analog to the C++ features of private and protected inheritance.

The keyword extends indicates that you are making a new class that derives from an existing class. The existing class is called the *superclass, base class,* or *parent class.* The new class is called the *subclass, derived class,* or *child class.* The terms superclass and subclass are those most commonly used by Java programmers, although some programmers prefer the parent/child analogy, which also ties in nicely with the "inheritance" theme.

The Employee class is a superclass, but not because it is superior to its subclass or contains more functionality. *In fact, the opposite is true:* Subclasses have *more* functionality than their superclasses. For example, as you will see when we go over the rest of the Manager class code, the Manager class encapsulates more data and has more functionality than its superclass Employee.

 NOTE: The prefixes *super* and *sub* come from the language of sets used in theoretical computer science and mathematics. The set of all employees contains the set of all managers, and thus is said to be a *superset* of the set of managers. Or, to put it another way, the set of all managers is a *subset* of the set of all employees.

Our Manager class has a new field to store the bonus, and a new method to set it:

```java
public class Manager extends Employee
{
    private double bonus;
    . . .
    public void setBonus(double bonus)
    {
        this.bonus = bonus;
    }
}
```

There is nothing special about these methods and fields. If you have a Manager object, you can simply apply the setBonus method.

```java
Manager boss = . . .;
boss.setBonus(5000);
```

Of course, if you have an Employee object, you cannot apply the setBonus method—it is not among the methods defined in the Employee class.

However, you *can* use methods such as getName and getHireDay with Manager objects. Even though these methods are not explicitly defined in the Manager class, they are automatically inherited from the Employee superclass.

Similarly, the fields name, salary, and hireDay are taken from the superclass. Every Manager object has four fields: name, salary, hireDay, and bonus.

When defining a subclass by extending its superclass, you only need to indicate the *differences* between the subclass and the superclass. When designing classes, you place the most general methods in the superclass and more specialized methods in its subclasses. Factoring out common functionality by moving it to a superclass is common in object-oriented programming.

5.1.2 Overriding Methods

Some of the superclass methods are not appropriate for the Manager subclass. In particular, the getSalary method should return the sum of the base salary and the bonus. You need to supply a new method to *override* the superclass method:

```
public class Manager extends Employee
{
   . . .
   public double getSalary()
   {
      . . .
   }
   . . .
}
```

How can you implement this method? At first glance, it appears to be simple—just return the sum of the salary and bonus fields:

```
public double getSalary()
{
   return salary + bonus; // won't work
}
```

However, that won't work. Recall that only the Employee methods have direct access to the private fields of the Employee class. This means that the getSalary method of the Manager class cannot directly access the salary field. If the Manager methods want to access those private fields, they have to do what every other method does—use the public interface, in this case the public getSalary method of the Employee class.

So, let's try again. You need to call getSalary instead of simply accessing the salary field:

```
public double getSalary()
{
   double baseSalary = getSalary(); // still won't work
   return baseSalary + bonus;
}
```

The problem is that the call to getSalary simply calls *itself*, because the Manager class has a getSalary method (namely, the method we are trying to implement). The consequence is an infinite chain of calls to the same method, leading to a program crash.

We need to indicate that we want to call the getSalary method of the Employee super-class, not the current class. You use the special keyword super for this purpose. The call

```
super.getSalary()
```

calls the getSalary method of the Employee class. Here is the correct version of the getSalary method for the Manager class:

```
public double getSalary()
{
   double baseSalary = super.getSalary();
   return baseSalary + bonus;
}
```

 NOTE: Some people think of super as being analogous to the this reference. However, that analogy is not quite accurate: super is not a reference to an object. For example, you cannot assign the value super to another object variable. Instead, super is a special keyword that directs the compiler to invoke the superclass method.

As you saw, a subclass can *add* fields, and it can *add* methods or *override* the methods of the superclass. However, inheritance can never take away any fields or methods.

 C++ NOTE: Java uses the keyword super to call a superclass method. In C++, you would use the name of the superclass with the :: operator instead. For example, the getSalary method of the Manager class would call Employee::getSalary instead of super.getSalary.

5.1.3 Subclass Constructors

To complete our example, let us supply a constructor.

```
public Manager(String name, double salary, int year, int month, int day)
{
   super(name, salary, year, month, day);
   bonus = 0;
}
```

Here, the keyword super has a different meaning. The instruction

```
super(n, s, year, month, day);
```

is shorthand for "call the constructor of the Employee superclass with n, s, year, month, and day as parameters."

Since the Manager constructor cannot access the private fields of the Employee class, it must initialize them through a constructor. The constructor is invoked with the special super syntax. The call using super must be the first statement in the constructor for the subclass.

If the subclass constructor does not call a superclass constructor explicitly, the no-argument constructor of the superclass is invoked. If the superclass does not have a no-argument constructor and the subclass constructor does not call another superclass constructor explicitly, the Java compiler reports an error.

NOTE: Recall that the this keyword has two meanings: to denote a reference to the implicit parameter and to call another constructor of the same class. Likewise, the super keyword has two meanings: to invoke a superclass method and to invoke a superclass constructor. When used to invoke constructors, the this and super keywords are closely related. The constructor calls can only occur as the first statement in another constructor. The constructor parameters are either passed to another constructor of the same class (this) or a constructor of the superclass (super).

C++ NOTE: In a C++ constructor, you do not call super, but you use the initializer list syntax to construct the superclass. The Manager constructor looks like this in C++:

```
Manager::Manager(String name, double salary, int year, int month, int day) // C++
: Employee(name, salary, year, month, day)
{
    bonus = 0;
}
```

After you redefine the getSalary method for Manager objects, managers will *automatically* have the bonus added to their salaries.

Here's an example of this at work. We make a new manager and set the manager's bonus:

```
Manager boss = new Manager("Carl Cracker", 80000, 1987, 12, 15);
boss.setBonus(5000);
```

We make an array of three employees:

```
Employee[] staff = new Employee[3];
```

We populate the array with a mix of managers and employees:

```
staff[0] = boss;
staff[1] = new Employee("Harry Hacker", 50000, 1989, 10, 1);
staff[2] = new Employee("Tony Tester", 40000, 1990, 3, 15);
```

We print out everyone's salary:

```
for (Employee e : staff)
    System.out.println(e.getName() + " " + e.getSalary());
```

This loop prints the following data:

```
Carl Cracker 85000.0
Harry Hacker 50000.0
Tommy Tester 40000.0
```

Now staff[1] and staff[2] each print their base salary because they are Employee objects. However, staff[0] is a Manager object whose getSalary method adds the bonus to the base salary.

What is remarkable is that the call

```
e.getSalary()
```

picks out the *correct* getSalary method. Note that the *declared* type of e is Employee, but the *actual* type of the object to which e refers can be either Employee or Manager.

When e refers to an Employee object, the call e.getSalary() calls the getSalary method of the Employee class. However, when e refers to a Manager object, then the getSalary method of the Manager class is called instead. The virtual machine knows about the actual type of the object to which e refers, and therefore can invoke the correct method.

The fact that an object variable (such as the variable e) can refer to multiple actual types is called *polymorphism.* Automatically selecting the appropriate method at runtime is called *dynamic binding.* We discuss both topics in more detail in this chapter.

 C++ NOTE: In C++, you need to declare a member function as virtual if you want dynamic binding. In Java, dynamic binding is the default behavior; if you do *not* want a method to be virtual, you tag it as final. (We discuss the final keyword later in this chapter.)

Listing 5.1 contains a program that shows how the salary computation differs for Employee (Listing 5.2) and Manager (Listing 5.3) objects.

Listing 5.1 inheritance/ManagerTest.java

```
1 package inheritance;
2
3 /**
4  * This program demonstrates inheritance.
5  * @version 1.21 2004-02-21
6  * @author Cay Horstmann
7  */
8 public class ManagerTest
9 {
10    public static void main(String[] args)
11    {
12       // construct a Manager object
13       Manager boss = new Manager("Carl Cracker", 80000, 1987, 12, 15);
14       boss.setBonus(5000);
15
16       Employee[] staff = new Employee[3];
17
18       // fill the staff array with Manager and Employee objects
19
20       staff[0] = boss;
21       staff[1] = new Employee("Harry Hacker", 50000, 1989, 10, 1);
22       staff[2] = new Employee("Tommy Tester", 40000, 1990, 3, 15);
23
24       // print out information about all Employee objects
25       for (Employee e : staff)
26          System.out.println("name=" + e.getName() + ",salary=" + e.getSalary());
27    }
28 }
```

Listing 5.2 inheritance/Employee.java

```
1 package inheritance;
2
3 import java.time.*;
4
5 public class Employee
6 {
7    private String name;
8    private double salary;
9    private LocalDate hireDay;
10
11    public Employee(String name, double salary, int year, int month, int day)
12    {
13       this.name = name;
14       this.salary = salary;
15       hireDay = LocalDate.of(year, month, day);
16    }
```

```
17
18    public String getName()
19    {
20       return name;
21    }
22
23    public double getSalary()
24    {
25       return salary;
26    }
27
28    public LocalDate getHireDay()
29    {
30       return hireDay;
31    }
32
33    public void raiseSalary(double byPercent)
34    {
35       double raise = salary * byPercent / 100;
36       salary += raise;
37    }
38 }
```

Listing 5.3 inheritance/Manager.java

```
1  package inheritance;
2
3  public class Manager extends Employee
4  {
5     private double bonus;
6
7     /**
8      * @param name the employee's name
9      * @param salary the salary
10     * @param year the hire year
11     * @param month the hire month
12     * @param day the hire day
13     */
14    public Manager(String name, double salary, int year, int month, int day)
15    {
16       super(name, salary, year, month, day);
17       bonus = 0;
18    }
19
```

(Continues)

Listing 5.3 *(Continued)*

```
20    public double getSalary()
21    {
22       double baseSalary = super.getSalary();
23       return baseSalary + bonus;
24    }
25
26    public void setBonus(double b)
27    {
28       bonus = b;
29    }
30 }
```

5.1.4 Inheritance Hierarchies

Inheritance need not stop at deriving one layer of classes. We could have an Executive class that extends Manager, for example. The collection of all classes extending a common superclass is called an *inheritance hierarchy,* as shown in Figure 5.1. The path from a particular class to its ancestors in the inheritance hierarchy is its *inheritance chain.*

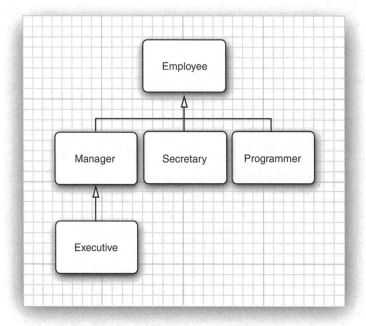

Figure 5.1 Employee inheritance hierarchy

There is usually more than one chain of descent from a distant ancestor class. You could form subclasses Programmer or Secretary that extend Employee, and they would have nothing to do with the Manager class (or with each other). This process can continue as long as is necessary.

C++ NOTE: In C++, a class can have multiple superclasses. Java does not support multiple inheritance. For ways to recover much of the functionality of multiple inheritance, see Section 6.1, "Interfaces," on p. 288.

5.1.5 Polymorphism

A simple rule can help you decide whether or not inheritance is the right design for your data. The "is–a" rule states that every object of the subclass is an object of the superclass. For example, every manager is an employee. Thus, it makes sense for the Manager class to be a subclass of the Employee class. Naturally, the opposite is not true—not every employee is a manager.

Another way of formulating the "is–a" rule is the *substitution principle.* That principle states that you can use a subclass object whenever the program expects a superclass object.

For example, you can assign a subclass object to a superclass variable.

```
Employee e;
e = new Employee(. . .);  // Employee object expected
e = new Manager(. . .); // OK, Manager can be used as well
```

In the Java programming language, object variables are *polymorphic.* A variable of type Employee can refer to an object of type Employee or to an object of any subclass of the Employee class (such as Manager, Executive, Secretary, and so on).

We took advantage of this principle in Listing 5.1:

```
Manager boss = new Manager(. . .);
Employee[] staff = new Employee[3];
staff[0] = boss;
```

In this case, the variables staff[0] and boss refer to the same object. However, staff[0] is considered to be only an Employee object by the compiler.

That means you can call

```
boss.setBonus(5000); // OK
```

but you can't call

```
staff[0].setBonus(5000); // Error
```

The declared type of staff[0] is Employee, and the setBonus method is not a method of the Employee class.

However, you cannot assign a superclass reference to a subclass variable. For example, it is not legal to make the assignment

```
Manager m = staff[i]; // Error
```

The reason is clear: Not all employees are managers. If this assignment were to succeed and m were to refer to an Employee object that is not a manager, then it would later be possible to call m.setBonus(. . .) and a runtime error would occur.

 CAUTION: In Java, arrays of subclass references can be converted to arrays of superclass references without a cast. For example, consider this array of managers:

```
Manager[] managers = new Manager[10];
```

It is legal to convert this array to an Employee[] array:

```
Employee[] staff = managers; // OK
```

Sure, why not, you may think. After all, if managers[i] is a Manager, it is also an Employee. But actually, something surprising is going on. Keep in mind that managers and staff are references to the same array. Now consider the statement

```
staff[0] = new Employee("Harry Hacker", . . .);
```

The compiler will cheerfully allow this assignment. But staff[0] and managers[0] are the same reference, so it looks as if we managed to smuggle a mere employee into the management ranks. That would be very bad—calling managers[0].setBonus(1000) would try to access a nonexistent instance field and would corrupt neighboring memory.

To make sure no such corruption can occur, all arrays remember the element type with which they were created, and they monitor that only compatible references are stored into them. For example, the array created as new Manager[10] remembers that it is an array of managers. Attempting to store an Employee reference causes an ArrayStoreException.

5.1.6 Understanding Method Calls

It is important to understand exactly how a method call is applied to an object. Let's say we call x.f(args), and the implicit parameter x is declared to be an object of class C. Here is what happens:

1. The compiler looks at the declared type of the object and the method name. Note that there may be multiple methods, all with the same name, f, but with different parameter types. For example, there may be a method f(int) and a method f(String). The compiler enumerates all methods called f in the class C and all accessible methods called f in the superclasses of C. (Private methods of the superclass are not accessible.)

    Now the compiler knows all possible candidates for the method to be called.

2. Next, the compiler determines the types of the arguments that are supplied in the method call. If among all the methods called f there is a unique method whose parameter types are a best match for the supplied arguments, that method is chosen to be called. This process is called *overloading resolution*. For example, in a call x.f("Hello"), the compiler picks f(String) and not f(int). The situation can get complex because of type conversions (int to double, Manager to Employee, and so on). If the compiler cannot find any method with matching parameter types or if multiple methods all match after applying conversions, the compiler reports an error.

    Now the compiler knows the name and parameter types of the method that needs to be called.

NOTE: Recall that the name and parameter type list for a method is called the method's *signature*. For example, f(int) and f(String) are two methods with the same name but different signatures. If you define a method in a subclass that has the same signature as a superclass method, you override the superclass method.

The return type is not part of the signature. However, when you override a method, you need to keep the return type compatible. A subclass may change the return type to a subtype of the original type. For example, suppose the Employee class has a method

```
public Employee getBuddy() { . . . }
```

A manager would never want to have a lowly employee as a buddy. To reflect that fact, the Manager subclass can override this method as

```
public Manager getBuddy() { . . . } // OK to change return type
```

We say that the two getBuddy methods have *covariant* return types.

---

3. If the method is private, static, final, or a constructor, then the compiler knows exactly which method to call. (The final modifier is explained in the next section.) This is called *static binding*. Otherwise, the method to be called

depends on the actual type of the implicit parameter, and dynamic binding must be used at runtime. In our example, the compiler would generate an instruction to call f(String) with dynamic binding.

4.   When the program runs and uses dynamic binding to call a method, the virtual machine must call the version of the method that is appropriate for the *actual* type of the object to which x refers. Let's say the actual type is D, a subclass of C. If the class D defines a method f(String), that method is called. If not, D's superclass is searched for a method f(String), and so on.

It would be time consuming to carry out this search every time a method is called. Therefore, the virtual machine precomputes for each class a *method table* that lists all method signatures and the actual methods to be called. When a method is actually called, the virtual machine simply makes a table lookup. In our example, the virtual machine consults the method table for the class D and looks up the method to call for f(String). That method may be D.f(String) or X.f(String), where X is some superclass of D. There is one twist to this scenario. If the call is super.f(param), then the compiler consults the method table of the superclass of the implicit parameter.

Let's look at this process in detail in the call e.getSalary() in Listing 5.1. The declared type of e is Employee. The Employee class has a single method, called getSalary, with no method parameters. Therefore, in this case, we don't worry about overloading resolution.

The getSalary method is not private, static, or final, so it is dynamically bound. The virtual machine produces method tables for the Employee and Manager classes. The Employee table shows that all methods are defined in the Employee class itself:

```
Employee:
    getName() -> Employee.getName()
    getSalary() -> Employee.getSalary()
    getHireDay() -> Employee.getHireDay()
    raiseSalary(double) -> Employee.raiseSalary(double)
```

Actually, that isn't the whole story—as you will see later in this chapter, the Employee class has a superclass Object from which it inherits a number of methods. We ignore the Object methods for now.

The Manager method table is slightly different. Three methods are inherited, one method is redefined, and one method is added.

```
Manager:
    getName() -> Employee.getName()
    getSalary() -> Manager.getSalary()
    getHireDay() -> Employee.getHireDay()
    raiseSalary(double) -> Employee.raiseSalary(double)
    setBonus(double) -> Manager.setBonus(double)
```

At runtime, the call `e.getSalary()` is resolved as follows:

1. First, the virtual machine fetches the method table for the actual type of `e`. That may be the table for `Employee`, `Manager`, or another subclass of `Employee`.
2. Then, the virtual machine looks up the defining class for the `getSalary()` signature. Now it knows which method to call.
3. Finally, the virtual machine calls the method.

Dynamic binding has a very important property: It makes programs *extensible* without the need for modifying existing code. Suppose a new class `Executive` is added and there is the possibility that the variable `e` refers to an object of that class. The code containing the call `e.getSalary()` need not be recompiled. The `Executive.getSalary()` method is called automatically if `e` happens to refer to an object of type `Executive`.

 CAUTION: When you override a method, the subclass method must be *at least as visible* as the superclass method. In particular, if the superclass method is `public`, the subclass method must also be declared `public`. It is a common error to accidentally omit the `public` specifier for the subclass method. The compiler then complains that you try to supply a more restrictive access privilege.

5.1.7 Preventing Inheritance: Final Classes and Methods

Occasionally, you want to prevent someone from forming a subclass from one of your classes. Classes that cannot be extended are called *final* classes, and you use the `final` modifier in the definition of the class to indicate this. For example, suppose we want to prevent others from subclassing the `Executive` class. Simply declare the class using the `final` modifier, as follows:

```
public final class Executive extends Manager
{
   . . .
}
```

You can also make a specific method in a class `final`. If you do this, then no subclass can override that method. (All methods in a `final` class are automatically `final`.) For example:

```
public class Employee
{
   . . .
   public final String getName()
   {
```

```
    return name;
  }
    . . .
}
```

 NOTE: Recall that fields can also be declared as final. A final field cannot be changed after the object has been constructed. However, if a class is declared final, only the methods, not the fields, are automatically final.

There is only one good reason to make a method or class final: to make sure its semantics cannot be changed in a subclass. For example, the getTime and setTime methods of the Calendar class are final. This indicates that the designers of the Calendar class have taken over responsibility for the conversion between the Date class and the calendar state. No subclass should be allowed to mess up this arrangement. Similarly, the String class is a final class. That means nobody can define a subclass of String. In other words, if you have a String reference, you know it refers to a String and nothing but a String.

Some programmers believe that you should declare all methods as final unless you have a good reason to want polymorphism. In fact, in C++ and C#, methods do not use polymorphism unless you specifically request it. That may be a bit extreme, but we agree that it is a good idea to think carefully about final methods and classes when you design a class hierarchy.

In the early days of Java, some programmers used the final keyword hoping to avoid the overhead of dynamic binding. If a method is not overridden, and it is short, then a compiler can optimize the method call away—a process called *inlining*. For example, inlining the call e.getName() replaces it with the field access e.name. This is a worthwhile improvement—CPUs hate branching because it interferes with their strategy of prefetching instructions while processing the current one. However, if getName can be overridden in another class, then the compiler cannot inline it because it has no way of knowing what the overriding code may do.

Fortunately, the just-in-time compiler in the virtual machine can do a better job than a traditional compiler. It knows exactly which classes extend a given class, and it can check whether any class actually overrides a given method. If a method is short, frequently called, and not actually overridden, the just-in-time compiler can inline the method. What happens if the virtual machine loads another subclass that overrides an inlined method? Then the optimizer must undo the inlining. That takes time, but it happens rarely.

5.1.8 Casting

Recall from Chapter 3 that the process of forcing a conversion from one type to another is called casting. The Java programming language has a special notation for casts. For example,

```
double x = 3.405;
int nx = (int) x;
```

converts the value of the expression x into an integer, discarding the fractional part.

Just as you occasionally need to convert a floating-point number to an integer, you may need to convert an object reference from one class to another. To actually make a cast of an object reference, use a syntax similar to what you use for casting a numeric expression. Surround the target class name with parentheses and place it before the object reference you want to cast. For example:

```
Manager boss = (Manager) staff[0];
```

There is only one reason why you would want to make a cast—to use an object in its full capacity after its actual type has been temporarily forgotten. For example, in the ManagerTest class, the staff array had to be an array of Employee objects because *some* of its elements were regular employees. We would need to cast the managerial elements of the array back to Manager to access any of its new variables. (Note that in the sample code for the first section, we made a special effort to avoid the cast. We initialized the boss variable with a Manager object before storing it in the array. We needed the correct type to set the bonus of the manager.)

As you know, in Java every variable has a type. The type describes the kind of object the variable refers to and what it can do. For example, staff[i] refers to an Employee object (so it can also refer to a Manager object).

The compiler checks that you do not promise too much when you store a value in a variable. If you assign a subclass reference to a superclass variable, you are promising less, and the compiler will simply let you do it. If you assign a superclass reference to a subclass variable, you are promising more. Then you must use a cast so that your promise can be checked at runtime.

What happens if you try to cast down an inheritance chain and are "lying" about what an object contains?

```
Manager boss = (Manager) staff[1]; // Error
```

When the program runs, the Java runtime system notices the broken promise and generates a ClassCastException. If you do not catch the exception, your program terminates. Thus, it is good programming practice to find out whether a cast will succeed before attempting it. Simply use the instanceof operator. For example:

```
if (staff[1] instanceof Manager)
{
   boss = (Manager) staff[1];
   . . .
}
```

Finally, the compiler will not let you make a cast if there is no chance for the cast to succeed. For example, the cast

```
String c = (String) staff[1];
```

is a compile-time error because String is not a subclass of Employee.

To sum up:

- You can cast only within an inheritance hierarchy.
- Use instanceof to check before casting from a superclass to a subclass.

 NOTE: The test

```
x instanceof C
```

does not generate an exception if x is null. It simply returns false. That makes sense: null refers to no object, so it certainly doesn't refer to an object of type C.

Actually, converting the type of an object by a cast is not usually a good idea. In our example, you do not need to cast an Employee object to a Manager object for most purposes. The getSalary method will work correctly on both objects of both classes. The dynamic binding that makes polymorphism work locates the correct method automatically.

The only reason to make the cast is to use a method that is unique to managers, such as setBonus. If for some reason you find yourself wanting to call setBonus on Employee objects, ask yourself whether this is an indication of a design flaw in the superclass. It may make sense to redesign the superclass and add a setBonus method. Remember, it takes only one uncaught ClassCastException to terminate your program. In general, it is best to minimize the use of casts and the instanceof operator.

C++ NOTE: Java uses the cast syntax from the "bad old days" of C, but it works like the safe `dynamic_cast` operation of C++. For example,

```
Manager boss = (Manager) staff[1]; // Java
```

is the same as

```
Manager* boss = dynamic_cast<Manager*>(staff[1]); // C++
```

with one important difference. If the cast fails, it does not yield a null object but throws an exception. In this sense, it is like a C++ cast of *references*. This is a pain in the neck. In C++, you can take care of the type test and type conversion in one operation.

```
Manager* boss = dynamic_cast<Manager*>(staff[1]); // C++
if (boss != NULL) . . .
```

In Java, you need to use a combination of the `instanceof` operator and a cast.

```
if (staff[1] instanceof Manager)
{
   Manager boss = (Manager) staff[1];
   . . .
}
```

5.1.9 Abstract Classes

As you move up the inheritance hierarchy, classes become more general and probably more abstract. At some point, the ancestor class becomes *so* general that you think of it more as a basis for other classes than as a class with specific instances you want to use. Consider, for example, an extension of our `Employee` class hierarchy. An employee is a person, and so is a student. Let us extend our class hierarchy to include classes `Person` and `Student`. Figure 5.2 shows the inheritance relationships between these classes.

Why bother with so high a level of abstraction? There are some attributes that make sense for every person, such as name. Both students and employees have names, and introducing a common superclass lets us factor out the `getName` method to a higher level in the inheritance hierarchy.

Now let's add another method, `getDescription`, whose purpose is to return a brief description of the person, such as

```
an employee with a salary of $50,000.00
a student majoring in computer science
```

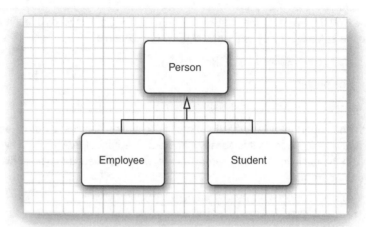

Figure 5.2 Inheritance diagram for Person and its subclasses

It is easy to implement this method for the Employee and Student classes. But what information can you provide in the Person class? The Person class knows nothing about the person except the name. Of course, you could implement Person.getDescription() to return an empty string. But there is a better way. If you use the abstract keyword, you do not need to implement the method at all.

```
public abstract String getDescription();
   // no implementation required
```

For added clarity, a class with one or more abstract methods must itself be declared abstract.

```
public abstract class Person
{
   . . .
   public abstract String getDescription();
}
```

In addition to abstract methods, abstract classes can have fields and concrete methods. For example, the Person class stores the name of the person and has a concrete method that returns it.

```
public abstract class Person
{
   private String name;
```

```
public Person(String name)
{
    this.name = name;
}

public abstract String getDescription();

public String getName()
{
    return name;
}
}
```

 TIP: Some programmers don't realize that abstract classes can have concrete methods. You should always move common fields and methods (whether abstract or not) to the superclass (whether abstract or not).

Abstract methods act as placeholders for methods that are implemented in the subclasses. When you extend an abstract class, you have two choices. You can leave some or all of the abstract methods undefined; then you must tag the subclass as abstract as well. Or you can define all methods, and the subclass is no longer abstract.

For example, we will define a Student class that extends the abstract Person class and implements the getDescription method. None of the methods of the Student class are abstract, so it does not need to be declared as an abstract class.

A class can even be declared as abstract though it has no abstract methods.

Abstract classes cannot be instantiated. That is, if a class is declared as abstract, no objects of that class can be created. For example, the expression

```
new Person("Vince Vu")
```

is an error. However, you can create objects of concrete subclasses.

Note that you can still create *object variables* of an abstract class, but such a variable must refer to an object of a nonabstract subclass. For example:

```
Person p = new Student("Vince Vu", "Economics");
```

Here p is a variable of the abstract type Person that refers to an instance of the nonabstract subclass Student.

C++ NOTE: In C++, an abstract method is called a *pure virtual function* and is tagged with a trailing = 0, such as in

```
class Person // C++
{
public:
   virtual string getDescription() = 0;
   . . .
};
```

A C++ class is abstract if it has at least one pure virtual function. In C++, there is no special keyword to denote abstract classes.

Let us define a concrete subclass Student that extends the abstract class Person:

```
public class Student extends Person
{
   private String major;

   public Student(String name, String major)
   {
      super(name);
      this.major = major;
   }

   public String getDescription()
   {
      return "a student majoring in " + major;
   }
}
```

The Student class defines the getDescription method. Therefore, all methods in the Student class are concrete, and the class is no longer an abstract class.

The program shown in Listing 5.4 defines the abstract superclass Person (Listing 5.5) and two concrete subclasses, Employee (Listing 5.6) and Student (Listing 5.7). We fill an array of Person references with employee and student objects:

```
Person[] people = new Person[2];
people[0] = new Employee(. . .);
people[1] = new Student(. . .);
```

We then print the names and descriptions of these objects:

```
for (Person p : people)
   System.out.println(p.getName() + ", " + p.getDescription());
```

Some people are baffled by the call

```
p.getDescription()
```

Isn't this a call to an undefined method? Keep in mind that the variable p never refers to a Person object because it is impossible to construct an object of the abstract Person class. The variable p always refers to an object of a concrete subclass such as Employee or Student. For these objects, the getDescription method is defined.

Could you have omitted the abstract method altogether from the Person superclass, simply defining the getDescription methods in the Employee and Student subclasses? If you did that, you wouldn't have been able to invoke the getDescription method on the variable p. The compiler ensures that you invoke only methods that are declared in the class.

Abstract methods are an important concept in the Java programming language. You will encounter them most commonly inside *interfaces*. For more information about interfaces, turn to Chapter 6.

Listing 5.4 abstractClasses/PersonTest.java

```java
1  package abstractClasses;
2
3  /**
4   * This program demonstrates abstract classes.
5   * @version 1.01 2004-02-21
6   * @author Cay Horstmann
7   */
8  public class PersonTest
9  {
10     public static void main(String[] args)
11     {
12        Person[] people = new Person[2];
13
14        // fill the people array with Student and Employee objects
15        people[0] = new Employee("Harry Hacker", 50000, 1989, 10, 1);
16        people[1] = new Student("Maria Morris", "computer science");
17
18        // print out names and descriptions of all Person objects
19        for (Person p : people)
20           System.out.println(p.getName() + ", " + p.getDescription());
21     }
22  }
```

Listing 5.5 abstractClasses/Person.java

```
1  package abstractClasses;
2
3  public abstract class Person
4  {
5     public abstract String getDescription();
6     private String name;
7
8     public Person(String name)
9     {
10       this.name = name;
11    }
12
13    public String getName()
14    {
15       return name;
16    }
17 }
```

Listing 5.6 abstractClasses/Employee.java

```
1  package abstractClasses;
2
3  import java.time.*;
4
5  public class Employee extends Person
6  {
7     private double salary;
8     private LocalDate hireDay;
9
10    public Employee(String name, double salary, int year, int month, int day)
11    {
12       super(name);
13       this.salary = salary;
14       hireDay = LocalDate.of(year, month, day);
15    }
16
17    public double getSalary()
18    {
19       return salary;
20    }
21
22    public LocalDate getHireDay()
23    {
24       return hireDay;
25    }
26
```

```
27    public String getDescription()
28    {
29        return String.format("an employee with a salary of $%.2f", salary);
30    }
31
32    public void raiseSalary(double byPercent)
33    {
34        double raise = salary * byPercent / 100;
35        salary += raise;
36    }
37 }
```

Listing 5.7 abstractClasses/Student.java

```
1 package abstractClasses;
2
3 public class Student extends Person
4 {
5    private String major;
6
7    /**
8     * @param nama the student's name
9     * @param major the student's major
10    */
11    public Student(String name, String major)
12    {
13        // pass n to superclass constructor
14        super(name);
15        this.major = major;
16    }
17
18    public String getDescription()
19    {
20        return "a student majoring in " + major;
21    }
22 }
```

5.1.10 Protected Access

As you know, fields in a class are best tagged as private, and methods are usually tagged as public. Any features declared private won't be visible to other classes. As we said at the beginning of this chapter, this is also true for subclasses: A subclass cannot access the private fields of its superclass.

There are times, however, when you want to restrict a method to subclasses only or, less commonly, to allow subclass methods to access a superclass field. In that case, you declare a class feature as protected. For example, if the superclass Employee declares the hireDay field as protected instead of private, then the Manager methods can access it directly.

However, the Manager class methods can peek inside the hireDay field of Manager objects only, not of other Employee objects. This restriction is made so that you can't abuse the protected mechanism by forming subclasses just to gain access to the protected fields.

In practice, use protected fields with caution. Suppose your class is used by other programmers and you designed it with protected fields. Unknown to you, other programmers may inherit classes from your class and start accessing your protected fields. In this case, you can no longer change the implementation of your class without upsetting those programmers. That is against the spirit of OOP, which encourages data encapsulation.

Protected methods make more sense. A class may declare a method as protected if it is tricky to use. This indicates that the subclasses (which, presumably, know their ancestor well) can be trusted to use the method correctly, but other classes cannot.

A good example of this kind of method is the clone method of the Object class—see Chapter 6 for more details.

 C++ NOTE: As it happens, protected features in Java are visible to all subclasses as well as to all other classes in the same package. This is slightly different from the C++ meaning of protected, and it makes the notion of protected in Java even less safe than in C++.

Here is a summary of the four access modifiers in Java that control visibility:

1. Visible to the class only (private).
2. Visible to the world (public).
3. Visible to the package and all subclasses (protected).
4. Visible to the package—the (unfortunate) default. No modifiers are needed.

5.2 Object: The Cosmic Superclass

The Object class is the ultimate ancestor—every class in Java extends Object. However, you never have to write

```
public class Employee extends Object
```

The ultimate superclass Object is taken for granted if no superclass is explicitly mentioned. Since *every* class in Java extends Object, it is important to be familiar with the services provided by the Object class. We go over the basic ones in this chapter; consult the later chapters or view the online documentation for what is not covered here. (Several methods of Object come up only when dealing with concurrency—see Chapter 14 for more on threads.)

You can use a variable of type Object to refer to objects of any type:

```
Object obj = new Employee("Harry Hacker", 35000);
```

Of course, a variable of type Object is only useful as a generic holder for arbitrary values. To do anything specific with the value, you need to have some knowledge about the original type and apply a cast:

```
Employee e = (Employee) obj;
```

In Java, only the values of *primitive types* (numbers, characters, and boolean values) are not objects.

All array types, no matter whether they are arrays of objects or arrays of primitive types, are class types that extend the Object class.

```
Employee[] staff = new Employee[10];
obj = staff; // OK
obj = new int[10]; // OK
```

 C++ NOTE: In C++, there is no cosmic root class. However, every pointer can be converted to a void* pointer.

5.2.1 The equals Method

The equals method in the Object class tests whether one object is considered equal to another. The equals method, as implemented in the Object class, determines whether two object references are identical. This is a pretty reasonable default—if two objects are identical, they should certainly be equal. For quite a few classes, nothing else is required. For example, it makes little sense to compare two PrintStream objects for equality. However, you will often want to implement state-based equality testing, in which two objects are considered equal when they have the same state.

For example, let us consider two employees equal if they have the same name, salary, and hire date. (In an actual employee database, it would be more sensible to compare IDs instead. We use this example to demonstrate the mechanics of implementing the equals method.)

```
public class Employee
{
    . . .
    public boolean equals(Object otherObject)
    {
        // a quick test to see if the objects are identical
        if (this == otherObject) return true;

        // must return false if the explicit parameter is null
        if (otherObject == null) return false;

        // if the classes don't match, they can't be equal
        if (getClass() != otherObject.getClass())
            return false;

        // now we know otherObject is a non-null Employee
        Employee other = (Employee) otherObject;

        // test whether the fields have identical values
        return name.equals(other.name)
            && salary == other.salary
            && hireDay.equals(other.hireDay);
    }
}
```

The getClass method returns the class of an object—we discuss this method in detail later in this chapter. In our test, two objects can only be equal when they belong to the same class.

TIP: To guard against the possibility that name or hireDay are null, use the Objects.equals method. The call Objects.equals(a, b) returns true if both arguments are null, false if only one is null, and calls a.equals(b) otherwise. With that method, the last statement of the Employee.equals method becomes

```
return Objects.equals(name, other.name)
    && salary == other.salary
    && Object.equals(hireDay, other.hireDay);
```

When you define the equals method for a subclass, first call equals on the superclass. If that test doesn't pass, then the objects can't be equal. If the superclass fields are equal, you are ready to compare the instance fields of the subclass.

```
public class Manager extends Employee
{
    . . .
    public boolean equals(Object otherObject)
    {
```

```
        if (!super.equals(otherObject)) return false;
        // super.equals checked that this and otherObject belong to the same class
        Manager other = (Manager) otherObject;
        return bonus == other.bonus;
    }
}
```

5.2.2 Equality Testing and Inheritance

How should the equals method behave if the implicit and explicit parameters don't belong to the same class? This has been an area of some controversy. In the preceding example, the equals method returns false if the classes don't match exactly. But many programmers use an instanceof test instead:

```
    if (!(otherObject instanceof Employee)) return false;
```

This leaves open the possibility that otherObject can belong to a subclass. However, this approach can get you into trouble. Here is why. The Java Language Specification requires that the equals method has the following properties:

1.   It is *reflexive*: For any non-null reference x, x.equals(x) should return true.

2.   It is *symmetric*: For any references x and y, x.equals(y) should return true if and only if y.equals(x) returns true.

3.   It is *transitive*: For any references x, y, and z, if x.equals(y) returns true and y.equals(z) returns true, then x.equals(z) should return true.

4.   It is *consistent*: If the objects to which x and y refer haven't changed, then repeated calls to x.equals(y) return the same value.

5.   For any non-null reference x, x.equals(null) should return false.

These rules are certainly reasonable. You wouldn't want a library implementor to ponder whether to call x.equals(y) or y.equals(x) when locating an element in a data structure.

However, the symmetry rule has subtle consequences when the parameters belong to different classes. Consider a call

```
    e.equals(m)
```

where e is an Employee object and m is a Manager object, both of which happen to have the same name, salary, and hire date. If Employee.equals uses an instanceof test, the call returns true. But that means that the reverse call

```
    m.equals(e)
```

also needs to return true—the symmetry rule does not allow it to return false or to throw an exception.

That leaves the Manager class in a bind. Its equals method must be willing to compare itself to any Employee, without taking manager-specific information into account! All of a sudden, the instanceof test looks less attractive.

Some authors have gone on record that the getClass test is wrong because it violates the substitution principle. A commonly cited example is the equals method in the AbstractSet class that tests whether two sets have the same elements. The AbstractSet class has two concrete subclasses, TreeSet and HashSet, that use different algorithms for locating set elements. You really want to be able to compare any two sets, no matter how they are implemented.

However, the set example is rather specialized. It would make sense to declare AbstractSet.equals as final, because nobody should redefine the semantics of set equality. (The method is not actually final. This allows a subclass to implement a more efficient algorithm for the equality test.)

The way we see it, there are two distinct scenarios:

- If subclasses can have their own notion of equality, then the symmetry requirement forces you to use the getClass test.
- If the notion of equality is fixed in the superclass, then you can use the instanceof test and allow objects of different subclasses to be equal to one another.

In the example with employees and managers, we consider two objects to be equal when they have matching fields. If we have two Manager objects with the same name, salary, and hire date, but with different bonuses, we want them to be different. Therefore, we used the getClass test.

But suppose we used an employee ID for equality testing. This notion of equality makes sense for all subclasses. Then we could use the instanceof test, and we should have declared Employee.equals as final.

 NOTE: The standard Java library contains over 150 implementations of equals methods, with a mishmash of using instanceof, calling getClass, catching a ClassCastException, or doing nothing at all. Check out the API documentation of the java.sql.Timestamp class, where the implementors note with some embarrassment that they have painted themselves in a corner. The Timestamp class inherits from java.util.Date, whose equals method uses an instanceof test, and it is impossible to override equals to be both symmetric and accurate.

Here is a recipe for writing the perfect equals method:

1. Name the explicit parameter otherObject—later, you will need to cast it to another variable that you should call other.

2. Test whether this happens to be identical to otherObject:

   ```
   if (this == otherObject) return true;
   ```

   This statement is just an optimization. In practice, this is a common case. It is much cheaper to check for identity than to compare the fields.

3. Test whether otherObject is null and return false if it is. This test is required.

   ```
   if (otherObject == null) return false;
   ```

4. Compare the classes of this and otherObject. If the semantics of equals can change in subclasses, use the getClass test:

   ```
   if (getClass() != otherObject.getClass()) return false;
   ```

   If the same semantics holds for *all* subclasses, you can use an instanceof test:

   ```
   if (!(otherObject instanceof ClassName)) return false;
   ```

5. Cast otherObject to a variable of your class type:

   ```
   ClassName other = (ClassName) otherObject
   ```

6. Now compare the fields, as required by your notion of equality. Use == for primitive type fields, Objects.equals for object fields. Return true if all fields match, false otherwise.

   ```
   return field1 == other.field1
       && Objects.equals(field2, other.field2)
       && . . .;
   ```

   If you redefine equals in a subclass, include a call to super.equals(other).

 TIP: If you have fields of array type, you can use the static Arrays.equals method to check that the corresponding array elements are equal.

CAUTION: Here is a common mistake when implementing the `equals` method. Can you spot the problem?

```
public class Employee
{
    public boolean equals(Employee other)
    {
        return other != null
            && getClass() == other.getClass()
            && Objects.equals(name, other.name)
            && salary == other.salary
            && Objects.equals(hireDay, other.hireDay);
    }
    . . .
}
```

This method declares the explicit parameter type as `Employee`. As a result, it does not override the `equals` method of the `Object` class but defines a completely unrelated method.

You can protect yourself against this type of error by tagging methods that are intended to override superclass methods with `@Override`:

```
@Override public boolean equals(Object other)
```

If you made a mistake and are defining a new method, the compiler reports an error. For example, suppose you add the following declaration to the `Employee` class:

```
@Override public boolean equals(Employee other)
```

An error is reported because this method doesn't override any method from the `Object` superclass.

---

java.util.Arrays 1.2

- `static boolean equals(type[] a, type[] b)` 5.0

  returns `true` if the arrays have equal lengths and equal elements in corresponding positions. The arrays can have component types `Object`, `int`, `long`, `short`, `char`, `byte`, `boolean`, `float`, or `double`.

```
java.util.Objects 7
```

- `static boolean equals(Object a, Object b)`

  returns `true` if a and b are both `null`, `false` if exactly one of them is `null`, and `a.equals(b)` otherwise.

5.2.3 The hashCode Method

A hash code is an integer that is derived from an object. Hash codes should be scrambled—if x and y are two distinct objects, there should be a high probability that x.hashCode() and y.hashCode() are different. Table 5.1 lists a few examples of hash codes that result from the hashCode method of the String class.

Table 5.1 Hash Codes Resulting from the hashCode Method

String	Hash Code
Hello	69609650
Harry	69496448
Hacker	-2141031506

The String class uses the following algorithm to compute the hash code:

```
int hash = 0;
for (int i = 0; i < length(); i++)
    hash = 31 * hash + charAt(i);
```

The hashCode method is defined in the Object class. Therefore, every object has a default hash code. That hash code is derived from the object's memory address. Consider this example:

```
String s = "Ok";
StringBuilder sb = new StringBuilder(s);
System.out.println(s.hashCode() + " " + sb.hashCode());
String t = new String("Ok");
StringBuilder tb = new StringBuilder(t);
System.out.println(t.hashCode() + " " + tb.hashCode());
```

Table 5.2 shows the result.

Table 5.2 Hash Codes of Strings and String Builders

Object	Hash Code
s	2556
sb	20526976
t	2556
tb	20527144

Note that the strings s and t have the same hash code because, for strings, the hash codes are derived from their *contents*. The string builders sb and tb have different hash codes because no hashCode method has been defined for the StringBuilder class and the default hashCode method in the Object class derives the hash code from the object's memory address.

If you redefine the equals method, you will also need to redefine the hashCode method for objects that users might insert into a hash table. (We discuss hash tables in Chapter 9.)

The hashCode method should return an integer (which can be negative). Just combine the hash codes of the instance fields so that the hash codes for different objects are likely to be widely scattered.

For example, here is a hashCode method for the Employee class:

```
public class Employee
{
   public int hashCode()
   {
      return 7 * name.hashCode()
         + 11 * new Double(salary).hashCode()
         + 13 * hireDay.hashCode();
   }
   . . .
}
```

However, you can do better. First, use the null-safe method Objects.hashCode. It returns 0 if its argument is null and the result of calling hashCode on the argument otherwise. Also, use the static Double.hashCode method to avoid creating a Double object:

```
public int hashCode()
{
   return 7 * Objects.hashCode(name)
      + 11 * Double.hashCode(salary)
      + 13 * Objects.hashCode(hireDay);
}
```

Even better, when you need to combine multiple hash values, call `Objects.hash` with all of them. It will call `Objects.hashCode` for each argument and combine the values. Then the `Employee.hashCode` method is simply

```
public int hashCode()
{
    return Objects.hash(name, salary, hireDay);
}
```

Your definitions of `equals` and `hashCode` must be compatible: If `x.equals(y)` is `true`, then `x.hashCode()` must return the same value as `y.hashCode()`. For example, if you define `Employee.equals` to compare employee IDs, then the `hashCode` method needs to hash the IDs, not employee names or memory addresses.

 TIP: If you have fields of an array type, you can use the static `Arrays.hashCode` method to compute a hash code composed of the hash codes of the array elements.

---

java.lang.Object 1.0

- `int hashCode()`

  returns a hash code for this object. A hash code can be any integer, positive or negative. Equal objects need to return identical hash codes.

---

java.util.Objects 7

- `static int hash(Object... objects)`

  returns a hash code that is combined from the hash codes of all supplied objects.

- `static int hashCode(Object a)`

  returns 0 if a is `null` or `a.hashCode()` otherwise.

---

java.lang.(Integer | Long | Short | Byte | Double | Float | Character | Boolean) 1.0

- `static int hashCode((int | long | short | byte | double | float | char | boolean) value)` 8

  returns the hash code of the given value.

---

java.util.Arrays 1.2

- static int hashCode(*type*[] a) 5.0

  computes the hash code of the array a, which can have component type Object, int, long, short, char, byte, boolean, float, or double.

5.2.4 The toString Method

Another important method in Object is the toString method that returns a string representing the value of this object. Here is a typical example. The toString method of the Point class returns a string like this:

```
java.awt.Point[x=10,y=20]
```

Most (but not all) toString methods follow this format: the name of the class, then the field values enclosed in square brackets. Here is an implementation of the toString method for the Employee class:

```
public String toString()
{
   return "Employee[name=" + name
      + ",salary=" + salary
      + ",hireDay=" + hireDay
      + "]";
}
```

Actually, you can do a little better. Instead of hardwiring the class name into the toString method, call getClass().getName() to obtain a string with the class name.

```
public String toString()
{
   return getClass().getName()
      + "[name=" + name
      + ",salary=" + salary
      + ",hireDay=" + hireDay
      + "]";
}
```

Such toString method will also work for subclasses.

Of course, the subclass programmer should define its own toString method and add the subclass fields. If the superclass uses getClass().getName(), then the subclass can simply call super.toString(). For example, here is a toString method for the Manager class:

```
public class Manager extends Employee
{
   . . .
   public String toString()
   {
      return super.toString()
        + "[bonus=" + bonus
        + "]";
   }
}
```

Now a Manager object is printed as

```
Manager[name=...,salary=...,hireDay=...][bonus=...]
```

The toString method is ubiquitous for an important reason: Whenever an object is concatenated with a string by the "+" operator, the Java compiler automatically invokes the toString method to obtain a string representation of the object. For example:

```
Point p = new Point(10, 20);
String message = "The current position is " + p;
  // automatically invokes p.toString()
```

 TIP: Instead of writing x.toString(), you can write "" + x. This statement concatenates the empty string with the string representation of x that is exactly x.toString(). Unlike toString, this statement even works if x is of primitive type.

If x is any object and you call

```
System.out.println(x);
```

then the println method simply calls x.toString() and prints the resulting string.

The Object class defines the toString method to print the class name and the hash code of the object. For example, the call

```
System.out.println(System.out)
```

produces an output that looks like this:

```
java.io.PrintStream@2f6684
```

The reason is that the implementor of the PrintStream class didn't bother to override the toString method.

CAUTION: Annoyingly, arrays inherit the `toString` method from `Object`, with the added twist that the array type is printed in an archaic format. For example,

```
int[] luckyNumbers = { 2, 3, 5, 7, 11, 13 };
String s = "" + luckyNumbers;
```

yields the string `"[I@1a46e30"`. (The prefix `[I` denotes an array of integers.) The remedy is to call the static `Arrays.toString` method instead. The code

```
String s = Arrays.toString(luckyNumbers);
```

yields the string `"[2, 3, 5, 7, 11, 13]"`.

To correctly print multidimensional arrays (that is, arrays of arrays), use `Arrays.deepToString`.

The `toString` method is a great tool for logging. Many classes in the standard class library define the `toString` method so that you can get useful information about the state of an object. This is particularly useful in logging messages like this:

```
System.out.println("Current position = " + position);
```

As we explain in Chapter 7, an even better solution is to use an object of the `Logger` class and call

```
Logger.global.info("Current position = " + position);
```

TIP: We strongly recommend that you add a `toString` method to each class that you write. You, as well as other programmers who use your classes, will be grateful for the logging support.

The program in Listing 5.8 implements the `equals`, `hashCode`, and `toString` methods for the classes `Employee` (Listing 5.9) and `Manager` (Listing 5.10).

Listing 5.8 equals/EqualsTest.java

```
1  package equals;
2
3  /**
4   * This program demonstrates the equals method.
5   * @version 1.12 2012-01-26
6   * @author Cay Horstmann
7   */
8  public class EqualsTest
9  {
```

```
10    public static void main(String[] args)
11    {
12       Employee alice1 = new Employee("Alice Adams", 75000, 1987, 12, 15);
13       Employee alice2 = alice1;
14       Employee alice3 = new Employee("Alice Adams", 75000, 1987, 12, 15);
15       Employee bob = new Employee("Bob Brandson", 50000, 1989, 10, 1);
16
17       System.out.println("alice1 == alice2: " + (alice1 == alice2));
18
19       System.out.println("alice1 == alice3: " + (alice1 == alice3));
20
21       System.out.println("alice1.equals(alice3): " + alice1.equals(alice3));
22
23       System.out.println("alice1.equals(bob): " + alice1.equals(bob));
24
25       System.out.println("bob.toString(): " + bob);
26
27       Manager carl = new Manager("Carl Cracker", 80000, 1987, 12, 15);
28       Manager boss = new Manager("Carl Cracker", 80000, 1987, 12, 15);
29       boss.setBonus(5000);
30       System.out.println("boss.toString(): " + boss);
31       System.out.println("carl.equals(boss): " + carl.equals(boss));
32       System.out.println("alice1.hashCode(): " + alice1.hashCode());
33       System.out.println("alice3.hashCode(): " + alice3.hashCode());
34       System.out.println("bob.hashCode(): " + bob.hashCode());
35       System.out.println("carl.hashCode(): " + carl.hashCode());
36    }
37 }
```

Listing 5.9 equals/Employee.java

```
1 package equals;
2
3 import java.time.*;
4 import java.util.Objects;
5
6 public class Employee
7 {
8    private String name;
9    private double salary;
10   private LocalDate hireDay;
11
12   public Employee(String name, double salary, int year, int month, int day)
13   {
14      this.name = name;
15      this.salary = salary;
16      hireDay = LocalDate.of(year, month, day);
17   }
```

(Continues)

Listing 5.9 *(Continued)*

```
18
19     public String getName()
20     {
21        return name;
22     }
23
24     public double getSalary()
25     {
26        return salary;
27     }
28
29     public LocalDate getHireDay()
30     {
31        return hireDay;
32     }
33
34     public void raiseSalary(double byPercent)
35     {
36        double raise = salary * byPercent / 100;
37        salary += raise;
38     }
39
40     public boolean equals(Object otherObject)
41     {
42        // a quick test to see if the objects are identical
43        if (this == otherObject) return true;
44
45        // must return false if the explicit parameter is null
46        if (otherObject == null) return false;
47
48        // if the classes don't match, they can't be equal
49        if (getClass() != otherObject.getClass()) return false;
50
51        // now we know otherObject is a non-null Employee
52        Employee other = (Employee) otherObject;
53
54        // test whether the fields have identical values
55        return Objects.equals(name, other.name) && salary == other.salary
56           && Objects.equals(hireDay, other.hireDay);
57     }
58
59     public int hashCode()
60     {
61        return Objects.hash(name, salary, hireDay);
62     }
63
```

```
64     public String toString()
65     {
66        return getClass().getName() + "[name=" + name + ",salary=" + salary + ",hireDay=" + hireDay
67           + "]";
68     }
69  }
```

Listing 5.10 equals/Manager.java

```
1  package equals;
2
3  public class Manager extends Employee
4  {
5     private double bonus;
6
7     public Manager(String name, double salary, int year, int month, int day)
8     {
9        super(name, salary, year, month, day);
10       bonus = 0;
11    }
12
13    public double getSalary()
14    {
15       double baseSalary = super.getSalary();
16       return baseSalary + bonus;
17    }
18
19    public void setBonus(double bonus)
20    {
21       this.bonus = bonus;
22    }
23
24    public boolean equals(Object otherObject)
25    {
26       if (!super.equals(otherObject)) return false;
27       Manager other = (Manager) otherObject;
28       // super.equals checked that this and other belong to the same class
29       return bonus == other.bonus;
30    }
31
32    public int hashCode()
33    {
34       return super.hashCode() + 17 * new Double(bonus).hashCode();
35    }
36
37    public String toString()
38    {
39       return super.toString() + "[bonus=" + bonus + "]";
40    }
41 }
```

---

java.lang.Object 1.0

- Class getClass()

  returns a class object that contains information about the object. As you will see later in this chapter, Java has a runtime representation for classes that is encapsulated in the Class class.

- boolean equals(Object otherObject)

  compares two objects for equality; returns true if the objects point to the same area of memory, and false otherwise. You should override this method in your own classes.

- String toString()

  returns a string that represents the value of this object. You should override this method in your own classes.

---

java.lang.Class 1.0

- String getName()

  returns the name of this class.

- Class getSuperclass()

  returns the superclass of this class as a Class object.

5.3 Generic Array Lists

In many programming languages—in particular, in C++—you have to fix the sizes of all arrays at compile time. Programmers hate this because it forces them into uncomfortable trade-offs. How many employees will be in a department? Surely no more than 100. What if there is a humongous department with 150 employees? Do we want to waste 90 entries for every department with just 10 employees?

In Java, the situation is much better. You can set the size of an array at runtime.

```
int actualSize = . . .;
Employee[] staff = new Employee[actualSize];
```

Of course, this code does not completely solve the problem of dynamically modifying arrays at runtime. Once you set the array size, you cannot change it easily. Instead, in Java you can deal with this common situation by using another Java class, called ArrayList. The ArrayList class is similar to an array, but it automatically adjusts its capacity as you add and remove elements, without any additional code.

ArrayList is a *generic class* with a *type parameter*. To specify the type of the element objects that the array list holds, you append a class name enclosed in angle brackets, such as ArrayList<Employee>. You will see in Chapter 8 how to define your own generic class, but you don't need to know any of those technicalities to use the ArrayList type.

Here we declare and construct an array list that holds Employee objects:

```
ArrayList<Employee> staff = new ArrayList<Employee>();
```

It is a bit tedious that the type parameter Employee is used on both sides. As of Java SE 7, you can omit the type parameter on the right-hand side:

```
ArrayList<Employee> staff = new ArrayList<>();
```

This is called the "diamond" syntax because the empty brackets <> resemble a diamond. Use the diamond syntax together with the new operator. The compiler checks what happens to the new value. If it is assigned to a variable, passed into a method, or returned from a method, then the compiler checks the generic type of the variable, parameter, or method. It then places that type into the <>. In our example, the new ArrayList<>() is assigned to a variable of type ArrayList<Employee>. Therefore, the generic type is Employee.

NOTE: Before Java SE 5.0, there were no generic classes. Instead, there was a single ArrayList class, a one-size-fits-all collection that holds elements of type Object. You can still use ArrayList without a <. . .> suffix. It is considered a "raw" type, with the type parameter erased.

NOTE: In even older versions of Java, programmers used the Vector class for dynamic arrays. However, the ArrayList class is more efficient, and there is no longer any good reason to use the Vector class.

Use the add method to add new elements to an array list. For example, here is how you populate an array list with employee objects:

```
staff.add(new Employee("Harry Hacker", . . .));
staff.add(new Employee("Tony Tester", . . .));
```

The array list manages an internal array of object references. Eventually, that array will run out of space. This is where array lists work their magic: If you call add and the internal array is full, the array list automatically creates a bigger array and copies all the objects from the smaller to the bigger array.

If you already know, or have a good guess, how many elements you want to store, call the ensureCapacity method before filling the array list:

```
staff.ensureCapacity(100);
```

That call allocates an internal array of 100 objects. Then, the first 100 calls to add will not involve any costly reallocation.

You can also pass an initial capacity to the ArrayList constructor:

```
ArrayList<Employee> staff = new ArrayList<>(100);
```

 CAUTION: Allocating an array list as

```
new ArrayList<>(100) // capacity is 100
```

is *not* the same as allocating a new array as

```
new Employee[100] // size is 100
```

There is an important distinction between the capacity of an array list and the size of an array. If you allocate an array with 100 entries, then the array has 100 slots, ready for use. An array list with a capacity of 100 elements has the *potential* of holding 100 elements (and, in fact, more than 100, at the cost of additional reallocations)—but at the beginning, even after its initial construction, an array list holds no elements at all.

The size method returns the actual number of elements in the array list. For example,

```
staff.size()
```

returns the current number of elements in the staff array list. This is the equivalent of

```
a.length
```

for an array a.

Once you are reasonably sure that the array list is at its permanent size, you can call the trimToSize method. This method adjusts the size of the memory block to use exactly as much storage space as is required to hold the current number of elements. The garbage collector will reclaim any excess memory.

Once you trim the size of an array list, adding new elements will move the block again, which takes time. You should only use trimToSize when you are sure you won't add any more elements to the array list.

C++ NOTE: The `ArrayList` class is similar to the C++ `vector` template. Both `ArrayList` and `vector` are generic types. But the C++ `vector` template overloads the [] operator for convenient element access. Java does not have operator overloading, so it must use explicit method calls instead. Moreover, C++ vectors are copied by value. If `a` and `b` are two vectors, then the assignment `a = b` makes `a` into a new vector with the same length as `b`, and all elements are copied from `b` to `a`. The same assignment in Java makes both `a` and `b` refer to the same array list.

---

java.util.ArrayList<E> 1.2

- `ArrayList<E>()`

  constructs an empty array list.

- `ArrayList<E>(int initialCapacity)`

  constructs an empty array list with the specified capacity.

  Parameters: `initialCapacity`   the initial storage capacity of the array list

- `boolean add(E obj)`

  appends an element at the end of the array list. Always returns `true`.

  Parameters: `obj`   the element to be added

- `int size()`

  returns the number of elements currently stored in the array list. (Of course, this is never larger than the array list's capacity.)

- `void ensureCapacity(int capacity)`

  ensures that the array list has the capacity to store the given number of elements without reallocating its internal storage array.

  Parameters: `capacity`   the desired storage capacity

- `void trimToSize()`

  reduces the storage capacity of the array list to its current size.

5.3.1 Accessing Array List Elements

Unfortunately, nothing comes for free. The automatic growth convenience that array lists give requires a more complicated syntax for accessing the elements. The reason is that the `ArrayList` class is not a part of the Java programming language; it is just a utility class programmed by someone and supplied in the standard library.

Instead of the pleasant [] syntax to access or change the element of an array, you use the `get` and `set` methods.

For example, to set the i th element, you use

```
staff.set(i, harry);
```

This is equivalent to

```
a[i] = harry;
```

for an array a. (As with arrays, the index values are zero based.)

CAUTION: Do not call list.set(i, x) until the *size* of the array list is larger than i. For example, the following code is wrong:

```
ArrayList<Employee> list = new ArrayList<>(100); // capacity 100, size 0
list.set(0, x); // no element 0 yet
```

Use the add method instead of set to fill up an array, and use set only to replace a previously added element.

To get an array list element, use

```
Employee e = staff.get(i);
```

This is equivalent to

```
Employee e = a[i];
```

NOTE: When there were no generic classes, the get method of the raw ArrayList class had no choice but to return an Object. Consequently, callers of get had to cast the returned value to the desired type:

```
Employee e = (Employee) staff.get(i);
```

The raw ArrayList is also a bit dangerous. Its add and set methods accept objects of any type. A call

```
staff.set(i, "Harry Hacker");
```

compiles without so much as a warning, and you run into grief only when you retrieve the object and try to cast it. If you use an ArrayList<Employee> instead, the compiler will detect this error.

You can sometimes get the best of both worlds—flexible growth and convenient element access—with the following trick. First, make an array list and add all the elements:

```
ArrayList<X> list = new ArrayList<>();
while (. . .)
{
   X = . . .;
   list.add(x);
}
```

When you are done, use the toArray method to copy the elements into an array:

```
X[] a = new X[list.size()];
list.toArray(a);
```

Sometimes, you need to add elements in the middle of an array list. Use the add method with an index parameter:

```
int n = staff.size() / 2;
staff.add(n, e);
```

The elements at locations n and above are shifted up to make room for the new entry. If the new size of the array list after the insertion exceeds the capacity, the array list reallocates its storage array.

Similarly, you can remove an element from the middle of an array list:

```
Employee e = staff.remove(n);
```

The elements located above it are copied down, and the size of the array is reduced by one.

Inserting and removing elements is not terribly efficient. It is probably not worth worrying about for small array lists. But if you store many elements and frequently insert and remove in the middle of a collection, consider using a linked list instead. We explain how to program with linked lists in Chapter 9.

You can use the "for each" loop to traverse the contents of an array list:

```
for (Employee e : staff)
   do something with e
```

This loop has the same effect as

```
for (int i = 0; i < staff.size(); i++)
{
   Employee e = staff.get(i);
   do something with e
}
```

Listing 5.11 is a modification of the EmployeeTest program of Chapter 4. The Employee[] array is replaced by an ArrayList<Employee>. Note the following changes:

- You don't have to specify the array size.
- You use add to add as many elements as you like.
- You use size() instead of length to count the number of elements.
- You use a.get(i) instead of a[i] to access an element.

Listing 5.11 arrayList/ArrayListTest.java

```java
1  package arrayList;
2
3  import java.util.*;
4
5  /**
6   * This program demonstrates the ArrayList class.
7   * @version 1.11 2012-01-26
8   * @author Cay Horstmann
9   */
10 public class ArrayListTest
11 {
12    public static void main(String[] args)
13    {
14       // fill the staff array list with three Employee objects
15       ArrayList<Employee> staff = new ArrayList<>();
16
17       staff.add(new Employee("Carl Cracker", 75000, 1987, 12, 15));
18       staff.add(new Employee("Harry Hacker", 50000, 1989, 10, 1));
19       staff.add(new Employee("Tony Tester", 40000, 1990, 3, 15));
20
21       // raise everyone's salary by 5%
22       for (Employee e : staff)
23          e.raiseSalary(5);
24
25       // print out information about all Employee objects
26       for (Employee e : staff)
27          System.out.println("name=" + e.getName() + ",salary=" + e.getSalary() + ",hireDay="
28             + e.getHireDay());
29    }
30 }
```

---

java.util.ArrayList<E> 1.2

- void set(int index, E obj)

  puts a value in the array list at the specified index, overwriting the previous contents.

Parameters:	index	the position (must be between 0 and size() - 1)
	obj	the new value

- E get(int index)

  gets the value stored at a specified index.

Parameters:	index	the index of the element to get (must be between 0 and size() - 1)

- void add(int index, E obj)

  shifts up elements to insert an element.

Parameters:	index	the insertion position (must be between 0 and size())
	obj	the new element

- E remove(int index)

  removes an element and shifts down all elements above it. The removed element is returned.

Parameters:	index	the position of the element to be removed (must be between 0 and size() - 1)

5.3.2 Compatibility between Typed and Raw Array Lists

In your own code, you will always want to use type parameters for added safety. In this section, you will see how to interoperate with legacy code that does not use type parameters.

Suppose you have the following legacy class:

```
public class EmployeeDB
{
   public void update(ArrayList list) { . . . }
   public ArrayList find(String query) { . . . }
}
```

You can pass a typed array list to the update method without any casts.

```
ArrayList<Employee> staff = . . .;
employeeDB.update(staff);
```

The staff object is simply passed to the update method.

CAUTION: Even though you get no error or warning from the compiler, this call is not completely safe. The `update` method might add elements into the array list that are not of type `Employee`. When these elements are retrieved, an exception occurs. This sounds scary, but if you think about it, the behavior is simply as it was before generics were added to Java. The integrity of the virtual machine is never jeopardized. In this situation, you do not lose security, but you also do not benefit from the compile-time checks.

Conversely, when you assign a raw `ArrayList` to a typed one, you get a warning.

```
ArrayList<Employee> result = employeeDB.find(query); // yields warning
```

 NOTE: To see the text of the warning, compile with the option `-Xlint:unchecked`.

Using a cast does not make the warning go away.

```
ArrayList<Employee> result = (ArrayList<Employee>) employeeDB.find(query);
   // yields another warning
```

Instead, you get a different warning, telling you that the cast is misleading.

This is the consequence of a somewhat unfortunate limitation of generic types in Java. For compatibility, the compiler translates all typed array lists into raw `ArrayList` objects after checking that the type rules were not violated. In a running program, all array lists are the same—there are no type parameters in the virtual machine. Thus, the casts (`ArrayList`) and (`ArrayList<Employee>`) carry out identical runtime checks.

There isn't much you can do about that situation. When you interact with legacy code, study the compiler warnings and satisfy yourself that the warnings are not serious.

Once you are satisfied, you can tag the variable that receives the cast with the `@SuppressWarnings("unchecked")` annotation, like this:

```
@SuppressWarnings("unchecked") ArrayList<Employee> result =
   (ArrayList<Employee>) employeeDB.find(query); // yields another warning
```

5.4 Object Wrappers and Autoboxing

Occasionally, you need to convert a primitive type like `int` to an object. All primitive types have class counterparts. For example, a class `Integer` corresponds to the primitive type `int`. These kinds of classes are usually called *wrappers*. The wrapper classes have obvious names: Integer, Long, Float, Double, Short, Byte, Character, and Boolean. (The first six inherit from the common superclass Number.) The wrapper classes are immutable—you cannot change a wrapped value after the wrapper has been constructed. They are also final, so you cannot subclass them.

Suppose we want an array list of integers. Unfortunately, the type parameter inside the angle brackets cannot be a primitive type. It is not possible to form an ArrayList<int>. Here, the Integer wrapper class comes in. It is OK to declare an array list of Integer objects.

```
ArrayList<Integer> list = new ArrayList<>();
```

 CAUTION: An ArrayList<Integer> is far less efficient than an int[] array because each value is separately wrapped inside an object. You would only want to use this construct for small collections when programmer convenience is more important than efficiency.

Fortunately, there is a useful feature that makes it easy to add an element of type int to an ArrayList<Integer>. The call

```
list.add(3);
```

is automatically translated to

```
list.add(Integer.valueOf(3));
```

This conversion is called *autoboxing*.

 NOTE: You might think that *autowrapping* would be more consistent, but the "boxing" metaphor was taken from C#.

Conversely, when you assign an Integer object to an int value, it is automatically unboxed. That is, the compiler translates

```
int n = list.get(i);
```

into

```
int n = list.get(i).intValue();
```

Automatic boxing and unboxing even works with arithmetic expressions. For example, you can apply the increment operator to a wrapper reference:

```
Integer n = 3;
n++;
```

The compiler automatically inserts instructions to unbox the object, increment the resulting value, and box it back.

In most cases, you get the illusion that the primitive types and their wrappers are one and the same. There is just one point in which they differ considerably: identity. As you know, the == operator, applied to wrapper objects, only tests whether the objects have identical memory locations. The following comparison would therefore probably fail:

```
Integer a = 1000;
Integer b = 1000;
if (a == b) . . .
```

However, a Java implementation *may*, if it chooses, wrap commonly occurring values into identical objects, and thus the comparison might succeed. This ambiguity is not what you want. The remedy is to call the equals method when comparing wrapper objects.

 NOTE: The autoboxing specification requires that boolean, byte, char <= 127, short, and int between -128 and 127 are wrapped into fixed objects. For example, if a and b had been initialized with 100 in the preceding example, then the comparison would have had to succeed.

There are a couple of other subtleties about autoboxing. First off, since wrapper class references can be null, it is possible for autounboxing to throw a NullPointerException:

```
Integer n = null;
System.out.println(2 * n); // Throws NullPointerException
```

Also, if you mix Integer and Double types in a conditional expression, then the Integer value is unboxed, promoted to double, and boxed into a Double:

```
Integer n = 1;
Double x = 2.0;
System.out.println(true ? n : x); // Prints 1.0
```

Finally, let us emphasize that boxing and unboxing is a courtesy of the *compiler*, not the virtual machine. The compiler inserts the necessary calls when it generates the bytecodes of a class. The virtual machine simply executes those bytecodes.

You will often see the number wrappers for another reason. The designers of Java found the wrappers a convenient place to put certain basic methods, such as those for converting strings of digits to numbers.

To convert a string to an integer, use the following statement:

```
int x = Integer.parseInt(s);
```

This has nothing to do with Integer objects—parseInt is a static method. But the Integer class was a good place to put it.

The API notes show some of the more important methods of the Integer class. The other number classes implement corresponding methods.

CAUTION: Some people think that the wrapper classes can be used to implement methods that can modify numeric parameters. However, that is not correct. Recall from Chapter 4 that it is impossible to write a Java method that increments an integer parameter because parameters to Java methods are always passed by value.

```
public static void triple(int x) // won't work
{
   x = 3 * x; // modifies local variable
}
```

Could we overcome this by using an Integer instead of an int?

```
public static void triple(Integer x) // won't work
{
   . . .
}
```

The problem is that Integer objects are *immutable*: The information contained inside the wrapper can't change. You cannot use these wrapper classes to create a method that modifies numeric parameters.

If you do want to write a method to change numeric parameters, you can use one of the *holder* types defined in the org.omg.CORBA package: IntHolder, BooleanHolder, and so on. Each holder type has a public (!) field value through which you can access the stored value.

```
public static void triple(IntHolder x)
{
   x.value = 3 * x.value;
}
```

---

java.lang.Integer 1.0

- int intValue()

  returns the value of this Integer object as an int (overrides the intValue method in the Number class).

(Continues)

---

java.lang.Integer 1.0 *(Continued)*

- `static String toString(int i)`

  returns a new `String` object representing the number i in base 10.
- `static String toString(int i, int radix)`

  lets you return a representation of the number i in the base specified by the `radix` parameter.
- `static int parseInt(String s)`
- `static int parseInt(String s, int radix)`

  returns the integer whose digits are contained in the string s. The string must represent an integer in base 10 (for the first method) or in the base given by the `radix` parameter (for the second method).
- `static Integer valueOf(String s)`
- `static Integer valueOf(String s, int radix)`

  returns a new `Integer` object initialized to the integer whose digits are contained in the string s. The string must represent an integer in base 10 (for the first method) or in the base given by the `radix` parameter (for the second method).

---

java.text.NumberFormat 1.1

- `Number parse(String s)`

  returns the numeric value, assuming the specified `String` represents a number.

5.5 Methods with a Variable Number of Parameters

It is possible to provide methods that can be called with a variable number of parameters. (These are sometimes called "varargs" methods.)

You have already seen such a method: `printf`. For example, the calls

```
System.out.printf("%d", n);
```

and

```
System.out.printf("%d %s", n, "widgets");
```

both call the same method, even though one call has two parameters and the other has three.

The `printf` method is defined like this:

```
public class PrintStream
{
   public PrintStream printf(String fmt, Object... args) { return format(fmt, args); }
}
```

Here, the ellipsis ... is part of the Java code. It denotes that the method can receive an arbitrary number of objects (in addition to the fmt parameter).

The printf method actually receives two parameters: the format string and an Object[] array that holds all other parameters. (If the caller supplies integers or other primitive type values, autoboxing turns them into objects.) It now faces the unenviable task of scanning the fmt string and matching up the ith format specifier with the value args[i].

In other words, for the implementor of printf, the Object... parameter type is exactly the same as Object[].

The compiler needs to transform each call to printf, bundling the parameters into an array and autoboxing as necessary:

```
System.out.printf("%d %s", new Object[] { new Integer(n), "widgets" } );
```

You can define your own methods with variable parameters, and you can specify any type for the parameters, even a primitive type. Here is a simple example: a function that computes the maximum of a variable number of values.

```
public static double max(double... values)
{
   double largest = Double.NEGATIVE_INFINITY;
   for (double v : values) if (v > largest) largest = v;
   return largest;
}
```

Simply call the function like this:

```
double m = max(3.1, 40.4, -5);
```

The compiler passes a new double[] { 3.1, 40.4, -5 } to the max function.

NOTE: It is legal to pass an array as the last parameter of a method with variable parameters. For example:

```
System.out.printf("%d %s", new Object[] { new Integer(1), "widgets" } );
```

Therefore, you can redefine an existing function whose last parameter is an array to a method with variable parameters, without breaking any existing code. For example, MessageFormat.format was enhanced in this way in Java SE 5.0. If you like, you can even declare the main method as

```
public static void main(String... args)
```

5.6 Enumeration Classes

You saw in Chapter 3 how to define enumerated types. Here is a typical example:

```
public enum Size { SMALL, MEDIUM, LARGE, EXTRA_LARGE };
```

The type defined by this declaration is actually a class. The class has exactly four instances—it is not possible to construct new objects.

Therefore, you never need to use `equals` for values of enumerated types. Simply use `==` to compare them.

You can, if you like, add constructors, methods, and fields to an enumerated type. Of course, the constructors are only invoked when the enumerated constants are constructed. Here is an example.

```
public enum Size
{
    SMALL("S"), MEDIUM("M"), LARGE("L"), EXTRA_LARGE("XL");

    private String abbreviation;

    private Size(String abbreviation) { this.abbreviation = abbreviation; }
    public String getAbbreviation() { return abbreviation; }
}
```

All enumerated types are subclasses of the class `Enum`. They inherit a number of methods from that class. The most useful one is `toString`, which returns the name of the enumerated constant. For example, `Size.SMALL.toString()` returns the string `"SMALL"`.

The converse of `toString` is the static `valueOf` method. For example, the statement

```
Size s = Enum.valueOf(Size.class, "SMALL");
```

sets `s` to `Size.SMALL`.

Each enumerated type has a static `values` method that returns an array of all values of the enumeration. For example, the call

```
Size[] values = Size.values();
```

returns the array with elements `Size.SMALL`, `Size.MEDIUM`, `Size.LARGE`, and `Size.EXTRA_LARGE`.

The `ordinal` method yields the position of an enumerated constant in the `enum` declaration, counting from zero. For example, `Size.MEDIUM.ordinal()` returns 1.

The short program in Listing 5.12 demonstrates how to work with enumerated types.

 NOTE: The `Enum` class has a type parameter that we have ignored for simplicity. For example, the enumerated type `Size` actually extends `Enum<Size>`. The type parameter is used in the `compareTo` method. (We discuss the `compareTo` method in Chapter 6 and type parameters in Chapter 8.)

Listing 5.12 enums/EnumTest.java

```
1  package enums;
2
3  import java.util.*;
4
5  /**
6   * This program demonstrates enumerated types.
7   * @version 1.0 2004-05-24
8   * @author Cay Horstmann
9   */
10 public class EnumTest
11 {
12    public static void main(String[] args)
13    {
14       Scanner in = new Scanner(System.in);
15       System.out.print("Enter a size: (SMALL, MEDIUM, LARGE, EXTRA_LARGE) ");
16       String input = in.next().toUpperCase();
17       Size size = Enum.valueOf(Size.class, input);
18       System.out.println("size=" + size);
19       System.out.println("abbreviation=" + size.getAbbreviation());
20       if (size == Size.EXTRA_LARGE)
21          System.out.println("Good job--you paid attention to the _.");
22    }
23 }
24
25 enum Size
26 {
27    SMALL("S"), MEDIUM("M"), LARGE("L"), EXTRA_LARGE("XL");
28
29    private Size(String abbreviation) { this.abbreviation = abbreviation; }
30    public String getAbbreviation() { return abbreviation; }
31
32    private String abbreviation;
33 }
```

`java.lang.Enum<E>` 5.0

- `static Enum valueOf(Class enumClass, String name)`

  returns the enumerated constant of the given class with the given name.

- `String toString()`

  returns the name of this enumerated constant.

- `int ordinal()`

  returns the zero-based position of this enumerated constant in the `enum` declaration.

- `int compareTo(E other)`

  returns a negative integer if this enumerated constant comes before `other`, zero if `this == other`, and a positive integer otherwise. The ordering of the constants is given by the `enum` declaration.

5.7 Reflection

The *reflection library* gives you a very rich and elaborate toolset to write programs that manipulate Java code dynamically. This feature is heavily used in *JavaBeans*, the component architecture for Java (see Volume II for more on JavaBeans). Using reflection, Java can support tools like those to which users of Visual Basic have grown accustomed. In particular, when new classes are added at design time or runtime, rapid application development tools can dynamically inquire about the capabilities of these classes.

A program that can analyze the capabilities of classes is called *reflective*. The reflection mechanism is extremely powerful. As the next sections show, you can use it to

- Analyze the capabilities of classes at runtime;
- Inspect objects at runtime—for example, to write a single `toString` method that works for *all* classes;
- Implement generic array manipulation code; and
- Take advantage of `Method` objects that work just like function pointers in languages such as C++.

Reflection is a powerful and complex mechanism; however, it is of interest mainly to tool builders, not application programmers. If you are interested in programming applications rather than tools for other Java programmers, you can safely skip the remainder of this chapter and return to it later.

5.7.1 The Class Class

While your program is running, the Java runtime system always maintains what is called *runtime type identification* on all objects. This information keeps track of the class to which each object belongs. Runtime type information is used by the virtual machine to select the correct methods to execute.

However, you can also access this information by working with a special Java class. The class that holds this information is called, somewhat confusingly, Class. The getClass() method in the Object class returns an instance of Class type.

```
Employee e;
. . .
Class cl = e.getClass();
```

Just like an Employee object describes the properties of a particular employee, a Class object describes the properties of a particular class. Probably the most commonly used method of Class is getName. This returns the name of the class. For example, the statement

```
System.out.println(e.getClass().getName() + " " + e.getName());
```

prints

```
Employee Harry Hacker
```

if e is an employee, or

```
Manager Harry Hacker
```

if e is a manager.

If the class is in a package, the package name is part of the class name:

```
Random generator = new Random();
Class cl = generator.getClass();
String name = cl.getName(); // name is set to "java.util.Random"
```

You can obtain a Class object corresponding to a class name by using the static forName method.

```
String className = "java.util.Random";
Class cl = Class.forName(className);
```

Use this method if the class name is stored in a string that varies at runtime. This works if className is the name of a class or interface. Otherwise, the forName method throws a *checked exception*. See Section 5.7.2, "A Primer on Catching Exceptions," on p. 263 for how to supply an *exception handler* whenever you use this method.

TIP: At startup, the class containing your `main` method is loaded. It loads all classes that it needs. Each of those loaded classes loads the classes that it needs, and so on. That can take a long time for a big application, frustrating the user. You can give the users of your program an illusion of a faster start with the following trick. Make sure the class containing the `main` method does not explicitly refer to other classes. In it, display a splash screen. Then manually force the loading of other classes by calling `Class.forName`.

A third method for obtaining an object of type `Class` is a convenient shorthand. If `T` is any Java type (or the `void` keyword), then `T.class` is the matching class object. For example:

```
Class cl1 = Random.class; // if you import java.util.*;
Class cl2 = int.class;
Class cl3 = Double[].class;
```

Note that a `Class` object really describes a *type*, which may or may not be a class. For example, `int` is not a class, but `int.class` is nevertheless an object of type `Class`.

 NOTE: The `Class` class is actually a generic class. For example, `Employee.class` is of type `Class<Employee>`. We are not dwelling on this issue because it would further complicate an already abstract concept. For most practical purposes, you can ignore the type parameter and work with the raw `Class` type. See Chapter 8 for more information on this issue.

 CAUTION: For historical reasons, the `getName` method returns somewhat strange names for array types:

- `Double[].class.getName()` returns `"[Ljava.lang.Double;"`.
- `int[].class.getName()` returns `"[I"`.

The virtual machine manages a unique `Class` object for each type. Therefore, you can use the `==` operator to compare class objects. For example:

```
if (e.getClass() == Employee.class) . . .
```

Another example of a useful method is one that lets you create an instance of a class on the fly. This method is called, naturally enough, `newInstance()`. For example,

```
e.getClass().newInstance();
```

creates a new instance of the same class type as `e`. The `newInstance` method calls the no-argument constructor to initialize the newly created object. An exception is thrown if the class does not have a no-argument constructor.

A combination of `forName` and `newInstance` lets you create an object from a class name stored in a string.

```
String s = "java.util.Random";
Object m = Class.forName(s).newInstance();
```

 NOTE: If you need to provide parameters for the constructor of a class you want to create by name in this manner, you can't use the above statements. Instead, you must use the `newInstance` method in the `Constructor` class.

 C++ NOTE: The `newInstance` method corresponds to the idiom of a *virtual constructor* in C++. However, virtual constructors in C++ are not a language feature but just an idiom that needs to be supported by a specialized library. The `Class` class is similar to the `type_info` class in C++, and the `getClass` method is equivalent to the `typeid` operator. The Java `Class` is quite a bit more versatile than `type_info`, though. The C++ `type_info` can only reveal a string with the name of the type, not create new objects of that type.

5.7.2 A Primer on Catching Exceptions

We cover exception handling fully in Chapter 7, but in the meantime you will occasionally encounter methods that threaten to throw exceptions.

When an error occurs at runtime, a program can "throw an exception." Throwing an exception is more flexible than terminating the program because you can provide a *handler* that "catches" the exception and deals with it.

If you don't provide a handler, the program still terminates and prints a message to the console, giving the type of the exception. You may have already seen exception reports when you accidentally used a `null` reference or overstepped the bounds of an array.

There are two kinds of exceptions: *unchecked* exceptions and *checked* exceptions. With checked exceptions, the compiler checks that you provide a handler. However, many common exceptions, such as accessing a null reference, are unchecked. The compiler does not check whether you provided a handler for these errors—after all, you should spend your mental energy on avoiding these mistakes rather than coding handlers for them.

But not all errors are avoidable. If an exception can occur despite your best efforts, then the compiler insists that you provide a handler. The Class.forName method is an example of a method that throws a checked exception. In Chapter 7, you will see several exception handling strategies. For now, we just show you the simplest handler implementation.

Place one or more statements that might throw checked exceptions inside a try block. Then provide the handler code in the catch clause.

```
try
{
    statements that might throw exceptions
}
catch (Exception e)
{
    handler action
}
```

Here is an example:

```
try
{
    String name = . . .; // get class name
    Class cl = Class.forName(name); // might throw exception
    do something with cl
}
catch (Exception e)
{
    e.printStackTrace();
}
```

If the class name doesn't exist, the remainder of the code in the try block is skipped and the program enters the catch clause. (Here, we print a stack trace by using the printStackTrace method of the Throwable class. Throwable is the superclass of the Exception class.) If none of the methods in the try block throws an exception, the handler code in the catch clause is skipped.

You only need to supply an exception handler for checked exceptions. It is easy to find out which methods throw checked exceptions—the compiler will complain whenever you call a method that threatens to throw a checked exception and you don't supply a handler.

---

java.lang.Class 1.0

- `static Class forName(String className)`

  returns the `Class` object representing the class with name `className`.
- `Object newInstance()`

  returns a new instance of this class.

---

java.lang.reflect.Constructor 1.1

- `Object newInstance(Object[] args)`

  constructs a new instance of the constructor's declaring class.

  Parameters: args   the parameters supplied to the constructor. See Section 5.7.6 for more information on how to supply parameters.

---

java.lang.Throwable 1.0

- `void printStackTrace()`

  prints the `Throwable` object and the stack trace to the standard error stream.

5.7.3 Using Reflection to Analyze the Capabilities of Classes

Here is a brief overview of the most important parts of the reflection mechanism for letting you examine the structure of a class.

The three classes `Field`, `Method`, and `Constructor` in the `java.lang.reflect` package describe the fields, methods, and constructors of a class, respectively. All three classes have a method called `getName` that returns the name of the item. The `Field` class has a method `getType` that returns an object, again of type `Class`, that describes the field type. The `Method` and `Constructor` classes have methods to report the types of the parameters, and the `Method` class also reports the return type. All three of these classes also have a method called `getModifiers` that returns an integer, with various bits turned on and off, that describes the modifiers used, such as `public` and `static`. You can then use the static methods in the `Modifier` class in the `java.lang.reflect` package to analyze the integer that `getModifiers` returns. Use methods like `isPublic`, `isPrivate`, or `isFinal` in the `Modifier` class to tell whether a method or constructor was `public`, `private`, or `final`. All you have to do is have the appropriate method in the `Modifier` class work on the integer that getModifiers returns. You can also use the Modifier.toString method to print the modifiers.

The getFields, getMethods, and getConstructors methods of the Class class return arrays of the *public* fields, methods, and constructors that the class supports. This includes public members of superclasses. The getDeclaredFields, getDeclaredMethods, and getDeclaredConstructors methods of the Class class return arrays consisting of all fields, methods, and constructors that are declared in the class. This includes private, package, and protected members, but not members of superclasses.

Listing 5.13 shows you how to print out all information about a class. The program prompts you for the name of a class and writes out the signatures of all methods and constructors as well as the names of all instance fields of a class. For example, if you enter

```
java.lang.Double
```

the program prints

```
public class java.lang.Double extends java.lang.Number
{
    public java.lang.Double(java.lang.String);
    public java.lang.Double(double);

    public int hashCode();
    public int compareTo(java.lang.Object);
    public int compareTo(java.lang.Double);
    public boolean equals(java.lang.Object);
    public java.lang.String toString();
    public static java.lang.String toString(double);
    public static java.lang.Double valueOf(java.lang.String);
    public static boolean isNaN(double);
    public boolean isNaN();
    public static boolean isInfinite(double);
    public boolean isInfinite();
    public byte byteValue();
    public short shortValue();
    public int intValue();
    public long longValue();
    public float floatValue();
    public double doubleValue();
    public static double parseDouble(java.lang.String);
    public static native long doubleToLongBits(double);
    public static native long doubleToRawLongBits(double);
    public static native double longBitsToDouble(long);

    public static final double POSITIVE_INFINITY;
    public static final double NEGATIVE_INFINITY;
    public static final double NaN;
    public static final double MAX_VALUE;
```

```
        public static final double MIN_VALUE;
        public static final java.lang.Class TYPE;
        private double value;
        private static final long serialVersionUID;
    }
```

What is remarkable about this program is that it can analyze any class that the Java interpreter can load, not just the classes that were available when the program was compiled. We will use this program in the next chapter to peek inside the inner classes that the Java compiler generates automatically.

Listing 5.13 reflection/ReflectionTest.java

```
 1  package reflection;
 2
 3  import java.util.*;
 4  import java.lang.reflect.*;
 5
 6  /**
 7   * This program uses reflection to print all features of a class.
 8   * @version 1.1 2004-02-21
 9   * @author Cay Horstmann
10   */
11  public class ReflectionTest
12  {
13      public static void main(String[] args)
14      {
15          // read class name from command line args or user input
16          String name;
17          if (args.length > 0) name = args[0];
18          else
19          {
20              Scanner in = new Scanner(System.in);
21              System.out.println("Enter class name (e.g. java.util.Date): ");
22              name = in.next();
23          }
24
25          try
26          {
27              // print class name and superclass name (if != Object)
28              Class cl = Class.forName(name);
29              Class supercl = cl.getSuperclass();
30              String modifiers = Modifier.toString(cl.getModifiers());
31              if (modifiers.length() > 0) System.out.print(modifiers + " ");
32              System.out.print("class " + name);
33              if (supercl != null && supercl != Object.class) System.out.print(" extends "
34                      + supercl.getName());
35
```

(Continues)

Listing 5.13 *(Continued)*

```
36          System.out.print("\n{\n");
37          printConstructors(cl);
38          System.out.println();
39          printMethods(cl);
40          System.out.println();
41          printFields(cl);
42          System.out.println("}");
43       }
44       catch (ClassNotFoundException e)
45       {
46          e.printStackTrace();
47       }
48       System.exit(0);
49    }
50
51    /**
52     * Prints all constructors of a class
53     * @param cl a class
54     */
55    public static void printConstructors(Class cl)
56    {
57       Constructor[] constructors = cl.getDeclaredConstructors();
58
59       for (Constructor c : constructors)
60       {
61          String name = c.getName();
62          System.out.print("   ");
63          String modifiers = Modifier.toString(c.getModifiers());
64          if (modifiers.length() > 0) System.out.print(modifiers + " ");
65          System.out.print(name + "(");
66
67          // print parameter types
68          Class[] paramTypes = c.getParameterTypes();
69          for (int j = 0; j < paramTypes.length; j++)
70          {
71             if (j > 0) System.out.print(", ");
72             System.out.print(paramTypes[j].getName());
73          }
74          System.out.println(");");
75       }
76    }
77
78    /**
79     * Prints all methods of a class
80     * @param cl a class
81     */
```

```
82    public static void printMethods(Class cl)
83    {
84       Method[] methods = cl.getDeclaredMethods();
85
86       for (Method m : methods)
87       {
88          Class retType = m.getReturnType();
89          String name = m.getName();
90
91          System.out.print("   ");
92          // print modifiers, return type and method name
93          String modifiers = Modifier.toString(m.getModifiers());
94          if (modifiers.length() > 0) System.out.print(modifiers + " ");
95          System.out.print(retType.getName() + " " + name + "(");
96
97          // print parameter types
98          Class[] paramTypes = m.getParameterTypes();
99          for (int j = 0; j < paramTypes.length; j++)
100         {
101            if (j > 0) System.out.print(", ");
102            System.out.print(paramTypes[j].getName());
103         }
104         System.out.println(");");
105      }
106   }
107
108   /**
109    * Prints all fields of a class
110    * @param cl a class
111    */
112   public static void printFields(Class cl)
113   {
114      Field[] fields = cl.getDeclaredFields();
115
116      for (Field f : fields)
117      {
118         Class type = f.getType();
119         String name = f.getName();
120         System.out.print("   ");
121         String modifiers = Modifier.toString(f.getModifiers());
122         if (modifiers.length() > 0) System.out.print(modifiers + " ");
123         System.out.println(type.getName() + " " + name + ";");
124      }
125   }
126 }
```

---

java.lang.Class 1.0

- Field[] getFields() 1.1
- Field[] getDeclaredFields() 1.1

  getFields returns an array containing Field objects for the public fields of this class or its superclasses; getDeclaredField returns an array of Field objects for all fields of this class. The methods return an array of length 0 if there are no such fields or if the Class object represents a primitive or array type.

- Method[] getMethods() 1.1
- Method[] getDeclaredMethods() 1.1

  returns an array containing Method objects: getMethods returns public methods and includes inherited methods; getDeclaredMethods returns all methods of this class or interface but does not include inherited methods.

- Constructor[] getConstructors() 1.1
- Constructor[] getDeclaredConstructors() 1.1

  returns an array containing Constructor objects that give you all the public constructors (for getConstructors) or all constructors (for getDeclaredConstructors) of the class represented by this Class object.

---

java.lang.reflect.Field 1.1
java.lang.reflect.Method 1.1
java.lang.reflect.Constructor 1.1

- Class getDeclaringClass()

  returns the Class object for the class that defines this constructor, method, or field.

- Class[] getExceptionTypes() (in Constructor and Method classes)

  returns an array of Class objects that represent the types of the exceptions thrown by the method.

- int getModifiers()

  returns an integer that describes the modifiers of this constructor, method, or field. Use the methods in the Modifier class to analyze the return value.

- String getName()

  returns a string that is the name of the constructor, method, or field.

- Class[] getParameterTypes() (in Constructor and Method classes)

  returns an array of Class objects that represent the types of the parameters.

- Class getReturnType() (in Method classes)

  returns a Class object that represents the return type.

---

java.lang.reflect.Modifier 1.1

- static String toString(int modifiers)

  returns a string with the modifiers that correspond to the bits set in modifiers.
- static boolean isAbstract(int modifiers)
- static boolean isFinal(int modifiers)
- static boolean isInterface(int modifiers)
- static boolean isNative(int modifiers)
- static boolean isPrivate(int modifiers)
- static boolean isProtected(int modifiers)
- static boolean isPublic(int modifiers)
- static boolean isStatic(int modifiers)
- static boolean isStrict(int modifiers)
- static boolean isSynchronized(int modifiers)
- static boolean isVolatile(int modifiers)

  tests the bit in the modifiers value that corresponds to the modifier in the method name.

5.7.4 Using Reflection to Analyze Objects at Runtime

In the preceding section, we saw how we can find out the *names* and *types* of the data fields of any object:

- Get the corresponding Class object.
- Call getDeclaredFields on the Class object.

In this section, we will go one step further and actually look at the *contents* of the fields. Of course, it is easy to look at the contents of a specific field of an object whose name and type are known when you write a program. But reflection lets you look at fields of objects that were not known at compile time.

The key method to achieve this is the get method in the Field class. If f is an object of type Field (for example, one obtained from getDeclaredFields) and obj is an object of the class of which f is a field, then f.get(obj) returns an object whose value is the current value of the field of obj. This is all a bit abstract, so let's run through an example.

```
Employee harry = new Employee("Harry Hacker", 35000, 10, 1, 1989);
Class cl = harry.getClass();
    // the class object representing Employee
Field f = cl.getDeclaredField("name");
    // the name field of the Employee class
```

```
Object v = f.get(harry);
   // the value of the name field of the harry object, i.e., the String object "Harry Hacker"
```

Actually, there is a problem with this code. Since the name field is a private field, the get method will throw an IllegalAccessException. You can only use get to get the values of accessible fields. The security mechanism of Java lets you find out what fields an object has, but it won't let you read the values of those fields unless you have access permission.

The default behavior of the reflection mechanism is to respect Java access control. However, if a Java program is not controlled by a security manager that disallows it, you can override access control. To do this, invoke the setAccessible method on a Field, Method, or Constructor object. For example:

```
f.setAccessible(true); // now OK to call f.get(harry);
```

The setAccessible method is a method of the AccessibleObject class, the common super-class of the Field, Method, and Constructor classes. This feature is provided for debuggers, persistent storage, and similar mechanisms. We use it for a generic toString method later in this section.

There is another issue with the get method that we need to deal with. The name field is a String, and so it is not a problem to return the value as an Object. But suppose we want to look at the salary field. That is a double, and in Java, number types are not objects. To handle this, you can either use the getDouble method of the Field class, or you can call get, whereby the reflection mechanism automatically wraps the field value into the appropriate wrapper class—in this case, Double.

Of course, you can also set the values that you can get. The call f.set(obj, value) sets the field represented by f of the object obj to the new value.

Listing 5.14 shows how to write a generic toString method that works for *any* class. It uses getDeclaredFields to obtain all data fields. It then uses the setAccessible convenience method to make all fields accessible. For each field, it obtains the name and the value. Each value is turned into a string by recursively invoking toString.

The generic toString method needs to address a couple of complexities. Cycles of references could cause an infinite recursion. Therefore, the ObjectAnalyzer keeps track of objects that were already visited. Also, to peek inside arrays, you need a different approach. You'll learn about the details in the next section.

You can use this toString method to peek inside any object. For example, the call

```
ArrayList<Integer> squares = new ArrayList<>();
for (int i = 1; i <= 5; i++) squares.add(i * i);
System.out.println(new ObjectAnalyzer().toString(squares));
```

yields the printout

java.util.ArrayList[elementData=class java.lang.Object[]{java.lang.Integer[value=1][][],
java.lang.Integer[value=4][][],java.lang.Integer[value=9][][],java.lang.Integer[value=16][][],
java.lang.Integer[value=25][][],null,null,null,null,null},size=5][modCount=5][][]

You can use this generic toString method to implement the toString methods of your own classes, like this:

```
public String toString()
{
    return new ObjectAnalyzer().toString(this);
}
```

This is a hassle-free method for supplying a toString method that you may find useful in your own programs.

Listing 5.14 objectAnalyzer/ObjectAnalyzerTest.java

```
1  package objectAnalyzer;
2
3  import java.util.ArrayList;
4
5  /**
6   * This program uses reflection to spy on objects.
7   * @version 1.12 2012-01-26
8   * @author Cay Horstmann
9   */
10 public class ObjectAnalyzerTest
11 {
12     public static void main(String[] args)
13     {
14         ArrayList<Integer> squares = new ArrayList<>();
15         for (int i = 1; i <= 5; i++)
16             squares.add(i * i);
17         System.out.println(new ObjectAnalyzer().toString(squares));
18     }
19 }
```

Listing 5.15 objectAnalyzer/ObjectAnalyzer.java

```
1  package objectAnalyzer;
2
3  import java.lang.reflect.AccessibleObject;
4  import java.lang.reflect.Array;
5  import java.lang.reflect.Field;
6  import java.lang.reflect.Modifier;
7  import java.util.ArrayList;
8
```

(Continues)

Listing 5.15 *(Continued)*

```
9   public class ObjectAnalyzer
10  {
11     private ArrayList<Object> visited = new ArrayList<>();
12
13     /**
14      * Converts an object to a string representation that lists all fields.
15      * @param obj an object
16      * @return a string with the object's class name and all field names and
17      * values
18      */
19     public String toString(Object obj)
20     {
21        if (obj == null) return "null";
22        if (visited.contains(obj)) return "...";
23        visited.add(obj);
24        Class cl = obj.getClass();
25        if (cl == String.class) return (String) obj;
26        if (cl.isArray())
27        {
28           String r = cl.getComponentType() + "[]{";
29           for (int i = 0; i < Array.getLength(obj); i++)
30           {
31              if (i > 0) r += ",";
32              Object val = Array.get(obj, i);
33              if (cl.getComponentType().isPrimitive()) r += val;
34              else r += toString(val);
35           }
36           return r + "}";
37        }
38
39        String r = cl.getName();
40        // inspect the fields of this class and all superclasses
41        do
42        {
43           r += "[";
44           Field[] fields = cl.getDeclaredFields();
45           AccessibleObject.setAccessible(fields, true);
46           // get the names and values of all fields
47           for (Field f : fields)
48           {
49              if (!Modifier.isStatic(f.getModifiers()))
50              {
51                 if (!r.endsWith("[")) r += ",";
52                 r += f.getName() + "=";
53                 try
54                 {
```

```
55          Class t = f.getType();
56          Object val = f.get(obj);
57          if (t.isPrimitive()) r += val;
58          else r += toString(val);
59       }
60       catch (Exception e)
61       {
62          e.printStackTrace();
63       }
64    }
65 }
66 r += "]";
67 cl = cl.getSuperclass();
68 }
69 while (cl != null);
70
71 return r;
72 }
73 }
```

---

java.lang.reflect.AccessibleObject 1.2

- void setAccessible(boolean flag)

  sets the accessibility flag for this reflection object. A value of true indicates that Java language access checking is suppressed and that the private properties of the object can be queried and set.

- boolean isAccessible()

  gets the value of the accessibility flag for this reflection object.

- static void setAccessible(AccessibleObject[] array, boolean flag)

  is a convenience method to set the accessibility flag for an array of objects.

---

java.lang.Class 1.1

- Field getField(String name)
- Field[] getFields()

  gets the public field with the given name, or an array of all fields.

- Field getDeclaredField(String name)
- Field[] getDeclaredFields()

  gets the field that is declared in this class with the given name, or an array of all fields.

---

java.lang.reflect.Field 1.1

- Object get(Object obj)

    gets the value of the field described by this Field object in the object obj.

- void set(Object obj, Object newValue)

    sets the field described by this Field object in the object obj to a new value.

5.7.5 Using Reflection to Write Generic Array Code

The Array class in the java.lang.reflect package allows you to create arrays dynamically. This is used, for example, in the implementation of the copyOf method in the Arrays class. Recall how this method can be used to grow an array that has become full.

```
Employee[] a = new Employee[100];
. . .
// array is full
a = Arrays.copyOf(a, 2 * a.length);
```

How can one write such a generic method? It helps that an Employee[] array can be converted to an Object[] array. That sounds promising. Here is a first attempt:

```
public static Object[] badCopyOf(Object[] a, int newLength) // not useful
{
   Object[] newArray = new Object[newLength];
   System.arraycopy(a, 0, newArray, 0, Math.min(a.length, newLength));
   return newArray;
}
```

However, there is a problem with actually *using* the resulting array. The type of array that this code returns is an array of *objects* (Object[]) because we created the array using the line of code

```
new Object[newLength]
```

An array of objects *cannot* be cast to an array of employees (Employee[]). The virtual machine would generate a ClassCastException at runtime. The point is that, as we mentioned earlier, a Java array remembers the type of its entries—that is, the element type used in the new expression that created it. It is legal to cast an Employee[] temporarily to an Object[] array and then cast it back, but an array that started its life as an Object[] array can never be cast into an Employee[] array. To write this kind of generic array code, we need to be able to make a new array of the *same* type as the original array. For this, we need the methods of the Array class in the java.lang.reflect package. The key is the static newInstance method of the Array class that constructs a new array. You must supply the type for the entries and the desired length as parameters to this method.

```
Object newArray = Array.newInstance(componentType, newLength);
```

To actually carry this out, we need to get the length and the component type of the new array.

We obtain the length by calling Array.getLength(a). The static getLength method of the Array class returns the length of an array. To get the component type of the new array:

1. First, get the class object of a.
2. Confirm that it is indeed an array.
3. Use the getComponentType method of the Class class (which is defined only for class objects that represent arrays) to find the right type for the array.

Why is getLength a method of Array but getComponentType a method of Class? We don't know—the distribution of the reflection methods seems a bit ad hoc at times.

Here's the code:

```
public static Object goodCopyOf(Object a, int newLength)
{
   Class cl = a.getClass();
   if (!cl.isArray()) return null;
   Class componentType = cl.getComponentType();
   int length = Array.getLength(a);
   Object newArray = Array.newInstance(componentType, newLength);
   System.arraycopy(a, 0, newArray, 0, Math.min(length, newLength));
   return newArray;
}
```

Note that this copyOf method can be used to grow arrays of any type, not just arrays of objects.

```
int[] a = { 1, 2, 3, 4, 5 };
a = (int[]) goodCopyOf(a, 10);
```

To make this possible, the parameter of goodCopyOf is declared to be of type Object, *not an array of objects* (Object[]). The integer array type int[] can be converted to an Object, but not to an array of objects!

Listing 5.16 shows both methods in action. Note that the cast of the return value of badcopyOf will throw an exception.

Listing 5.16 arrays/CopyOfTest.java

```
1   package arrays;
2
3   import java.lang.reflect.*;
4   import java.util.*;
5
6   /**
7    * This program demonstrates the use of reflection for manipulating arrays.
8    * @version 1.2 2012-05-04
9    * @author Cay Horstmann
10   */
11  public class CopyOfTest
12  {
13     public static void main(String[] args)
14     {
15        int[] a = { 1, 2, 3 };
16        a = (int[]) goodCopyOf(a, 10);
17        System.out.println(Arrays.toString(a));
18
19        String[] b = { "Tom", "Dick", "Harry" };
20        b = (String[]) goodCopyOf(b, 10);
21        System.out.println(Arrays.toString(b));
22
23        System.out.println("The following call will generate an exception.");
24        b = (String[]) badCopyOf(b, 10);
25     }
26
27     /**
28      * This method attempts to grow an array by allocating a new array and copying all elements.
29      * @param a the array to grow
30      * @param newLength the new length
31      * @return a larger array that contains all elements of a. However, the returned array has
32      * type Object[], not the same type as a
33      */
34     public static Object[] badCopyOf(Object[] a, int newLength) // not useful
35     {
36        Object[] newArray = new Object[newLength];
37        System.arraycopy(a, 0, newArray, 0, Math.min(a.length, newLength));
38        return newArray;
39     }
40
41     /**
42      * This method grows an array by allocating a new array of the same type and
43      * copying all elements.
44      * @param a the array to grow. This can be an object array or a primitive
45      * type array
46      * @return a larger array that contains all elements of a.
47      */
```

```
48      public static Object goodCopyOf(Object a, int newLength)
49      {
50          Class cl = a.getClass();
51          if (!cl.isArray()) return null;
52          Class componentType = cl.getComponentType();
53          int length = Array.getLength(a);
54          Object newArray = Array.newInstance(componentType, newLength);
55          System.arraycopy(a, 0, newArray, 0, Math.min(length, newLength));
56          return newArray;
57      }
58  }
```

---

java.lang.reflect.Array 1.1

- static Object get(Object array, int index)
- static *xxx* get*Xxx*(Object array, int index)

  (*xxx* is one of the primitive types boolean, byte, char, double, float, int, long, or short.) These methods return the value of the given array that is stored at the given index.

- static void set(Object array, int index, Object newValue)
- static set*Xxx*(Object array, int index, *xxx* newValue)

  (*xxx* is one of the primitive types boolean, byte, char, double, float, int, long, or short.) These methods store a new value into the given array at the given index.

- static int getLength(Object array)

  returns the length of the given array.

- static Object newInstance(Class componentType, int length)
- static Object newInstance(Class componentType, int[] lengths)

  returns a new array of the given component type with the given dimensions.

5.7.6 Invoking Arbitrary Methods

In C and C++, you can execute an arbitrary function through a function pointer. On the surface, Java does not have method pointers—that is, ways of giving the location of a method to another method, so that the second method can invoke it later. In fact, the designers of Java have said that method pointers are dangerous and error-prone, and that Java *interfaces* (discussed in the next chapter) are a superior solution. However, the reflection mechanism allows you to call arbitrary methods.

NOTE: Among the nonstandard language extensions that Microsoft added to its Java derivatives, J++ and C#, is another method pointer type, called a *delegate*, that is different from the Method class that we discuss in this section. However, inner classes (which we will introduce in the next chapter) are a more useful construct than delegates.

Recall that you can inspect a field of an object with the get method of the Field class. Similarly, the Method class has an invoke method that lets you call the method that is wrapped in the current Method object. The signature for the invoke method is

```
Object invoke(Object obj, Object... args)
```

The first parameter is the implicit parameter, and the remaining objects provide the explicit parameters.

For a static method, the first parameter is ignored—you can set it to null.

For example, if m1 represents the getName method of the Employee class, the following code shows how you can call it:

```
String n = (String) m1.invoke(harry);
```

If the return type is a primitive type, the invoke method will return the wrapper type instead. For example, suppose that m2 represents the getSalary method of the Employee class. Then, the returned object is actually a Double, and you must cast it accordingly. Use automatic unboxing to turn it into a double:

```
double s = (Double) m2.invoke(harry);
```

How do you obtain a Method object? You can, of course, call getDeclaredMethods and search through the returned array of Method objects until you find the method you want. Or, you can call the getMethod method of the Class class. This is similar to the getField method that takes a string with the field name and returns a Field object. However, there may be several methods with the same name, so you need to be careful that you get the right one. For that reason, you must also supply the parameter types of the desired method. The signature of getMethod is

```
Method getMethod(String name, Class... parameterTypes)
```

For example, here is how you can get method pointers to the getName and raiseSalary methods of the Employee class:

```
Method m1 = Employee.class.getMethod("getName");
Method m2 = Employee.class.getMethod("raiseSalary", double.class);
```

Now that you have seen the rules for using Method objects, let's put them to work. Listing 5.17 is a program that prints a table of values for a mathematical function such as Math.sqrt or Math.sin. The printout looks like this:

```
public static native double java.lang.Math.sqrt(double)
     1.0000 |    1.0000
     2.0000 |    1.4142
     3.0000 |    1.7321
     4.0000 |    2.0000
     5.0000 |    2.2361
     6.0000 |    2.4495
     7.0000 |    2.6458
     8.0000 |    2.8284
     9.0000 |    3.0000
    10.0000 |    3.1623
```

The code for printing a table is, of course, independent of the actual function that is being tabulated.

```
double dx = (to - from) / (n - 1);
for (double x = from; x <= to; x += dx)
{
    double y = (Double) f.invoke(null, x);
    System.out.printf("%10.4f | %10.4f%n", x, y);
}
```

Here, f is an object of type Method. The first parameter of invoke is null because we are calling a static method.

To tabulate the Math.sqrt function, we set f to

```
Math.class.getMethod("sqrt", double.class)
```

That is the method of the Math class that has the name sqrt and a single parameter of type double.

Listing 5.17 shows the complete code of the generic tabulator and a couple of test runs.

As this example clearly shows, you can do anything with Method objects that you can do with function pointers in C (or delegates in C#). Just as in C, this style of programming is usually quite inconvenient, and always error-prone. What happens if you invoke a method with the wrong parameters? The invoke method throws an exception.

Also, the parameters and return values of invoke are necessarily of type Object. That means you must cast back and forth a lot. As a result, the compiler is deprived of the chance to check your code, so errors surface only during testing, when they are more tedious to find and fix. Moreover, code that uses reflection to get at method pointers is significantly slower than code that simply calls methods directly.

For that reason, we suggest that you use Method objects in your own programs only when absolutely necessary. Using interfaces and, as of Java SE 8, lambda expressions (the subject of the next chapter) is almost always a better idea. In particular, we echo the developers of Java and suggest not using Method objects for callback functions. Using interfaces for the callbacks leads to code that runs faster and is a lot more maintainable.

Listing 5.17 methods/MethodTableTest.java

```
1  package methods;
2
3  import java.lang.reflect.*;
4
5  /**
6   * This program shows how to invoke methods through reflection.
7   * @version 1.2 2012-05-04
8   * @author Cay Horstmann
9   */
10 public class MethodTableTest
11 {
12    public static void main(String[] args) throws Exception
13    {
14       // get method pointers to the square and sqrt methods
15       Method square = MethodTableTest.class.getMethod("square", double.class);
16       Method sqrt = Math.class.getMethod("sqrt", double.class);
17
18       // print tables of x- and y-values
19
20       printTable(1, 10, 10, square);
21       printTable(1, 10, 10, sqrt);
22    }
23
24    /**
25     * Returns the square of a number
26     * @param x a number
27     * @return x squared
28     */
29    public static double square(double x)
30    {
31       return x * x;
32    }
33
34    /**
35     * Prints a table with x- and y-values for a method
36     * @param from the lower bound for the x-values
37     * @param to the upper bound for the x-values
38     * @param n the number of rows in the table
39     * @param f a method with a double parameter and double return value
40     */
```

```
41    public static void printTable(double from, double to, int n, Method f)
42    {
43       // print out the method as table header
44       System.out.println(f);
45
46       double dx = (to - from) / (n - 1);
47
48       for (double x = from; x <= to; x += dx)
49       {
50          try
51          {
52             double y = (Double) f.invoke(null, x);
53             System.out.printf("%10.4f | %10.4f%n", x, y);
54          }
55          catch (Exception e)
56          {
57             e.printStackTrace();
58          }
59       }
60    }
61 }
```

---

java.lang.reflect.Method 1.1

- `public Object invoke(Object implicitParameter, Object[] explicitParameters)`

  invokes the method described by this object, passing the given parameters and returning the value that the method returns. For static methods, pass `null` as the implicit parameter. Pass primitive type values by using wrappers. Primitive type return values must be unwrapped.

5.8 Design Hints for Inheritance

We want to end this chapter with some hints that we have found useful when using inheritance.

1. *Place common operations and fields in the superclass.*

   This is why we put the name field into the Person class instead of replicating it in the Employee and Student classes.

2. *Don't use protected fields.*

   Some programmers think it is a good idea to define most instance fields as protected, "just in case," so that subclasses can access these fields if they need to. However, the protected mechanism doesn't give much protection, for two reasons. First, the set of subclasses is unbounded—anyone can form a subclass of your classes and then write code that directly accesses protected instance fields, thereby breaking encapsulation. And second, in the Java programming language, all classes in the same package have access to protected fields, whether or not they are subclasses.

However, protected methods can be useful to indicate methods that are not ready for general use and should be redefined in subclasses.

3. *Use inheritance to model the "is–a" relationship.*

Inheritance is a handy code-saver, but sometimes people overuse it. For example, suppose we need a Contractor class. Contractors have names and hire dates, but they do not have salaries. Instead, they are paid by the hour, and they do not stay around long enough to get a raise. There is the temptation to form a subclass Contractor from Employee and add an hourlyWage field.

```
public class Contractor extends Employee
{
   private double hourlyWage;
   . . .
}
```

This is *not* a good idea, however, because now each contractor object has both a salary and hourly wage field. It will cause you no end of grief when you implement methods for printing paychecks or tax forms. You will end up writing more code than you would have written by not inheriting in the first place.

The contractor-employee relationship fails the "is–a" test. A contractor is not a special case of an employee.

4. *Don't use inheritance unless all inherited methods make sense.*

Suppose we want to write a Holiday class. Surely every holiday is a day, and days can be expressed as instances of the GregorianCalendar class, so we can use inheritance.

```
class Holiday extends GregorianCalendar { . . . }
```

Unfortunately, the set of holidays is not *closed* under the inherited operations. One of the public methods of GregorianCalendar is add. And add can turn holidays into nonholidays:

```
Holiday christmas;
christmas.add(Calendar.DAY_OF_MONTH, 12);
```

Therefore, inheritance is not appropriate in this example.

Note that this problem does not arise if you extend LocalDate. Because that class is immutable, there is no method that could turn a holiday into a nonholiday.

5. *Don't change the expected behavior when you override a method.*

The substitution principle applies not just to syntax but, more importantly, to behavior. When you override a method, you should not unreasonably change its behavior. The compiler can't help you—it cannot check whether your redefinitions make sense. For example, you can "fix" the issue of the add method in the Holiday class by redefining add, perhaps to do nothing, or to throw an exception, or to move on to the next holiday.

However, such a fix violates the substitution principle. The sequence of statements

```
int d1 = x.get(Calendar.DAY_OF_MONTH);
x.add(Calendar.DAY_OF_MONTH, 1);
int d2 = x.get(Calendar.DAY_OF_MONTH);
System.out.println(d2 - d1);
```

should have the *expected behavior*, no matter whether x is of type GregorianCalendar or Holiday.

Of course, therein lies the rub. Reasonable and unreasonable people can argue at length about what the expected behavior is. For example, some authors argue that the substitution principle requires Manager.equals to ignore the bonus field because Employee.equals ignores it. These discussions are pointless if they occur in a vacuum. Ultimately, what matters is that you do not circumvent the intent of the original design when you override methods in subclasses.

6. *Use polymorphism, not type information.*

Whenever you find code of the form

```
if (x is of type 1)
    action₁(x);
else if (x is of type 2)
    action₂(x);
```

think polymorphism.

Do $action_1$ and $action_2$ represent a common concept? If so, make the concept a method of a common superclass or interface of both types. Then, you can simply call

```
x.action();
```

and have the dynamic dispatch mechanism inherent in polymorphism launch the correct action.

Code that uses polymorphic methods or interface implementations is much easier to maintain and extend than code using multiple type tests.

7. *Don't overuse reflection.*

The reflection mechanism lets you write programs with amazing generality, by detecting fields and methods at runtime. This capability can be extremely useful for systems programming, but it is usually not appropriate in applications. Reflection is fragile—with it, the compiler cannot help you find programming errors. Any errors are found at runtime and result in exceptions.

You have now seen how Java supports the fundamentals of object-oriented programming: classes, inheritance, and polymorphism. In the next chapter, we will tackle two advanced topics that are very important for using Java effectively: interfaces and lambda expressions.

CHAPTER **6**

Interfaces, Lambda Expressions, and Inner Classes

In this chapter

You have now seen all the basic tools for object-oriented programming in Java. This chapter shows you several advanced techniques that are commonly used. Despite their less obvious nature, you will need to master them to complete your Java tool chest.

The first technique, called *interfaces*, is a way of describing *what* classes should do, without specifying *how* they should do it. A class can *implement* one or more interfaces. You can then use objects of these implementing classes whenever conformance to the interface is required. After we cover interfaces, we move on to *lambda expressions*, a concise way for expressing a block of code that can be executed at a later point in time. Using lambda expressions, you can express code that uses callbacks or variable behavior in an elegant and concise fashion.

We then discuss the mechanism of *inner classes*. Inner classes are technically somewhat complex—they are defined inside other classes, and their methods can access the fields of the surrounding class. Inner classes are useful when you design collections of cooperating classes.

This chapter concludes with a discussion of *proxies*, objects that implement arbitrary interfaces. A proxy is a very specialized construct that is useful for building system-level tools. You can safely skip that section on first reading.

6.1 Interfaces

In the following sections, you will learn what Java interfaces are and how to use them. You will also find out how interfaces have been made more powerful in Java SE 8.

6.1.1 The Interface Concept

In the Java programming language, an interface is not a class but a set of *requirements* for the classes that want to conform to the interface.

Typically, the supplier of some service states: "If your class conforms to a particular interface, then I'll perform the service." Let's look at a concrete example. The sort method of the Arrays class promises to sort an array of objects, but under one condition: The objects must belong to classes that implement the Comparable interface.

Here is what the Comparable interface looks like:

```
public interface Comparable
{
    int compareTo(Object other);
}
```

This means that any class that implements the Comparable interface is required to have a compareTo method, and the method must take an Object parameter and return an integer.

NOTE: As of Java SE 5.0, the `Comparable` interface has been enhanced to be a generic type.

```
public interface Comparable<T>
{
    int compareTo(T other); // parameter has type T
}
```

For example, a class that implements `Comparable<Employee>` must supply a method

```
int compareTo(Employee other)
```

You can still use the "raw" `Comparable` type without a type parameter. Then the `compareTo` method has a parameter of type `Object`, and you have to manually cast that parameter of the `compareTo` method to the desired type. We will do just that for a little while so that you don't have to worry about two new concepts at the same time.

All methods of an interface are automatically `public`. For that reason, it is not necessary to supply the keyword `public` when declaring a method in an interface.

Of course, there is an additional requirement that the interface cannot spell out: When calling `x.compareTo(y)`, the `compareTo` method must actually be able to *compare* the two objects and return an indication whether x or y is larger. The method is supposed to return a negative number if x is smaller than y, zero if they are equal, and a positive number otherwise.

This particular interface has a single method. Some interfaces have multiple methods. As you will see later, interfaces can also define constants. What is more important, however, is what interfaces *cannot* supply. Interfaces never have instance fields. Before Java SE 8, methods were never implemented in interfaces. (As you will see in Section 6.1.4, "Static Methods," on p. 298 and Section 6.1.5, "Default Methods," on p. 298, it is now possible to supply simple methods in interfaces. Of course, those methods cannot refer to instance fields—interfaces don't have any.)

Supplying instance fields and methods that operate on them is the job of the classes that implement the interface. You can think of an interface as being similar to an abstract class with no instance fields. However, there are some differences between these two concepts—we look at them later in some detail.

Now suppose we want to use the sort method of the Arrays class to sort an array of Employee objects. Then the Employee class must *implement* the Comparable interface.

To make a class implement an interface, you carry out two steps:

1. You declare that your class intends to implement the given interface.
2. You supply definitions for all methods in the interface.

To declare that a class implements an interface, use the implements keyword:

```
class Employee implements Comparable
```

Of course, now the Employee class needs to supply the compareTo method. Let's suppose that we want to compare employees by their salary. Here is an implementation of the compareTo method:

```
public int compareTo(Object otherObject)
{
   Employee other = (Employee) otherObject;
   return Double.compare(salary, other.salary);
}
```

Here, we use the static Double.compare method that returns a negative if the first argument is less than the second argument, 0 if they are equal, and a positive value otherwise.

 CAUTION: In the interface declaration, the compareTo method was not declared public because all methods in an *interface* are automatically public. However, when implementing the interface, you must declare the method as public. Otherwise, the compiler assumes that the method has package visibility—the default for a *class*. The compiler then complains that you're trying to supply a more restrictive access privilege.

We can do a little better by supplying a type parameter for the generic Comparable interface:

```
class Employee implements Comparable<Employee>
{
   public int compareTo(Employee other)
   {
      return Double.compare(salary, other.salary);
   }
   . . .
}
```

Note that the unsightly cast of the Object parameter has gone away.

TIP: The compareTo method of the Comparable interface returns an integer. If the objects are not equal, it does not matter what negative or positive value you return. This flexibility can be useful when you are comparing integer fields. For example, suppose each employee has a unique integer id and you want to sort by the employee ID number. Then you can simply return id - other.id. That value will be some negative value if the first ID number is less than the other, 0 if they are the same ID, and some positive value otherwise. However, there is one caveat: The range of the integers must be small enough so that the subtraction does not overflow. If you know that the IDs are not negative or that their absolute value is at most (Integer.MAX_VALUE - 1) / 2, you are safe. Otherwise, call the static Integer.compare method.

Of course, the subtraction trick doesn't work for floating-point numbers. The difference salary - other.salary can round to 0 if the salaries are close together but not identical. The call Double.compare(x, y) simply returns -1 if x < y or 1 if x > y.

 NOTE: The documentation of the Comparable interface suggests that the compareTo method should be compatible with the equals method. That is, x.compareTo(y) should be zero exactly when x.equals(y). Most classes in the Java API that implement Comparable follow this advice. A notable exception is BigDecimal. Consider x = new BigDecimal("1.0") and y = new BigDecimal("1.00"). Then x.equals(y) is false because the numbers differ in precision. But x.compareTo(y) is zero. Ideally, it shouldn't be, but there was no obvious way of deciding which one should come first.

Now you saw what a class must do to avail itself of the sorting service—it must implement a compareTo method. That's eminently reasonable. There needs to be some way for the sort method to compare objects. But why can't the Employee class simply provide a compareTo method without implementing the Comparable interface?

The reason for interfaces is that the Java programming language is *strongly typed*. When making a method call, the compiler needs to be able to check that the method actually exists. Somewhere in the sort method will be statements like this:

```
if (a[i].compareTo(a[j]) > 0)
{
   // rearrange a[i] and a[j]
   . . .
}
```

The compiler must know that a[i] actually has a compareTo method. If a is an array of Comparable objects, then the existence of the method is assured because every class that implements the Comparable interface must supply the method.

NOTE: You would expect that the sort method in the Arrays class is defined to accept a Comparable[] array so that the compiler can complain if anyone ever calls sort with an array whose element type doesn't implement the Comparable interface. Sadly, that is not the case. Instead, the sort method accepts an Object[] array and uses a clumsy cast:

```
// Approach used in the standard library--not recommended
if ((((Comparable) a[i]).compareTo(a[j]) > 0)
{
   // rearrange a[i] and a[j]
   . . .
}
```

If a[i] does not belong to a class that implements the Comparable interface, the virtual machine throws an exception.

Listing 6.1 presents the full code for sorting an array of instances of the class Employee (Listing 6.2) for sorting an employee array.

Listing 6.1 interfaces/EmployeeSortTest.java

```
1  package interfaces;
2
3  import java.util.*;
4
5  /**
6   * This program demonstrates the use of the Comparable interface.
7   * @version 1.30 2004-02-27
8   * @author Cay Horstmann
9   */
10 public class EmployeeSortTest
11 {
12    public static void main(String[] args)
13    {
14       Employee[] staff = new Employee[3];
15
16       staff[0] = new Employee("Harry Hacker", 35000);
17       staff[1] = new Employee("Carl Cracker", 75000);
18       staff[2] = new Employee("Tony Tester", 38000);
19
20       Arrays.sort(staff);
21
22       // print out information about all Employee objects
23       for (Employee e : staff)
24          System.out.println("name=" + e.getName() + ",salary=" + e.getSalary());
25    }
26 }
```

Listing 6.2 interfaces/Employee.java

```
1  package interfaces;
2
3  public class Employee implements Comparable<Employee>
4  {
5     private String name;
6     private double salary;
7
8     public Employee(String name, double salary)
9     {
10       this.name = name;
11       this.salary = salary;
12    }
13
14    public String getName()
15    {
16       return name;
17    }
18
19    public double getSalary()
20    {
21       return salary;
22    }
23
24    public void raiseSalary(double byPercent)
25    {
26       double raise = salary * byPercent / 100;
27       salary += raise;
28    }
29
30    /**
31     * Compares employees by salary
32     * @param other another Employee object
33     * @return a negative value if this employee has a lower salary than
34     * otherObject, 0 if the salaries are the same, a positive value otherwise
35     */
36    public int compareTo(Employee other)
37    {
38       return Double.compare(salary, other.salary);
39    }
40 }
```

---

java.lang.Comparable<T> 1.0

- int compareTo(T other)

  compares this object with other and returns a negative integer if this object is less than other, zero if they are equal, and a positive integer otherwise.

---

java.util.Arrays 1.2

- `static void sort(Object[] a)`

  sorts the elements in the array a. All elements in the array must belong to classes that implement the Comparable interface, and they must all be comparable to each other.

---

java.lang.Integer 1.0

- `static int compare(int x, int y)` 7

  returns a negative integer if x < y, zero if x and y are equal, and a positive integer otherwise.

---

java.lang.Double 1.0

- `static int compare(double x, double y)` 1.4

  returns a negative integer if x < y, zero if x and y are equal, and a positive integer otherwise.

 NOTE: According to the language standard: "The implementor must ensure `sgn(x.compareTo(y)) = -sgn(y.compareTo(x))` for all x and y. (This implies that `x.compareTo(y)` must throw an exception if `y.compareTo(x)` throws an exception.)" Here, sgn is the *sign* of a number: sgn(n) is −1 if n is negative, 0 if n equals 0, and 1 if n is positive. In plain English, if you flip the parameters of compareTo, the sign (but not necessarily the actual value) of the result must also flip.

As with the equals method, problems can arise when inheritance comes into play.

Since Manager extends Employee, it implements Comparable<Employee> and not Comparable<Manager>. If Manager chooses to override compareTo, it must be prepared to compare managers to employees. It can't simply cast an employee to a manager:

```
class Manager extends Employee
{
   public int compareTo(Employee other)
   {
      Manager otherManager = (Manager) other; // NO
      . . .
   }
   . . .
}
```

That violates the "antisymmetry" rule. If x is an Employee and y is a Manager, then the call x.compareTo(y) doesn't throw an exception—it simply compares x and y as employees. But the reverse, y.compareTo(x), throws a ClassCastException.

This is the same situation as with the equals method that we discussed in Chapter 5, and the remedy is the same. There are two distinct scenarios.

If subclasses have different notions of comparison, then you should outlaw comparison of objects that belong to different classes. Each compareTo method should start out with the test

```
if (getClass() != other.getClass()) throw new ClassCastException();
```

If there is a common algorithm for comparing subclass objects, simply provide a single compareTo method in the superclass and declare it as final.

For example, suppose you want managers to be better than regular employees, regardless of salary. What about other subclasses such as Executive and Secretary? If you need to establish a pecking order, supply a method such as rank in the Employee class. Have each subclass override rank, and implement a single compareTo method that takes the rank values into account.

6.1.2 Properties of Interfaces

Interfaces are not classes. In particular, you can never use the new operator to instantiate an interface:

```
x = new Comparable(. . .); // ERROR
```

However, even though you can't construct interface objects, you can still declare interface variables.

```
Comparable x; // OK
```

An interface variable must refer to an object of a class that implements the interface:

```
x = new Employee(. . .); // OK provided Employee implements Comparable
```

Next, just as you use instanceof to check whether an object is of a specific class, you can use instanceof to check whether an object implements an interface:

```
if (anObject instanceof Comparable) { . . . }
```

Just as you can build hierarchies of classes, you can extend interfaces. This allows for multiple chains of interfaces that go from a greater degree of generality to a greater degree of specialization. For example, suppose you had an interface called Moveable.

```
public interface Moveable
{
   void move(double x, double y);
}
```

Then, you could imagine an interface called Powered that extends it:

```
public interface Powered extends Moveable
{
   double milesPerGallon();
}
```

Although you cannot put instance fields or static methods in an interface, you can supply constants in them. For example:

```
public interface Powered extends Moveable
{
   double milesPerGallon();
   double SPEED_LIMIT = 95; // a public static final constant
}
```

Just as methods in an interface are automatically public, fields are always public static final.

 NOTE: It is legal to tag interface methods as public, and fields as public static final. Some programmers do that, either out of habit or for greater clarity. However, the Java Language Specification recommends that the redundant keywords not be supplied, and we follow that recommendation.

Some interfaces define just constants and no methods. For example, the standard library contains an interface SwingConstants that defines constants NORTH, SOUTH, HORIZONTAL, and so on. Any class that chooses to implement the SwingConstants interface automatically inherits these constants. Its methods can simply refer to NORTH rather than the more cumbersome SwingConstants.NORTH. However, this use of interfaces seems rather degenerate, and we do not recommend it.

While each class can have only one superclass, classes can implement *multiple* interfaces. This gives you the maximum amount of flexibility in defining a class's behavior. For example, the Java programming language has an important interface built into it, called Cloneable. (We will discuss this interface in detail in Section 6.2.3, "Object Cloning," on p. 306.) If your class implements Cloneable, the clone method in the Object class will make an exact copy of your class's objects. If you want both cloneability and comparability, simply implement both interfaces. Use commas to separate the interfaces that you want to implement:

```
class Employee implements Cloneable, Comparable
```

6.1.3 Interfaces and Abstract Classes

If you read the section about abstract classes in Chapter 5, you may wonder why the designers of the Java programming language bothered with introducing the concept of interfaces. Why can't Comparable simply be an abstract class:

```
abstract class Comparable // why not?
{
    public abstract int compareTo(Object other);
}
```

The Employee class would then simply extend this abstract class and supply the compareTo method:

```
class Employee extends Comparable // why not?
{
    public int compareTo(Object other) { . . . }
}
```

There is, unfortunately, a major problem with using an abstract base class to express a generic property. A class can only extend a single class. Suppose the Employee class already extends a different class, say, Person. Then it can't extend a second class.

```
class Employee extends Person, Comparable // Error
```

But each class can implement as many interfaces as it likes:

```
class Employee extends Person implements Comparable // OK
```

Other programming languages, in particular C++, allow a class to have more than one superclass. This feature is called *multiple inheritance*. The designers of Java chose not to support multiple inheritance, because it makes the language either very complex (as in C++) or less efficient (as in Eiffel).

Instead, interfaces afford most of the benefits of multiple inheritance while avoiding the complexities and inefficiencies.

 C++ NOTE: C++ has multiple inheritance and all the complications that come with it, such as virtual base classes, dominance rules, and transverse pointer casts. Few C++ programmers use multiple inheritance, and some say it should never be used. Other programmers recommend using multiple inheritance only for the "mix-in" style of inheritance. In the mix-in style, a primary base class describes the parent object, and additional base classes (the so-called mix-ins) may supply auxiliary characteristics. That style is similar to a Java class with a single superclass and additional interfaces.

6.1.4 Static Methods

As of Java SE 8, you are allowed to add static methods to interfaces. There was never a technical reason why this should be outlawed. It simply seemed to be against the spirit of interfaces as abstract specifications.

Up to now, it has been common to place static methods in companion classes. In the standard library, you find pairs of interfaces and utility classes such as `Collection`/`Collections` or `Path`/`Paths`.

Have a look at the `Paths` class. It only has a couple of factory methods. You can construct a path to a file or directory from a sequence of strings, such as `Paths.get("jdk1.8.0", "jre", "bin")`. In Java SE 8, one could have added this method to the `Path` interface:

```
public interface Path
{
   public static Path get(String first, String... more) {
      return FileSystems.getDefault().getPath(first, more);
   }
   . . .
}
```

Then the `Paths` class is no longer necessary.

It is unlikely that the Java library will be refactored in this way, but when you implement your own interfaces, there is no longer a reason to provide a separate companion class for utility methods.

6.1.5 Default Methods

You can supply a *default* implementation for any interface method. You must tag such a method with the `default` modifier.

```
public interface Comparable<T>
{
   default int compareTo(T other) { return 0; }
      // By default, all elements are the same
}
```

Of course, that is not very useful since every realistic implementation of `Comparable` would override this method. But there are other situations where default methods can be useful. For example, as you will see in Chapter 11, if you want to be notified when a mouse click happens, you are supposed to implement an interface that has five methods:

```
public interface MouseListener
{
    void mouseClicked(MouseEvent event);
    void mousePressed(MouseEvent event);
    void mouseReleased(MouseEvent event);
    void mouseEntered(MouseEvent event);
    void mouseExited(MouseEvent event);
}
```

Most of the time, you only care about one or two of these event types. As of Java SE 8, you can declare all of the methods as default methods that do nothing.

```
public interface MouseListener
{
    default void mouseClicked(MouseEvent event) {}
    default void mousePressed(MouseEvent event) {}
    default void mouseReleased(MouseEvent event) {}
    default void mouseEntered(MouseEvent event) {}
    default void mouseExited(MouseEvent event) {}
}
```

Then programmers who implement this interface only need to override the listeners for the events they actually care about.

A default method can call other methods. For example, a Collection interface can define a convenience method

```
public interface Collection
{
    int size(); // An abstract method
    default boolean isEmpty()
    {
        return size() == 0;
    }
    . . .
}
```

Then a programmer implementing Collection doesn't have to worry about implementing an isEmpty method.

 NOTE: In the Java API, you will find a number of interfaces with companion classes that implement some or all of its methods, such as Collection/ AbstractCollection or MouseListener/MouseAdapter. With Java SE 8, this technique is obsolete. Just implement the methods in the interface.

An important use for default methods is *interface evolution*. Consider for example the Collection interface that has been a part of Java for many years. Suppose that a long time ago, you provided a class

```
public class Bag implements Collection
```

Later, in Java SE 8, a `stream` method was added to the interface.

Suppose the `stream` method was not a default method. Then the `Bag` class no longer compiles since it doesn't implement the new method. Adding a nondefault method to an interface is not *source compatible*.

But suppose you don't recompile the class and simply use an old JAR file containing it. The class will still load, even with the missing method. Programs can still construct `Bag` instances, and nothing bad will happen. (Adding a method to an interface is *binary compatible*.) However, if a program calls the `stream` method on a `Bag` instance, an `AbstractMethodError` occurs.

Making the method a `default` method solves both problems. The `Bag` class will again compile. And if the class is loaded without being recompiled and the `stream` method is invoked on a `Bag` instance, the `Collection.stream` method is called.

6.1.6 Resolving Default Method Conflicts

What happens if the exact same method is defined as a default method in one interface and then again as a method of a superclass or another interface? Languages such as Scala and C++ have complex rules for resolving such ambiguities. Fortunately, the rules in Java are much simpler. Here they are:

1. Superclasses win. If a superclass provides a concrete method, default methods with the same name and parameter types are simply ignored.

2. Interfaces clash. If a superinterface provides a default method, and another interface supplies a method with the same name and parameter types (default or not), then you must resolve the conflict by overriding that method.

Let's look at the second rule. Consider another interface with a `getName` method:

```
interface Named
{
    default String getName() { return getClass().getName() + "_" + hashCode(); }
}
```

What happens if you form a class that implements both of them?

```
class Student implements Person, Named
{
    . . .
}
```

The class inherits two inconsistent `getName` methods provided by the `Person` and `Named` interfaces. Instead of choosing one over the other, the Java compiler reports an error and leaves it up to the programmer to resolve the ambiguity. Simply provide a getName method in the Student class. In that method, you can choose one of the two conflicting methods, like this:

```
class Student implements Person, Named
{
    public String getName() { return Person.super.getName(); }
    . . .
}
```

Now assume that the Named interface does not provide a default implementation for getName:

```
interface Named
{
    String getName();
}
```

Can the Student class inherit the default method from the Person interface? This might be reasonable, but the Java designers decided in favor of uniformity. It doesn't matter how two interfaces conflict. If at least one interface provides an implementation, the compiler reports an error, and the programmer must resolve the ambiguity.

 NOTE: Of course, if neither interface provides a default for a shared method, then we are in the situation before Java SE 8, and there is no conflict. An implementing class has two choices: implement the method, or leave it unimplemented. In the latter case, the class is itself abstract.

We just discussed name clashes between two interfaces. Now consider a class that extends a superclass and implements an interface, inheriting the same method from both. For example, suppose that Person is a class and Student is defined as

```
class Student extends Person implements Named { . . . }
```

In that case, only the superclass method matters, and any default method from the interface is simply ignored. In our example, Student inherits the getName method from Person, and it doesn't make any difference whether the Named interface provides a default for getName or not. This is the "class wins" rule.

The "class wins" rule ensures compatibility with Java SE 7. If you add default methods to an interface, it has no effect on code that worked before there were default methods.

CAUTION: You can never make a default method that redefines one of the methods in the `Object` class. For example, you can't define a default method for `toString` or `equals`, even though that might be attractive for interfaces such as `List`. As a consequence of the "classes win" rule, such a method could never win against `Object.toString` or `Objects.equals`.

6.2 Examples of Interfaces

In the next three sections, we give additional examples of interfaces so you can see how they are used in practice.

6.2.1 Interfaces and Callbacks

A common pattern in programming is the *callback* pattern. In this pattern, you specify the action that should occur whenever a particular event happens. For example, you may want a particular action to occur when a button is clicked or a menu item is selected. However, as you have not yet seen how to implement user interfaces, we will consider a similar but simpler situation.

The `javax.swing` package contains a `Timer` class that is useful if you want to be notified whenever a time interval has elapsed. For example, if a part of your program contains a clock, you can ask to be notified every second so that you can update the clock face.

When you construct a timer, you set the time interval and you tell it what it should do whenever the time interval has elapsed.

How do you tell the timer what it should do? In many programming languages, you supply the name of a function that the timer should call periodically. However, the classes in the Java standard library take an object-oriented approach. You pass an object of some class. The timer then calls one of the methods on that object. Passing an object is more flexible than passing a function because the object can carry additional information.

Of course, the timer needs to know what method to call. The timer requires that you specify an object of a class that implements the `ActionListener` interface of the `java.awt.event` package. Here is that interface:

```
public interface ActionListener
{
    void actionPerformed(ActionEvent event);
}
```

The timer calls the `actionPerformed` method when the time interval has expired.

Suppose you want to print a message "At the tone, the time is . . .", followed by a beep, once every 10 seconds. You would define a class that implements the `ActionListener` interface. You would then place whatever statements you want to have executed inside the `actionPerformed` method.

```
class TimePrinter implements ActionListener
{
   public void actionPerformed(ActionEvent event)
   {
      System.out.println("At the tone, the time is " + new Date());
      Toolkit.getDefaultToolkit().beep();
   }
}
```

Note the `ActionEvent` parameter of the `actionPerformed` method. This parameter gives information about the event, such as the source object that generated it—see Chapter 11 for more information. However, detailed information about the event is not important in this program, and you can safely ignore the parameter.

Next, you construct an object of this class and pass it to the `Timer` constructor.

```
ActionListener listener = new TimePrinter();
Timer t = new Timer(10000, listener);
```

The first parameter of the `Timer` constructor is the time interval that must elapse between notifications, measured in milliseconds. We want to be notified every 10 seconds. The second parameter is the listener object.

Finally, you start the timer.

```
t.start();
```

Every 10 seconds, a message like

```
At the tone, the time is Wed Apr 13 23:29:08 PDT 2016
```

is displayed, followed by a beep.

Listing 6.3 puts the timer and its action listener to work. After the timer is started, the program puts up a message dialog and waits for the user to click the OK button to stop. While the program waits for the user, the current time is displayed at 10-second intervals.

Be patient when running the program. The "Quit program?" dialog box appears right away, but the first timer message is displayed after 10 seconds.

Note that the program imports the `javax.swing.Timer` class by name, in addition to importing `javax.swing.*` and `java.util.*`. This breaks the ambiguity between `javax.swing.Timer` and `java.util.Timer`, an unrelated class for scheduling background tasks.

Listing 6.3 timer/TimerTest.java

```
1  package timer;
2
3  /**
4     @version 1.01 2015-05-12
5     @author Cay Horstmann
6  */
7
8  import java.awt.*;
9  import java.awt.event.*;
10 import java.util.*;
11 import javax.swing.*;
12 import javax.swing.Timer;
13 // to resolve conflict with java.util.Timer
14
15 public class TimerTest
16 {
17    public static void main(String[] args)
18    {
19       ActionListener listener = new TimePrinter();
20
21       // construct a timer that calls the listener
22       // once every 10 seconds
23       Timer t = new Timer(10000, listener);
24       t.start();
25
26       JOptionPane.showMessageDialog(null, "Quit program?");
27       System.exit(0);
28    }
29 }
30
31 class TimePrinter implements ActionListener
32 {
33    public void actionPerformed(ActionEvent event)
34    {
35       System.out.println("At the tone, the time is " + new Date());
36       Toolkit.getDefaultToolkit().beep();
37    }
38 }
```

---

javax.swing.JOptionPane 1.2

- static void showMessageDialog(Component parent, Object message)

  displays a dialog box with a message prompt and an OK button. The dialog is centered over the parent component. If parent is null, the dialog is centered on the screen.

`javax.swing.Timer` 1.2

- `Timer(int interval, ActionListener listener)`

  constructs a timer that notifies `listener` whenever `interval` milliseconds have elapsed.

- `void start()`

  starts the timer. Once started, the timer calls `actionPerformed` on its listeners.

- `void stop()`

  stops the timer. Once stopped, the timer no longer calls `actionPerformed` on its listeners.

`java.awt.Toolkit` 1.0

- `static Toolkit getDefaultToolkit()`

  gets the default toolkit. A toolkit contains information about the GUI environment.

- `void beep()`

  emits a beep sound.

6.2.2 The Comparator Interface

In Section 6.1.1, "The Interface Concept," on p. 288, you have seen how you can sort an array of objects, provided they are instances of classes that implement the `Comparable` interface. For example, you can sort an array of strings since the `String` class implements `Comparable<String>`, and the `String.compareTo` method compares strings in dictionary order.

Now suppose we want to sort strings by increasing length, not in dictionary order. We can't have the `String` class implement the `compareTo` method in two ways—and at any rate, the `String` class isn't ours to modify.

To deal with this situation, there is a second version of the `Arrays.sort` method whose parameters are an array and a *comparator*—an instance of a class that implements the `Comparator` interface.

```
public interface Comparator<T>
{
    int compare(T first, T second);
}
```

To compare strings by length, define a class that implements `Comparator<String>`:

```
class LengthComparator implements Comparator<String>
{
    public int compare(String first, String second) {
        return first.length() - second.length();
    }
}
```

To actually do the comparison, you need to make an instance:

```
Comparator<String> comp = new LengthComparator();
if (comp.compare(words[i], words[j]) > 0) . . .
```

Contrast this call with `words[i].compareTo(words[j])`. The `compare` method is called on the comparator object, not the string itself.

 NOTE: Even though the `LengthComparator` object has no state, you still need to make an instance of it. You need the instance to call the `compare` method—it is not a static method.

To sort an array, pass a `LengthComparator` object to the `Arrays.sort` method:

```
String[] friends = { "Peter", "Paul", "Mary" };
Arrays.sort(friends, new LengthComparator());
```

Now the array is either `["Paul", "Mary", "Peter"]` or `["Mary", "Paul", "Peter"]`.

You will see in Section 6.3, "Lambda Expressions," on p. 314 how to use a `Comparator` much more easily with a lambda expression.

6.2.3 Object Cloning

In this section, we discuss the `Cloneable` interface that indicates that a class has provided a safe `clone` method. Since cloning is not all that common, and the details are quite technical, you may just want to glance at this material until you need it.

To understand what cloning means, recall what happens when you make a copy of a variable holding an object reference. The original and the copy are references to the same object (see Figure 6.1). This means a change to either variable also affects the other.

```
Employee original = new Employee("John Public", 50000);
Employee copy = original;
copy.raiseSalary(10); // oops--also changed original
```

If you would like `copy` to be a new object that begins its life being identical to `original` but whose state can diverge over time, use the `clone` method.

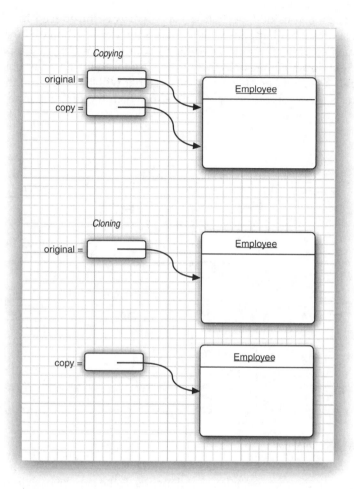

Figure 6.1 Copying and cloning

```
Employee copy = original.clone();
copy.raiseSalary(10); // OK--original unchanged
```

But it isn't quite so simple. The clone method is a protected method of Object, which means that your code cannot simply call it. Only the Employee class can clone Employee objects. There is a reason for this restriction. Think about the way in which the Object class can implement clone. It knows nothing about the object at all, so it can make only a field-by-field copy. If all data fields in the object are numbers or other basic types, copying the fields is just fine. But if the object contains references to subobjects, then copying the field gives you another reference to the same subobject, so the original and the cloned objects still share some information.

To visualize that, consider the Employee class that was introduced in Chapter 4. Figure 6.2 shows what happens when you use the clone method of the Object class to clone such an Employee object. As you can see, the default cloning operation is "shallow"—it doesn't clone objects that are referenced inside other objects. (The figure shows a shared Date object. For reasons that will become clear shortly, this example uses a version of the Employee class in which the hire day is represented as a Date.)

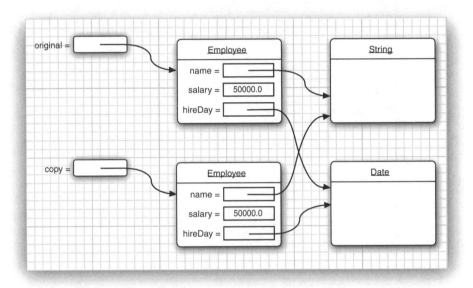

Figure 6.2 A shallow copy

Does it matter if the copy is shallow? It depends. If the subobject shared between the original and the shallow clone is *immutable*, then the sharing is safe. This certainly happens if the subobject belongs to an immutable class, such as String. Alternatively, the subobject may simply remain constant throughout the lifetime of the object, with no mutators touching it and no methods yielding a reference to it.

Quite frequently, however, subobjects are mutable, and you must redefine the clone method to make a *deep copy* that clones the subobjects as well. In our example, the hireDay field is a Date, which is mutable, so it too must be cloned. (For that reason, this example uses a field of type Date, not LocalDate, to demonstrate the cloning process. Had hireDay been an instance of the immutable LocalDate class, no further action would have been required.)

For every class, you need to decide whether

1. The default clone method is good enough;
2. The default clone method can be patched up by calling clone on the mutable subobjects; and
3. clone should not be attempted.

The third option is actually the default. To choose either the first or the second option, a class must

1. Implement the Cloneable interface; and
2. Redefine the clone method with the public access modifier.

 NOTE: The clone method is declared protected in the Object class, so that your code can't simply call anObject.clone(). But aren't protected methods accessible from any subclass, and isn't every class a subclass of Object? Fortunately, the rules for protected access are more subtle (see Chapter 5). A subclass can call a protected clone method only to clone *its own* objects. You must redefine clone to be public to allow objects to be cloned by any method.

In this case, the appearance of the Cloneable interface has nothing to do with the normal use of interfaces. In particular, it does *not* specify the clone method—that method is inherited from the Object class. The interface merely serves as a tag, indicating that the class designer understands the cloning process. Objects are so paranoid about cloning that they generate a checked exception if an object requests cloning but does not implement that interface.

 NOTE: The Cloneable interface is one of a handful of *tagging interfaces* that Java provides. (Some programmers call them *marker interfaces*.) Recall that the usual purpose of an interface such as Comparable is to ensure that a class implements a particular method or set of methods. A tagging interface has no methods; its only purpose is to allow the use of instanceof in a type inquiry:

```
if (obj instanceof Cloneable) . . .
```

We recommend that you do not use tagging interfaces in your own programs.

Even if the default (shallow copy) implementation of clone is adequate, you still need to implement the Cloneable interface, redefine clone to be public, and call super.clone(). Here is an example:

```
class Employee implements Cloneable
{
   // raise visibility level to public, change return type
   public Employee clone() throws CloneNotSupportedException
   {
      return (Employee) super.clone();
   }
   . . .
}
```

 NOTE: Up to Java SE 1.4, the clone method always had return type Object. Nowadays, you can specify the correct return type for your clone methods. This is an example of covariant return types (see Chapter 5).

The clone method that you just saw adds no functionality to the shallow copy provided by Object.clone. It merely makes the method public. To make a deep copy, you have to work harder and clone the mutable instance fields.

Here is an example of a clone method that creates a deep copy:

```
class Employee implements Cloneable
{
   . . .
   public Employee clone() throws CloneNotSupportedException
   {
      // call Object.clone()
      Employee cloned = (Employee) super.clone();

      // clone mutable fields
      cloned.hireDay = (Date) hireDay.clone();

      return cloned;
   }
}
```

The clone method of the Object class threatens to throw a CloneNotSupportedException—it does that whenever clone is invoked on an object whose class does not implement the Cloneable interface. Of course, the Employee and Date classes implement the Cloneable interface, so the exception won't be thrown. However, the compiler does not know that. Therefore, we declared the exception:

```
public Employee clone() throws CloneNotSupportedException
```

Would it be better to catch the exception instead?

```
public Employee clone()
{
   try
   {
      Employee cloned = (Employee) super.clone();
      . . .
   }
   catch (CloneNotSupportedException e) { return null; }
   // this won't happen, since we are Cloneable
}
```

This is appropriate for final classes. Otherwise, it is a good idea to leave the throws specifier in place. That gives subclasses the option of throwing a CloneNotSupportedException if they can't support cloning.

You have to be careful about cloning of subclasses. For example, once you have defined the clone method for the Employee class, anyone can use it to clone Manager objects. Can the Employee clone method do the job? It depends on the fields of the Manager class. In our case, there is no problem because the bonus field has primitive type. But Manager might have acquired fields that require a deep copy or are not cloneable. There is no guarantee that the implementor of the subclass has fixed clone to do the right thing. For that reason, the clone method is declared as protected in the Object class. But you don't have that luxury if you want users of your classes to invoke clone.

Should you implement clone in your own classes? If your clients need to make deep copies, then you probably should. Some authors feel that you should avoid clone altogether and instead implement another method for the same purpose. We agree that clone is rather awkward, but you'll run into the same issues if you shift the responsibility to another method. At any rate, cloning is less common than you may think. Less than 5 percent of the classes in the standard library implement clone.

The program in Listing 6.4 clones an instance of the class Employee (Listing 6.5), then invokes two mutators. The raiseSalary method changes the value of the salary field, whereas the setHireDay method changes the state of the hireDay field. Neither mutation affects the original object because clone has been defined to make a deep copy.

 NOTE: All array types have a clone method that is public, not protected. You can use it to make a new array that contains copies of all elements. For example:

```
int[] luckyNumbers = { 2, 3, 5, 7, 11, 13 };
int[] cloned = luckyNumbers.clone();
cloned[5] = 12; // doesn't change luckyNumbers[5]
```

NOTE: Chapter 2 of Volume II shows an alternate mechanism for cloning objects, using the object serialization feature of Java. That mechanism is easy to implement and safe, but not very efficient.

Listing 6.4 clone/CloneTest.java

```java
1  package clone;
2
3  /**
4   * This program demonstrates cloning.
5   * @version 1.10 2002-07-01
6   * @author Cay Horstmann
7   */
8  public class CloneTest
9  {
10    public static void main(String[] args)
11    {
12       try
13       {
14          Employee original = new Employee("John Q. Public", 50000);
15          original.setHireDay(2000, 1, 1);
16          Employee copy = original.clone();
17          copy.raiseSalary(10);
18          copy.setHireDay(2002, 12, 31);
19          System.out.println("original=" + original);
20          System.out.println("copy=" + copy);
21       }
22       catch (CloneNotSupportedException e)
23       {
24          e.printStackTrace();
25       }
26    }
27 }
```

Listing 6.5 clone/Employee.java

```java
1  package clone;
2
3  import java.util.Date;
4  import java.util.GregorianCalendar;
5
6  public class Employee implements Cloneable
7  {
```

```
 8     private String name;
 9     private double salary;
10     private Date hireDay;
11
12     public Employee(String name, double salary)
13     {
14        this.name = name;
15        this.salary = salary;
16        hireDay = new Date();
17     }
18
19     public Employee clone() throws CloneNotSupportedException
20     {
21        // call Object.clone()
22        Employee cloned = (Employee) super.clone();
23
24        // clone mutable fields
25        cloned.hireDay = (Date) hireDay.clone();
26
27        return cloned;
28     }
29
30     /**
31      * Set the hire day to a given date.
32      * @param year the year of the hire day
33      * @param month the month of the hire day
34      * @param day the day of the hire day
35      */
36     public void setHireDay(int year, int month, int day)
37     {
38        Date newHireDay = new GregorianCalendar(year, month - 1, day).getTime();
39
40        // Example of instance field mutation
41        hireDay.setTime(newHireDay.getTime());
42     }
43
44     public void raiseSalary(double byPercent)
45     {
46        double raise = salary * byPercent / 100;
47        salary += raise;
48     }
49
50     public String toString()
51     {
52        return "Employee[name=" + name + ",salary=" + salary + ",hireDay=" + hireDay + "]";
53     }
54  }
```

6.3 Lambda Expressions

Now you are ready to learn about lambda expressions, the most exciting change to the Java language in many years. You will see how to use lambda expressions for defining blocks of code with a concise syntax, and how to write code that consumes lambda expressions.

6.3.1 Why Lambdas?

A lambda expression is a block of code that you can pass around so it can be executed later, once or multiple times. Before getting into the syntax (or even the curious name), let's step back and observe where we have used such code blocks in Java.

In Section 6.2.1, "Interfaces and Callbacks," on p. 302, you saw how to do work in timed intervals. Put the work into the `actionPerformed` method of an `ActionListener`:

```
class Worker implements ActionListener
{
    public void actionPerformed(ActionEvent event)
    {
        // do some work
    }
}
```

Then, when you want to repeatedly execute this code, you construct an instance of the `Worker` class. You then submit the instance to a `Timer` object.

The key point is that the `actionPerformed` method contains code that you want to execute later.

Or consider sorting with a custom comparator. If you want to sort strings by length instead of the default dictionary order, you can pass a `Comparator` object to the `sort` method:

```
class LengthComparator implements Comparator<String>
{
    public int compare(String first, String second)
    {
        return first.length() - second.length();
    }
}
. . .
Arrays.sort(strings, new LengthComparator());
```

The `compare` method isn't called right away. Instead, the `sort` method keeps calling the `compare` method, rearranging the elements if they are out of order, until the array is sorted. You give the `sort` method a snippet of code needed to compare elements, and that code is integrated into the rest of the sorting logic, which you'd probably not care to reimplement.

Both examples have something in common. A block of code was passed to someone—a timer, or a `sort` method. That code block was called at some later time.

Up to now, giving someone a block of code hasn't been easy in Java. You couldn't just pass code blocks around. Java is an object-oriented language, so you had to construct an object belonging to a class that has a method with the desired code.

In other languages, it is possible to work with blocks of code directly. The Java designers have resisted adding this feature for a long time. After all, a great strength of Java is its simplicity and consistency. A language can become an unmaintainable mess if it includes every feature that yields marginally more concise code. However, in those other languages it isn't just easier to spawn a thread or to register a button click handler; large swaths of their APIs are simpler, more consistent, and more powerful. In Java, one could have written similar APIs that take objects of classes implementing a particular function, but such APIs would be unpleasant to use.

For some time now, the question was not whether to augment Java for functional programming, but how to do it. It took several years of experimentation before a design emerged that is a good fit for Java. In the next section, you will see how you can work with blocks of code in Java SE 8.

6.3.2 The Syntax of Lambda Expressions

Consider again the sorting example from the preceding section. We pass code that checks whether one string is shorter than another. We compute

```
first.length() - second.length()
```

What are `first` and `second`? They are both strings. Java is a strongly typed language, and we must specify that as well:

```
(String first, String second)
    -> first.length() - second.length()
```

You have just seen your first *lambda expression*. Such an expression is simply a block of code, together with the specification of any variables that must be passed to the code.

Why the name? Many years ago, before there were any computers, the logician Alonzo Church wanted to formalize what it means for a mathematical function to be effectively computable. (Curiously, there are functions that are known to exist, but nobody knows how to compute their values.) He used the Greek letter lambda (λ) to mark parameters. Had he known about the Java API, he would have written

```
λfirst.λsecond.first.length() - second.length()
```

 NOTE: Why the letter λ? Did Church run out of other letters of the alphabet? Actually, the venerable *Principia Mathematica* used the ^ accent to denote free variables, which inspired Church to use an uppercase lambda Λ for parameters. But in the end, he switched to the lowercase version. Ever since, an expression with parameter variables has been called a lambda expression.

You have just seen one form of lambda expressions in Java: parameters, the -> arrow, and an expression. If the code carries out a computation that doesn't fit in a single expression, write it exactly like you would have written a method: enclosed in {} and with explicit return statements. For example,

```
(String first, String second) ->
    {
        if (first.length() < second.length()) return -1;
        else if (first.length() > second.length()) return 1;
        else return 0;
    }
```

If a lambda expression has no parameters, you still supply empty parentheses, just as with a parameterless method:

```
() -> { for (int i = 100; i >= 0; i--) System.out.println(i); }
```

If the parameter types of a lambda expression can be inferred, you can omit them. For example,

```
Comparator<String> comp
    = (first, second) // Same as (String first, String second)
        -> first.length() - second.length();
```

Here, the compiler can deduce that first and second must be strings because the lambda expression is assigned to a string comparator. (We will have a closer look at this assignment in the next section.)

If a method has a single parameter with inferred type, you can even omit the parentheses:

```
ActionListener listener = event ->
    System.out.println("The time is " + new Date()");
        // Instead of (event) -> . . . or (ActionEvent event) -> . . .
```

You never specify the result type of a lambda expression. It is always inferred from context. For example, the expression

```
(String first, String second) -> first.length() - second.length()
```

can be used in a context where a result of type int is expected.

> **NOTE:** It is illegal for a lambda expression to return a value in some branches but not in others. For example, (int x) -> { if (x >= 0) return 1; } is invalid.

The program in Listing 6.6 shows how to use lambda expressions for a comparator and an action listener.

Listing 6.6 lambda/LambdaTest.java

```
1  package lambda;
2
3  import java.util.*;
4
5  import javax.swing.*;
6  import javax.swing.Timer;
7
8  /**
9   * This program demonstrates the use of lambda expressions.
10  * @version 1.0 2015-05-12
11  * @author Cay Horstmann
12  */
13 public class LambdaTest
14 {
15    public static void main(String[] args)
16    {
17       String[] planets = new String[] { "Mercury", "Venus", "Earth", "Mars",
18          "Jupiter", "Saturn", "Uranus", "Neptune" };
19       System.out.println(Arrays.toString(planets));
20       System.out.println("Sorted in dictionary order:");
21       Arrays.sort(planets);
22       System.out.println(Arrays.toString(planets));
23       System.out.println("Sorted by length:");
24       Arrays.sort(planets, (first, second) -> first.length() - second.length());
25       System.out.println(Arrays.toString(planets));
26
27       Timer t = new Timer(1000, event ->
28          System.out.println("The time is " + new Date()));
29       t.start();
30
31       // keep program running until user selects "Ok"
32       JOptionPane.showMessageDialog(null, "Quit program?");
33       System.exit(0);
34    }
35 }
```

6.3.3 Functional Interfaces

As we discussed, there are many existing interfaces in Java that encapsulate blocks of code, such as ActionListener or Comparator. Lambdas are compatible with these interfaces.

You can supply a lambda expression whenever an object of an interface with a single abstract method is expected. Such an interface is called a *functional interface*.

 NOTE: You may wonder why a functional interface must have a single *abstract* method. Aren't all methods in an interface abstract? Actually, it has always been possible for an interface to redeclare methods from the Object class such as toString or clone, and these declarations do not make the methods abstract. (Some interfaces in the Java API redeclare Object methods in order to attach javadoc comments. Check out the Comparator API for an example.) More importantly, as you saw in Section 6.1.5, "Default Methods," on p. 298, in Java SE 8, interfaces can declare nonabstract methods.

To demonstrate the conversion to a functional interface, consider the Arrays.sort method. Its second parameter requires an instance of Comparator, an interface with a single method. Simply supply a lambda:

```
Arrays.sort(words,
    (first, second) -> first.length() - second.length());
```

Behind the scenes, the Arrays.sort method receives an object of some class that implements Comparator<String>. Invoking the compare method on that object executes the body of the lambda expression. The management of these objects and classes is completely implementation dependent, and it can be much more efficient than using traditional inner classes. It is best to think of a lambda expression as a function, not an object, and to accept that it can be passed to a functional interface.

This conversion to interfaces is what makes lambda expressions so compelling. The syntax is short and simple. Here is another example:

```
Timer t = new Timer(1000, event ->
    {
        System.out.println("At the tone, the time is " + new Date());
        Toolkit.getDefaultToolkit().beep();
    });
```

That's a lot easier to read than the alternative with a class that implements the ActionListener interface.

In fact, conversion to a functional interface is the *only* thing that you can do with a lambda expression in Java. In other programming languages that support function literals, you can declare function types such as `(String, String) -> int`, declare variables of those types, and use the variables to save function expressions. However, the Java designers decided to stick with the familiar concept of interfaces instead of adding function types to the language.

 NOTE: You can't even assign a lambda expression to a variable of type `Object`—`Object` is not a functional interface.

The Java API defines a number of very generic functional interfaces in the `java.util.function` package. One of the interfaces, `BiFunction<T, U, R>`, describes functions with parameter types `T` and `U` and return type `R`. You can save our string comparison lambda in a variable of that type:

```
BiFunction<String, String, Integer> comp
   = (first, second) -> first.length() - second.length();
```

However, that does not help you with sorting. There is no `Arrays.sort` method that wants a `BiFunction`. If you have used a functional programming language before, you may find this curious. But for Java programmers, it's pretty natural. An interface such as `Comparator` has a specific purpose, not just a method with given parameter and return types. Java SE 8 retains this flavor. When you want to do something with lambda expressions, you still want to keep the purpose of the expression in mind, and have a specific functional interface for it.

A particularly useful interface in the `java.util.function` package is `Predicate`:

```
public interface Predicate<T>
{
   boolean test(T t);
   // Additional default and static methods
}
```

The `ArrayList` class has a `removeIf` method whose parameter is a `Predicate`. It is specifically designed to pass a lambda expression. For example, the following statement removes all null values from an array list:

```
list.removeIf(e -> e == null);
```

6.3.4 Method References

Sometimes, there is already a method that carries out exactly the action that you'd like to pass on to some other code. For example, suppose you simply want to print the event object whenever a timer event occurs. Of course, you could call

```
Timer t = new Timer(1000, event -> System.out.println(event));
```

It would be nicer if you could just pass the `println` method to the `Timer` constructor. Here is how you do that:

```
Timer t = new Timer(1000, System.out::println);
```

The expression `System.out::println` is a *method reference* that is equivalent to the lambda expression `x -> System.out.println(x)`.

As another example, suppose you want to sort strings regardless of letter case. You can pass this method expression:

```
Arrays.sort(strings, String::compareToIgnoreCase)
```

As you can see from these examples, the `::` operator separates the method name from the name of an object or class. There are three principal cases:

- *object*`::`*instanceMethod*
- *Class*`::`*staticMethod*
- *Class*`::`*instanceMethod*

In the first two cases, the method reference is equivalent to a lambda expression that supplies the parameters of the method. As already mentioned, `System.out::println` is equivalent to `x -> System.out.println(x)`. Similarly, `Math::pow` is equivalent to `(x, y) -> Math.pow(x, y)`.

In the third case, the first parameter becomes the target of the method. For example, `String::compareToIgnoreCase` is the same as `(x, y) -> x.compareToIgnoreCase(y)`.

 NOTE: When there are multiple overloaded methods with the same name, the compiler will try to find from the context which one you mean. For example, there are two versions of the `Math.max` method, one for integers and one for `double` values. Which one gets picked depends on the method parameters of the functional interface to which `Math::max` is converted. Just like lambda expressions, method references don't live in isolation. They are always turned into instances of functional interfaces.

You can capture the `this` parameter in a method reference. For example, `this::equals` is the same as `x -> this.equals(x)`. It is also valid to use `super`. The method expression

```
super::instanceMethod
```

uses `this` as the target and invokes the superclass version of the given method. Here is an artificial example that shows the mechanics:

```
class Greeter
{
   public void greet()
   {
      System.out.println("Hello, world!");
   }
}

class TimedGreeter extends Greeter
{
   public void greet()
   {
      Timer t = new Timer(1000, super::greet);
      t.start();
   }
}
```

When the TimedGreeter.greet method starts, a Timer is constructed that executes the super::greet method on every timer tick. That method calls the greet method of the superclass.

6.3.5 Constructor References

Constructor references are just like method references, except that the name of the method is new. For example, Person::new is a reference to a Person constructor. Which constructor? It depends on the context. Suppose you have a list of strings. Then you can turn it into an array of Person objects, by calling the constructor on each of the strings, with the following invocation:

```
ArrayList<String> names = . . .;
Stream<Person> stream = names.stream().map(Person::new);
List<Person> people = stream.collect(Collectors.toList());
```

We will discuss the details of the stream, map, and collect methods in Chapter 1 of Volume II. For now, what's important is that the map method calls the Person(String) constructor for each list element. If there are multiple Person constructors, the compiler picks the one with a String parameter because it infers from the context that the constructor is called with a string.

You can form constructor references with array types. For example, int[]::new is a constructor reference with one parameter: the length of the array. It is equivalent to the lambda expression x -> new int[x].

Array constructor references are useful to overcome a limitation of Java. It is not possible to construct an array of a generic type T. The expression new T[n] is an error since it would be erased to new Object[n]. That is a problem for library authors. For example, suppose we want to have an array of Person objects. The Stream interface has a toArray method that returns an Object array:

```
Object[] people = stream.toArray();
```

But that is unsatisfactory. The user wants an array of references to Person, not references to Object. The stream library solves that problem with constructor references. Pass Person[]::new to the toArray method:

```
Person[] people = stream.toArray(Person[]::new);
```

The toArray method invokes this constructor to obtain an array of the correct type. Then it fills and returns the array.

6.3.6 Variable Scope

Often, you want to be able to access variables from an enclosing method or class in a lambda expression. Consider this example:

```
public static void repeatMessage(String text, int delay)
{
    ActionListener listener = event ->
        {
            System.out.println(text);
            Toolkit.getDefaultToolkit().beep();
        };
    new Timer(delay, listener).start();
}
```

Consider a call

```
repeatMessage("Hello", 1000); // Prints Hello every 1,000 milliseconds
```

Now look at the variable text inside the lambda expression. Note that this variable is *not* defined in the lambda expression. Instead, it is a parameter variable of the repeatMessage method.

If you think about it, something nonobvious is going on here. The code of the lambda expression may run long after the call to repeatMessage has returned and the parameter variables are gone. How does the text variable stay around?

To understand what is happening, we need to refine our understanding of a lambda expression. A lambda expression has three ingredients:

1. A block of code
2. Parameters
3. Values for the *free* variables, that is, the variables that are not parameters and not defined inside the code

In our example, the lambda expression has one free variable, text. The data structure representing the lambda expression must store the values for the free variables, in our case, the string `"Hello"`. We say that such values have been *captured* by the lambda expression. (It's an implementation detail how that is done. For example, one can translate a lambda expression into an object with a single method, so that the values of the free variables are copied into instance variables of that object.)

 NOTE: The technical term for a block of code together with the values of the free variables is a *closure*. If someone gloats that their language has closures, rest assured that Java has them as well. In Java, lambda expressions are closures.

As you have seen, a lambda expression can capture the value of a variable in the enclosing scope. In Java, to ensure that the captured value is well-defined, there is an important restriction. In a lambda expression, you can only reference variables whose value doesn't change. For example, the following is illegal:

```
public static void countDown(int start, int delay)
{
   ActionListener listener = event ->
      {
         start--; // Error: Can't mutate captured variable
         System.out.println(start);
      };
   new Timer(delay, listener).start();
}
```

There is a reason for this restriction. Mutating variables in a lambda expression is not safe when multiple actions are executed concurrently. This won't happen for the kinds of actions that we have seen so far, but in general, it is a serious problem. See Chapter 14 for more information on this important issue.

It is also illegal to refer to variable in a lambda expression that is mutated outside. For example, the following is illegal:

```
public static void repeat(String text, int count)
{
   for (int i = 1; i <= count; i++)
   {
      ActionListener listener = event ->
         {
            System.out.println(i + ": " + text);
               // Error: Cannot refer to changing i
         };
      new Timer(1000, listener).start();
   }
}
```

The rule is that any captured variable in a lambda expression must be *effectively final*. An effectively final variable is a variable that is never assigned a new value after it has been initialized. In our case, text always refers to the same String object, and it is OK to capture it. However, the value of i is mutated, and therefore i cannot be captured.

The body of a lambda expression has *the same scope as a nested block*. The same rules for name conflicts and shadowing apply. It is illegal to declare a parameter or a local variable in the lambda that has the same name as a local variable.

```
Path first = Paths.get("/usr/bin");
Comparator<String> comp =
   (first, second) -> first.length() - second.length();
   // Error: Variable first already defined
```

Inside a method, you can't have two local variables with the same name, and therefore, you can't introduce such variables in a lambda expression either.

When you use the this keyword in a lambda expression, you refer to the this parameter of the method that creates the lambda. For example, consider

```
public class Application()
{
   public void init()
   {
      ActionListener listener = event ->
         {
            System.out.println(this.toString());
            . . .
         }
      . . .
   }
}
```

The expression this.toString() calls the toString method of the Application object, *not* the ActionListener instance. There is nothing special about the use of this in a lambda expression. The scope of the lambda expression is nested inside the init method, and this has the same meaning anywhere in that method.

6.3.7 Processing Lambda Expressions

Up to now, you have seen how to produce lambda expressions and pass them to a method that expects a functional interface. Now let us see how to write methods that can consume lambda expressions.

The point of using lambdas is *deferred execution*. After all, if you wanted to execute some code right now, you'd do that, without wrapping it inside a lambda. There are many reasons for executing code later, such as:

- Running the code in a separate thread
- Running the code multiple times
- Running the code at the right point in an algorithm (for example, the comparison operation in sorting)
- Running the code when something happens (a button was clicked, data has arrived, and so on)
- Running the code only when necessary

Let's look at a simple example. Suppose you want to repeat an action n times. The action and the count are passed to a repeat method:

```
repeat(10, () -> System.out.println("Hello, World!"));
```

To accept the lambda, we need to pick (or, in rare cases, provide) a functional interface. Table 6.1 lists the most important functional interfaces that are provided in the Java API. In this case, we can use the Runnable interface:

```
public static void repeat(int n, Runnable action)
{
    for (int i = 0; i < n; i++) action.run();
}
```

Note that the body of the lambda expression is executed when action.run() is called.

Now let's make this example a bit more sophisticated. We want to tell the action in which iteration it occurs. For that, we need to pick a functional interface that has a method with an int parameter and a void return. The standard interface for processing int values is

```
public interface IntConsumer
{
    void accept(int value);
}
```

Here is the improved version of the repeat method:

```
public static void repeat(int n, IntConsumer action)
{
    for (int i = 0; i < n; i++) action.accept(i);
}
```

And here is how you call it:

```
repeat(10, i -> System.out.println("Countdown: " + (9 - i)));
```

Table 6.1 Common Functional Interfaces

Functional Interface	Parameter Types	Return Type	Abstract Method Name	Description	Other Methods
Runnable	none	void	run	Runs an action without arguments or return value	
Supplier<T>	none	T	get	Supplies a value of type T	
Consumer<T>	T	void	accept	Consumes a value of type T	andThen
BiConsumer<T, U>	T, U	void	accept	Consumes values of types T and U	andThen
Function<T, R>	T	R	apply	A function with argument of type T	compose, andThen, identity
BiFunction<T, U, R>	T, U	R	apply	A function with arguments of types T and U	andThen
UnaryOperator<T>	T	T	apply	A unary operator on the type T	compose, andThen, identity
BinaryOperator<T>	T, T	T	apply	A binary operator on the type T	andThen, maxBy, minBy
Predicate<T>	T	boolean	test	A boolean-valued function	and, or, negate, isEqual
BiPredicate<T, U>	T, U	boolean	test	A boolean-valued function with two arguments	and, or, negate

Table 6.2 lists the 34 available specializations for primitive types int, long, and double. It is a good idea to use these specializations to reduce autoboxing. For that reason, I used an IntConsumer instead of a Consumer<Integer> in the example of the preceding section.

Table 6.2 Functional Interfaces for Primitive Types
p, q is int, long, double; P, Q is Int, Long, Double

Functional Interface	Parameter Types	Return Type	Abstract Method Name
BooleanSupplier	none	boolean	getAsBoolean
PSupplier	none	p	getAsP
PConsumer	p	void	accept
ObjPConsumer<T>	T, p	void	accept
PFunction<T>	p	T	apply
PToQFunction	p	q	applyAsQ
ToPFunction<T>	T	p	applyAsP
ToPBiFunction<T, U>	T, U	p	applyAsP
PUnaryOperator	p	p	applyAsP
PBinaryOperator	p, p	p	applyAsP
PPredicate	p	boolean	test

TIP: It is a good idea to use an interface from Tables 6.1 or 6.2 whenever you can. For example, suppose you write a method to process files that match a certain criterion. There is a legacy interface java.io.FileFilter, but it is better to use the standard Predicate<File>. The only reason not to do so would be if you already have many useful methods producing FileFilter instances.

NOTE: Most of the standard functional interfaces have nonabstract methods for producing or combining functions. For example, Predicate.isEqual(a) is the same as a::equals, but it also works if a is null. There are default methods and, or, negate for combining predicates. For example, Predicate.isEqual(a).or(Predicate.isEqual(b)) is the same as x -> a.equals(x) || b.equals(x).

NOTE: If you design your own interface with a single abstract method, you can tag it with the `@FunctionalInterface` annotation. This has two advantages. The compiler gives an error message if you accidentally add another nonabstract method. And the javadoc page includes a statement that your interface is a functional interface.

It is not required to use the annotation. Any interface with a single abstract method is, by definition, a functional interface. But using the `@FunctionalInterface` annotation is a good idea.

6.3.8 More about Comparators

The `Comparator` interface has a number of convenient static methods for creating comparators. These methods are intended to be used with lambda expressions or method references.

The static `comparing` method takes a "key extractor" function that maps a type `T` to a comparable type (such as `String`). The function is applied to the objects to be compared, and the comparison is then made on the returned keys. For example, suppose you have an array of `Person` objects. Here is how you can sort them by name:

```
Arrays.sort(people, Comparator.comparing(Person::getName));
```

This is certainly much easier than implementing a `Comparator` by hand. Moreover, the code is clearer since it is obvious that we want to compare people by name.

You can chain comparators with the `thenComparing` method for breaking ties. For example,

```
Arrays.sort(people,
    Comparator.comparing(Person::getLastName)
    .thenComparing(Person::getFirstName));
```

If two people have the same last name, then the second comparator is used.

There are a few variations of these methods. You can specify a comparator to be used for the keys that the `comparing` and `thenComparing` methods extract. For example, here we sort people by the length of their names:

```
Arrays.sort(people, Comparator.comparing(Person::getName,
    (s, t) -> Integer.compare(s.length(), t.length())));
```

Moreover, both the `comparing` and `thenComparing` methods have variants that avoid boxing of `int`, `long`, or `double` values. An easier way of producing the preceding operation would be

```
Arrays.sort(people, Comparator.comparingInt(p -> p.getName().length()));
```

If your key function can return `null`, you will like the `nullsFirst` and `nullsLast` adapters. These static methods take an existing comparator and modify it so that it doesn't throw an exception when encountering `null` values but ranks them as smaller or larger than regular values. For example, suppose `getMiddleName` returns a `null` when a person has no middle name. Then you can use `Comparator.comparing(Person::getMiddleName(), Comparator.nullsFirst(...))`.

The `nullsFirst` method needs a comparator—in this case, one that compares two strings. The `naturalOrder` method makes a comparator for any class implementing `Comparable`. A `Comparator.<String>naturalOrder()` is what we need. Here is the complete call for sorting by potentially null middle names. I use a static import of `java.util.Comparator.*`, to make the expression more legible. Note that the type for `naturalOrder` is inferred.

```
Arrays.sort(people, comparing(Person::getMiddleName, nullsFirst(naturalOrder())));
```

The static `reverseOrder` method gives the reverse of the natural order. To reverse any comparator, use the `reversed` instance method. For example, `naturalOrder().reversed()` is the same as `reverseOrder()`.

6.4 Inner Classes

An *inner class* is a class that is defined inside another class. Why would you want to do that? There are three reasons:

- Inner class methods can access the data from the scope in which they are defined—including the data that would otherwise be private.
- Inner classes can be hidden from other classes in the same package.
- *Anonymous* inner classes are handy when you want to define callbacks without writing a lot of code.

We will break up this rather complex topic into several steps.

1. Starting on page 331, you will see a simple inner class that accesses an instance field of its outer class.
2. On page 334, we cover the special syntax rules for inner classes.
3. Starting on page 335, we peek inside inner classes to see how they are translated into regular classes. Squeamish readers may want to skip that section.
4. Starting on page 339, we discuss *local inner classes* that can access local variables of the enclosing scope.
5. Starting on page 342, we introduce *anonymous inner classes* and show how they were commonly used to implement callbacks before Java had lambda expressions.

6.   Finally, starting on page 346, you will see how *static inner classes* can be used for nested helper classes.

 C++ NOTE: C++ has *nested classes*. A nested class is contained inside the scope of the enclosing class. Here is a typical example: A linked list class defines a class to hold the links, and a class to define an iterator position.

```
class LinkedList
{
public:
   class Iterator // a nested class
   {
   public:
      void insert(int x);
      int erase();
      . . .
   };
   . . .
private:
   class Link // a nested class
   {
   public:
      Link* next;
      int data;
   };
   . . .
};
```

The nesting is a relationship between *classes,* not *objects.* A LinkedList object does *not* have subobjects of type Iterator or Link.

There are two benefits: *name control* and *access control.* The name Iterator is nested inside the LinkedList class, so it is known externally as LinkedList::Iterator and cannot conflict with another class called Iterator. In Java, this benefit is not as important because Java *packages* give the same kind of name control. Note that the Link class is in the *private* part of the LinkedList class. It is completely hidden from all other code. For that reason, it is safe to make its data fields public. They can be accessed by the methods of the LinkedList class (which has a legitimate need to access them) but they are not visible elsewhere. In Java, this kind of control was not possible until inner classes were introduced.

However, the Java inner classes have an additional feature that makes them richer and more useful than nested classes in C++. An object that comes from an inner class has an implicit reference to the outer class object that instantiated it. Through this pointer, it gains access to the total state of the outer object. You will see the details of the Java mechanism later in this chapter.

In Java, static inner classes do not have this added pointer. They are the Java analog to nested classes in C++.

6.4.1 Use of an Inner Class to Access Object State

The syntax for inner classes is rather complex. For that reason, we present a simple but somewhat artificial example to demonstrate the use of inner classes. We refactor the TimerTest example and extract a TalkingClock class. A talking clock is constructed with two parameters: the interval between announcements and a flag to turn beeps on or off.

```
public class TalkingClock
{
   private int interval;
   private boolean beep;

   public TalkingClock(int interval, boolean beep) { . . . }
   public void start() { . . . }

   public class TimePrinter implements ActionListener
      // an inner class
   {
      . . .
   }
}
```

Note that the TimePrinter class is now located inside the TalkingClock class. This does *not* mean that every TalkingClock has a TimePrinter instance field. As you will see, the TimePrinter objects are constructed by methods of the TalkingClock class.

Here is the TimePrinter class in greater detail. Note that the actionPerformed method checks the beep flag before emitting a beep.

```
public class TimePrinter implements ActionListener
{
   public void actionPerformed(ActionEvent event)
   {
      System.out.println("At the tone, the time is " + new Date());
      if (beep) Toolkit.getDefaultToolkit().beep();
   }
}
```

Something surprising is going on. The TimePrinter class has no instance field or variable named beep. Instead, beep refers to the field of the TalkingClock object that created this TimePrinter. This is quite innovative. Traditionally, a method could refer to the data fields of the object invoking the method. An inner class method gets to access both its own data fields *and* those of the outer object creating it.

For this to work, an object of an inner class always gets an implicit reference to the object that created it (see Figure 6.3).

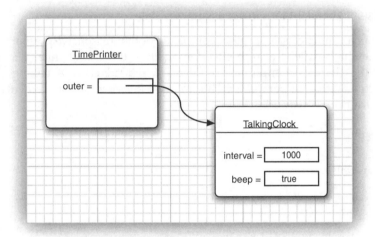

Figure 6.3 An inner class object has a reference to an outer class object

This reference is invisible in the definition of the inner class. However, to illuminate the concept, let us call the reference to the outer object *outer*. Then the actionPerformed method is equivalent to the following:

```
public void actionPerformed(ActionEvent event)
{
    System.out.println("At the tone, the time is " + new Date());
    if (outer.beep) Toolkit.getDefaultToolkit().beep();
}
```

The outer class reference is set in the constructor. The compiler modifies all inner class constructors, adding a parameter for the outer class reference. The TimePrinter class defines no constructors; therefore, the compiler synthesizes a no-argument constructor, generating code like this:

```
public TimePrinter(TalkingClock clock) // automatically generated code
{
    outer = clock;
}
```

Again, please note that *outer* is not a Java keyword. We just use it to illustrate the mechanism involved in an inner class.

When a TimePrinter object is constructed in the start method, the compiler passes the this reference to the current talking clock into the constructor:

```
ActionListener listener = new TimePrinter(this); // parameter automatically added
```

Listing 6.7 shows the complete program that tests the inner class. Have another look at the access control. Had the TimePrinter class been a regular class, it would have needed to access the beep flag through a public method of the TalkingClock class. Using an inner class is an improvement. There is no need to provide accessors that are of interest only to one other class.

 NOTE: We could have declared the TimePrinter class as private. Then only TalkingClock methods would be able to construct TimePrinter objects. Only inner classes can be private. Regular classes always have either package or public visibility.

Listing 6.7 innerClass/InnerClassTest.java

```
 1  package innerClass;
 2
 3  import java.awt.*;
 4  import java.awt.event.*;
 5  import java.util.*;
 6  import javax.swing.*;
 7  import javax.swing.Timer;
 8
 9  /**
10   * This program demonstrates the use of inner classes.
11   * @version 1.11 2015-05-12
12   * @author Cay Horstmann
13   */
14  public class InnerClassTest
15  {
16     public static void main(String[] args)
17     {
18        TalkingClock clock = new TalkingClock(1000, true);
19        clock.start();
20
21        // keep program running until user selects "Ok"
22        JOptionPane.showMessageDialog(null, "Quit program?");
23        System.exit(0);
24     }
25  }
26
27  /**
28   * A clock that prints the time in regular intervals.
29   */
```

(Continues)

Listing 6.7 *(Continued)*

```
30  class TalkingClock
31  {
32     private int interval;
33     private boolean beep;
34
35     /**
36      * Constructs a talking clock
37      * @param interval the interval between messages (in milliseconds)
38      * @param beep true if the clock should beep
39      */
40     public TalkingClock(int interval, boolean beep)
41     {
42        this.interval = interval;
43        this.beep = beep;
44     }
45
46     /**
47      * Starts the clock.
48      */
49     public void start()
50     {
51        ActionListener listener = new TimePrinter();
52        Timer t = new Timer(interval, listener);
53        t.start();
54     }
55
56     public class TimePrinter implements ActionListener
57     {
58        public void actionPerformed(ActionEvent event)
59        {
60           System.out.println("At the tone, the time is " + new Date());
61           if (beep) Toolkit.getDefaultToolkit().beep();
62        }
63     }
64  }
```

6.4.2 Special Syntax Rules for Inner Classes

In the preceding section, we explained the outer class reference of an inner class by calling it `outer`. Actually, the proper syntax for the outer reference is a bit more complex. The expression

> *OuterClass*.`this`

denotes the outer class reference. For example, you can write the `actionPerformed` method of the `TimePrinter` inner class as

```
public void actionPerformed(ActionEvent event)
{
   . . .
   if (TalkingClock.this.beep) Toolkit.getDefaultToolkit().beep();
}
```

Conversely, you can write the inner object constructor more explicitly, using the syntax

outerObject.new *InnerClass*(*construction parameters*)

For example:

```
ActionListener listener = this.new TimePrinter();
```

Here, the outer class reference of the newly constructed `TimePrinter` object is set to the `this` reference of the method that creates the inner class object. This is the most common case. As always, the `this.` qualifier is redundant. However, it is also possible to set the outer class reference to another object by explicitly naming it. For example, since `TimePrinter` is a public inner class, you can construct a `TimePrinter` for any talking clock:

```
TalkingClock jabberer = new TalkingClock(1000, true);
TalkingClock.TimePrinter listener = jabberer.new TimePrinter();
```

Note that you refer to an inner class as

OuterClass.InnerClass

when it occurs outside the scope of the outer class.

 NOTE: Any static fields declared in an inner class must be `final`. There is a simple reason. One expects a unique instance of a static field, but there is a separate instance of the inner class for each outer object. If the field was not `final`, it might not be unique.

An inner class cannot have `static` methods. The Java Language Specification gives no reason for this limitation. It would have been possible to allow static methods that only access static fields and methods from the enclosing class. Apparently, the language designers decided that the complexities outweighed the benefits.

6.4.3 Are Inner Classes Useful? Actually Necessary? Secure?

When inner classes were added to the Java language in Java 1.1, many programmers considered them a major new feature that was out of character with the Java philosophy of being simpler than C++. The inner class syntax is undeniably complex. (It gets more complex as we study anonymous inner classes later in this chapter.) It is not obvious how inner classes interact with other features of the language, such as access control and security.

By adding a feature that was elegant and interesting rather than needed, has Java started down the road to ruin which has afflicted so many other languages?

While we won't try to answer this question completely, it is worth noting that inner classes are a phenomenon of the *compiler*, not the virtual machine. Inner classes are translated into regular class files with $ (dollar signs) delimiting outer and inner class names, and the virtual machine does not have any special knowledge about them.

For example, the `TimePrinter` class inside the `TalkingClock` class is translated to a class file `TalkingClock$TimePrinter.class`. To see this at work, try the following experiment: run the `ReflectionTest` program of Chapter 5, and give it the class `TalkingClock$TimePrinter` to reflect upon. Alternatively, simply use the `javap` utility:

```
javap -private ClassName
```

NOTE: If you use UNIX, remember to escape the $ character when you supply the class name on the command line. That is, run the `ReflectionTest` or `javap` program as

```
java reflection.ReflectionTest innerClass.TalkingClock\$TimePrinter
```

or

```
javap -private innerClass.TalkingClock\$TimePrinter
```

You will get the following printout:

```
public class TalkingClock$TimePrinter
{
    public TalkingClock$TimePrinter(TalkingClock);

    public void actionPerformed(java.awt.event.ActionEvent);

    final TalkingClock this$0;
}
```

You can plainly see that the compiler has generated an additional instance field, `this$0`, for the reference to the outer class. (The name `this$0` is synthesized by the compiler—you cannot refer to it in your code.) You can also see the `TalkingClock` parameter for the constructor.

If the compiler can automatically do this transformation, couldn't you simply program the same mechanism by hand? Let's try it. We would make `TimePrinter` a regular class, outside the TalkingClock class. When constructing a TimePrinter object, we pass it the this reference of the object that is creating it.

```
class TalkingClock
{
   . . .
   public void start()
   {
      ActionListener listener = new TimePrinter(this);
      Timer t = new Timer(interval, listener);
      t.start();
   }
}

class TimePrinter implements ActionListener
{
   private TalkingClock outer;
   . . .
   public TimePrinter(TalkingClock clock)
   {
      outer = clock;
   }
}
```

Now let us look at the actionPerformed method. It needs to access outer.beep.

```
if (outer.beep) . . . // Error
```

Here we run into a problem. The inner class can access the private data of the outer class, but our external TimePrinter class cannot.

Thus, inner classes are genuinely more powerful than regular classes because they have more access privileges.

You may well wonder how inner classes manage to acquire those added access privileges, if they are translated to regular classes with funny names—the virtual machine knows nothing at all about them. To solve this mystery, let's again use the ReflectionTest program to spy on the TalkingClock class:

```
class TalkingClock
{
   private int interval;
   private boolean beep;

   public TalkingClock(int, boolean);

   static boolean access$0(TalkingClock);
   public void start();
}
```

Notice the static access$0 method that the compiler added to the outer class. It returns the beep field of the object that is passed as a parameter. (The method name might be slightly different, such as access$000, depending on your compiler.)

The inner class methods call that method. The statement

```
if (beep)
```

in the actionPerformed method of the TimePrinter class effectively makes the following call:

```
if (TalkingClock.access$0(outer))
```

Is this a security risk? You bet it is. It is an easy matter for someone else to invoke the access$0 method to read the private beep field. Of course, access$0 is not a legal name for a Java method. However, hackers who are familiar with the structure of class files can easily produce a class file with virtual machine instructions to call that method, for example, by using a hex editor. Since the secret access methods have package visibility, the attack code would need to be placed inside the same package as the class under attack.

To summarize, if an inner class accesses a private data field, then it is possible to access that data field through other classes added to the package of the outer class, but to do so requires skill and determination. A programmer cannot accidentally obtain access but must intentionally build or modify a class file for that purpose.

 NOTE: The synthesized constructors and methods can get quite convoluted. (Skip this note if you are squeamish.) Suppose we turn TimePrinter into a private inner class. There are no private classes in the virtual machine, so the compiler produces the next best thing: a package-visible class with a private constructor

```
private TalkingClock$TimePrinter(TalkingClock);
```

Of course, nobody can call that constructor, so there is a second package-visible constructor

```
TalkingClock$TimePrinter(TalkingClock, TalkingClock$1);
```

that calls the first one. The TalkingClock$1 class is synthesized solely to distinguish this constructor from others.

The compiler translates the constructor call in the start method of the TalkingClock class to

```
new TalkingClock$TimePrinter(this, null)
```

6.4.4 Local Inner Classes

If you look carefully at the code of the TalkingClock example, you will find that you need the name of the type TimePrinter only once: when you create an object of that type in the start method.

In a situation like this, you can define the class *locally in a single method*.

```java
public void start()
{
    class TimePrinter implements ActionListener
    {
        public void actionPerformed(ActionEvent event)
        {
            System.out.println("At the tone, the time is " + new Date());
            if (beep) Toolkit.getDefaultToolkit().beep();
        }
    }

    ActionListener listener = new TimePrinter();
    Timer t = new Timer(interval, listener);
    t.start();
}
```

Local classes are never declared with an access specifier (that is, public or private). Their scope is always restricted to the block in which they are declared.

Local classes have one great advantage: They are completely hidden from the outside world—not even other code in the TalkingClock class can access them. No method except start has any knowledge of the TimePrinter class.

6.4.5 Accessing Variables from Outer Methods

Local classes have another advantage over other inner classes. Not only can they access the fields of their outer classes; they can even access local variables! However, those local variables must be *effectively final*. That means, they may never change once they have been assigned.

Here is a typical example. Let's move the interval and beep parameters from the TalkingClock constructor to the start method.

```java
public void start(int interval, boolean beep)
{
    class TimePrinter implements ActionListener
    {
        public void actionPerformed(ActionEvent event)
        {
```

```
            System.out.println("At the tone, the time is " + new Date());
                if (beep) Toolkit.getDefaultToolkit().beep();
        }
    }

    ActionListener listener = new TimePrinter();
    Timer t = new Timer(interval, listener);
    t.start();
}
```

Note that the `TalkingClock` class no longer needs to store a `beep` instance field. It simply refers to the `beep` parameter variable of the `start` method.

Maybe this should not be so surprising. The line

```
if (beep) . . .
```

is, after all, ultimately inside the `start` method, so why shouldn't it have access to the value of the `beep` variable?

To see why there is a subtle issue here, let's consider the flow of control more closely.

1. The `start` method is called.
2. The object variable `listener` is initialized by a call to the constructor of the inner class `TimePrinter`.
3. The `listener` reference is passed to the `Timer` constructor, the timer is started, and the `start` method exits. At this point, the `beep` parameter variable of the `start` method no longer exists.
4. A second later, the `actionPerformed` method executes `if (beep) . . .`

For the code in the `actionPerformed` method to work, the `TimePrinter` class must have copied the `beep` field as a local variable of the `start` method, before the `beep` parameter value went away. That is indeed exactly what happens. In our example, the compiler synthesizes the name `TalkingClock$1TimePrinter` for the local inner class. If you use the `ReflectionTest` program again to spy on the `TalkingClock$1TimePrinter` class, you will get the following output:

```
class TalkingClock$1TimePrinter
{
    TalkingClock$1TimePrinter(TalkingClock, boolean);

    public void actionPerformed(java.awt.event.ActionEvent);

    final boolean val$beep;
    final TalkingClock this$0;
}
```

Note the `boolean` parameter to the constructor and the `val$beep` instance variable. When an object is created, the value `beep` is passed into the constructor and stored in the `val$beep` field. The compiler detects access of local variables, makes matching instance fields for each one, and copies the local variables into the constructor so that the instance fields can be initialized.

From the programmer's point of view, local variable access is quite pleasant. It makes your inner classes simpler by reducing the instance fields that you need to program explicitly.

As we already mentioned, the methods of a local class can refer only to local variables that are declared `final`. For that reason, the `beep` parameter was declared `final` in our example. A local variable that is declared `final` cannot be modified after it has been initialized. Thus, it is guaranteed that the local variable and the copy made inside the local class will always have the same value.

 NOTE: Before Java SE 8, it was necessary to declare any local variables that are accessed from local classes as `final`. For example, this is how the `start` method would have been declared so that the inner class can access the `beep` parameter:

```
public void start(int interval, final boolean beep)
```

The "effectively `final`" restriction is sometimes inconvenient. Suppose, for example, that you want to update a counter in the enclosing scope. Here, we want to count how often the `compareTo` method is called during sorting:

```
int counter = 0;
Date[] dates = new Date[100];
for (int i = 0; i < dates.length; i++)
   dates[i] = new Date()
      {
         public int compareTo(Date other)
         {
            counter++; // Error
            return super.compareTo(other);
         }
      };
Arrays.sort(dates);
System.out.println(counter + " comparisons.");
```

You can't declare `counter` as `final` because you clearly need to update it. You can't replace it with an `Integer` because `Integer` objects are immutable. A remedy is to use an array of length 1:

```
int[] counter = new int[1];
for (int i = 0; i < dates.length; i++)
   dates[i] = new Date()
      {
         public int compareTo(Date other)
         {
            counter[0]++;
            return super.compareTo(other);
         }
      };
```

When inner classes were first invented, a prototype version of the compiler automatically made this transformation for all local variables that were modified in the inner class. However, this was later abandoned. After all, there is a danger. When the code in the inner class is executed at the same time in multiple threads, the concurrent updates can lead to race conditions—see Chapter 14.

6.4.6 Anonymous Inner Classes

When using local inner classes, you can often go a step further. If you want to make only a single object of this class, you don't even need to give the class a name. Such a class is called an *anonymous inner class*.

```
public void start(int interval, boolean beep)
{
   ActionListener listener = new ActionListener()
   {
      public void actionPerformed(ActionEvent event)
      {
         System.out.println("At the tone, the time is " + new Date());
         if (beep) Toolkit.getDefaultToolkit().beep();
      }
   };
   Timer t = new Timer(interval, listener);
   t.start();
}
```

This syntax is very cryptic indeed. What it means is this: Create a new object of a class that implements the ActionListener interface, where the required method actionPerformed is the one defined inside the braces { }.

In general, the syntax is

```
new SuperType(construction parameters)
   {
      inner class methods and data
   }
```

Here, *SuperType* can be an interface, such as ActionListener; then, the inner class implements that interface. *SuperType* can also be a class; then, the inner class extends that class.

An anonymous inner class cannot have constructors because the name of a constructor must be the same as the name of a class, and the class has no name. Instead, the construction parameters are given to the *superclass* constructor. In particular, whenever an inner class implements an interface, it cannot have any construction parameters. Nevertheless, you must supply a set of parentheses as in

```
new InterfaceType()
    {
        methods and data
    }
```

You have to look carefully to see the difference between the construction of a new object of a class and the construction of an object of an anonymous inner class extending that class.

```
Person queen = new Person("Mary");
    // a Person object
Person count = new Person("Dracula") { . . . };
    // an object of an inner class extending Person
```

If the closing parenthesis of the construction parameter list is followed by an opening brace, then an anonymous inner class is being defined.

Listing 6.8 contains the complete source code for the talking clock program with an anonymous inner class. If you compare this program with Listing 6.7, you will see that in this case, the solution with the anonymous inner class is quite a bit shorter and, hopefully, with some practice, as easy to comprehend.

For many years, Java programmers routinely used anonymous inner classes for event listeners and other callbacks. Nowadays, you are better off using a lambda expression. For example, the start method from the beginning of this section can be written much more concisely with a lambda expression like this:

```
public void start(int interval, boolean beep)
{
    Timer t = new Timer(interval, event ->
        {
            System.out.println("At the tone, the time is " + new Date());
            if (beep) Toolkit.getDefaultToolkit().beep();
        });
    t.start();
}
```

NOTE: The following trick, called *double brace initialization*, takes advantage of the inner class syntax. Suppose you want to construct an array list and pass it to a method:

```
ArrayList<String> friends = new ArrayList<>();
friends.add("Harry");
friends.add("Tony");
invite(friends);
```

If you don't need the array list again, it would be nice to make it anonymous. But then how can you add the elements? Here is how:

```
invite(new ArrayList<String>() {{ add("Harry"); add("Tony"); }});
```

Note the double braces. The outer braces make an anonymous subclass of ArrayList. The inner braces are an object construction block (see Chapter 4).

 CAUTION: It is often convenient to make an anonymous subclass that is almost, but not quite, like its superclass. But you need to be careful with the equals method. In Chapter 5, we recommended that your equals methods use a test

```
if (getClass() != other.getClass()) return false;
```

An anonymous subclass will fail this test.

 TIP: When you produce logging or debugging messages, you often want to include the name of the current class, such as

```
System.err.println("Something awful happened in " + getClass());
```

But that fails in a static method. After all, the call to getClass calls this.getClass(), and a static method has no this. Use the following expression instead:

```
new Object(){}.getClass().getEnclosingClass() // gets class of static method
```

Here, new Object(){} makes an anonymous object of an anonymous subclass of Object, and getEnclosingClass gets its enclosing class—that is, the class containing the static method.

Listing 6.8 anonymousInnerClass/AnonymousInnerClassTest.java

```
1  package anonymousInnerClass;
2
3  import java.awt.*;
4  import java.awt.event.*;
```

```
5   import java.util.*;
6   import javax.swing.*;
7   import javax.swing.Timer;
8
9   /**
10   * This program demonstrates anonymous inner classes.
11   * @version 1.11 2015-05-12
12   * @author Cay Horstmann
13   */
14  public class AnonymousInnerClassTest
15  {
16     public static void main(String[] args)
17     {
18        TalkingClock clock = new TalkingClock();
19        clock.start(1000, true);
20
21        // keep program running until user selects "Ok"
22        JOptionPane.showMessageDialog(null, "Quit program?");
23        System.exit(0);
24     }
25  }
26
27  /**
28   * A clock that prints the time in regular intervals.
29   */
30  class TalkingClock
31  {
32     /**
33      * Starts the clock.
34      * @param interval the interval between messages (in milliseconds)
35      * @param beep true if the clock should beep
36      */
37     public void start(int interval, boolean beep)
38     {
39        ActionListener listener = new ActionListener()
40           {
41              public void actionPerformed(ActionEvent event)
42              {
43                 System.out.println("At the tone, the time is " + new Date());
44                 if (beep) Toolkit.getDefaultToolkit().beep();
45              }
46           };
47        Timer t = new Timer(interval, listener);
48        t.start();
49     }
50  }
```

6.4.7 Static Inner Classes

Occasionally, you may want to use an inner class simply to hide one class inside another—but you don't need the inner class to have a reference to the outer class object. You can suppress the generation of that reference by declaring the inner class static.

Here is a typical example of where you would want to do this. Consider the task of computing the minimum and maximum value in an array. Of course, you write one method to compute the minimum and another method to compute the maximum. When you call both methods, the array is traversed twice. It would be more efficient to traverse the array only once, computing both the minimum and the maximum simultaneously.

```
double min = Double.POSITIVE_INFINITY;
double max = Double.NEGATIVE_INFINITY;
for (double v : values)
{
   if (min > v) min = v;
   if (max < v) max = v;
}
```

However, the method must return two numbers. We can achieve that by defining a class Pair that holds two values:

```
class Pair
{
   private double first;
   private double second;

   public Pair(double f, double s)
   {
      first = f;
      second = s;
   }
   public double getFirst() { return first; }
   public double getSecond() {  return second; }
}
```

The minmax method can then return an object of type Pair.

```
class ArrayAlg
{
   public static Pair minmax(double[] values)
   {
      . . .
      return new Pair(min, max);
   }
}
```

The caller of the method uses the getFirst and getSecond methods to retrieve the answers:

```
Pair p = ArrayAlg.minmax(d);
System.out.println("min = " + p.getFirst());
System.out.println("max = " + p.getSecond());
```

Of course, the name Pair is an exceedingly common name, and in a large project, it is quite possible that some other programmer had the same bright idea—but made a Pair class that contains a pair of strings. We can solve this potential name clash by making Pair a public inner class inside ArrayAlg. Then the class will be known to the public as ArrayAlg.Pair:

```
ArrayAlg.Pair p = ArrayAlg.minmax(d);
```

However, unlike the inner classes that we used in previous examples, we do not want to have a reference to any other object inside a Pair object. That reference can be suppressed by declaring the inner class static:

```
class ArrayAlg
{
    public static class Pair
    {
        . . .
    }
    . . .
}
```

Of course, only inner classes can be declared static. A static inner class is exactly like any other inner class, except that an object of a static inner class does not have a reference to the outer class object that generated it. In our example, we must use a static inner class because the inner class object is constructed inside a static method:

```
public static Pair minmax(double[] d)
{
    . . .
    return new Pair(min, max);
}
```

Had the Pair class not been declared as static, the compiler would have complained that there was no implicit object of type ArrayAlg available to initialize the inner class object.

 NOTE: Use a static inner class whenever the inner class does not need to access an outer class object. Some programmers use the term *nested class* to describe static inner classes.

NOTE: Unlike regular inner classes, static inner classes can have static fields and methods.

 NOTE: Inner classes that are declared inside an interface are automatically `static` and `public`.

Listing 6.9 contains the complete source code of the `ArrayAlg` class and the nested `Pair` class.

Listing 6.9 staticInnerClass/StaticInnerClassTest.java

```java
package staticInnerClass;

/**
 * This program demonstrates the use of static inner classes.
 * @version 1.02 2015-05-12
 * @author Cay Horstmann
 */
public class StaticInnerClassTest
{
   public static void main(String[] args)
   {
      double[] d = new double[20];
      for (int i = 0; i < d.length; i++)
         d[i] = 100 * Math.random();
      ArrayAlg.Pair p = ArrayAlg.minmax(d);
      System.out.println("min = " + p.getFirst());
      System.out.println("max = " + p.getSecond());
   }
}

class ArrayAlg
{
   /**
    * A pair of floating-point numbers
    */
   public static class Pair
   {
      private double first;
      private double second;

```

```
31        /**
32         * Constructs a pair from two floating-point numbers
33         * @param f the first number
34         * @param s the second number
35         */
36        public Pair(double f, double s)
37        {
38           first = f;
39           second = s;
40        }
41
42        /**
43         * Returns the first number of the pair
44         * @return the first number
45         */
46        public double getFirst()
47        {
48           return first;
49        }
50
51        /**
52         * Returns the second number of the pair
53         * @return the second number
54         */
55        public double getSecond()
56        {
57           return second;
58        }
59     }
60
61     /**
62      * Computes both the minimum and the maximum of an array
63      * @param values an array of floating-point numbers
64      * @return a pair whose first element is the minimum and whose second element
65      * is the maximum
66      */
67     public static Pair minmax(double[] values)
68     {
69        double min = Double.POSITIVE_INFINITY;
70        double max = Double.NEGATIVE_INFINITY;
71        for (double v : values)
72        {
73           if (min > v) min = v;
74           if (max < v) max = v;
75        }
76        return new Pair(min, max);
77     }
78  }
```

6.5 Proxies

In the final section of this chapter, we discuss *proxies*. You can use a proxy to create, at runtime, new classes that implement a given set of interfaces. Proxies are only necessary when you don't yet know at compile time which interfaces you need to implement. This is not a common situation for application programmers, and you should feel free to skip this section if you are not interested in advanced wizardry. However, for certain systems programming applications, the flexibility that proxies offer can be very important.

6.5.1 When to Use Proxies

Suppose you want to construct an object of a class that implements one or more interfaces whose exact nature you may not know at compile time. This is a difficult problem. To construct an actual class, you can simply use the `newInstance` method or use reflection to find a constructor. But you can't instantiate an interface. You need to define a new class in a running program.

To overcome this problem, some programs generate code, place it into a file, invoke the compiler, and then load the resulting class file. Naturally, this is slow, and it also requires deployment of the compiler together with the program. The *proxy* mechanism is a better solution. The proxy class can create brand-new classes at runtime. Such a proxy class implements the interfaces that you specify. In particular, the proxy class has the following methods:

- All methods required by the specified interfaces; and
- All methods defined in the `Object` class (`toString`, `equals`, and so on).

However, you cannot define new code for these methods at runtime. Instead, you must supply an *invocation handler*. An invocation handler is an object of any class that implements the `InvocationHandler` interface. That interface has a single method:

```
Object invoke(Object proxy, Method method, Object[] args)
```

Whenever a method is called on the proxy object, the `invoke` method of the invocation handler gets called, with the `Method` object and parameters of the original call. The invocation handler must then figure out how to handle the call.

6.5.2 Creating Proxy Objects

To create a proxy object, use the `newProxyInstance` method of the `Proxy` class. The method has three parameters:

- A *class loader*. As part of the Java security model, different class loaders can be used for system classes, classes that are downloaded from the Internet, and so on. We will discuss class loaders in Chapter 9 of Volume II. For now, we specify null to use the default class loader.
- An array of Class objects, one for each interface to be implemented.
- An invocation handler.

There are two remaining questions. How do we define the handler? And what can we do with the resulting proxy object? The answers depend, of course, on the problem that we want to solve with the proxy mechanism. Proxies can be used for many purposes, such as

- Routing method calls to remote servers
- Associating user interface events with actions in a running program
- Tracing method calls for debugging purposes

In our example program, we use proxies and invocation handlers to trace method calls. We define a TraceHandler wrapper class that stores a wrapped object. Its invoke method simply prints the name and parameters of the method to be called and then calls the method with the wrapped object as the implicit parameter.

```
class TraceHandler implements InvocationHandler
{
   private Object target;

   public TraceHandler(Object t)
   {
      target = t;
   }

   public Object invoke(Object proxy, Method m, Object[] args)
      throws Throwable
   {
      // print method name and parameters
      . . .
      // invoke actual method
      return m.invoke(target, args);
   }
}
```

Here is how you construct a proxy object that causes the tracing behavior whenever one of its methods is called:

```
Object value = . . .;
// construct wrapper
InvocationHandler handler = new TraceHandler(value);
// construct proxy for one or more interfaces
```

```
Class[] interfaces = new Class[] { Comparable.class};
Object proxy = Proxy.newProxyInstance(null, interfaces, handler);
```

Now, whenever a method from one of the interfaces is called on proxy, the method name and parameters are printed out and the method is then invoked on value.

In the program shown in Listing 6.10, we use proxy objects to trace a binary search. We fill an array with proxies to the integers 1 . . . 1000. Then we invoke the binarySearch method of the Arrays class to search for a random integer in the array. Finally, we print the matching element.

```
Object[] elements = new Object[1000];
// fill elements with proxies for the integers 1 . . . 1000
for (int i = 0; i < elements.length; i++)
{
   Integer value = i + 1;
   elements[i] = Proxy.newProxyInstance(. . .); // proxy for value;
}

// construct a random integer
Integer key = new Random().nextInt(elements.length) + 1;

// search for the key
int result = Arrays.binarySearch(elements, key);

// print match if found
if (result >= 0) System.out.println(elements[result]);
```

The Integer class implements the Comparable interface. The proxy objects belong to a class that is defined at runtime. (It has a name such as $Proxy0.) That class also implements the Comparable interface. However, its compareTo method calls the invoke method of the proxy object's handler.

 NOTE: As you saw earlier in this chapter, the Integer class actually implements Comparable<Integer>. However, at runtime, all generic types are erased and the proxy is constructed with the class object for the raw Comparable class.

The binarySearch method makes calls like this:

```
if (elements[i].compareTo(key) < 0) . . .
```

Since we filled the array with proxy objects, the compareTo calls call the invoke method of the TraceHandler class. That method prints the method name and parameters and then invokes compareTo on the wrapped Integer object.

Finally, at the end of the sample program, we call

```
System.out.println(elements[result]);
```

The println method calls toString on the proxy object, and that call is also redirected to the invocation handler.

Here is the complete trace of a program run:

```
500.compareTo(288)
250.compareTo(288)
375.compareTo(288)
312.compareTo(288)
281.compareTo(288)
296.compareTo(288)
288.compareTo(288)
288.toString()
```

You can see how the binary search algorithm homes in on the key by cutting the search interval in half in every step. Note that the toString method is proxied even though it does not belong to the Comparable interface—as you will see in the next section, certain Object methods are always proxied.

Listing 6.10 proxy/ProxyTest.java

```
1  package proxy;
2
3  import java.lang.reflect.*;
4  import java.util.*;
5
6  /**
7   * This program demonstrates the use of proxies.
8   * @version 1.00 2000-04-13
9   * @author Cay Horstmann
10  */
11  public class ProxyTest
12  {
13     public static void main(String[] args)
14     {
15        Object[] elements = new Object[1000];
16
17        // fill elements with proxies for the integers 1 ... 1000
18        for (int i = 0; i < elements.length; i++)
19        {
20           Integer value = i + 1;
21           InvocationHandler handler = new TraceHandler(value);
22           Object proxy = Proxy.newProxyInstance(null, new Class[] { Comparable.class } , handler);
23           elements[i] = proxy;
24        }
25
26        // construct a random integer
27        Integer key = new Random().nextInt(elements.length) + 1;
```

(Continues)

Listing 6.10   *(Continued)*

```
28
29        // search for the key
30        int result = Arrays.binarySearch(elements, key);
31
32        // print match if found
33        if (result >= 0) System.out.println(elements[result]);
34     }
35  }
36
37  /**
38   * An invocation handler that prints out the method name and parameters, then
39   * invokes the original method
40   */
41  class TraceHandler implements InvocationHandler
42  {
43     private Object target;
44
45     /**
46      * Constructs a TraceHandler
47      * @param t the implicit parameter of the method call
48      */
49     public TraceHandler(Object t)
50     {
51        target = t;
52     }
53
54     public Object invoke(Object proxy, Method m, Object[] args) throws Throwable
55     {
56        // print implicit argument
57        System.out.print(target);
58        // print method name
59        System.out.print("." + m.getName() + "(");
60        // print explicit arguments
61        if (args != null)
62        {
63           for (int i = 0; i < args.length; i++)
64           {
65              System.out.print(args[i]);
66              if (i < args.length - 1) System.out.print(", ");
67           }
68        }
69        System.out.println(")");
70
71        // invoke actual method
72        return m.invoke(target, args);
73     }
74  }
```

6.5.3 Properties of Proxy Classes

Now that you have seen proxy classes in action, let's go over some of their properties. Remember that proxy classes are created on the fly in a running program. However, once they are created, they are regular classes, just like any other classes in the virtual machine.

All proxy classes extend the class Proxy. A proxy class has only one instance field—the invocation handler, which is defined in the Proxy superclass. Any additional data required to carry out the proxy objects' tasks must be stored in the invocation handler. For example, when we proxied Comparable objects in the program shown in Listing 6.10, the TraceHandler wrapped the actual objects.

All proxy classes override the toString, equals, and hashCode methods of the Object class. Like all proxy methods, these methods simply call invoke on the invocation handler. The other methods of the Object class (such as clone and getClass) are not redefined.

The names of proxy classes are not defined. The Proxy class in Oracle's virtual machine generates class names that begin with the string $Proxy.

There is only one proxy class for a particular class loader and ordered set of interfaces. That is, if you call the newProxyInstance method twice with the same class loader and interface array, you get two objects of the same class. You can also obtain that class with the getProxyClass method:

```
Class proxyClass = Proxy.getProxyClass(null, interfaces);
```

A proxy class is always public and final. If all interfaces that the proxy class implements are public, the proxy class does not belong to any particular package. Otherwise, all non-public interfaces must belong to the same package, and the proxy class will also belong to that package.

You can test whether a particular Class object represents a proxy class by calling the isProxyClass method of the Proxy class.

---

java.lang.reflect.InvocationHandler 1.3

- Object invoke(Object proxy, Method method, Object[] args)

  define this method to contain the action that you want carried out whenever a method was invoked on the proxy object.

`java.lang.reflect.Proxy` 1.3

- `static Class<?> getProxyClass(ClassLoader loader, Class<?>... interfaces)`

  returns the proxy class that implements the given interfaces.

- `static Object newProxyInstance(ClassLoader loader, Class<?>[] interfaces, InvocationHandler handler)`

  constructs a new instance of the proxy class that implements the given interfaces. All methods call the `invoke` method of the given handler object.

- `static boolean isProxyClass(Class<?> cl)`

  returns `true` if `cl` is a proxy class.

This ends our final chapter on the fundamentals of the Java programming language. Interfaces, lambda expressions, and inner classes are concepts that you will encounter frequently. However, as we already mentioned, cloning and proxies are advanced techniques that are of interest mainly to library designers and tool builders, not application programmers. You are now ready to learn how to deal with exceptional situations in your programs in Chapter 7.

CHAPTER

7

Exceptions, Assertions, and Logging

In this chapter

In a perfect world, users would never enter data in the wrong form, files they choose to open would always exist, and code would never have bugs. So far, we have mostly presented code as if we lived in this kind of perfect world. It is now time to turn to the mechanisms the Java programming language has for dealing with the real world of bad data and buggy code.

Encountering errors is unpleasant. If a user loses all the work he or she did during a program session because of a programming mistake or some external circumstance, that user may forever turn away from your program. At the very least, you must:

- Notify the user of an error;
- Save all work; and
- Allow users to gracefully exit the program.

For exceptional situations, such as bad input data with the potential to bomb the program, Java uses a form of error trapping called, naturally enough, *exception handling*. Exception handling in Java is similar to that in C++ or Delphi. The first part of this chapter covers Java's exceptions.

During testing, you need to run lots of checks to make sure your program does the right thing. But those checks can be time consuming and unnecessary after testing has completed. You could just remove the checks and stick them back in when additional testing is required—but that is tedious. The second part of this chapter shows you how to use the assertion facility for selectively activating checks.

When your program does the wrong thing, you can't always communicate with the user or terminate. Instead, you may want to record the problem for later analysis. The third part of this chapter discusses the standard Java logging framework.

7.1 Dealing with Errors

Suppose an error occurs while a Java program is running. The error might be caused by a file containing wrong information, a flaky network connection, or (we hate to mention it) use of an invalid array index or an attempt to use an object reference that hasn't yet been assigned to an object. Users expect that programs will act sensibly when errors happen. If an operation cannot be completed because of an error, the program ought to either

- Return to a safe state and enable the user to execute other commands; or
- Allow the user to save all work and terminate the program gracefully.

This may not be easy to do, because the code that detects (or even causes) the error condition is usually far removed from the code that can roll back the data to a safe state or the code that can save the user's work and exit cheerfully. The mission of exception handling is to transfer control from where the error occurred to an error handler that can deal with the situation. To handle exceptional situations in your program, you must take into account the errors and problems that may occur. What sorts of problems do you need to consider?

- *User input errors.* In addition to the inevitable typos, some users like to blaze their own trail instead of following directions. Suppose, for example, that a user asks to connect to a URL that is syntactically wrong. Your code should check the syntax, but suppose it does not. Then the network layer will complain.

- *Device errors.* Hardware does not always do what you want it to. The printer may be turned off. A web page may be temporarily unavailable. Devices will often fail in the middle of a task. For example, a printer may run out of paper during printing.

- *Physical limitations.* Disks can fill up; you can run out of available memory.

- *Code errors.* A method may not perform correctly. For example, it could deliver wrong answers or use other methods incorrectly. Computing an invalid array index, trying to find a nonexistent entry in a hash table, or trying to pop an empty stack are all examples of a code error.

The traditional reaction to an error in a method is to return a special error code that the calling method analyzes. For example, methods that read information back from files often return a -1 end-of-file value marker rather than a standard character. This can be an efficient method for dealing with many exceptional conditions. Another common return value to denote an error condition is the null reference.

Unfortunately, it is not always possible to return an error code. There may be no obvious way of distinguishing valid and invalid data. A method returning an integer cannot simply return -1 to denote the error; the value -1 might be a perfectly valid result.

Instead, as we mentioned back in Chapter 5, Java allows every method an alternative exit path if it is unable to complete its task in the normal way. In this situation, the method does not return a value. Instead, it *throws* an object that encapsulates the error information. Note that the method exits immediately; it does not return its normal (or any) value. Moreover, execution does not resume at the code that called the method; instead, the exception-handling mechanism begins its search for an *exception handler* that can deal with this particular error condition.

Exceptions have their own syntax and are part of a special inheritance hierarchy. We'll take up the syntax first and then give a few hints on how to use this language feature effectively.

7.1.1 The Classification of Exceptions

In the Java programming language, an exception object is always an instance of a class derived from Throwable. As you will soon see, you can create your own exception classes if the ones built into Java do not suit your needs.

Figure 7.1 is a simplified diagram of the exception hierarchy in Java.

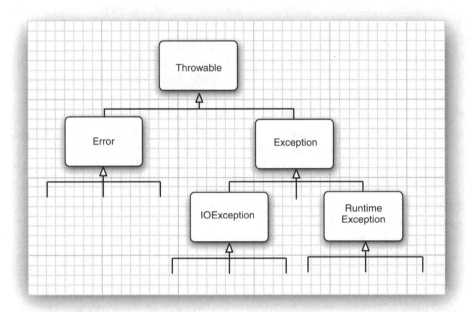

Figure 7.1 Exception hierarchy in Java

Notice that all exceptions descend from Throwable, but the hierarchy immediately splits into two branches: Error and Exception.

The Error hierarchy describes internal errors and resource exhaustion situations inside the Java runtime system. You should not throw an object of this type. There is little you can do if such an internal error occurs, beyond notifying the user and trying to terminate the program gracefully. These situations are quite rare.

When doing Java programming, focus on the Exception hierarchy. The Exception hierarchy also splits into two branches: exceptions that derive from RuntimeException and those that do not. The general rule is this: A RuntimeException happens because you made a programming error. Any other exception occurs because a bad thing, such as an I/O error, happened to your otherwise good program.

Exceptions that inherit from RuntimeException include such problems as

- A bad cast
- An out-of-bounds array access
- A null pointer access

Exceptions that do not inherit from RuntimeException include

- Trying to read past the end of a file
- Trying to open a file that doesn't exist
- Trying to find a `Class` object for a string that does not denote an existing class

The rule "If it is a `RuntimeException`, it was your fault" works pretty well. You could have avoided that `ArrayIndexOutOfBoundsException` by testing the array index against the array bounds. The `NullPointerException` would not have happened had you checked whether the variable was `null` before using it.

How about a file that doesn't exist? Can't you first check whether the file exists, and then open it? Well, the file might be deleted right after you checked for its existence. Thus, the notion of "existence" depends on the environment, not just on your code.

The Java Language Specification calls any exception that derives from the class `Error` or the class `RuntimeException` an *unchecked* exception. All other exceptions are called *checked* exceptions. This is useful terminology that we also adopt. The compiler checks that you provide exception handlers for all checked exceptions.

NOTE: The name `RuntimeException` is somewhat confusing. Of course, all of the errors we are discussing occur at runtime.

C++ NOTE: If you are familiar with the (much more limited) exception hierarchy of the standard C++ library, you may be really confused at this point. C++ has two fundamental exception classes, `runtime_error` and `logic_error`. The `logic_error` class is the equivalent of Java's `RuntimeException` and also denotes logical errors in the program. The `runtime_error` class is the base class for exceptions caused by unpredictable problems. It is equivalent to those exceptions in Java that are not of type `RuntimeException`.

7.1.2 Declaring Checked Exceptions

A Java method can throw an exception if it encounters a situation it cannot handle. The idea is simple: A method will not only tell the Java compiler what values it can return, *it is also going to tell the compiler what can go wrong*. For example, code that attempts to read from a file knows that the file might not exist or that it might be empty. The code that tries to process the information in a file therefore will need to notify the compiler that it can throw some sort of `IOException`.

The place in which you advertise that your method can throw an exception is the header of the method; the header changes to reflect the checked exceptions the method can throw. For example, here is the declaration of one of the constructors of the `FileInputStream` class from the standard library. (See Chapter 2 of Volume II for more on input and output.)

```
public FileInputStream(String name) throws FileNotFoundException
```

The declaration says that this constructor produces a `FileInputStream` object from a `String` parameter but that it *also* can go wrong in a special way—by throwing a `FileNotFoundException`. If this sad state should come to pass, the constructor call will not initialize a new `FileInputStream` object but instead will throw an object of the `FileNotFoundException` class. If it does, the runtime system will begin to search for an exception handler that knows how to deal with `FileNotFoundException` objects.

When you write your own methods, you don't have to advertise every possible throwable object that your method might actually throw. To understand when (and what) you have to advertise in the `throws` clause of the methods you write, keep in mind that an exception is thrown in any of the following four situations:

- You call a method that throws a checked exception—for example, the `FileInputStream` constructor.

- You detect an error and throw a checked exception with the `throw` statement (we cover the `throw` statement in the next section).

- You make a programming error, such as a[-1] = 0 that gives rise to an unchecked exception (in this case, an `ArrayIndexOutOfBoundsException`).

- An internal error occurs in the virtual machine or runtime library.

If either of the first two scenarios occurs, you must tell the programmers who will use your method about the possibility of an exception. Why? Any method that throws an exception is a potential death trap. If no handler catches the exception, the current thread of execution terminates.

As with Java methods that are part of the supplied classes, you declare that your method may throw an exception with an *exception specification* in the method header.

```
class MyAnimation
{
   . . .
   public Image loadImage(String s) throws IOException
   {
      . . .
   }
}
```

If a method might throw more than one checked exception type, you must list all exception classes in the header. Separate them by commas, as in the following example:

```
class MyAnimation
{
    . . .
    public Image loadImage(String s) throws FileNotFoundException, EOFException
    {
        . . .
    }
}
```

However, you do not need to advertise internal Java errors—that is, exceptions inheriting from Error. Any code could potentially throw those exceptions, and they are entirely beyond your control.

Similarly, you should not advertise unchecked exceptions inheriting from RuntimeException.

```
class MyAnimation
{
    . . .
    void drawImage(int i) throws ArrayIndexOutOfBoundsException // bad style
    {
        . . .
    }
}
```

These runtime errors are completely under your control. If you are so concerned about array index errors, you should spend your time fixing them instead of advertising the possibility that they can happen.

In summary, a method must declare all the *checked* exceptions that it might throw. Unchecked exceptions are either beyond your control (Error) or result from conditions that you should not have allowed in the first place (RuntimeException). If your method fails to faithfully declare all checked exceptions, the compiler will issue an error message.

Of course, as you have already seen in quite a few examples, instead of declaring the exception, you can also catch it. Then the exception won't be thrown out of the method, and no throws specification is necessary. You will see later in this chapter how to decide whether to catch an exception or to enable someone else to catch it.

CAUTION: If you override a method from a superclass, the checked exceptions that the subclass method declares cannot be more general than those of the superclass method. (It is OK to throw more specific exceptions, or not to throw any exceptions in the subclass method.) In particular, if the superclass method throws no checked exception at all, neither can the subclass. For example, if you override JComponent.paintComponent, your paintComponent method must not throw any checked exceptions, because the superclass method doesn't throw any.

When a method in a class declares that it throws an exception that is an instance of a particular class, it may throw an exception of that class or of any of its subclasses. For example, the FileInputStream constructor could have declared that it throws an IOException. In that case, you would not have known what kind of IOException it is; it could be a plain IOException or an object of one of the various subclasses, such as FileNotFoundException.

C++ NOTE: The throws specifier is the same as the throw specifier in C++, with one important difference. In C++, throw specifiers are enforced at runtime, not at compile time. That is, the C++ compiler pays no attention to exception specifications. But if an exception is thrown in a function that is not part of the throw list, the unexpected function is called, and, by default, the program terminates.

Also, in C++, a function may throw any exception if no throw specification is given. In Java, a method without a throws specifier may not throw any checked exceptions at all.

7.1.3 How to Throw an Exception

Now, suppose something terrible has happened in your code. You have a method, readData, that is reading in a file whose header promised

```
Content-length: 1024
```

but you got an end of file after 733 characters. You may decide this situation is so abnormal that you want to throw an exception.

You need to decide what exception type to throw. Some kind of IOException would be a good choice. Perusing the Java API documentation, you find an EOFException with the description "Signals that an EOF has been reached unexpectedly during input." Perfect. Here is how you throw it:

```
throw new EOFException();
```

or, if you prefer,

```
EOFException e = new EOFException();
throw e;
```

Here is how it all fits together:

```
String readData(Scanner in) throws EOFException
{
  . . .
  while (. . .)
  {
    if (!in.hasNext()) // EOF encountered
    {
      if (n < len)
        throw new EOFException();
    }
    . . .
  }
  return s;
}
```

The `EOFException` has a second constructor that takes a string argument. You can put this to good use by describing the exceptional condition more carefully.

```
String gripe = "Content-length: " + len + ", Received: " + n;
throw new EOFException(gripe);
```

As you can see, throwing an exception is easy if one of the existing exception classes works for you. In this case:

1. Find an appropriate exception class.
2. Make an object of that class.
3. Throw it.

Once a method throws an exception, it does not return to its caller. This means you do not have to worry about cooking up a default return value or an error code.

 C++ NOTE: Throwing an exception is the same in C++ and in Java, with one small difference. In Java, you can throw only objects of subclasses of `Throwable`. In C++, you can throw values of any type.

7.1.4 Creating Exception Classes

Your code may run into a problem which is not adequately described by any of the standard exception classes. In this case, it is easy enough to create your own exception class. Just derive it from `Exception`, or from a child class of `Exception` such as `IOException`. It is customary to give both a default constructor and a constructor that contains a detailed message. (The `toString` method of the `Throwable` superclass returns a string containing that detailed message, which is handy for debugging.)

```
class FileFormatException extends IOException
{
    public FileFormatException() {}
    public FileFormatException(String gripe)
    {
        super(gripe);
    }
}
```

Now you are ready to throw your very own exception type.

```
String readData(BufferedReader in) throws FileFormatException
{
    . . .
    while (. . .)
    {
        if (ch == -1) // EOF encountered

        {
            if (n < len)
                throw new FileFormatException();
        }
        . . .
    }
    return s;
}
```

---

java.lang.Throwable 1.0

- `Throwable()`

  constructs a new `Throwable` object with no detailed message.

- `Throwable(String message)`

  constructs a new `Throwable` object with the specified detailed message. By convention, all derived exception classes support both a default constructor and a constructor with a detailed message.

- `String getMessage()`

  gets the detailed message of the `Throwable` object.

7.2 Catching Exceptions

You now know how to throw an exception. It is pretty easy: You throw it and you forget it. Of course, some code has to catch the exception. Catching exceptions requires more planning. That's what the next sections will cover.

7.2.1 Catching an Exception

If an exception occurs that is not caught anywhere, the program will terminate and print a message to the console, giving the type of the exception and a stack trace. GUI programs (both applets and applications) catch exceptions, print stack trace messages, and then go back to the user interface processing loop. (When you are debugging a GUI program, it is a good idea to keep the console on the screen and not minimized.)

To catch an exception, set up a try/catch block. The simplest form of the try block is as follows:

```
try
{
    code
    more code
    more code
}
catch (ExceptionType e)
{
    handler for this type
}
```

If any code inside the try block throws an exception of the class specified in the catch clause, then

1. The program skips the remainder of the code in the try block.
2. The program executes the handler code inside the catch clause.

If none of the code inside the try block throws an exception, then the program skips the catch clause.

If any of the code in a method throws an exception of a type other than the one named in the catch clause, this method exits immediately. (Hopefully, one of its callers has already provided a catch clause for that type.)

To show this at work, here's some fairly typical code for reading in data:

```
public void read(String filename)
{
    try
    {
```

```
      InputStream in = new FileInputStream(filename);
      int b;
      while ((b = in.read()) != -1)
      {
         process input
      }
   }
   catch (IOException exception)
   {
      exception.printStackTrace();
   }
}
```

Notice that most of the code in the try clause is straightforward: It reads and processes bytes until we encounter the end of the file. As you can see by looking at the Java API, there is the possibility that the read method will throw an IOException. In that case, we skip out of the entire while loop, enter the catch clause, and generate a stack trace. For a toy program, that seems like a reasonable way to deal with this exception. What other choice do you have?

Often, the best choice is to do nothing at all and simply pass the exception on to the caller. If an error occurs in the read method, let the caller of the read method worry about it! If we take that approach, then we have to advertise the fact that the method may throw an IOException.

```
public void read(String filename) throws IOException
{
   InputStream in = new FileInputStream(filename);
   int b;
   while ((b = in.read()) != -1)
   {
      process input
   }
}
```

Remember, the compiler strictly enforces the throws specifiers. If you call a method that throws a checked exception, you must either handle it or pass it on.

Which of the two is better? As a general rule, you should catch those exceptions that you know how to handle and propagate those that you do not know how to handle.

When you propagate an exception, you must add a throws specifier to alert the caller that an exception may be thrown.

Look at the Java API documentation to see what methods throw which exceptions. Then decide whether you should handle them or add them to the throws list. There is nothing embarrassing about the latter choice. It is better to direct an exception to a competent handler than to squelch it.

Please keep in mind that there is, as we mentioned earlier, one exception to this rule. If you are writing a method that overrides a superclass method which throws no exceptions (such as paintComponent in JComponent), then you *must* catch each checked exception in the method's code. You are not allowed to add more throws specifiers to a subclass method than are present in the superclass method.

 C++ NOTE: Catching exceptions is almost the same in Java and in C++. Strictly speaking, the analog of

```
catch (Exception e) // Java
```

is

```
catch (Exception& e) // C++
```

There is no analog to the C++ catch (. . .). This is not needed in Java because all exceptions derive from a common superclass.

7.2.2 Catching Multiple Exceptions

You can catch multiple exception types in a try block and handle each type differently. Use a separate catch clause for each type as in the following example:

```
try
{
    code that might throw exceptions
}
catch (FileNotFoundException e)
{
    emergency action for missing files
}
catch (UnknownHostException e)
{
    emergency action for unknown hosts
}
catch (IOException e)
{
    emergency action for all other I/O problems
}
```

The exception object may contain information about the nature of the exception. To find out more about the object, try

```
e.getMessage()
```

to get the detailed error message (if there is one), or

```
e.getClass().getName()
```

to get the actual type of the exception object.

As of Java SE7, you can catch multiple exception types in the same catch clause. For example, suppose that the action for missing files and unknown hosts is the same. Then you can combine the catch clauses:

```
try
{
    code that might throw exceptions
}
catch (FileNotFoundException | UnknownHostException e)
{
    emergency action for missing files and unknown hosts
}
catch (IOException e)
{
    emergency action for all other I/O problems
}
```

This feature is only needed when catching exception types that are not subclasses of one another.

 NOTE: When you catch multiple exceptions, the exception variable is implicitly final. For example, you cannot assign a different value to e in the body of the clause

```
catch (FileNotFoundException | UnknownHostException e) { . . . }
```

 NOTE: Catching multiple exceptions doesn't just make your code look simpler but also more efficient. The generated bytecodes contain a single block for the shared catch clause.

7.2.3 Rethrowing and Chaining Exceptions

You can throw an exception in a catch clause. Typically, you do this when you want to change the exception type. If you build a subsystem that other program-mers use, it makes a lot of sense to use an exception type that indicates a failure of the subsystem. An example of such an exception type is the ServletException. The code that executes a servlet may not want to know in minute detail what went wrong, but it definitely wants to know that the servlet was at fault.

Here is how you can catch an exception and rethrow it:

```
try
{
    access the database
```

```
}
catch (SQLException e)
{
    throw new ServletException("database error: " + e.getMessage());
}
```

Here, the ServletException is constructed with the message text of the exception.

However, it is a better idea to set the original exception as the "cause" of the new exception:

```
try
{
    access the database
}
catch (SQLException e)
{
    Throwable se = new ServletException("database error");
    se.initCause(e);
    throw se;
}
```

When the exception is caught, the original exception can be retrieved:

```
Throwable e = se.getCause();
```

This wrapping technique is highly recommended. It allows you to throw high-level exceptions in subsystems without losing the details of the original failure.

 TIP: The wrapping technique is also useful if a checked exception occurs in a method that is not allowed to throw a checked exception. You can catch the checked exception and wrap it into a runtime exception.

Sometimes, you just want to log an exception and rethrow it without any change:

```
try
{
    access the database
}
catch (Exception e)
{
    logger.log(level, message, e);
    throw e;
}
```

Before Java SE 7, there was a problem with this approach. Suppose the code is inside a method

```
public void updateRecord() throws SQLException
```

The Java compiler looked at the `throw` statement inside the `catch` block, then at the type of `e`, and complained that this method might throw any `Exception`, not just a `SQLException`. This has now been improved. The compiler now tracks the fact that `e` originates from the `try` block. Provided that the only checked exceptions in that block are `SQLException` instances, and provided that `e` is not changed in the `catch` block, it is valid to declare the enclosing method as `throws SQLException`.

7.2.4 The finally Clause

When your code throws an exception, it stops processing the remaining code in your method and exits the method. This is a problem if the method has acquired some local resource, which only this method knows about, and that resource must be cleaned up. One solution is to catch and rethrow all exceptions. But this solution is tedious because you need to clean up the resource allocation in two places—in the normal code and in the exception code.

Java has a better solution: the `finally` clause. Here we show you how to properly close a file in Java. If you do any database programming, you will need to use the same technique to close connections to the database. As you will see in Chapter 4 of Volume II, it is very important to close all database connections properly, even when exceptions occur.

The code in the `finally` clause executes whether or not an exception was caught. In the following example, the program will dispose of the graphics context *under all circumstances*:

```
InputStream in = new FileInputStream(. . .);
try
{
   // 1
   code that might throw exceptions
   // 2
}
catch (IOException e)
{
   // 3
   show error message
   // 4
}
finally
{
   // 5
   in.close();
}
// 6
```

Let us look at the three possible situations in which the program will execute the finally clause.

1. The code throws no exceptions. In this case, the program first executes all the code in the try block. Then, it executes the code in the finally clause. Afterwards, execution continues with the first statement after the finally clause. In other words, execution passes through points 1, 2, 5, and 6.

2. The code throws an exception that is caught in a catch clause—in our case, an IOException. For this, the program executes all code in the try block, up to the point at which the exception was thrown. The remaining code in the try block is skipped. The program then executes the code in the matching catch clause, and then the code in the finally clause.

   If the catch clause does not throw an exception, the program executes the first line after the finally clause. In this scenario, execution passes through points 1, 3, 4, 5, and 6.

   If the catch clause throws an exception, then the exception is thrown back to the caller of this method, and execution passes through points 1, 3, and 5 only.

3. The code throws an exception that is not caught in any catch clause. Here, the program executes all code in the try block until the exception is thrown. The remaining code in the try block is skipped. Then, the code in the finally clause is executed, and the exception is thrown back to the caller of this method. Execution passes through points 1 and 5 only.

You can use the finally clause without a catch clause. For example, consider the following try statement:

```
InputStream in = . . .;
try
{
    code that might throw exceptions
}
finally
{
    in.close();
}
```

The in.close() statement in the finally clause is executed whether or not an exception is encountered in the try block. Of course, if an exception is encountered, it is rethrown and must be caught in another catch clause.

In fact, as explained in the following tip, we think it is a very good idea to use the finally clause in this way whenever you need to close a resource.

TIP: We strongly suggest that you *decouple* try/catch and try/finally blocks. This makes your code far less confusing. For example:

```
InputStream in = . . .;
try
{
   try
   {
      code that might throw exceptions
   }
   finally
   {
      in.close();
   }
}
catch (IOException e)
{
   show error message
}
```

The inner try block has a single responsibility: to make sure that the input stream is closed. The outer try block has a single responsibility: to ensure that errors are reported. Not only is this solution clearer, it is also more functional: Errors in the finally clause are reported.

CAUTION: A finally clause can yield unexpected results when it contains return statements. Suppose you exit the middle of a try block with a return statement. Before the method returns, the finally block is executed. If the finally block also contains a return statement, then it masks the original return value. Consider this contrived example:

```
public static int f(int n)
{
   try
   {
      int r = n * n;
      return r;
   }
   finally
   {
      if (n == 2) return 0;
   }
}
```

If you call f(2), then the try block computes r = 4 and executes the return statement. However, the finally clause is executed before the method actually returns and causes the method to return 0, ignoring the original return value of 4.

Sometimes the `finally` clause gives you grief—namely, if the cleanup method can also throw an exception. Suppose you want to make sure that you close a stream when an exception hits in the stream processing code.

```
InputStream in = . . .;
try
{
    code that might throw exceptions
}
finally
{
    in.close();
}
```

Now suppose that the code in the `try` block throws some exception *other than* an `IOException` which is of interest to the caller of the code. The `finally` block executes, and the `close` method is called. That method can itself throw an `IOException`! When it does, the original exception is lost and the exception of the `close` method is thrown instead.

This is a problem because the first exception is likely to be more interesting. If you want to do the right thing and rethrow the original exception, the code becomes incredibly tedious. Here is one way of setting it up:

```
InputStream in = . . .;
Exception ex = null;
try
{
    try
    {
        code that might throw exceptions
    }
    catch (Exception e)
    {
        ex = e;
        throw e;
    }
}
finally
{
    try
    {
        in.close();
    }
    catch (Exception e)
    {
        if (ex == null) throw e;
    }
}
```

Fortunately, Java SE 7 has made it much easier to deal with closing resources, as you will see in the next section.

7.2.5 The Try-with-Resources Statement

Java SE 7 provides a useful shortcut to the code pattern

```
open a resource
try
{
    work with the resource
}
finally
{
    close the resource
}
```

provided the resource belongs to a class that implements the `AutoCloseable` interface. That interface has a single method

```
void close() throws Exception
```

 NOTE: There is also a `Closeable` interface. It is a subinterface of `AutoCloseable`, also with a single `close` method. However, that method is declared to throw an `IOException`.

In its simplest variant, the try-with-resources statement has the form

```
try (Resource res = . . .)
{
    work with res
}
```

When the `try` block exits, then `res.close()` is called automatically. Here is a typical example—reading all words of a file:

```
try (Scanner in = new Scanner(new FileInputStream("/usr/share/dict/words")), "UTF-8")
{
    while (in.hasNext())
        System.out.println(in.next());
}
```

When the block exits normally, or when there was an exception, the `in.close()` method is called, exactly as if you had used a `finally` block.

You can specify multiple resources. For example,

```
try (Scanner in = new Scanner(new FileInputStream("/usr/share/dict/words"), "UTF-8");
   PrintWriter out = new PrintWriter("out.txt"))
{
   while (in.hasNext())
      out.println(in.next().toUpperCase());
}
```

No matter how the block exits, both in and out are closed. If you programmed this by hand, you would need two nested try/finally statements.

As you have seen in the preceding section, a difficulty arises when the try block throws an exception and the close method also throws an exception. The try-with-resources statement handles this situation quite elegantly. The original exception is rethrown, and any exceptions thrown by close methods are considered "suppressed." They are automatically caught and added to the original exception with the addSuppressed method. If you are interested in them, call the getSuppressed method which yields an array of the suppressed expressions from close methods.

You don't want to program this by hand. Use the try-with-resources statement whenever you need to close a resource.

 NOTE: A try-with-resources statement can itself have catch clauses and a finally clause. These are executed after closing the resources. In practice, it's probably not a good idea to pile so much onto a single try statement.

7.2.6 Analyzing Stack Trace Elements

A *stack trace* is a listing of all pending method calls at a particular point in the execution of a program. You have almost certainly seen stack trace listings—they are displayed whenever a Java program terminates with an uncaught exception.

You can access the text description of a stack trace by calling the printStackTrace method of the Throwable class.

```
Throwable t = new Throwable();
StringWriter out = new StringWriter();
t.printStackTrace(new PrintWriter(out));
String description = out.toString();
```

A more flexible approach is the getStackTrace method that yields an array of StackTraceElement objects, which you can analyze in your program. For example:

```
Throwable t = new Throwable();
StackTraceElement[] frames = t.getStackTrace();
for (StackTraceElement frame : frames)
   analyze frame
```

The `StackTraceElement` class has methods to obtain the file name and line number, as well as the class and method name, of the executing line of code. The `toString` method yields a formatted string containing all of this information.

The static `Thread.getAllStackTraces` method yields the stack traces of all threads. Here is how you use that method:

```
Map<Thread, StackTraceElement[]> map = Thread.getAllStackTraces();
for (Thread t : map.keySet())
{
    StackTraceElement[] frames = map.get(t);
    analyze frames
}
```

See Chapters 9 and 14 for more information on the `Map` interface and threads.

Listing 7.1 prints the stack trace of a recursive factorial function. For example, if you compute `factorial(3)`, the printout is

```
factorial(3):
StackTraceTest.factorial(StackTraceTest.java:18)
StackTraceTest.main(StackTraceTest.java:34)
factorial(2):
StackTraceTest.factorial(StackTraceTest.java:18)
StackTraceTest.factorial(StackTraceTest.java:24)
StackTraceTest.main(StackTraceTest.java:34)
factorial(1):
StackTraceTest.factorial(StackTraceTest.java:18)
StackTraceTest.factorial(StackTraceTest.java:24)
StackTraceTest.factorial(StackTraceTest.java:24)
StackTraceTest.main(StackTraceTest.java:34)
return 1
return 2
return 6
```

Listing 7.1 stackTrace/StackTraceTest.java

```java
1  package stackTrace;
2
3  import java.util.*;
4
5  /**
6   * A program that displays a trace feature of a recursive method call.
7   * @version 1.01 2004-05-10
8   * @author Cay Horstmann
9   */
10 public class StackTraceTest
11 {
```

```
12      /**
13       * Computes the factorial of a number
14       * @param n a non-negative integer
15       * @return n! = 1 * 2 * . . . * n
16       */
17      public static int factorial(int n)
18      {
19         System.out.println("factorial(" + n + "):");
20         Throwable t = new Throwable();
21         StackTraceElement[] frames = t.getStackTrace();
22         for (StackTraceElement f : frames)
23            System.out.println(f);
24         int r;
25         if (n <= 1) r = 1;
26         else r = n * factorial(n - 1);
27         System.out.println("return " + r);
28         return r;
29      }
30
31      public static void main(String[] args)
32      {
33         Scanner in = new Scanner(System.in);
34         System.out.print("Enter n: ");
35         int n = in.nextInt();
36         factorial(n);
37      }
38   }
```

---

java.lang.Throwable 1.0

- Throwable(Throwable cause) 1.4
- Throwable(String message, Throwable cause) 1.4

  constructs a Throwable with a given cause.

- Throwable initCause(Throwable cause) 1.4

  sets the cause for this object or throws an exception if this object already has a cause. Returns this.

- Throwable getCause() 1.4

  gets the exception object that was set as the cause for this object, or null if no cause was set.

- StackTraceElement[] getStackTrace() 1.4

  gets the trace of the call stack at the time this object was constructed.

(Continues)

---

java.lang.Throwable 1.0 *(Continued)*

- void addSuppressed(Throwable t) 7

  adds a "suppressed" exception to this exception. This happens in a try-with-resources statement where t is an exception thrown by a close method.
- Throwable[] getSuppressed() 7

  gets all "suppressed" exceptions of this exception. Typically, these are exceptions thrown by a close method in a try-with-resources statement.

---

java.lang.Exception 1.0

- Exception(Throwable cause) 1.4
- Exception(String message, Throwable cause)

  constructs an Exception with a given cause.

---

java.lang.RuntimeException 1.0

- RuntimeException(Throwable cause) 1.4
- RuntimeException(String message, Throwable cause) 1.4

  constructs a RuntimeException with a given cause.

---

java.lang.StackTraceElement 1.4

- String getFileName()

  gets the name of the source file containing the execution point of this element, or null if the information is not available.
- int getLineNumber()

  gets the line number of the source file containing the execution point of this element, or -1 if the information is not available.
- String getClassName()

  gets the fully qualified name of the class containing the execution point of this element.
- String getMethodName()

  gets the name of the method containing the execution point of this element. The name of a constructor is <init>. The name of a static initializer is <clinit>. You can't distinguish between overloaded methods with the same name.

(Continues)

---

java.lang.StackTraceElement 1.4 *(Continued)*

- `boolean isNativeMethod()`

  returns true if the execution point of this element is inside a native method.
- `String toString()`

  returns a formatted string containing the class and method name and the file name and line number, if available.

7.3 Tips for Using Exceptions

There is a certain amount of controversy about the proper use of exceptions. Some programmers believe that all checked exceptions are a nuisance, others can't seem to throw enough of them. We think that exceptions (even checked exceptions) have their place, and offer you these tips for their proper use.

1. *Exception handling is not supposed to replace a simple test.*

   As an example of this, we wrote some code that tries 10,000,000 times to pop an empty stack. It first does this by finding out whether the stack is empty.

   ```
   if (!s.empty()) s.pop();
   ```

   Next, we force it to pop the stack no matter what and then catch the `EmptyStackException` that tells us we should not have done that.

   ```
   try
   {
      s.pop();
   }
   catch (EmptyStackException e)
   {
   }
   ```

   On our test machine, the version that calls `isEmpty` ran in 646 milliseconds. The version that catches the `EmptyStackException` ran in 21,739 milliseconds.

   As you can see, it took far longer to catch an exception than to perform a simple test. The moral is: Use exceptions for exceptional circumstances only.

2. *Do not micromanage exceptions.*

   Many programmers wrap every statement in a separate `try` block.

   ```
   PrintStream out;
   Stack s;
   ```

```
for (i = 0; i < 100; i++)
{
   try
   {
      n = s.pop();
   }
   catch (EmptyStackException e)
   {
      // stack was empty
   }
   try
   {
      out.writeInt(n);
   }
   catch (IOException e)
   {
      // problem writing to file
   }
}
```

This approach blows up your code dramatically. Think about the task that you want the code to accomplish. Here, we want to pop 100 numbers off a stack and save them to a file. (Never mind why—it is just a toy example.) There is nothing we can do if a problem rears its ugly head. If the stack is empty, it will not become occupied. If the file contains an error, the error will not magically go away. It therefore makes sense to wrap the *entire task* in a try block. If any one operation fails, you can then abandon the task.

```
try
{
   for (i = 0; i < 100; i++)
   {
      n = s.pop();
      out.writeInt(n);
   }
}
catch (IOException e)
{
   // problem writing to file
}
catch (EmptyStackException e)
{
   // stack was empty
}
```

This code looks much cleaner. It fulfills one of the promises of exception handling: to *separate* normal processing from error handling.

3. *Make good use of the exception hierarchy.*

   Don't just throw a RuntimeException. Find an appropriate subclass or create your own.

   Don't just catch Throwable. It makes your code hard to read and maintain.

   Respect the difference between checked and unchecked exceptions. Checked exceptions are inherently burdensome—don't throw them for logic errors. (For example, the reflection library gets this wrong. Callers often need to catch exceptions that they know can never happen.)

   Do not hesitate to turn an exception into another exception that is more appropriate. For example, when you parse an integer in a file, catch the NumberFormatException and turn it into a subclass of IOException or MySubsystemException.

4. *Do not squelch exceptions.*

   In Java, there is a tremendous temptation to shut up exceptions. If you're writing a method that calls a method that might throw an exception once a century, the compiler whines because you have not declared the exception in the throws list of your method. You do not want to put it in the throws list because then the compiler will whine about all the methods that call your method. So you just shut it up:

   ```
   public Image loadImage(String s)
   {
      try
      {
         // code that threatens to throw checked exceptions
      }
      catch (Exception e)
      {} // so there
   }
   ```

   Now your code will compile without a hitch. It will run fine, except when an exception occurs. Then, the exception will be silently ignored. If you believe that exceptions are at all important, you should make some effort to handle them right.

5. *When you detect an error, "tough love" works better than indulgence.*

   Some programmers worry about throwing exceptions when they detect errors. Maybe it would be better to return a dummy value rather than throw an exception when a method is called with invalid parameters? For example, should Stack.pop return null, or throw an exception when a stack is empty? We think it is better to throw a EmptyStackException at the point of failure than to have a NullPointerException occur at later time.

6. *Propagating exceptions is not a sign of shame.*

Many programmers feel compelled to catch all exceptions that are thrown. If they call a method that throws an exception, such as the `FileInputStream` constructor or the `readLine` method, they instinctively catch the exception that may be generated. Often, it is actually better to *propagate* the exception instead of catching it:

```
public void readStuff(String filename) throws IOException // not a sign of shame!
{
    InputStream in = new FileInputStream(filename);
    . . .
}
```

Higher-level methods are often better equipped to inform the user of errors or to abandon unsuccessful commands.

 NOTE: Rules 5 and 6 can be summarized as "throw early, catch late."

7.4 Using Assertions

Assertions are a commonly used idiom of defensive programming. In the following sections, you will learn how to use them effectively.

7.4.1 The Assertion Concept

Suppose you are convinced that a particular property is fulfilled, and you rely on that property in your code. For example, you may be computing

```
double y = Math.sqrt(x);
```

You are certain that x is not negative. Perhaps it is the result of another computation that can't have a negative result, or it is a parameter of a method that requires its callers to supply only positive inputs. Still, you want to double-check rather than allow confusing "not a number" floating-point values creep into your computation. You could, of course, throw an exception:

```
if (x < 0) throw new IllegalArgumentException("x < 0");
```

But this code stays in the program, even after testing is complete. If you have lots of checks of this kind, the program may run quite a bit slower than it should.

The assertion mechanism allows you to put in checks during testing and to have them automatically removed in the production code.

The Java language has a keyword `assert`. There are two forms:

> `assert` *condition*;

and

> `assert` *condition* : *expression*;

Both statements evaluate the condition and throw an `AssertionError` if it is `false`. In the second statement, the expression is passed to the constructor of the `AssertionError` object and turned into a message string.

NOTE: The sole purpose of the *expression* part is to produce a message string. The `AssertionError` object does not store the actual expression value, so you can't query it later. As the JDK documentation states with paternalistic charm, doing so "would encourage programmers to attempt to recover from assertion failure, which defeats the purpose of the facility."

To assert that `x` is non-negative, you can simply use the statement

> `assert x >= 0;`

Or you can pass the actual value of `x` into the `AssertionError` object, so that it gets displayed later.

> `assert x >= 0 : x;`

C++ NOTE: The `assert` macro of the C language turns the assertion condition into a string that is printed if the assertion fails. For example, if `assert(x >= 0)` fails, it prints that `"x >= 0"` is the failing condition. In Java, the condition is not automatically part of the error report. If you want to see it, you have to pass it as a string into the `AssertionError` object: `assert x >= 0 : "x >= 0"`.

7.4.2 Assertion Enabling and Disabling

By default, assertions are disabled. Enable them by running the program with the `-enableassertions` or `-ea` option:

> `java -enableassertions MyApp`

Note that you do not have to recompile your program to enable or disable assertions. Enabling or disabling assertions is a function of the *class loader*. When assertions are disabled, the class loader strips out the assertion code so that it won't slow execution.

You can even turn on assertions in specific classes or in entire packages. For example:

```
java -ea:MyClass -ea:com.mycompany.mylib... MyApp
```

This command turns on assertions for the class `MyClass` and all classes in the `com.mycompany.mylib` package *and its subpackages*. The option `-ea...` turns on assertions in all classes of the default package.

You can also disable assertions in certain classes and packages with the `-disableassertions` or `-da` option:

```
java -ea:... -da:MyClass MyApp
```

Some classes are not loaded by a class loader but directly by the virtual machine. You can use these switches to selectively enable or disable assertions in those classes.

However, the `-ea` and `-da` switches that enable or disable all assertions do not apply to the "system classes" without class loaders. Use the `-enablesystemassertions/-esa` switch to enable assertions in system classes.

It is also possible to programmatically control the assertion status of class loaders. See the API notes at the end of this section.

7.4.3 Using Assertions for Parameter Checking

The Java language gives you three mechanisms to deal with system failures:

* Throwing an exception
* Logging
* Using assertions

When should you choose assertions? Keep these points in mind:

* Assertion failures are intended to be fatal, unrecoverable errors.
* Assertion checks are turned on only during development and testing. (This is sometimes jokingly described as "wearing a life jacket when you are close to shore, and throwing it overboard once you are in the middle of the ocean.")

Therefore, you would not use assertions for signaling recoverable conditions to another part of the program or for communicating problems to the program user. Assertions should only be used to locate internal program errors during testing.

Let's look at a common scenario—the checking of method parameters. Should you use assertions to check for illegal index values or `null` references? To answer that question, you have to look at the documentation of the method. Suppose you implement a sorting method.

```
/**
    Sorts the specified range of the specified array in ascending numerical order.
    The range to be sorted extends from fromIndex, inclusive, to toIndex, exclusive.
    @param a the array to be sorted.
    @param fromIndex the index of the first element (inclusive) to be sorted.
    @param toIndex the index of the last element (exclusive) to be sorted.
    @throws IllegalArgumentException if fromIndex > toIndex
    @throws ArrayIndexOutOfBoundsException if fromIndex < 0 or toIndex > a.length
*/
static void sort(int[] a, int fromIndex, int toIndex)
```

The documentation states that the method throws an exception if the index values are incorrect. That behavior is part of the contract that the method makes with its callers. If you implement the method, you have to respect that contract and throw the indicated exceptions. It would not be appropriate to use assertions instead.

Should you assert that a is not null? That is not appropriate either. The method documentation is silent on the behavior of the method when a is null. The callers have the right to assume that the method will return successfully in that case and not throw an assertion error.

However, suppose the method contract had been slightly different:

```
@param a the array to be sorted (must not be null).
```

Now the callers of the method have been put on notice that it is illegal to call the method with a null array. Then the method may start with the assertion

```
assert a != null;
```

Computer scientists call this kind of contract a *precondition*. The original method had no preconditions on its parameters—it promised a well-defined behavior in all cases. The revised method has a single precondition: that a is not null. If the caller fails to fulfill the precondition, then all bets are off and the method can do anything it wants. In fact, with the assertion in place, the method has a rather unpredictable behavior when it is called illegally. It sometimes throws an assertion error, and sometimes a null pointer exception, depending on how its class loader is configured.

7.4.4 Using Assertions for Documenting Assumptions

Many programmers use comments to document their underlying assumptions. Consider this example from http://docs.oracle.com/javase/6/docs/technotes/guides/language/assert.html:

```
if (i % 3 == 0)
    . . .
else if (i % 3 == 1)
    . . .
else // (i % 3 == 2)
    . . .
```

In this case, it makes a lot of sense to use an assertion instead.

```
if (i % 3 == 0)
    . . .
else if (i % 3 == 1)
    . . .
else
{
    assert i % 3 == 2;
    . . .
}
```

Of course, it would make even more sense to think through the issue thoroughly. What are the possible values of i % 3? If i is positive, the remainders must be 0, 1, or 2. If i is negative, then the remainders can be -1 or -2. Thus, the real assumption is that i is not negative. A better assertion would be

```
assert i >= 0;
```

before the if statement.

At any rate, this example shows a good use of assertions as a self-check for the programmer. As you can see, assertions are a tactical tool for testing and debugging. In contrast, logging is a strategic tool for the entire lifecycle of a program. We will examine logging in the next section.

---

java.lang.ClassLoader 1.0

- void setDefaultAssertionStatus(boolean b) 1.4

  enables or disables assertions for all classes loaded by this class loader that don't have an explicit class or package assertion status.

- void setClassAssertionStatus(String className, boolean b) 1.4

  enables or disables assertions for the given class and its inner classes.

- void setPackageAssertionStatus(String packageName, boolean b) 1.4

  enables or disables assertions for all classes in the given package and its subpackages.

- void clearAssertionStatus() 1.4

  removes all explicit class and package assertion status settings and disables assertions for all classes loaded by this class loader.

7.5 Logging

Every Java programmer is familiar with the process of inserting calls to System.out.println into troublesome code to gain insight into program behavior. Of course, once you have figured out the cause of trouble, you remove the print statements, only to put them back in when the next problem surfaces. The logging API is designed to overcome this problem. Here are the principal advantages of the API:

- It is easy to suppress all log records or just those below a certain level, and just as easy to turn them back on.
- Suppressed logs are very cheap, so that there is only a minimal penalty for leaving the logging code in your application.
- Log records can be directed to different handlers—for displaying in the console, writing to a file, and so on.
- Both loggers and handlers can filter records. Filters can discard boring log entries, using any criteria supplied by the filter implementor.
- Log records can be formatted in different ways—for example, in plain text or XML.
- Applications can use multiple loggers, with hierarchical names such as com.mycompany.myapp, similar to package names.
- By default, the logging configuration is controlled by a configuration file. Applications can replace this mechanism if desired.

7.5.1 Basic Logging

For simple logging, use the global logger and call its info method:

```
Logger.getGlobal().info("File->Open menu item selected");
```

By default, the record is printed like this:

```
May 10, 2013 10:12:15 PM LoggingImageViewer fileOpen
INFO: File->Open menu item selected
```

But if you call

```
Logger.getGlobal().setLevel(Level.OFF);
```

at an appropriate place (such as the beginning of main), all logging is suppressed.

7.5.2 Advanced Logging

Now that you have seen "logging for dummies," let's go on to industrial-strength logging. In a professional application, you wouldn't want to log all records to a single global logger. Instead, you can define your own loggers.

Call the `getLogger` method to create or retrieve a logger:

```
private static final Logger myLogger = Logger.getLogger("com.mycompany.myapp");
```

 TIP: A logger that is not referenced by any variable can be garbage collected. To prevent this, save a reference to the logger with a static variable, as in the example above.

Similar to package names, logger names are hierarchical. In fact, they are *more* hierarchical than packages. There is no semantic relationship between a package and its parent, but logger parents and children share certain properties. For example, if you set the log level on the logger `"com.mycompany"`, then the child loggers inherit that level.

There are seven logging levels:

- SEVERE
- WARNING
- INFO
- CONFIG
- FINE
- FINER
- FINEST

By default, the top three levels are actually logged. You can set a different level—for example,

```
logger.setLevel(Level.FINE);
```

Now FINE and all levels above it are logged.

You can also use `Level.ALL` to turn on logging for all levels or `Level.OFF` to turn all logging off.

There are logging methods for all levels, such as

```
logger.warning(message);
logger.fine(message);
```

and so on. Alternatively, you can use the `log` method and supply the level, such as

```
logger.log(Level.FINE, message);
```

 TIP: The default logging configuration logs all records with the level of INFO or higher. Therefore, you should use the levels CONFIG, FINE, FINER, and FINEST for debugging messages that are useful for diagnostics but meaningless to the user.

 CAUTION: If you set the logging level to a value finer than INFO, you also need to change the log handler configuration. The default log handler suppresses messages below INFO. See the next section for details.

The default log record shows the name of the class and method that contain the logging call, as inferred from the call stack. However, if the virtual machine optimizes execution, accurate call information may not be available. You can use the logp method to give the precise location of the calling class and method. The method signature is

```
void logp(Level 1, String className, String methodName, String message)
```

There are convenience methods for tracing execution flow:

```
void entering(String className, String methodName)
void entering(String className, String methodName, Object param)
void entering(String className, String methodName, Object[] params)
void exiting(String className, String methodName)
void exiting(String className, String methodName, Object result)
```

For example:

```
int read(String file, String pattern)
{
    logger.entering("com.mycompany.mylib.Reader", "read",
        new Object[] { file, pattern });
    . . .
    logger.exiting("com.mycompany.mylib.Reader", "read", count);
    return count;
}
```

These calls generate log records of level FINER that start with the strings ENTRY and RETURN.

 NOTE: At some point in the future, the logging methods with an Object[] parameter will be rewritten to support variable parameter lists ("varargs"). Then, you will be able to make calls such as logger.entering("com.mycompany.mylib.Reader", "read", file, pattern).

A common use for logging is to log unexpected exceptions. Two convenience methods include a description of the exception in the log record.

```
void throwing(String className, String methodName, Throwable t)
void log(Level l, String message, Throwable t)
```

Typical uses are

```
if (. . .)
{
   IOException exception = new IOException(". . .");
   logger.throwing("com.mycompany.mylib.Reader", "read", exception);
   throw exception;
}
```

and

```
try
{
   . . .
}
catch (IOException e)
{
   Logger.getLogger("com.mycompany.myapp").log(Level.WARNING, "Reading image", e);
}
```

The `throwing` call logs a record with level `FINER` and a message that starts with `THROW`.

7.5.3 Changing the Log Manager Configuration

You can change various properties of the logging system by editing a configuration file. The default configuration file is located at

```
jre/lib/logging.properties
```

To use another file, set the `java.util.logging.config.file` property to the file location by starting your application with

```
java -Djava.util.logging.config.file=configFile MainClass
```

 CAUTION: The log manager is initialized during VM startup, before `main` executes. If you call `System.setProperty("java.util.logging.config.file", file)` in `main`, also call `LogManager.readConfiguration()` to reinitialize the log manager.

To change the default logging level, edit the configuration file and modify the line

```
.level=INFO
```

You can specify the logging levels for your own loggers by adding lines such as

```
com.mycompany.myapp.level=FINE
```

That is, append the .level suffix to the logger name.

As you will see later in this section, the loggers don't actually send the messages to the console—that is the job of the handlers. Handlers also have levels. To see FINE messages on the console, you also need to set

```
java.util.logging.ConsoleHandler.level=FINE
```

 CAUTION: The settings in the log manager configuration are *not* system properties. Starting a program with -Dcom.mycompany.myapp.level=FINE does not have any effect on the logger.

 CAUTION: At least up to Java SE 7, the API documentation of the LogManager class claims that you can set the java.util.logging.config.class and java.util.logging.config.file properties via the Preferences API. This is false—see bug 4691587 in the Java bug database (http://bugs.sun.com/bugdatabase).

 NOTE: The logging properties file is processed by the java.util.logging.LogManager class. It is possible to specify a different log manager by setting the java.util.logging.manager system property to the name of a subclass. Alternatively, you can keep the standard log manager and still bypass the initialization from the logging properties file. Set the java.util.logging.config.class system property to the name of a class that sets log manager properties in some other way. See the API documentation for the LogManager class for more information.

It is also possible to change logging levels in a running program by using the jconsole program. See www.oracle.com/technetwork/articles/java/jconsole-1564139.html #LoggingControl for information.

7.5.4 Localization

You may want to localize logging messages so that they are readable for international users. Internationalization of applications is the topic of Chapter 5 of Volume II. Briefly, here are the points to keep in mind when localizing logging messages.

Localized applications contain locale-specific information in *resource bundles*. A resource bundle consists of a set of mappings for various locales (such as United

States or Germany). For example, a resource bundle may map the string `"readingFile"` into strings `"Reading file"` in English or `"Achtung! Datei wird eingelesen"` in German.

A program may contain multiple resource bundles—for example, one for menus and another for log messages. Each resource bundle has a name (such as `"com.mycompany.logmessages"`). To add mappings to a resource bundle, supply a file for each locale. English message mappings are in a file `com/mycompany/logmessages_en.properties`, and German message mappings are in a file `com/mycompany/logmessages_de.properties`. (The `en` and `de` are the language codes.) You place the files together with the class files of your application, so that the `ResourceBundle` class will automatically locate them. These files are plain text files, consisting of entries such as

```
readingFile=Achtung! Datei wird eingelesen
renamingFile=Datei wird umbenannt
. . .
```

When requesting a logger, you can specify a resource bundle:

```
Logger logger = Logger.getLogger(loggerName, "com.mycompany.logmessages");
```

Then you specify the resource bundle key, not the actual message string, for the log message.

```
logger.info("readingFile");
```

You often need to include arguments into localized messages. A message may contain placeholders: {0}, {1}, and so on. For example, to include the file name with a log message, use the placeholder like this:

```
Reading file {0}.
Achtung! Datei {0} wird eingelesen.
```

Then, to pass values into the placeholders, call one of the following methods:

```
logger.log(Level.INFO, "readingFile", fileName);
logger.log(Level.INFO, "renamingFile", new Object[] { oldName, newName });
```

7.5.5 Handlers

By default, loggers send records to a `ConsoleHandler` that prints them to the `System.err` stream. Specifically, the logger sends the record to the parent handler, and the ultimate ancestor (with name `""`) has a `ConsoleHandler`.

Like loggers, handlers have a logging level. For a record to be logged, its logging level must be above the threshold of *both* the logger and the handler. The log manager configuration file sets the logging level of the default console handler as

```
java.util.logging.ConsoleHandler.level=INFO
```

To log records with level FINE, change both the default logger level and the handler level in the configuration. Alternatively, you can bypass the configuration file altogether and install your own handler.

```
Logger logger = Logger.getLogger("com.mycompany.myapp");
logger.setLevel(Level.FINE);
logger.setUseParentHandlers(false);
Handler handler = new ConsoleHandler();
handler.setLevel(Level.FINE);
logger.addHandler(handler);
```

By default, a logger sends records both to its own handlers and the handlers of the parent. Our logger is a child of the primordial logger (with name "") that sends all records with level INFO and above to the console. We don't want to see those records twice, however, so we set the useParentHandlers property to false.

To send log records elsewhere, add another handler. The logging API provides two useful handlers for this purpose: a FileHandler and a SocketHandler. The SocketHandler sends records to a specified host and port. Of greater interest is the FileHandler that collects records in a file.

You can simply send records to a default file handler, like this:

```
FileHandler handler = new FileHandler();
logger.addHandler(handler);
```

The records are sent to a file java*n*.log in the user's home directory, where *n* is a number to make the file unique. If a user's system has no concept of the user's home directory (for example, in Windows 95/98/Me), then the file is stored in a default location such as C:\Windows. By default, the records are formatted in XML. A typical log record has the form

```
<record>
  <date>2002-02-04T07:45:15</date>
  <millis>1012837515710</millis>
  <sequence>1</sequence>
  <logger>com.mycompany.myapp</logger>
  <level>INFO</level>
  <class>com.mycompany.mylib.Reader</class>
  <method>read</method>
  <thread>10</thread>
  <message>Reading file corejava.gif</message>
</record>
```

You can modify the default behavior of the file handler by setting various parameters in the log manager configuration (see Table 7.1) or by using another constructor (see the API notes at the end of this section).

You probably don't want to use the default log file name. Therefore, you should use another pattern, such as %h/myapp.log. (See Table 7.2 for an explanation of the pattern variables.)

Table 7.1 File Handler Configuration Parameters

Configuration Property	Description	Default
java.util.logging.FileHandler.level	The handler level	Level.ALL
java.util.logging.FileHandler.append	Controls whether the handler should append to an existing file, or open a new file for each program run	false
java.util.logging.FileHandler.limit	The approximate maximum number of bytes to write in a file before opening another (0 = no limit)	0 (no limit) in the FileHandler class, 50000 in the default log manager configuration
java.util.logging.FileHandler.pattern	The pattern for the log file name. See Table 7.2 for pattern variables.	%h/java%u.log
java.util.logging.FileHandler.count	The number of logs in a rotation sequence	1 (no rotation)
java.util.logging.FileHandler.filter	The filter class to use	No filtering
java.util.logging.FileHandler.encoding	The character encoding to use	The platform encoding
java.util.logging.FileHandler.formatter	The record formatter	java.util.logging.XMLFormatter

Table 7.2 Log File Pattern Variables

Variable	Description
%h	The value of the user.home system property
%t	The system temporary directory
%u	A unique number to resolve conflicts
%g	The generation number for rotated logs. (A .%g suffix is used if rotation is specified and the pattern doesn't contain %g.)
%%	The % character

If multiple applications (or multiple copies of the same application) use the same log file, you should turn the append flag on. Alternatively, use %u in the file name pattern so that each application creates a unique copy of the log.

It is also a good idea to turn file rotation on. Log files are kept in a rotation sequence, such as myapp.log.0, myapp.log.1, myapp.log.2, and so on. Whenever a file exceeds the size limit, the oldest log is deleted, the other files are renamed, and a new file with generation number 0 is created.

 TIP: Many programmers use logging as an aid for the technical support staff. If a program misbehaves in the field, the user can send back the log files for inspection. In that case, you should turn the append flag on, use rotating logs, or both.

You can also define your own handlers by extending the Handler or the StreamHandler class. We define such a handler in the example program at the end of this section. That handler displays the records in a window (see Figure 7.2).

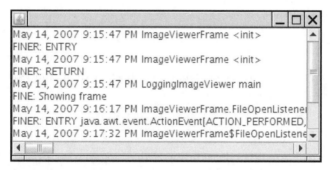

Figure 7.2 A log handler that displays records in a window

The handler extends the StreamHandler class and installs a stream whose write methods display the stream output in a text area.

```
class WindowHandler extends StreamHandler
{
    public WindowHandler()
    {
        . . .
        final JTextArea output = new JTextArea();
```

```
setOutputStream(new
   OutputStream()
   {
      public void write(int b) {} // not called
      public void write(byte[] b, int off, int len)
      {
         output.append(new String(b, off, len));
      }
   });
}
   . . .
}
```

There is just one problem with this approach—the handler buffers the records
and only writes them to the stream when the buffer is full. Therefore, we override
the publish method to flush the buffer after each record:

```
class WindowHandler extends StreamHandler
{
   . . .
   public void publish(LogRecord record)
   {
      super.publish(record);
      flush();
   }
}
```

If you want to write more exotic stream handlers, extend the Handler class and
define the publish, flush, and close methods.

7.5.6 Filters

By default, records are filtered according to their logging levels. Each logger and
handler can have an optional filter to perform additional filtering. To define a
filter, implement the Filter interface and define the method

```
boolean isLoggable(LogRecord record)
```

Analyze the log record, using any criteria that you desire, and return true for those
records that should be included in the log. For example, a particular filter may
only be interested in the messages generated by the entering and exiting methods.
The filter should then call record.getMessage() and check whether it starts with ENTRY
or RETURN.

To install a filter into a logger or handler, simply call the setFilter method. Note
that you can have at most one filter at a time.

7.5.7 Formatters

The ConsoleHandler and FileHandler classes emit the log records in text and XML formats. However, you can define your own formats as well. You need to extend the Formatter class and override the method

```
String format(LogRecord record)
```

Format the information in the record in any way you like and return the resulting string. In your format method, you may want to call the method

```
String formatMessage(LogRecord record)
```

That method formats the message part of the record, substituting parameters and applying localization.

Many file formats (such as XML) require a head and tail parts that surround the formatted records. To achieve this, override the methods

```
String getHead(Handler h)
String getTail(Handler h)
```

Finally, call the setFormatter method to install the formatter into the handler.

7.5.8 A Logging Recipe

With so many options for logging, it is easy to lose track of the fundamentals. The following recipe summarizes the most common operations.

1. For a simple application, choose a single logger. It is a good idea to give the logger the same name as your main application package, such as com.mycompany.myprog. You can always get the logger by calling

    ```
    Logger logger = Logger.getLogger("com.mycompany.myprog");
    ```

    For convenience, you may want to add static fields

    ```
    private static final Logger logger = Logger.getLogger("com.mycompany.myprog");
    ```

    to classes with a lot of logging activity.

2. The default logging configuration logs all messages of level INFO or higher to the console. Users can override the default configuration, but as you have seen, the process is a bit involved. Therefore, it is a good idea to install a more reasonable default in your application.

    The following code ensures that all messages are logged to an application-specific file. Place the code into the main method of your application.

```
if (System.getProperty("java.util.logging.config.class") == null
    && System.getProperty("java.util.logging.config.file") == null)
{
   try
   {
      Logger.getLogger("").setLevel(Level.ALL);
      final int LOG_ROTATION_COUNT = 10;
      Handler handler = new FileHandler("%h/myapp.log", 0, LOG_ROTATION_COUNT);
      Logger.getLogger("").addHandler(handler);
   }
   catch (IOException e)
   {
      logger.log(Level.SEVERE, "Can't create log file handler", e);
   }
}
```

3. Now you are ready to log to your heart's content. Keep in mind that all
    messages with level INFO, WARNING, and SEVERE show up on the console. Therefore,
    reserve these levels for messages that are meaningful to the users of your
    program. The level FINE is a good choice for logging messages that are intended
    for programmers.

    Whenever you are tempted to call System.out.println, emit a log message instead:

    ```
    logger.fine("File open dialog canceled");
    ```

    It is also a good idea to log unexpected exceptions. For example:

    ```
    try
    {
       . . .
    }
    catch (SomeException e)
    {
       logger.log(Level.FINE, "explanation", e);
    }
    ```

    Listing 7.2 puts this recipe to use with an added twist: Logging messages are
    also displayed in a log window.

Listing 7.2 logging/LoggingImageViewer.java

```
1  package logging;
2
3  import java.awt.*;
4  import java.awt.event.*;
5  import java.io.*;
6  import java.util.logging.*;
7  import javax.swing.*;
8
```

```
 9    /**
10     * A modification of the image viewer program that logs various events.
11     * @version 1.03 2015-08-20
12     * @author Cay Horstmann
13     */
14    public class LoggingImageViewer
15    {
16       public static void main(String[] args)
17       {
18          if (System.getProperty("java.util.logging.config.class") == null
19                && System.getProperty("java.util.logging.config.file") == null)
20          {
21             try
22             {
23                Logger.getLogger("com.horstmann.corejava").setLevel(Level.ALL);
24                final int LOG_ROTATION_COUNT = 10;
25                Handler handler = new FileHandler("%h/LoggingImageViewer.log", 0, LOG_ROTATION_COUNT);
26                Logger.getLogger("com.horstmann.corejava").addHandler(handler);
27             }
28             catch (IOException e)
29             {
30                Logger.getLogger("com.horstmann.corejava").log(Level.SEVERE,
31                      "Can't create log file handler", e);
32             }
33          }
34
35          EventQueue.invokeLater(() ->
36                {
37                   Handler windowHandler = new WindowHandler();
38                   windowHandler.setLevel(Level.ALL);
39                   Logger.getLogger("com.horstmann.corejava").addHandler(windowHandler);
40
41                   JFrame frame = new ImageViewerFrame();
42                   frame.setTitle("LoggingImageViewer");
43                   frame.setDefaultCloseOperation(JFrame.EXIT_ON_CLOSE);
44
45                   Logger.getLogger("com.horstmann.corejava").fine("Showing frame");
46                   frame.setVisible(true);
47                });
48       }
49    }
50
51    /**
52     * The frame that shows the image.
53     */
54    class ImageViewerFrame extends JFrame
55    {
56       private static final int DEFAULT_WIDTH = 300;
57       private static final int DEFAULT_HEIGHT = 400;
```

(Continues)

Listing 7.2 *(Continued)*

```
58
59    private JLabel label;
60    private static Logger logger = Logger.getLogger("com.horstmann.corejava");
61
62    public ImageViewerFrame()
63    {
64       logger.entering("ImageViewerFrame", "<init>");
65       setSize(DEFAULT_WIDTH, DEFAULT_HEIGHT);
66
67       // set up menu bar
68       JMenuBar menuBar = new JMenuBar();
69       setJMenuBar(menuBar);
70
71       JMenu menu = new JMenu("File");
72       menuBar.add(menu);
73
74       JMenuItem openItem = new JMenuItem("Open");
75       menu.add(openItem);
76       openItem.addActionListener(new FileOpenListener());
77
78       JMenuItem exitItem = new JMenuItem("Exit");
79       menu.add(exitItem);
80       exitItem.addActionListener(new ActionListener()
81          {
82             public void actionPerformed(ActionEvent event)
83             {
84                logger.fine("Exiting.");
85                System.exit(0);
86             }
87          });
88
89       // use a label to display the images
90       label = new JLabel();
91       add(label);
92       logger.exiting("ImageViewerFrame", "<init>");
93    }
94
95    private class FileOpenListener implements ActionListener
96    {
97       public void actionPerformed(ActionEvent event)
98       {
99          logger.entering("ImageViewerFrame.FileOpenListener", "actionPerformed", event);
100
101         // set up file chooser
102         JFileChooser chooser = new JFileChooser();
103         chooser.setCurrentDirectory(new File("."));
```

```
104
105        // accept all files ending with .gif
106        chooser.setFileFilter(new javax.swing.filechooser.FileFilter()
107           {
108              public boolean accept(File f)
109              {
110                 return f.getName().toLowerCase().endsWith(".gif") || f.isDirectory();
111              }
112
113              public String getDescription()
114              {
115                 return "GIF Images";
116              }
117           });
118
119        // show file chooser dialog
120        int r = chooser.showOpenDialog(ImageViewerFrame.this);
121
122        // if image file accepted, set it as icon of the label
123        if (r == JFileChooser.APPROVE_OPTION)
124        {
125           String name = chooser.getSelectedFile().getPath();
126           logger.log(Level.FINE, "Reading file {0}", name);
127           label.setIcon(new ImageIcon(name));
128        }
129        else logger.fine("File open dialog canceled.");
130        logger.exiting("ImageViewerFrame.FileOpenListener", "actionPerformed");
131     }
132  }
133 }
134
135 /**
136  * A handler for displaying log records in a window.
137  */
138 class WindowHandler extends StreamHandler
139 {
140    private JFrame frame;
141
142    public WindowHandler()
143    {
144       frame = new JFrame();
145       final JTextArea output = new JTextArea();
146       output.setEditable(false);
147       frame.setSize(200, 200);
148       frame.add(new JScrollPane(output));
149       frame.setFocusableWindowState(false);
150       frame.setVisible(true);
```

(Continues)

Listing 7.2 *(Continued)*

```
151        setOutputStream(new OutputStream()
152           {
153              public void write(int b)
154              {
155              } // not called
156
157              public void write(byte[] b, int off, int len)
158              {
159                 output.append(new String(b, off, len));
160              }
161           });
162     }
163
164     public void publish(LogRecord record)
165     {
166        if (!frame.isVisible()) return;
167        super.publish(record);
168        flush();
169     }
170  }
```

---

java.util.logging.Logger 1.4

- Logger getLogger(String loggerName)
- Logger getLogger(String loggerName, String bundleName)

  gets the logger with the given name. If the logger doesn't exist, it is created.

  | *Parameters:* | loggerName | The hierarchical logger name, such as com.mycompany.myapp |
  | | bundleName | The name of the resource bundle for looking up localized messages |

- void severe(String message)
- void warning(String message)
- void info(String message)
- void config(String message)
- void fine(String message)
- void finer(String message)
- void finest(String message)

  logs a record with the level indicated by the method name and the given message.

(Continues)

`java.util.logging.Logger` 1.4 *(Continued)*

- void entering(String className, String methodName)
- void entering(String className, String methodName, Object param)
- void entering(String className, String methodName, Object[] param)
- void exiting(String className, String methodName)
- void exiting(String className, String methodName, Object result)

logs a record that describes entering or exiting a method with the given parameter(s) or return value.

- void throwing(String className, String methodName, Throwable t)

logs a record that describes throwing of the given exception object.

- void log(Level level, String message)
- void log(Level level, String message, Object obj)
- void log(Level level, String message, Object[] objs)
- void log(Level level, String message, Throwable t)

logs a record with the given level and message, optionally including objects or a throwable. To include objects, the message must contain formatting placeholders ({0}, {1}, and so on).

- void logp(Level level, String className, String methodName, String message)
- void logp(Level level, String className, String methodName, String message, Object obj)
- void logp(Level level, String className, String methodName, String message, Object[] objs)
- void logp(Level level, String className, String methodName, String message, Throwable t)

logs a record with the given level, precise caller information, and message, optionally including objects or a throwable.

- void logrb(Level level, String className, String methodName, String bundleName, String message)
- void logrb(Level level, String className, String methodName, String bundleName, String message, Object obj)
- void logrb(Level level, String className, String methodName, String bundleName, String message, Object[] objs)
- void logrb(Level level, String className, String methodName, String bundleName, String message, Throwable t)

logs a record with the given level, precise caller information, resource bundle name, and message, optionally including objects or a throwable.

- Level getLevel()
- void setLevel(Level l)

gets and sets the level of this logger.

(Continues)

`java.util.logging.Logger` 1.4 *(Continued)*

- `Logger getParent()`
- `void setParent(Logger l)`

  gets and sets the parent logger of this logger.

- `Handler[] getHandlers()`

  gets all handlers of this logger.

- `void addHandler(Handler h)`
- `void removeHandler(Handler h)`

  adds or removes a handler for this logger.

- `boolean getUseParentHandlers()`
- `void setUseParentHandlers(boolean b)`

  gets and sets the "use parent handler" property. If this property is true, the logger forwards all logged records to the handlers of its parent.

- `Filter getFilter()`
- `void setFilter(Filter f)`

  gets and sets the filter of this logger.

`java.util.logging.Handler` 1.4

- `abstract void publish(LogRecord record)`

  sends the record to the intended destination.

- `abstract void flush()`

  flushes any buffered data.

- `abstract void close()`

  flushes any buffered data and releases all associated resources.

- `Filter getFilter()`
- `void setFilter(Filter f)`

  gets and sets the filter of this handler.

- `Formatter getFormatter()`
- `void setFormatter(Formatter f)`

  gets and sets the formatter of this handler.

- `Level getLevel()`
- `void setLevel(Level l)`

  gets and sets the level of this handler.

`java.util.logging.ConsoleHandler` 1.4

- `ConsoleHandler()`

  constructs a new console handler.

`java.util.logging.FileHandler` 1.4

- `FileHandler(String pattern)`
- `FileHandler(String pattern, boolean append)`
- `FileHandler(String pattern, int limit, int count)`
- `FileHandler(String pattern, int limit, int count, boolean append)`

  constructs a file handler.

Parameters:	pattern	The pattern for constructing the log file name. See Table 7.2 for pattern variables.
	limit	The approximate maximum number of bytes before a new log file is opened.
	count	The number of files in a rotation sequence.
	append	true if a newly constructed file handler object should append to an existing log file.

`java.util.logging.LogRecord` 1.4

- `Level getLevel()`

  gets the logging level of this record.

- `String getLoggerName()`

  gets the name of the logger that is logging this record.

- `ResourceBundle getResourceBundle()`
- `String getResourceBundleName()`

  gets the resource bundle, or its name, to be used for localizing the message, or `null` if none is provided.

- `String getMessage()`

  gets the "raw" message before localization or formatting.

- `Object[] getParameters()`

  gets the parameter objects, or `null` if none is provided.

(Continues)

---

java.util.logging.LogRecord 1.4 *(Continued)*

- `Throwable getThrown()`

  gets the thrown object, or `null` if none is provided.

- `String getSourceClassName()`
- `String getSourceMethodName()`

  gets the location of the code that logged this record. This information may be supplied by the logging code or automatically inferred from the runtime stack. It might be inaccurate if the logging code supplied the wrong value or if the running code was optimized so that the exact location cannot be inferred.

- `long getMillis()`

  gets the creation time, in milliseconds, since 1970.

- `long getSequenceNumber()`

  gets the unique sequence number of this record.

- `int getThreadID()`

  gets the unique ID for the thread in which this record was created. These IDs are assigned by the `LogRecord` class and have no relationship to other thread IDs.

---

java.util.logging.Filter 1.4

- `boolean isLoggable(LogRecord record)`

  returns `true` if the given log record should be logged.

---

java.util.logging.Formatter 1.4

- `abstract String format(LogRecord record)`

  returns the string that results from formatting the given log record.

- `String getHead(Handler h)`
- `String getTail(Handler h)`

  returns the strings that should appear at the head and tail of the document containing the log records. The `Formatter` superclass defines these methods to return the empty string; override them if necessary.

- `String formatMessage(LogRecord record)`

  returns the localized and formatted message part of the log record.

7.6 Debugging Tips

Suppose you wrote your program and made it bulletproof by catching and properly handling all exceptions. Then you run it, and it does not work right. Now what? (If you never have this problem, you can skip the remainder of this chapter.)

Of course, it is best if you have a convenient and powerful debugger. Debuggers are available as a part of professional development environments such as Eclipse and NetBeans. In this section, we offer you a number of tips that may be worth trying before you launch the debugger.

1. You can print or log the value of any variable with code like this:

   ```
   System.out.println("x=" + x);
   ```

   or

   ```
   Logger.getGlobal().info("x=" + x);
   ```

   If x is a number, it is converted to its string equivalent. If x is an object, Java calls its toString method. To get the state of the implicit parameter object, print the state of the this object.

   ```
   Logger.getGlobal().info("this=" + this);
   ```

   Most of the classes in the Java library are very conscientious about overriding the toString method to give you useful information about the class. This is a real boon for debugging. You should make the same effort in your classes.

2. One seemingly little-known but very useful trick is putting a separate main method in each class. Inside it, you can put a unit test stub that lets you test the class in isolation.

   ```
   public class MyClass
   {
       methods and fields
       . . .
       public static void main(String[] args)
       {
           test code
       }
   }
   ```

   Make a few objects, call all methods, and check that each of them does the right thing. You can leave all these main methods in place and launch the Java virtual machine separately on each of the files to run the tests. When you run an applet, none of these main methods are ever called. When you run an application, the Java virtual machine calls only the main method of the startup class.

3. If you liked the preceding tip, you should check out JUnit from http://junit.org. JUnit is a very popular unit testing framework that makes it easy to organize suites of test cases. Run the tests whenever you make changes to a class, and add another test case whenever you find a bug.

4. A *logging proxy* is an object of a subclass that intercepts method calls, logs them, and then calls the superclass. For example, if you have trouble with the nextDouble method of the Random class, you can create a proxy object as an instance of an anonymous subclass:

```
Random generator = new
   Random()
   {
      public double nextDouble()
      {
         double result = super.nextDouble();
         Logger.getGlobal().info("nextDouble: " + result);
         return result;
      }
   };
```

Whenever the nextDouble method is called, a log message is generated.

To find out who called the method, generate a stack trace.

5. You can get a stack trace from any exception object with the printStackTrace method in the Throwable class. The following code catches any exception, prints the exception object and the stack trace, and rethrows the exception so it can find its intended handler.

```
try
{
   . . .
}
catch (Throwable t)
{
   t.printStackTrace();
   throw t;
}
```

You don't even need to catch an exception to generate a stack trace. Simply insert the statement

```
Thread.dumpStack();
```

anywhere into your code to get a stack trace.

6. Normally, the stack trace is displayed on System.err. If you want to log or display the stack trace, here is how you can capture it into a string:

```
StringWriter out = new StringWriter();
new Throwable().printStackTrace(new PrintWriter(out));
String description = out.toString();
```

7. It is often handy to trap program errors in a file. However, errors are sent to System.err, not System.out. Therefore, you cannot simply trap them by running

```
java MyProgram > errors.txt
```

Instead, capture the error stream as

```
java MyProgram 2> errors.txt
```

To capture both System.err and System.out in the same file, use

```
java MyProgram 1> errors.txt 2>&1
```

This works in bash and the Windows shell.

8. Having the stack traces of uncaught exceptions show up in System.err is not ideal. These messages are confusing to end users if they happen to see them, and they are not available for diagnostic purposes when you need them. A better approach is to log them to a file. You can change the handler for uncaught exceptions with the static Thread.setDefaultUncaughtExceptionHandler method:

```
Thread.setDefaultUncaughtExceptionHandler(
    new Thread.UncaughtExceptionHandler()
    {
        public void uncaughtException(Thread t, Throwable e)
        {
            save information in log file
        };
    });
```

9. To watch class loading, launch the Java virtual machine with the -verbose flag. You will get a printout such as the following:

```
[Opened /usr/local/jdk5.0/jre/lib/rt.jar]
[Opened /usr/local/jdk5.0/jre/lib/jsse.jar]
[Opened /usr/local/jdk5.0/jre/lib/jce.jar]
[Opened /usr/local/jdk5.0/jre/lib/charsets.jar]
[Loaded java.lang.Object from shared objects file]
[Loaded java.io.Serializable from shared objects file]
[Loaded java.lang.Comparable from shared objects file]
[Loaded java.lang.CharSequence from shared objects file]
[Loaded java.lang.String from shared objects file]
[Loaded java.lang.reflect.GenericDeclaration from shared objects file]
[Loaded java.lang.reflect.Type from shared objects file]
```

```
[Loaded java.lang.reflect.AnnotatedElement from shared objects file]
[Loaded java.lang.Class from shared objects file]
[Loaded java.lang.Cloneable from shared objects file]
. . .
```

This can occasionally be helpful to diagnose class path problems.

10. The `-Xlint` option tells the compiler to spot common code problems. For example, if you compile with the command

```
javac -Xlint:fallthrough
```

the compiler will report missing `break` statements in `switch` statements. (The term "lint" originally described a tool for locating potential problems in C programs, but is now generically applied to any tools that flag constructs that are questionable but not illegal.)

The following options are available:

`-Xlint` or `-Xlint:all`	Carries out all checks
`-Xlint:deprecation`	Same as `-deprecation`, checks for deprecated methods
`-Xlint:fallthrough`	Checks for missing `break` statements in `switch` statements
`-Xlint:finally`	Warns about `finally` clauses that cannot complete normally
`-Xlint:none`	Carries out none of the checks
`-Xlint:path`	Checks that all directories on the class path and source path exist
`-Xlint:serial`	Warns about serializable classes without `serialVersionUID` (see Chapter 1 of Volume II)
`-Xlint:unchecked`	Warns of unsafe conversions between generic and raw types (see Chapter 8)

11. The Java VM has support for *monitoring and management* of Java applications, allowing the installation of agents in the virtual machine that track memory consumption, thread usage, class loading, and so on. This feature is particularly important for large and long-running Java programs, such as application servers. As a demonstration of these capabilities, the JDK ships with a graphical tool called `jconsole` that displays statistics about the performance of a virtual machine (see Figure 7.3). Find out the ID of the operating system process that runs the virtual machine. In UNIX/Linux, run the `ps` utility; in Windows, use the task manager. Then launch the `jconsole` program:

```
jconsole processID
```

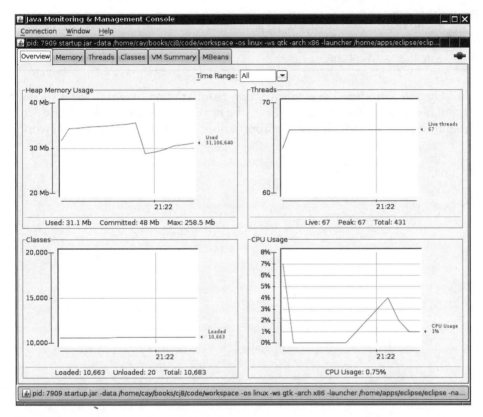

Figure 7.3 The jconsole program

The console gives you a wealth of information about your running program. See www.oracle.com/technetwork/articles/java/jconsole-1564139.html for more information.

12. You can use the jmap utility to get a heap dump that shows you every object on the heap. Use these commands:

```
jmap -dump:format=b,file=dumpFileName processID
jhat dumpFileName
```

Then, point your browser to localhost:7000. You will get a web application that lets you drill down into the contents of the heap at the time of the dump.

13. If you launch the Java virtual machine with the -Xprof flag, it runs a rudimentary *profiler* that keeps track of the methods in your code that were executed most often. The profiling information is sent to System.out. The output also tells you which methods were compiled by the just-in-time compiler.

CAUTION: The -X options of the compiler are not officially supported and may not be present in all versions of the JDK. Run `java -X` to get a listing of all nonstandard options.

This chapter introduced you to exception handling and logging. You also saw useful hints for testing and debugging. The next two chapters cover generic programming and its most important application: the Java collections framework.

Generic Programming

In this chapter

Generic classes constitute the most significant change in the Java programming language since the 1.0 release. The addition of generics to Java SE 5.0 was the result of one of the first Java Specification Requests, JSR 14, that was formulated in 1999. The expert group spent about five years on specifications and test implementations.

Generic classes are desirable because they let you write code that is safer and easier to read than code littered with `Object` variables and casts. Generics are particularly useful for collection classes, such as the ubiquitous `ArrayList`.

Generic classes are—at least on the surface—similar to templates in C++. In C++, as in Java, templates were first added to the language to support strongly typed collections. However, over the years, many other uses were discovered. After reading this chapter, you may find novel uses for Java generics in your programs.

8.1 Why Generic Programming?

Generic programming means writing code that can be reused for objects of many different types. For example, you don't want to program separate classes to collect String and File objects. And you don't have to—the single class ArrayList collects objects of any class. This is one example of generic programming.

Actually, Java had an ArrayList class before it had generic classes. Let us investigate how the mechanism for generic programming has evolved, and what that means for users and implementors.

8.1.1 The Advantage of Type Parameters

Before generic classes were added to Java, generic programming was achieved with *inheritance*. The ArrayList class simply maintained an array of Object references:

```
public class ArrayList // before generic classes
{
   private Object[] elementData;
   . . .
   public Object get(int i) { . . . }
   public void add(Object o) { . . . }
}
```

This approach has two problems. A cast is necessary whenever you retrieve a value:

```
ArrayList files = new ArrayList();
. . .
String filename = (String) files.get(0);
```

Moreover, there is no error checking. You can add values of any class:

```
files.add(new File(". . ."));
```

This call compiles and runs without error. Elsewhere, casting the result of get to a String will cause an error.

Generics offer a better solution: *type parameters*. The ArrayList class now has a type parameter that indicates the element type:

```
ArrayList<String> files = new ArrayList<String>();
```

This makes your code easier to read. You can tell right away that this particular array list contains String objects.

NOTE: As we already mentioned, in Java SE 7 and beyond, you can omit the generic type in the constructor:

```
ArrayList<String> files = new ArrayList<>();
```

The omitted type is inferred from the type of the variable.

The compiler can make good use of the type information too. No cast is required for calling get. The compiler knows that the return type is String, not Object:

```
String filename = files.get(0);
```

The compiler also knows that the add method of an ArrayList<String> has a parameter of type String. That is a lot safer than having an Object parameter. Now the compiler can check that you don't insert objects of the wrong type. For example, the statement

```
files.add(new File(". . .")); // can only add String objects to an ArrayList<String>
```

will not compile. A compiler error is much better than a class cast exception at runtime.

This is the appeal of type parameters: They make your programs easier to read and safer.

8.1.2 Who Wants to Be a Generic Programmer?

It is easy to use a generic class such as ArrayList. Most Java programmers will simply use types such as ArrayList<String> as if they had been built into the language, just like String[] arrays. (Of course, array lists are better than arrays because they can expand automatically.)

However, it is not so easy to implement a generic class. The programmers who use your code will want to plug in all sorts of classes for your type parameters. They will expect everything to work without onerous restrictions and confusing error messages. Your job as a generic programmer, therefore, is to anticipate all the potential future uses of your class.

How hard can this get? Here is a typical issue that the designers of the standard class library had to grapple with. The ArrayList class has a method addAll to add all elements of another collection. A programmer may want to add all elements from an ArrayList<Manager> to an ArrayList<Employee>. But, of course, doing it the other way round should not be legal. How do you allow one call and disallow the other? The Java language designers invented an ingenious new concept, the *wildcard type*, to solve this problem. Wildcard types are rather abstract, but they allow a library builder to make methods as flexible as possible.

Generic programming falls into three skill levels. At a basic level, you just use generic classes—typically, collections such as ArrayList—without thinking how and why they work. Most application programmers will want to stay at that level until something goes wrong. You may encounter a confusing error message when mixing different generic classes, or when interfacing with legacy code that knows nothing about type parameters; at that point, you need to learn enough about Java generics to solve problems systematically rather than through random tinkering. Finally, of course, you may want to implement your own generic classes and methods.

Application programmers probably won't write lots of generic code. The JDK developers have already done the heavy lifting and supplied type parameters for all the collection classes. As a rule of thumb, only code that traditionally involved lots of casts from very general types (such as Object or the Comparable interface) will benefit from using type parameters.

In this chapter, we will show you everything you need to know to implement your own generic code. However, we expect that most readers will use this knowledge primarily for help with troubleshooting and to satisfy their curiosity about the inner workings of the parameterized collection classes.

8.2 Defining a Simple Generic Class

A *generic class* is a class with one or more type variables. In this chapter, we will use a simple Pair class as an example. This class allows us to focus on generics without being distracted by data storage details. Here is the code for the generic Pair class:

```
public class Pair<T>
{
   private T first;
   private T second;

   public Pair() { first = null; second = null; }
   public Pair(T first, T second) { this.first = first; this.second = second; }

   public T getFirst() { return first; }
   public T getSecond() { return second; }

   public void setFirst(T newValue) { first = newValue; }
   public void setSecond(T newValue) { second = newValue; }
}
```

The Pair class introduces a type variable T, enclosed in angle brackets < >, after the class name. A generic class can have more than one type variable. For example, we could have defined the Pair class with separate types for the first and second field:

```
public class Pair<T, U> { . . . }
```

The type variables are used throughout the class definition to specify method return types and the types of fields and local variables. For example:

```
private T first; // uses the type variable
```

NOTE: It is common practice to use uppercase letters for type variables, and to keep them short. The Java library uses the variable E for the element type of a collection, K and V for key and value types of a table, and T (and the neighboring letters U and S, if necessary) for "any type at all."

You *instantiate* the generic type by substituting types for the type variables, such as

```
Pair<String>
```

You can think of the result as an ordinary class with constructors

```
Pair<String>()
Pair<String>(String, String)
```

and methods

```
String getFirst()
String getSecond()
void setFirst(String)
void setSecond(String)
```

In other words, the generic class acts as a factory for ordinary classes.

The program in Listing 8.1 puts the Pair class to work. The static minmax method traverses an array and simultaneously computes the minimum and maximum value. It uses a Pair object to return both results. Recall that the compareTo method compares two strings, returning 0 if the strings are identical, a negative integer if the first string comes before the second in dictionary order, and a positive integer otherwise.

C++ NOTE: Superficially, generic classes in Java are similar to template classes in C++. The only obvious difference is that Java has no special `template` keyword. However, as you will see throughout this chapter, there are substantial differences between these two mechanisms.

Listing 8.1   pair1/PairTest1.java

```
1  package pair1;
2
3  /**
4   * @version 1.01 2012-01-26
5   * @author Cay Horstmann
6   */
7  public class PairTest1
8  {
9     public static void main(String[] args)
10    {
11       String[] words = { "Mary", "had", "a", "little", "lamb" };
12       Pair<String> mm = ArrayAlg.minmax(words);
13       System.out.println("min = " + mm.getFirst());
14       System.out.println("max = " + mm.getSecond());
15    }
16 }
17
18 class ArrayAlg
19 {
20    /**
21     * Gets the minimum and maximum of an array of strings.
22     * @param a an array of strings
23     * @return a pair with the min and max value, or null if a is null or empty
24     */
25    public static Pair<String> minmax(String[] a)
26    {
27       if (a == null || a.length == 0) return null;
28       String min = a[0];
29       String max = a[0];
30       for (int i = 1; i < a.length; i++)
31       {
32          if (min.compareTo(a[i]) > 0) min = a[i];
33          if (max.compareTo(a[i]) < 0) max = a[i];
34       }
35       return new Pair<>(min, max);
36    }
37 }
```

8.3 Generic Methods

In the preceding section, you have seen how to define a generic class. You can also define a single method with type parameters.

```
class ArrayAlg
{
   public static <T> T getMiddle(T... a)
   {
      return a[a.length / 2];
   }
}
```

This method is defined inside an ordinary class, not inside a generic class. However, it is a generic method, as you can see from the angle brackets and the type variable. Note that the type variables are inserted after the modifiers (public static, in our case) and before the return type.

You can define generic methods both inside ordinary classes and inside generic classes.

When you call a generic method, you can place the actual types, enclosed in angle brackets, before the method name:

```
String middle = ArrayAlg.<String>getMiddle("John", "Q.", "Public");
```

In this case (and indeed in most cases), you can omit the <String> type parameter from the method call. The compiler has enough information to infer the method that you want. It matches the type of names (that is, String[]) against the generic type T[] and deduces that T must be String. That is, you can simply call

```
String middle = ArrayAlg.getMiddle("John", "Q.", "Public");
```

In almost all cases, type inference for generic methods works smoothly. Occasionally, the compiler gets it wrong, and you'll need to decipher an error report. Consider this example:

```
double middle = ArrayAlg.getMiddle(3.14, 1729, 0);
```

The error message complains, in cryptic terms that vary from one compiler version to another, that there are two ways of interpreting this code, both equally valid. In a nutshell, the compiler autoboxed the parameters into a Double and two Integer objects, and then it tried to find a common supertype of these classes. It actually found two: Number and the Comparable interface, which is itself a generic type. In this case, the remedy is to write all parameters as double values.

TIP: Peter von der Ahé recommends this trick if you want to see which type the compiler infers for a generic method call: Purposefully introduce an error and study the resulting error message. For example, consider the call `ArrayAlg.getMiddle("Hello", 0, null)`. Assign the result to a `JButton`, which can't possibly be right. You will get an error report:

```
found:
java.lang.Object&java.io.Serializable&java.lang.Comparable<? extends
java.lang.Object&java.io.Serializable&java.lang.Comparable<?>>
```

In plain English, you can assign the result to `Object`, `Serializable`, or `Comparable`.

C++ NOTE: In C++, you place the type parameters after the method name. That can lead to nasty parsing ambiguities. For example, `g(f<a,b>(c))` can mean "call g with the result of `f<a,b>(c)`", or "call g with the two `boolean` values `f<a` and `b>(c)`".

8.4 Bounds for Type Variables

Sometimes, a class or a method needs to place restrictions on type variables. Here is a typical example. We want to compute the smallest element of an array:

```
class ArrayAlg
{
   public static <T> T min(T[] a) // almost correct
   {
      if (a == null || a.length == 0) return null;
      T smallest = a[0];
      for (int i = 1; i < a.length; i++)
         if (smallest.compareTo(a[i]) > 0) smallest = a[i];
      return smallest;
   }
}
```

But there is a problem. Look inside the code of the `min` method. The variable `smallest` has type `T`, which means that it could be an object of an arbitrary class. How do we know that the class to which `T` belongs has a `compareTo` method?

The solution is to restrict `T` to a class that implements the `Comparable` interface—a standard interface with a single method, `compareTo`. You can achieve this by giving a *bound* for the type variable `T`:

```
public static <T extends Comparable> T min(T[] a) . . .
```

Actually, the `Comparable` interface is itself a generic type. For now, we will ignore that complexity and the warnings that the compiler generates. Section 8.8,

"Wildcard Types," on p. 442 discusses how to properly use type parameters with the Comparable interface.

Now, the generic min method can only be called with arrays of classes that implement the Comparable interface, such as String, LocalDate, and so on. Calling min with a Rectangle array is a compile-time error because the Rectangle class does not implement Comparable.

 C++ NOTE: In C++, you cannot restrict the types of template parameters. If a programmer instantiates a template with an inappropriate type, an (often obscure) error message is reported inside the template code.

You may wonder why we use the extends keyword rather than the implements keyword in this situation—after all, Comparable is an interface. The notation

```
<T extends BoundingType>
```

expresses that T should be a *subtype* of the bounding type. Both T and the bounding type can be either a class or an interface. The extends keyword was chosen because it is a reasonable approximation of the subtype concept, and the Java designers did not want to add a new keyword (such as sub) to the language.

A type variable or wildcard can have multiple bounds. For example:

```
T extends Comparable & Serializable
```

The bounding types are separated by ampersands (&) because commas are used to separate type variables.

As with Java inheritance, you can have as many interface supertypes as you like, but at most one of the bounds can be a class. If you have a class as a bound, it must be the first one in the bounds list.

In the next sample program (Listing 8.2), we rewrite the minmax method to be generic. The method computes the minimum and maximum of a generic array, returning a Pair<T>.

Listing 8.2 pair2/PairTest2.java

```
1  package pair2;
2
3  import java.time.*;
4
```

(Continues)

Listing 8.2 *(Continued)*

```
5   /**
6    * @version 1.02 2015-06-21
7    * @author Cay Horstmann
8    */
9   public class PairTest2
10  {
11     public static void main(String[] args)
12     {
13        LocalDate[] birthdays =
14           {
15              LocalDate.of(1906, 12, 9), // G. Hopper
16              LocalDate.of(1815, 12, 10), // A. Lovelace
17              LocalDate.of(1903, 12, 3), // J. von Neumann
18              LocalDate.of(1910, 6, 22), // K. Zuse
19           };
20        Pair<LocalDate> mm = ArrayAlg.minmax(birthdays);
21        System.out.println("min = " + mm.getFirst());
22        System.out.println("max = " + mm.getSecond());
23     }
24  }
25
26  class ArrayAlg
27  {
28     /**
29        Gets the minimum and maximum of an array of objects of type T.
30        @param a an array of objects of type T
31        @return a pair with the min and max value, or null if a is
32        null or empty
33     */
34     public static <T extends Comparable> Pair<T> minmax(T[] a)
35     {
36        if (a == null || a.length == 0) return null;
37        T min = a[0];
38        T max = a[0];
39        for (int i = 1; i < a.length; i++)
40        {
41           if (min.compareTo(a[i]) > 0) min = a[i];
42           if (max.compareTo(a[i]) < 0) max = a[i];
43        }
44        return new Pair<>(min, max);
45     }
46  }
```

8.5 Generic Code and the Virtual Machine

The virtual machine does not have objects of generic types—all objects belong to ordinary classes. An earlier version of the generics implementation was even able to compile a program that used generics into class files that executed on 1.0 virtual machines! In the following sections, you will see how the compiler "erases" type parameters, and what implication that process has for Java programmers.

8.5.1 Type Erasure

Whenever you define a generic type, a corresponding *raw* type is automatically provided. The name of the raw type is simply the name of the generic type, with the type parameters removed. The type variables are *erased* and replaced by their bounding types (or Object for variables without bounds).

For example, the raw type for Pair<T> looks like this:

```
public class Pair
{
   private Object first;
   private Object second;

   public Pair(Object first, Object second)
   {
      this.first = first;
      this.second = second;
   }

   public Object getFirst() { return first; }
   public Object getSecond() { return second; }

   public void setFirst(Object newValue) { first = newValue; }
   public void setSecond(Object newValue) { second = newValue; }
}
```

Since T is an unbounded type variable, it is simply replaced by Object.

The result is an ordinary class, just as you might have implemented it before generics were added to Java.

Your programs may contain different kinds of Pair, such as Pair<String> or Pair<LocalDate>, but erasure turns them all into raw Pair types.

C++ NOTE: In this regard, Java generics are very different from C++ templates. C++ produces different types for each template instantiation—a phenomenon called "template code bloat." Java does not suffer from this problem.

The raw type replaces type variables with the first bound, or `Object` if no bounds are given. For example, the type variable in the class `Pair<T>` has no explicit bounds, hence the raw type replaces `T` with `Object`. Suppose we declare a slightly different type:

```
public class Interval<T extends Comparable & Serializable> implements Serializable
{
   private T lower;
   private T upper;
   . . .
   public Interval(T first, T second)
   {
      if (first.compareTo(second) <= 0) { lower = first; upper = second; }
      else { lower = second; upper = first; }
   }
}
```

The raw type `Interval` looks like this:

```
public class Interval implements Serializable
{
   private Comparable lower;
   private Comparable upper;
   . . .
   public Interval(Comparable first, Comparable second) { . . . }
}
```

NOTE: You may wonder what happens if you switch the bounds: `class Interval<T extends Serializable & Comparable>`. In that case, the raw type replaces `T` with `Serializable`, and the compiler inserts casts to `Comparable` when necessary. For efficiency, you should therefore put tagging interfaces (that is, interfaces without methods) at the end of the bounds list.

8.5.2 Translating Generic Expressions

When you program a call to a generic method, the compiler inserts casts when the return type has been erased. For example, consider the sequence of statements

```
Pair<Employee> buddies = . . .;
Employee buddy = buddies.getFirst();
```

The erasure of `getFirst` has return type `Object`. The compiler automatically inserts the cast to `Employee`. That is, the compiler translates the method call into two virtual machine instructions:

- A call to the raw method `Pair.getFirst`
- A cast of the returned `Object` to the type `Employee`

Casts are also inserted when you access a generic field. Suppose the `first` and `second` fields of the `Pair` class were public. (Not a good programming style, perhaps, but it is legal Java.) Then the expression

```
Employee buddy = buddies.first;
```

also has a cast inserted in the resulting byte codes.

8.5.3 Translating Generic Methods

Type erasure also happens for generic methods. Programmers usually think of a generic method such as

```
public static <T extends Comparable> T min(T[] a)
```

as a whole family of methods, but after erasure, only a single method is left:

```
public static Comparable min(Comparable[] a)
```

Note that the type parameter `T` has been erased, leaving only its bounding type `Comparable`.

Erasure of methods brings up a couple of complexities. Consider this example:

```
class DateInterval extends Pair<LocalDate>
{
   public void setSecond(LocalDate second)
   {
      if (second.compareTo(getFirst()) >= 0)
         super.setSecond(second);
   }
   . . .
}
```

A date interval is a pair of `LocalDate` objects, and we'll want to override the methods to ensure that the second value is never smaller than the first. This class is erased to

```
class DateInterval extends Pair // after erasure
{
   public void setSecond(LocalDate second) { . . . }
   . . .
}
```

Perhaps surprisingly, there is another setSecond method, inherited from Pair, namely

```
public void setSecond(Object second)
```

This is clearly a different method because it has a parameter of a different type—Object instead of LocalDate. But it *shouldn't* be different. Consider this sequence of statements:

```
DateInterval interval = new DateInterval(. . .);
Pair<LocalDate> pair = interval; // OK--assignment to superclass
pair.setSecond(aDate);
```

Our expectation is that the call to setSecond is polymorphic and that the appropriate method is called. Since pair refers to a DateInterval object, that should be DateInterval.setSecond. The problem is that the type erasure interferes with polymorphism. To fix this problem, the compiler generates a *bridge method* in the DateInterval class:

```
public void setSecond(Object second) { setSecond((Date) second); }
```

To see why this works, let us carefully follow the execution of the statement

```
pair.setSecond(aDate)
```

The variable pair has declared type Pair<LocalDate>, and that type only has a single method called setSecond, namely setSecond(Object). The virtual machine calls that method on the object to which pair refers. That object is of type DateInterval. Therefore, the method DateInterval.setSecond(Object) is called. That method is the synthesized bridge method. It calls DateInterval.setSecond(Date), which is what we want.

Bridge methods can get even stranger. Suppose the DateInterval method also overrides the getSecond method:

```
class DateInterval extends Pair<LocalDate>
{
    public LocalDate getSecond() { return (Date) super.getSecond().clone(); }
    . . .
}
```

In the DateInterval class, there are two getSecond methods:

```
LocalDate getSecond() // defined in DateInterval
Object getSecond() // overrides the method defined in Pair to call the first method
```

You could not write Java code like that; it would be illegal to have two methods with the same parameter types—here, with no parameters. However, in the virtual machine, the parameter types *and the return type* specify a method. Therefore, the compiler can produce bytecodes for two methods that differ only in their return type, and the virtual machine will handle this situation correctly.

NOTE: Bridge methods are not limited to generic types. We already noted in Chapter 5 that it is legal for a method to specify a more restrictive return type when overriding another method. For example:

```
public class Employee implements Cloneable
{
    public Employee clone() throws CloneNotSupportedException { . . . }
}
```

The `Object.clone` and `Employee.clone` methods are said to have *covariant return types*.

Actually, the `Employee` class has *two* clone methods:

```
Employee clone() // defined above
Object clone() // synthesized bridge method, overrides Object.clone
```

The synthesized bridge method calls the newly defined method.

In summary, you need to remember these facts about translation of Java generics:

- There are no generics in the virtual machine, only ordinary classes and methods.
- All type parameters are replaced by their bounds.
- Bridge methods are synthesized to preserve polymorphism.
- Casts are inserted as necessary to preserve type safety.

8.5.4 Calling Legacy Code

When Java generics were designed, a major goal was to allow interoperability between generics and legacy code. Let us look at a concrete example. To set the labels of a `JSlider`, you use the method

```
void setLabelTable(Dictionary table)
```

Here, `Dictionary` is the raw type, since the `JSlider` class was implemented before generics existed in Java. However, when you populate the dictionary, you should use the generic type.

```
Dictionary<Integer, Component> labelTable = new Hashtable<>();
labelTable.put(0, new JLabel(new ImageIcon("nine.gif")));
labelTable.put(20, new JLabel(new ImageIcon("ten.gif")));
. . .
```

When you pass the `Dictionary<Integer, Component>` object to `setLabelTable`, the compiler issues a warning.

```
slider.setLabelTable(labelTable); // Warning
```

After all, the compiler has no assurance about what the setLabelTable might do to the Dictionary object. That method might replace all the keys with strings. That breaks the guarantee that the keys have type Integer, and future operations may cause bad cast exceptions.

There isn't much you can do with this warning, except ponder it and ask what the JSlider is likely going to do with this Dictionary object. In our case, it is pretty clear that the JSlider only reads the information, so we can ignore the warning.

Now consider the opposite case, in which you get an object of a raw type from a legacy class. You can assign it to a variable whose type uses generics, but of course you will get a warning. For example:

```
Dictionary<Integer, Components> labelTable = slider.getLabelTable(); // Warning
```

That's OK—review the warning and make sure that the label table really contains Integer and Component objects. Of course, there never is an absolute guarantee. A malicious coder might have installed a different Dictionary in the slider. But again, the situation is no worse than it was before generics. In the worst case, your program will throw an exception.

After you are done pondering the warning, you can use an *annotation* to make it disappear. You can annotate a local variable:

```
@SuppressWarnings("unchecked")
Dictionary<Integer, Components> labelTable = slider.getLabelTable(); // No warning
```

Or you can annotate an entire method, like this:

```
@SuppressWarnings("unchecked")
public void configureSlider() { . . . }
```

This annotation turns off checking for all code inside the method.

8.6 Restrictions and Limitations

In the following sections, we discuss a number of restrictions that you need to consider when working with Java generics. Most of these restrictions are a consequence of type erasure.

8.6.1 Type Parameters Cannot Be Instantiated with Primitive Types

You cannot substitute a primitive type for a type parameter. Thus, there is no Pair<double>, only Pair<Double>. The reason is, of course, type erasure. After erasure, the Pair class has fields of type Object, and you can't use them to store double values.

This is an annoyance, to be sure, but it is consistent with the separate status of primitive types in the Java language. It is not a fatal flaw—there are only eight primitive types, and you can always handle them with separate classes and methods when wrapper types are not an acceptable substitute.

8.6.2 Runtime Type Inquiry Only Works with Raw Types

Objects in the virtual machine always have a specific nongeneric type. Therefore, all type inquiries yield only the raw type. For example,

```
if (a instanceof Pair<String>) // Error
```

could only test whether a is a Pair of any type. The same is true for the test

```
if (a instanceof Pair<T>) // Error
```

or the cast

```
Pair<String> p = (Pair<String>) a; // Warning--can only test that a is a Pair
```

To remind you of the risk, you will get a compiler error (with instanceof) or warning (with casts) when you try to inquire whether an object belongs to a generic type.

In the same spirit, the getClass method always returns the raw type. For example:

```
Pair<String> stringPair = . . .;
Pair<Employee> employeePair = . . .;
if (stringPair.getClass() == employeePair.getClass()) // they are equal
```

The comparison yields true because both calls to getClass return Pair.class.

8.6.3 You Cannot Create Arrays of Parameterized Types

You cannot instantiate arrays of parameterized types, such as

```
Pair<String>[] table = new Pair<String>[10]; // Error
```

What's wrong with that? After erasure, the type of table is Pair[]. You can convert it to Object[]:

```
Object[] objarray = table;
```

An array remembers its component type and throws an ArrayStoreException if you try to store an element of the wrong type:

```
objarray[0] = "Hello"; // Error--component type is Pair
```

But erasure renders this mechanism ineffective for generic types. The assignment

```
objarray[0] = new Pair<Employee>();
```

would pass the array store check but still result in a type error. For this reason, arrays of parameterized types are outlawed.

Note that only the creation of these arrays is outlawed. You can declare a variable of type `Pair<String>[]`. But you can't initialize it with a `new Pair<String>[10]`.

> **NOTE:** You can declare arrays of wildcard types and then cast them:
>
>   Pair<String>[] table = (Pair<String>[]) new Pair<?>[10];
>
> The result is not safe. If you store a `Pair<Employee>` in `table[0]` and then call a `String` method on `table[0].getFirst()`, you get a `ClassCastException`.

> **TIP:** If you need to collect parameterized type objects, simply use an `ArrayList`: `ArrayList<Pair<String>>` is safe and effective.

8.6.4 Varargs Warnings

In the preceding section, you saw that Java doesn't support arrays of generic types. In this section, we discuss a related issue: passing instances of a generic type to a method with a variable number of arguments.

Consider this simple method with variable arguments:

```
public static <T> void addAll(Collection<T> coll, T... ts)
{
    for (t : ts) coll.add(t);
}
```

Recall that the parameter `ts` is actually an array that holds all supplied arguments.

Now consider this call:

```
Collection<Pair<String>> table = . . .;
Pair<String> pair1 = . . .;
Pair<String> pair2 = . . .;
addAll(table, pair1, pair2);
```

In order to call this method, the Java virtual machine must make an array of `Pair<String>`, which is against the rules. However, the rules have been relaxed for this situation, and you only get a warning, not an error.

You can suppress the warning in one of two ways. You can add the annotation `@SuppressWarnings("unchecked")` to the method containing the call to `addAll`. Or, as of Java SE 7, you can annotate the `addAll` method itself with `@SafeVarargs`:

```
@SafeVarargs
public static <T> void addAll(Collection<T> coll, T... ts)
```

This method can now be called with generic types. You can use this annotation for any methods that merely read the elements of the parameter array, which is bound to be the most common use case.

 NOTE: You can use the @SafeVarargs annotation to defeat the restriction against generic array creation, using this method:

```
@SafeVarargs static <E> E[] array(E... array) { return array; }
```

Now you can call

```
Pair<String>[] table = array(pair1, pair2);
```

This seems convenient, but there is a hidden danger. The code

```
Object[] objarray = table;
objarray[0] = new Pair<Employee>();
```

will run without an ArrayStoreException (because the array store only checks the erased type), and you'll get an exception elsewhere when you work with table[0].

8.6.5 You Cannot Instantiate Type Variables

You cannot use type variables in an expression such as new T(...). For example, the following Pair<T> constructor is illegal:

```
public Pair() { first = new T(); second = new T(); } // Error
```

Type erasure would change T to Object, and surely you don't want to call new Object().

The best workaround, available since Java SE 8, is to make the caller provide a constructor expression. For example:

```
Pair<String> p = Pair.makePair(String::new);
```

The makePair method receives a Supplier<T>, the functional interface for a function with no arguments and a result of type T:

```
public static <T> Pair<T> makePair(Supplier<T> constr)
{
    return new Pair<>(constr.get(), constr.get());
}
```

A more traditional workaround is to construct generic objects through reflection, by calling the Class.newInstance method.

Unfortunately, the details are a bit complex. You cannot call

```
first = T.class.newInstance(); // Error
```

The expression T.class is not legal because it would erase to Object.class. Instead, you must design the API so that you are handed a Class object, like this:

```
public static <T> Pair<T> makePair(Class<T> cl)
{
    try { return new Pair<>(cl.newInstance(), cl.newInstance()); }
    catch (Exception ex) { return null; }
}
```

This method could be called as follows:

```
Pair<String> p = Pair.makePair(String.class);
```

Note that the Class class is itself generic. For example, String.class is an instance (indeed, the sole instance) of Class<String>. Therefore, the makePair method can infer the type of the pair that it is making.

8.6.6 You Cannot Construct a Generic Array

Just as you cannot instantiate a single generic instance, you cannot instantiate an array. The reasons are different—an array is, after all, filled with null values, which would seem safe to construct. But an array also carries a type, which is used to monitor array stores in the virtual machine. That type is erased. For example, consider

```
public static <T extends Comparable> T[] minmax(T[] a) { T[] mm = new T[2]; . . . } // Error
```

Type erasure would cause this method to always construct an array Comparable[2].

If the array is only used as a private instance field of a class, you can declare the array as Object[] and use casts when retrieving elements. For example, the ArrayList class could be implemented as follows:

```
public class ArrayList<E>
{
    private Object[] elements;
    . . .
    @SuppressWarnings("unchecked") public E get(int n) { return (E) elements[n]; }
    public void set(int n, E e) { elements[n] = e; } // no cast needed
}
```

The actual implementation is not quite as clean:

```
public class ArrayList<E>
{
    private E[] elements;
    . . .
```

```
    public ArrayList() { elements = (E[]) new Object[10]; }
}
```

Here, the cast E[] is an outright lie, but type erasure makes it undetectable.

This technique does not work for our minmax method since we are returning a T[] array, and a runtime error results if we lie about its type. Suppose we implement

```
public static <T extends Comparable> T[] minmax(T... a)
{
    Object[] mm = new Object[2];
    . . .
    return (T[]) mm; // compiles with warning
}
```

The call

```
String[] ss = ArrayAlg.minmax("Tom", "Dick", "Harry");
```

compiles without any warning. A ClassCastException occurs when the Object[] reference is cast to Comparable[] as the method returns.

In this situation, it is best to ask the user to provide an array constructor expression:

```
String[] ss = ArrayAlg.minmax(String[]::new, "Tom", "Dick", "Harry");
```

The constructor expression String::new denotes a function that, given the desired length, constructs a String array of that length.

The method uses that parameter to produce an array of the correct type:

```
public static <T extends Comparable> T[] minmax(IntFunction<T[]> constr, T... a)
{
    T[] mm = constr.apply(2);
    . . .
}
```

A more old-fashioned approach is to use reflection and call Array.newInstance:

```
public static <T extends Comparable> T[] minmax(T... a)
{
    T[] mm = (T[]) Array.newInstance(a.getClass().getComponentType(), 2);
    . . .
}
```

The toArray method of the ArrayList class is not so lucky. It needs to produce a T[] array, but it doesn't have the component type. Therefore, there are two variants:

```
Object[] toArray()
T[] toArray(T[] result)
```

The second method receives an array parameter. If the array is large enough, it is used. Otherwise, a new array of sufficient size is created, using the component type of result.

8.6.7 Type Variables Are Not Valid in Static Contexts of Generic Classes

You cannot reference type variables in static fields or methods. For example, the following clever idea won't work:

```
public class Singleton<T>
{
   private static T singleInstance; // Error

   public static T getSingleInstance() // Error
   {
      if (singleInstance == null) construct new instance of T
      return singleInstance;
   }
}
```

If this could be done, then a program could declare a Singleton<Random> to share a random number generator and a Singleton<JFileChooser> to share a file chooser dialog. But it can't work. After type erasure there is only one Singleton class, and only one singleInstance field. For that reason, static fields and methods with type variables are simply outlawed.

8.6.8 You Cannot Throw or Catch Instances of a Generic Class

You can neither throw nor catch objects of a generic class. In fact, it is not even legal for a generic class to extend Throwable. For example, the following definition will not compile:

```
public class Problem<T> extends Exception { /* . . . */ } // Error--can't extend Throwable
```

You cannot use a type variable in a catch clause. For example, the following method will not compile:

```
public static <T extends Throwable> void doWork(Class<T> t)
{
   try
   {
      do work
   }
   catch (T e) // Error--can't catch type variable
   {
      Logger.global.info(...)
   }
}
```

However, it is OK to use type variables in exception specifications. The following method is legal:

```
public static <T extends Throwable> void doWork(T t) throws T // OK
{
   try
   {
      do work
   }
   catch (Throwable realCause)
   {
      t.initCause(realCause);
      throw t;
   }
}
```

8.6.9 You Can Defeat Checked Exception Checking

A bedrock principle of Java exception handling is that you must provide a handler for all checked exceptions. You can use generics to defeat this scheme. The key ingredient is this method:

```
@SuppressWarnings("unchecked")
public static <T extends Throwable> void throwAs(Throwable e) throws T
{
   throw (T) e;
}
```

Suppose this method is contained in a class Block. When you call

```
Block.<RuntimeException>throwAs(t);
```

then the compiler will believe that t becomes an unchecked exception. The following turns all exceptions into those that the compiler believes to be unchecked:

```
try
{
   do work
}
catch (Throwable t)
{
   Block.<RuntimeException>throwAs(t);
}
```

Let's package this in an abstract class. The user will override the body method to supply a particular action. When calling toThread, you get an object of the Thread class whose run method doesn't mind checked exceptions.

```
public abstract class Block
{
   public abstract void body() throws Exception;

   public Thread toThread()
   {
      return new Thread()
         {
            public void run()
            {
               try
               {
                  body();
               }
               catch (Throwable t)
               {
                  Block.<RuntimeException>throwAs(t);
               }
            }
         };
   }

   @SuppressWarnings("unchecked")
   public static <T extends Throwable> void throwAs(Throwable e) throws T
   {
      throw (T) e;
   }
}
```

For example, this program runs a thread that will throw a checked exception:

```
public class Test
{
   public static void main(String[] args)
   {
      new Block()
         {
            public void body() throws Exception
            {
               Scanner in = new Scanner(new File("ququx"), "UTF-8");
               while (in.hasNext())
                  System.out.println(in.next());
            }
         }
      .toThread().start();
   }
}
```

When you run the program, you will get a stack trace with a FileNotFoundException (assuming that you didn't provide a file named ququx, of course).

What's so remarkable about that? Normally, you have to catch all checked exceptions inside the `run` method of a thread and *wrap them* into unchecked exceptions—the `run` method is declared to throw no checked exceptions.

But here, we don't wrap. We simply throw the exception, tricking the compiler into believing that it is not a checked exception.

Using generic classes, erasure, and the `@SuppressWarnings` annotation, we were able to defeat an essential part of the Java type system.

8.6.10 Beware of Clashes after Erasure

It is illegal to create conditions that cause clashes when generic types are erased. Here is an example. Suppose we add an `equals` method to the `Pair` class, like this:

```
public class Pair<T>
{
    public boolean equals(T value) { return first.equals(value) && second.equals(value); }
    . . .
}
```

Consider a `Pair<String>`. Conceptually, it has two `equals` methods:

```
boolean equals(String) // defined in Pair<T>
boolean equals(Object) // inherited from Object
```

But the intuition leads us astray. The erasure of the method

```
boolean equals(T)
```

is

```
boolean equals(Object)
```

which clashes with the `Object.equals` method.

The remedy is, of course, to rename the offending method.

The generics specification cites another rule: "To support translation by erasure, we impose the restriction that a class or type variable may not at the same time be a subtype of two interface types which are different parameterizations of the same interface." For example, the following is illegal:

```
class Employee implements Comparable<Employee> { . . . }
class Manager extends Employee implements Comparable<Manager>
    { . . . } // Error
```

`Manager` would then implement both `Comparable<Employee>` and `Comparable<Manager>`, which are different parameterizations of the same interface.

It is not obvious what this restriction has to do with type erasure. After all, the nongeneric version

```
class Employee implements Comparable { . . . }
class Manager extends Employee implements Comparable { . . . }
```

is legal. The reason is far more subtle. There would be a conflict with the synthesized bridge methods. A class that implements Comparable<X> gets a bridge method

```
public int compareTo(Object other) { return compareTo((X) other); }
```

You cannot have two such methods for different types X.

8.7 Inheritance Rules for Generic Types

When you work with generic classes, you need to learn a few rules about inheritance and subtypes. Let's start with a situation which many programmers find unintuitive. Consider a class and a subclass, such as Employee and Manager. Is Pair<Manager> a subclass of Pair<Employee>? Perhaps surprisingly, the answer is "no." For example, the following code will not compile:

```
Manager[] topHonchos = . . .;
Pair<Employee> result = ArrayAlg.minmax(topHonchos); // Error
```

The minmax method returns a Pair<Manager>, not a Pair<Employee>, and it is illegal to assign one to the other.

In general, there is *no* relationship between Pair<S> and Pair<T>, no matter how S and T are related (see Figure 8.1).

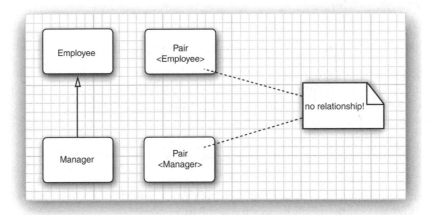

Figure 8.1 No inheritance relationship between pair classes

This seems like a cruel restriction, but it is necessary for type safety. Suppose we were allowed to convert a Pair<Manager> to a Pair<Employee>. Consider this code:

```
Pair<Manager> managerBuddies = new Pair<>(ceo, cfo);
Pair<Employee> employeeBuddies = managerBuddies; // illegal, but suppose it wasn't
employeeBuddies.setFirst(lowlyEmployee);
```

Clearly, the last statement is legal. But employeeBuddies and managerBuddies refer to the *same object*. We now managed to pair up the CFO with a lowly employee, which should not be possible for a Pair<Manager>.

NOTE: You just saw an important difference between generic types and Java arrays. You can assign a Manager[] array to a variable of type Employee[]:

```
Manager[] managerBuddies = { ceo, cfo };
Employee[] employeeBuddies = managerBuddies; // OK
```

However, arrays come with special protection. If you try to store a lowly employee into employeeBuddies[0], the virtual machine throws an ArrayStoreException.

You can always convert a parameterized type to a raw type. For example, Pair<Employee> is a subtype of the raw type Pair. This conversion is necessary for interfacing with legacy code.

Can you convert to the raw type and then cause a type error? Unfortunately, you can. Consider this example:

```
Pair<Manager> managerBuddies = new Pair<>(ceo, cfo);
Pair rawBuddies = managerBuddies; // OK
rawBuddies.setFirst(new File(". . .")); // only a compile-time warning
```

This sounds scary. However, keep in mind that you are no worse off than you were with older versions of Java. The security of the virtual machine is not at stake. When the foreign object is retrieved with getFirst and assigned to a Manager variable, a ClassCastException is thrown, just as in the good old days. You merely lose the added safety that generic programming normally provides.

Finally, generic classes can extend or implement other generic classes. In this regard, they are no different from ordinary classes. For example, the class ArrayList<T> implements the interface List<T>. That means an ArrayList<Manager> can be converted to a List<Manager>. However, as you just saw, an ArrayList<Manager> is *not* an ArrayList<Employee> or List<Employee>. Figure 8.2 shows these relationships.

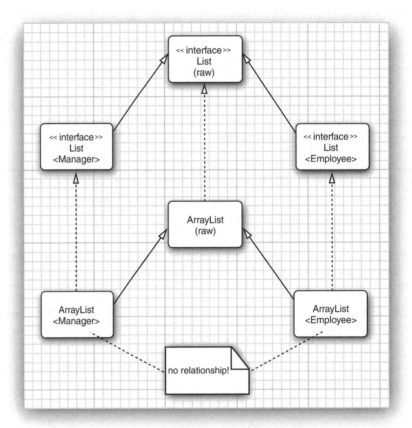

Figure 8.2 Subtype relationships among generic list types

8.8 Wildcard Types

It was known for some time among researchers of type systems that a rigid system of generic types is quite unpleasant to use. The Java designers invented an ingenious (but nevertheless safe) "escape hatch": the *wildcard type*. The following sections show you how to work with wildcards.

8.8.1 The Wildcard Concept

In a wildcard type, a type parameter is allowed to vary. For example, the wildcard type

```
Pair<? extends Employee>
```

denotes any generic Pair type whose type parameter is a subclass of Employee, such as Pair<Manager>, but not Pair<String>.

Let's say you want to write a method that prints out pairs of employees, like this:

```
public static void printBuddies(Pair<Employee> p)
{
    Employee first = p.getFirst();
    Employee second = p.getSecond();
    System.out.println(first.getName() + " and " + second.getName() + " are buddies.");
}
```

As you saw in the preceding section, you cannot pass a Pair<Manager> to that method, which is rather limiting. But the solution is simple—use a wildcard type:

```
public static void printBuddies(Pair<? extends Employee> p)
```

The type Pair<Manager> is a subtype of Pair<? extends Employee> (see Figure 8.3).

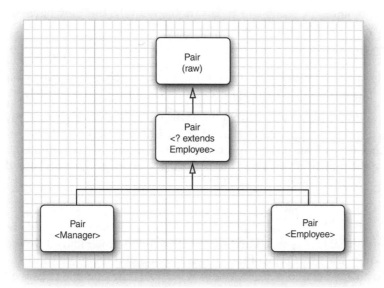

Figure 8.3 Subtype relationships with wildcards

Can we use wildcards to corrupt a Pair<Manager> through a Pair<? extends Employee> reference?

```
Pair<Manager> managerBuddies = new Pair<>(ceo, cfo);
Pair<? extends Employee> wildcardBuddies = managerBuddies; // OK
wildcardBuddies.setFirst(lowlyEmployee); // compile-time error
```

No corruption is possible. The call to setFirst is a type error. To see why, let us have a closer look at the type Pair<? extends Employee>. Its methods look like this:

```
? extends Employee getFirst()
void setFirst(? extends Employee)
```

This makes it impossible to call the setFirst method. The compiler only knows that it needs some subtype of Employee, but it doesn't know which type. It refuses to pass any specific type—after all, ? might not match it.

We don't have this problem with getFirst: It is perfectly legal to assign the return value of getFirst to an Employee reference.

This is the key idea behind bounded wildcards. We now have a way of distinguishing between the safe accessor methods and the unsafe mutator methods.

8.8.2 Supertype Bounds for Wildcards

Wildcard bounds are similar to type variable bounds, but they have an added capability—you can specify a *supertype bound*, like this:

```
? super Manager
```

This wildcard is restricted to all supertypes of Manager. (It was a stroke of good luck that the existing super keyword describes the relationship so accurately.)

Why would you want to do this? A wildcard with a supertype bound gives you a behavior that is opposite to that of the wildcards described in Section 8.8, "Wildcard Types," on p. 442. You can supply parameters to methods, but you can't use the return values. For example, Pair<? super Manager> has methods that can be described as follows:

```
void setFirst(? super Manager)
? super Manager getFirst()
```

This is not actual Java syntax, but it shows what the compiler knows. The compiler cannot know the exact type of the setFirst method and therefore cannot accept a call with an argument of type Employee or Object. It is only possible to pass an object of type Manager or a subtype such as Executive. Moreover, if you call getFirst, there is no guarantee about the type of the returned object. You can only assign it to an Object.

Here is a typical example. We have an array of managers and want to put the manager with the lowest and highest bonus into a Pair object. What kind of Pair? A Pair<Employee> should be fair game or, for that matter, a Pair<Object> (see Figure 8.4). The following method will accept any appropriate Pair:

```
public static void minmaxBonus(Manager[] a, Pair<? super Manager> result)
{
   if (a.length == 0) return;
   Manager min = a[0];
   Manager max = a[0];
   for (int i = 1; i < a.length; i++)
   {
      if (min.getBonus() > a[i].getBonus()) min = a[i];
      if (max.getBonus() < a[i].getBonus()) max = a[i];
   }
   result.setFirst(min);
   result.setSecond(max);
}
```

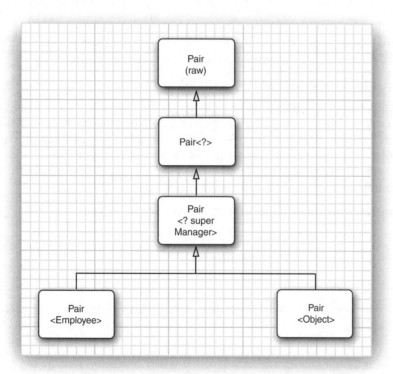

Figure 8.4 A wildcard with a supertype bound

Intuitively speaking, wildcards with supertype bounds let you write to a generic object, while wildcards with subtype bounds let you read from a generic object.

Here is another use for supertype bounds. The Comparable interface is itself a generic type. It is declared as follows:

```
public interface Comparable<T>
{
    public int compareTo(T other);
}
```

Here, the type variable indicates the type of the other parameter. For example, the String class implements Comparable<String>, and its compareTo method is declared as

```
public int compareTo(String other)
```

This is nice—the explicit parameter has the correct type. Before the interface was generic, other was an Object, and a cast was necessary in the implementation of the method.

Now that Comparable is a generic type, perhaps we should have done a better job with the min method of the ArrayAlg class? We could have declared it as

```
public static <T extends Comparable<T>> T min(T[] a)
```

This looks more thorough than just using T extends Comparable, and it would work fine for many classes. For example, if you compute the minimum of a String array, then T is the type String, and String is a subtype of Comparable<String>. But we run into a problem when processing an array of LocalDate objects. As it happens, LocalDate implements ChronoLocalDate, and ChronoLocalDate extends Comparable<ChronoLocalDate>. Thus, LocalDate implements Comparable<ChronoLocalDate> but *not* Comparable<LocalDate>.

In a situation such as this one, supertypes come to the rescue:

```
public static <T extends Comparable<? super T>> T min(T[] a) . . .
```

Now the compareTo method has the form

```
int compareTo(? super T)
```

Maybe it is declared to take an object of type T, or—for example, when T is LocalDate—a supertype of T. At any rate, it is safe to pass an object of type T to the compareTo method.

To the uninitiated, a declaration such as <T extends Comparable<? super T>> is bound to look intimidating. This is unfortunate, because the intent of this declaration is to help application programmers by removing unnecessary restrictions on the call parameters. Application programmers with no interest in generics will probably learn quickly to gloss over these declarations and just take for granted that library programmers will do the right thing. If you are a library programmer, you'll need to get used to wildcards, or your users will curse you and throw random casts at their code until it compiles.

NOTE: Another common use for supertype bounds is an argument type of a functional interface. For example, the Collection interface has a method

```
default boolean removeIf(Predicate<? super E> filter)
```

The method removes all elements that fulfill the given predicate. For example, if you hate employees with odd hash codes, you can remove them like this:

```
ArrayList<Employee> staff = . . .;
Predicate<Object> oddHashCode = obj -> obj.hashCode() %2 != 0;
staff.removeIf(oddHashCode);
```

You want to be able to pass a Predicate<Object>, not just a Predicate<Employee>. The super wildcard makes that possible.

8.8.3 Unbounded Wildcards

You can even use wildcards with no bounds at all—for example, Pair<?>. At first glance, this looks identical to the raw Pair type. Actually, the types are very different. The type Pair<?> has methods such as

```
? getFirst()
void setFirst(?)
```

The return value of getFirst can only be assigned to an Object. The setFirst method can never be called, *not even with an* Object. That's the essential difference between Pair<?> and Pair: you can call the setFirst method of the raw Pair class with *any* Object.

 NOTE: You can call setFirst(null).

Why would you ever want such a wimpy type? It is useful for very simple operations. For example, the following method tests whether a pair contains a null reference. It never needs the actual type.

```
public static boolean hasNulls(Pair<?> p)
{
    return p.getFirst() == null || p.getSecond() == null;
}
```

You could have avoided the wildcard type by turning hasNulls into a generic method:

```
public static <T> boolean hasNulls(Pair<T> p)
```

However, the version with the wildcard type seems easier to read.

8.8.4 Wildcard Capture

Let us write a method that swaps the elements of a pair:

```
public static void swap(Pair<?> p)
```

A wildcard is not a type variable, so we can't write code that uses ? as a type. In other words, the following would be illegal:

```
? t = p.getFirst(); // Error
p.setFirst(p.getSecond());
p.setSecond(t);
```

That's a problem because we need to temporarily hold the first element when we do the swapping. Fortunately, there is an interesting solution to this problem. We can write a helper method, swapHelper, like this:

```
public static <T> void swapHelper(Pair<T> p)
{
   T t = p.getFirst();
   p.setFirst(p.getSecond());
   p.setSecond(t);
}
```

Note that swapHelper is a generic method, whereas swap is not—it has a fixed parameter of type Pair<?>.

Now we can call swapHelper from swap:

```
public static void swap(Pair<?> p) { swapHelper(p); }
```

In this case, the parameter T of the swapHelper method *captures the wildcard*. It isn't known what type the wildcard denotes, but it is a definite type, and the definition of <T>swapHelper makes perfect sense when T denotes that type.

Of course, in this case, we were not compelled to use a wildcard. We could have directly implemented <T> void swap(Pair<T> p) as a generic method without wildcards. However, consider this example in which a wildcard type occurs naturally in the middle of a computation:

```
public static void maxminBonus(Manager[] a, Pair<? super Manager> result)
{
   minmaxBonus(a, result);
   PairAlg.swap(result); // OK--swapHelper captures wildcard type
}
```

Here, the wildcard capture mechanism cannot be avoided.

Wildcard capture is only legal in very limited circumstances. The compiler must be able to guarantee that the wildcard represents a single, definite type. For example, the `T` in `ArrayList<Pair<T>>` can never capture the wildcard in `ArrayList<Pair<?>>`. The array list might hold two `Pair<?>`, each of which has a different type for `?`.

The test program in Listing 8.3 gathers up the various methods that we discussed in the preceding sections, so that you can see them in context.

Listing 8.3 pair3/PairTest3.java

```java
 1  package pair3;
 2
 3  /**
 4   * @version 1.01 2012-01-26
 5   * @author Cay Horstmann
 6   */
 7  public class PairTest3
 8  {
 9     public static void main(String[] args)
10     {
11        Manager ceo = new Manager("Gus Greedy", 800000, 2003, 12, 15);
12        Manager cfo = new Manager("Sid Sneaky", 600000, 2003, 12, 15);
13        Pair<Manager> buddies = new Pair<>(ceo, cfo);
14        printBuddies(buddies);
15
16        ceo.setBonus(1000000);
17        cfo.setBonus(500000);
18        Manager[] managers = { ceo, cfo };
19
20        Pair<Employee> result = new Pair<>();
21        minmaxBonus(managers, result);
22        System.out.println("first: " + result.getFirst().getName()
23           + ", second: " + result.getSecond().getName());
24        maxminBonus(managers, result);
25        System.out.println("first: " + result.getFirst().getName()
26           + ", second: " + result.getSecond().getName());
27     }
28
29     public static void printBuddies(Pair<? extends Employee> p)
30     {
31        Employee first = p.getFirst();
32        Employee second = p.getSecond();
33        System.out.println(first.getName() + " and " + second.getName() + " are buddies.");
34     }
35
36     public static void minmaxBonus(Manager[] a, Pair<? super Manager> result)
37     {
38        if (a.length == 0) return;
39        Manager min = a[0];
40        Manager max = a[0];
```

(Continues)

Listing 8.3 *(Continued)*

```
41        for (int i = 1; i < a.length; i++)
42        {
43           if (min.getBonus() > a[i].getBonus()) min = a[i];
44           if (max.getBonus() < a[i].getBonus()) max = a[i];
45        }
46        result.setFirst(min);
47        result.setSecond(max);
48     }
49
50     public static void maxminBonus(Manager[] a, Pair<? super Manager> result)
51     {
52        minmaxBonus(a, result);
53        PairAlg.swapHelper(result); // OK--swapHelper captures wildcard type
54     }
55  }
56
57  class PairAlg
58  {
59     public static boolean hasNulls(Pair<?> p)
60     {
61        return p.getFirst() == null || p.getSecond() == null;
62     }
63
64     public static void swap(Pair<?> p) { swapHelper(p); }
65
66     public static <T> void swapHelper(Pair<T> p)
67     {
68        T t = p.getFirst();
69        p.setFirst(p.getSecond());
70        p.setSecond(t);
71     }
72  }
```

8.9 Reflection and Generics

Reflection lets you analyze arbitrary objects at runtime. If the objects are instances of generic classes, you don't get much information about the generic type parameters because they have been erased. In the following sections, you will learn what you can nevertheless find out about generic classes with reflection.

8.9.1 The Generic Class Class

The Class class is now generic. For example, String.class is actually an object (in fact, the sole object) of the class Class<String>.

The type parameter is useful because it allows the methods of Class<T> to be more specific about their return types. The following methods of Class<T> take advantage of the type parameter:

```
T newInstance()
T cast(Object obj)
T[] getEnumConstants()
Class<? super T> getSuperclass()
Constructor<T> getConstructor(Class... parameterTypes)
Constructor<T> getDeclaredConstructor(Class... parameterTypes)
```

The newInstance method returns an instance of the class, obtained from the no-argument constructor. Its return type can now be declared to be T, the same type as the class that is being described by Class<T>. That saves a cast.

The cast method returns the given object, now declared as type T if its type is indeed a subtype of T. Otherwise, it throws a BadCastException.

The getEnumConstants method returns null if this class is not an enum class or an array of the enumeration values which are known to be of type T.

Finally, the getConstructor and getDeclaredConstructor methods return a Constructor<T> object. The Constructor class has also been made generic so that its newInstance method has the correct return type.

---

java.lang.Class<T> 1.0

- T newInstance()

  returns a new instance constructed with the no-argument constructor.

- T cast(Object obj)

  returns obj if it is null or can be converted to the type T, or throws a BadCastException otherwise.

- T[] getEnumConstants() 5.0

  returns an array of all values if T is an enumerated type, null otherwise.

- Class<? super T> getSuperclass()

  returns the superclass of this class, or null if T is not a class or the class Object.

- Constructor<T> getConstructor(Class... parameterTypes) 1.1
- Constructor<T> getDeclaredConstructor(Class... parameterTypes) 1.1

  gets the public constructor, or the constructor with the given parameter types.

---

java.lang.reflect.Constructor<T> 1.1

- T newInstance(Object... parameters)

  returns a new instance constructed with the given parameters.

8.9.2 Using Class<T> Parameters for Type Matching

It is sometimes useful to match the type variable of a Class<T> parameter in a generic method. Here is the canonical example:

```
public static <T> Pair<T> makePair(Class<T> c) throws InstantiationException,
    IllegalAccessException
{
    return new Pair<>(c.newInstance(), c.newInstance());
}
```

If you call

```
makePair(Employee.class)
```

then Employee.class is an object of type Class<Employee>. The type parameter T of the makePair method matches Employee, and the compiler can infer that the method returns a Pair<Employee>.

8.9.3 Generic Type Information in the Virtual Machine

One of the notable features of Java generics is the erasure of generic types in the virtual machine. Perhaps surprisingly, the erased classes still retain some faint memory of their generic origin. For example, the raw Pair class knows that it originated from the generic class Pair<T>, even though an object of type Pair can't tell whether it was constructed as a Pair<String> or Pair<Employee>.

Similarly, consider a method

```
public static Comparable min(Comparable[] a)
```

that is the erasure of a generic method

```
public static <T extends Comparable<? super T>> T min(T[] a)
```

You can use the reflection API to determine that

- The generic method has a type parameter called T;
- The type parameter has a subtype bound that is itself a generic type;

- The bounding type has a wildcard parameter;
- The wildcard parameter has a supertype bound; and
- The generic method has a generic array parameter.

In other words, you can reconstruct everything about generic classes and methods that their implementors declared. However, you won't know how the type parameters were resolved for specific objects or method calls.

In order to express generic type declarations, use the interface Type in the java.lang.reflect package. The interface has the following subtypes:

- The Class class, describing concrete types
- The TypeVariable interface, describing type variables (such as T extends Comparable<? super T>)
- The WildcardType interface, describing wildcards (such as ? super T)
- The ParameterizedType interface, describing generic class or interface types (such as Comparable<? super T>)
- The GenericArrayType interface, describing generic arrays (such as T[])

Figure 8.5 shows the inheritance hierarchy. Note that the last four subtypes are interfaces—the virtual machine instantiates suitable classes that implement these interfaces.

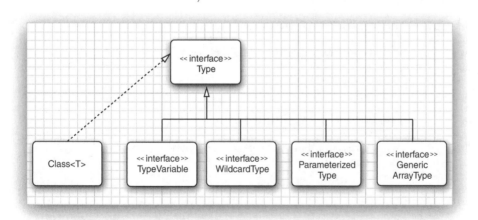

Figure 8.5 The Type interface and its descendants

Listing 8.4 uses the generic reflection API to print out what it discovers about a given class. If you run it with the Pair class, you get this report:

```
class Pair<T> extends java.lang.Object
public T getFirst()
public T getSecond()
public void setFirst(T)
public void setSecond(T)
```

If you run it with `ArrayAlg` in the `PairTest2` directory, the report displays the following method:

```
public static <T extends java.lang.Comparable> Pair<T> minmax(T[])
```

The API notes at the end of this section describe the methods used in the example program.

Listing 8.4 genericReflection/GenericReflectionTest.java

```java
 1  package genericReflection;
 2
 3  import java.lang.reflect.*;
 4  import java.util.*;
 5
 6  /**
 7   * @version 1.10 2007-05-15
 8   * @author Cay Horstmann
 9   */
10  public class GenericReflectionTest
11  {
12     public static void main(String[] args)
13     {
14        // read class name from command line args or user input
15        String name;
16        if (args.length > 0) name = args[0];
17        else
18        {
19           try (Scanner in = new Scanner(System.in))
20           {
21              System.out.println("Enter class name (e.g. java.util.Collections): ");
22              name = in.next();
23           }
24        }
25
26        try
27        {
28           // print generic info for class and public methods
29           Class<?> cl = Class.forName(name);
30           printClass(cl);
31           for (Method m : cl.getDeclaredMethods())
32              printMethod(m);
33        }
```

```
34          catch (ClassNotFoundException e)
35          {
36             e.printStackTrace();
37          }
38       }
39
40       public static void printClass(Class<?> cl)
41       {
42          System.out.print(cl);
43          printTypes(cl.getTypeParameters(), "<", ", ", ">", true);
44          Type sc = cl.getGenericSuperclass();
45          if (sc != null)
46          {
47             System.out.print(" extends ");
48             printType(sc, false);
49          }
50          printTypes(cl.getGenericInterfaces(), " implements ", ", ", "", false);
51          System.out.println();
52       }
53
54       public static void printMethod(Method m)
55       {
56          String name = m.getName();
57          System.out.print(Modifier.toString(m.getModifiers()));
58          System.out.print(" ");
59          printTypes(m.getTypeParameters(), "<", ", ", "> ", true);
60
61          printType(m.getGenericReturnType(), false);
62          System.out.print(" ");
63          System.out.print(name);
64          System.out.print("(");
65          printTypes(m.getGenericParameterTypes(), "", ", ", "", false);
66          System.out.println(")");
67       }
68
69       public static void printTypes(Type[] types, String pre, String sep, String suf,
70             boolean isDefinition)
71       {
72          if (pre.equals(" extends ") && Arrays.equals(types, new Type[] { Object.class })) return;
73          if (types.length > 0) System.out.print(pre);
74          for (int i = 0; i < types.length; i++)
75          {
76             if (i > 0) System.out.print(sep);
77             printType(types[i], isDefinition);
78          }
79          if (types.length > 0) System.out.print(suf);
80       }
81
```

(Continues)

Listing 8.4 *(Continued)*

```
82    public static void printType(Type type, boolean isDefinition)
83    {
84       if (type instanceof Class)
85       {
86          Class<?> t = (Class<?>) type;
87          System.out.print(t.getName());
88       }
89       else if (type instanceof TypeVariable)
90       {
91          TypeVariable<?> t = (TypeVariable<?>) type;
92          System.out.print(t.getName());
93          if (isDefinition)
94             printTypes(t.getBounds(), " extends ", " & ", "", false);
95       }
96       else if (type instanceof WildcardType)
97       {
98          WildcardType t = (WildcardType) type;
99          System.out.print("?");
100         printTypes(t.getUpperBounds(), " extends ", " & ", "", false);
101         printTypes(t.getLowerBounds(), " super ", " & ", "", false);
102      }
103      else if (type instanceof ParameterizedType)
104      {
105         ParameterizedType t = (ParameterizedType) type;
106         Type owner = t.getOwnerType();
107         if (owner != null)
108         {
109            printType(owner, false);
110            System.out.print(".");
111         }
112         printType(t.getRawType(), false);
113         printTypes(t.getActualTypeArguments(), "<", ", ", ">", false);
114      }
115      else if (type instanceof GenericArrayType)
116      {
117         GenericArrayType t = (GenericArrayType) type;
118         System.out.print("");
119         printType(t.getGenericComponentType(), isDefinition);
120         System.out.print("[]");
121      }
122   }
123 }
```

---

java.lang.Class<T> 1.0

- TypeVariable[] getTypeParameters() 5.0

  gets the generic type variables if this type was declared as a generic type, or an array of length 0 otherwise.

- Type getGenericSuperclass() 5.0

  gets the generic type of the superclass that was declared for this type, or null if this type is Object or not a class type.

- Type[] getGenericInterfaces() 5.0

  gets the generic types of the interfaces that were declared for this type, in declaration order, or an array of length 0 if this type doesn't implement interfaces.

---

java.lang.reflect.Method 1.1

- TypeVariable[] getTypeParameters() 5.0

  gets the generic type variables if this method was declared as a generic method, or an array of length 0 otherwise.

- Type getGenericReturnType() 5.0

  gets the generic return type with which this method was declared.

- Type[] getGenericParameterTypes() 5.0

  gets the generic parameter types with which this method was declared. If the method has no parameters, an array of length 0 is returned.

---

java.lang.reflect.TypeVariable 5.0

- String getName()

  gets the name of this type variable.

- Type[] getBounds()

  gets the subclass bounds of this type variable, or an array of length 0 if the variable is unbounded.

`java.lang.reflect.WildcardType` 5.0

- `Type[] getUpperBounds()`

  gets the subclass (`extends`) bounds of this type variable, or an array of length 0 if the variable has no subclass bounds.

- `Type[] getLowerBounds()`

  gets the superclass (`super`) bounds of this type variable, or an array of length 0 if the variable has no superclass bounds.

`java.lang.reflect.ParameterizedType` 5.0

- `Type getRawType()`

  gets the raw type of this parameterized type.

- `Type[] getActualTypeArguments()`

  gets the type parameters with which this parameterized type was declared.

- `Type getOwnerType()`

  gets the outer class type if this is an inner type, or `null` if this is a top-level type.

`java.lang.reflect.GenericArrayType` 5.0

- `Type getGenericComponentType()`

  gets the generic component type with which this array type was declared.

You now know how to use generic classes and how to program your own generic classes and methods if the need arises. Just as importantly, you know how to decipher the generic type declarations that you may encounter in the API documentation and in error messages. For an exhaustive discussion of everything there is to know about Java generics, turn to Angelika Langer's excellent list of frequently (and not so frequently) asked questions at `http://angelikalanger.com/GenericsFAQ/JavaGenericsFAQ.html`.

In the next chapter, you will see how the Java collections framework puts generics to work.

9

Collections

In this chapter

The data structures that you choose can make a big difference when you try to implement methods in a natural style or are concerned with performance. Do you need to search quickly through thousands (or even millions) of sorted items? Do you need to rapidly insert and remove elements in the middle of an ordered sequence? Do you need to establish associations between keys and values?

This chapter shows how the Java library can help you accomplish the traditional data structuring needed for serious programming. In college computer science programs, a course called *Data Structures* usually takes a semester to complete, and there are many, many books devoted to this important topic. Our coverage differs from that of a college course; we will skip the theory and just show you how to use the collection classes in the standard library.

9.1 The Java Collections Framework

The initial release of Java supplied only a small set of classes for the most useful data structures: Vector, Stack, Hashtable, BitSet, and the Enumeration interface that provides an abstract mechanism for visiting elements in an arbitrary container. That was certainly a wise choice—it takes time and skill to come up with a comprehensive collection class library.

With the advent of Java SE 1.2, the designers felt that the time had come to roll out a full-fledged set of data structures. They faced a number of conflicting design challenges. They wanted the library to be small and easy to learn. They did not want the complexity of the Standard Template Library (or STL) of C++, but they wanted the benefit of "generic algorithms" that STL pioneered. They wanted the legacy classes to fit into the new framework. As all designers of collections libraries do, they had to make some hard choices, and they came up with a number of idiosyncratic design decisions along the way. In this section, we will explore the basic design of the Java collections framework, show you how to put it to work, and explain the reasoning behind some of the more controversial features.

9.1.1 Separating Collection Interfaces and Implementation

As is common with modern data structure libraries, the Java collection library separates *interfaces* and *implementations*. Let us look at that separation with a familiar data structure, the *queue*.

A *queue interface* specifies that you can add elements at the tail end of the queue, remove them at the head, and find out how many elements are in the queue. You use a queue when you need to collect objects and retrieve them in a "first in, first out" fashion (see Figure 9.1).

A minimal form of a queue interface might look like this:

```
public interface Queue<E> // a simplified form of the interface in the standard library
{
   void add(E element);
   E remove();
   int size();
}
```

The interface tells you nothing about how the queue is implemented. Of the two common implementations of a queue, one uses a "circular array" and one uses a linked list (see Figure 9.2).

Each implementation can be expressed by a class that implements the Queue interface.

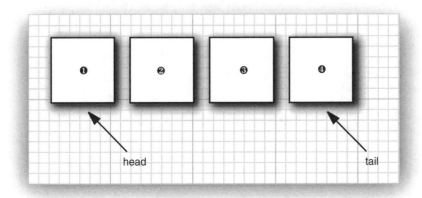

Figure 9.1 A queue

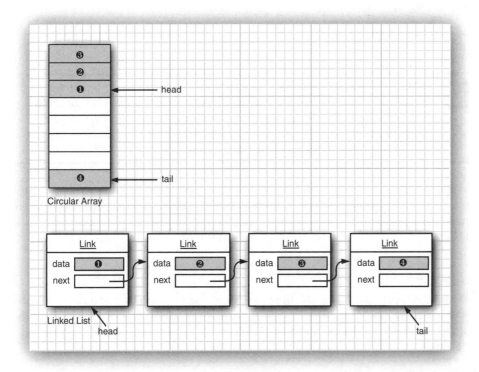

Figure 9.2 Queue implementations

```
public class CircularArrayQueue<E> implements Queue<E> // not an actual library class
{
   private int head;
   private int tail;

   CircularArrayQueue(int capacity) { . . . }
   public void add(E element) { . . . }
   public E remove() { . . . }
   public int size() { . . . }
   private E[] elements;
}

public class LinkedListQueue<E> implements Queue<E> // not an actual library class
{
   private Link head;
   private Link tail;

   LinkedListQueue() { . . . }
   public void add(E element) { . . . }
   public E remove() { . . . }
   public int size() { . . . }
}
```

 NOTE: The Java library doesn't actually have classes named `CircularArrayQueue` and `LinkedListQueue`. We use these classes as examples to explain the conceptual distinction between collection interfaces and implementations. If you need a circular array queue, use the `ArrayDeque` class. For a linked list queue, simply use the `LinkedList` class—it implements the `Queue` interface.

When you use a queue in your program, you don't need to know which implementation is actually used once the collection has been constructed. Therefore, it makes sense to use the concrete class *only* when you construct the collection object. Use the *interface type* to hold the collection reference.

```
Queue<Customer> expressLane = new CircularArrayQueue<>(100);
expressLane.add(new Customer("Harry"));
```

With this approach, if you change your mind, you can easily use a different implementation. You only need to change your program in one place—in the constructor call. If you decide that a `LinkedListQueue` is a better choice after all, your code becomes

```
Queue<Customer> expressLane = new LinkedListQueue<>();
expressLane.add(new Customer("Harry"));
```

Why would you choose one implementation over another? The interface says nothing about the efficiency of an implementation. A circular array is somewhat more efficient than a linked list, so it is generally preferable. However, as usual, there is a price to pay.

The circular array is a *bounded* collection—it has a finite capacity. If you don't have an upper limit on the number of objects that your program will collect, you may be better off with a linked list implementation after all.

When you study the API documentation, you will find another set of classes whose name begins with Abstract, such as AbstractQueue. These classes are intended for library implementors. In the (perhaps unlikely) event that you want to implement your own queue class, you will find it easier to extend AbstractQueue than to implement all the methods of the Queue interface.

9.1.2 The Collection Interface

The fundamental interface for collection classes in the Java library is the Collection interface. The interface has two fundamental methods:

```java
public interface Collection<E>
{
    boolean add(E element);
    Iterator<E> iterator();
    . . .
}
```

There are several methods in addition to these two; we will discuss them later.

The add method adds an element to the collection. The add method returns true if adding the element actually changes the collection, and false if the collection is unchanged. For example, if you try to add an object to a set and the object is already present, the add request has no effect because sets reject duplicates.

The iterator method returns an object that implements the Iterator interface. You can use the iterator object to visit the elements in the collection one by one. We discuss iterators in the next section.

9.1.3 Iterators

The Iterator interface has four methods:

```java
public interface Iterator<E>
{
    E next();
    boolean hasNext();
    void remove();
    default void forEachRemaining(Consumer<? super E> action);
}
```

By repeatedly calling the next method, you can visit the elements from the collection one by one. However, if you reach the end of the collection, the next method throws a NoSuchElementException. Therefore, you need to call the hasNext method before calling next. That method returns true if the iterator object still has more elements to visit. If you want to inspect all elements in a collection, request an iterator and then keep calling the next method while hasNext returns true. For example:

```
Collection<String> c = . . .;
Iterator<String> iter = c.iterator();
while (iter.hasNext())
{
    String element = iter.next();
    do something with element
}
```

You can write such a loop more concisely as the "for each" loop:

```
for (String element : c)
{
    do something with element
}
```

The compiler simply translates the "for each" loop into a loop with an iterator.

The "for each" loop works with any object that implements the Iterable interface, an interface with a single abstract method:

```
public interface Iterable<E>
{
    Iterator<E> iterator();
    . . .
}
```

The Collection interface extends the Iterable interface. Therefore, you can use the "for each" loop with any collection in the standard library.

As of Java SE 8, you don't even have to write a loop. You can call the forEachRemaining method with a lambda expression that consumes an element. The lambda expression is invoked with each element of the iterator, until there are none left.

```
iterator.forEachRemaining(element -> do something with element);
```

The order in which the elements are visited depends on the collection type. If you iterate over an ArrayList, the iterator starts at index 0 and increments the index in each step. However, if you visit the elements in a HashSet, you will get them in an essentially random order. You can be assured that you will encounter all elements of the collection during the course of the iteration, but you cannot make any assumptions about their ordering. This is usually not a problem because the ordering does not matter for computations such as computing totals or counting matches.

NOTE: Old-timers will notice that the `next` and `hasNext` methods of the `Iterator` interface serve the same purpose as the `nextElement` and `hasMoreElements` methods of an `Enumeration`. The designers of the Java collections library could have chosen to make use of the `Enumeration` interface. But they disliked the cumbersome method names and instead introduced a new interface with shorter method names.

There is an important conceptual difference between iterators in the Java collections library and iterators in other libraries. In traditional collections libraries, such as the Standard Template Library of C++, iterators are modeled after array indexes. Given such an iterator, you can look up the element that is stored at that position, much like you can look up an array element a[i] if you have an array index i. Independently of the lookup, you can advance the iterator to the next position. This is the same operation as advancing an array index by calling i++, without performing a lookup. However, the Java iterators do not work like that. The lookup and position change are tightly coupled. The only way to look up an element is to call `next`, and that lookup advances the position.

Instead, think of Java iterators as being *between elements*. When you call `next`, the iterator *jumps over* the next element, and it returns a reference to the element that it just passed (see Figure 9.3).

 NOTE: Here is another useful analogy. You can think of `Iterator.next` as the equivalent of `InputStream.read`. Reading a byte from a stream automatically "consumes" the byte. The next call to `read` consumes and returns the next byte from the input. Similarly, repeated calls to `next` let you read all elements in a collection.

The `remove` method of the `Iterator` interface removes the element that was returned by the last call to `next`. In many situations, that makes sense—you need to see the element before you can decide that it is the one that should be removed. But if you want to remove an element in a particular position, you still need to skip past the element. For example, here is how you remove the first element in a collection of strings:

```
Iterator<String> it = c.iterator();
it.next(); // skip over the first element
it.remove(); // now remove it
```

More importantly, there is a dependency between the calls to the `next` and `remove` methods. It is illegal to call `remove` if it wasn't preceded by a call to `next`. If you try, an `IllegalStateException` is thrown.

If you want to remove two adjacent elements, you cannot simply call

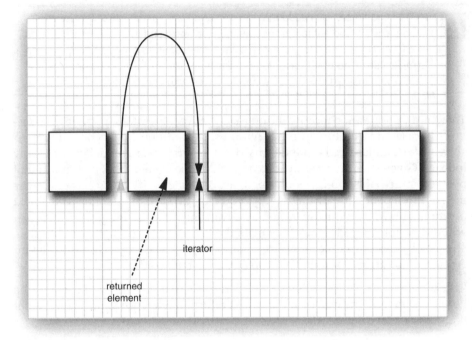

Figure 9.3 Advancing an iterator

```
it.remove();
it.remove(); // Error!
```

Instead, you must first call next to jump over the element to be removed.

```
it.remove();
it.next();
it.remove(); // OK
```

9.1.4 Generic Utility Methods

The Collection and Iterator interfaces are generic, which means you can write utility methods that operate on any kind of collection. For example, here is a generic method that tests whether an arbitrary collection contains a given element:

```
public static <E> boolean contains(Collection<E> c, Object obj)
{
    for (E element : c)
        if (element.equals(obj))
            return true;
    return false;
}
```

The designers of the Java library decided that some of these utility methods are so useful that the library should make them available. That way, library users don't have to keep reinventing the wheel. The contains method is one such method.

In fact, the Collection interface declares quite a few useful methods that all implementing classes must supply. Among them are

```
int size()
boolean isEmpty()
boolean contains(Object obj)
boolean containsAll(Collection<?> c)
boolean equals(Object other)
boolean addAll(Collection<? extends E> from)
boolean remove(Object obj)
boolean removeAll(Collection<?> c)
void clear()
boolean retainAll(Collection<?> c)
Object[] toArray()
<T> T[] toArray(T[] arrayToFill)
```

Many of these methods are self-explanatory; you will find full documentation in the API notes at the end of this section.

Of course, it is a bother if every class that implements the Collection interface has to supply so many routine methods. To make life easier for implementors, the library supplies a class AbstractCollection that leaves the fundamental methods size and iterator abstract but implements the routine methods in terms of them. For example:

```
public abstract class AbstractCollection<E>
    implements Collection<E>
{
    . . .
    public abstract Iterator<E> iterator();

    public boolean contains(Object obj)
    {
        for (E element : this) // calls iterator()
            if (element.equals(obj))
                return = true;
        return false;
    }
    . . .
}
```

A concrete collection class can now extend the AbstractCollection class. It is up to the concrete collection class to supply an iterator method, but the contains method has been taken care of by the AbstractCollection superclass. However, if the subclass has a more efficient way of implementing contains, it is free to do so.

With Java SE 8, this approach is a bit outdated. It would be nicer if the methods were default methods of the Collection interface. This has not happened. However, several default methods have been added. Most of them deal with streams (which we will discuss in Volume II). In addition, there is a useful method

```
default boolean removeIf(Predicate<? super E> filter)
```

for removing elements that fulfill a condition.

---

java.util.Collection<E> 1.2

- Iterator<E> iterator()

  returns an iterator that can be used to visit the elements in the collection.

- int size()

  returns the number of elements currently stored in the collection.

- boolean isEmpty()

  returns true if this collection contains no elements.

- boolean contains(Object obj)

  returns true if this collection contains an object equal to obj.

- boolean containsAll(Collection<?> other)

  returns true if this collection contains all elements in the other collection.

- boolean add(Object element)

  adds an element to the collection. Returns true if the collection changed as a result of this call.

- boolean addAll(Collection<? extends E> other)

  adds all elements from the other collection to this collection. Returns true if the collection changed as a result of this call.

- boolean remove(Object obj)

  removes an object equal to obj from this collection. Returns true if a matching object was removed.

- boolean removeAll(Collection<?> other)

  removes from this collection all elements from the other collection. Returns true if the collection changed as a result of this call.

- default boolean removeIf(Predicate<? super E> filter) 8

  removes all elements for which filter returns true. Returns true if the collection changed as a result of this call.

(Continues)

---

java.util.Collection<E> 1.2 *(Continued)*

- void clear()

  removes all elements from this collection.

- boolean retainAll(Collection<?> other)

  removes all elements from this collection that do not equal one of the elements in the other collection. Returns true if the collection changed as a result of this call.

- Object[] toArray()

  returns an array of the objects in the collection.

- <T> T[] toArray(T[] arrayToFill)

  returns an array of the objects in the collection. If arrayToFill has sufficient length, it is filled with the elements of this collection. If there is space, a null element is appended. Otherwise, a new array with the same component type as arrayToFill and the same length as the size of this collection is allocated and filled.

---

java.util.Iterator<E> 1.2

- boolean hasNext()

  returns true if there is another element to visit.

- E next()

  returns the next object to visit. Throws a NoSuchElementException if the end of the collection has been reached.

- void remove()

  removes the last visited object. This method must immediately follow an element visit. If the collection has been modified since the last element visit, this method throws an IllegalStateException.

9.1.5 Interfaces in the Collections Framework

The Java collections framework defines a number of interfaces for different types of collections, shown in Figure 9.4.

There are two fundamental interfaces for collections: Collection and Map. As you already saw, you insert elements into a collection with a method

```
boolean add(E element)
```

However, maps hold key/value pairs, and you use the put method to insert them:

```
V put(K key, V value)
```

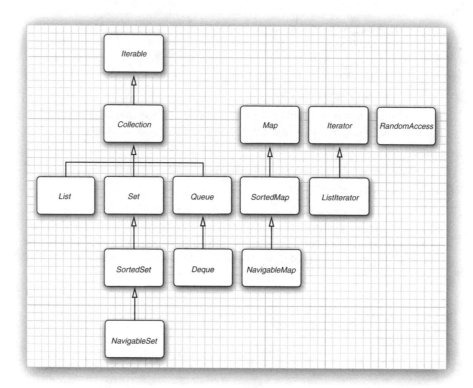

Figure 9.4 The interfaces of the collections framework

To read elements from a collection, visit them with an iterator. However, you can read values from a map with the get method:

```
V get(K key)
```

A List is an *ordered collection*. Elements are added into a particular position in the container. An element can be accessed in two ways: by an iterator or by an integer index. The latter is called *random access* because elements can be visited in any order. In contrast, when using an iterator, one must visit them sequentially.

The List interface defines several methods for random access:

```
void add(int index, E element)
void remove(int index)
E get(int index)
E set(int index, E element)
```

The ListIterator interface is a subinterface of Iterator. It defines a method for adding an element before the iterator position:

```
void add(E element)
```

Frankly, this aspect of the collections framework is poorly designed. In practice, there are two kinds of ordered collections, with very different performance tradeoffs. An ordered collection that is backed by an array has fast random access, and it makes sense to use the List methods with an integer index. In contrast, a linked list, while also ordered, has slow random access, and it is best traversed with an iterator. It would have been an easy matter to provide two interfaces.

NOTE: To avoid carrying out random access operations for linked lists, Java SE 1.4 introduced a tagging interface, RandomAccess. That interface has no methods, but you can use it to test whether a particular collection supports efficient random access:

```
if (c instanceof RandomAccess)
{
    use random access algorithm
}
else
{
    use sequential access algorithm
}
```

The Set interface is identical to the Collection interface, but the behavior of the methods is more tightly defined. The add method of a set should reject duplicates. The equals method of a set should be defined so that two sets are identical if they have the same elements, but not necessarily in the same order. The hashCode method should be defined so that two sets with the same elements yield the same hash code.

Why make a separate interface if the method signatures are the same? Conceptually, not all collections are sets. Making a Set interface enables programmers to write methods that accept only sets.

The SortedSet and SortedMap interfaces expose the comparator object used for sorting, and they define methods to obtain views of subsets of the collections. We discuss these in Section 9.4, "Views and Wrappers," on p. 509.

Finally, Java SE 6 introduced interfaces NavigableSet and NavigableMap that contain additional methods for searching and traversal in sorted sets and maps. (Ideally, these methods should have simply been included in the SortedSet and SortedMap interface.) The TreeSet and TreeMap classes implement these interfaces.

9.2 Concrete Collections

Table 9.1 shows the collections in the Java library and briefly describes the purpose of each collection class. (For simplicity, we omit the thread-safe collections that will be discussed in Chapter 14.) All classes in Table 9.1 implement the `Collection` interface, with the exception of the classes with names ending in `Map`. Those classes implement the `Map` interface instead. We will discuss maps in Section 9.3, "Maps," on p. 497.

Figure 9.5 shows the relationships between these classes.

Table 9.1 Concrete Collections in the Java Library

Collection Type	Description	See Page
ArrayList	An indexed sequence that grows and shrinks dynamically	484
LinkedList	An ordered sequence that allows efficient insertion and removal at any location	474
ArrayDeque	A double-ended queue that is implemented as a circular array	494
HashSet	An unordered collection that rejects duplicates	485
TreeSet	A sorted set	489
EnumSet	A set of enumerated type values	506
LinkedHashSet	A set that remembers the order in which elements were inserted	504
PriorityQueue	A collection that allows efficient removal of the smallest element	495
HashMap	A data structure that stores key/value associations	504
TreeMap	A map in which the keys are sorted	497
EnumMap	A map in which the keys belong to an enumerated type	506
LinkedHashMap	A map that remembers the order in which entries were added	504
WeakHashMap	A map with values that can be reclaimed by the garbage collector if they are not used elsewhere	504
IdentityHashMap	A map with keys that are compared by ==, not equals	507

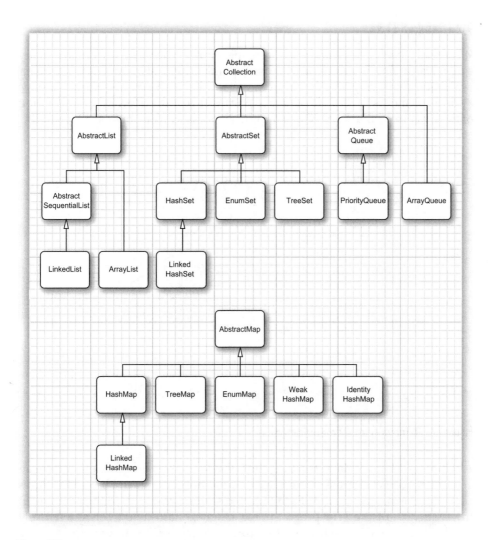

Figure 9.5 Classes in the collections framework

9.2.1 Linked Lists

We already used arrays and their dynamic cousin, the ArrayList class, for many examples in this book. However, arrays and array lists suffer from a major drawback. Removing an element from the middle of an array is expensive since all array elements beyond the removed one must be moved toward the beginning of the array (see Figure 9.6). The same is true for inserting elements in the middle.

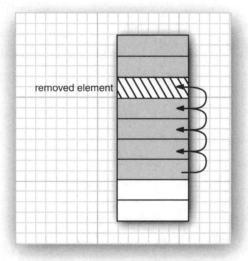

Figure 9.6 Removing an element from an array

Another well-known data structure, the *linked list*, solves this problem. Where an array stores object references in consecutive memory locations, a linked list stores each object in a separate *link*. Each link also stores a reference to the next link in the sequence. In the Java programming language, all linked lists are actually *doubly linked*; that is, each link also stores a reference to its predecessor (see Figure 9.7).

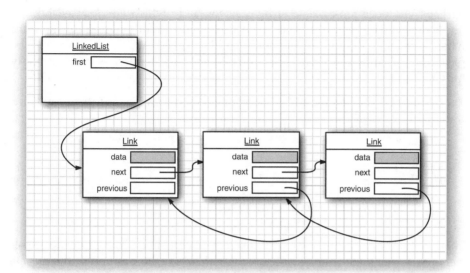

Figure 9.7 A doubly linked list

Removing an element from the middle of a linked list is an inexpensive operation—only the links around the element to be removed need to be updated (see Figure 9.8).

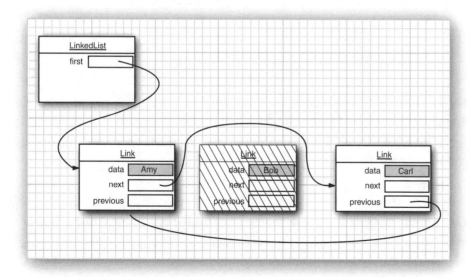

Figure 9.8 Removing an element from a linked list

Perhaps you once took a data structures course in which you learned how to implement linked lists. You may have bad memories of tangling up the links when removing or adding elements in the linked list. If so, you will be pleased to learn that the Java collections library supplies a class LinkedList ready for you to use.

The following code example adds three elements and then removes the second one:

```
List<String> staff = new LinkedList<>(); // LinkedList implements List
staff.add("Amy");
staff.add("Bob");
staff.add("Carl");
Iterator iter = staff.iterator();
String first = iter.next(); // visit first element
String second = iter.next(); // visit second element
iter.remove(); // remove last visited element
```

There is, however, an important difference between linked lists and generic collections. A linked list is an *ordered collection* in which the position of the objects matters. The LinkedList.add method adds the object to the end of the list. But you will often want to add objects somewhere in the middle of a list. This position-dependent add method is the responsibility of an iterator, since iterators describe positions in collections. Using iterators to add elements makes sense only for collections that have a natural ordering. For example, the *set* data type that we discuss in the next section does not impose any ordering on its elements. Therefore, there is no add method in the Iterator interface. Instead, the collections library supplies a subinterface ListIterator that contains an add method:

```
interface ListIterator<E> extends Iterator<E>
{
    void add(E element);
    . . .
}
```

Unlike Collection.add, this method does not return a boolean—it is assumed that the add operation always modifies the list.

In addition, the ListIterator interface has two methods that you can use for traversing a list backwards.

```
E previous()
boolean hasPrevious()
```

Like the next method, the previous method returns the object that it skipped over.

The listIterator method of the LinkedList class returns an iterator object that implements the ListIterator interface.

```
ListIterator<String> iter = staff.listIterator();
```

The add method adds the new element *before* the iterator position. For example, the following code skips past the first element in the linked list and adds "Juliet" before the second element (see Figure 9.9):

```
List<String> staff = new LinkedList<>();
staff.add("Amy");
staff.add("Bob");
staff.add("Carl");
ListIterator<String> iter = staff.listIterator();
iter.next(); // skip past first element
iter.add("Juliet");
```

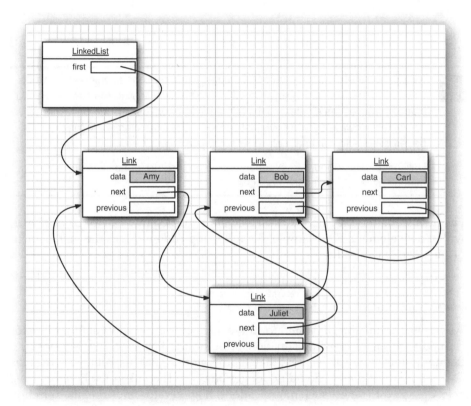

Figure 9.9 Adding an element to a linked list

If you call the add method multiple times, the elements are simply added in the order in which you supplied them. They are all added in turn before the current iterator position.

When you use the add operation with an iterator that was freshly returned from the listIterator method and that points to the beginning of the linked list, the newly added element becomes the new head of the list. When the iterator has passed the last element of the list (that is, when hasNext returns false), the added element becomes the new tail of the list. If the linked list has n elements, there are $n + 1$ spots for adding a new element. These spots correspond to the $n + 1$ possible positions of the iterator. For example, if a linked list contains three elements, A, B, and C, there are four possible positions (marked as |) for inserting a new element:

```
|ABC
A|BC
AB|C
ABC|
```

 NOTE: Be careful with the "cursor" analogy. The remove operation does not work exactly like the Backspace key. Immediately after a call to next, the remove method indeed removes the element to the left of the iterator, just like the Backspace key would. However, if you have just called previous, the element to the right will be removed. And you can't call remove twice in a row.

Unlike the add method, which depends only on the iterator position, the remove method depends on the iterator state.

Finally, a set method replaces the last element, returned by a call to next or previous, with a new element. For example, the following code replaces the first element of a list with a new value:

```
ListIterator<String> iter = list.listIterator();
String oldValue = iter.next(); // returns first element
iter.set(newValue); // sets first element to newValue
```

As you might imagine, if an iterator traverses a collection while another iterator is modifying it, confusing situations can occur. For example, suppose an iterator points before an element that another iterator has just removed. The iterator is now invalid and should no longer be used. The linked list iterators have been designed to detect such modifications. If an iterator finds that its collection has been modified by another iterator or by a method of the collection itself, it throws a ConcurrentModificationException. For example, consider the following code:

```
List<String> list = . . .;
ListIterator<String> iter1 = list.listIterator();
ListIterator<String> iter2 = list.listIterator();
iter1.next();
iter1.remove();
iter2.next(); // throws ConcurrentModificationException
```

The call to iter2.next throws a ConcurrentModificationException since iter2 detects that the list was modified externally.

To avoid concurrent modification exceptions, follow this simple rule: You can attach as many iterators to a collection as you like, provided that all of them are only readers. Alternatively, you can attach a single iterator that can both read and write.

Concurrent modification detection is done in a simple way. The collection keeps track of the number of mutating operations (such as adding and removing elements). Each iterator keeps a separate count of the number of mutating operations that *it* was responsible for. At the beginning of each iterator method, the iterator simply checks whether its own mutation count equals that of the collection. If not, it throws a ConcurrentModificationException.

 NOTE: There is, however, a curious exception to the detection of concurrent modifications. The linked list only keeps track of *structural* modifications to the list, such as adding and removing links. The set method does *not* count as a structural modification. You can attach multiple iterators to a linked list, all of which call set to change the contents of existing links. This capability is required for a number of algorithms in the Collections class that we discuss later in this chapter.

Now you have seen the fundamental methods of the LinkedList class. Use a ListIterator to traverse the elements of the linked list in either direction and to add and remove elements.

As you saw in the preceding section, many other useful methods for operating on linked lists are declared in the Collection interface. These are, for the most part, implemented in the AbstractCollection superclass of the LinkedList class. For example, the toString method invokes toString on all elements and produces one long string of the format [A, B, C]. This is handy for debugging. Use the contains method to check whether an element is present in a linked list. For example, the call staff.contains("Harry") returns true if the linked list already contains a string equal to the string "Harry".

The library also supplies a number of methods that are, from a theoretical perspective, somewhat dubious. Linked lists do not support fast random access. If you want to see the *n*th element of a linked list, you have to start at the beginning and skip past the first $n - 1$ elements. There is no shortcut. For that reason, programmers don't usually use linked lists in situations where elements need to be accessed by an integer index.

Nevertheless, the LinkedList class supplies a get method that lets you access a particular element:

```
LinkedList<String> list = . . .;
String obj = list.get(n);
```

Of course, this method is not very efficient. If you find yourself using it, you are probably using a wrong data structure for your problem.

You should *never* use this illusory random access method to step through a linked list. The code

```
for (int i = 0; i < list.size(); i++)
    do something with list.get(i);
```

is staggeringly inefficient. Each time you look up another element, the search starts again from the beginning of the list. The LinkedList object makes no effort to cache the position information.

 NOTE: The get method has one slight optimization: If the index is at least size() / 2, the search for the element starts at the end of the list.

The list iterator interface also has a method to tell you the index of the current position. In fact, since Java iterators conceptually point between elements, it has two of them: The nextIndex method returns the integer index of the element that would be returned by the next call to next; the previousIndex method returns the index of the element that would be returned by the next call to previous. Of course, that is simply one less than nextIndex. These methods are efficient—an iterator keeps a count of its current position. Finally, if you have an integer index n, then list.listIterator(n) returns an iterator that points just before the element with index n. That is, calling next yields the same element as list.get(n); obtaining that iterator is inefficient.

If you have a linked list with only a handful of elements, you don't have to be overly paranoid about the cost of the get and set methods. But then, why use a linked list in the first place? The only reason to use a linked list is to minimize the cost of insertion and removal in the middle of the list. If you have only a few elements, you can just use an ArrayList.

We recommend that you simply stay away from all methods that use an integer index to denote a position in a linked list. If you want random access into a collection, use an array or ArrayList, not a linked list.

The program in Listing 9.1 puts linked lists to work. It simply creates two lists, merges them, then removes every second element from the second list, and finally tests the removeAll method. We recommend that you trace the program flow and pay special attention to the iterators. You may find it helpful to draw diagrams of the iterator positions, like this:

```
|ACE   |BDFG
A|CE   |BDFG
AB|CE B|DFG
. . .
```

Note that the call

```
System.out.println(a);
```

prints all elements in the linked list a by invoking the toString method in AbstractCollection.

Listing 9.1 linkedList/LinkedListTest.java

```java
1  package linkedList;
2
3  import java.util.*;
4
5  /**
6   * This program demonstrates operations on linked lists.
7   * @version 1.11 2012-01-26
8   * @author Cay Horstmann
9   */
10 public class LinkedListTest
11 {
12    public static void main(String[] args)
13    {
14       List<String> a = new LinkedList<>();
15       a.add("Amy");
16       a.add("Carl");
17       a.add("Erica");
18
19       List<String> b = new LinkedList<>();
20       b.add("Bob");
21       b.add("Doug");
22       b.add("Frances");
23       b.add("Gloria");
24
25       // merge the words from b into a
26
27       ListIterator<String> aIter = a.listIterator();
28       Iterator<String> bIter = b.iterator();
29
30       while (bIter.hasNext())
31       {
```

(Continues)

Listing 9.1 *(Continued)*

```
32        if (aIter.hasNext()) aIter.next();
33        aIter.add(bIter.next());
34      }
35
36      System.out.println(a);
37
38      // remove every second word from b
39
40      bIter = b.iterator();
41      while (bIter.hasNext())
42      {
43        bIter.next(); // skip one element
44        if (bIter.hasNext())
45        {
46          bIter.next(); // skip next element
47          bIter.remove(); // remove that element
48        }
49      }
50
51      System.out.println(b);
52
53      // bulk operation: remove all words in b from a
54
55      a.removeAll(b);
56
57      System.out.println(a);
58    }
59 }
```

---

java.util.List<E> 1.2

- ListIterator<E> listIterator()

  returns a list iterator for visiting the elements of the list.

- ListIterator<E> listIterator(int index)

  returns a list iterator for visiting the elements of the list whose first call to next will return the element with the given index.

- void add(int i, E element)

  adds an element at the specified position.

- void addAll(int i, Collection<? extends E> elements)

  adds all elements from a collection to the specified position.

(Continues)

---

java.util.List<E> 1.2 *(Continued)*

- `E remove(int i)`

  removes and returns the element at the specified position.

- `E get(int i)`

  gets the element at the specified position.

- `E set(int i, E element)`

  replaces the element at the specified position with a new element and returns the old element.

- `int indexOf(Object element)`

  returns the position of the first occurrence of an element equal to the specified element, or -1 if no matching element is found.

- `int lastIndexOf(Object element)`

  returns the position of the last occurrence of an element equal to the specified element, or -1 if no matching element is found.

---

java.util.ListIterator<E> 1.2

- `void add(E newElement)`

  adds an element before the current position.

- `void set(E newElement)`

  replaces the last element visited by next or previous with a new element. Throws an IllegalStateException if the list structure was modified since the last call to next or previous.

- `boolean hasPrevious()`

  returns true if there is another element to visit when iterating backwards through the list.

- `E previous()`

  returns the previous object. Throws a NoSuchElementException if the beginning of the list has been reached.

- `int nextIndex()`

  returns the index of the element that would be returned by the next call to next.

- `int previousIndex()`

  returns the index of the element that would be returned by the next call to previous.

---

java.util.LinkedList<E> 1.2

- `LinkedList()`

  constructs an empty linked list.

- `LinkedList(Collection<? extends E> elements)`

  constructs a linked list and adds all elements from a collection.

- `void addFirst(E element)`
- `void addLast(E element)`

  adds an element to the beginning or the end of the list.

- `E getFirst()`
- `E getLast()`

  returns the element at the beginning or the end of the list.

- `E removeFirst()`
- `E removeLast()`

  removes and returns the element at the beginning or the end of the list.

9.2.2 Array Lists

In the preceding section, you saw the List interface and the LinkedList class that implements it. The List interface describes an ordered collection in which the position of elements matters. There are two protocols for visiting the elements: through an iterator and by random access with methods get and set. The latter is not appropriate for linked lists, but of course get and set make a lot of sense for arrays. The collections library supplies the familiar ArrayList class that also implements the List interface. An ArrayList encapsulates a dynamically reallocated array of objects.

 NOTE: If you are a veteran Java programmer, you may have used the Vector class whenever you need a dynamic array. Why use an ArrayList instead of a Vector? For one simple reason: All methods of the Vector class are *synchronized*. It is safe to access a Vector object from two threads. But if you access a vector from only a single thread—by far the more common case—your code wastes quite a bit of time with synchronization. In contrast, the ArrayList methods are not synchronized. We recommend that you use an ArrayList instead of a Vector whenever you don't need synchronization.

9.2.3 Hash Sets

Linked lists and arrays let you specify the order in which you want to arrange the elements. However, if you are looking for a particular element and don't remember its position, you need to visit all elements until you find a match. That can be time consuming if the collection contains many elements. If you don't care about the ordering of the elements, there are data structures that let you find elements much faster. The drawback is that those data structures give you no control over the order in which the elements appear. These data structures organize the elements in an order that is convenient for their own purposes.

A well-known data structure for finding objects quickly is the *hash table*. A hash table computes an integer, called the *hash code*, for each object. A hash code is somehow derived from the instance fields of an object, preferably in such a way that objects with different data yield different codes. Table 9.2 lists a few examples of hash codes that result from the hashCode method of the String class.

Table 9.2 Hash Codes Resulting from the hashCode Method

String	Hash Code
"Lee"	76268
"lee"	107020
"eel"	100300

If you define your own classes, you are responsible for implementing your own hashCode method—see Chapter 5 for more information. Your implementation needs to be compatible with the equals method: If a.equals(b), then a and b must have the same hash code.

What's important for now is that hash codes can be computed quickly and that the computation depends only on the state of the object that needs to be hashed, not on the other objects in the hash table.

In Java, hash tables are implemented as arrays of linked lists. Each list is called a *bucket* (see Figure 9.10). To find the place of an object in the table, compute its hash code and reduce it modulo the total number of buckets. The resulting number is the index of the bucket that holds the element. For example, if an object has hash code 76268 and there are 128 buckets, then the object is placed in bucket 108 (because the remainder 76268 % 128 is 108). Perhaps you are lucky and there is no other element in that bucket. Then, you simply insert the element into that bucket. Of course, sometimes you will hit a bucket that is already filled. This is called a *hash collision*. Then, compare the new object with all objects in that bucket to see if it is already present. If the hash codes are reasonably randomly distributed

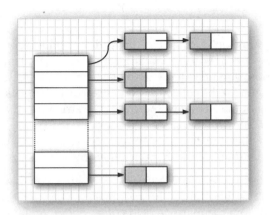

Figure 9.10 A hash table

and the number of buckets is large enough, only a few comparisons should be necessary.

 NOTE: As of Java SE 8, the buckets change from linked lists into balanced binary trees when they get full. This improves performance if a hash function was poorly chosen and yields many collisions, or if malicious code tries to flood a hash table with many values that have identical hash codes.

If you want more control over the performance of the hash table, you can specify the initial bucket count. The bucket count gives the number of buckets used to collect objects with identical hash values. If too many elements are inserted into a hash table, the number of collisions increases and retrieval performance suffers.

If you know how many elements, approximately, will eventually be in the table, you can set the bucket count. Typically, you should set it to somewhere between 75% and 150% of the expected element count. Some researchers believe that it is a good idea to make the bucket count a prime number to prevent a clustering of keys. The evidence for this isn't conclusive, however. The standard library uses bucket counts that are powers of 2, with a default of 16. (Any value you supply for the table size is automatically rounded to the next power of 2.)

Of course, you do not always know how many elements you need to store, or your initial guess may be too low. If the hash table gets too full, it needs to be *rehashed*. To rehash the table, a table with more buckets is created, all elements are inserted into the new table, and the original table is discarded. The *load factor* determines when a hash table is rehashed. For example, if the load factor is 0.75

(which is the default) and the table is more than 75% full, it is automatically re-hashed with twice as many buckets. For most applications, it is reasonable to leave the load factor at 0.75.

Hash tables can be used to implement several important data structures. The simplest among them is the *set* type. A set is a collection of elements without duplicates. The add method of a set first tries to find the object to be added, and adds it only if it is not yet present.

The Java collections library supplies a HashSet class that implements a set based on a hash table. You add elements with the add method. The contains method is re-defined to make a fast lookup to see if an element is already present in the set. It checks only the elements in one bucket and not all elements in the collection.

The hash set iterator visits all buckets in turn. Since hashing scatters the elements around in the table, they are visited in a seemingly random order. You would only use a HashSet if you don't care about the ordering of the elements in the collection.

The sample program at the end of this section (Listing 9.2) reads words from System.in, adds them to a set, and finally prints out the first twenty words in the set. For example, you can feed the program the text from *Alice in Wonderland* (which you can obtain from www.gutenberg.org) by launching it from a command shell as

```
java SetTest < alice30.txt
```

The program reads all words from the input and adds them to the hash set. It then iterates through the unique words in the set and finally prints out a count. (*Alice in Wonderland* has 5,909 unique words, including the copyright notice at the beginning.) The words appear in random order.

 CAUTION: Be careful when you mutate set elements. If the hash code of an element were to change, the element would no longer be in the correct position in the data structure.

Listing 9.2 set/SetTest.java

```
1  package set;
2
3  import java.util.*;
4
5  /**
6   * This program uses a set to print all unique words in System.in.
```

(Continues)

Listing 9.2 *(Continued)*

```
7    * @version 1.12 2015-06-21
8    * @author Cay Horstmann
9    */
10   public class SetTest
11   {
12      public static void main(String[] args)
13      {
14         Set<String> words = new HashSet<>(); // HashSet implements Set
15         long totalTime = 0;
16
17         try (Scanner in = new Scanner(System.in))
18         {
19            while (in.hasNext())
20            {
21               String word = in.next();
22               long callTime = System.currentTimeMillis();
23               words.add(word);
24               callTime = System.currentTimeMillis() - callTime;
25               totalTime += callTime;
26            }
27         }
28
29         Iterator<String> iter = words.iterator();
30         for (int i = 1; i <= 20 && iter.hasNext(); i++)
31            System.out.println(iter.next());
32         System.out.println(". . .");
33         System.out.println(words.size() + " distinct words. " + totalTime + " milliseconds.");
34      }
35   }
```

---

java.util.HashSet<E> 1.2

- HashSet()

  constructs an empty hash set.

- HashSet(Collection<? extends E> elements)

  constructs a hash set and adds all elements from a collection.

- HashSet(int initialCapacity)

  constructs an empty hash set with the specified capacity (number of buckets).

- HashSet(int initialCapacity, float loadFactor)

  constructs an empty hash set with the specified capacity and load factor (a number between 0.0 and 1.0 that determines at what percentage of fullness the hash table will be rehashed into a larger one).

---

java.lang.Object 1.0

- int hashCode()

  returns a hash code for this object. A hash code can be any integer, positive or negative. The definitions of equals and hashCode must be compatible: If x.equals(y) is true, then x.hashCode() must be the same value as y.hashCode().

9.2.4 Tree Sets

The TreeSet class is similar to the hash set, with one added improvement. A tree set is a *sorted collection.* You insert elements into the collection in any order. When you iterate through the collection, the values are automatically presented in sorted order. For example, suppose you insert three strings and then visit all elements that you added.

```
SortedSet<String> sorter = new TreeSet<>(); // TreeSet implements SortedSet
sorter.add("Bob");
sorter.add("Amy");
sorter.add("Carl");
for (String s : sorter) System.println(s);
```

Then, the values are printed in sorted order: Amy Bob Carl. As the name of the class suggests, the sorting is accomplished by a tree data structure. (The current implementation uses a *red-black tree.* For a detailed description of red-black trees see, for example, *Introduction to Algorithms* by Thomas Cormen, Charles Leiserson, Ronald Rivest, and Clifford Stein, The MIT Press, 2009.) Every time an element is added to a tree, it is placed into its proper sorting position. Therefore, the iterator always visits the elements in sorted order.

Adding an element to a tree is slower than adding it to a hash table—see Table 9.3 for a comparison. But it is still much faster than checking for duplicates in an array or linked list. If the tree contains n elements, then an average of $\log_2 n$ comparisons are required to find the correct position for the new element. For example, if the tree already contains 1,000 elements, adding a new element requires about 10 comparisons.

NOTE: In order to use a tree set, you must be able to compare the elements. The elements must implement the Comparable interface (see Section 6.1.1, "The Interface Concept," on p. 288), or you must supply a Comparator when constructing the set (see Section 6.2.2, "The Comparator Interface," on p. 305 and Section 6.3.8, "More about Comparators," on p. 328).

Table 9.3 Adding Elements into Hash and Tree Sets

Document	Total Number of Words	Number of Distinct Words	HashSet	TreeSet
Alice in Wonderland	28195	5909	5 sec	7 sec
The Count of Monte Cristo	466300	37545	75 sec	98 sec

If you look back at Table 9.3, you may well wonder if you should always use a tree set instead of a hash set. After all, adding elements does not seem to take much longer, and the elements are automatically sorted. The answer depends on the data that you are collecting. If you don't need the data sorted, there is no reason to pay for the sorting overhead. More important, with some data it is much more difficult to come up with a sort order than a hash function. A hash function only needs to do a reasonably good job of scrambling the objects, whereas a comparison function must tell objects apart with complete precision.

To make this distinction more concrete, consider the task of collecting a set of rectangles. If you use a TreeSet, you need to supply a Comparator<Rectangle>. How do you compare two rectangles? By area? That doesn't work. You can have two different rectangles with different coordinates but the same area. The sort order for a tree must be a *total ordering*. Any two elements must be comparable, and the comparison can only be zero if the elements are equal. There is such a sort order for rectangles (the lexicographic ordering on its coordinates), but it is unnatural and cumbersome to compute. In contrast, a hash function is already defined for the Rectangle class. It simply hashes the coordinates.

 NOTE: As of Java SE 6, the TreeSet class implements the NavigableSet interface. That interface adds several convenient methods for locating elements and for backward traversal. See the API notes for details.

The program in Listing 9.3 builds two tree sets of Item objects. The first one is sorted by part number, the default sort order of Item objects. The second set is sorted by description, using a custom comparator.

Listing 9.3 treeSet/TreeSetTest.java

```
1 package treeSet;
2
3 import java.util.*;
4
```

```
 5   /**
 6    * This program sorts a set of item by comparing their descriptions.
 7    * @version 1.12 2015-06-21
 8    * @author Cay Horstmann
 9    */
10   public class TreeSetTest
11   {
12      public static void main(String[] args)
13      {
14         SortedSet<Item> parts = new TreeSet<>();
15         parts.add(new Item("Toaster", 1234));
16         parts.add(new Item("Widget", 4562));
17         parts.add(new Item("Modem", 9912));
18         System.out.println(parts);
19
20         NavigableSet<Item> sortByDescription = new TreeSet<>(
21               Comparator.comparing(Item::getDescription));
22
23         sortByDescription.addAll(parts);
24         System.out.println(sortByDescription);
25      }
26   }
```

Listing 9.4 treeSet/Item.java

```
 1   package treeSet;
 2
 3   import java.util.*;
 4
 5   /**
 6    * An item with a description and a part number.
 7    */
 8   public class Item implements Comparable<Item>
 9   {
10      private String description;
11      private int partNumber;
12
13      /**
14       * Constructs an item.
15       *
16       * @param aDescription
17       *            the item's description
18       * @param aPartNumber
19       *            the item's part number
20       */
```

(Continues)

Listing 9.4 *(Continued)*

```java
21     public Item(String aDescription, int aPartNumber)
22     {
23        description = aDescription;
24        partNumber = aPartNumber;
25     }
26
27     /**
28      * Gets the description of this item.
29      *
30      * @return the description
31      */
32     public String getDescription()
33     {
34        return description;
35     }
36
37     public String toString()
38     {
39        return "[descripion=" + description + ", partNumber=" + partNumber + "]";
40     }
41
42     public boolean equals(Object otherObject)
43     {
44        if (this == otherObject) return true;
45        if (otherObject == null) return false;
46        if (getClass() != otherObject.getClass()) return false;
47        Item other = (Item) otherObject;
48        return Objects.equals(description, other.description) && partNumber == other.partNumber;
49     }
50
51     public int hashCode()
52     {
53        return Objects.hash(description, partNumber);
54     }
55
56     public int compareTo(Item other)
57     {
58        int diff = Integer.compare(partNumber, other.partNumber);
59        return diff != 0 ? diff : description.compareTo(other.description);
60     }
61  }
```

---

java.util.TreeSet<E> 1.2

- TreeSet()
- TreeSet(Comparator<? super E> comparator)

constructs an empty tree set.

- TreeSet(Collection<? extends E> elements)
- TreeSet(SortedSet<E> s)

constructs a tree set and adds all elements from a collection or sorted set (in the latter case, using the same ordering).

---

java.util.SortedSet<E> 1.2

- Comparator<? super E> comparator()

returns the comparator used for sorting the elements, or null if the elements are compared with the compareTo method of the Comparable interface.

- E first()
- E last()

returns the smallest or largest element in the sorted set.

---

java.util.NavigableSet<E> 6

- E higher(E value)
- E lower(E value)

returns the least element > value or the largest element < value, or null if there is no such element.

- E ceiling(E value)
- E floor(E value)

returns the least element >= value or the largest element <= value, or null if there is no such element.

- E pollFirst()
- E pollLast

removes and returns the smallest or largest element in this set, or null if the set is empty.

- Iterator<E> descendingIterator()

returns an iterator that traverses this set in descending direction.

9.2.5 Queues and Deques

As we already discussed, a queue lets you efficiently add elements at the tail and remove elements from the head. A double-ended queue, or *deque*, lets you efficiently add or remove elements at the head and tail. Adding elements in the middle is not supported. Java SE 6 introduced a Deque interface. It is implemented by the ArrayDeque and LinkedList classes, both of which provide deques whose size grows as needed. In Chapter 14, you will see bounded queues and deques.

---

java.util.Queue<E> 5.0

- • boolean add(E element)
- • boolean offer(E element)

  adds the given element to the tail of this deque and returns true, provided the queue is not full. If the queue is full, the first method throws an IllegalStateException, whereas the second method returns false.

- • E remove()
- • E poll()

  removes and returns the element at the head of this queue, provided the queue is not empty. If the queue is empty, the first method throws a NoSuchElementException, whereas the second method returns null.

- • E element()
- • E peek()

  returns the element at the head of this queue without removing it, provided the queue is not empty. If the queue is empty, the first method throws a NoSuchElementException, whereas the second method returns null.

---

java.util.Deque<E> 6

- • void addFirst(E element)
- • void addLast(E element)
- • boolean offerFirst(E element)
- • boolean offerLast(E element)

  adds the given element to the head or tail of this deque. If the queue is full, the first two methods throw an IllegalStateException, whereas the last two methods return false.

(Continues)

---

java.util.Deque<E> 6 *(Continued)*

- E removeFirst()
- E removeLast()
- E pollFirst()
- E pollLast()

removes and returns the element at the head of this queue, provided the queue is not empty. If the queue is empty, the first two methods throw a NoSuchElementException, whereas the last two methods return null.

- E getFirst()
- E getLast()
- E peekFirst()
- E peekLast()

returns the element at the head of this queue without removing it, provided the queue is not empty. If the queue is empty, the first two methods throw a NoSuchElementException, whereas the last two methods return null.

---

java.util.ArrayDeque<E> 6

- ArrayDeque()
- ArrayDeque(int initialCapacity)

constructs an unbounded deque with an initial capacity of 16 or the given initial capacity.

9.2.6 Priority Queues

A priority queue retrieves elements in sorted order after they were inserted in arbitrary order. That is, whenever you call the remove method, you get the smallest element currently in the priority queue. However, the priority queue does not sort all its elements. If you iterate over the elements, they are not necessarily sorted. The priority queue makes use of an elegant and efficient data structure called a *heap*. A heap is a self-organizing binary tree in which the add and remove operations cause the smallest element to gravitate to the root, without wasting time on sorting all elements.

Just like a TreeSet, a priority queue can either hold elements of a class that implements the Comparable interface or a Comparator object you supply in the constructor.

A typical use for a priority queue is job scheduling. Each job has a priority. Jobs are added in random order. Whenever a new job can be started, the highest priority job is removed from the queue. (Since it is traditional for priority 1 to be the "highest" priority, the remove operation yields the minimum element.)

Listing 9.5 shows a priority queue in action. Unlike iteration in a TreeSet, the iteration here does not visit the elements in sorted order. However, removal always yields the smallest remaining element.

Listing 9.5 priorityQueue/PriorityQueueTest.java

```
 1  package priorityQueue;
 2
 3  import java.util.*;
 4  import java.time.*;
 5
 6  /**
 7   * This program demonstrates the use of a priority queue.
 8   * @version 1.01 2012-01-26
 9   * @author Cay Horstmann
10   */
11  public class PriorityQueueTest
12  {
13     public static void main(String[] args)
14     {
15        PriorityQueue<LocalDate> pq = new PriorityQueue<>();
16        pq.add(LocalDate.of(1906, 12, 9)); // G. Hopper
17        pq.add(LocalDate.of(1815, 12, 10)); // A. Lovelace
18        pq.add(LocalDate.of(1903, 12, 3)); // J. von Neumann
19        pq.add(LocalDate.of(1910, 6, 22)); // K. Zuse
20
21        System.out.println("Iterating over elements...");
22        for (LocalDate date : pq)
23           System.out.println(date);
24        System.out.println("Removing elements...");
25        while (!pq.isEmpty())
26           System.out.println(pq.remove());
27     }
28  }
```

---

java.util.PriorityQueue 5.0

- PriorityQueue()
- PriorityQueue(int initialCapacity)

  constructs a priority queue for storing Comparable objects.

- PriorityQueue(int initialCapacity, Comparator<? super E> c)

  constructs a priority queue and uses the specified comparator for sorting its elements.

9.3 Maps

A set is a collection that lets you quickly find an existing element. However, to look up an element, you need to have an exact copy of the element to find. That isn't a very common lookup—usually, you have some key information, and you want to look up the associated element. The *map* data structure serves that purpose. A map stores key/value pairs. You can find a value if you provide the key. For example, you may store a table of employee records, where the keys are the employee IDs and the values are Employee objects. In the following sections, you will learn how to work with maps.

9.3.1 Basic Map Operations

The Java library supplies two general-purpose implementations for maps: HashMap and TreeMap. Both classes implement the Map interface.

A hash map hashes the keys, and a tree map uses an ordering on the keys to organize them in a search tree. The hash or comparison function is applied *only to the keys*. The values associated with the keys are not hashed or compared.

Should you choose a hash map or a tree map? As with sets, hashing is usually a bit faster, and it is the preferred choice if you don't need to visit the keys in sorted order.

Here is how you set up a hash map for storing employees:

```
Map<String, Employee> staff = new HashMap<>(); // HashMap implements Map
Employee harry = new Employee("Harry Hacker");
staff.put("987-98-9996", harry);
. . .
```

Whenever you add an object to a map, you must supply a key as well. In our case, the key is a string, and the corresponding value is an Employee object.

To retrieve an object, you must use (and, therefore, remember) the key.

```
String id = "987-98-9996";
e = staff.get(id); // gets harry
```

If no information is stored in the map with the particular key specified, get returns null.

The null return value can be inconvenient. Sometimes, you have a good default that can be used for keys that are not present in the map. Then use the getOrDefault method.

```
Map<String, Integer> scores = . . .;
int score = scores.get(id, 0); // Gets 0 if the id is not present
```

Keys must be unique. You cannot store two values with the same key. If you call the put method twice with the same key, the second value replaces the first one. In fact, put returns the previous value associated with its key parameter.

The remove method removes an element with a given key from the map. The size method returns the number of entries in the map.

The easiest way of iterating over the keys and values of a map is the forEach method. Provide a lambda expression that receives a key and a value. That expression is invoked for each map entry in turn.

```
scores.forEach((k, v) ->
   System.out.println("key=" + k + ", value=" + v));
```

Listing 9.6 illustrates a map at work. We first add key/value pairs to a map. Then, we remove one key from the map, which removes its associated value as well. Next, we change the value that is associated with a key and call the get method to look up a value. Finally, we iterate through the entry set.

Listing 9.6   map/MapTest.java

```java
1  package map;
2
3  import java.util.*;
4
5  /**
6   * This program demonstrates the use of a map with key type String and value type Employee.
7   * @version 1.11 2012-01-26
8   * @author Cay Horstmann
9   */
10 public class MapTest
11 {
12    public static void main(String[] args)
13    {
14       Map<String, Employee> staff = new HashMap<>();
15       staff.put("144-25-5464", new Employee("Amy Lee"));
16       staff.put("567-24-2546", new Employee("Harry Hacker"));
17       staff.put("157-62-7935", new Employee("Gary Cooper"));
18       staff.put("456-62-5527", new Employee("Francesca Cruz"));
19
20       // print all entries
21
22       System.out.println(staff);
23
24       // remove an entry
25
```

```
26          staff.remove("567-24-2546");
27
28          // replace an entry
29
30          staff.put("456-62-5527", new Employee("Francesca Miller"));
31
32          // look up a value
33
34          System.out.println(staff.get("157-62-7935"));
35
36          // iterate through all entries
37
38          staff.forEach((k, v) ->
39              System.out.println("key=" + k + ", value=" + v));
40      }
41 }
```

---

java.util.Map<K, V> 1.2

- V get(Object key)

  gets the value associated with the key; returns the object associated with the key, or null if the key is not found in the map. Implementing classes may forbid null keys.

- default V getOrDefault(Object key, V defaultValue)

  gets the value associated with the key; returns the object associated with the key, or defaultValue if the key is not found in the map.

- V put(K key, V value)

  puts the association of a key and a value into the map. If the key is already present, the new object replaces the old one previously associated with the key. This method returns the old value of the key, or null if the key was not previously present. Implementing classes may forbid null keys or values.

- void putAll(Map<? extends K, ? extends V> entries)

  adds all entries from the specified map to this map.

- boolean containsKey(Object key)

  returns true if the key is present in the map.

- boolean containsValue(Object value)

  returns true if the value is present in the map.

- default void forEach(BiConsumer<? super K,? super V> action) 8

  Applies the action to all key/value pairs of this map.

---

java.util.HashMap<K, V> 1.2

- HashMap()
- HashMap(int initialCapacity)
- HashMap(int initialCapacity, float loadFactor)

  constructs an empty hash map with the specified capacity and load factor (a number between 0.0 and 1.0 that determines at what percentage of fullness the hash table will be rehashed into a larger one). The default load factor is 0.75.

---

java.util.TreeMap<K,V> 1.2

- TreeMap()

  constructs an empty tree map for keys that implement the Comparable interface.

- TreeMap(Comparator<? super K> c)

  constructs a tree map and uses the specified comparator for sorting its keys.

- TreeMap(Map<? extends K, ? extends V> entries)

  constructs a tree map and adds all entries from a map.

- TreeMap(SortedMap<? extends K, ? extends V> entries)

  constructs a tree map, adds all entries from a sorted map, and uses the same element comparator as the given sorted map.

---

java.util.SortedMap<K, V> 1.2

- Comparator<? super K> comparator()

  returns the comparator used for sorting the keys, or null if the keys are compared with the compareTo method of the Comparable interface.

- K firstKey()
- K lastKey()

  returns the smallest or largest key in the map.

9.3.2 Updating Map Entries

A tricky part of dealing with maps is updating an entry. Normally, you get the old value associated with a key, update it, and put back the updated value. But you have to worry about the special case of the first occurrence of a key. Consider using a map for counting how often a word occurs in a file. When we see a word, we'd like to increment a counter like this:

```
counts.put(word, counts.get(word) + 1);
```

That works, except in the case when word is encountered for the first time. Then get returns null, and a NullPointerException occurs.

A simple remedy is to use the getOrDefault method:

```
counts.put(word, counts.getOrDefault(word, 0) + 1);
```

Another approach is to first call the putIfAbsent method. It only puts a value if the key was previously absent.

```
counts.putIfAbsent(word, 0);
counts.put(word, counts.get(word) + 1); // Now we know that get will succeed
```

But you can do better than that. The merge method simplifies this common operation. The call

```
counts.merge(word, 1, Integer::sum);
```

associates word with 1 if the key wasn't previously present, and otherwise combines the previous value and 1, using the Integer::sum function.

The API notes describe other methods for updating map entries that are less commonly used.

---

java.util.Map<K, V> 1.2

- default V merge(K key, V value, BiFunction<? super V,? super V,? extends V> remappingFunction) 8

  If key is associated with a non-null value v, applies the function to v and value and either associates key with the result or, if the result is null, removes the key. Otherwise, associates key with value. Returns get(key).

- default V compute(K key, BiFunction<? super K,? super V,? extends V> remappingFunction) 8

  Applies the function to key and get(key). Either associates key with the result or, if the result is null, removes the key. Returns get(key).

- default V computeIfPresent(K key, BiFunction<? super K,? super V,? extends V> remappingFunction) 8

  If key is associated with a non-null value v, applies the function to key and v and either associates key with the result or, if the result is null, removes the key. Returns get(key).

- default V computeIfAbsent(K key, Function<? super K,? extends V> mappingFunction) 8

  Applies the function to key unless key is associated with a non-null value. Either associates key with the result or, if the result is null, removes the key. Returns get(key).

(Continues)

---

java.util.Map<K, V> 1.2 *(Continued)*

- default void replaceAll(BiFunction<? super K,? super V,? extends V> function) 8

  Calls the function on all entries. Associates keys with non-null results and removes keys with null results.

9.3.3 Map Views

The collections framework does not consider a map itself as a collection. (Other frameworks for data structures consider a map as a collection of key/value pairs, or as a collection of values indexed by the keys.) However, you can obtain *views* of the map—objects that implement the Collection interface or one of its subinterfaces.

There are three views: the set of keys, the collection of values (which is not a set), and the set of key/value pairs. The keys and key/value pairs form a set because there can be only one copy of a key in a map. The methods

```
Set<K> keySet()
Collection<V> values()
Set<Map.Entry<K, V>> entrySet()
```

return these three views. (The elements of the entry set are objects of a class implementing the Map.Entry interface.)

Note that the keySet is *not* a HashSet or TreeSet, but an object of some other class that implements the Set interface. The Set interface extends the Collection interface. Therefore, you can use a keySet as you would use any collection.

For example, you can enumerate all keys of a map:

```
Set<String> keys = map.keySet();
for (String key : keys)
{
    do something with key
}
```

If you want to look at both keys and values, you can avoid value lookups by enumerating the *entries*. Use the following code skeleton:

```
for (Map.Entry<String, Employee> entry : staff.entrySet())
{
    String k = entry.getKey();
    Employee v = entry.getValue();
    do something with k, v
}
```

TIP: This used to be the most efficient way of visiting all map entries. Nowadays, simply use the forEach method:

```
counts.forEach((k, v) -> {
    do something with k, v
});
```

If you invoke the remove method of the iterator on the key set view, you actually remove the key *and its associated value* from the map. However, you cannot *add* an element to the key set view. It makes no sense to add a key without also adding a value. If you try to invoke the add method, it throws an UnsupportedOperationException. The entry set view has the same restriction, even though it would make conceptual sense to add a new key/value pair.

---

java.util.Map<K, V> 1.2

- Set<Map.Entry<K, V>> entrySet()

  returns a set view of Map.Entry objects, the key/value pairs in the map. You can remove elements from this set and they are removed from the map, but you cannot add any elements.

- Set<K> keySet()

  returns a set view of all keys in the map. You can remove elements from this set and the keys and associated values are removed from the map, but you cannot add any elements.

- Collection<V> values()

  returns a collection view of all values in the map. You can remove elements from this set and the removed value and its key are removed from the map, but you cannot add any elements.

---

java.util.Map.Entry<K, V> 1.2

- K getKey()
- V getValue()

  returns the key or value of this entry.

- V setValue(V newValue)

  changes the value *in the associated map* to the new value and returns the old value.

9.3.4 Weak Hash Maps

The collection class library has several map classes for specialized needs that we briefly discuss in this and the following sections.

The WeakHashMap class was designed to solve an interesting problem. What happens with a value whose key is no longer used anywhere in your program? Suppose the last reference to a key has gone away. Then, there is no longer any way to refer to the value object. But, as no part of the program has the key any more, the key/value pair cannot be removed from the map. Why can't the garbage collector remove it? Isn't it the job of the garbage collector to remove unused objects?

Unfortunately, it isn't quite so simple. The garbage collector traces *live* objects. As long as the map object is live, *all* buckets in it are live and won't be reclaimed. Thus, your program should take care to remove unused values from long-lived maps. Or, you can use a WeakHashMap instead. This data structure cooperates with the garbage collector to remove key/value pairs when the only reference to the key is the one from the hash table entry.

Here are the inner workings of this mechanism. The WeakHashMap uses *weak references* to hold keys. A WeakReference object holds a reference to another object—in our case, a hash table key. Objects of this type are treated in a special way by the garbage collector. Normally, if the garbage collector finds that a particular object has no references to it, it simply reclaims the object. However, if the object is reachable *only* by a WeakReference, the garbage collector still reclaims the object, but places the weak reference that led to it into a queue. The operations of the WeakHashMap periodically check that queue for newly arrived weak references. The arrival of a weak reference in the queue signifies that the key was no longer used by anyone and has been collected. The WeakHashMap then removes the associated entry.

9.3.5 Linked Hash Sets and Maps

The LinkedHashSet and LinkedHashMap classes remember in which order you inserted items. That way, you can avoid the seemingly random order of items in a hash table. As entries are inserted into the table, they are joined in a doubly linked list (see Figure 9.11).

For example, consider the following map insertions from Listing 9.6:

```
Map<String, Employee> staff = new LinkedHashMap<>();
staff.put("144-25-5464", new Employee("Amy Lee"));
staff.put("567-24-2546", new Employee("Harry Hacker"));
staff.put("157-62-7935", new Employee("Gary Cooper"));
staff.put("456-62-5527", new Employee("Francesca Cruz"));
```

Then, staff.keySet().iterator() enumerates the keys in this order:

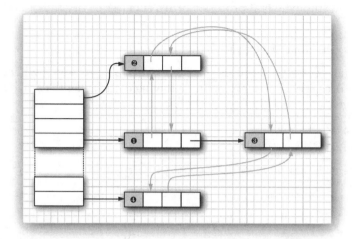

Figure 9.11 A linked hash table

```
144-25-5464
567-24-2546
157-62-7935
456-62-5527
```

and `staff.values().iterator()` enumerates the values in this order:

```
Amy Lee
Harry Hacker
Gary Cooper
Francesca Cruz
```

A linked hash map can alternatively use *access order*, not insertion order, to iterate through the map entries. Every time you call `get` or `put`, the affected entry is removed from its current position and placed at the *end* of the linked list of entries. (Only the position in the linked list of entries is affected, not the hash table bucket. An entry always stays in the bucket that corresponds to the hash code of the key.) To construct such a hash map, call

```
LinkedHashMap<K, V>(initialCapacity, loadFactor, true)
```

Access order is useful for implementing a "least recently used" discipline for a cache. For example, you may want to keep frequently accessed entries in memory and read less frequently accessed objects from a database. When you don't find an entry in the table, and the table is already pretty full, you can get an iterator into the table and remove the first few elements that it enumerates. Those entries were the least recently used ones.

You can even automate that process. Form a subclass of LinkedHashMap and override the method

```
protected boolean removeEldestEntry(Map.Entry<K, V> eldest)
```

Adding a new entry then causes the eldest entry to be removed whenever your method returns true. For example, the following cache is kept at a size of at most 100 elements:

```
Map<K, V> cache = new
    LinkedHashMap<>(128, 0.75F, true)
    {
        protected boolean removeEldestEntry(Map.Entry<K, V> eldest)
        {
            return size() > 100;
        }
    }();
```

Alternatively, you can consider the eldest entry to decide whether to remove it. For example, you may want to check a time stamp stored with the entry.

9.3.6 Enumeration Sets and Maps

The EnumSet is an efficient set implementation with elements that belong to an enumerated type. Since an enumerated type has a finite number of instances, the EnumSet is internally implemented simply as a sequence of bits. A bit is turned on if the corresponding value is present in the set.

The EnumSet class has no public constructors. Use a static factory method to construct the set:

```
enum Weekday { MONDAY, TUESDAY, WEDNESDAY, THURSDAY, FRIDAY, SATURDAY, SUNDAY };
EnumSet<Weekday> always = EnumSet.allOf(Weekday.class);
EnumSet<Weekday> never = EnumSet.noneOf(Weekday.class);
EnumSet<Weekday> workday = EnumSet.range(Weekday.MONDAY, Weekday.FRIDAY);
EnumSet<Weekday> mwf = EnumSet.of(Weekday.MONDAY, Weekday.WEDNESDAY, Weekday.FRIDAY);
```

You can use the usual methods of the Set interface to modify an EnumSet.

An EnumMap is a map with keys that belong to an enumerated type. It is simply and efficiently implemented as an array of values. You need to specify the key type in the constructor:

```
EnumMap<Weekday, Employee> personInCharge = new EnumMap<>(Weekday.class);
```

NOTE: In the API documentation for `EnumSet`, you will see odd-looking type parameters of the form `E extends Enum<E>`. This simply means "E is an enumerated type." All enumerated types extend the generic `Enum` class. For example, `Weekday` extends `Enum<Weekday>`.

9.3.7 Identity Hash Maps

The `IdentityHashMap` has a quite specialized purpose. Here, the hash values for the keys should not be computed by the `hashCode` method but by the `System.identityHashCode` method. That's the method that `Object.hashCode` uses to compute a hash code from the object's memory address. Also, for comparison of objects, the `IdentityHashMap` uses `==`, not `equals`.

In other words, different key objects are considered distinct even if they have equal contents. This class is useful for implementing object traversal algorithms, such as object serialization, in which you want to keep track of which objects have already been traversed.

---

java.util.WeakHashMap<K, V> 1.2

- `WeakHashMap()`
- `WeakHashMap(int initialCapacity)`
- `WeakHashMap(int initialCapacity, float loadFactor)`

  constructs an empty hash map with the specified capacity and load factor.

---

java.util.LinkedHashSet<E> 1.4

- `LinkedHashSet()`
- `LinkedHashSet(int initialCapacity)`
- `LinkedHashSet(int initialCapacity, float loadFactor)`

  constructs an empty linked hash set with the specified capacity and load factor.

---

java.util.LinkedHashMap<K, V> 1.4

- LinkedHashMap()
- LinkedHashMap(int initialCapacity)
- LinkedHashMap(int initialCapacity, float loadFactor)
- LinkedHashMap(int initialCapacity, float loadFactor, boolean accessOrder)

  constructs an empty linked hash map with the specified capacity, load factor, and ordering. The accessOrder parameter is true for access order, false for insertion order.

- protected boolean removeEldestEntry(Map.Entry<K, V> eldest)

  should be overridden to return true if you want the eldest entry to be removed. The eldest parameter is the entry whose removal is being contemplated. This method is called after an entry has been added to the map. The default implementation returns false—old elements are not removed by default. However, you can redefine this method to selectively return true—for example, if the eldest entry fits a certain condition or if the map exceeds a certain size.

---

java.util.EnumSet<E extends Enum<E>> 5.0

- static <E extends Enum<E>> EnumSet<E> allOf(Class<E> enumType)

  returns a set that contains all values of the given enumerated type.

- static <E extends Enum<E>> EnumSet<E> noneOf(Class<E> enumType)

  returns an empty set, capable of holding values of the given enumerated type.

- static <E extends Enum<E>> EnumSet<E> range(E from, E to)

  returns a set that contains all values between from and to (inclusive).

- static <E extends Enum<E>> EnumSet<E> of(E value)
- static <E extends Enum<E>> EnumSet<E> of(E value, E... values)

  returns a set that contains the given values.

---

java.util.EnumMap<K extends Enum<K>, V> 5.0

- EnumMap(Class<K> keyType)

  constructs an empty map whose keys have the given type.

`java.util.IdentityHashMap<K, V>` 1.4

- `IdentityHashMap()`
- `IdentityHashMap(int expectedMaxSize)`

  constructs an empty identity hash map whose capacity is the smallest power of 2 exceeding 1.5 × `expectedMaxSize`. (The default for `expectedMaxSize` is 21.)

`java.lang.System` 1.0

- `static int identityHashCode(Object obj)` 1.1

  returns the same hash code (derived from the object's memory address) that `Object.hashCode` computes, even if the class to which `obj` belongs has redefined the hashCode method.

9.4 Views and Wrappers

If you look at Figures 9.4 and 9.5, you might think it is overkill to have lots of interfaces and abstract classes to implement a modest number of concrete collection classes. However, these figures don't tell the whole story. By using *views*, you can obtain other objects that implement the `Collection` or `Map` interfaces. You saw one example of this with the `keySet` method of the map classes. At first glance, it appears as if the method creates a new set, fills it with all the keys of the map, and returns it. However, that is not the case. Instead, the `keySet` method returns an object of a class that implements the `Set` interface and whose methods manipulate the original map. Such a collection is called a *view*.

The technique of views has a number of useful applications in the collections framework. We will discuss these applications in the following sections.

9.4.1 Lightweight Collection Wrappers

The static `asList` method of the `Arrays` class returns a `List` wrapper around a plain Java array. This method lets you pass the array to a method that expects a list or collection argument. For example:

```
Card[] cardDeck = new Card[52];
. . .
List<Card> cardList = Arrays.asList(cardDeck);
```

The returned object is *not* an `ArrayList`. It is a view object with `get` and `set` methods that access the underlying array. All methods that would change the size of the array (such as the add and remove methods of the associated iterator) throw an UnsupportedOperationException.

The asList method can receive a variable number of arguments. For example:

```
List<String> names = Arrays.asList("Amy", "Bob", "Carl");
```

The method call

```
Collections.nCopies(n, anObject)
```

returns an immutable object that implements the List interface and gives the illusion of having n elements, each of which appears as anObject.

For example, the following call creates a List containing 100 strings, all set to "DEFAULT":

```
List<String> settings = Collections.nCopies(100, "DEFAULT");
```

There is very little storage cost—the object is stored only once. This is a cute application of the view technique.

 NOTE: The Collections class contains a number of utility methods with parameters or return values that are collections. Do not confuse it with the Collection interface.

The method call

```
Collections.singleton(anObject)
```

returns a view object that implements the Set interface (unlike nCopies, which produces a List). The returned object implements an immutable single-element set without the overhead of data structure. The methods singletonList and singletonMap behave similarly.

Similarly, there are methods that produce an empty set, list, map, and so on, for every interface in the collections framework. Impressively, the type of the set is inferred:

```
Set<String> deepThoughts = Collections.emptySet();
```

9.4.2 Subranges

You can form subrange views for a number of collections. For example, suppose you have a list staff and want to extract elements 10 to 19. Use the subList method to obtain a view into the subrange of the list:

```
List group2 = staff.subList(10, 20);
```

The first index is inclusive, the second exclusive—just like the parameters for the substring operation of the String class.

You can apply any operations to the subrange, and they automatically reflect the entire list. For example, you can erase the entire subrange:

```
group2.clear(); // staff reduction
```

The elements get automatically cleared from the staff list, and group2 becomes empty.

For sorted sets and maps, you use the sort order, not the element position, to form subranges. The SortedSet interface declares three methods:

```
SortedSet<E> subSet(E from, E to)
SortedSet<E> headSet(E to)
SortedSet<E> tailSet(E from)
```

These return the subsets of all elements that are larger than or equal to from and strictly smaller than to. For sorted maps, the similar methods

```
SortedMap<K, V> subMap(K from, K to)
SortedMap<K, V> headMap(K to)
SortedMap<K, V> tailMap(K from)
```

return views into the maps consisting of all entries in which the *keys* fall into the specified ranges.

The NavigableSet interface introduced in Java SE 6 gives more control over these subrange operations. You can specify whether the bounds are included:

```
NavigableSet<E> subSet(E from, boolean fromInclusive, E to, boolean toInclusive)
NavigableSet<E> headSet(E to, boolean toInclusive)
NavigableSet<E> tailSet(E from, boolean fromInclusive)
```

9.4.3 Unmodifiable Views

The Collections class has methods that produce *unmodifiable views* of collections. These views add a runtime check to an existing collection. If an attempt to modify the collection is detected, an exception is thrown and the collection remains untouched.

You obtain unmodifiable views by eight methods:

```
Collections.unmodifiableCollection
Collections.unmodifiableList
Collections.unmodifiableSet
Collections.unmodifiableSortedSet
Collections.unmodifiableNavigableSet
Collections.unmodifiableMap
```

```
Collections.unmodifiableSortedMap
Collections.unmodifiableNavigableMap
```

Each method is defined to work on an interface. For example, `Collections.unmodifiableList` works with an `ArrayList`, a `LinkedList`, or any other class that implements the `List` interface.

For example, suppose you want to let some part of your code look at, but not touch, the contents of a collection. Here is what you could do:

```
List<String> staff = new LinkedList<>();
. . .
lookAt(Collections.unmodifiableList(staff));
```

The `Collections.unmodifiableList` method returns an object of a class implementing the `List` interface. Its accessor methods retrieve values from the `staff` collection. Of course, the `lookAt` method can call all methods of the `List` interface, not just the accessors. But all mutator methods (such as `add`) have been redefined to throw an `UnsupportedOperationException` instead of forwarding the call to the underlying collection.

The unmodifiable view does not make the collection itself immutable. You can still modify the collection through its original reference (`staff`, in our case). And you can still call mutator methods on the elements of the collection.

The views wrap the *interface* and not the actual collection object, so you only have access to those methods that are defined in the interface. For example, the `LinkedList` class has convenience methods, `addFirst` and `addLast`, that are not part of the `List` interface. These methods are not accessible through the unmodifiable view.

 CAUTION: The `unmodifiableCollection` method (as well as the `synchronizedCollection` and `checkedCollection` methods discussed later in this section) returns a collection whose `equals` method does *not* invoke the `equals` method of the underlying collection. Instead, it inherits the `equals` method of the `Object` class, which just tests whether the objects are identical. If you turn a set or list into just a collection, you can no longer test for equal contents. The view acts in this way because equality testing is not well defined at this level of the hierarchy. The views treat the `hashCode` method in the same way.

However, the `unmodifiableSet` and `unmodifiableList` methods use the `equals` and `hashCode` methods of the underlying collections.

9.4.4 Synchronized Views

If you access a collection from multiple threads, you need to ensure that the collection is not accidentally damaged. For example, it would be disastrous if one thread tried to add to a hash table while another thread was rehashing the elements.

Instead of implementing thread-safe collection classes, the library designers used the view mechanism to make regular collections thread safe. For example, the static synchronizedMap method in the Collections class can turn any map into a Map with synchronized access methods:

```
Map<String, Employee> map = Collections.synchronizedMap(new HashMap<String, Employee>());
```

You can now access the map object from multiple threads. The methods such as get and put are serialized—each method call must be finished completely before another thread can call another method. We discuss the issue of synchronized access to data structures in greater detail in Chapter 14.

9.4.5 Checked Views

Checked views are intended as debugging support for a problem that can occur with generic types. As explained in Chapter 8, it is actually possible to smuggle elements of the wrong type into a generic collection. For example:

```
ArrayList<String> strings = new ArrayList<>();
ArrayList rawList = strings; // warning only, not an error, for compatibility with legacy code
rawList.add(new Date()); // now strings contains a Date object!
```

The erroneous add command is not detected at runtime. Instead, a class cast exception will happen later when another part of the code calls get and casts the result to a String.

A checked view can detect this problem. Define a safe list as follows:

```
List<String> safeStrings = Collections.checkedList(strings, String.class);
```

The view's add method checks that the inserted object belongs to the given class and immediately throws a ClassCastException if it does not. The advantage is that the error is reported at the correct location:

```
ArrayList rawList = safeStrings;
rawList.add(new Date()); // checked list throws a ClassCastException
```

 CAUTION: The checked views are limited by the runtime checks that the virtual machine can carry out. For example, if you have an ArrayList<Pair<String>>, you cannot protect it from inserting a Pair<Date> since the virtual machine has a single "raw" Pair class.

9.4.6 A Note on Optional Operations

A view usually has some restriction—it may be read-only, it may not be able to change the size, or it may support removal but not insertion (as is the case for the key view of a map). A restricted view throws an `UnsupportedOperationException` if you attempt an inappropriate operation.

In the API documentation for the collection and iterator interfaces, many methods are described as "optional operations." This seems to be in conflict with the notion of an interface. After all, isn't the purpose of an interface to lay out the methods that a class *must* implement? Indeed, this arrangement is unsatisfactory from a theoretical perspective. A better solution might have been to design separate interfaces for read-only views and views that can't change the size of a collection. However, that would have tripled the number of interfaces, which the designers of the library found unacceptable.

Should you extend the technique of "optional" methods to your own designs? We think not. Even though collections are used frequently, the coding style for implementing them is not typical for other problem domains. The designers of a collection class library have to resolve a particularly brutal set of conflicting requirements. Users want the library to be easy to learn, convenient to use, completely generic, idiot-proof, and at the same time as efficient as hand-coded algorithms. It is plainly impossible to achieve all these goals simultaneously, or even to come close. But in your own programming problems, you will rarely encounter such an extreme set of constraints. You should be able to find solutions that do not rely on the extreme measure of "optional" interface operations.

---

java.util.Collections 1.2

- static <E> Collection unmodifiableCollection(Collection<E> c)
- static <E> List unmodifiableList(List<E> c)
- static <E> Set unmodifiableSet(Set<E> c)
- static <E> SortedSet unmodifiableSortedSet(SortedSet<E> c)
- static <E> SortedSet unmodifiableNavigableSet(NavigableSet<E> c) 8
- static <K, V> Map unmodifiableMap(Map<K, V> c)
- static <K, V> SortedMap unmodifiableSortedMap(SortedMap<K, V> c)
- static <K, V> SortedMap unmodifiableNavigableMap(NavigableMap<K, V> c) 8

    constructs a view of the collection; the view's mutator methods throw an `UnsupportedOperationException`.

(Continues)

`java.util.Collections` 1.2 *(Continued)*

- static <E> Collection<E> synchronizedCollection(Collection<E> c)
- static <E> List synchronizedList(List<E> c)
- static <E> Set synchronizedSet(Set<E> c)
- static <E> SortedSet synchronizedSortedSet(SortedSet<E> c)
- static <E> NavigableSet synchronizedNavigableSet(NavigableSet<E> c) 8
- static <K, V> Map<K, V> synchronizedMap(Map<K, V> c)
- static <K, V> SortedMap<K, V> synchronizedSortedMap(SortedMap<K, V> c)
- static <K, V> NavigableMap<K, V> synchronizedNavigableMap(NavigableMap<K, V> c) 8

  constructs a view of the collection; the view's methods are synchronized.

- static <E> Collection checkedCollection(Collection<E> c, Class<E> elementType)
- static <E> List checkedList(List<E> c, Class<E> elementType)
- static <E> Set checkedSet(Set<E> c, Class<E> elementType)
- static <E> SortedSet checkedSortedSet(SortedSet<E> c, Class<E> elementType)
- static <E> NavigableSet checkedNavigableSet(NavigableSet<E> c, Class<E> elementType) 8
- static <K, V> Map checkedMap(Map<K, V> c, Class<K> keyType, Class<V> valueType)
- static <K, V> SortedMap checkedSortedMap(SortedMap<K, V> c, Class<K> keyType, Class<V> valueType)
- static <K, V> NavigableMap checkedNavigableMap(NavigableMap<K, V> c, Class<K> keyType, Class<V> valueType) 8
- static <E> Queue<E> checkedQueue(Queue<E> queue, Class<E> elementType) 8

  constructs a view of the collection; the view's methods throw a ClassCastException if an element of the wrong type is inserted.

- static <E> List<E> nCopies(int n, E value)
- static <E> Set<E> singleton(E value)
- static <E> List<E> singletonList(E value)
- static <K, V> Map<K, V> singletonMap(K key, V value)

  constructs a view of the object as either an unmodifiable list with n identical elements or a singleton set, list, or map.

- static <E> List<E> emptyList()
- static <T> Set<T> emptySet()
- static <E> SortedSet<E> emptySortedSet()
- static NavigableSet<E> emptyNavigableSet()
- static <K,V> Map<K,V> emptyMap()
- static <K,V> SortedMap<K,V> emptySortedMap()
- static <K,V> NavigableMap<K,V> emptyNavigableMap()
- static <T> Enumeration<T> emptyEnumeration()
- static <T> Iterator<T> emptyIterator()
- static <T> ListIterator<T> emptyListIterator()

  Yields an empty collection, map, or iterator.

---

java.util.Arrays 1.2

- `static <E> List<E> asList(E... array)`

  returns a list view of the elements in an array that is modifiable but not resizable.

---

java.util.List<E> 1.2

- `List<E> subList(int firstIncluded, int firstExcluded)`

  returns a list view of the elements within a range of positions.

---

java.util.SortedSet<E> 1.2

- `SortedSet<E> subSet(E firstIncluded, E firstExcluded)`
- `SortedSet<E> headSet(E firstExcluded)`
- `SortedSet<E> tailSet(E firstIncluded)`

  returns a view of the elements within a range.

---

java.util.NavigableSet<E> 6

- `NavigableSet<E> subSet(E from, boolean fromIncluded, E to, boolean toIncluded)`
- `NavigableSet<E> headSet(E to, boolean toIncluded)`
- `NavigableSet<E> tailSet(E from, boolean fromIncluded)`

  returns a view of the elements within a range. The `boolean` flags determine whether the bounds are included in the view.

---

java.util.SortedMap<K, V> 1.2

- `SortedMap<K, V> subMap(K firstIncluded, K firstExcluded)`
- `SortedMap<K, V> headMap(K firstExcluded)`
- `SortedMap<K, V> tailMap(K firstIncluded)`

  returns a map view of the entries whose keys are within a range.

---

java.util.NavigableMap<K, V> 6

- NavigableMap<K, V> subMap(K from, boolean fromIncluded, K to, boolean toIncluded)
- NavigableMap<K, V> headMap(K from, boolean fromIncluded)
- NavigableMap<K, V> tailMap(K to, boolean toIncluded)

   returns a map view of the entries whose keys are within a range. The boolean flags determine whether the bounds are included in the view.

9.5 Algorithms

Generic collection interfaces have a great advantage—you only need to implement your algorithms once. For example, consider a simple algorithm to compute the maximum element in a collection. Traditionally, programmers would implement such an algorithm as a loop. Here is how you can find the largest element of an array.

```
if (a.length == 0) throw new NoSuchElementException();
T largest = a[0];
for (int i = 1; i < a.length; i++)
   if (largest.compareTo(a[i]) < 0)
      largest = a[i];
```

Of course, to find the maximum of an array list, you would write the code slightly differently.

```
if (v.size() == 0) throw new NoSuchElementException();
T largest = v.get(0);
for (int i = 1; i < v.size(); i++)
   if (largest.compareTo(v.get(i)) < 0)
      largest = v.get(i);
```

What about a linked list? You don't have efficient random access in a linked list, but you can use an iterator.

```
if (l.isEmpty()) throw new NoSuchElementException();
Iterator<T> iter = l.iterator();
T largest = iter.next();
while (iter.hasNext())
{
   T next = iter.next();
   if (largest.compareTo(next) < 0)
      largest = next;
}
```

These loops are tedious to write, and just a bit error-prone. Is there an off-by-one error? Do the loops work correctly for empty containers? For containers with only one element? You don't want to test and debug this code every time, but you also don't want to implement a whole slew of methods, such as these:

```
static <T extends Comparable> T max(T[] a)
static <T extends Comparable> T max(ArrayList<T> v)
static <T extends Comparable> T max(LinkedList<T> l)
```

That's where the collection interfaces come in. Think of the *minimal* collection interface that you need to efficiently carry out the algorithm. Random access with get and set comes higher in the food chain than simple iteration. As you have seen in the computation of the maximum element in a linked list, random access is not required for this task. Computing the maximum can be done simply by iterating through the elements. Therefore, you can implement the max method to take *any* object that implements the Collection interface.

```
public static <T extends Comparable> T max(Collection<T> c)
{
    if (c.isEmpty()) throw new NoSuchElementException();
    Iterator<T> iter = c.iterator();
    T largest = iter.next();
    while (iter.hasNext())
    {
        T next = iter.next();
        if (largest.compareTo(next) < 0)
            largest = next;
    }
    return largest;
}
```

Now you can compute the maximum of a linked list, an array list, or an array, with a single method.

That's a powerful concept. In fact, the standard C++ library has dozens of useful algorithms, each operating on a generic collection. The Java library is not quite so rich, but it does contain the basics: sorting, binary search, and some utility algorithms.

9.5.1 Sorting and Shuffling

Computer old-timers will sometimes reminisce about how they had to use punched cards and to actually program, by hand, algorithms for sorting. Nowadays, of course, sorting algorithms are part of the standard library for most programming languages, and the Java programming language is no exception.

The sort method in the Collections class sorts a collection that implements the List interface.

```
List<String> staff = new LinkedList<>();
fill collection
Collections.sort(staff);
```

This method assumes that the list elements implement the Comparable interface. If you want to sort the list in some other way, you can use the sort method of the List interface and pass a Comparator object. Here is how you can sort a list of employees by salary:

```
staff.sort(Comparator.comparingDouble(Employee::getSalary));
```

If you want to sort a list in *descending* order, use the static convenience method Comparator.reverseOrder(). It returns a comparator that returns b.compareTo(a). For example,

```
staff.sort(Comparator.reverseOrder())
```

sorts the elements in the list staff in reverse order, according to the ordering given by the compareTo method of the element type. Similarly,

```
staff.sort(Comparator.comparingDouble(Employee::getSalary).reversed())
```

sorts by descending salary.

You may wonder how the sort method sorts a list. Typically, when you look at a sorting algorithm in a book on algorithms, it is presented for arrays and uses random element access. However, random access in a linked list is inefficient. You can actually sort linked lists efficiently by using a form of merge sort. However, the implementation in the Java programming language does not do that. It simply dumps all elements into an array, sorts the array, and then copies the sorted sequence back into the list.

The sort algorithm used in the collections library is a bit slower than QuickSort, the traditional choice for a general-purpose sorting algorithm. However, it has one major advantage: It is *stable*, that is, it doesn't switch equal elements. Why do you care about the order of equal elements? Here is a common scenario. Suppose you have an employee list that you already sorted by name. Now you sort by salary. What happens to employees with equal salary? With a stable sort, the ordering by name is preserved. In other words, the outcome is a list that is sorted first by salary, then by name.

Collections need not implement all of their "optional" methods, so all methods that receive collection parameters must describe when it is safe to pass a collection to an algorithm. For example, you clearly cannot pass an unmodifiableList list to the sort algorithm. What kind of list *can* you pass? According to the documentation, the list must be modifiable but need not be resizable.

The terms are defined as follows:

- A list is *modifiable* if it supports the set method.
- A list is *resizable* if it supports the add and remove operations.

The Collections class has an algorithm shuffle that does the opposite of sorting—it randomly permutes the order of the elements in a list. For example:

```
ArrayList<Card> cards = . . .;
Collections.shuffle(cards);
```

If you supply a list that does not implement the RandomAccess interface, the shuffle method copies the elements into an array, shuffles the array, and copies the shuffled elements back into the list.

The program in Listing 9.7 fills an array list with 49 Integer objects containing the numbers 1 through 49. It then randomly shuffles the list and selects the first six values from the shuffled list. Finally, it sorts the selected values and prints them.

Listing 9.7 shuffle/ShuffleTest.java

```
1  package shuffle;
2
3  import java.util.*;
4
5  /**
6   * This program demonstrates the random shuffle and sort algorithms.
7   * @version 1.11 2012-01-26
8   * @author Cay Horstmann
9   */
10 public class ShuffleTest
11 {
12    public static void main(String[] args)
13    {
14       List<Integer> numbers = new ArrayList<>();
15       for (int i = 1; i <= 49; i++)
16          numbers.add(i);
17       Collections.shuffle(numbers);
18       List<Integer> winningCombination = numbers.subList(0, 6);
19       Collections.sort(winningCombination);
20       System.out.println(winningCombination);
21    }
22 }
```

---

java.util.Collections 1.2

- static <T extends Comparable<? super T>> void sort(List<T> elements)

  sorts the elements in the list, using a stable sort algorithm. The algorithm is guaranteed to run in $O(n \log n)$ time, where n is the length of the list.
- static void shuffle(List<?> elements)
- static void shuffle(List<?> elements, Random r)

  randomly shuffles the elements in the list. This algorithm runs in $O(n \, a(n))$ time, where n is the length of the list and $a(n)$ is the average time to access an element.

---

java.util.List<E> 1.2

- default void sort(Comparator<? super T> comparator) 8

  Sorts this list, using the given comparator.

---

java.util.Comparator<T> 1.2

- static <T extends Comparable<? super T>> Comparator<T> reverseOrder() 8

  Yields a comparator that reverses the ordering provided by the Comparable interface.
- default Comparator<T> reversed() 8

  Yields a comparator that reverses the ordering provided by this comparator.

9.5.2 Binary Search

To find an object in an array, you normally visit all elements until you find a match. However, if the array is sorted, you can look at the middle element and check whether it is larger than the element that you are trying to find. If so, keep looking in the first half of the array; otherwise, look in the second half. That cuts the problem in half, and you keep going in the same way. For example, if the array has 1024 elements, you will locate the match (or confirm that there is none) after 10 steps, whereas a linear search would have taken you an average of 512 steps if the element is present, and 1024 steps to confirm that it is not.

The binarySearch of the Collections class implements this algorithm. Note that the collection must already be sorted, or the algorithm will return the wrong answer. To find an element, supply the collection (which must implement the List interface—more on that in the note below) and the element to be located. If the collection is not sorted by the compareTo element of the Comparable interface, supply a comparator object as well.

```
i = Collections.binarySearch(c, element);
i = Collections.binarySearch(c, element, comparator);
```

A non-negative return value from the `binarySearch` method denotes the index of the matching object. That is, `c.get(i)` is equal to `element` under the comparison order. If the value is negative, then there is no matching element. However, you can use the return value to compute the location where you *should* insert `element` into the collection to keep it sorted. The insertion location is

```
insertionPoint = -i - 1;
```

It isn't simply `-i` because then the value of `0` would be ambiguous. In other words, the operation

```
if (i < 0)
   c.add(-i - 1, element);
```

adds the element in the correct place.

To be worthwhile, binary search requires random access. If you have to iterate one by one through half of a linked list to find the middle element, you have lost all advantage of the binary search. Therefore, the `binarySearch` algorithm reverts to a linear search if you give it a linked list.

`java.util.Collections` 1.2

- `static <T extends Comparable<? super T>> int binarySearch(List<T> elements, T key)`
- `static <T> int binarySearch(List<T> elements, T key, Comparator<? super T> c)`

  searches for a key in a sorted list, using a linear search if the element type implements the `RandomAccess` interface, and a binary search in all other cases. The methods are guaranteed to run in $O(a(n) \log n)$ time, where n is the length of the list and $a(n)$ is the average time to access an element. The methods return either the index of the key in the list, or a negative value i if the key is not present in the list. In that case, the key should be inserted at index $-i - 1$ for the list to stay sorted.

9.5.3 Simple Algorithms

The `Collections` class contains several simple but useful algorithms. Among them is the example from the beginning of this section—finding the maximum value of a collection. Others include copying elements from one list to another, filling a container with a constant value, and reversing a list.

Why supply such simple algorithms in the standard library? Surely most programmers could easily implement them with simple loops. We like the algorithms because they make life easier for the programmer *reading* the code. When you read a loop that was implemented by someone else, you have to decipher the original programmer's intentions. For example, look at this loop:

```
for (int i = 0; i < words.size(); i++)
    if (words.get(i).equals("C++")) words.set(i, "Java");
```

Now compare the loop with the call

```
Collections.replaceAll("C++", "Java");
```

When you see the method call, you know right away what the code does.

The API notes at the end of this section describe the simple algorithms in the Collections class.

Java SE 8 adds default methods Collection.removeIf and List.replaceAll that are just a bit more complex. You provide a lambda expression to test or transform elements. For example, here we remove all short words and change the remaining ones to lowercase:

```
words.removeIf(w -> w.length() <= 3);
words.replaceAll(String::toLowerCase);
```

---

java.util.Collections 1.2

- static <T extends Comparable<? super T>> T min(Collection<T> elements)
- static <T extends Comparable<? super T>> T max(Collection<T> elements)
- static <T> min(Collection<T> elements, Comparator<? super T> c)
- static <T> max(Collection<T> elements, Comparator<? super T> c)

  returns the smallest or largest element in the collection. (The parameter bounds are simplified for clarity.)

- static <T> void copy(List<? super T> to, List<T> from)

  copies all elements from a source list to the same positions in the target list. The target list must be at least as long as the source list.

- static <T> void fill(List<? super T> l, T value)

  sets all positions of a list to the same value.

- static <T> boolean addAll(Collection<? super T> c, T... values) 5.0

  adds all values to the given collection and returns true if the collection changed as a result.

- static <T> boolean replaceAll(List<T> l, T oldValue, T newValue) 1.4

  replaces all elements equal to oldValue with newValue.

(Continues)

`java.util.Collections` 1.2 *(Continued)*

- `static int indexOfSubList(List<?> l, List<?> s)` 1.4
- `static int lastIndexOfSubList(List<?> l, List<?> s)` 1.4

  returns the index of the first or last sublist of l equaling s, or -1 if no sublist of l equals s. For example, if l is [s, t, a, r] and s is [t, a, r], then both methods return the index 1.

- `static void swap(List<?> l, int i, int j)` 1.4

  swaps the elements at the given offsets.

- `static void reverse(List<?> l)`

  reverses the order of the elements in a list. For example, reversing the list [t, a, r] yields the list [r, a, t]. This method runs in $O(n)$ time, where n is the length of the list.

- `static void rotate(List<?> l, int d)` 1.4

  rotates the elements in the list, moving the entry with index i to position (i + d) % l.size(). For example, rotating the list [t, a, r] by 2 yields the list [a, r, t]. This method runs in $O(n)$ time, where n is the length of the list.

- `static int frequency(Collection<?> c, Object o)` 5.0

  returns the count of elements in c that equal the object o.

- `boolean disjoint(Collection<?> c1, Collection<?> c2)` 5.0

  returns true if the collections have no elements in common.

`java.util.Collection<T>` 1.2

- `default boolean removeIf(Predicate<? super E> filter)` 8

  Removes all matching elements.

`java.util.List<E>` 1.2

- `default void replaceAll(UnaryOperator<E> op)` 8

  Applies the operation to all elements of this list.

9.5.4 Bulk Operations

There are several operations that copy or remove elements "in bulk." The call

```
coll1.removeAll(coll2);
```

removes all elements from `coll1` that are present in `coll2`. Conversely,

```
coll1.retainAll(coll2);
```

removes all elements from `coll1` that are *not* present in `coll2`. Here is a typical application.

Suppose you want to find the *intersection* of two sets—the elements that two sets have in common. First, make a new set to hold the result.

```
Set<String> result = new HashSet<>(a);
```

Here, we use the fact that every collection has a constructor whose parameter is another collection that holds the initialization values.

Now, use the `retainAll` method:

```
result.retainAll(b);
```

It retains all elements that also happen to be in `b`. You have formed the intersection without programming a loop.

You can carry this idea further and apply a bulk operation to a *view*. For example, suppose you have a map that maps employee IDs to employee objects and you have a set of the IDs of all employees that are to be terminated.

```
Map<String, Employee> staffMap = . . .;
Set<String> terminatedIDs = . . .;
```

Simply form the key set and remove all IDs of terminated employees.

```
staffMap.keySet().removeAll(terminatedIDs);
```

Since the key set is a view into the map, the keys and associated employee names are automatically removed from the map.

By using a subrange view, you can restrict bulk operations to sublists and subsets. For example, suppose you want to add the first ten elements of a list to another container. Form a sublist to pick out the first ten:

```
relocated.addAll(staff.subList(0, 10));
```

The subrange can also be a target of a mutating operation.

```
staff.subList(0, 10).clear();
```

9.5.5 Converting between Collections and Arrays

Large portions of the Java platform API were designed before the collections framework was created. As a result, you will occasionally need to translate between traditional arrays and the more modern collections.

If you have an array that you need to turn into a collection, the `Arrays.asList` wrapper serves this purpose. For example:

```
String[] values = . . .;
HashSet<String> staff = new HashSet<>(Arrays.asList(values));
```

Obtaining an array from a collection is a bit trickier. Of course, you can use the `toArray` method:

```
Object[] values = staff.toArray();
```

But the result is an array of *objects*. Even if you know that your collection contained objects of a specific type, you cannot use a cast:

```
String[] values = (String[]) staff.toArray(); // Error!
```

The array returned by the `toArray` method was created as an `Object[]` array, and you cannot change its type. Instead, use a variant of the `toArray` method and give it an array of length 0 of the type that you'd like. The returned array is then created *as the same array type*:

```
String[] values = staff.toArray(new String[0]);
```

If you like, you can construct the array to have the correct size:

```
staff.toArray(new String[staff.size()]);
```

In this case, no new array is created.

 NOTE: You may wonder why you can't simply pass a `Class` object (such as `String.class`) to the `toArray` method. However, this method does "double duty"—both to fill an existing array (provided it is long enough) and to create a new array.

9.5.6 Writing Your Own Algorithms

If you write your own algorithm (or, in fact, any method that has a collection as a parameter), you should work with *interfaces*, not concrete implementations, whenever possible. For example, suppose you want to fill a `JMenu` with a set of menu items. Traditionally, such a method might have been implemented like this:

```
void fillMenu(JMenu menu, ArrayList<JMenuItem> items)
{
   for (JMenuItem item : items)
      menu.add(item);
}
```

However, you now constrained the caller of your method—the caller must supply the choices in an ArrayList. If the choices happen to be in another container, they first need to be repackaged. It is much better to accept a more general collection.

You should ask yourself this: What is the most general collection interface that can do the job? In this case, you just need to visit all elements, a capability of the basic Collection interface. Here is how you can rewrite the fillMenu method to accept collections of any kind:

```
void fillMenu(JMenu menu, Collection<JMenuItem> items)
{
    for (JMenuItem item : items)
        menu.add(item);
}
```

Now, anyone can call this method with an ArrayList or a LinkedList, or even with an array wrapped with the Arrays.asList wrapper.

NOTE: If it is such a good idea to use collection interfaces as method parameters, why doesn't the Java library follow this rule more often? For example, the JComboBox class has two constructors:

```
JComboBox(Object[] items)
JComboBox(Vector<?> items)
```

The reason is simply timing. The Swing library was created before the collections library.

If you write a method that *returns* a collection, you may also want to return an interface instead of a class because you can then change your mind and reimplement the method later with a different collection.

For example, let's write a method getAllItems that returns all items of a menu.

```
List<JMenuItem> getAllItems(JMenu menu)
{
    List<JMenuItem> items = new ArrayList<>()
    for (int i = 0; i < menu.getItemCount(); i++)
        items.add(menu.getItem(i));
    return items;
}
```

Later, you may decide that you don't want to *copy* the items but simply provide a view into them. You can achieve this by returning an anonymous subclass of AbstractList.

```
List<JMenuItem> getAllItems(final JMenu menu)
{
    return new
        AbstractList<>()
        {
            public JMenuItem get(int i)
            {
                return menu.getItem(i);
            }
            public int size()
            {
                return menu.getItemCount();
            }
        };
}
```

Of course, this is an advanced technique. If you employ it, be careful to document exactly which "optional" operations are supported. In this case, you must advise the caller that the returned object is an unmodifiable list.

9.6 Legacy Collections

A number of "legacy" container classes have been present since the first release of Java, before there was a collections framework.

They have been integrated into the collections framework—see Figure 9.12. We briefly introduce them in the following sections.

9.6.1 The Hashtable Class

The classic Hashtable class serves the same purpose as the HashMap class and has essentially the same interface. Just like methods of the Vector class, the Hashtable methods are synchronized. If you do not require compatibility with legacy code, you should use a HashMap instead. If you need concurrent access, use a ConcurrentHashMap—see Chapter 14.

9.6.2 Enumerations

The legacy collections use the Enumeration interface for traversing sequences of elements. The Enumeration interface has two methods, hasMoreElements and nextElement. These are entirely analogous to the hasNext and next methods of the Iterator interface.

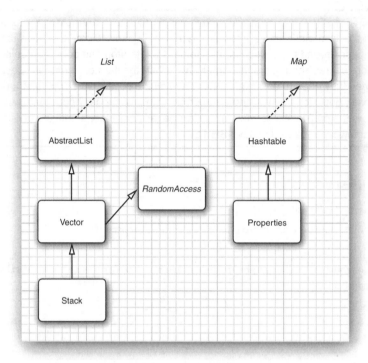

Figure 9.12 Legacy classes in the collections framework

For example, the `elements` method of the `Hashtable` class yields an object for enumerating the values in the table:

```
Enumeration<Employee> e = staff.elements();
while (e.hasMoreElements())
{
    Employee e = e.nextElement();
    . . .
}
```

You will occasionally encounter a legacy method that expects an enumeration parameter. The static method `Collections.enumeration` yields an enumeration object that enumerates the elements in the collection. For example:

```
List<InputStream> streams = . . .;
SequenceInputStream in = new SequenceInputStream(Collections.enumeration(streams));
    // the SequenceInputStream constructor expects an enumeration
```

NOTE: In C++, it is quite common to use iterators as parameters. Fortunately, on the Java platform, very few programmers use this idiom. It is much smarter to pass around the collection than to pass an iterator. The collection object is more useful. The recipients can always obtain the iterator from the collection when they need to do so, plus they have all the collection methods at their disposal. However, you will find enumerations in some legacy code because they were the only available mechanism for generic collections until the collections framework appeared in Java SE 1.2.

---

java.util.Enumeration<E> 1.0

- boolean hasMoreElements()

  returns true if there are more elements yet to be inspected.

- E nextElement()

  returns the next element to be inspected. Do not call this method if hasMoreElements() returned false.

---

java.util.Hashtable<K, V> 1.0

- Enumeration<K> keys()

  returns an enumeration object that traverses the keys of the hash table.

- Enumeration<V> elements()

  returns an enumeration object that traverses the elements of the hash table.

---

java.util.Vector<E> 1.0

- Enumeration<E> elements()

  returns an enumeration object that traverses the elements of the vector.

9.6.3 Property Maps

A *property map* is a map structure of a very special type. It has three particular characteristics:

- The keys and values are strings.
- The table can be saved to a file and loaded from a file.
- A secondary table for defaults is used.

The Java platform class that implements a property map is called `Properties`.

Property maps are commonly used in specifying configuration options for programs—see Chapter 13.

---

java.util.Properties 1.0

- `Properties()`

  creates an empty property map.
- `Properties(Properties defaults)`

  creates an empty property map with a set of defaults.
- `String getProperty(String key)`

  gets a property association: returns the string associated with the key, or the string associated with the key in the default table if it wasn't present in the map.
- `String getProperty(String key, String defaultValue)`

  gets a property with a default value if the key is not found; returns the string associated with the key, or the default string if it wasn't present in the map.
- `void load(InputStream in)`

  loads a property map from an `InputStream`.
- `void store(OutputStream out, String commentString)`

  stores a property map to an `OutputStream`.

9.6.4 Stacks

Since version 1.0, the standard library had a `Stack` class with the familiar `push` and `pop` methods. However, the `Stack` class extends the `Vector` class, which is not satisfactory from a theoretical perspective—you can apply such un-stack-like operations as `insert` and `remove` to insert and remove values anywhere, not just at the top of the stack.

---

java.util.Stack<E> 1.0

- E push(E item)

  pushes item onto the stack and returns item.

- E pop()

  pops and returns the top item of the stack. Don't call this method if the stack is empty.

- E peek()

  returns the top of the stack without popping it. Don't call this method if the stack is empty.

9.6.5 Bit Sets

The Java platform's BitSet class stores a sequence of bits. (It is not a *set* in the mathematical sense—bit *vector* or bit *array* would have been more appropriate terms.) Use a bit set if you need to store a sequence of bits (for example, flags) efficiently. A bit set packs the bits into bytes, so it is far more efficient to use a bit set than an ArrayList of Boolean objects.

The BitSet class gives you a convenient interface for reading, setting, and resetting individual bits. Using this interface avoids the masking and other bit-fiddling operations that are necessary if you store bits in int or long variables.

For example, for a BitSet named bucketOfBits,

```
bucketOfBits.get(i)
```

returns true if the ith bit is on, and false otherwise. Similarly,

```
bucketOfBits.set(i)
```

turns the ith bit on. Finally,

```
bucketOfBits.clear(i)
```

turns the ith bit off.

 C++ NOTE: The C++ bitset template has the same functionality as the Java platform BitSet.

---

java.util.BitSet 1.0

- BitSet(int initialCapacity)

  constructs a bit set.

- int length()

  returns the "logical length" of the bit set: 1 plus the index of the highest set bit.

- boolean get(int bit)

  gets a bit.

- void set(int bit)

  sets a bit.

- void clear(int bit)

  clears a bit.

- void and(BitSet set)

  logically ANDs this bit set with another.

- void or(BitSet set)

  logically ORs this bit set with another.

- void xor(BitSet set)

  logically XORs this bit set with another.

- void andNot(BitSet set)

  clears all bits in this bit set that are set in the other bit set.

As an example of using bit sets, we want to show you an implementation of the "sieve of Eratosthenes" algorithm for finding prime numbers. (A prime number is a number like 2, 3, or 5 that is divisible only by itself and 1, and the sieve of Eratosthenes was one of the first methods discovered to enumerate these fundamental building blocks.) This isn't a terribly good algorithm for finding the primes, but for some reason it has become a popular benchmark for compiler performance. (It isn't a good benchmark either, because it mainly tests bit operations.)

Oh well, we bow to tradition and present an implementation. This program counts all prime numbers between 2 and 2,000,000. (There are 148,933 primes in this interval, so you probably don't want to print them all out.)

Without going into too many details of this program, the idea is to march through a bit set with 2 million bits. First, we turn on all the bits. After that, we turn off the bits that are multiples of numbers known to be prime. The positions of the bits that remain after this process are themselves prime numbers. Listing 9.8 lists this program in the Java programming language, and Listing 9.9 is the C++ code.

 NOTE: Even though the sieve isn't a good benchmark, we couldn't resist timing the two implementations of the algorithm. Here are the timing results on a 2.9-GHz dual core ThinkPad with 8 GB of RAM, running Ubuntu 14.04.

- C++ (g++ 4.6.3): 390 milliseconds
- Java (Java SE 8): 119 milliseconds

We have run this test for nine editions of *Core Java*, and in the last five editions, Java easily beat C++. In all fairness, if one cranks up the optimization level in the C++ compiler, it beats Java with a time of 33 milliseconds. Java could only match that if the program ran long enough to trigger the Hotspot just-in-time compiler.

Listing 9.8 sieve/Sieve.java

```java
1  package sieve;
2
3  import java.util.*;
4
5  /**
6   * This program runs the Sieve of Erathostenes benchmark. It computes all primes up to 2,000,000.
7   * @version 1.21 2004-08-03
8   * @author Cay Horstmann
9   */
10 public class Sieve
11 {
12    public static void main(String[] s)
13    {
14       int n = 2000000;
15       long start = System.currentTimeMillis();
16       BitSet b = new BitSet(n + 1);
17       int count = 0;
18       int i;
19       for (i = 2; i <= n; i++)
20          b.set(i);
21       i = 2;
22       while (i * i <= n)
23       {
24          if (b.get(i))
25          {
26             count++;
27             int k = 2 * i;
```

```
28              while (k <= n)
29              {
30                  b.clear(k);
31                  k += i;
32              }
33          }
34          i++;
35      }
36      while (i <= n)
37      {
38          if (b.get(i)) count++;
39          i++;
40      }
41      long end = System.currentTimeMillis();
42      System.out.println(count + " primes");
43      System.out.println((end - start) + " milliseconds");
44   }
45 }
```

Listing 9.9 sieve/sieve.cpp

```
1  /**
2     @version 1.21 2004-08-03
3     @author Cay Horstmann
4  */
5
6  #include <bitset>
7  #include <iostream>
8  #include <ctime>
9
10 using namespace std;
11
12 int main()
13 {
14    const int N = 2000000;
15    clock_t cstart = clock();
16
17    bitset<N + 1> b;
18    int count = 0;
19    int i;
20    for (i = 2; i <= N; i++)
21       b.set(i);
22    i = 2;
23    while (i * i <= N)
24    {
25       if (b.test(i))
26       {
```

(Continues)

Listing 9.9   *(Continued)*

```
27          count++;
28          int k = 2 * i;
29          while (k <= N)
30          {
31              b.reset(k);
32              k += i;
33          }
34      }
35      i++;
36  }
37  while (i <= N)
38  {
39      if (b.test(i))
40          count++;
41      i++;
42  }
43
44  clock_t cend = clock();
45  double millis = 1000.0 * (cend - cstart) / CLOCKS_PER_SEC;
46
47  cout << count << " primes\n" << millis << " milliseconds\n";
48
49  return 0;
50  }
```

This completes our tour through the Java collections framework. As you have seen, the Java library offers a wide variety of collection classes for your programming needs. In the next chapter, you will learn how to write graphical user interfaces.

Graphics Programming

In this chapter

To this point, you have seen only how to write programs that take input from the keyboard, fuss with it, and display the results on a console screen. This is not what most users want now. Modern programs don't work this way and neither do web pages. This chapter starts you on the road to writing Java programs that use a graphical user interface (GUI). In particular, you will learn how to write programs that size and locate windows on the screen, display text with multiple fonts in a window, display images, and so on. This gives you a useful, valuable repertoire of skills that you will put to good use in subsequent chapters as you write interesting programs.

The next two chapters show you how to process events, such as keystrokes and mouse clicks, and how to add interface elements, such as menus and buttons, to your applications. When you finish these three chapters, you will know the essentials of writing graphical applications. For more sophisticated graphics programming techniques, we refer you to Volume II.

If, on the other hand, you intend to use Java for server-side programming only and are not interested in writing GUI programming, you can safely skip these chapters.

10.1 Introducing Swing

When Java 1.0 was introduced, it contained a class library, which Sun called the Abstract Window Toolkit (AWT), for basic GUI programming. The basic AWT library deals with user interface elements by delegating their creation and behavior to the native GUI toolkit on each target platform (Windows, Solaris, Macintosh, and so on). For example, if you used the original AWT to put a text box on a Java window, an underlying "peer" text box actually handled the text input. The resulting program could then, in theory, run on any of these platforms, with the "look-and-feel" of the target platform—hence Sun's trademarked slogan: "Write Once, Run Anywhere."

The peer-based approach worked well for simple applications, but it soon became apparent that it was fiendishly difficult to write a high-quality portable graphics library depending on native user interface elements. User interface elements such as menus, scrollbars, and text fields can have subtle differences in behavior on different platforms. It was hard, therefore, to give users a consistent and predictable experience with this approach. Moreover, some graphical environments (such as X11/Motif) do not have as rich a collection of user interface components as does Windows or the Macintosh. This, in turn, further limits a portable library based on a "lowest common denominator" approach. As a result, GUI applications built with the AWT simply did not look as nice as native Windows or Macintosh applications, nor did they have the kind of functionality that users of those platforms had come to expect. More depressingly, there were *different* bugs in the AWT user interface library on the different platforms. Developers complained that they had to test their applications on each platform—a practice derisively called "write once, debug everywhere."

In 1996, Netscape created a GUI library they called the IFC (Internet Foundation Classes) that used an entirely different approach. User interface elements, such as buttons, menus, and so on, were *painted* onto blank windows. The only functionality required from the underlying windowing system was a way to put up windows and to paint on the window. Thus, Netscape's IFC widgets looked and behaved the same no matter which platform the program ran on. Sun worked with Netscape to perfect this approach, creating a user interface library with the code name "Swing." Swing was available as an extension to Java 1.1 and became a part of the standard library in Java SE 1.2.

Since, as Duke Ellington said, "It Don't Mean a Thing If It Ain't Got That Swing," Swing is now the official name for the non-peer-based GUI toolkit. Swing is part of the Java Foundation Classes (JFC). The full JFC is vast and contains far more than the Swing GUI toolkit; besides the Swing components, it also has an accessibility API, a 2D API, and a drag-and-drop API.

 NOTE: Swing is not a complete replacement for the AWT—it is built on top of the AWT architecture. Swing simply gives you more capable user interface components. Whenever you write a Swing program, you use the foundations of the AWT—in particular, event handling. From now on, we say "Swing" when we mean the "painted" user interface classes, and we say "AWT" when we mean the underlying mechanisms of the windowing toolkit, such as event handling.

Of course, Swing-based user interface elements will be somewhat slower to appear on the user's screen than the peer-based components used by the AWT. In our experience, on any reasonably modern machine the speed difference shouldn't be a problem. On the other hand, the reasons to choose Swing are overwhelming:

- Swing has a rich and convenient set of user interface elements.
- Swing has few dependencies on the underlying platform; it is therefore less prone to platform-specific bugs.
- Swing gives a consistent user experience across platforms.

Still, the third plus is also a potential drawback: If the user interface elements look the same on all platforms, they look *different* from the native controls, so users will be less familiar with them.

Swing solves this problem in a very elegant way. Programmers writing Swing programs can give the program a specific "look-and-feel." For example, Figures 10.1 and 10.2 show the same program running with the Windows and the GTK look-and-feel.

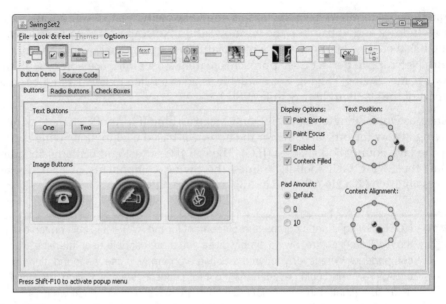

Figure 10.1 The Windows look-and-feel of Swing

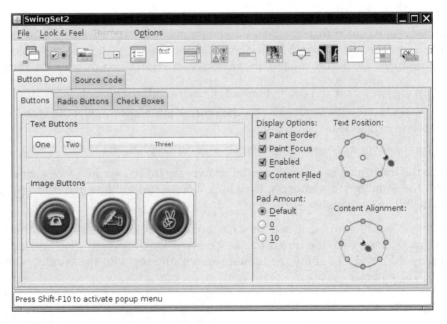

Figure 10.2 The GTK look-and-feel of Swing

Furthermore, Sun developed a platform-independent look-and-feel that was called "Metal" until the marketing folks renamed it into "Java look-and-feel." However, most programmers continue to use the term "Metal," and we will do the same in this book.

Some people criticized Metal for being stodgy, and the look was freshened up for the Java SE 5.0 release (see Figure 10.3). Now the Metal look supports multiple themes—minor variations in colors and fonts. The default theme is called "Ocean."

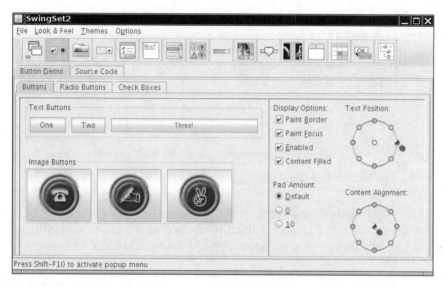

Figure 10.3 The Ocean theme of the Metal look-and-feel

In Java SE 6, Sun improved the support for the native look-and-feel for Windows and GTK. A Swing application will now pick up the color scheme customizations and faithfully render the throbbing buttons and scrollbars that have become fashionable.

A new look-and-feel, called Nimbus (Figure 10.4), is offered since Java SE 7, but it is not available by default. Nimbus uses vector drawings, not bitmaps, and is therefore independent of the screen resolution.

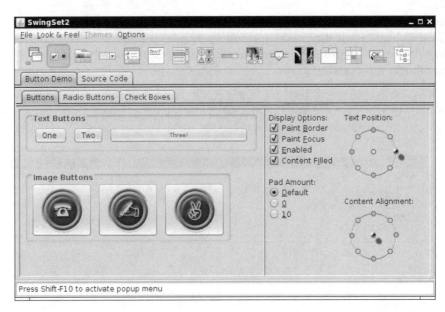

Figure 10.4 The Nimbus look-and-feel

Some users prefer their Java applications to use the native look-and-feel of their platforms, others like Metal or a third-party look-and-feel. As you will see in Chapter 11, it is very easy to let your users choose their favorite look-and-feel.

NOTE: Although we won't have space in this book to tell you how to do it, Java programmers can extend an existing look-and-feel or even design a totally new one. This is a tedious process that involves specifying how each Swing component is painted. Some developers have done just that, especially when porting Java to nontraditional platforms such as kiosk terminals or handheld devices. See www.javootoo.com for a collection of interesting look-and-feel implementations.

Java SE 5.0 introduced a look-and-feel, called Synth, that makes this process easier. In Synth, you can define a new look-and-feel by providing image files and XML descriptors, without doing any programming.

TIP: The Napkin look-and-feel (http://napkinlaf.sourceforge.net) gives a hand-drawn appearance to all user interface elements. This is very useful when you show prototypes to your customers, sending a clear message that you're not giving them a finished product.

NOTE: Most Java user interface programming is nowadays done in Swing, with one notable exception. The Eclipse integrated development environment uses a graphics toolkit called SWT that is similar to the AWT, mapping to the native components on various platforms. You can find articles describing SWT at www.eclipse.org/articles.

Oracle is developing an alternate technology, called JavaFX, as a replacement for Swing. We do not discuss JavaFX in this book. See http://docs.oracle.com/javase/8/javafx/get-started-tutorial/jfx-overview.htm for more information.

If you have programmed Microsoft Windows applications with Visual Basic or C#, you know about the ease of use that comes with the graphical layout tools and resource editors these products provide. These tools let you design the visual appearance of your application, and then they generate much (often all) of the GUI code for you. GUI builders are available for Java programming too, but we feel that in order to use these tools effectively, you should know how to build a user interface manually. The remainder of this chapter shows you the basics of displaying windows and painting their contents.

10.2 Creating a Frame

A top-level window (that is, a window that is not contained inside another window) is called a *frame* in Java. The AWT library has a class, called Frame, for this top level. The Swing version of this class is called JFrame and extends the Frame class. The JFrame is one of the few Swing components that is not painted on a canvas. Thus, the decorations (buttons, title bar, icons, and so on) are drawn by the user's windowing system, not by Swing.

CAUTION: Most Swing component classes start with a "J": JButton, JFrame, and so on. There are classes such as Button and Frame, but they are AWT components. If you accidentally omit a "J", your program may still compile and run, but the mixture of Swing and AWT components can lead to visual and behavioral inconsistencies.

In this section, we will go over the most common methods for working with a Swing JFrame. Listing 10.1 lists a simple program that displays an empty frame on the screen, as illustrated in Figure 10.5.

Figure 10.5 The simplest visible frame

Listing 10.1 simpleframe/SimpleFrameTest.java

```
1  package simpleFrame;
2
3  import java.awt.*;
4  import javax.swing.*;
5
6  /**
7   * @version 1.33 2015-05-12
8   * @author Cay Horstmann
9   */
10 public class SimpleFrameTest
11 {
12    public static void main(String[] args)
13    {
14       EventQueue.invokeLater(() ->
15          {
16             SimpleFrame frame = new SimpleFrame();
17             frame.setDefaultCloseOperation(JFrame.EXIT_ON_CLOSE);
18             frame.setVisible(true);
19          });
20    }
21 }
22
23 class SimpleFrame extends JFrame
24 {
25    private static final int DEFAULT_WIDTH = 300;
26    private static final int DEFAULT_HEIGHT = 200;
27
28    public SimpleFrame()
29    {
30       setSize(DEFAULT_WIDTH, DEFAULT_HEIGHT);
31    }
32 }
```

Let's work through this program, line by line.

The Swing classes are placed in the javax.swing package. The package name javax indicates a Java extension package, not a core package. For historical reasons, Swing is considered an extension. However, it is present in every Java SE implementation since version 1.2.

By default, a frame has a rather useless size of 0 × 0 pixels. We define a subclass SimpleFrame whose constructor sets the size to 300 × 200 pixels. This is the only difference between a SimpleFrame and a JFrame.

In the main method of the SimpleFrameTest class, we construct a SimpleFrame object and make it visible.

There are two technical issues that we need to address in every Swing program.

First, all Swing components must be configured from the *event dispatch thread*, the thread of control that passes events such as mouse clicks and keystrokes to the user interface components. The following code fragment is used to execute statements in the event dispatch thread:

```
EventQueue.invokeLater(() ->
   {
      statements
   });
```

We discuss the details in Chapter 14. For now, you should simply consider it a magic incantation that is used to start a Swing program.

 NOTE: You will see many Swing programs that do not initialize the user interface in the event dispatch thread. It used to be perfectly acceptable to carry out the initialization in the main thread. Sadly, as Swing components got more complex, the developers of the JDK were no longer able to guarantee the safety of that approach. The probability of an error is extremely low, but you would not want to be one of the unlucky few who encounter an intermittent problem. It is better to do the right thing, even if the code looks rather mysterious.

Next, we define what should happen when the user closes the application's frame. For this particular program, we want the program to exit. To select this behavior, we use the statement

```
frame.setDefaultCloseOperation(JFrame.EXIT_ON_CLOSE);
```

In other programs with multiple frames, you would not want the program to exit just because the user closes one of the frames. By default, a frame is hidden when the user closes it, but the program does not terminate. (It might have been nice if the program terminated once the *last* frame becomes invisible, but that is not how Swing works.)

Simply constructing a frame does not automatically display it. Frames start their life invisible. That gives the programmer the chance to add components into the frame before showing it for the first time. To show the frame, the main method calls the setVisible method of the frame.

 NOTE: Before Java SE 5.0, it was possible to use the show method that the JFrame class inherits from the superclass Window. The Window class has a superclass Component that also has a show method. The Component.show method was deprecated in Java SE 1.2. You are supposed to call setVisible(true) instead if you want to show a component. However, until Java SE 1.4, the Window.show method was *not* deprecated. In fact, it was quite useful, making the window visible *and* bringing it to the front. Sadly, that benefit was lost on the deprecation police, and Java SE 5.0 deprecated the show method for windows as well.

After scheduling the initialization statements, the main method exits. Note that exiting main does not terminate the program—just the main thread. The event dispatch thread keeps the program alive until it is terminated, either by closing the frame or by calling the System.exit method.

The running program is shown in Figure 10.5—it is a truly boring top-level window. As you can see in the figure, the title bar and the surrounding decorations, such as resize corners, are drawn by the operating system and not the Swing library. If you run the same program in Windows, GTK, and the Mac, the frame decorations will be different. The Swing library draws everything inside the frame. In this program, it just fills the frame with a default background color.

 NOTE: You can turn off all frame decorations by calling frame.setUndecorated(true).

10.3 Positioning a Frame

The JFrame class itself has only a few methods for changing how frames look. Of course, through the magic of inheritance, most of the methods for working with the size and position of a frame come from the various superclasses of JFrame. Here are some of the most important methods:

•   The setLocation and setBounds methods for setting the position of the frame

- The setIconImage method, which tells the windowing system which icon to display in the title bar, task switcher window, and so on
- The setTitle method for changing the text in the title bar
- The setResizable method, which takes a boolean to determine if a frame will be resizeable by the user

Figure 10.6 illustrates the inheritance hierarchy for the JFrame class.

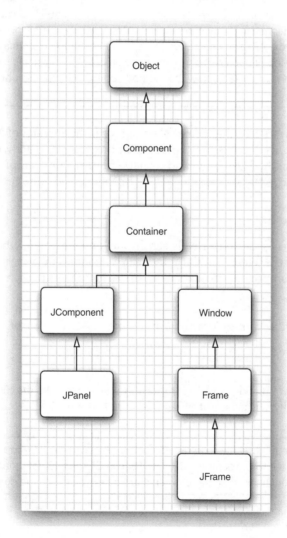

Figure 10.6 Inheritance hierarchy for the frame and component classes in AWT and Swing

TIP: The API notes for this section list what we think are the most important methods for giving frames the proper look-and-feel. Some of these methods are defined in the JFrame class. Others come from the various superclasses of JFrame. At some point, you may need to search the API docs to see if there are methods for some special purpose. Unfortunately, that is a bit tedious to do with inherited methods. For example, the toFront method is applicable to objects of type JFrame, but since it's simply inherited from the Window class, the JFrame documentation doesn't explain it. If you feel that there should be a method to do something and it isn't mentioned in the documentation for the class you are working with, try looking at the API documentation for the methods of the *superclasses* of that class. The top of each API page has hyperlinks to the superclasses, and inherited methods are listed below the method summary for the new and overridden methods.

As the API notes indicate, the Component class (which is the ancestor of all GUI objects) and the Window class (which is the superclass of the Frame class) are where you need to look for the methods to resize and reshape frames. For example, the setLocation method in the Component class is one way to reposition a component. If you make the call

```
setLocation(x, y)
```

the top left corner is located x pixels across and y pixels down, where (0, 0) is the top left corner of the screen. Similarly, the setBounds method in Component lets you resize and relocate a component (in particular, a JFrame) in one step, as

```
setBounds(x, y, width, height)
```

Alternatively, you can give the windowing system control over window placement. If you call

```
setLocationByPlatform(true);
```

before displaying the window, the windowing system picks the location (but not the size), typically with a slight offset from the last window.

 NOTE: For a frame, the coordinates of the setLocation and setBounds are taken relative to the whole screen. As you will see in Chapter 12, for other components inside a container, the measurements are taken relative to the container.

10.3.1 Frame Properties

Many methods of component classes come in getter/setter pairs, such as the following methods of the Frame class:

```
public String getTitle()
public void setTitle(String title)
```

Such a getter/setter pair is called a *property*. A property has a name and a type. The name is obtained by changing the first letter after the get or set to lowercase. For example, the Frame class has a property with name title and type String.

Conceptually, title is a property of the frame. When we set the property, we expect the title to change on the user's screen. When we get the property, we expect to get back the value that we have set.

We do not know (or care) how the Frame class implements this property. Perhaps it simply uses its peer frame to store the title. Perhaps it has an instance field

```
private String title; // not required for property
```

If the class does have a matching instance field, we don't know (or care) how the getter and setter methods are implemented. Perhaps they just read and write the instance field. Perhaps they do more, such as notifying the windowing system whenever the title changes.

There is one exception to the get/set convention: For properties of type boolean, the getter starts with is. For example, the following two methods define the locationByPlatform property:

```
public boolean isLocationByPlatform()
public void setLocationByPlatform(boolean b)
```

10.3.2 Determining a Good Frame Size

Remember: If you don't explicitly size a frame, all frames will default to 0 by 0 pixels. To keep our example programs simple, we resize the frames to a size that we hope works acceptably on most displays. However, in a professional application, you should check the resolution of the user's screen and write code that resizes the frames accordingly: A window that looks nice on the screen of a low-end laptop will look like a postage stamp on a high-resolution screen.

To find out the screen size, use the following steps. Call the static getDefaultToolkit method of the Toolkit class to get the Toolkit object. (The Toolkit class is a dumping ground for a variety of methods interfacing with the native windowing system.)

Then call the getScreenSize method, which returns the screen size as a Dimension object. A Dimension object simultaneously stores a width and a height, in public (!) instance variables width and height. Here is the code:

```
Toolkit kit = Toolkit.getDefaultToolkit();
Dimension screenSize = kit.getScreenSize();
int screenWidth = screenSize.width;
int screenHeight = screenSize.height;
```

We use 50% of these values for the frame size, and tell the windowing system to position the frame:

```
setSize(screenWidth / 2, screenHeight / 2);
setLocationByPlatform(true);
```

We also supply an icon. The ImageIcon class is convenient for loading images. Here is how you use it:

```
Image img = new ImageIcon("icon.gif").getImage();
setIconImage(img);
```

Depending on your operating system, you can see the icon in various places. For example, in Windows, the icon is displayed in the top left corner of the window, and you can see it in the list of active tasks when you press Alt+Tab.

Listing 10.2 is the complete program. When you run the program, pay attention to the "Core Java" icon.

Here are a few additional tips for dealing with frames:

- If your frame contains only standard components such as buttons and text fields, you can simply call the pack method to set the frame size. The frame will be set to the smallest size that contains all components. You can maximize a frame by calling

  ```
  frame.setExtendedState(Frame.MAXIMIZED_BOTH);
  ```

- It is also a good idea to remember how the user positions and sizes the frame of your application, and restore those bounds when you start the application again. You will see in Chapter 13 how to use the Preferences API for this purpose.

- If you write an application that takes advantage of multiple display screens, use the GraphicsEnvironment and GraphicsDevice classes to find the dimensions of the display screens.

- The GraphicsDevice class also lets you execute your application in full-screen mode.

Listing 10.2 sizedFrame/SizedFrameTest.java

```
1  package sizedFrame;
2
3  import java.awt.*;
4  import javax.swing.*;
5
6  /**
7   * @version 1.33 2007-05-12
8   * @author Cay Horstmann
9   */
10 public class SizedFrameTest
11 {
12    public static void main(String[] args)
13    {
14       EventQueue.invokeLater(() ->
15          {
16             JFrame frame = new SizedFrame();
17             frame.setTitle("SizedFrame");
18             frame.setDefaultCloseOperation(JFrame.EXIT_ON_CLOSE);
19             frame.setVisible(true);
20          });
21    }
22 }
23
24 class SizedFrame extends JFrame
25 {
26    public SizedFrame()
27    {
28       // get screen dimensions
29
30       Toolkit kit = Toolkit.getDefaultToolkit();
31       Dimension screenSize = kit.getScreenSize();
32       int screenHeight = screenSize.height;
33       int screenWidth = screenSize.width;
34
35       // set frame width, height and let platform pick screen location
36
37       setSize(screenWidth / 2, screenHeight / 2);
38       setLocationByPlatform(true);
39
40       // set frame icon
41
42       Image img = new ImageIcon("icon.gif").getImage();
43       setIconImage(img);
44    }
45 }
```

`java.awt.Component` 1.0

- boolean isVisible()
- void setVisible(boolean b)

  gets or sets the visible property. Components are initially visible, with the exception of top-level components such as JFrame.

- void setSize(int width, int height) 1.1

  resizes the component to the specified width and height.

- void setLocation(int x, int y) 1.1

  moves the component to a new location. The x and y coordinates use the coordinates of the container if the component is not a top-level component, or the coordinates of the screen if the component is top level (for example, a JFrame).

- void setBounds(int x, int y, int width, int height) 1.1

  moves and resizes this component.

- Dimension getSize() 1.1
- void setSize(Dimension d) 1.1

  gets or sets the size property of this component.

`java.awt.Window` 1.0

- void toFront()

  shows this window on top of any other windows.

- void toBack()

  moves this window to the back of the stack of windows on the desktop and rearranges all other visible windows accordingly.

- boolean isLocationByPlatform() 5.0
- void setLocationByPlatform(boolean b) 5.0

  gets or sets the locationByPlatform property. When the property is set before this window is displayed, the platform picks a suitable location.

---

java.awt.Frame 1.0

- boolean isResizable()
- void setResizable(boolean b)

  gets or sets the resizable property. When the property is set, the user can resize the frame.

- String getTitle()
- void setTitle(String s)

  gets or sets the title property that determines the text in the title bar for the frame.

- Image getIconImage()
- void setIconImage(Image image)

  gets or sets the iconImage property that determines the icon for the frame. The windowing system may display the icon as part of the frame decoration or in other locations.

- boolean isUndecorated() 1.4
- void setUndecorated(boolean b) 1.4

  gets or sets the undecorated property. When the property is set, the frame is displayed without decorations such as a title bar or close button. This method must be called before the frame is displayed.

- int getExtendedState() 1.4
- void setExtendedState(int state) 1.4

  gets or sets the extended window state. The state is one of

  ```
  Frame.NORMAL
  Frame.ICONIFIED
  Frame.MAXIMIZED_HORIZ
  Frame.MAXIMIZED_VERT
  Frame.MAXIMIZED_BOTH
  ```

---

java.awt.Toolkit 1.0

- static Toolkit getDefaultToolkit()

  returns the default toolkit.

- Dimension getScreenSize()

  gets the size of the user's screen.

`javax.swing.ImageIcon` 1.2

- `ImageIcon(String filename)`
  constructs an icon whose image is stored in a file.
- `Image getImage()`
  gets the image of this icon.

10.4 Displaying Information in a Component

In this section, we will show you how to display information inside a frame. For example, instead of displaying "Not a Hello World program" in text mode in a console window as we did in Chapter 3, we display the message in a frame, as shown in Figure 10.7.

Figure 10.7 A frame that displays information

You could draw the message string directly onto a frame, but that is not considered good programming practice. In Java, frames are really designed to be containers for components, such as a menu bar and other user interface elements. You normally draw on another component which you add to the frame.

The structure of a JFrame is surprisingly complex. Look at Figure 10.8 which shows the makeup of a JFrame. As you can see, four panes are layered in a JFrame. The root pane, layered pane, and glass pane are of no interest to us; they are required to organize the menu bar and content pane and to implement the look-and-feel. The part that most concerns Swing programmers is the *content pane*. When designing a frame, you add components into the content pane, using code such as the following:

```
Container contentPane = frame.getContentPane();
Component c = . . .;
contentPane.add(c);
```

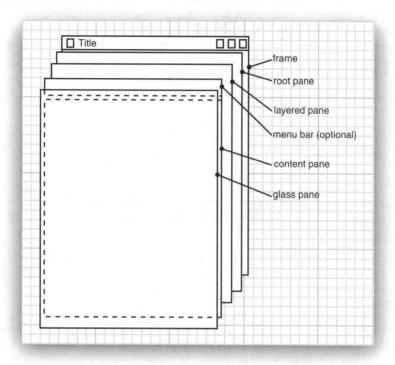

Figure 10.8 Internal structure of a JFrame

Up to Java SE 1.4, the add method of the JFrame class was defined to throw an exception with the message "Do not use JFrame.add(). Use JFrame.getContentPane().add() instead." Nowadays, the JFrame.add method has given up trying to reeducate programmers, and simply calls add on the content pane.

Thus, you can simply use the call

```
frame.add(c);
```

In our case, we want to add a single component to the frame onto which we will draw our message. To draw on a component, you define a class that extends JComponent and override the paintComponent method in that class.

The paintComponent method takes one parameter of type Graphics. A Graphics object remembers a collection of settings for drawing images and text, such as the font you set or the current color. All drawing in Java must go through a Graphics object. It has methods that draw patterns, images, and text.

 NOTE: The Graphics parameter is similar to a device context in Windows or a graphics context in X11 programming.

Here's how to make a component onto which you can draw:

```
class MyComponent extends JComponent
{
    public void paintComponent(Graphics g)
    {
        code for drawing
    }
}
```

Each time a window needs to be redrawn, no matter what the reason, the event handler notifies the component. This causes the paintComponent methods of all components to be executed.

Never call the paintComponent method yourself. It is called automatically whenever a part of your application needs to be redrawn, and you should not interfere with this automatic process.

What sorts of actions trigger this automatic response? For example, painting occurs when the user increases the size of the window, or minimizes and then restores the window. If the user popped up another window that covered an existing window and then made the overlaid window disappear, the window that was covered is now corrupted and will need to be repainted. (The graphics system does not save the pixels underneath.) And, of course, when the window is displayed for the first time, it needs to process the code that specifies how and where it should draw the initial elements.

 TIP: If you need to force repainting of the screen, call the repaint method instead of paintComponent. The repaint method will cause paintComponent to be called for all components, with a properly configured Graphics object.

As you saw in the code fragment above, the paintComponent method takes a single parameter of type Graphics. Measurement on a Graphics object for screen display is done in pixels. The (0, 0) coordinate denotes the top left corner of the component on whose surface you are drawing.

Displaying text is considered a special kind of drawing. The Graphics class has a drawString method that has the following syntax:

```
g.drawString(text, x, y)
```

In our case, we want to draw the string "Not a Hello World Program" in our original window, roughly one-quarter of the way across and halfway down. Although we don't yet know how to measure the size of the string, we'll start the string at coordinates (75, 100). This means the first character in the string will start at a position 75 pixels to the right and 100 pixels down. (Actually, it is the baseline for the text that is 100 pixels down—see p. 576 for more on how text is measured.) Thus, our paintComponent method looks like this:

```
public class NotHelloWorldComponent extends JComponent
{
   public static final int MESSAGE_X = 75;
   public static final int MESSAGE_Y = 100;

   public void paintComponent(Graphics g)
   {
      g.drawString("Not a Hello World program", MESSAGE_X, MESSAGE_Y);
   }
   . . .
}
```

Finally, a component should tell its users how big it would like to be. Override the getPreferredSize method and return an object of the Dimension class with the preferred width and height:

```
public class NotHelloWorldComponent extends JComponent
{
   private static final int DEFAULT_WIDTH = 300;
   private static final int DEFAULT_HEIGHT = 200;
   . . .
   public Dimension getPreferredSize() { return new Dimension(DEFAULT_WIDTH, DEFAULT_HEIGHT); }
}
```

When you fill a frame with one or more components, and you simply want to use their preferred size, call the pack method instead of the setSize method:

```
class NotHelloWorldFrame extends JFrame
{
   public NotHelloWorldFrame()
   {
      add(new NotHelloWorldComponent());
      pack();
   }
}
```

Listing 10.3 shows the complete code.

NOTE: Instead of extending JComponent, some programmers prefer to extend the JPanel class. A JPanel is intended to be a *container* that can contain other components, but it is also possible to paint on it. There is just one difference. A panel is *opaque*, which means it is responsible for painting all pixels within its bounds. The easiest way to achieve that is to paint the panel with the background color, by calling super.paintComponent in the paintComponent method of each panel subclass:

```
class NotHelloWorldPanel extends JPanel
{
    public void paintComponent(Graphics g)
    {
        super.paintComponent(g);

        code for drawing
    }
}
```

Listing 10.3 notHelloWorld/NotHelloWorld.java

```
1  package notHelloWorld;
2
3  import javax.swing.*;
4  import java.awt.*;
5
6  /**
7   * @version 1.33 2015-05-12
8   * @author Cay Horstmann
9   */
10 public class NotHelloWorld
11 {
12    public static void main(String[] args)
13    {
14       EventQueue.invokeLater(() ->
15          {
16             JFrame frame = new NotHelloWorldFrame();
17             frame.setTitle("NotHelloWorld");
18             frame.setDefaultCloseOperation(JFrame.EXIT_ON_CLOSE);
19             frame.setVisible(true);
20          });
21    }
22 }
23
24 /**
25  * A frame that contains a message panel
26  */
```

```
27  class NotHelloWorldFrame extends JFrame
28  {
29     public NotHelloWorldFrame()
30     {
31        add(new NotHelloWorldComponent());
32        pack();
33     }
34  }
35
36  /**
37   * A component that displays a message.
38   */
39  class NotHelloWorldComponent extends JComponent
40  {
41     public static final int MESSAGE_X = 75;
42     public static final int MESSAGE_Y = 100;
43
44     private static final int DEFAULT_WIDTH = 300;
45     private static final int DEFAULT_HEIGHT = 200;
46
47     public void paintComponent(Graphics g)
48     {
49        g.drawString("Not a Hello, World program", MESSAGE_X, MESSAGE_Y);
50     }
51
52     public Dimension getPreferredSize() { return new Dimension(DEFAULT_WIDTH, DEFAULT_HEIGHT); }
53  }
```

---

javax.swing.JFrame 1.2

- Container getContentPane()

  returns the content pane object for this JFrame.

- Component add(Component c)

  adds and returns the given component to the content pane of this frame. (Before Java SE 5.0, this method threw an exception.)

---

java.awt.Component 1.0

- void repaint()

  causes a repaint of the component "as soon as possible."

- Dimension getPreferredSize()

  is the method to override to return the preferred size of this component.

---

javax.swing.JComponent 1.2

- void paintComponent(Graphics g)

  is the method to override to describe how your component needs to be painted.

---

java.awt.Window 1.0

- void pack()
  resizes this window, taking into account the preferred sizes of its components.

10.5 Working with 2D Shapes

Starting with Java 1.0, the Graphics class has methods to draw lines, rectangles, ellipses, and so on. But those drawing operations are very limited. For example, you cannot vary the line thickness and cannot rotate the shapes.

Java SE 1.2 introduced the *Java 2D* library, which implements a powerful set of graphical operations. In this chapter, we only look at the basics of the Java 2D library—see Chapter 7 in Volume II for more information on the advanced features.

To draw shapes in the Java 2D library, you need to obtain an object of the Graphics2D class. This class is a subclass of the Graphics class. Ever since Java SE 2, methods such as paintComponent automatically receive an object of the Graphics2D class. Simply use a cast, as follows:

```
public void paintComponent(Graphics g)
{
   Graphics2D g2 = (Graphics2D) g;
   . . .
}
```

The Java 2D library organizes geometric shapes in an object-oriented fashion. In particular, there are classes to represent lines, rectangles, and ellipses:

```
Line2D
Rectangle2D
Ellipse2D
```

These classes all implement the Shape interface.

 NOTE: The Java 2D library supports more complex shapes—in particular, arcs, quadratic and cubic curves, and general paths. See Chapter 7 of Volume II for more information.

To draw a shape, you first create an object of a class that implements the Shape interface and then call the draw method of the Graphics2D class. For example:

```
Rectangle2D rect = . . .;
g2.draw(rect);
```

 NOTE: Before the Java 2D library appeared, programmers used methods of the Graphics class, such as drawRectangle, to draw shapes. Superficially, the old-style method calls look a bit simpler. However, by using the Java 2D library, you keep your options open—you can later enhance your drawings with some of the many tools that the Java 2D library supplies.

Using the Java 2D shape classes introduces some complexity. Unlike the 1.0 draw methods, which used integer pixel coordinates, Java 2D shapes use floating-point coordinates. In many cases, that is a great convenience because it allows you to specify your shapes in coordinates that are meaningful to you (such as millimeters or inches) and then translate them to pixels. The Java 2D library uses single-precision float quantities for many of its internal floating-point calculations. Single precision is sufficient—after all, the ultimate purpose of the geometric computations is to set pixels on the screen or printer. As long as any roundoff errors stay within one pixel, the visual outcome is not affected.

However, manipulating float values is sometimes inconvenient for the programmer because Java is adamant about requiring casts when converting double values into float values. For example, consider the following statement:

```
float f = 1.2; // Error
```

This statement does not compile because the constant 1.2 has type double, and the compiler is nervous about loss of precision. The remedy is to add an F suffix to the floating-point constant:

```
float f = 1.2F; // Ok
```

Now consider this statement:

```
Rectangle2D r = . . .
float f = r.getWidth(); // Error
```

This statement does not compile either, for the same reason. The getWidth method returns a double. This time, the remedy is to provide a cast:

```
float f = (float) r.getWidth(); // OK
```

These suffixes and casts are a bit of a pain, so the designers of the 2D library decided to supply *two versions* of each shape class: one with float coordinates for frugal programmers, and one with double coordinates for the lazy ones. (In this book, we fall into the second camp and use double coordinates whenever we can.)

The library designers chose a curious, and initially confusing, method for packaging these choices. Consider the Rectangle2D class. This is an abstract class with two concrete subclasses, which are also static inner classes:

```
Rectangle2D.Float
Rectangle2D.Double
```

Figure 10.9 shows the inheritance diagram.

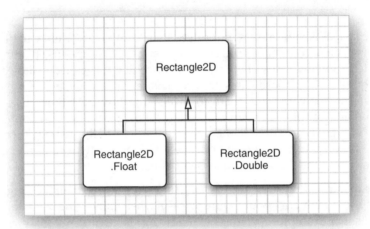

Figure 10.9 2D rectangle classes

It is best to ignore the fact that the two concrete classes are static inner classes—that is just a gimmick to avoid names such as FloatRectangle2D and DoubleRectangle2D. (For more information on static inner classes, see Chapter 6.)

When you construct a Rectangle2D.Float object, you supply the coordinates as float numbers. For a Rectangle2D.Double object, you supply them as double numbers.

```
Rectangle2D.Float floatRect = new Rectangle2D.Float(10.0F, 25.0F, 22.5F, 20.0F);
Rectangle2D.Double doubleRect = new Rectangle2D.Double(10.0, 25.0, 22.5, 20.0);
```

Actually, since both Rectangle2D.Float and Rectangle2D.Double extend the common Rectangle2D class and the methods in the subclasses simply override those in the Rectangle2D superclass, there is no benefit in remembering the exact shape type. You can simply use Rectangle2D variables to hold the rectangle references.

```
Rectangle2D floatRect = new Rectangle2D.Float(10.0F, 25.0F, 22.5F, 20.0F);
Rectangle2D doubleRect = new Rectangle2D.Double(10.0, 25.0, 22.5, 20.0);
```

That is, you only need to use the pesky inner classes when you construct the shape objects.

The construction parameters denote the top left corner, width, and height of the rectangle.

 NOTE: Actually, the `Rectangle2D.Float` class has one additional method that is not inherited from `Rectangle2D`—namely, `setRect(float x, float y, float h, float w)`. You lose that method if you store the `Rectangle2D.Float` reference in a `Rectangle2D` variable. But it is not a big loss—the `Rectangle2D` class has a `setRect` method with `double` parameters.

The `Rectangle2D` methods use `double` parameters and return values. For example, the `getWidth` method returns a `double` value, even if the width is stored as a `float` in a `Rectangle2D.Float` object.

 TIP: Simply use the `Double` shape classes to avoid dealing with `float` values altogether. However, if you are constructing thousands of shape objects, consider using the `Float` classes to conserve memory.

What we just discussed for the `Rectangle2D` classes holds for the other shape classes as well. Furthermore, there is a `Point2D` class with subclasses `Point2D.Float` and `Point2D.Double`. Here is how to make a point object:

```
Point2D p = new Point2D.Double(10, 20);
```

 TIP: The `Point2D` class is very useful—it is more object oriented to work with `Point2D` objects than with separate *x* and *y* values. Many constructors and methods accept `Point2D` parameters. We suggest that you use `Point2D` objects when you can—they usually make geometric computations easier to understand.

The classes `Rectangle2D` and `Ellipse2D` both inherit from the common superclass `RectangularShape`. Admittedly, ellipses are not rectangular, but they have a *bounding rectangle* (see Figure 10.10).

The `RectangularShape` class defines over 20 methods that are common to these shapes, among them such useful methods as `getWidth`, `getHeight`, `getCenterX`, and `getCenterY` (but, sadly, at the time of this writing, not a `getCenter` method that would return the center as a `Point2D` object).

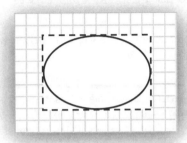

Figure 10.10 The bounding rectangle of an ellipse

Finally, a couple of legacy classes from Java 1.0 have been fitted into the shape class hierarchy. The `Rectangle` and `Point` classes, which store a rectangle and a point with integer coordinates, extend the `Rectangle2D` and `Point2D` classes.

Figure 10.11 shows the relationships between the shape classes. However, the `Double` and `Float` subclasses are omitted. Legacy classes are marked with a gray fill.

`Rectangle2D` and `Ellipse2D` objects are simple to construct. You need to specify

- The x and y coordinates of the top left corner; and
- The width and height.

For ellipses, these refer to the bounding rectangle. For example,

```
Ellipse2D e = new Ellipse2D.Double(150, 200, 100, 50);
```

constructs an ellipse that is bounded by a rectangle with the top left corner at (150, 200), width of 100, and height of 50.

However, sometimes you don't have the top left corner readily available. It is quite common to have two diagonal corner points of a rectangle, but perhaps they aren't the top left and bottom right corners. You can't simply construct a rectangle as

```
Rectangle2D rect = new Rectangle2D.Double(px, py, qx - px, qy - py); // Error
```

If `p` isn't the top left corner, one or both of the coordinate differences will be negative and the rectangle will come out empty. In that case, first create a blank rectangle and use the `setFrameFromDiagonal` method, as follows:

```
Rectangle2D rect = new Rectangle2D.Double();
rect.setFrameFromDiagonal(px, py, qx, qy);
```

Or, even better, if you have the corner points as `Point2D` objects p and q, use

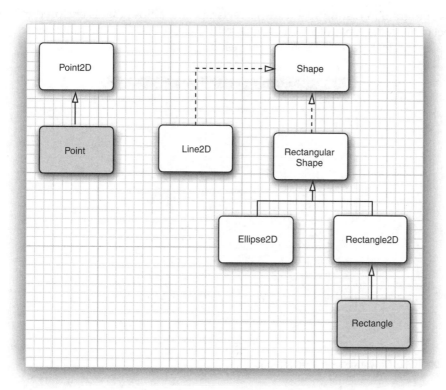

Figure 10.11 Relationships between the shape classes

```
rect.setFrameFromDiagonal(p, q);
```

When constructing an ellipse, you usually know the center, width, and height, but not the corner points of the bounding rectangle (which don't even lie on the ellipse). The setFrameFromCenter method uses the center point, but it still requires one of the four corner points. Thus, you will usually end up constructing an ellipse as follows:

```
Ellipse2D ellipse = new Ellipse2D.Double(centerX - width / 2, centerY - height / 2, width, height);
```

To construct a line, you supply the start and end points, either as Point2D objects or as pairs of numbers:

```
Line2D line = new Line2D.Double(start, end);
```

or

```
Line2D line = new Line2D.Double(startX, startY, endX, endY);
```

The program in Listing 10.4 draws a rectangle, the ellipse that is enclosed in the rectangle, a diagonal of the rectangle, and a circle that has the same center as the rectangle. Figure 10.12 shows the result.

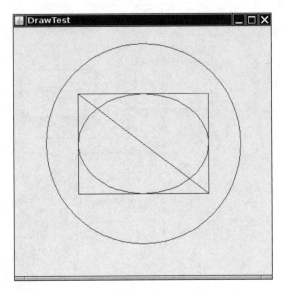

Figure 10.12 Drawing geometric shapes

Listing 10.4 draw/DrawTest.java

```
 1  package draw;
 2
 3  import java.awt.*;
 4  import java.awt.geom.*;
 5  import javax.swing.*;
 6
 7  /**
 8   * @version 1.33 2007-05-12
 9   * @author Cay Horstmann
10   */
11  public class DrawTest
12  {
13     public static void main(String[] args)
14     {
15        EventQueue.invokeLater(() ->
16           {
17              JFrame frame = new DrawFrame();
18              frame.setTitle("DrawTest");
```

```
19              frame.setDefaultCloseOperation(JFrame.EXIT_ON_CLOSE);
20              frame.setVisible(true);
21          });
22      }
23  }
24
25  /**
26   * A frame that contains a panel with drawings
27   */
28  class DrawFrame extends JFrame
29  {
30      public DrawFrame()
31      {
32          add(new DrawComponent());
33          pack();
34      }
35  }
36
37  /**
38   * A component that displays rectangles and ellipses.
39   */
40  class DrawComponent extends JComponent
41  {
42      private static final int DEFAULT_WIDTH = 400;
43      private static final int DEFAULT_HEIGHT = 400;
44
45      public void paintComponent(Graphics g)
46      {
47          Graphics2D g2 = (Graphics2D) g;
48
49          // draw a rectangle
50
51          double leftX = 100;
52          double topY = 100;
53          double width = 200;
54          double height = 150;
55
56          Rectangle2D rect = new Rectangle2D.Double(leftX, topY, width, height);
57          g2.draw(rect);
58
59          // draw the enclosed ellipse
60
61          Ellipse2D ellipse = new Ellipse2D.Double();
62          ellipse.setFrame(rect);
63          g2.draw(ellipse);
64
65          // draw a diagonal line
66
```

(Continues)

Listing 10.4 *(Continued)*

```
67      g2.draw(new Line2D.Double(leftX, topY, leftX + width, topY + height));
68
69      // draw a circle with the same center
70
71      double centerX = rect.getCenterX();
72      double centerY = rect.getCenterY();
73      double radius = 150;
74
75      Ellipse2D circle = new Ellipse2D.Double();
76      circle.setFrameFromCenter(centerX, centerY, centerX + radius, centerY + radius);
77      g2.draw(circle);
78   }
79
80   public Dimension getPreferredSize() { return new Dimension(DEFAULT_WIDTH, DEFAULT_HEIGHT); }
81 }
```

---

java.awt.geom.RectangularShape 1.2

- `double getCenterX()`
- `double getCenterY()`
- `double getMinX()`
- `double getMinY()`
- `double getMaxX()`
- `double getMaxY()`

  returns the center, minimum, or maximum *x* or *y* value of the enclosing rectangle.

- `double getWidth()`
- `double getHeight()`

  returns the width or height of the enclosing rectangle.

- `double getX()`
- `double getY()`

  returns the *x* or *y* coordinate of the top left corner of the enclosing rectangle.

---

java.awt.geom.Rectangle2D.Double 1.2

- `Rectangle2D.Double(double x, double y, double w, double h)`

  constructs a rectangle with the given top left corner, width, and height.

---

java.awt.geom.Rectangle2D.Float 1.2

- Rectangle2D.Float(float x, float y, float w, float h)

  constructs a rectangle with the given top left corner, width, and height.

---

java.awt.geom.Ellipse2D.Double 1.2

- Ellipse2D.Double(double x, double y, double w, double h)

  constructs an ellipse whose bounding rectangle has the given top left corner, width, and height.

---

java.awt.geom.Point2D.Double 1.2

- Point2D.Double(double x, double y)

  constructs a point with the given coordinates.

---

java.awt.geom.Line2D.Double 1.2

- Line2D.Double(Point2D start, Point2D end)
- Line2D.Double(double startX, double startY, double endX, double endY)

  constructs a line with the given start and end points.

10.6 Using Color

The setPaint method of the Graphics2D class lets you select a color that is used for all subsequent drawing operations on the graphics context. For example:

```
g2.setPaint(Color.RED);
g2.drawString("Warning!", 100, 100);
```

You can fill the interiors of closed shapes (such as rectangles or ellipses) with a color. Simply call fill instead of draw:

```
Rectangle2D rect = . . .;
g2.setPaint(Color.RED);
g2.fill(rect); // fills rect with red
```

To draw in multiple colors, select a color, draw or fill, then select another color, and draw or fill again.

 NOTE: The `fill` method paints one fewer pixel to the right and the bottom. For example, if you draw a `new Rectangle2D.Double(0, 0, 10, 20)`, then the drawing includes the pixels with $x = 10$ and $y = 20$. If you fill the same rectangle, those pixels are not painted.

Define colors with the `Color` class. The `java.awt.Color` class offers predefined constants for the following 13 standard colors:

BLACK, BLUE, CYAN, DARK_GRAY, GRAY, GREEN, LIGHT_GRAY, MAGENTA, ORANGE, PINK, RED, WHITE, YELLOW

 NOTE: Before Java SE 1.4, color constant names were lowercase, such as `Color.red`. This is odd because the standard coding convention is to write constants in uppercase. You can now write the standard color names in uppercase or, for backward compatibility, lowercase.

You can specify a custom color by creating a `Color` object by its red, green, and blue components. Using a scale of 0–255 (that is, one byte) for the redness, blueness, and greenness, call the `Color` constructor like this:

```
Color(int redness, int greenness, int blueness)
```

Here is an example of setting a custom color:

```
g2.setPaint(new Color(0, 128, 128)); // a dull blue-green
g2.drawString("Welcome!", 75, 125);
```

 NOTE: In addition to solid colors, you can select more complex "paint" settings, such as varying hues or images. See the Advanced AWT chapter in Volume II for more details. If you use a `Graphics` object instead of a `Graphics2D` object, you need to use the `setColor` method to set colors.

To set the *background color*, use the `setBackground` method of the `Component` class, an ancestor of `JComponent`.

```
MyComponent p = new MyComponent();
p.setBackground(Color.PINK);
```

There is also a `setForeground` method. It specifies the default color that is used for drawing on the component.

TIP: The brighter() and darker() methods of the Color class produce, as their names suggest, either brighter or darker versions of the current color. Using the brighter method is also a good way to highlight an item. Actually, brighter() is just a little bit brighter. To make a color really stand out, apply it three times: c.brighter().brighter().brighter().

Java gives you predefined names for many more colors in its SystemColor class. The constants in this class encapsulate the colors used for various elements of the user's system. For example,

```
p.setBackground(SystemColor.window)
```

sets the background color of the component to the default used by all windows on the user's desktop. (The background is filled in whenever the window is repainted.) Using the colors in the SystemColor class is particularly useful when you want to draw user interface elements so that the colors match those already found on the user's desktop. Table 10.1 lists the system color names and their meanings.

Table 10.1 System Colors

Name	Purpose
desktop	Background color of desktop
activeCaption	Background color for captions
activeCaptionText	Text color for captions
activeCaptionBorder	Border color for caption text
inactiveCaption	Background color for inactive captions
inactiveCaptionText	Text color for inactive captions
inactiveCaptionBorder	Border color for inactive captions
window	Background for windows
windowBorder	Color of window border frame
windowText	Text color inside windows
menu	Background for menus
menuText	Text color for menus
text	Background color for text
textText	Text color for text

(Continues)

Table 10.1 *(Continued)*

Name	Purpose
textInactiveText	Text color for inactive controls
textHighlight	Background color for highlighted text
textHighlightText	Text color for highlighted text
control	Background color for controls
controlText	Text color for controls
controlLtHighlight	Light highlight color for controls
controlHighlight	Highlight color for controls
controlShadow	Shadow color for controls
controlDkShadow	Dark shadow color for controls
scrollbar	Background color for scrollbars
info	Background color for spot-help text
infoText	Text color for spot-help text

---

java.awt.Color 1.0

- Color(int r, int g, int b)

  creates a color object.

Parameters:	r	The red value (0–255)
	g	The green value (0–255)
	b	The blue value (0–255)

---

java.awt.Graphics 1.0

- Color getColor()
- void setColor(Color c)

  gets or sets the current color. All subsequent graphics operations will use the new color.

Parameters:	c	The new color

---

java.awt.Graphics2D 1.2

- `Paint getPaint()`
- `void setPaint(Paint p)`

  gets or sets the paint property of this graphics context. The `Color` class implements the `Paint` interface. Therefore, you can use this method to set the paint attribute to a solid color.

- `void fill(Shape s)`

  fills the shape with the current paint.

---

java.awt.Component 1.0

- `Color getBackground()`
- `void setBackground(Color c)`

  gets or sets the background color.

  Parameters: c   The new background color

- `Color getForeground()`
- `void setForeground(Color c)`

  gets or sets the foreground color.

  Parameters: c   The new foreground color

10.7 Using Special Fonts for Text

The "Not a Hello World" program at the beginning of this chapter displayed a string in the default font. Sometimes, you will want to show your text in a different font. You can specify a font by its *font face name*. A font face name is composed of a *font family name*, such as "Helvetica," and an optional suffix such as "Bold." For example, the font faces "Helvetica" and "Helvetica Bold" are both considered to be part of the family named "Helvetica."

To find out which fonts are available on a particular computer, call the `getAvailableFontFamilyNames` method of the `GraphicsEnvironment` class. The method returns an array of strings containing the names of all available fonts. To obtain an instance of the `GraphicsEnvironment` class that describes the graphics environment of the user's system, use the static `getLocalGraphicsEnvironment` method. The following program prints the names of all fonts on your system:

```
import java.awt.*;

public class ListFonts
{
   public static void main(String[] args)
   {
      String[] fontNames = GraphicsEnvironment
         .getLocalGraphicsEnvironment()
         .getAvailableFontFamilyNames();
      for (String fontName : fontNames)
         System.out.println(fontName);
   }
}
```

On one system, the list starts out like this:

```
Abadi MT Condensed Light
Arial
Arial Black
Arial Narrow
Arioso
Baskerville
Binner Gothic
. . .
```

and goes on for another seventy or so fonts.

Font face names can be trademarked, and font designs can be copyrighted in some jurisdictions. Thus, the distribution of fonts often involves royalty payments to a font foundry. Of course, just as there are inexpensive imitations of famous perfumes, there are lookalikes for name-brand fonts. For example, the Helvetica imitation that is shipped with Windows is called Arial.

To establish a common baseline, the AWT defines five *logical* font names:

```
SansSerif
Serif
Monospaced
Dialog
DialogInput
```

These names are always mapped to some fonts that actually exist on the client machine. For example, on a Windows system, SansSerif is mapped to Arial.

In addition, the Oracle JDK always includes three font families named "Lucida Sans," "Lucida Bright," and "Lucida Sans Typewriter."

To draw characters in a font, you must first create an object of the class Font. Specify the font face name, the font style, and the point size. Here is an example of how you construct a Font object:

```
Font sansbold14 = new Font("SansSerif", Font.BOLD, 14);
```

The third argument is the point size. Points are commonly used in typography to indicate the size of a font. There are 72 points per inch.

You can use a logical font name in place of the font face name in the Font constructor. Specify the style (plain, **bold**, *italic*, or ***bold italic***) by setting the second Font constructor argument to one of the following values:

```
Font.PLAIN
Font.BOLD
Font.ITALIC
Font.BOLD + Font.ITALIC
```

 NOTE: The mapping from logical to physical font names is defined in the fontconfig.properties file in the jre/lib subdirectory of the Java installation. See http://docs.oracle.com/javase/8/docs/technotes/guides/intl/fontconfig.html for information on this file.

You can read font files in TrueType, OpenType, or PostScript Type 1 formats. You need an input stream for the font—typically from a file or URL. (See Chapter 1 of Volume II for more information on streams.) Then, call the static Font.createFont method:

```
URL url = new URL("http://www.fonts.com/Wingbats.ttf");
InputStream in = url.openStream();
Font f1 = Font.createFont(Font.TRUETYPE_FONT, in);
```

The font is plain with a font size of 1 point. Use the deriveFont method to get a font of the desired size:

```
Font f = f1.deriveFont(14.0F);
```

 CAUTION: There are two overloaded versions of the deriveFont method. One of them (with a float parameter) sets the font size, the other (with an int parameter) sets the font style. Thus, f1.deriveFont(14) sets the style and not the size! (The result is an italic font because it happens that the binary representation of 14 has the ITALIC bit but not the BOLD bit set.)

The Java fonts contain the usual ASCII characters as well as symbols. For example, if you print the character '\u2297' in the Dialog font, you get a ⊗ character. Only the symbols defined in the Unicode character set are available.

Here's the code that displays the string "Hello, World!" in the standard sans serif font on your system, using 14-point bold type:

```
Font sansbold14 = new Font("SansSerif", Font.BOLD, 14);
g2.setFont(sansbold14);
String message = "Hello, World!";
g2.drawString(message, 75, 100);
```

Next, let's *center* the string in its component instead of drawing it at an arbitrary position. We need to know the width and height of the string in pixels. These dimensions depend on three factors:

- The font used (in our case, sans serif, bold, 14 point);
- The string (in our case, "Hello, World!"); and
- The device on which the font is drawn (in our case, the user's screen).

To obtain an object that represents the font characteristics of the screen device, call the getFontRenderContext method of the Graphics2D class. It returns an object of the FontRenderContext class. Simply pass that object to the getStringBounds method of the Font class:

```
FontRenderContext context = g2.getFontRenderContext();
Rectangle2D bounds = sansbold14..getStringBounds(message, context);
```

The getStringBounds method returns a rectangle that encloses the string.

To interpret the dimensions of that rectangle, you should know some basic typesetting terms (see Figure 10.13). The *baseline* is the imaginary line where, for example, the bottom of a character like "e" rests. The *ascent* is the distance from the baseline to the top of an *ascender*, which is the upper part of a letter like "b" or "k," or an uppercase character. The *descent* is the distance from the baseline to a *descender*, which is the lower portion of a letter like 'p' or 'g'.

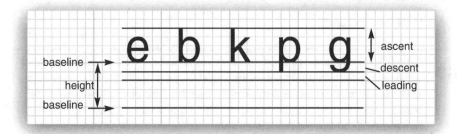

Figure 10.13 Typesetting terms illustrated

Leading is the space between the descent of one line and the ascent of the next line. (The term has its origin from the strips of lead that typesetters used to separate lines.) The *height* of a font is the distance between successive baselines, which is the same as descent + leading + ascent.

The width of the rectangle that the getStringBounds method returns is the horizontal extent of the string. The height of the rectangle is the sum of ascent, descent, and leading. The rectangle has its origin at the baseline of the string. The top *y* coordinate of the rectangle is negative. Thus, you can obtain string width, height, and ascent as follows:

```
double stringWidth = bounds.getWidth();
double stringHeight = bounds.getHeight();
double ascent = -bounds.getY();
```

If you need to know the descent or leading, use the getLineMetrics method of the Font class. That method returns an object of the LineMetrics class, which has methods to obtain the descent and leading:

```
LineMetrics metrics = f.getLineMetrics(message, context);
float descent = metrics.getDescent();
float leading = metrics.getLeading();
```

The following code uses all this information to center a string in its surrounding component:

```
FontRenderContext context = g2.getFontRenderContext();
Rectangle2D bounds = f.getStringBounds(message, context);

// (x,y) = top left corner of text
double x = (getWidth() - bounds.getWidth()) / 2;
double y = (getHeight() - bounds.getHeight()) / 2;

// add ascent to y to reach the baseline
double ascent = -bounds.getY();
double baseY = y + ascent;
g2.drawString(message, (int) x, (int) baseY);
```

To understand the centering, consider that getWidth() returns the width of the component. A portion of that width, namely bounds.getWidth(), is occupied by the message string. The remainder should be equally distributed on both sides. Therefore, the blank space on each side is half the difference. The same reasoning applies to the height.

 NOTE: When you need to compute layout dimensions outside the paintComponent method, you can't obtain the font render context from the Graphics2D object. Instead, call the getFontMetrics method of the JComponent class and then call getFontRenderContext.

```
FontRenderContext context = getFontMetrics(f).getFontRenderContext();
```

To show that the positioning is accurate, the sample program also draws the baseline and the bounding rectangle. Figure 10.14 shows the screen display; Listing 10.5 is the program listing.

Figure 10.14 Drawing the baseline and string bounds

Listing 10.5   font/FontTest.java

```
1  package font;
2
3  import java.awt.*;
4  import java.awt.font.*;
5  import java.awt.geom.*;
6  import javax.swing.*;
7
8  /**
9   * @version 1.34 2015-05-12
10  * @author Cay Horstmann
11  */
12 public class FontTest
13 {
14    public static void main(String[] args)
15    {
16       EventQueue.invokeLater(() ->
17          {
18             JFrame frame = new FontFrame();
19             frame.setTitle("FontTest");
20             frame.setDefaultCloseOperation(JFrame.EXIT_ON_CLOSE);
21             frame.setVisible(true);
22          });
23    }
24 }
25
26 /**
27  * A frame with a text message component
28  */
```

```
29  class FontFrame extends JFrame
30  {
31     public FontFrame()
32     {
33        add(new FontComponent());
34        pack();
35     }
36  }
37
38  /**
39   * A component that shows a centered message in a box.
40   */
41  class FontComponent extends JComponent
42  {
43     private static final int DEFAULT_WIDTH = 300;
44     private static final int DEFAULT_HEIGHT = 200;
45
46     public void paintComponent(Graphics g)
47     {
48        Graphics2D g2 = (Graphics2D) g;
49
50        String message = "Hello, World!";
51
52        Font f = new Font("Serif", Font.BOLD, 36);
53        g2.setFont(f);
54
55        // measure the size of the message
56
57        FontRenderContext context = g2.getFontRenderContext();
58        Rectangle2D bounds = f.getStringBounds(message, context);
59
60        // set (x,y) = top left corner of text
61
62        double x = (getWidth() - bounds.getWidth()) / 2;
63        double y = (getHeight() - bounds.getHeight()) / 2;
64
65        // add ascent to y to reach the baseline
66
67        double ascent = -bounds.getY();
68        double baseY = y + ascent;
69
70        // draw the message
71
72        g2.drawString(message, (int) x, (int) baseY);
73
74        g2.setPaint(Color.LIGHT_GRAY);
75
76        // draw the baseline
77
```

(Continues)

Listing 10.5 *(Continued)*

```
78        g2.draw(new Line2D.Double(x, baseY, x + bounds.getWidth(), baseY));
79
80        // draw the enclosing rectangle
81
82        Rectangle2D rect = new Rectangle2D.Double(x, y, bounds.getWidth(), bounds.getHeight());
83        g2.draw(rect);
84     }
85
86     public Dimension getPreferredSize() { return new Dimension(DEFAULT_WIDTH, DEFAULT_HEIGHT); }
87  }
```

---

java.awt.Font 1.0

- Font(String name, int style, int size)

  creates a new font object.

Parameters:	name	The font name. This is either a font face name (such as "Helvetica Bold") or a logical font name (such as "Serif", "SansSerif")
	style	The style (Font.PLAIN, Font.BOLD, Font.ITALIC, or Font.BOLD + Font.ITALIC)
	size	The point size (for example, 12)

- String getFontName()

  gets the font face name (such as "Helvetica Bold").

- String getFamily()

  gets the font family name (such as "Helvetica").

- String getName()

  gets the logical name (such as "SansSerif") if the font was created with a logical font name; otherwise, gets the font face name.

- Rectangle2D getStringBounds(String s, FontRenderContext context) 1.2

  returns a rectangle that encloses the string. The origin of the rectangle falls on the baseline. The top y coordinate of the rectangle equals the negative of the ascent. The height of the rectangle equals the sum of ascent, descent, and leading. The width equals the string width.

- LineMetrics getLineMetrics(String s, FontRenderContext context) 1.2

  returns a line metrics object to determine the extent of the string.

(Continues)

`java.awt.Font` `1.0` *(Continued)*

- Font deriveFont(int style) `1.2`
- Font deriveFont(float size) `1.2`
- Font deriveFont(int style, float size) `1.2`

  returns a new font that is equal to this font, except that it has the given size and style.

`java.awt.font.LineMetrics` `1.2`

- float getAscent()

  gets the font ascent—the distance from the baseline to the tops of uppercase characters.

- float getDescent()

  gets the font descent—the distance from the baseline to the bottoms of descenders.

- float getLeading()

  gets the font leading—the space between the bottom of one line of text and the top of the next line.

- float getHeight()

  gets the total height of the font—the distance between the two baselines of text (descent + leading + ascent).

`java.awt.Graphics` `1.0`

- Font getFont()
- void setFont(Font font)

  gets or sets the current font. That font will be used for subsequent text-drawing operations.

  Parameters: font   A font

- void drawString(String str, int x, int y)

  draws a string in the current font and color.

  Parameters: str   The string to be drawn

                       x   The x coordinate of the start of the string

                       y   The y coordinate of the baseline of the string

---

java.awt.Graphics2D 1.2

- FontRenderContext getFontRenderContext()

  gets a font render context that specifies font characteristics in this graphics context.
- void drawString(String str, float x, float y)

  draws a string in the current font and color.

Parameters:	str	The string to be drawn
	x	The *x* coordinate of the start of the string
	y	The *y* coordinate of the baseline of the string

---

javax.swing.JComponent 1.2

- FontMetrics getFontMetrics(Font f) 5.0

  gets the font metrics for the given font. The FontMetrics class is a precursor to the LineMetrics class.

---

java.awt.FontMetrics 1.0

- FontRenderContext getFontRenderContext() 1.2

  gets a font render context for the font.

10.8 Displaying Images

You have already seen how to build up simple drawings by painting lines and shapes. Complex images, such as photographs, are usually generated externally—for example, with a scanner or special image-manipulation software. As you will see in Volume II, it is also possible to produce an image, pixel by pixel.

Once images are stored in local files or someplace on the Internet, you can read them into a Java application and display them on Graphics objects. There are many ways of reading images. Here, we use the ImageIcon class that you already saw:

```
Image image = new ImageIcon(filename).getImage();
```

Now the variable image contains a reference to an object that encapsulates the image data. You can display the image with the drawImage method of the Graphics class.

```
public void paintComponent(Graphics g)
{
   . . .
   g.drawImage(image, x, y, null);
}
```

Listing 10.6 takes this a little bit further and *tiles* the window with the graphics image. The result looks like the screen shown in Figure 10.15. We do the tiling in the `paintComponent` method. We first draw one copy of the image in the top left corner and then use the `copyArea` call to copy it into the entire window:

```
for (int i = 0; i * imageWidth <= getWidth(); i++)
   for (int j = 0; j * imageHeight <= getHeight(); j++)
      if (i + j > 0)
         g.copyArea(0, 0, imageWidth, imageHeight, i * imageWidth, j * imageHeight);
```

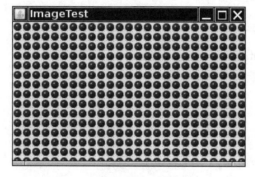

Figure 10.15 Window with tiled graphics image

Listing 10.6 shows the full source code of the image display program.

Listing 10.6 `image/ImageTest.java`

```
1  package image;
2
3  import java.awt.*;
4  import javax.swing.*;
5
6  /**
7   * @version 1.34 2015-05-12
8   * @author Cay Horstmann
9   */
10 public class ImageTest
11 {
```

(Continues)

Listing 10.6 *(Continued)*

```
12    public static void main(String[] args)
13    {
14       EventQueue.invokeLater(() ->
15          {
16             JFrame frame = new ImageFrame();
17             frame.setTitle("ImageTest");
18             frame.setDefaultCloseOperation(JFrame.EXIT_ON_CLOSE);
19             frame.setVisible(true);
20          });
21    }
22 }
23
24 /**
25  * A frame with an image component
26  */
27 class ImageFrame extends JFrame
28 {
29    public ImageFrame()
30    {
31       add(new ImageComponent());
32       pack();
33    }
34 }
35
36 /**
37  * A component that displays a tiled image
38  */
39 class ImageComponent extends JComponent
40 {
41    private static final int DEFAULT_WIDTH = 300;
42    private static final int DEFAULT_HEIGHT = 200;
43
44    private Image image;
45
46    public ImageComponent()
47    {
48       image = new ImageIcon("blue-ball.gif").getImage();
49    }
50
51    public void paintComponent(Graphics g)
52    {
53       if (image == null) return;
54
```

```
55        int imageWidth = image.getWidth(this);
56        int imageHeight = image.getHeight(this);
57
58        // draw the image in the upper-left corner
59
60        g.drawImage(image, 0, 0, null);
61
62        // tile the image across the component
63
64        for (int i = 0; i * imageWidth <= getWidth(); i++)
65           for (int j = 0; j * imageHeight <= getHeight(); j++)
66              if (i + j > 0)
67                 g.copyArea(0, 0, imageWidth, imageHeight, i * imageWidth, j * imageHeight);
68     }
69
70     public Dimension getPreferredSize() { return new Dimension(DEFAULT_WIDTH, DEFAULT_HEIGHT); }
71  }
```

---

java.awt.Graphics 1.0

- `boolean drawImage(Image img, int x, int y, ImageObserver observer)`

  draws an unscaled image. Note: This call may return before the image is drawn.

  Parameters: `img`   The image to be drawn

                     `x`   The x coordinate of the top left corner

                     `y`   The y coordinate of the top left corner

                     `observer`   The object to notify of the progress of the rendering process (may be `null`)

- `boolean drawImage(Image img, int x, int y, int width, int height, ImageObserver observer)`

  draws a scaled image. The system scales the image to fit into a region with the given width and height. Note: This call may return before the image is drawn.

  Parameters: `img`   The image to be drawn

                     `x`   The x coordinate of the top left corner

                     `y`   The y coordinate of the top left corner

                     `width`   The desired width of image

                     `height`   The desired height of image

                     `observer`   The object to notify of the progress of the rendering process (may be `null`)

(Continues)

`java.awt.Graphics` 1.0 *(Continued)*

- `void copyArea(int x, int y, int width, int height, int dx, int dy)`

  copies an area of the screen.

Parameters:	x	The *x* coordinate of the top left corner of the source area
	y	The *y* coordinate of the top left corner of the source area
	width	The width of the source area
	height	The height of the source area
	dx	The horizontal distance from the source area to the target area
	dy	The vertical distance from the source area to the target area

---

This concludes our introduction to Java graphics programming. For more advanced techniques, refer to the discussion of 2D graphics and image manipulation in Volume II. In the next chapter, you will learn how your programs can react to user input.

Event Handling

In this chapter

Event handling is of fundamental importance to programs with a graphical user interface. To implement user interfaces, you have to master the way in which Java handles events. This chapter explains how the Java AWT event model works. You will see how to capture events from user interface components and input devices. We will also show you how to work with *actions*, which represent a more structured approach for processing action events.

11.1 Basics of Event Handling

Any operating environment that supports GUIs constantly monitors events such as keystrokes or mouse clicks. The operating environment reports these events to the programs that are running. Each program then decides what, if anything, to do in response to these events. In languages like Visual Basic, the correspondence between events and code is obvious. One writes code for each specific event of interest and places the code in what is usually called an *event procedure*. For example, a Visual Basic button named "HelpButton" would have a `HelpButton_Click` event procedure associated with it. The code in this procedure executes whenever

587

that button is clicked. Each Visual Basic GUI component responds to a fixed set of events, and it is impossible to change the events to which it responds.

On the other hand, if you use a language like raw C to do event-driven programming, you need to write the code that constantly checks the event queue for what the operating environment is reporting. This is usually done by encasing your code in a loop with a massive switch statement. This technique is obviously ugly and, in any case, much more difficult to code. Its advantage is that the events you can respond to are not as limited as in the languages which, like Visual Basic, go to great lengths to hide the event queue from the programmer.

The Java programming environment takes an approach somewhere in between the Visual Basic and the raw C in terms of power and the resulting complexity. Within the limits of the events that the AWT knows about, you completely control how events are transmitted from the *event sources* (such as buttons or scrollbars) to *event listeners*. You can designate *any* object to be an event listener—in practice, you pick an object that can conveniently carry out the desired response to the event. This *event delegation model* gives you much more flexibility than is possible with Visual Basic, in which the listener is predetermined.

Event sources have methods that allow you to register event listeners with them. When an event happens to the source, the source sends a notification of that event to all the listener objects that were registered for that event.

As one would expect in an object-oriented language like Java, the information about the event is encapsulated in an *event object*. In Java, all event objects ultimately derive from the class `java.util.EventObject`. Of course, there are subclasses for each event type, such as `ActionEvent` and `WindowEvent`.

Different event sources can produce different kinds of events. For example, a button can send `ActionEvent` objects, whereas a window can send `WindowEvent` objects.

To sum up, here's an overview of how event handling in the AWT works:

- A listener object is an instance of a class that implements a special interface called (naturally enough) a *listener interface*.

- An event source is an object that can register listener objects and send them event objects.

- The event source sends out event objects to all registered listeners when that event occurs.

- The listener objects will then use the information in the event object to determine their reaction to the event.

Figure 11.1 shows the relationship between the event handling classes and interfaces.

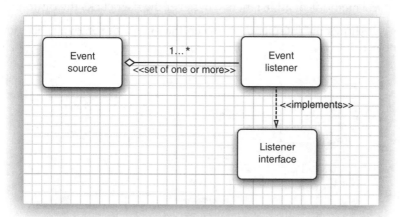

Figure 11.1 Relationship between event sources and listeners

Here is an example for specifying a listener:

```
ActionListener listener = . . .;
JButton button = new JButton("OK");
button.addActionListener(listener);
```

Now the `listener` object is notified whenever an "action event" occurs in the button. For buttons, as you might expect, an action event is a button click.

To implement the `ActionListener` interface, the listener class must have a method called `actionPerformed` that receives an `ActionEvent` object as a parameter.

```
class MyListener implements ActionListener
{
   . . .
   public void actionPerformed(ActionEvent event)
   {
      // reaction to button click goes here
      . . .
   }
}
```

Whenever the user clicks the button, the JButton object creates an ActionEvent object and calls listener.actionPerformed(event), passing that event object. An event source such as a button can have multiple listeners. In that case, the button calls the actionPerformed methods of all listeners whenever the user clicks the button.

Figure 11.2 shows the interaction between the event source, event listener, and event object.

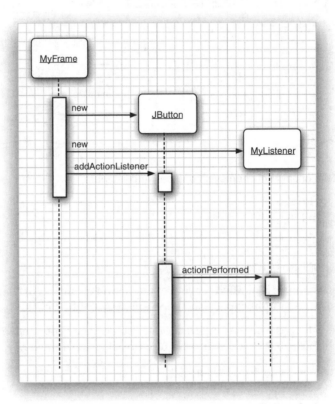

Figure 11.2 Event notification

11.1.1 Example: Handling a Button Click

As a way of getting comfortable with the event delegation model, let's work through all the details needed for the simple example of responding to a button click. For this example, we will show a panel populated with three buttons. Three listener objects are added as action listeners to the buttons.

With this scenario, each time a user clicks on any of the buttons on the panel, the associated listener object receives an ActionEvent that indicates a button click. In our sample program, the listener object will then change the background color of the panel.

Before we can show you the program that listens to button clicks, we first need to explain how to create buttons and how to add them to a panel. (For more on GUI elements, see Chapter 12.)

To create a button, specify a label string, an icon, or both in the button constructor. Here are two examples:

```
JButton yellowButton = new JButton("Yellow");
JButton blueButton = new JButton(new ImageIcon("blue-ball.gif"));
```

Call the add method to add the buttons to a panel:

```
JButton yellowButton = new JButton("Yellow");
JButton blueButton = new JButton("Blue");
JButton redButton = new JButton("Red");

buttonPanel.add(yellowButton);
buttonPanel.add(blueButton);
buttonPanel.add(redButton);
```

Figure 11.3 shows the result.

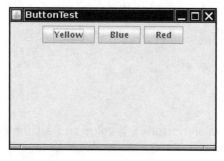

Figure 11.3 A panel filled with buttons

Next, we need to add code that listens to these buttons. This requires classes that implement the `ActionListener` interface, which, as we just mentioned, has one method: `actionPerformed`, whose signature looks like this:

```
public void actionPerformed(ActionEvent event)
```

 NOTE: The `ActionListener` interface we used in the button example is not restricted to button clicks. It is used in many separate situations:

- When an item is selected from a list box with a double click
- When a menu item is selected
- When the Enter key is pressed in a text field
- When a certain amount of time has elapsed for a `Timer` component

You will see more details in this chapter and the next.

The way to use the `ActionListener` interface is the same in all situations: The `actionPerformed` method (which is the only method in `ActionListener`) takes an object of type `ActionEvent` as a parameter. This event object gives you information about the event that happened.

When a button is clicked, we want the background color of the panel to change to a particular color. We store the desired color in our listener class.

```
class ColorAction implements ActionListener
{
   private Color backgroundColor;

   public ColorAction(Color c)
   {
      backgroundColor = c;
   }

   public void actionPerformed(ActionEvent event)
   {
      // set panel background color
      . . .
   }
}
```

We then construct one object for each color and set the objects as the button listeners.

```
ColorAction yellowAction = new ColorAction(Color.YELLOW);
ColorAction blueAction = new ColorAction(Color.BLUE);
ColorAction redAction = new ColorAction(Color.RED);

yellowButton.addActionListener(yellowAction);
blueButton.addActionListener(blueAction);
redButton.addActionListener(redAction);
```

For example, if a user clicks on the button marked "Yellow," the actionPerformed method of the yellowAction object is called. Its backgroundColor instance field is set to Color.YELLOW, and it can now proceed to set the panel's background color.

Just one issue remains. The ColorAction object doesn't have access to the buttonPanel variable. You can solve this problem in two ways. You can store the panel in the ColorAction object and set it in the ColorAction constructor. Or, more conveniently, you can make ColorAction into an inner class of the ButtonFrame class. Its methods can then access the outer panel automatically. (For more information on inner classes, see Chapter 6.)

We follow the latter approach. Here is how you place the ColorAction class inside the ButtonFrame class:

```
class ButtonFrame extends JFrame
{
   private JPanel buttonPanel;
   . . .
   private class ColorAction implements ActionListener
   {
      private Color backgroundColor;
      . . .
      public void actionPerformed(ActionEvent event)
      {
         buttonPanel.setBackground(backgroundColor);
      }
   }
}
```

Look closely at the actionPerformed method. The ColorAction class doesn't have a buttonPanel field. But the outer ButtonFrame class does.

This situation is very common. Event listener objects usually need to carry out some action that affects other objects. You can often strategically place the listener class inside the class whose state the listener should modify.

Listing 11.1 contains the complete frame class. Whenever you click one of the buttons, the appropriate action listener changes the background color of the panel.

Listing 11.1 button/ButtonFrame.java

```
1  package button;
2
3  import java.awt.*;
4  import java.awt.event.*;
5  import javax.swing.*;
6
7  /**
8   * A frame with a button panel
9   */
10 public class ButtonFrame extends JFrame
11 {
12    private JPanel buttonPanel;
13    private static final int DEFAULT_WIDTH = 300;
14    private static final int DEFAULT_HEIGHT = 200;
15
16    public ButtonFrame()
17    {
18       setSize(DEFAULT_WIDTH, DEFAULT_HEIGHT);
19
20       // create buttons
21       JButton yellowButton = new JButton("Yellow");
22       JButton blueButton = new JButton("Blue");
23       JButton redButton = new JButton("Red");
24
25       buttonPanel = new JPanel();
26
27       // add buttons to panel
28       buttonPanel.add(yellowButton);
29       buttonPanel.add(blueButton);
30       buttonPanel.add(redButton);
31
32       // add panel to frame
33       add(buttonPanel);
34
35       // create button actions
36       ColorAction yellowAction = new ColorAction(Color.YELLOW);
37       ColorAction blueAction = new ColorAction(Color.BLUE);
38       ColorAction redAction = new ColorAction(Color.RED);
39
40       // associate actions with buttons
```

```
41        yellowButton.addActionListener(yellowAction);
42        blueButton.addActionListener(blueAction);
43        redButton.addActionListener(redAction);
44     }
45
46     /**
47      * An action listener that sets the panel's background color.
48      */
49     private class ColorAction implements ActionListener
50     {
51        private Color backgroundColor;
52
53        public ColorAction(Color c)
54        {
55           backgroundColor = c;
56        }
57
58        public void actionPerformed(ActionEvent event)
59        {
60           buttonPanel.setBackground(backgroundColor);
61        }
62     }
63  }
```

---

javax.swing.JButton 1.2

- JButton(String label)
- JButton(Icon icon)
- JButton(String label, Icon icon)

  constructs a button. The label string can be plain text or, starting with Java SE 1.3, HTML; for example, "<html>Ok</html>".

---

java.awt.Container 1.0

- Component add(Component c)

  adds the component c to this container.

11.1.2 Specifying Listeners Concisely

In the preceding section, we defined a class for the event listener and constructed three objects of that class. It is not all that common to have multiple instances of a listener class. Most commonly, each listener carries out a separate action. In that case, there is no need to make a separate class. Simply use a lambda expression:

```
exitButton.addActionListener(event -> System.exit(0));
```

Now consider the case in which we have multiple related actions, such as the color buttons of the preceding section. In such a case, implement a helper method:

```
public void makeButton(String name, Color backgroundColor)
{
   JButton button = new JButton(name);
   buttonPanel.add(button);
   button.addActionListener(event ->
      buttonPanel.setBackground(backgroundColor));
}
```

Note that the lambda expression refers to the parameter variable backgroundColor.

Then we simply call

```
makeButton("yellow", Color.YELLOW);
makeButton("blue", Color.BLUE);
makeButton("red", Color.RED);
```

Here, we construct three listener objects, one for each color, without explicitly defining a class. Each time the helper method is called, it makes an instance of a class that implements the ActionListener interface. Its actionPerformed action references the backGroundColor value that is, in fact, stored with the listener object. However, all this happens without having to explicitly define listener classes, instance variables, or constructors that set them.

 NOTE: In older code, you will often see the use of anonymous classes:

```
exitButton.addActionListener(new ActionListener()
   {
      public void actionPerformed(new ActionEvent)
      {
         System.exit(0);
      }
   });
```

Of course, this rather verbose code is no longer necessary. Using a lambda expression is simpler and clearer.

NOTE: Some programmers are not comfortable with inner classes or lambda expressions and instead make the container of the event sources implement the ActionListener interface. Then, the container sets *itself* as the listener, like this:

```
yellowButton.addActionListener(this);
blueButton.addActionListener(this);
redButton.addActionListener(this);
```

Now the three buttons no longer have individual listeners. They share a single listener object—namely, the frame. Therefore, the actionPerformed method must figure out which button was clicked.

```
class ButtonFrame extends JFrame implements ActionListener
{
   . . .
   public void actionPerformed(ActionEvent event)
   {
      Object source = event.getSource();
      if (source == yellowButton) . . .
      else if (source == blueButton) . . .
      else if (source == redButton ) . . .
      else . . .
   }
}
```

We do not recommend this strategy.

NOTE: Before lambda expressions were available, there was another mechanism for specifying event listeners whose event handler contains a single method call. Suppose, for example, that a button listener needs to execute the call

```
frame.loadData();
```

The EventHandler class can create such a listener with the call

```
EventHandler.create(ActionListener.class, frame, "loadData")
```

This is now only of historical interest. With lambda expressions, it is much easier to use

```
event -> frame.loadData();
```

The EventHandler mechanism is also inefficient and somewhat error-prone. It uses reflection to invoke the method. For that reason, the second argument in the call to EventHandler.create must belong to a *public* class. Otherwise, the reflection mechanism will not be able to locate and invoke the target method.

`java.awt.event.ActionEvent` 1.1

- `String getActionCommand()`

  returns the command string associated with this action event. If the action event originated from a button, the command string equals the button label, unless it has been changed with the `setActionCommand` method.

`java.beans.EventHandler` 1.4

- `static <T> T create(Class<T> listenerInterface, Object target, String action)`
- `static <T> T create(Class<T> listenerInterface, Object target, String action, String eventProperty)`
- `static <T> T create(Class<T> listenerInterface, Object target, String action, String eventProperty, String listenerMethod)`

  constructs an object of a proxy class that implements the given interface. Either the named method or all methods of the interface carry out the given action on the target object.

  The action can be a method name or a property of the target. If it is a property, its setter method is executed. For example, an action `"text"` is turned into a call of the `setText` method.

  The event property consists of one or more dot-separated property names. The first property is read from the parameter of the listener method, the second property is read from the resulting object, and so on. The final result becomes the parameter of the action. For example, the property `"source.text"` is turned into calls to the `getSource` and `getText` methods.

`java.util.EventObject` 1.1

- `Object getSource()`

  returns a reference to the object where the event occurred.

11.1.3 Example: Changing the Look-and-Feel

By default, Swing programs use the Metal look-and-feel. There are two ways to change to a different look-and-feel. The first is to supply a file `swing.properties` in the jre/lib subdirectory of your Java installation. In that file, set the property swing.defaultlaf to the class name of the look-and-feel that you want. For example:

```
swing.defaultlaf=com.sun.java.swing.plaf.motif.MotifLookAndFeel
```

Note that the Metal and Nimbus look-and-feels are located in the javax.swing package. The other look-and-feel packages are located in the com.sun.java package and need not be present in every Java implementation. For example, for copyright reasons, the Windows and Macintosh look-and-feel packages are only shipped with the Windows and Macintosh versions of the Java runtime environment.

 TIP: Lines starting with a # character are ignored in property files, so you can supply several look-and-feel selections in the swing.properties file and move around the # to select one of them:

```
#swing.defaultlaf=javax.swing.plaf.metal.MetalLookAndFeel
swing.defaultlaf=com.sun.java.swing.plaf.motif.MotifLookAndFeel
#swing.defaultlaf=com.sun.java.swing.plaf.windows.WindowsLookAndFeel
```

You must restart your program to switch the look-and-feel in this way. A Swing program reads the swing.properties file only once, at startup.

The second way is to change the look-and-feel dynamically. Call the static UIManager.setLookAndFeel method and give it the name of the look-and-feel class that you want. Then call the static method SwingUtilities.updateComponentTreeUI to refresh the entire set of components. You need to supply one component to that method; it will find all others.

Here is an example showing how you can switch to the Motif look-and-feel in your program:

```
String className = "com.sun.java.swing.plaf.motif.MotifLookAndFeel";
try
{
   UIManager.setLookAndFeel(className);
   SwingUtilities.updateComponentTreeUI(frame);
   pack();
}
catch(Exception e) { e.printStackTrace(); }
```

To enumerate all installed look-and-feel implementations, call

```
UIManager.LookAndFeelInfo[] infos = UIManager.getInstalledLookAndFeels();
```

Then you can get the name and class name for each look-and-feel as

```
String name = infos[i].getName();
String className = infos[i].getClassName();
```

Listing 11.2 is a complete program that demonstrates how to switch the look-and-feel (see Figure 11.4). The program is similar to Listing 11.1. Following the advice of the preceding section, we use a helper method makeButton and a lambda expression to specify the button action—namely, to switch the look-and-feel.

```
public class PlafFrame extends JFrame
{
    . . .
    private void makeButton(String name, String className)
    {
        JButton button = new JButton(name);
        buttonPanel.add(button);
        button.addActionListener(event -> {
            . . .
            UIManager.setLookAndFeel(className);
            SwingUtilities.updateComponentTreeUI(this);
            . . .
        });
    }
}
```

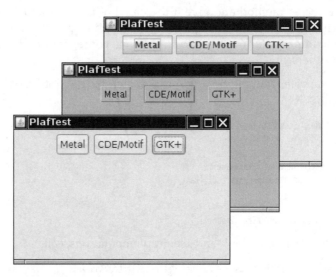

Figure 11.4 Switching the look-and-feel

NOTE: In previous editions of this book, we used an anonymous inner class to define this listener. At that time, we had to be careful to pass PlafFrame.this (and not the this reference of the inner class) to SwingUtilities.updateComponentTreeUI:

```
public class PlafFrame extends JFrame
{
    . . .
    private void makeButton(String name, final String className)
    {
        . . .
        button.addActionListener(new ActionListener()
            {
                public void actionPerformed(ActionEvent event)
                {
                    . . .
                    SwingUtilities.updateComponentTreeUI(PlafFrame.this);
                    . . .
                }
            });
    }
}
```

This problem goes away with lambda expressions. Inside a lambda expression, this refers to the enclosing object.

Listing 11.2 plaf/PlafFrame.java

```
1  package plaf;
2
3  import javax.swing.JButton;
4  import javax.swing.JFrame;
5  import javax.swing.JPanel;
6  import javax.swing.SwingUtilities;
7  import javax.swing.UIManager;
8
9  /**
10  * A frame with a button panel for changing look-and-feel
11  */
12  public class PlafFrame extends JFrame
13  {
14     private JPanel buttonPanel;
15
16     public PlafFrame()
17     {
18        buttonPanel = new JPanel();
19
20        UIManager.LookAndFeelInfo[] infos = UIManager.getInstalledLookAndFeels();
```

(Continues)

Listing 11.2 *(Continued)*

```
21        for (UIManager.LookAndFeelInfo info : infos)
22           makeButton(info.getName(), info.getClassName());
23
24        add(buttonPanel);
25        pack();
26     }
27
28     /**
29      * Makes a button to change the pluggable look-and-feel.
30      * @param name the button name
31      * @param className the name of the look-and-feel class
32      */
33     private void makeButton(String name, String className)
34     {
35        // add button to panel
36
37        JButton button = new JButton(name);
38        buttonPanel.add(button);
39
40        // set button action
41
42        button.addActionListener(event -> {
43           // button action: switch to the new look-and-feel
44           try
45           {
46              UIManager.setLookAndFeel(className);
47              SwingUtilities.updateComponentTreeUI(this);
48              pack();
49           }
50           catch (Exception e)
51           {
52              e.printStackTrace();
53           }
54        });
55     }
56  }
```

---

javax.swing.UIManager 1.2

- `static UIManager.LookAndFeelInfo[] getInstalledLookAndFeels()`

  gets an array of objects that describe the installed look-and-feel implementations.

- `static setLookAndFeel(String className)`

  sets the current look-and-feel, using the given class name (such as "javax.swing.plaf.metal.MetalLookAndFeel").

---

javax.swing.UIManager.LookAndFeelInfo 1.2

- `String getName()`

  returns the display name for the look-and-feel.
- `String getClassName()`

  returns the name of the implementation class for the look-and-feel.

11.1.4 Adapter Classes

Not all events are as simple to handle as button clicks. In a non-toy program, you will want to monitor when the user tries to close the main frame because you don't want your users to lose unsaved work. When the user closes the frame, you want to put up a dialog and exit the program only when the user agrees.

When the user tries to close a window, the `JFrame` object is the source of a `WindowEvent`. If you want to catch that event, you must have an appropriate listener object and add it to the frame's list of window listeners.

```
WindowListener listener = . . .;
frame.addWindowListener(listener);
```

The window listener must be an object of a class that implements the `WindowListener` interface. There are actually seven methods in the `WindowListener` interface. The frame calls them as the responses to seven distinct events that could happen to a window. The names are self-explanatory, except that "iconified" is usually called "minimized" under Windows. Here is the complete `WindowListener` interface:

```
public interface WindowListener
{
    void windowOpened(WindowEvent e);
    void windowClosing(WindowEvent e);
    void windowClosed(WindowEvent e);
    void windowIconified(WindowEvent e);
    void windowDeiconified(WindowEvent e);
    void windowActivated(WindowEvent e);
    void windowDeactivated(WindowEvent e);
}
```

 NOTE: To find out whether a window has been maximized, install a `WindowStateListener` and override the `windowStateChanged` method.

As is always the case in Java, any class that implements an interface must implement all its methods; in this case, that means implementing *seven* methods. Recall that we are only interested in one of these seven methods, namely the windowClosing method.

Of course, we can define a class that implements the interface, add a call to System.exit(0) in the windowClosing method, and write do-nothing functions for the other six methods:

```
class Terminator implements WindowListener
{
   public void windowClosing(WindowEvent e)
   {
     if (user agrees)
        System.exit(0);
   }

   public void windowOpened(WindowEvent e) {}
   public void windowClosed(WindowEvent e) {}
   public void windowIconified(WindowEvent e) {}
   public void windowDeiconified(WindowEvent e) {}
   public void windowActivated(WindowEvent e) {}
   public void windowDeactivated(WindowEvent e) {}
}
```

Typing code for six methods that don't do anything is the kind of tedious busy-work that nobody likes. To simplify this task, each of the AWT listener interfaces that have more than one method comes with a companion *adapter* class that implements all the methods in the interface but does nothing with them. For example, the WindowAdapter class has seven do-nothing methods. This means the adapter class automatically satisfies the technical requirements that Java imposes for implementing the associated listener interface. You can extend the adapter class to specify the desired reactions to some, but not all, of the event types in the interface. (An interface such as ActionListener that has only a single method does not need an adapter class.)

Let us make use of the window adapter. We can extend the WindowAdapter class, inherit six of the do-nothing methods, and override the windowClosing method:

```
class Terminator extends WindowAdapter
{
   public void windowClosing(WindowEvent e)
   {
     if (user agrees)
        System.exit(0);
   }
}
```

Now you can register an object of type Terminator as the event listener:

```
WindowListener listener = new Terminator();
frame.addWindowListener(listener);
```

Whenever the frame generates a window event, it passes it to the `listener` object by calling one of its seven methods (see Figure 11.5). Six of those methods do nothing; the `windowClosing` method calls `System.exit(0)`, terminating the application.

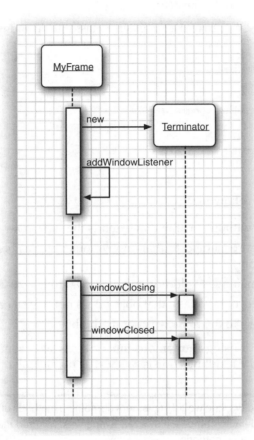

Figure 11.5 A window listener

 CAUTION: If you misspell the name of a method when extending an adapter class, the compiler won't catch your error. For example, if you define a method `windowIsClosing` in a `WindowAdapter` class, you will get a class with eight methods, and the `windowClosing` method will do nothing. Use the `@Override` annotation (which was described in Chapter 5) to protect against this error.

Creating a listener class that extends the WindowAdapter is an improvement, but we can go even further. There is no need to give a name to the listener object. Simply write

```
frame.addWindowListener(new Terminator());
```

But why stop there? We can make the listener class into an anonymous inner class of the frame.

```
frame.addWindowListener(new
    WindowAdapter()
    {
        public void windowClosing(WindowEvent e)
        {
            if (user agrees)
                System.exit(0);
        }
    });
```

This code does the following:

- Defines a class without a name that extends the WindowAdapter class
- Adds a windowClosing method to that anonymous class (as before, this method exits the program)
- Inherits the remaining six do-nothing methods from WindowAdapter
- Creates an object of this class; that object does not have a name, either
- Passes that object to the addWindowListener method

Again, the syntax for using anonymous inner classes takes some getting used to. The payoff is that the resulting code is as short as possible.

 NOTE: Nowadays, one would implement do-nothing methods of the WindowListener interface as default methods. However, Swing was invented many years before there were default methods.

---

java.awt.event.WindowListener 1.1

- void windowOpened(WindowEvent e)

    is called after the window has been opened.

- void windowClosing(WindowEvent e)

    is called when the user has issued a window manager command to close the window. Note that the window will close only if its hide or dispose method is called.

(Continues)

---

java.awt.event.WindowListener 1.1 *(Continued)*

- void windowClosed(WindowEvent e)

  is called after the window has closed.

- void windowIconified(WindowEvent e)

  is called after the window has been iconified.

- void windowDeiconified(WindowEvent e)

  is called after the window has been deiconified.

- void windowActivated(WindowEvent e)

  is called after the window has become active. Only a frame or dialog can be active. Typically, the window manager decorates the active window—for example, by highlighting the title bar.

- void windowDeactivated(WindowEvent e)

  is called after the window has become deactivated.

---

java.awt.event.WindowStateListener 1.4

- void windowStateChanged(WindowEvent event)

  is called after the window has been maximized, iconified, or restored to normal size.

---

java.awt.event.WindowEvent 1.1

- int getNewState() 1.4
- int getOldState() 1.4

  return the new and old state of a window in a window state change event. The returned integer is one of the following values:

  ```
  Frame.NORMAL
  Frame.ICONIFIED
  Frame.MAXIMIZED_HORIZ
  Frame.MAXIMIZED_VERT
  Frame.MAXIMIZED_BOTH
  ```

11.2 Actions

It is common to have multiple ways to activate the same command. The user can choose a certain function through a menu, a keystroke, or a button on a toolbar.

This is easy to achieve in the AWT event model: link all events to the same listener. For example, suppose blueAction is an action listener whose actionPerformed method changes the background color to blue. You can attach the same object as a listener to several event sources:

- A toolbar button labeled "Blue"
- A menu item labeled "Blue"
- A keystroke Ctrl+B

The color change command will now be handled in a uniform way, no matter whether it was caused by a button click, a menu selection, or a key press.

The Swing package provides a very useful mechanism to encapsulate commands and to attach them to multiple event sources: the Action interface. An *action* is an object that encapsulates

- A description of the command (as a text string and an optional icon); and
- Parameters that are necessary to carry out the command (such as the requested color in our example).

The Action interface has the following methods:

```
void actionPerformed(ActionEvent event)
void setEnabled(boolean b)
boolean isEnabled()
void putValue(String key, Object value)
Object getValue(String key)
void addPropertyChangeListener(PropertyChangeListener listener)
void removePropertyChangeListener(PropertyChangeListener listener)
```

The first method is the familiar method in the ActionListener interface; in fact, the Action interface extends the ActionListener interface. Therefore, you can use an Action object whenever an ActionListener object is expected.

The next two methods let you enable or disable the action and check whether the action is currently enabled. When an action is attached to a menu or toolbar and the action is disabled, the option is grayed out.

The putValue and getValue methods let you store and retrieve arbitrary name/value pairs in the action object. A couple of important predefined strings, namely Action.NAME and Action.SMALL_ICON, store action names and icons into an action object:

```
action.putValue(Action.NAME, "Blue");
action.putValue(Action.SMALL_ICON, new ImageIcon("blue-ball.gif"));
```

Table 11.1 shows all predefined action table names.

Table 11.1 Predefined Action Table Names

Name	Value
NAME	The name of the action; displayed on buttons and menu items.
SMALL_ICON	A place to store a small icon for display in a button, menu item, or toolbar.
SHORT_DESCRIPTION	A short description of the icon for display in a tooltip.
LONG_DESCRIPTION	A long description of the icon for potential use in online help. No Swing component uses this value.
MNEMONIC_KEY	A mnemonic abbreviation for display in menu items (see Chapter 12).
ACCELERATOR_KEY	A place to store an accelerator keystroke. No Swing component uses this value.
ACTION_COMMAND_KEY	Historically, used in the now-obsolete registerKeyboardAction method.
DEFAULT	Potentially useful catch-all property. No Swing component uses this value.

If the action object is added to a menu or toolbar, the name and icon are automatically retrieved and displayed in the menu item or toolbar button. The SHORT_DESCRIPTION value turns into a tooltip.

The final two methods of the Action interface allow other objects, in particular menus or toolbars that trigger the action, to be notified when the properties of the action object change. For example, if a menu is added as a property change listener of an action object and the action object is subsequently disabled, the menu is called and can gray out the action name. Property change listeners are a general construct that is a part of the "JavaBeans" component model. You can find out more about beans and their properties in Volume II.

Note that Action is an *interface*, not a class. Any class implementing this interface must implement the seven methods we just discussed. Fortunately, a friendly soul has provided a class AbstractAction that implements all methods except for actionPerformed. That class takes care of storing all name/value pairs and managing the property change listeners. You simply extend AbstractAction and supply an actionPerformed method.

Let's build an action object that can execute color change commands. We store the name of the command, an icon, and the desired color. We store the color in the table of name/value pairs that the AbstractAction class provides. Here is the code for the ColorAction class. The constructor sets the name/value pairs, and the actionPerformed method carries out the color change action.

```
public class ColorAction extends AbstractAction
{
   public ColorAction(String name, Icon icon, Color c)
   {
      putValue(Action.NAME, name);
      putValue(Action.SMALL_ICON, icon);
      putValue("color", c);
      putValue(Action.SHORT_DESCRIPTION, "Set panel color to " + name.toLowerCase());
   }

   public void actionPerformed(ActionEvent event)
   {
      Color c = (Color) getValue("color");
      buttonPanel.setBackground(c);
   }
}
```

Our test program creates three objects of this class, such as

```
Action blueAction = new ColorAction("Blue", new ImageIcon("blue-ball.gif"), Color.BLUE);
```

Next, let's associate this action with a button. That is easy because we can use a `JButton` constructor that takes an `Action` object.

```
JButton blueButton = new JButton(blueAction);
```

That constructor reads the name and icon from the action, sets the short description as the tooltip, and sets the action as the listener. You can see the icons and a tooltip in Figure 11.6.

As we demonstrate in the next chapter, it is just as easy to add the same action to a menu.

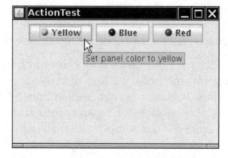

Figure 11.6 Buttons display the icons from the action objects.

Finally, we want to add the action objects to keystrokes so that an action is carried out when the user types a keyboard command. To associate actions with keystrokes, you first need to generate objects of the `KeyStroke` class. This is a convenience class that encapsulates the description of a key. To generate a KeyStroke object, you don't call a constructor but instead use the static getKeyStroke method of the KeyStroke class.

```
KeyStroke ctrlBKey = KeyStroke.getKeyStroke("ctrl B");
```

To understand the next step, you need to understand the concept of *keyboard focus*. A user interface can have many buttons, menus, scrollbars, and other components. When you hit a key, it is sent to the component that has focus. That component is usually (but not always) visually distinguished. For example, in the Java look-and-feel, a button with focus has a thin rectangular border around the button text. You can use the Tab key to move the focus between components. When you press the space bar, the button with focus is clicked. Other keys carry out different actions; for example, the arrow keys can move a scrollbar.

However, in our case, we do not want to send the keystroke to the component that has focus. Otherwise, each of the buttons would need to know how to handle the Ctrl+Y, Ctrl+B, and Ctrl+R keys.

This is a common problem, and the Swing designers came up with a convenient solution. Every JComponent has three *input maps*, each mapping KeyStroke objects to associated actions. The three input maps correspond to three different conditions (see Table 11.2).

Table 11.2 Input Map Conditions

Flag	Invoke Action
WHEN_FOCUSED	When this component has keyboard focus
WHEN_ANCESTOR_OF_FOCUSED_COMPONENT	When this component contains the component that has keyboard focus
WHEN_IN_FOCUSED_WINDOW	When this component is contained in the same window as the component that has keyboard focus

Keystroke processing checks these maps in the following order:

1. Check the WHEN_FOCUSED map of the component with input focus. If the keystroke exists, execute the corresponding action. If the action is enabled, stop processing.

2. Starting from the component with input focus, check the WHEN_ANCESTOR_OF_FOCUSED_COMPONENT maps of its parent components. As soon as a map with the keystroke is found, execute the corresponding action. If the action is enabled, stop processing.

3. Look at all *visible* and *enabled* components, in the window with input focus, that have this keystroke registered in a WHEN_IN_FOCUSED_WINDOW map. Give these components (in the order of their keystroke registration) a chance to execute the corresponding action. As soon as the first enabled action is executed, stop processing. This part of the process is somewhat fragile if a keystroke appears in more than one WHEN_IN_FOCUSED_WINDOW map.

To obtain an input map from the component, use the getInputMap method. Here is an example:

```
InputMap imap = panel.getInputMap(JComponent.WHEN_FOCUSED);
```

The WHEN_FOCUSED condition means that this map is consulted when the current component has the keyboard focus. In our situation, that isn't the map we want. One of the buttons, not the panel, has the input focus. Either of the other two map choices works fine for inserting the color change keystrokes. We use WHEN_ANCESTOR_OF_FOCUSED_COMPONENT in our example program.

The InputMap doesn't directly map KeyStroke objects to Action objects. Instead, it maps to arbitrary objects, and a second map, implemented by the ActionMap class, maps objects to actions. That makes it easier to share the same actions among keystrokes that come from different input maps.

Thus, each component has three input maps and one action map. To tie them together, you need to come up with names for the actions. Here is how you can tie a key to an action:

```
imap.put(KeyStroke.getKeyStroke("ctrl Y"), "panel.yellow");
ActionMap amap = panel.getActionMap();
amap.put("panel.yellow", yellowAction);
```

It is customary to use the string "none" for a do-nothing action. That makes it easy to deactivate a key:

```
imap.put(KeyStroke.getKeyStroke("ctrl C"), "none");
```

 CAUTION: The JDK documentation suggests using the action name as the action's key. We don't think that is a good idea. The action name is displayed on buttons and menu items; thus, it can change at the whim of the UI designer and may be translated into multiple languages. Such unstable strings are poor choices for lookup keys, so we recommend that you come up with action names that are independent of the displayed names.

To summarize, here is what you do to carry out the same action in response to a button, a menu item, or a keystroke:

1. Implement a class that extends the AbstractAction class. You may be able to use the same class for multiple related actions.

2. Construct an object of the action class.

3. Construct a button or menu item from the action object. The constructor will read the label text and icon from the action object.

4. For actions that can be triggered by keystrokes, you have to carry out additional steps. First, locate the top-level component of the window, such as a panel that contains all other components.

5. Then, get the WHEN_ANCESTOR_OF_FOCUSED_COMPONENT input map of the top-level component. Make a KeyStroke object for the desired keystroke. Make an action key object, such as a string that describes your action. Add the pair (keystroke, action key) into the input map.

6. Finally, get the action map of the top-level component. Add the pair (action key, action object) into the map.

Listing 11.3 shows the complete code of the program that maps both buttons and keystrokes to action objects. Try it out—both clicking the buttons and pressing Ctrl+Y, Ctrl+B, or Ctrl+R changes the panel color.

Listing 11.3 action/ActionFrame.java

```java
1  package action;
2
3  import java.awt.*;
4  import java.awt.event.*;
5  import javax.swing.*;
6
7  /**
8   * A frame with a panel that demonstrates color change actions.
9   */
10 public class ActionFrame extends JFrame
11 {
12    private JPanel buttonPanel;
13    private static final int DEFAULT_WIDTH = 300;
14    private static final int DEFAULT_HEIGHT = 200;
15
16    public ActionFrame()
17    {
18       setSize(DEFAULT_WIDTH, DEFAULT_HEIGHT);
19       buttonPanel = new JPanel();
20
21       // define actions
22       Action yellowAction = new ColorAction("Yellow", new ImageIcon("yellow-ball.gif"),
23             Color.YELLOW);
```

(Continues)

Listing 11.3 *(Continued)*

```
24        Action blueAction = new ColorAction("Blue", new ImageIcon("blue-ball.gif"), Color.BLUE);
25        Action redAction = new ColorAction("Red", new ImageIcon("red-ball.gif"), Color.RED);
26
27        // add buttons for these actions
28        buttonPanel.add(new JButton(yellowAction));
29        buttonPanel.add(new JButton(blueAction));
30        buttonPanel.add(new JButton(redAction));
31
32        // add panel to frame
33        add(buttonPanel);
34
35        // associate the Y, B, and R keys with names
36        InputMap imap = buttonPanel.getInputMap(JComponent.WHEN_ANCESTOR_OF_FOCUSED_COMPONENT);
37        imap.put(KeyStroke.getKeyStroke("ctrl Y"), "panel.yellow");
38        imap.put(KeyStroke.getKeyStroke("ctrl B"), "panel.blue");
39        imap.put(KeyStroke.getKeyStroke("ctrl R"), "panel.red");
40
41        // associate the names with actions
42        ActionMap amap = buttonPanel.getActionMap();
43        amap.put("panel.yellow", yellowAction);
44        amap.put("panel.blue", blueAction);
45        amap.put("panel.red", redAction);
46     }
47
48     public class ColorAction extends AbstractAction
49     {
50        /**
51         * Constructs a color action.
52         * @param name the name to show on the button
53         * @param icon the icon to display on the button
54         * @param c the background color
55         */
56        public ColorAction(String name, Icon icon, Color c)
57        {
58           putValue(Action.NAME, name);
59           putValue(Action.SMALL_ICON, icon);
60           putValue(Action.SHORT_DESCRIPTION, "Set panel color to " + name.toLowerCase());
61           putValue("color", c);
62        }
63
64        public void actionPerformed(ActionEvent event)
65        {
66           Color c = (Color) getValue("color");
67           buttonPanel.setBackground(c);
68        }
69     }
70  }
```

---

javax.swing.Action 1.2

- boolean isEnabled()
- void setEnabled(boolean b)

  gets or sets the enabled property of this action.

- void putValue(String key, Object value)

  places a name/value pair inside the action object.

  | *Parameters:* | key | The name of the feature to store with the action object. This can be any string, but several names have predefined meanings—see Table 11.1. |
  | | value | The object associated with the name. |

- Object getValue(String key)

  returns the value of a stored name/value pair.

---

javax.swing.KeyStroke 1.2

- static KeyStroke getKeyStroke(String description)

  constructs a keystroke from a human-readable description (a sequence of whitespace-delimited strings). The description starts with zero or more modifiers shift control ctrl meta alt altGraph and ends with either the string typed, followed by a one-character string (for example, "typed a"), or an optional event specifier (pressed or released, with pressed being the default), followed by a key code. The key code, when prefixed with VK_, should correspond to a KeyEvent constant; for example, "INSERT" corresponds to KeyEvent.VK_INSERT.

---

javax.swing.JComponent 1.2

- ActionMap getActionMap() 1.3

  returns the map that associates action map keys (which can be arbitrary objects) with Action objects.

- InputMap getInputMap(int flag) 1.3

  gets the input map that maps key strokes to action map keys.

  | *Parameters:* | flag | A condition on the keyboard focus to trigger the action, one of the values in Table 11.2. |

11.3 Mouse Events

You do not need to handle mouse events explicitly if you just want the user to be able to click on a button or menu. These mouse operations are handled internally by the various components in the user interface. However, if you want to enable the user to draw with the mouse, you will need to trap the mouse move, click, and drag events.

In this section, we will show you a simple graphics editor application that allows the user to place, move, and erase squares on a canvas (see Figure 11.7).

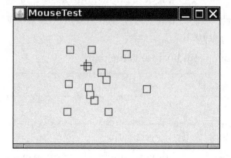

Figure 11.7 A mouse test program

When the user clicks a mouse button, three listener methods are called: mousePressed when the mouse is first pressed, mouseReleased when the mouse is released, and, finally, mouseClicked. If you are only interested in complete clicks, you can ignore the first two methods. By using the getX and getY methods on the MouseEvent argument, you can obtain the *x* and *y* coordinates of the mouse pointer when the mouse was clicked. To distinguish between single, double, and triple (!) clicks, use the getClickCount method.

Some user interface designers inflict mouse click and keyboard modifier combinations, such as Ctrl+Shift+click, on their users. We find this practice reprehensible, but if you disagree, you will find that checking for mouse buttons and keyboard modifiers is a mess.

Use bit masks to test which modifiers have been set. In the original API, two of the button masks equal two keyboard modifier masks, namely

```
BUTTON2_MASK == ALT_MASK
BUTTON3_MASK == META_MASK
```

This was done so that users with a one-button mouse could simulate the other mouse buttons by holding down modifier keys instead. However, as of Java SE 1.4, a different approach is recommended. There are now masks

```
BUTTON1_DOWN_MASK
BUTTON2_DOWN_MASK
BUTTON3_DOWN_MASK
SHIFT_DOWN_MASK
CTRL_DOWN_MASK
ALT_DOWN_MASK
ALT_GRAPH_DOWN_MASK
META_DOWN_MASK
```

The getModifiersEx method accurately reports the mouse buttons and keyboard modifiers of a mouse event.

Note that BUTTON3_DOWN_MASK tests for the right (nonprimary) mouse button under Windows. For example, you can use code like this to detect whether the right mouse button is down:

```
if ((event.getModifiersEx() & InputEvent.BUTTON3_DOWN_MASK) != 0)
    . . . // code for right click
```

In our sample program, we supply both a mousePressed and a mouseClicked methods. When you click on a pixel that is not inside any of the squares that have been drawn, a new square is added. We implemented this in the mousePressed method so that the user receives immediate feedback and does not have to wait until the mouse button is released. When a user double-clicks inside an existing square, it is erased. We implemented this in the mouseClicked method because we need the click count.

```
public void mousePressed(MouseEvent event)
{
    current = find(event.getPoint());
    if (current == null) // not inside a square
        add(event.getPoint());
}

public void mouseClicked(MouseEvent event)
{
    current = find(event.getPoint());
    if (current != null && event.getClickCount() >= 2)
        remove(current);
}
```

As the mouse moves over a window, the window receives a steady stream of mouse movement events. Note that there are separate MouseListener and MouseMotionListener interfaces. This is done for efficiency—there are a lot of mouse events as the user moves the mouse around, and a listener that just cares about mouse *clicks* will not be bothered with unwanted mouse *moves*.

Our test application traps mouse motion events to change the cursor to a different shape (a cross hair) when it is over a square. This is done with the getPredefinedCursor method of the Cursor class. Table 11.3 lists the constants to use with this method along with what the cursors look like under Windows.

Table 11.3 Sample Cursor Shapes

Icon	Constant	Icon	Constant
	DEFAULT_CURSOR		NE_RESIZE_CURSOR
	CROSSHAIR_CURSOR		E_RESIZE_CURSOR
	HAND_CURSOR		SE_RESIZE_CURSOR
	MOVE_CURSOR		S_RESIZE_CURSOR
	TEXT_CURSOR		SW_RESIZE_CURSOR
	WAIT_CURSOR		W_RESIZE_CURSOR
	N_RESIZE_CURSOR		NW_RESIZE_CURSOR

Here is the mouseMoved method of the MouseMotionListener in our example program:

```
public void mouseMoved(MouseEvent event)
{
   if (find(event.getPoint()) == null)
      setCursor(Cursor.getDefaultCursor());
   else
      setCursor(Cursor.getPredefinedCursor(Cursor.CROSSHAIR_CURSOR));
}
```

NOTE: You can also define your own cursor types through the use of the createCustomCursor method in the Toolkit class:

```
Toolkit tk = Toolkit.getDefaultToolkit();
Image img = tk.getImage("dynamite.gif");
Cursor dynamiteCursor = tk.createCustomCursor(img, new Point(10, 10), "dynamite stick");
```

The first parameter of the createCustomCursor points to the cursor image. The second parameter gives the offset of the "hot spot" of the cursor. The third parameter is a string that describes the cursor. This string can be used for accessibility support. For example, a screen reader program can read the cursor shape description to a user who is visually impaired or who simply is not facing the screen.

If the user presses a mouse button while the mouse is in motion, mouseDragged calls are generated instead of mouseMoved calls. Our test application lets a user drag the square under the cursor. We simply update the currently dragged rectangle to be centered under the mouse position. Then, we repaint the canvas to show the new mouse position.

```
public void mouseDragged(MouseEvent event)
{
   if (current != null)
   {
      int x = event.getX();
      int y = event.getY();

      current.setFrame(x - SIDELENGTH / 2, y - SIDELENGTH / 2, SIDELENGTH, SIDELENGTH);
      repaint();
   }
}
```

 NOTE: The mouseMoved method is only called as long as the mouse stays inside the component. However, the mouseDragged method keeps getting called even when the mouse is being dragged outside the component.

There are two other mouse event methods: mouseEntered and mouseExited. These methods are called when the mouse enters or exits a component.

Finally, we explain how to listen to mouse events. Mouse clicks are reported through the mouseClicked procedure, which is part of the MouseListener interface. Many applications are only interested in mouse clicks and not in mouse moves; with the mouse move events occurring so frequently, the mouse move and drag events are defined in a separate interface called MouseMotionListener.

In our program we are interested in both types of mouse events. We define two inner classes: MouseHandler and MouseMotionHandler. The MouseHandler class extends the MouseAdapter class because it defines only two of the five MouseListener methods. The MouseMotionHandler implements the MouseMotionListener and defines both methods of that interface. Listing 11.4 is the program listing.

Listing 11.4 mouse/MouseFrame.java

```
1  package mouse;
2
3  import javax.swing.*;
4
```

(Continues)

Listing 11.4 *(Continued)*

```
5  /**
6   * A frame containing a panel for testing mouse operations
7   */
8  public class MouseFrame extends JFrame
9  {
10    public MouseFrame()
11    {
12       add(new MouseComponent());
13       pack();
14    }
15 }
```

Listing 11.5 mouse/MouseComponent.java

```
1  package mouse;
2
3  import java.awt.*;
4  import java.awt.event.*;
5  import java.awt.geom.*;
6  import java.util.*;
7  import javax.swing.*;
8
9  /**
10  * A component with mouse operations for adding and removing squares.
11  */
12 public class MouseComponent extends JComponent
13 {
14    private static final int DEFAULT_WIDTH = 300;
15    private static final int DEFAULT_HEIGHT = 200;
16
17    private static final int SIDELENGTH = 10;
18    private ArrayList<Rectangle2D> squares;
19    private Rectangle2D current; // the square containing the mouse cursor
20
21    public MouseComponent()
22    {
23       squares = new ArrayList<>();
24       current = null;
25
26       addMouseListener(new MouseHandler());
27       addMouseMotionListener(new MouseMotionHandler());
28    }
29
30    public Dimension getPreferredSize() { return new Dimension(DEFAULT_WIDTH, DEFAULT_HEIGHT); }
31
```

```
32    public void paintComponent(Graphics g)
33    {
34       Graphics2D g2 = (Graphics2D) g;
35
36       // draw all squares
37       for (Rectangle2D r : squares)
38          g2.draw(r);
39    }
40
41    /**
42     * Finds the first square containing a point.
43     * @param p a point
44     * @return the first square that contains p
45     */
46    public Rectangle2D find(Point2D p)
47    {
48       for (Rectangle2D r : squares)
49       {
50          if (r.contains(p)) return r;
51       }
52       return null;
53    }
54
55    /**
56     * Adds a square to the collection.
57     * @param p the center of the square
58     */
59    public void add(Point2D p)
60    {
61       double x = p.getX();
62       double y = p.getY();
63
64       current = new Rectangle2D.Double(x - SIDELENGTH / 2, y - SIDELENGTH / 2, SIDELENGTH,
65             SIDELENGTH);
66       squares.add(current);
67       repaint();
68    }
69
70    /**
71     * Removes a square from the collection.
72     * @param s the square to remove
73     */
74    public void remove(Rectangle2D s)
75    {
76       if (s == null) return;
77       if (s == current) current = null;
78       squares.remove(s);
79       repaint();
80    }
```

(Continues)

Listing 11.5 *(Continued)*

```
81
82    private class MouseHandler extends MouseAdapter
83    {
84       public void mousePressed(MouseEvent event)
85       {
86          // add a new square if the cursor isn't inside a square
87          current = find(event.getPoint());
88          if (current == null) add(event.getPoint());
89       }
90
91       public void mouseClicked(MouseEvent event)
92       {
93          // remove the current square if double clicked
94          current = find(event.getPoint());
95          if (current != null && event.getClickCount() >= 2) remove(current);
96       }
97    }
98
99    private class MouseMotionHandler implements MouseMotionListener
100   {
101      public void mouseMoved(MouseEvent event)
102      {
103         // set the mouse cursor to cross hairs if it is inside
104         // a rectangle
105
106         if (find(event.getPoint()) == null) setCursor(Cursor.getDefaultCursor());
107         else setCursor(Cursor.getPredefinedCursor(Cursor.CROSSHAIR_CURSOR));
108      }
109
110      public void mouseDragged(MouseEvent event)
111      {
112         if (current != null)
113         {
114            int x = event.getX();
115            int y = event.getY();
116
117            // drag the current rectangle to center it at (x, y)
118            current.setFrame(x - SIDELENGTH / 2, y - SIDELENGTH / 2, SIDELENGTH, SIDELENGTH);
119            repaint();
120         }
121      }
122   }
123 }
```

---

java.awt.event.MouseEvent 1.1

- int getX()
- int getY()
- Point getPoint()

returns the *x* (horizontal) and *y* (vertical) coordinates of the point where the event happened, measured from the top left corner of the component that is the event source.

- int getClickCount()

returns the number of consecutive mouse clicks associated with this event. (The time interval for what constitutes "consecutive" is system dependent.)

---

java.awt.event.InputEvent 1.1

- int getModifiersEx() 1.4

returns the extended or "down" modifiers for this event. Use the following mask values to test the returned value:

```
BUTTON1_DOWN_MASK
BUTTON2_DOWN_MASK
BUTTON3_DOWN_MASK
SHIFT_DOWN_MASK
CTRL_DOWN_MASK
ALT_DOWN_MASK
ALT_GRAPH_DOWN_MASK
META_DOWN_MASK
```

- static String getModifiersExText(int modifiers) 1.4

returns a string such as "Shift+Button1" describing the extended or "down" modifiers in the given flag set.

---

java.awt.Toolkit 1.0

- public Cursor createCustomCursor(Image image, Point hotSpot, String name) 1.2

creates a new custom cursor object.

Parameters:	image	The image to display when the cursor is active
	hotSpot	The cursor's hot spot (such as the tip of an arrow or the center of crosshairs)
	name	A description of the cursor, to support special accessibility environments

---

java.awt.Component 1.0

- public void setCursor(Cursor cursor) 1.1

  sets the cursor image to the specified cursor.

11.4 The AWT Event Hierarchy

Having given you a taste of how event handling works, we finish this chapter with an overview of the AWT event-handling architecture.

As we briefly mentioned earlier, event handling in Java is object oriented, with all events descending from the EventObject class in the java.util package. (The common superclass is not called Event because that is the name of the event class in the old event model. Although the old model is now deprecated, its classes are still a part of the Java library.)

The EventObject class has a subclass AWTEvent, which is the parent of all AWT event classes. Figure 11.8 shows the inheritance diagram of the AWT events.

Some of the Swing components generate event objects of yet more event types; these directly extend EventObject, not AWTEvent.

The event objects encapsulate information about the event that the event source communicates to its listeners. When necessary, you can then analyze the event objects that were passed to the listener object, as we did in the button example with the getSource and getActionCommand methods.

Some of the AWT event classes are of no practical use for the Java programmer. For example, the AWT inserts PaintEvent objects into the event queue, but these objects are not delivered to listeners. Java programmers don't listen to paint events; instead, they override the paintComponent method to control repainting. The AWT also generates a number of events that are needed only by systems programmers, to provide input systems for ideographic languages, automated testing robots, and so on. We do not discuss these specialized event types.

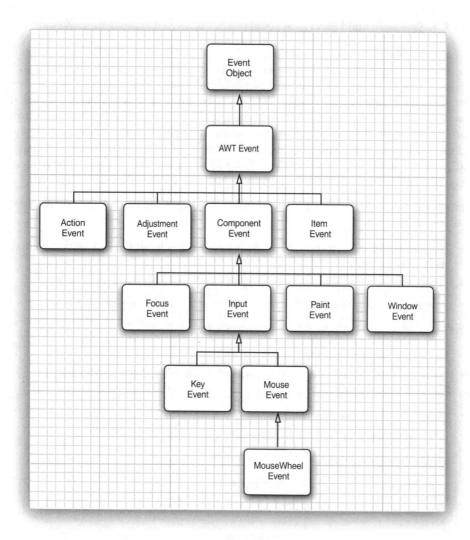

Figure 11.8 Inheritance diagram of AWT event classes

11.4.1 Semantic and Low–Level Events

The AWT makes a useful distinction between *low-level* and *semantic* events. A semantic event is one that expresses what the user is doing, such as "clicking that button"; an ActionEvent is a semantic event. Low-level events are those events that make this possible. In the case of a button click, this is a mouse down, a series of mouse moves, and a mouse up (but only if the mouse up is inside the button area). Or it might be a keystroke, which happens if the user selects the button with the Tab key and then activates it with the space bar. Similarly, adjusting a scrollbar is a semantic event, but dragging the mouse is a low-level event.

Here are the most commonly used semantic event classes in the java.awt.event package:

- ActionEvent (for a button click, a menu selection, selecting a list item, or Enter typed in a text field)
- AdjustmentEvent (the user adjusted a scrollbar)
- ItemEvent (the user made a selection from a set of checkbox or list items)

Five low-level event classes are commonly used:

- KeyEvent (a key was pressed or released)
- MouseEvent (the mouse button was pressed, released, moved, or dragged)
- MouseWheelEvent (the mouse wheel was rotated)
- FocusEvent (a component got focus or lost focus)
- WindowEvent (the window state changed)

The following interfaces listen to these events:

```
ActionListener          MouseMotionListener
AdjustmentListener      MouseWheelListener
FocusListener           WindowListener
ItemListener            WindowFocusListener
KeyListener             WindowStateListener
MouseListener
```

Several of the AWT listener interfaces, namely those that have more than one method, come with a companion adapter class that implements all the methods in the interface to do nothing. (The other interfaces have only a single method each, so there is no benefit in having adapter classes for these interfaces.) Here are the commonly used adapter classes:

```
FocusAdapter            MouseMotionAdapter
KeyAdapter              WindowAdapter
MouseAdapter
```

Table 11.4 shows the most important AWT listener interfaces, events, and event sources.

The `javax.swing.event` package contains additional events that are specific to Swing components. We cover some of them in the next chapter.

Table 11.4 Event Handling Summary

Interface	Methods	Parameter/Accessors	Events Generated By
ActionListener	actionPerformed	ActionEvent • getActionCommand • getModifiers	AbstractButton JComboBox JTextField Timer
AdjustmentListener	adjustmentValueChanged	AdjustmentEvent • getAdjustable • getAdjustmentType • getValue	JScrollbar
ItemListener	itemStateChanged	ItemEvent • getItem • getItemSelectable • getStateChange	AbstractButton JComboBox
FocusListener	focusGained focusLost	FocusEvent • isTemporary	Component
KeyListener	keyPressed keyReleased keyTyped	KeyEvent • getKeyChar • getKeyCode • getKeyModifiersText • getKeyText • isActionKey	Component
MouseListener	mousePressed mouseReleased mouseEntered mouseExited mouseClicked	MouseEvent • getClickCount • getX • getY • getPoint • translatePoint	Component

(Continues)

Table 11.4 *(Continued)*

Interface	Methods	Parameter/Accessors	Events Generated By
MouseMotionListener	mouseDragged mouseMoved	MouseEvent	Component
MouseWheelListener	mouseWheelMoved	MouseWheelEvent • getWheelRotation • getScrollAmount	Component
WindowListener	windowClosing windowOpened windowIconified windowDeiconified windowClosed windowActivated windowDeactivated	WindowEvent • getWindow	Window
WindowFocusListener	windowGainedFocus windowLostFocus	WindowEvent • getOppositeWindow	Window
WindowStateListener	windowStateChanged	WindowEvent • getOldState • getNewState	Window

This concludes our discussion of AWT event handling. The next chapter shows you how to put together the most common Swing components, along with a detailed coverage of the events they generate.

User Interface Components with Swing

The previous chapter was written primarily to show you how to use the event model in Java. In the process, you took the first steps toward learning how to build a graphical user interface. This chapter shows you the most important tools you'll need to build more full-featured GUIs.

We start out with a tour of the architectural underpinnings of Swing. Knowing what goes on "under the hood" is important in understanding how to use some of the more advanced components effectively. We then show you how to use the most common user interface components in Swing, such as text fields, radio buttons, and menus. Next, you will learn how to use the nifty layout manager features of Java to arrange these components in a window, regardless of the look-and-feel of a particular user interface. Finally, you'll see how to implement dialog boxes in Swing.

This chapter covers the basic Swing components such as text components, buttons, and sliders. These are the essential user interface components that you will need most frequently. We will cover advanced Swing components in Volume II.

12.1 Swing and the Model-View-Controller Design Pattern

As promised, we start this chapter with a description of the architecture of Swing components. We first discuss the concept of *design patterns* and then look at the "model-view-controller" pattern that has greatly influenced the design of the Swing framework.

12.1.1 Design Patterns

When solving a problem, you don't usually figure out a solution from first principles. Instead, you are likely to be guided by your past experience, or you may ask other experts for advice on what has worked for them. Design patterns are a method for presenting this expertise in a structured way.

In recent years, software engineers have begun to assemble catalogs of such patterns. The pioneers in this area were inspired by the architectural design patterns of the architect Christopher Alexander. In his book, *The Timeless Way of Building* (Oxford University Press, 1979), Alexander gives a catalog of patterns for designing public and private living spaces. Here is a typical example:

Window Place

Everybody loves window seats, bay windows, and big windows with low sills and comfortable chairs drawn up to them. . . A room which does not have a place like this seldom allows you to feel comfortable or perfectly at ease. . .

If the room contains no window which is a "place," a person in the room will be torn between two forces: (1) He wants to sit down and be comfortable, and (2) he is drawn toward the light.

Obviously, if the comfortable places—those places in the room where you most want to sit—are away from the windows, there is no way of overcoming this conflict. . .

Therefore: In every room where you spend any length of time during the day, make at least one window into a "window place." (Figure 12.1.)

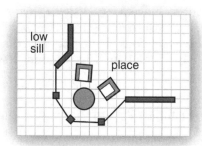

Figure 12.1 A window place

Each pattern in Alexander's catalog, as well as those in the catalogs of software patterns, follows a particular format. The pattern first describes a context, a situation that gives rise to a design problem. Then, the problem is explained, usually as a set of conflicting forces. Finally, the solution shows a configuration that balances these forces.

In the "window place" pattern, the context is a room in which you spend any length of time during the day. The conflicting forces are that you want to sit down and be comfortable and that you are drawn to the light. The solution is to make a "window place."

In the "model-view-controller" pattern, which we will describe in the next section, the context is a user interface system that presents information and receives user input. There are several forces. There may be multiple visual representations of the same data that need to be updated together. The visual representations may change—for example, to accommodate various look-and-feel standards. The interaction mechanisms may change—for example, to support voice commands. The solution is to distribute responsibilities into three separate interacting components: the model, the view, and the controller.

The model-view-controller pattern is not the only pattern used in the design of AWT and Swing. Here are several additonal examples:

- Containers and components are examples of the "composite" pattern.
- The scroll pane is a "decorator."
- Layout managers follow the "strategy" pattern.

One important aspect of design patterns is that they become part of the culture. Programmers all over the world know what you mean when you talk about the model-view-controller pattern or the decorator pattern. Thus, patterns become an efficient way of talking about design problems.

You will find a formal description of numerous useful software patterns in the seminal book of the pattern movement, *Design Patterns—Elements of Reusable Object-Oriented Software*, by Erich Gamma et al. (Addison-Wesley, 1995). We also highly recommend the excellent book *A System of Patterns* by Frank Buschmann et al. (John Wiley & Sons, 1996), which we find less seminal and more approachable.

12.1.2 The Model–View–Controller Pattern

Let's step back for a minute and think about the pieces that make up a user interface component such as a button, a checkbox, a text field, or a sophisticated tree control. Every component has three characteristics:

- Its *content*, such as the state of a button (pushed in or not), or the text in a text field
- Its *visual appearance* (color, size, and so on)
- Its *behavior* (reaction to events)

Even a seemingly simple component such as a button exhibits some moderately complex interaction among these characteristics. Obviously, the visual appearance of a button depends on the look-and-feel. A Metal button looks different from a Windows button or a Motif button. In addition, the appearance depends on the button state; when a button is pushed in, it needs to be redrawn to look different. The state depends on the events that the button receives. When the user depresses the mouse inside the button, the button is pushed in.

Of course, when you use a button in your programs, you simply consider it as a *button*; you don't think too much about the inner workings and characteristics. That, after all, is the job of the programmer who implemented the button. However, programmers who implement buttons and all other user interface components are motivated to think a little harder about them, so that they work well no matter what look-and-feel is in effect.

To do this, the Swing designers turned to a well-known design pattern: the *model-view-controller* pattern. This pattern, like many other design patterns, goes back to one of the principles of object-oriented design that we mentioned way back in Chapter 5: Don't make one object responsible for too much. Don't have a single button class do everything. Instead, have the look-and-feel of the component associated with one object and store the content in *another* object. The model-view-controller (MVC) design pattern teaches how to accomplish this. Implement three separate classes:

- The *model*, which stores the content
- The *view*, which displays the content
- The *controller*, which handles user input

The pattern specifies precisely how these three objects interact. The model stores the content and has *no user interface*. For a button, the content is pretty trivial—just a small set of flags that tells whether the button is currently pushed in or out, whether it is active or inactive, and so on. For a text field, the content is a bit more interesting. It is a string object that holds the current text. This is *not the same* as the view of the content—if the content is larger than the text field, the user sees only a portion of the text displayed (see Figure 12.2).

Figure 12.2 Model and view of a text field

The model must implement methods to change the content and to discover what the content is. For example, a text model has methods to add or remove characters in the current text and to return the current text as a string. Again, keep in mind that the model is completely nonvisual. It is the job of a view to draw the data stored in the model.

 NOTE: The term "model" is perhaps unfortunate because we often think of a model as a representation of an abstract concept. Car and airplane designers build models to simulate real cars and planes. But that analogy really leads you astray when thinking about the model-view-controller pattern. In this design pattern, the model stores the complete content, and the view gives a (complete or incomplete) visual representation of the content. A better analogy might be the model who poses for an artist. It is up to the artist to look at the model and create a view. Depending on the artist, that view might be a formal portrait, an impressionist painting, or a cubist drawing that shows the limbs in strange contortions.

One of the advantages of the model-view-controller pattern is that a model can have multiple views, each showing a different part or aspect of the full content. For example, an HTML editor can offer two *simultaneous* views of the same content: a WYSIWYG view and a "raw tag" view (see Figure 12.3). When the model is updated through the controller of one of the views, it tells both attached views about the change. When the views are notified, they refresh themselves automatically. Of course, for a simple user interface component such as a button, you won't have multiple views of the same model.

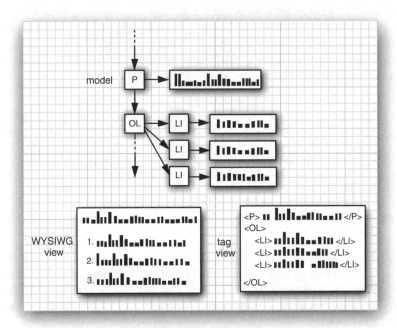

Figure 12.3 Two separate views of the same model

The controller handles the user-input events, such as mouse clicks and keystrokes. It then decides whether to translate these events into changes in the model or the view. For example, if the user presses a character key in a text box, the controller calls the "insert character" command of the model. The model then tells the view to update itself. The view never knows why the text changed. But if the user presses a cursor key, the controller may tell the view to scroll. Scrolling the view has no effect on the underlying text, so the model never knows that this event happened.

Figure 12.4 shows the interactions among model, view, and controller objects.

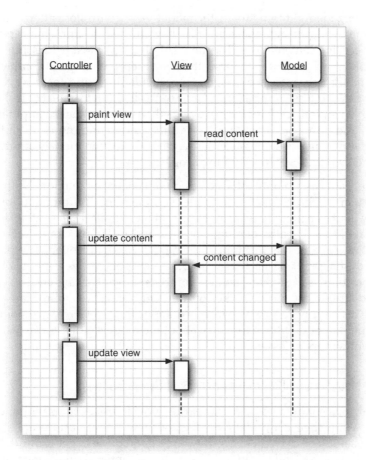

Figure 12.4 Interactions among model, view, and controller objects

As a programmer using Swing components, you generally don't need to think about the model-view-controller architecture. Each user interface component has a wrapper class (such as JButton or JTextField) that stores the model and the view. When you want to inquire about the content (for example, the text in a text field), the wrapper class asks the model and returns the answer to you. When you want to change the view (for example, move the caret position in a text field), the wrapper class forwards that request to the view. However, occasionally the wrapper class doesn't work hard enough on forwarding commands. Then, you have to ask it to retrieve the model and work directly with it. (You don't have to work directly with the view—that is the job of the look-and-feel code.)

Besides being the right thing to do, the model-view-controller pattern was attractive for the Swing designers because it allowed them to implement pluggable look-and-feel implementations. The model of a button or text field is independent of the look-and-feel—but, of course, the visual representation is completely dependent on the user interface design of a particular look-and-feel. The controller can vary as well. For example, in a voice-controlled device, the controller must cope with an entirely different set of events than on a standard computer with a keyboard and a mouse. By separating out the underlying model from the user interface, the Swing designers can reuse the code for the models and can even switch the look-and-feel in a running program.

Of course, patterns are only intended as guidance, not as religion. No pattern is applicable in all situations. For example, you may find it difficult to follow the "window places" pattern to rearrange your cubicle. Similarly, the Swing designers found that the harsh reality of pluggable look-and-feel implementations does not always allow for a neat realization of the model-view-controller pattern. Models are easy to separate, and each user interface component has a model class. But the responsibilities of the view and the controller are not always clearly separated and are distributed over a number of different classes. Of course, as a user of these classes, you need not be concerned about this. In fact, as we pointed out before, you often don't have to worry about the models either—you just use the component wrapper classes.

12.1.3 A Model–View–Controller Analysis of Swing Buttons

In the previous chapter, you already learned how to use buttons without having to worry about their controllers, models, or views. Still, buttons are about the simplest user interface elements, so they are a good place to get comfortable with the model-view-controller pattern. You will encounter similar kinds of classes and interfaces for the more sophisticated Swing components.

For most components, the model class implements an interface whose name ends in `Model`; in this case, the interface is called `ButtonModel`. Classes implementing that interface can define the state of the various kinds of buttons. Actually, buttons aren't all that complicated, and the Swing library contains a single class, called `DefaultButtonModel`, that implements this interface.

You can get a sense of the sort of data maintained by a button model by looking at the properties of the `ButtonModel` interface—see Table 12.1.

Table 12.1 Properties of the `ButtonModel` Interface

Property Name	Value
`actionCommand`	The action command string associated with this button
`mnemonic`	The keyboard mnemonic for this button
`armed`	true if the button was pressed and the mouse is still over the button
`enabled`	true if the button is selectable
`pressed`	true if the button was pressed but the mouse button hasn't yet been released
`rollover`	true if the mouse is over the button
`selected`	true if the button has been toggled on (used for checkboxes and radio buttons)

Each `JButton` object stores a button model object which you can retrieve.

```
JButton button = new JButton("Blue");
ButtonModel model = button.getModel();
```

In practice, you won't care—the minutiae of the button state are only of interest to the view that draws it. All the important information—such as whether a button is enabled—is available from the `JButton` class. (Of course, the `JButton` then asks its model to retrieve that information.)

Have another look at the `ButtonModel` interface to see what *isn't* there. The model does *not* store the button label or icon. There is no way to find out what's on the face of a button just by looking at its model. (Actually, as you will see in Section 12.4.2, "Radio Buttons," on p. 660, purity of design is the source of some grief for the programmer.)

It is also worth noting that the *same* model (namely, `DefaultButtonModel`) is used for push buttons, radio buttons, checkboxes, and even menu items. Of course, each of these button types has different views and controllers. When using the Metal look-and-feel, the `JButton` uses a class called `BasicButtonUI` for the view and a class called `ButtonUIListener` as controller. In general, each Swing component has an associated view object that ends in `UI`. But not all Swing components have dedicated controller objects.

So, having read this short introduction to what is going on under the hood in a JButton, you may be wondering: Just what is a JButton really? It is simply a wrapper class inheriting from JComponent that holds the DefaultButtonModel object, some view data (such as the button label and icons), and a BasicButtonUI object that is responsible for the button view.

12.2 Introduction to Layout Management

Before we go on to discussing individual Swing components, such as text fields and radio buttons, we briefly cover how to arrange these components inside a frame. Unlike Visual Basic, the JDK has no form designer. You need to write code to position (lay out) the user interface components where you want them to be.

Of course, if you have a Java-enabled development environment, it will probably have a layout tool that automates some or all of these tasks. Nevertheless, it is important to know exactly what goes on "under the hood" because even the best of these tools will usually require hand-tweaking.

Let's start by reviewing the program from Chapter 11 that used buttons to change the background color of a frame (see Figure 12.5).

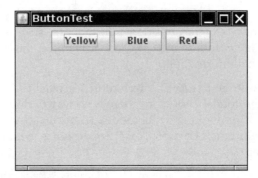

Figure 12.5 A panel with three buttons

The buttons are contained in a JPanel object and are managed by the *flow layout manager*, the default layout manager for a panel. Figure 12.6 shows what happens when you add more buttons to the panel. As you can see, a new row is started when there is no more room.

Figure 12.6 A panel with six buttons managed by a flow layout

Moreover, the buttons stay centered in the panel, even when the user resizes the frame (see Figure 12.7).

Figure 12.7 Changing the panel size rearranges the buttons automatically.

In general, *components* are placed inside *containers*, and a *layout manager* determines the positions and sizes of components in a container.

Buttons, text fields, and other user interface elements extend the class Component. Components can be placed inside containers, such as panels. Containers can themselves be put inside other containers, so the class Container extends Component. Figure 12.8 shows the inheritance hierarchy for Component.

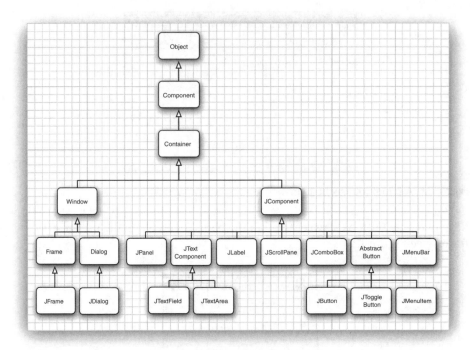

Figure 12.8 Inheritance hierarchy for the Component class

 NOTE: Unfortunately, the inheritance hierarchy is somewhat unclean in two respects. First, top-level windows, such as JFrame, are subclasses of Container and hence Component, but they cannot be placed inside other containers. Moreover, JComponent is a subclass of Container, not Component. Therefore one can add other components into a JButton. (However, those components would not be displayed.)

Each container has a default layout manager, but you can always set your own. For example, the statement

```
panel.setLayout(new GridLayout(4, 4));
```

uses the GridLayout class to lay out the components in four rows and four columns. When you add components to the container, the add method of the container passes the component and any placement directions to the layout manager.

---

java.awt.Container 1.0

- void setLayout(LayoutManager m)

  sets the layout manager for this container.

- Component add(Component c)
- Component add(Component c, Object constraints) 1.1

  adds a component to this container and returns the component reference.

  Parameters: c   The component to add

                  constraints   An identifier understood by the layout manager

---

java.awt.FlowLayout 1.0

- FlowLayout()
- FlowLayout(int align)
- FlowLayout(int align, int hgap, int vgap)

  constructs a new FlowLayout.

  Parameters: align   One of LEFT, CENTER, or RIGHT

                  hgap   The horizontal gap to use in pixels (negative values force
                          an overlap)

                  vgap   The vertical gap to use in pixels (negative values force
                          an overlap)

12.2.1 Border Layout

The *border layout manager* is the default layout manager of the content pane of every JFrame. Unlike the flow layout manager, which completely controls the position of each component, the border layout manager lets you choose where you want to place each component. You can choose to place the component in the center, north, south, east, or west of the content pane (see Figure 12.9).

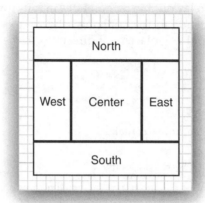

Figure 12.9 Border layout

For example:

```
frame.add(component, BorderLayout.SOUTH);
```

The edge components are laid out first, and the remaining available space is occupied by the center. When the container is resized, the dimensions of the edge components are unchanged, but the center component changes its size. Add components by specifying a constant CENTER, NORTH, SOUTH, EAST, or WEST of the BorderLayout class. Not all of the positions need to be occupied. If you don't supply any value, CENTER is assumed.

 NOTE: The BorderLayout constants are defined as strings. For example, BorderLayout.SOUTH is defined as the string "South". This is safer than using strings. If you accidentally misspell a string, for example, frame.add(component, "south"), the compiler won't catch that error.

Unlike the flow layout, the border layout grows all components to fill the available space. (The flow layout leaves each component at its preferred size.) This is a problem when you add a button:

```
frame.add(yellowButton, BorderLayout.SOUTH); // don't
```

Figure 12.10 shows what happens when you use the preceding code fragment. The button has grown to fill the entire southern region of the frame. And, if you were to add another button to the southern region, it would just displace the first button.

Figure 12.10 A single button managed by a border layout

To solve this problem, use additional panels. For example, look at Figure 12.11. The three buttons at the bottom of the screen are all contained in a panel. The panel is put into the southern region of the content pane.

Figure 12.11 Panel placed at the southern region of the frame

To achieve this configuration, first create a new JPanel object, then add the individual buttons to the panel. The default layout manager for a panel is a FlowLayout, which is a good choice for this situation. Add the individual buttons to the panel, using the add method you have seen before. The position and size of the buttons is under the control of the FlowLayout manager. This means the buttons stay centered within the panel and do not expand to fill the entire panel area. Finally, add the panel to the content pane of the frame.

```
JPanel panel = new JPanel();
panel.add(yellowButton);
panel.add(blueButton);
panel.add(redButton);
frame.add(panel, BorderLayout.SOUTH);
```

The border layout expands the size of the panel to fill the entire southern region.

---

java.awt.BorderLayout 1.0

- BorderLayout()
- BorderLayout(int hgap, int vgap)

constructs a new BorderLayout.

| *Parameters*: | hgap | The horizontal gap to use in pixels (negative values force an overlap) |
| | vgap | The vertical gap to use in pixels (negative values force an overlap) |

12.2.2 Grid Layout

The grid layout arranges all components in rows and columns like a spreadsheet. All components are given the same size. The calculator program in Figure 12.12 uses a grid layout to arrange the calculator buttons. When you resize the window, the buttons grow and shrink, but all buttons have identical sizes.

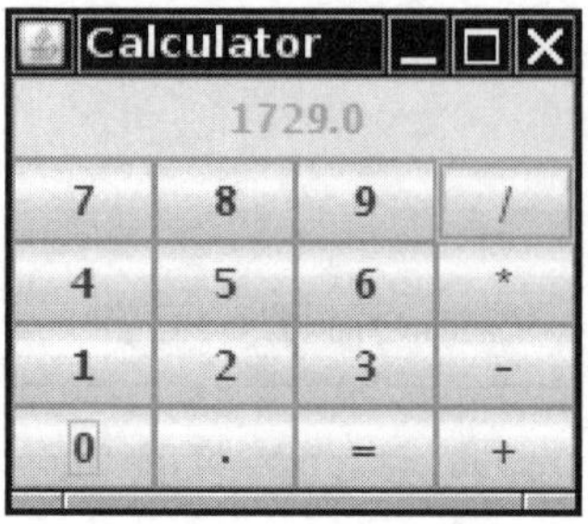

Figure 12.12 A calculator

In the constructor of the grid layout object, you specify how many rows and columns you need.

```
panel.setLayout(new GridLayout(4, 4));
```

Add the components, starting with the first entry in the first row, then the second entry in the first row, and so on.

```
panel.add(new JButton("1"));
panel.add(new JButton("2"));
```

Listing 12.1 shows the panel class of the calculator program. This is a regular calculator, not the "reverse Polish" variety that is so oddly popular in Java tutorials. In this program, we call the `pack` method after adding the component to the frame. This method uses the preferred sizes of all components to compute the width and height of the frame.

Of course, few applications have as rigid a layout as the face of a calculator. In practice, small grids (usually with just one row or one column) can be useful to organize partial areas of a window. For example, if you want to have a row of buttons of identical sizes, you can put the buttons inside a panel that is governed by a grid layout with a single row.

Listing 12.1 `calculator/CalculatorPanel.java`

```
1  package calculator;
2
3  import java.awt.*;
4  import java.awt.event.*;
5  import javax.swing.*;
6
7  /**
8   * A panel with calculator buttons and a result display.
9   */
10 public class CalculatorPanel extends JPanel
11 {
12    private JButton display;
13    private JPanel panel;
14    private double result;
15    private String lastCommand;
16    private boolean start;
17
18    public CalculatorPanel()
19    {
20       setLayout(new BorderLayout());
21
22       result = 0;
23       lastCommand = "=";
24       start = true;
25
26       // add the display
27
28       display = new JButton("0");
29       display.setEnabled(false);
30       add(display, BorderLayout.NORTH);
31
32       ActionListener insert = new InsertAction();
33       ActionListener command = new CommandAction();
```

(Continues)

Listing 12.1 *(Continued)*

```
34       // add the buttons in a 4 x 4 grid
35
36       panel = new JPanel();
37       panel.setLayout(new GridLayout(4, 4));
38
39       addButton("7", insert);
40       addButton("8", insert);
41       addButton("9", insert);
42       addButton("/", command);
43
44       addButton("4", insert);
45       addButton("5", insert);
46       addButton("6", insert);
47       addButton("*", command);
48
49       addButton("1", insert);
50       addButton("2", insert);
51       addButton("3", insert);
52       addButton("-", command);
53
54       addButton("0", insert);
55       addButton(".", insert);
56       addButton("=", command);
57       addButton("+", command);
58
59       add(panel, BorderLayout.CENTER);
60    }
61
62    /**
63     * Adds a button to the center panel.
64     * @param label the button label
65     * @param listener the button listener
66     */
67    private void addButton(String label, ActionListener listener)
68    {
69       JButton button = new JButton(label);
70       button.addActionListener(listener);
71       panel.add(button);
72    }
73
74    /**
75     * This action inserts the button action string to the end of the display text.
76     */
77    private class InsertAction implements ActionListener
78    {
79       public void actionPerformed(ActionEvent event)
80       {
81          String input = event.getActionCommand();
```

```
82          if (start)
83          {
84              display.setText("");
85              start = false;
86          }
87          display.setText(display.getText() + input);
88      }
89  }
90
91  /**
92   * This action executes the command that the button action string denotes.
93   */
94  private class CommandAction implements ActionListener
95  {
96      public void actionPerformed(ActionEvent event)
97      {
98          String command = event.getActionCommand();
99
100         if (start)
101         {
102             if (command.equals("-"))
103             {
104                 display.setText(command);
105                 start = false;
106             }
107             else lastCommand = command;
108         }
109         else
110         {
111             calculate(Double.parseDouble(display.getText()));
112             lastCommand = command;
113             start = true;
114         }
115     }
116 }
117
118 /**
119  * Carries out the pending calculation.
120  * @param x the value to be accumulated with the prior result.
121  */
122 public void calculate(double x)
123 {
124     if (lastCommand.equals("+")) result += x;
125     else if (lastCommand.equals("-")) result -= x;
126     else if (lastCommand.equals("*")) result *= x;
127     else if (lastCommand.equals("/")) result /= x;
128     else if (lastCommand.equals("=")) result = x;
129     display.setText("" + result);
130 }
131 }
```

---

java.awt.GridLayout 1.0

- GridLayout(int rows, int columns)
- GridLayout(int rows, int columns, int hgap, int vgap)

  constructs a new GridLayout. One of rows and columns (but not both) may be zero, denoting an arbitrary number of components per row or column.

Parameters:	rows	The number of rows in the grid
	columns	The number of columns in the grid
	hgap	The horizontal gap to use in pixels (negative values force an overlap)
	vgap	The vertical gap to use in pixels (negative values force an overlap)

12.3 Text Input

We are finally ready to start introducing the Swing user interface components. We begin with the components that let a user input and edit text. You can use the JTextField and JTextArea components for text input. A text field can accept only one line of text; a text area can accept multiple lines of text. A JPasswordField accepts one line of text without showing the contents.

All three of these classes inherit from a class called JTextComponent. You will not be able to construct a JTextComponent yourself because it is an abstract class. On the other hand, as is so often the case in Java, when you go searching through the API documentation, you may find that the methods you are looking for are actually in the parent class JTextComponent rather than the derived class. For example, the methods that get or set the text in a text field or text area are actually in JTextComponent.

---

javax.swing.text.JTextComponent 1.2

- String getText()
- void setText(String text)

  gets or sets the text of this text component.

- boolean isEditable()
- void setEditable(boolean b)

  gets or sets the editable property that determines whether the user can edit the content of this text component.

12.3.1 Text Fields

The usual way to add a text field to a window is to add it to a panel or other container—just as you would add a button:

```
JPanel panel = new JPanel();
JTextField textField = new JTextField("Default input", 20);
panel.add(textField);
```

This code adds a text field and initializes it by placing the string `"Default input"` inside it. The second parameter of this constructor sets the width. In this case, the width is 20 "columns." Unfortunately, a column is a rather imprecise measurement. One column is the expected width of one character in the font you are using for the text. The idea is that if you expect the inputs to be n characters or less, you are supposed to specify n as the column width. In practice, this measurement doesn't work out too well, and you should add 1 or 2 to the maximum input length to be on the safe side. Also, keep in mind that the number of columns is only a hint to the AWT that gives the *preferred* size. If the layout manager needs to grow or shrink the text field, it can adjust its size. The column width that you set in the `JTextField` constructor is not an upper limit on the number of characters the user can enter. The user can still type in longer strings, but the input scrolls when the text exceeds the length of the field. Users tend to find scrolling text fields irritating, so you should size the fields generously. If you need to reset the number of columns at runtime, you can do that with the `setColumns` method.

 TIP: After changing the size of a text box with the `setColumns` method, call the `revalidate` method of the surrounding container.

```
textField.setColumns(10);
panel.revalidate();
```

The `revalidate` method recomputes the size and layout of all components in a container. After you use the `revalidate` method, the layout manager resizes the container, and the changed size of the text field will be visible.

The `revalidate` method belongs to the `JComponent` class. It doesn't immediately resize the component but merely marks it for resizing. This approach avoids repetitive calculations if multiple components request to be resized. However, if you want to recompute all components inside a `JFrame`, you have to call the `validate` method—`JFrame` doesn't extend `JComponent`.

In general, users add text (or edit an existing text) in a text field. Quite often these text fields start out blank. To make a blank text field, just leave out the string as a parameter for the JTextField constructor:

```
JTextField textField = new JTextField(20);
```

You can change the content of the text field at any time by using the setText method from the JTextComponent parent class mentioned in the previous section. For example:

```
textField.setText("Hello!");
```

And, as was mentioned in the previous section, you can find out what the user typed by calling the getText method. This method returns the exact text that the user has typed. To trim any extraneous leading and trailing spaces from the data in a text field, apply the trim method to the return value of getText:

```
String text = textField.getText().trim();
```

To change the font in which the user text appears, use the setFont method.

---

javax.swing.JTextField 1.2

- JTextField(int cols)

  constructs an empty JTextField with the specified number of columns.

- JTextField(String text, int cols)

  constructs a new JTextField with an initial string and the specified number of columns.

- int getColumns()
- void setColumns(int cols)

  gets or sets the number of columns that this text field should use.

---

javax.swing.JComponent 1.2

- void revalidate()

  causes the position and size of a component to be recomputed.

- void setFont(Font f)

  sets the font of this component.

---

java.awt.Component 1.0

- void validate()

  recomputes the position and size of a component. If the component is a container, the positions and sizes of its components are recomputed.

- Font getFont()

  gets the font of this component.

12.3.2 Labels and Labeling Components

Labels are components that hold text. They have no decorations (for example, no boundaries). They also do not react to user input. You can use a label to identify components. For example, unlike buttons, text fields have no label to identify them. To label a component that does not itself come with an identifier:

1. Construct a JLabel component with the correct text.
2. Place it close enough to the component you want to identify so that the user can see that the label identifies the correct component.

The constructor for a JLabel lets you specify the initial text or icon and, optionally, the alignment of the content. You use constants from the SwingConstants interface to specify alignment. That interface defines a number of useful constants such as LEFT, RIGHT, CENTER, NORTH, EAST, and so on. The JLabel class is one of several Swing classes that implement this interface. Therefore, you can specify a right-aligned label either as

```
JLabel label = new JLabel("User name: ", SwingConstants.RIGHT);
```

or

```
JLabel label = new JLabel("User name: ", JLabel.RIGHT);
```

The setText and setIcon methods let you set the text and icon of the label at runtime.

 TIP: You can use both plain and HTML text in buttons, labels, and menu items. We don't recommend HTML in buttons—it interferes with the look-and-feel. But HTML in labels can be very effective. Simply surround the label string with <html>. . .</html>, like this:

```
label = new JLabel("<html><b>Required</b> entry:</html>");
```

Note that the first component with an HTML label may take some time to be displayed because the rather complex HTML rendering code must be loaded.

Labels can be positioned inside a container like any other component. This means you can use the techniques you have seen before to place your labels where you need them.

`javax.swing.JLabel` 1.2

- `JLabel(String text)`
- `JLabel(Icon icon)`
- `JLabel(String text, int align)`
- `JLabel(String text, Icon icon, int align)`

  constructs a label.

  Parameters: text   The text in the label

                  icon   The icon in the label

                  align   One of the `SwingConstants` constants `LEFT` (default), `CENTER`, or `RIGHT`

- `String getText()`
- `void setText(String text)`

  gets or sets the text of this label.

- `Icon getIcon()`
- `void setIcon(Icon icon)`

  gets or sets the icon of this label.

12.3.3 Password Fields

Password fields are a special kind of text field. To prevent nosy bystanders from seeing your password, the characters that the user enters are not actually displayed. Instead, each typed character is represented by an *echo character,* typically an asterisk (*). Swing supplies a `JPasswordField` class that implements such a text field.

The password field is another example of the power of the model-view-controller architecture pattern. The password field uses the same model to store the data as a regular text field, but its view has been changed to display all characters as echo characters.

---

javax.swing.JPasswordField 1.2

- `JPasswordField(String text, int columns)`

  constructs a new password field.

- `void setEchoChar(char echo)`

  sets the echo character for this password field. This is advisory; a particular look-and-feel may insist on its own choice of echo character. A value of 0 resets the echo character to the default.

- `char[] getPassword()`

  returns the text contained in this password field. For stronger security, you should overwrite the content of the returned array after use. (The password is not returned as a `String` because a string would stay in the virtual machine until it is garbage-collected.)

12.3.4 Text Areas

Sometimes, you need to collect user input that is more than one line long. As mentioned earlier, you can use the `JTextArea` component for this. When you place a text area component in your program, a user can enter any number of lines of text, using the Enter key to separate them. Each line ends with a `'\n'`. Figure 12.13 shows a text area at work.

Figure 12.13 Text components

In the constructor for the `JTextArea` component, specify the number of rows and columns for the text area. For example,

```
textArea = new JTextArea(8, 40); // 8 lines of 40 columns each
```

where the `columns` parameter works as before—and you still need to add a few more columns for safety's sake. Also, as before, the user is not restricted to the number of rows and columns; the text simply scrolls when the user inputs too much. You can also use the `setColumns` method to change the number of columns and the `setRows` method to change the number of rows. These numbers only indicate the preferred size—the layout manager can still grow or shrink the text area.

If there is more text than the text area can display, the remaining text is simply clipped. You can avoid clipping long lines by turning on line wrapping:

```
textArea.setLineWrap(true); // long lines are wrapped
```

This wrapping is a visual effect only; the text in the document is not changed—no automatic `'\n'` characters are inserted into the text.

12.3.5 Scroll Panes

In Swing, a text area does not have scrollbars. If you want scrollbars, you have to place the text area inside a *scroll pane.*

```
textArea = new JTextArea(8, 40);
JScrollPane scrollPane = new JScrollPane(textArea);
```

The scroll pane now manages the view of the text area. Scrollbars automatically appear if there is more text than the text area can display, and they vanish again if text is deleted and the remaining text fits inside the area. The scrolling is handled internally by the scroll pane—your program does not need to process scroll events.

This is a general mechanism that works for any component, not just text areas. To add scrollbars to a component, put them inside a scroll pane.

Listing 12.2 demonstrates the various text components. This program shows a text field, a password field, and a text area with scrollbars. The text field and password field are labeled. Click on "Insert" to insert the field contents into the text area.

 NOTE: The `JTextArea` component displays plain text only, without special fonts or formatting. To display formatted text (such as HTML), you can use the `JEditorPane` class that is discussed in Volume II.

Listing 12.2 text/TextComponentFrame.java

```
1  package text;
2
3  import java.awt.BorderLayout;
4  import java.awt.GridLayout;
5
6  import javax.swing.JButton;
7  import javax.swing.JFrame;
8  import javax.swing.JLabel;
9  import javax.swing.JPanel;
10 import javax.swing.JPasswordField;
11 import javax.swing.JScrollPane;
12 import javax.swing.JTextArea;
13 import javax.swing.JTextField;
14 import javax.swing.SwingConstants;
15
16 /**
17  * A frame with sample text components.
18  */
19 public class TextComponentFrame extends JFrame
20 {
21    public static final int TEXTAREA_ROWS = 8;
22    public static final int TEXTAREA_COLUMNS = 20;
23
24    public TextComponentFrame()
25    {
26       JTextField textField = new JTextField();
27       JPasswordField passwordField = new JPasswordField();
28
29       JPanel northPanel = new JPanel();
30       northPanel.setLayout(new GridLayout(2, 2));
31       northPanel.add(new JLabel("User name: ", SwingConstants.RIGHT));
32       northPanel.add(textField);
33       northPanel.add(new JLabel("Password: ", SwingConstants.RIGHT));
34       northPanel.add(passwordField);
35
36       add(northPanel, BorderLayout.NORTH);
37
38       JTextArea textArea = new JTextArea(TEXTAREA_ROWS, TEXTAREA_COLUMNS);
39       JScrollPane scrollPane = new JScrollPane(textArea);
40
41       add(scrollPane, BorderLayout.CENTER);
42
43       // add button to append text into the text area
44
45       JPanel southPanel = new JPanel();
46
47       JButton insertButton = new JButton("Insert");
```

(Continues)

Listing 12.2 *(Continued)*

```
48        southPanel.add(insertButton);
49        insertButton.addActionListener(event ->
50          textArea.append("User name: " + textField.getText() + " Password: "
51            + new String(passwordField.getPassword()) + "\n"));
52
53        add(southPanel, BorderLayout.SOUTH);
54        pack();
55      }
56    }
```

---

javax.swing.JTextArea 1.2

- JTextArea()
- JTextArea(int rows, int cols)
- JTextArea(String text, int rows, int cols)

  constructs a new text area.

- void setColumns(int cols)

  tells the text area the preferred number of columns it should use.

- void setRows(int rows)

  tells the text area the preferred number of rows it should use.

- void append(String newText)

  appends the given text to the end of the text already in the text area.

- void setLineWrap(boolean wrap)

  turns line wrapping on or off.

- void setWrapStyleWord(boolean word)

  If word is true, long lines are wrapped at word boundaries. If it is false, long lines are broken without taking word boundaries into account.

- void setTabSize(int c)

  sets tab stops every c columns. Note that the tabs aren't converted to spaces but cause alignment with the next tab stop.

---

javax.swing.JScrollPane 1.2

- JScrollPane(Component c)

  creates a scroll pane that displays the content of the specified component. Scrollbars are supplied when the component is larger than the view.

12.4 Choice Components

You now know how to collect text input from users, but there are many occasions where you would rather give users a finite set of choices than have them enter the data in a text component. Using a set of buttons or a list of items tells your users what choices they have. (It also saves you the trouble of error checking.) In this section, you will learn how to program checkboxes, radio buttons, lists of choices, and sliders.

12.4.1 Checkboxes

If you want to collect just a "yes" or "no" input, use a checkbox component. Checkboxes automatically come with labels that identify them. The user can check the box by clicking inside it and turn off the checkmark by clicking inside the box again. Pressing the space bar when the focus is in the checkbox also toggles the checkmark.

Figure 12.14 shows a simple program with two checkboxes, one for turning the italic attribute of a font on or off, and the other for boldface. Note that the second checkbox has focus, as indicated by the rectangle around the label. Each time the user clicks one of the checkboxes, the screen is refreshed, using the new font attributes.

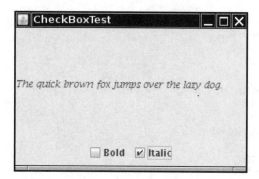

Figure 12.14 Checkboxes

Checkboxes need a label next to them to identify their purpose. Give the label text in the constructor:

```
bold = new JCheckBox("Bold");
```

Use the `setSelected` method to turn a checkbox on or off. For example:

```
bold.setSelected(true);
```

The isSelected method then retrieves the current state of each checkbox. It is false if unchecked, true if checked.

When the user clicks on a checkbox, this triggers an action event. As always, you attach an action listener to the checkbox. In our program, the two checkboxes share the same action listener.

```
ActionListener listener = . . .
bold.addActionListener(listener);
italic.addActionListener(listener);
```

The listener queries the state of the bold and italic checkboxes and sets the font of the panel to plain, bold, italic, or both bold and italic.

```
ActionListener listener = event -> {
   int mode = 0;
   if (bold.isSelected()) mode += Font.BOLD;
   if (italic.isSelected()) mode += Font.ITALIC;
   label.setFont(new Font(Font.SERIF, mode, FONTSIZE));
};
```

Listing 12.3 is the program listing for the checkbox example.

Listing 12.3 checkBox/CheckBoxFrame.java

```
1  package checkBox;
2
3  import java.awt.*;
4  import java.awt.event.*;
5  import javax.swing.*;
6
7  /**
8   * A frame with a sample text label and check boxes for selecting font
9   * attributes.
10  */
11 public class CheckBoxFrame extends JFrame
12 {
13    private JLabel label;
14    private JCheckBox bold;
15    private JCheckBox italic;
16    private static final int FONTSIZE = 24;
17
18    public CheckBoxFrame()
19    {
20       // add the sample text label
21
```

```
22      label = new JLabel("The quick brown fox jumps over the lazy dog.");
23      label.setFont(new Font("Serif", Font.BOLD, FONTSIZE));
24      add(label, BorderLayout.CENTER);
25
26      // this listener sets the font attribute of
27      // the label to the check box state
28
29      ActionListener listener = event -> {
30         int mode = 0;
31         if (bold.isSelected()) mode += Font.BOLD;
32         if (italic.isSelected()) mode += Font.ITALIC;
33         label.setFont(new Font("Serif", mode, FONTSIZE));
34      };
35
36      // add the check boxes
37
38      JPanel buttonPanel = new JPanel();
39
40      bold = new JCheckBox("Bold");
41      bold.addActionListener(listener);
42      bold.setSelected(true);
43      buttonPanel.add(bold);
44
45      italic = new JCheckBox("Italic");
46      italic.addActionListener(listener);
47      buttonPanel.add(italic);
48
49      add(buttonPanel, BorderLayout.SOUTH);
50      pack();
51   }
52 }
```

---

javax.swing.JCheckBox 1.2

- JCheckBox(String label)
- JCheckBox(String label, Icon icon)

  constructs a checkbox that is initially unselected.

- JCheckBox(String label, boolean state)

  constructs a checkbox with the given label and initial state.

- boolean isSelected()
- void setSelected(boolean state)

  gets or sets the selection state of the checkbox.

12.4.2 Radio Buttons

In the previous example, the user could check either, both, or neither of the two checkboxes. In many cases, we want the user to check only one of several boxes. When another box is checked, the previous box is automatically unchecked. Such a group of boxes is often called a *radio button group* because the buttons work like the station selector buttons on a radio. When you push in one button, the previously depressed button pops out. Figure 12.15 shows a typical example. We allow the user to select a font size from among the choices—Small, Medium, Large, or Extra large—but, of course, we will allow selecting only one size at a time.

Figure 12.15 A radio button group

Implementing radio button groups is easy in Swing. You construct one object of type ButtonGroup for every group of buttons. Then, you add objects of type JRadioButton to the button group. The button group object is responsible for turning off the previously set button when a new button is clicked.

```
ButtonGroup group = new ButtonGroup();

JRadioButton smallButton = new JRadioButton("Small", false);
group.add(smallButton);

JRadioButton mediumButton = new JRadioButton("Medium", true);
group.add(mediumButton);
. . .
```

The second argument of the constructor is true for the button that should be checked initially and false for all others. Note that the button group controls only the *behavior* of the buttons; if you want to group the buttons for layout purposes, you also need to add them to a container such as a JPanel.

If you look again at Figures 12.14 and 12.15, you will note that the appearance of the radio buttons is different from that of checkboxes. Checkboxes are square and contain a checkmark when selected. Radio buttons are round and contain a dot when selected.

The event notification mechanism for radio buttons is the same as for any other buttons. When the user checks a radio button, the button generates an action event. In our example program, we define an action listener that sets the font size to a particular value:

```
ActionListener listener = event ->
   label.setFont(new Font("Serif", Font.PLAIN, size));
```

Compare this listener setup to that of the checkbox example. Each radio button gets a different listener object. Each listener object knows exactly what it needs to do—set the font size to a particular value. With checkboxes, we used a different approach: Both checkboxes have the same action listener that calls a method looking at the current state of both checkboxes.

Could we follow the same approach here? We could have a single listener that computes the size as follows:

```
if (smallButton.isSelected()) size = 8;
else if (mediumButton.isSelected()) size = 12;
. . .
```

However, we prefer to use separate action listener objects because they tie the size values more closely to the buttons.

 NOTE: If you have a group of radio buttons, you know that only one of them is selected. It would be nice to be able to quickly find out which, without having to query all the buttons in the group. The ButtonGroup object controls all buttons, so it would be convenient if this object could give us a reference to the selected button. Indeed, the ButtonGroup class has a getSelection method, but that method doesn't return the radio button that is selected. Instead, it returns a ButtonModel reference to the model attached to the button. Unfortunately, none of the ButtonModel methods are very helpful. The ButtonModel interface inherits a method getSelectedObjects from the ItemSelectable interface that, rather uselessly, returns null. The getActionCommand method looks promising because the "action command" of a radio button is its text label. But the action command of its model is null. Only if you explicitly set the action commands of all radio buttons with the setActionCommand method do the action command values of the models also get set. Then you can retrieve the action command of the currently selected button with buttonGroup.getSelection().getActionCommand().

Listing 12.4 is the complete program for font size selection that puts a set of radio buttons to work.

Listing 12.4 radioButton/RadioButtonFrame.java

```
1  package radioButton;
2
3  import java.awt.*;
4  import java.awt.event.*;
5  import javax.swing.*;
6
7  /**
8   * A frame with a sample text label and radio buttons for selecting font sizes.
9   */
10 public class RadioButtonFrame extends JFrame
11 {
12    private JPanel buttonPanel;
13    private ButtonGroup group;
14    private JLabel label;
15    private static final int DEFAULT_SIZE = 36;
16
17    public RadioButtonFrame()
18    {
19       // add the sample text label
20
21       label = new JLabel("The quick brown fox jumps over the lazy dog.");
22       label.setFont(new Font("Serif", Font.PLAIN, DEFAULT_SIZE));
23       add(label, BorderLayout.CENTER);
24
25       // add the radio buttons
26
27       buttonPanel = new JPanel();
28       group = new ButtonGroup();
29
30       addRadioButton("Small", 8);
31       addRadioButton("Medium", 12);
32       addRadioButton("Large", 18);
33       addRadioButton("Extra large", 36);
34
35       add(buttonPanel, BorderLayout.SOUTH);
36       pack();
37    }
38
39    /**
40     * Adds a radio button that sets the font size of the sample text.
41     * @param name the string to appear on the button
42     * @param size the font size that this button sets
43     */
44    public void addRadioButton(String name, int size)
45    {
```

```
46      boolean selected = size == DEFAULT_SIZE;
47      JRadioButton button = new JRadioButton(name, selected);
48      group.add(button);
49      buttonPanel.add(button);
50
51      // this listener sets the label font size
52
53      ActionListener listener = event -> label.setFont(new Font("Serif", Font.PLAIN, size));
54
55      button.addActionListener(listener);
56   }
57 }
```

---

javax.swing.JRadioButton 1.2

- JRadioButton(String label, Icon icon)

  constructs a radio button that is initially unselected.

- JRadioButton(String label, boolean state)

  constructs a radio button with the given label and initial state.

---

javax.swing.ButtonGroup 1.2

- void add(AbstractButton b)

  adds the button to the group.

- ButtonModel getSelection()

  returns the button model of the selected button.

---

javax.swing.ButtonModel 1.2

- String getActionCommand()

  returns the action command for this button model.

---

javax.swing.AbstractButton 1.2

- void setActionCommand(String s)

  sets the action command for this button and its model.

12.4.3 Borders

If you have multiple groups of radio buttons in a window, you will want to visually indicate which buttons are grouped. Swing provides a set of useful *borders* for this purpose. You can apply a border to any component that extends JComponent. The most common usage is to place a border around a panel and fill that panel with other user interface elements, such as radio buttons.

You can choose from quite a few borders, but you need to follow the same steps for all of them.

1. Call a static method of the BorderFactory to create a border. You can choose among the following styles (see Figure 12.16):

   - Lowered bevel
   - Raised bevel
   - Etched
   - Line
   - Matte
   - Empty (just to create some blank space around the component)

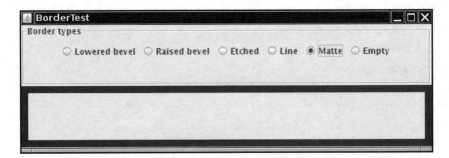

Figure 12.16 Testing border types

2. If you like, add a title to your border by passing your border to BorderFactory.createTitledBorder.

3. If you really want to go all out, combine several borders with a call to BorderFactory.createCompoundBorder.

4. Add the resulting border to your component by calling the setBorder method of the JComponent class.

For example, here is how you add an etched border with a title to a panel:

```
Border etched = BorderFactory.createEtchedBorder();
Border titled = BorderFactory.createTitledBorder(etched, "A Title");
panel.setBorder(titled);
```

Run the program in Listing 12.5 to get an idea what the various borders look like.

Different borders have different options for setting border widths and colors; see the API notes for details. True border enthusiasts will appreciate that there is also a SoftBevelBorder class for beveled borders with softened corners and that a LineBorder can have rounded corners as well. You can construct these borders only by using one of the class constructors—there is no BorderFactory method for them.

Listing 12.5 border/BorderFrame.java

```
1  package border;
2
3  import java.awt.*;
4  import javax.swing.*;
5  import javax.swing.border.*;
6
7  /**
8   * A frame with radio buttons to pick a border style.
9   */
10  public class BorderFrame extends JFrame
11  {
12     private JPanel demoPanel;
13     private JPanel buttonPanel;
14     private ButtonGroup group;
15
16     public BorderFrame()
17     {
18        demoPanel = new JPanel();
19        buttonPanel = new JPanel();
20        group = new ButtonGroup();
21
22        addRadioButton("Lowered bevel", BorderFactory.createLoweredBevelBorder());
23        addRadioButton("Raised bevel", BorderFactory.createRaisedBevelBorder());
24        addRadioButton("Etched", BorderFactory.createEtchedBorder());
25        addRadioButton("Line", BorderFactory.createLineBorder(Color.BLUE));
26        addRadioButton("Matte", BorderFactory.createMatteBorder(10, 10, 10, 10, Color.BLUE));
27        addRadioButton("Empty", BorderFactory.createEmptyBorder());
28
29        Border etched = BorderFactory.createEtchedBorder();
```

(Continues)

Listing 12.5 *(Continued)*

```
30        Border titled = BorderFactory.createTitledBorder(etched, "Border types");
31        buttonPanel.setBorder(titled);
32
33        setLayout(new GridLayout(2, 1));
34        add(buttonPanel);
35        add(demoPanel);
36        pack();
37     }
38
39     public void addRadioButton(String buttonName, Border b)
40     {
41        JRadioButton button = new JRadioButton(buttonName);
42        button.addActionListener(event -> demoPanel.setBorder(b));
43        group.add(button);
44        buttonPanel.add(button);
45     }
46  }
```

---

javax.swing.BorderFactory 1.2

- static Border createLineBorder(Color color)
- static. Border createLineBorder(Color color, int thickness)

  creates a simple line border.

- static MatteBorder createMatteBorder(int top, int left, int bottom, int right, Color color)
- static MatteBorder createMatteBorder(int top, int left, int bottom, int right, Icon tileIcon)

  creates a thick border that is filled with a color or a repeating icon.

- static Border createEmptyBorder()
- static Border createEmptyBorder(int top, int left, int bottom, int right)

  creates an empty border.

- static Border createEtchedBorder()
- static Border createEtchedBorder(Color highlight, Color shadow)
- static Border createEtchedBorder(int type)
- static Border createEtchedBorder(int type, Color highlight, Color shadow)

  creates a line border with a 3D effect.

Parameters:	highlight, shadow	Colors for 3D effect
	type	One of EtchedBorder.RAISED, EtchedBorder.LOWERED

(Continues)

---

javax.swing.BorderFactory 1.2 *(Continued)*

- `static Border createBevelBorder(int type)`
- `static Border createBevelBorder(int type, Color highlight, Color shadow)`
- `static Border createLoweredBevelBorder()`
- `static Border createRaisedBevelBorder()`

creates a border that gives the effect of a lowered or raised surface.

Parameters: highlight, shadow   Colors for 3D effect

            type   One of BevelBorder.RAISED, BevelBorder.LOWERED

- `static TitledBorder createTitledBorder(String title)`
- `static TitledBorder createTitledBorder(Border border)`
- `static TitledBorder createTitledBorder(Border border, String title)`
- `static TitledBorder createTitledBorder(Border border, String title, int justification, int position)`
- `static TitledBorder createTitledBorder(Border border, String title, int justification, int position, Font font)`
- `static TitledBorder createTitledBorder(Border border, String title, int justification, int position, Font font, Color color)`

creates a titled border with the specified properties.

Parameters: title   The title string

            border   The border to decorate with the title

            justification   One of the TitledBorder constants LEFT, CENTER, RIGHT, LEADING, TRAILING, or DEFAULT_JUSTIFICATION (left)

            position   One of the TitledBorder constants ABOVE_TOP, TOP, BELOW_TOP, ABOVE_BOTTOM, BOTTOM, BELOW_BOTTOM, or DEFAULT_POSITION (top)

            font   The font for the title

            color   The color of the title

- `static CompoundBorder createCompoundBorder(Border outsideBorder, Border insideBorder)`

combines two borders to a new border.

---

javax.swing.border.SoftBevelBorder 1.2

- `SoftBevelBorder(int type)`
- `SoftBevelBorder(int type, Color highlight, Color shadow)`

creates a bevel border with softened corners.

Parameters: highlight, shadow   Colors for 3D effect

            type   One of EtchedBorder.RAISED, EtchedBorder.LOWERED

`javax.swing.border.LineBorder` 1.2

- `public LineBorder(Color color, int thickness, boolean roundedCorners)`

  creates a line border with the given color and thickness. If `roundedCorners` is `true`, the border has rounded corners.

`javax.swing.JComponent` 1.2

- `void setBorder(Border border)`

  sets the border of this component.

12.4.4 Combo Boxes

If you have more than a handful of alternatives, radio buttons are not a good choice because they take up too much screen space. Instead, you can use a combo box. When the user clicks on this component, a list of choices drops down, and the user can then select one of them (see Figure 12.17).

Figure 12.17 A combo box

If the drop-down list box is set to be *editable*, you can edit the current selection as if it were a text field. For that reason, this component is called a *combo box*—it combines the flexibility of a text field with a set of predefined choices. The `JComboBox` class provides a combo box component.

As of Java SE 7, the JComboBox class is a generic class. For example, a JComboBox<String> holds objects of type String, and a JComboBox<Integer> holds integers.

Call the setEditable method to make the combo box editable. Note that editing affects only the selected item. It does not change the list of choices in any way.

You can obtain the current selection, which may have been edited if the combo box is editable, by calling the getSelectedItem method. However, for an editable combo box, that item may have any type, depending on the editor that takes the user edits and turns the result into an object. (See Volume II, Chapter 6 for a discussion of editors.) If your combo box isn't editable, you are better off calling

```
combo.getItemAt(combo.getSelectedIndex())
```

which gives you the selected item with the correct type.

In the example program, the user can choose a font style from a list of styles (Serif, SansSerif, Monospaced, etc.). The user can also type in another font.

Add the choice items with the addItem method. In our program, addItem is called only in the constructor, but you can call it any time.

```
JComboBox<String> faceCombo = new JComboBox<>();
faceCombo.addItem("Serif");
faceCombo.addItem("SansSerif");
. . .
```

This method adds the string to the end of the list. You can add new items anywhere in the list with the insertItemAt method:

```
faceCombo.insertItemAt("Monospaced", 0); // add at the beginning
```

You can add items of any type—the combo box invokes each item's toString method to display it.

If you need to remove items at runtime, use the removeItem or removeItemAt method, depending on whether you supply the item to be removed or its position.

```
faceCombo.removeItem("Monospaced");
faceCombo.removeItemAt(0); // remove first item
```

The removeAllItems method removes all items at once.

 TIP: If you need to add a large number of items to a combo box, the addItem method will perform poorly. Instead, construct a DefaultComboBoxModel, populate it by calling addElement, and then call the setModel method of the JComboBox class.

When the user selects an item from a combo box, the combo box generates an action event. To find out which item was selected, call getSource on the event parameter to get a reference to the combo box that sent the event. Then call the getSelectedItem method to retrieve the currently selected item. You will need to cast the returned value to the appropriate type, usually String.

```
ActionListener listener = event ->
    label.setFont(new Font(
        faceCombo.getItemAt(faceCombo.setSelectedIndex()),
        Font.PLAIN,
        DEFAULT_SIZE));
```

Listing 12.6 shows the complete program.

> **NOTE:** If you want to show a permanently displayed list instead of a drop-down list, use the JList component. We cover JList in Chapter 6 of Volume II.

Listing 12.6 comboBox/ComboBoxFrame.java

```
1  package comboBox;
2
3  import java.awt.BorderLayout;
4  import java.awt.Font;
5
6  import javax.swing.JComboBox;
7  import javax.swing.JFrame;
8  import javax.swing.JLabel;
9  import javax.swing.JPanel;
10
11 /**
12  * A frame with a sample text label and a combo box for selecting font faces.
13  */
14 public class ComboBoxFrame extends JFrame
15 {
16    private JComboBox<String> faceCombo;
17    private JLabel label;
18    private static final int DEFAULT_SIZE = 24;
19
20    public ComboBoxFrame()
21    {
22       // add the sample text label
23
24       label = new JLabel("The quick brown fox jumps over the lazy dog.");
25       label.setFont(new Font("Serif", Font.PLAIN, DEFAULT_SIZE));
26       add(label, BorderLayout.CENTER);
27
```

```
28        // make a combo box and add face names
29
30        faceCombo = new JComboBox<>();
31        faceCombo.addItem("Serif");
32        faceCombo.addItem("SansSerif");
33        faceCombo.addItem("Monospaced");
34        faceCombo.addItem("Dialog");
35        faceCombo.addItem("DialogInput");
36
37        // the combo box listener changes the label font to the selected face name
38
39        faceCombo.addActionListener(event ->
40           label.setFont(
41              new Font(faceCombo.getItemAt(faceCombo.getSelectedIndex()),
42                 Font.PLAIN, DEFAULT_SIZE)));
43
44        // add combo box to a panel at the frame's southern border
45
46        JPanel comboPanel = new JPanel();
47        comboPanel.add(faceCombo);
48        add(comboPanel, BorderLayout.SOUTH);
49        pack();
50     }
51  }
```

---

javax.swing.JComboBox 1.2

- boolean isEditable()
- void setEditable(boolean b)

  gets or sets the editable property of this combo box.

- void addItem(Object item)

  adds an item to the item list.

- void insertItemAt(Object item, int index)

  inserts an item into the item list at a given index.

- void removeItem(Object item)

  removes an item from the item list.

- void removeItemAt(int index)

  removes the item at an index.

- void removeAllItems()

  removes all items from the item list.

- Object getSelectedItem()

  returns the currently selected item.

12.4.5 Sliders

Combo boxes let users choose from a discrete set of values. Sliders offer a choice from a continuum of values—for example, any number between 1 and 100.

The most common way of constructing a slider is as follows:

```
JSlider slider = new JSlider(min, max, initialValue);
```

If you omit the minimum, maximum, and initial values, they are initialized with 0, 100, and 50, respectively.

Or if you want the slider to be vertical, use the following constructor call:

```
JSlider slider = new JSlider(SwingConstants.VERTICAL, min, max, initialValue);
```

These constructors create a plain slider, such as the top slider in Figure 12.18. You will see presently how to add decorations to a slider.

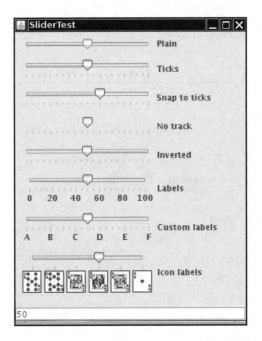

Figure 12.18 Sliders

As the user slides the slider bar, the *value* of the slider moves between the minimum and the maximum values. When the value changes, a ChangeEvent is sent to all change listeners. To be notified of the change, call the addChangeListener method and install an object that implements the functional ChangeListener interface. In the callback, retrieve the slider value:

```
ChangeListener listener = event -> {
   JSlider slider = (JSlider) event.getSource();
   int value = slider.getValue();
   . . .
};
```

You can embellish the slider by showing *ticks*. For example, in the sample program, the second slider uses the following settings:

```
slider.setMajorTickSpacing(20);
slider.setMinorTickSpacing(5);
```

The slider is decorated with large tick marks every 20 units and small tick marks every 5 units. The units refer to slider values, not pixels.

These instructions only set the units for the tick marks. To actually have the tick marks appear, call

```
slider.setPaintTicks(true);
```

The major and minor tick marks are independent. For example, you can set major tick marks every 20 units and minor tick marks every 7 units, but that will give you a very messy scale.

You can force the slider to *snap to ticks*. Whenever the user has finished dragging a slider in snap mode, it is immediately moved to the closest tick. You activate this mode with the call

```
slider.setSnapToTicks(true);
```

CAUTION: The "snap to ticks" behavior doesn't work as well as you might imagine. Until the slider has actually snapped, the change listener still reports slider values that don't correspond to ticks. And if you click next to the slider—an action that normally advances the slider a bit in the direction of the click—a slider with "snap to ticks" does not move to the next tick.

You can display *tick mark labels* for the major tick marks by calling

```
slider.setPaintLabels(true);
```

For example, with a slider ranging from 0 to 100 and major tick spacing of 20, the ticks are labeled 0, 20, 40, 60, 80, and 100.

You can also supply other tick mark labels, such as strings or icons (see Figure 12.18). The process is a bit convoluted. You need to fill a hash table with keys of type Integer and values of type Component. You then call the setLabelTable method. The components are placed under the tick marks. Usually, JLabel objects are used. Here is how you can label ticks as A, B, C, D, E, and F:

```
Hashtable<Integer, Component> labelTable = new Hashtable<Integer, Component>();
labelTable.put(0, new JLabel("A"));
labelTable.put(20, new JLabel("B"));
. . .
labelTable.put(100, new JLabel("F"));
slider.setLabelTable(labelTable);
```

See Chapter 9 for more information about hash tables.

Listing 12.7 also shows a slider with icons as tick labels.

 TIP: If your tick marks or labels don't show, double-check that you called setPaintTicks(true) and setPaintLabels(true).

The fourth slider in Figure 12.18 has no track. To suppress the "track" in which the slider moves, call

```
slider.setPaintTrack(false);
```

The fifth slider has its direction reversed by a call to

```
slider.setInverted(true);
```

The example program shows all these visual effects with a collection of sliders. Each slider has a change event listener installed that places the current slider value into the text field at the bottom of the frame.

Listing 12.7 slider/SliderFrame.java

```
1  package slider;
2
3  import java.awt.*;
4  import java.util.*;
5  import javax.swing.*;
6  import javax.swing.event.*;
7
8  /**
9   * A frame with many sliders and a text field to show slider values.
10  */
```

```
11  public class SliderFrame extends JFrame
12  {
13      private JPanel sliderPanel;
14      private JTextField textField;
15      private ChangeListener listener;
16
17      public SliderFrame()
18      {
19         sliderPanel = new JPanel();
20         sliderPanel.setLayout(new GridBagLayout());
21
22         // common listener for all sliders
23         listener = event -> {
24            // update text field when the slider value changes
25            JSlider source = (JSlider) event.getSource();
26            textField.setText("" + source.getValue());
27         };
28
29         // add a plain slider
30
31         JSlider slider = new JSlider();
32         addSlider(slider, "Plain");
33
34         // add a slider with major and minor ticks
35
36         slider = new JSlider();
37         slider.setPaintTicks(true);
38         slider.setMajorTickSpacing(20);
39         slider.setMinorTickSpacing(5);
40         addSlider(slider, "Ticks");
41
42         // add a slider that snaps to ticks
43
44         slider = new JSlider();
45         slider.setPaintTicks(true);
46         slider.setSnapToTicks(true);
47         slider.setMajorTickSpacing(20);
48         slider.setMinorTickSpacing(5);
49         addSlider(slider, "Snap to ticks");
50
51         // add a slider with no track
52
53         slider = new JSlider();
54         slider.setPaintTicks(true);
55         slider.setMajorTickSpacing(20);
56         slider.setMinorTickSpacing(5);
57         slider.setPaintTrack(false);
```

(Continues)

Listing 12.7 *(Continued)*

```
58        addSlider(slider, "No track");
59
60        // add an inverted slider
61
62        slider = new JSlider();
63        slider.setPaintTicks(true);
64        slider.setMajorTickSpacing(20);
65        slider.setMinorTickSpacing(5);
66        slider.setInverted(true);
67        addSlider(slider, "Inverted");
68
69        // add a slider with numeric labels
70
71        slider = new JSlider();
72        slider.setPaintTicks(true);
73        slider.setPaintLabels(true);
74        slider.setMajorTickSpacing(20);
75        slider.setMinorTickSpacing(5);
76        addSlider(slider, "Labels");
77
78        // add a slider with alphabetic labels
79
80        slider = new JSlider();
81        slider.setPaintLabels(true);
82        slider.setPaintTicks(true);
83        slider.setMajorTickSpacing(20);
84        slider.setMinorTickSpacing(5);
85
86        Dictionary<Integer, Component> labelTable = new Hashtable<>();
87        labelTable.put(0, new JLabel("A"));
88        labelTable.put(20, new JLabel("B"));
89        labelTable.put(40, new JLabel("C"));
90        labelTable.put(60, new JLabel("D"));
91        labelTable.put(80, new JLabel("E"));
92        labelTable.put(100, new JLabel("F"));
93
94        slider.setLabelTable(labelTable);
95        addSlider(slider, "Custom labels");
96
97        // add a slider with icon labels
98
99        slider = new JSlider();
100       slider.setPaintTicks(true);
```

```
101        slider.setPaintLabels(true);
102        slider.setSnapToTicks(true);
103        slider.setMajorTickSpacing(20);
104        slider.setMinorTickSpacing(20);
105
106        labelTable = new Hashtable<Integer, Component>();
107
108        // add card images
109
110        labelTable.put(0, new JLabel(new ImageIcon("nine.gif")));
111        labelTable.put(20, new JLabel(new ImageIcon("ten.gif")));
112        labelTable.put(40, new JLabel(new ImageIcon("jack.gif")));
113        labelTable.put(60, new JLabel(new ImageIcon("queen.gif")));
114        labelTable.put(80, new JLabel(new ImageIcon("king.gif")));
115        labelTable.put(100, new JLabel(new ImageIcon("ace.gif")));
116
117        slider.setLabelTable(labelTable);
118        addSlider(slider, "Icon labels");
119
120        // add the text field that displays the slider value
121
122        textField = new JTextField();
123        add(sliderPanel, BorderLayout.CENTER);
124        add(textField, BorderLayout.SOUTH);
125        pack();
126     }
127
128     /**
129      * Adds a slider to the slider panel and hooks up the listener
130      * @param s the slider
131      * @param description the slider description
132      */
133     public void addSlider(JSlider s, String description)
134     {
135        s.addChangeListener(listener);
136        JPanel panel = new JPanel();
137        panel.add(s);
138        panel.add(new JLabel(description));
139        panel.setAlignmentX(Component.LEFT_ALIGNMENT);
140        GridBagConstraints gbc = new GridBagConstraints();
141        gbc.gridy = sliderPanel.getComponentCount();
142        gbc.anchor = GridBagConstraints.WEST;
143        sliderPanel.add(panel, gbc);
144     }
145 }
```

---

javax.swing.JSlider 1.2

- JSlider()
- JSlider(int direction)
- JSlider(int min, int max)
- JSlider(int min, int max, int initialValue)
- JSlider(int direction, int min, int max, int initialValue)

    constructs a horizontal slider with the given direction and minimum, maximum, and initial values.

Parameters:	direction	One of SwingConstants.HORIZONTAL or SwingConstants.VERTICAL. The default is horizontal.
	min, max	The minimum and maximum for the slider values. Defaults are 0 and 100.
	initialValue	The initial value for the slider. The default is 50.

- void setPaintTicks(boolean b)

    displays ticks if b is true.

- void setMajorTickSpacing(int units)
- void setMinorTickSpacing(int units)

    sets major or minor ticks at multiples of the given slider units.

- void setPaintLabels(boolean b)

    displays tick labels if b is true.

- void setLabelTable(Dictionary table)

    sets the components to use for the tick labels. Each key/value pair in the table has the form new Integer(*value*)/*component*.

- void setSnapToTicks(boolean b)

    if b is true, then the slider snaps to the closest tick after each adjustment.

- void setPaintTrack(boolean b)

    if b is true, a track is displayed in which the slider runs.

12.5 Menus

We started this chapter by introducing the most common components that you might want to place into a window, such as various kinds of buttons, text fields, and combo boxes. Swing also supports another type of user interface element—pull-down menus that are familiar from GUI applications.

A *menu bar* at the top of a window contains the names of the pull-down menus. Clicking on a name opens the menu containing *menu items* and *submenus*. When the user clicks on a menu item, all menus are closed and a message is sent to the program. Figure 12.19 shows a typical menu with a submenu.

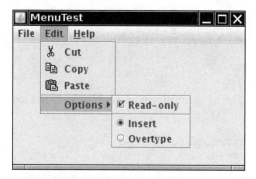

Figure 12.19 A menu with a submenu

12.5.1 Menu Building

Building menus is straightforward. First, create a menu bar:

```
JMenuBar menuBar = new JMenuBar();
```

A menu bar is just a component that you can add anywhere you like. Normally, you want it to appear at the top of a frame. You can add it there with the setJMenuBar method:

```
frame.setJMenuBar(menuBar);
```

For each menu, you create a menu object:

```
JMenu editMenu = new JMenu("Edit");
```

Add the top-level menus to the menu bar:

```
menuBar.add(editMenu);
```

Add menu items, separators, and submenus to the menu object:

```
JMenuItem pasteItem = new JMenuItem("Paste");
editMenu.add(pasteItem);
editMenu.addSeparator();
JMenu optionsMenu = . . .; // a submenu
editMenu.add(optionsMenu);
```

You can see separators in Figure 12.19 below the Paste and Read-only menu items.

When the user selects a menu, an action event is triggered. You need to install an action listener for each menu item:

```
ActionListener listener = . . .;
pasteItem.addActionListener(listener);
```

The method `JMenu.add(String s)` conveniently adds a menu item to the end of a menu. For example:

```
editMenu.add("Paste");
```

The `add` method returns the created menu item, so you can capture it and add the listener, as follows:

```
JMenuItem pasteItem = editMenu.add("Paste");
pasteItem.addActionListener(listener);
```

It often happens that menu items trigger commands that can also be activated through other user interface elements such as toolbar buttons. In Chapter 11, you saw how to specify commands through `Action` objects. You define a class that implements the `Action` interface, usually by extending the `AbstractAction` convenience class, specify the menu item label in the constructor of the `AbstractAction` object, and override the `actionPerformed` method to hold the menu action handler. For example:

```
Action exitAction = new AbstractAction("Exit") // menu item text goes here
   {
      public void actionPerformed(ActionEvent event)
      {
         // action code goes here
         System.exit(0);
      }
   };
```

You can then add the action to the menu:

```
JMenuItem exitItem = fileMenu.add(exitAction);
```

This command adds a menu item to the menu, using the action name. The action object becomes its listener. This is just a convenient shortcut for

```
JMenuItem exitItem = new JMenuItem(exitAction);
fileMenu.add(exitItem);
```

---

javax.swing.JMenu 1.2

- JMenu(String label)

  constructs a menu with the given label.

- JMenuItem add(JMenuItem item)

  adds a menu item (or a menu).

- JMenuItem add(String label)

  adds a menu item with the given label to this menu and returns the item.

- JMenuItem add(Action a)

  adds a menu item with the given action to this menu and returns the item.

- void addSeparator()

  adds a separator line to the menu.

- JMenuItem insert(JMenuItem menu, int index)

  adds a new menu item (or submenu) to the menu at a specific index.

- JMenuItem insert(Action a, int index)

  adds a new menu item with the given action at a specific index.

- void insertSeparator(int index)

  adds a separator to the menu.

  Parameters: index   Where to add the separator

- void remove(int index)
- void remove(JMenuItem item)

  removes a specific item from the menu.

---

javax.swing.JMenuItem 1.2

- JMenuItem(String label)

  constructs a menu item with a given label.

- JMenuItem(Action a) 1.3

  constructs a menu item for the given action.

---

javax.swing.AbstractButton 1.2

- void setAction(Action a) 1.3

  sets the action for this button or menu item.

`javax.swing.JFrame` 1.2

- void setJMenuBar(JMenuBar menubar)

  sets the menu bar for this frame.

12.5.2 Icons in Menu Items

Menu items are very similar to buttons. In fact, the `JMenuItem` class extends the `AbstractButton` class. Just like buttons, menus can have just a text label, just an icon, or both. You can specify the icon with the `JMenuItem(String, Icon)` or `JMenuItem(Icon)` constructor, or you can set it with the `setIcon` method that the `JMenuItem` class inherits from the `AbstractButton` class. Here is an example:

```
JMenuItem cutItem = new JMenuItem("Cut", new ImageIcon("cut.gif"));
```

In Figure 12.19, you can see icons next to several menu items. By default, the menu item text is placed to the right of the icon. If you prefer the text to be placed on the left, call the `setHorizontalTextPosition` method that the `JMenuItem` class inherits from the `AbstractButton` class. For example, the call

```
cutItem.setHorizontalTextPosition(SwingConstants.LEFT);
```

moves the menu item text to the left of the icon.

You can also add an icon to an action:

```
cutAction.putValue(Action.SMALL_ICON, new ImageIcon("cut.gif"));
```

Whenever you construct a menu item out of an action, the `Action.NAME` value becomes the text of the menu item and the `Action.SMALL_ICON` value becomes the icon.

Alternatively, you can set the icon in the `AbstractAction` constructor:

```
cutAction = new
   AbstractAction("Cut", new ImageIcon("cut.gif"))
   {
      public void actionPerformed(ActionEvent event)
      {
         . . .
      }
   };
```

`javax.swing.JMenuItem` 1.2

- JMenuItem(String label, Icon icon)

  constructs a menu item with the given label and icon.

---

javax.swing.AbstractButton 1.2

- void setHorizontalTextPosition(int pos)

  sets the horizontal position of the text relative to the icon.

  Parameters: pos   SwingConstants.RIGHT (text is to the right of icon) or
  SwingConstants.LEFT

---

javax.swing.AbstractAction 1.2

- AbstractAction(String name, Icon smallIcon)

  constructs an abstract action with the given name and icon.

12.5.3 Checkbox and Radio Button Menu Items

Checkbox and *radio button* menu items display a checkbox or radio button next to the name (see Figure 12.19). When the user selects the menu item, the item automatically toggles between checked and unchecked.

Apart from the button decoration, treat these menu items just as you would any others. For example, here is how you create a checkbox menu item:

```
JCheckBoxMenuItem readonlyItem = new JCheckBoxMenuItem("Read-only");
optionsMenu.add(readonlyItem);
```

The radio button menu items work just like regular radio buttons. You must add them to a button group. When one of the buttons in a group is selected, all others are automatically deselected.

```
ButtonGroup group = new ButtonGroup();
JRadioButtonMenuItem insertItem = new JRadioButtonMenuItem("Insert");
insertItem.setSelected(true);
JRadioButtonMenuItem overtypeItem = new JRadioButtonMenuItem("Overtype");
group.add(insertItem);
group.add(overtypeItem);
optionsMenu.add(insertItem);
optionsMenu.add(overtypeItem);
```

With these menu items, you don't necessarily want to be notified when the user selects the item. Instead, you can simply use the isSelected method to test the current state of the menu item. (Of course, that means you should keep a reference to the menu item stored in an instance field.) Use the setSelected method to set the state.

---

javax.swing.JCheckBoxMenuItem 1.2

- `JCheckBoxMenuItem(String label)`

  constructs the checkbox menu item with the given label.

- `JCheckBoxMenuItem(String label, boolean state)`

  constructs the checkbox menu item with the given label and the given initial state (`true` is checked).

---

javax.swing.JRadioButtonMenuItem 1.2

- `JRadioButtonMenuItem(String label)`

  constructs the radio button menu item with the given label.

- `JRadioButtonMenuItem(String label, boolean state)`

  constructs the radio button menu item with the given label and the given initial state (`true` is checked).

---

javax.swing.AbstractButton 1.2

- `boolean isSelected()`
- `void setSelected(boolean state)`

  gets or sets the selection state of this item (`true` is checked).

12.5.4 Pop-Up Menus

A *pop-up menu* is a menu that is not attached to a menu bar but floats somewhere (see Figure 12.20).

Create a pop-up menu just as you create a regular menu, except that a pop-up menu has no title.

```
JPopupMenu popup = new JPopupMenu();
```

Then, add your menu items as usual:

```
JMenuItem item = new JMenuItem("Cut");
item.addActionListener(listener);
popup.add(item);
```

Unlike the regular menu bar that is always shown at the top of the frame, you must explicitly display a pop-up menu by using the show method. Specify the

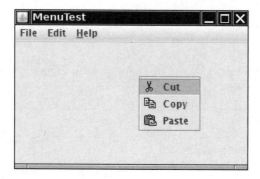

Figure 12.20 A pop-up menu

parent component and the location of the pop-up, using the coordinate system of the parent. For example:

```
popup.show(panel, x, y);
```

Usually, you want to pop up a menu when the user clicks a particular mouse button—the so-called *pop-up trigger*. In Windows and Linux, the pop-up trigger is the nonprimary (usually, the right) mouse button. To pop up a menu when the user clicks on a component, using the pop-up trigger, simply call the method

```
component.setComponentPopupMenu(popup);
```

Very occasionally, you may place a component inside another component that has a pop-up menu. The child component can inherit the parent component's pop-up menu by calling

```
child.setInheritsPopupMenu(true);
```

---

javax.swing.JPopupMenu 1.2

- `void show(Component c, int x, int y)`

  shows the pop-up menu.

  Parameters: c   The component over which the pop-up menu is to appear

  x, y   The coordinates (in the coordinate space of c) of the top left
  corner of the pop-up menu

- `boolean isPopupTrigger(MouseEvent event)` 1.3

  returns `true` if the mouse event is the pop-up menu trigger.

---

java.awt.event.MouseEvent 1.1

- `boolean isPopupTrigger()`

  returns `true` if this mouse event is the pop-up menu trigger.

---

javax.swing.JComponent 1.2

- `JPopupMenu getComponentPopupMenu()` 5.0
- `void setComponentPopupMenu(JPopupMenu popup)` 5.0

  gets or sets the pop-up menu for this component.

- `boolean getInheritsPopupMenu()` 5.0
- `void setInheritsPopupMenu(boolean b)` 5.0

  gets or sets the `inheritsPopupMenu` property. If the property is set and this component's pop-up menu is `null`, it uses its parent's pop-up menu.

12.5.5 Keyboard Mnemonics and Accelerators

It is a real convenience for the experienced user to select menu items by *keyboard mnemonics*. You can create a keyboard mnemonic for a menu item by specifying a mnemonic letter in the menu item constructor:

```
JMenuItem aboutItem = new JMenuItem("About", 'A');
```

The keyboard mnemonic is displayed automatically in the menu, with the mnemonic letter underlined (see Figure 12.21). For example, in the item defined in the last example, the label will be displayed as "About" with an underlined letter "A". When the menu is displayed, the user just needs to press the A key, and the menu item is selected. (If the mnemonic letter is not part of the menu string, then typing it still selects the item, but the mnemonic is not displayed in the menu. Naturally, such invisible mnemonics are of dubious utility.)

Sometimes, you don't want to underline the first letter of the menu item that matches the mnemonic. For example, if you have a mnemonic "A" for the menu item "Save As," then it makes more sense to underline the second "A" (Save As). You can specify which character you want to have underlined by calling the `setDisplayedMnemonicIndex` method.

If you have an `Action` object, you can add the mnemonic as the value of the `Action.MNEMONIC_KEY` key, as follows:

```
cutAction.putValue(Action.MNEMONIC_KEY, new Integer('A'));
```

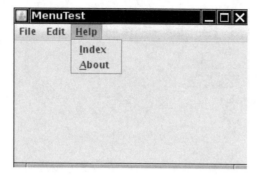

Figure 12.21 Keyboard mnemonics

You can supply a mnemonic letter only in the constructor of a menu item, not in the constructor for a menu. To attach a mnemonic to a menu, call the `setMnemonic` method:

```
JMenu helpMenu = new JMenu("Help");
helpMenu.setMnemonic('H');
```

To select a top-level menu from the menu bar, press the Alt key together with the mnemonic letter. For example, press Alt+H to select the Help menu from the menu bar.

Keyboard mnemonics let you select a submenu or menu item from the currently open menu. In contrast, *accelerators* are keyboard shortcuts that let you select menu items without ever opening a menu. For example, many programs attach the accelerators Ctrl+O and Ctrl+S to the Open and Save items in the File menu. Use the `setAccelerator` method to attach an accelerator key to a menu item. The `setAccelerator` method takes an object of type `KeyStroke`. For example, the following call attaches the accelerator Ctrl+O to the `openItem` menu item:

```
openItem.setAccelerator(KeyStroke.getKeyStroke("ctrl O"));
```

Typing the accelerator key combination automatically selects the menu option and fires an action event, as if the user had selected the menu option manually.

You can attach accelerators only to menu items, not to menus. Accelerator keys don't actually open the menu. Instead, they directly fire the action event associated with a menu.

Conceptually, adding an accelerator to a menu item is similar to the technique of adding an accelerator to a Swing component. (We discussed that technique in Chapter 11.) However, when the accelerator is added to a menu item, the key combination is automatically displayed in the menu (see Figure 12.22).

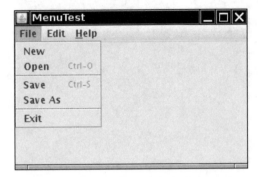

Figure 12.22 Accelerators

 NOTE: Under Windows, Alt+F4 closes a window. But this is not an accelerator to be programmed in Java. It is a shortcut defined by the operating system. This key combination will always trigger the `WindowClosing` event for the active window regardless of whether there is a Close item on the menu.

`javax.swing.JMenuItem` 1.2

- `JMenuItem(String label, int mnemonic)`

  constructs a menu item with a given label and mnemonic.

  Parameters: `label`   The label for this menu item

  `mnemonic`   The mnemonic character for the item; this character will be underlined in the label

- `void setAccelerator(KeyStroke k)`

  sets the keystroke k as accelerator for this menu item. The accelerator key is displayed next to the label.

`javax.swing.AbstractButton` 1.2

- `void setMnemonic(int mnemonic)`

  sets the mnemonic character for the button. This character will be underlined in the label.

- `void setDisplayedMnemonicIndex(int index)` 1.4

  sets the index of the character to be underlined in the button text. Use this method if you don't want the first occurrence of the mnemonic character to be underlined.

12.5.6 Enabling and Disabling Menu Items

Occasionally, a particular menu item should be selected only in certain contexts. For example, when a document is opened in read-only mode, the Save menu item is not meaningful. Of course, we could remove the item from the menu with the `JMenu.remove` method, but users would react with some surprise to menus whose content keeps changing. Instead, it is better to deactivate the menu items that lead to temporarily inappropriate commands. A deactivated menu item is shown in gray, and it cannot be selected (see Figure 12.23).

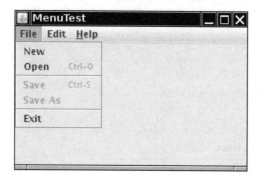

Figure 12.23 Disabled menu items

To enable or disable a menu item, use the `setEnabled` method:

```
saveItem.setEnabled(false);
```

There are two strategies for enabling and disabling menu items. Each time circumstances change, you can call `setEnabled` on the relevant menu items or actions. For example, as soon as a document has been set to read-only mode, you can locate the Save and Save As menu items and disable them. Alternatively, you can disable items just before displaying the menu. To do this, you must register a listener for the "menu selected" event. The `javax.swing.event` package defines a `MenuListener` interface with three methods:

```
void menuSelected(MenuEvent event)
void menuDeselected(MenuEvent event)
void menuCanceled(MenuEvent event)
```

The `menuSelected` method is called *before* the menu is displayed. It can therefore be used to disable or enable menu items. The following code shows how to disable the Save and Save As actions whenever the Read Only checkbox menu item is selected:

```
public void menuSelected(MenuEvent event)
{
   saveAction.setEnabled(!readonlyItem.isSelected());
   saveAsAction.setEnabled(!readonlyItem.isSelected());
}
```

 CAUTION: Disabling menu items just before displaying the menu is a clever idea, but it does not work for menu items that also have accelerator keys. Since the menu is never opened when the accelerator key is pressed, the action is never disabled, and is still triggered by the accelerator key.

`javax.swing.JMenuItem` 1.2

- void setEnabled(boolean b)

  enables or disables the menu item.

`javax.swing.event.MenuListener` 1.2

- void menuSelected(MenuEvent e)

  is called when the menu has been selected, before it is opened.

- void menuDeselected(MenuEvent e)

  is called when the menu has been deselected, after it has been closed.

- void menuCanceled(MenuEvent e)

  is called when the menu has been canceled, for example, by a user clicking outside the menu.

Listing 12.8 is a sample program that generates a set of menus. It shows all the features that you saw in this section: nested menus, disabled menu items, checkbox and radio button menu items, a pop-up menu, and keyboard mnemonics and accelerators.

Listing 12.8   menu/MenuFrame.java

```
1  package menu;
2
3  import java.awt.event.*;
4  import javax.swing.*;
5
```

```
 6   /**
 7    * A frame with a sample menu bar.
 8    */
 9   public class MenuFrame extends JFrame
10   {
11      private static final int DEFAULT_WIDTH = 300;
12      private static final int DEFAULT_HEIGHT = 200;
13      private Action saveAction;
14      private Action saveAsAction;
15      private JCheckBoxMenuItem readonlyItem;
16      private JPopupMenu popup;
17
18      /**
19       * A sample action that prints the action name to System.out
20       */
21      class TestAction extends AbstractAction
22      {
23         public TestAction(String name)
24         {
25            super(name);
26         }
27
28         public void actionPerformed(ActionEvent event)
29         {
30            System.out.println(getValue(Action.NAME) + " selected.");
31         }
32      }
33
34      public MenuFrame()
35      {
36         setSize(DEFAULT_WIDTH, DEFAULT_HEIGHT);
37
38         JMenu fileMenu = new JMenu("File");
39         fileMenu.add(new TestAction("New"));
40
41         // demonstrate accelerators
42
43         JMenuItem openItem = fileMenu.add(new TestAction("Open"));
44         openItem.setAccelerator(KeyStroke.getKeyStroke("ctrl O"));
45
46         fileMenu.addSeparator();
47
48         saveAction = new TestAction("Save");
49         JMenuItem saveItem = fileMenu.add(saveAction);
50         saveItem.setAccelerator(KeyStroke.getKeyStroke("ctrl S"));
51
52         saveAsAction = new TestAction("Save As");
```

(Continues)

Listing 12.8 *(Continued)*

```
53      fileMenu.add(saveAsAction);
54      fileMenu.addSeparator();
55
56      fileMenu.add(new AbstractAction("Exit")
57         {
58            public void actionPerformed(ActionEvent event)
59            {
60               System.exit(0);
61            }
62         });
63
64      // demonstrate checkbox and radio button menus
65
66      readonlyItem = new JCheckBoxMenuItem("Read-only");
67      readonlyItem.addActionListener(new ActionListener()
68         {
69            public void actionPerformed(ActionEvent event)
70            {
71               boolean saveOk = !readonlyItem.isSelected();
72               saveAction.setEnabled(saveOk);
73               saveAsAction.setEnabled(saveOk);
74            }
75         });
76
77      ButtonGroup group = new ButtonGroup();
78
79      JRadioButtonMenuItem insertItem = new JRadioButtonMenuItem("Insert");
80      insertItem.setSelected(true);
81      JRadioButtonMenuItem overtypeItem = new JRadioButtonMenuItem("Overtype");
82
83      group.add(insertItem);
84      group.add(overtypeItem);
85
86      // demonstrate icons
87
88      Action cutAction = new TestAction("Cut");
89      cutAction.putValue(Action.SMALL_ICON, new ImageIcon("cut.gif"));
90      Action copyAction = new TestAction("Copy");
91      copyAction.putValue(Action.SMALL_ICON, new ImageIcon("copy.gif"));
92      Action pasteAction = new TestAction("Paste");
93      pasteAction.putValue(Action.SMALL_ICON, new ImageIcon("paste.gif"));
94
95      JMenu editMenu = new JMenu("Edit");
96      editMenu.add(cutAction);
97      editMenu.add(copyAction);
98      editMenu.add(pasteAction);
99
```

```
100        // demonstrate nested menus
101
102        JMenu optionMenu = new JMenu("Options");
103
104        optionMenu.add(readonlyItem);
105        optionMenu.addSeparator();
106        optionMenu.add(insertItem);
107        optionMenu.add(overtypeItem);
108
109        editMenu.addSeparator();
110        editMenu.add(optionMenu);
111
112        // demonstrate mnemonics
113
114        JMenu helpMenu = new JMenu("Help");
115        helpMenu.setMnemonic('H');
116
117        JMenuItem indexItem = new JMenuItem("Index");
118        indexItem.setMnemonic('I');
119        helpMenu.add(indexItem);
120
121        // you can also add the mnemonic key to an action
122        Action aboutAction = new TestAction("About");
123        aboutAction.putValue(Action.MNEMONIC_KEY, new Integer('A'));
124        helpMenu.add(aboutAction);
125
126        // add all top-level menus to menu bar
127
128        JMenuBar menuBar = new JMenuBar();
129        setJMenuBar(menuBar);
130
131        menuBar.add(fileMenu);
132        menuBar.add(editMenu);
133        menuBar.add(helpMenu);
134
135        // demonstrate pop-ups
136
137        popup = new JPopupMenu();
138        popup.add(cutAction);
139        popup.add(copyAction);
140        popup.add(pasteAction);
141
142        JPanel panel = new JPanel();
143        panel.setComponentPopupMenu(popup);
144        add(panel);
145    }
146 }
```

12.5.7 Toolbars

A toolbar is a button bar that gives quick access to the most commonly used commands in a program (see Figure 12.24).

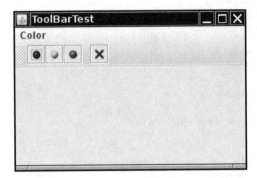

Figure 12.24 A toolbar

What makes toolbars special is that you can move them elsewhere. You can drag the toolbar to one of the four borders of the frame (see Figure 12.25). When you release the mouse button, the toolbar is dropped into the new location (see Figure 12.26).

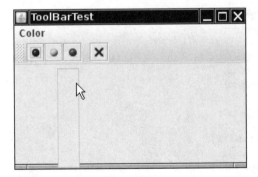

Figure 12.25 Dragging the toolbar

 NOTE: Toolbar dragging works if the toolbar is inside a container with a border layout, or any other layout manager that supports the North, East, South, and West constraints.

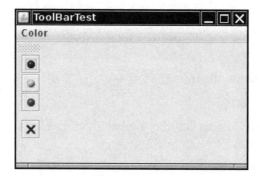

Figure 12.26 The toolbar has been dragged to another border

The toolbar can even be completely detached from the frame. A detached toolbar is contained in its own frame (see Figure 12.27). When you close the frame containing a detached toolbar, the toolbar jumps back into the original frame.

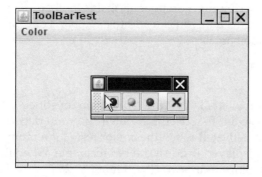

Figure 12.27 Detaching the toolbar

Toolbars are straightforward to program. Add components into the toolbar:

```
JToolBar bar = new JToolBar();
bar.add(blueButton);
```

The JToolBar class also has a method to add an Action object. Simply populate the toolbar with Action objects, like this:

```
bar.add(blueAction);
```

The small icon of the action is displayed in the toolbar.

You can separate groups of buttons with a separator:

```
bar.addSeparator();
```

For example, the toolbar in Figure 12.24 has a separator between the third and fourth button.

Then, add the toolbar to the frame:

```
add(bar, BorderLayout.NORTH);
```

You can also specify a title for the toolbar that appears when the toolbar is undocked:

```
bar = new JToolBar(titleString);
```

By default, toolbars are initially horizontal. To have a toolbar start out vertical, use

```
bar = new JToolBar(SwingConstants.VERTICAL)
```

or

```
bar = new JToolBar(titleString, SwingConstants.VERTICAL)
```

Buttons are the most common components inside toolbars. But there is no restriction on the components that you can add to a toolbar. For example, you can add a combo box to a toolbar.

12.5.8 Tooltips

A disadvantage of toolbars is that users are often mystified by the meanings of the tiny icons in toolbars. To solve this problem, user interface designers invented *tooltips*. A tooltip is activated when the cursor rests for a moment over a button. The tooltip text is displayed inside a colored rectangle. When the user moves the mouse away, the tooltip disappears. (See Figure 12.28.)

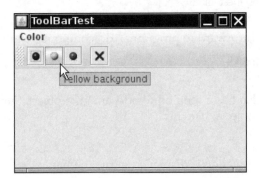

Figure 12.28 A tooltip

In Swing, you can add tooltips to any JComponent simply by calling the setToolTipText method:

```
exitButton.setToolTipText("Exit");
```

Alternatively, if you use Action objects, you associate the tooltip with the SHORT_DESCRIPTION key:

```
exitAction.putValue(Action.SHORT_DESCRIPTION, "Exit");
```

Listing 12.9 shows how the same Action objects can be added to a menu and a toolbar. Note that the action names show up as the menu item names in the menu, and the short descriptions as the tooltips in the toolbar.

Listing 12.9 toolBar/ToolBarFrame.java

```
 1  package toolBar;
 2
 3  import java.awt.*;
 4  import java.awt.event.*;
 5  import javax.swing.*;
 6
 7  /**
 8   * A frame with a toolbar and menu for color changes.
 9   */
10  public class ToolBarFrame extends JFrame
11  {
12     private static final int DEFAULT_WIDTH = 300;
13     private static final int DEFAULT_HEIGHT = 200;
14     private JPanel panel;
15
16     public ToolBarFrame()
17     {
18        setSize(DEFAULT_WIDTH, DEFAULT_HEIGHT);
19
20        // add a panel for color change
21
22        panel = new JPanel();
23        add(panel, BorderLayout.CENTER);
24
25        // set up actions
26
27        Action blueAction = new ColorAction("Blue", new ImageIcon("blue-ball.gif"), Color.BLUE);
28        Action yellowAction = new ColorAction("Yellow", new ImageIcon("yellow-ball.gif"),
29              Color.YELLOW);
30        Action redAction = new ColorAction("Red", new ImageIcon("red-ball.gif"), Color.RED);
31
```

(Continues)

Listing 12.9 *(Continued)*

```
32      Action exitAction = new AbstractAction("Exit", new ImageIcon("exit.gif"))
33         {
34            public void actionPerformed(ActionEvent event)
35            {
36               System.exit(0);
37            }
38         };
39      exitAction.putValue(Action.SHORT_DESCRIPTION, "Exit");
40
41      // populate toolbar
42
43      JToolBar bar = new JToolBar();
44      bar.add(blueAction);
45      bar.add(yellowAction);
46      bar.add(redAction);
47      bar.addSeparator();
48      bar.add(exitAction);
49      add(bar, BorderLayout.NORTH);
50
51      // populate menu
52
53      JMenu menu = new JMenu("Color");
54      menu.add(yellowAction);
55      menu.add(blueAction);
56      menu.add(redAction);
57      menu.add(exitAction);
58      JMenuBar menuBar = new JMenuBar();
59      menuBar.add(menu);
60      setJMenuBar(menuBar);
61   }
62
63   /**
64    * The color action sets the background of the frame to a given color.
65    */
66   class ColorAction extends AbstractAction
67   {
68      public ColorAction(String name, Icon icon, Color c)
69      {
70         putValue(Action.NAME, name);
71         putValue(Action.SMALL_ICON, icon);
72         putValue(Action.SHORT_DESCRIPTION, name + " background");
73         putValue("Color", c);
74      }
75
```

```
76      public void actionPerformed(ActionEvent event)
77      {
78         Color c = (Color) getValue("Color");
79         panel.setBackground(c);
80      }
81   }
82 }
```

---

javax.swing.JToolBar 1.2

- JToolBar()
- JToolBar(String titleString)
- JToolBar(int orientation)
- JToolBar(String titleString, int orientation)

  constructs a toolbar with the given title string and orientation. orientation is one of SwingConstants.HORIZONTAL (the default) or SwingConstants.VERTICAL.

- JButton add(Action a)

  constructs a new button inside the toolbar with name, icon, short description, and action callback from the given action, and adds the button to the end of the toolbar.

- void addSeparator()

  adds a separator to the end of the toolbar.

---

javax.swing.JComponent 1.2

- void setToolTipText(String text)

  sets the text that should be displayed as a tooltip when the mouse hovers over the component.

12.6 Sophisticated Layout Management

So far we've been using only the border layout, flow layout, and grid layout for the user interface of our sample applications. For more complex tasks, this is not going to be enough. In this section, we will discuss advanced layout management in detail.

Windows programmers may well wonder why Java makes so much fuss about layout managers. After all, in Windows, layout management is not a big deal; you just use a dialog editor to drag and drop your components onto the surface of a dialog, and then use editor tools to line up components, to space them equally, to center them, and so on. If you are working on a big project, you probably don't have to worry about component layout at all—a skilled user interface designer does all this for you.

The problem with this approach is that the resulting layout must be manually updated if the sizes of the components change. Why would the component sizes change? This can happen when the strings in an application are translated to a foreign language. For example, the German word for "Cancel" is "Abbrechen." If a button has been designed with just enough room for the string "Cancel", the German version will look broken, with a clipped string.

Why don't the buttons simply grow to accommodate the labels? When you drop buttons in a dialog editor, there is no indication in which direction they should grow. After the dragging and dropping and arranging, the dialog editor merely remembers the pixel position and size of each component. It does not remember *why* the components were arranged in this fashion.

The Java layout managers are a much better approach to component layout. With a layout manager, the layout comes with instructions about the relationships among the components. This was particularly important in the original AWT, which used native user interface elements. The size of a button or a list box in Motif, Windows, and the Macintosh could vary widely, and an application or applet would not know *a priori* on which platform it would display its user interface. To some extent, that degree of variability has gone away with Swing. If your application forces a particular look-and-feel, such as Metal, it looks identical on all platforms. However, if you let users of your application choose their favorite look-and-feel, then you again need to rely on the flexibility of layout managers to arrange the components.

Since Java 1.0, the AWT includes the *grid bag layout* that lays out components in rows and columns. The row and column sizes are flexible, and components can span multiple rows and columns. This layout manager is very flexible, but also very complex. The mere mention of the words "grid bag layout" has been known to strike fear in the hearts of Java programmers.

In an unsuccessful attempt to design a layout manager that would free programmers from the tyranny of the grid bag layout, the Swing designers came up with the *box layout*. According to the JDK documentation of the BoxLayout class: "Nesting multiple panels with different combinations of horizontal and vertical [*sic*] gives an effect similar to GridBagLayout, without the complexity." However, as each box is laid out independently, you cannot use box layouts to arrange neighboring components both horizontally and vertically.

Java SE 1.4 saw yet another attempt to design a replacement for the grid bag layout—the *spring layout*. You use imaginary springs to connect the components in a container. As the container is resized, the springs stretch or shrink, thereby adjusting the positions of the components. This sounds tedious and confusing, and it is. The spring layout quickly sank into obscurity.

In 2005, the NetBeans team invented the Matisse technology, which combines a layout tool and a layout manager. A user interface designer uses the tool to drop components into a container and to indicate which components should line up. The tool translates the designer's intentions into instructions for the *group layout manager.* This is much more convenient than writing the layout management code by hand. The group layout manager became a part of Java SE 6. Even if you don't use NetBeans as your IDE, we think you should consider using its GUI builder tool. You can design your GUI in NetBeans and paste the resulting code into your IDE of choice.

In the coming sections, we will cover the grid bag layout because it is commonly used and is still the easiest mechanism for producing layout code for older Java versions. We will show you a strategy that makes grid bag layouts relatively painless in common situations.

Next, we will cover the Matisse tool and the group layout manager. You will want to know how the group layout manager works so that you can check whether Matisse recorded the correct instructions when you visually positioned your components.

Finally, we will show you how you can bypass layout management altogether and place your components manually, and how you can write your own layout manager.

12.6.1 The Grid Bag Layout

The grid bag layout is the mother of all layout managers. You can think of a grid bag layout as a grid layout without the limitations. In a grid bag layout, the rows and columns can have variable sizes. You can join adjacent cells to make room for larger components. (Many word processors, as well as HTML, provide similar capabilities for tables: You can start out with a grid and then merge adjacent cells as necessary.) The components need not fill the entire cell area, and you can specify their alignment within cells.

Consider the font selector of Figure 12.29. It consists of the following components:

- Two combo boxes to specify the font face and size
- Labels for these two combo boxes
- Two checkboxes to select bold and italic
- A text area for the sample string

Figure 12.29 A font selector

Now, chop up the container into a grid of cells, as shown in Figure 12.30. (The rows and columns need not have equal size.) Each checkbox spans two columns, and the text area spans four rows.

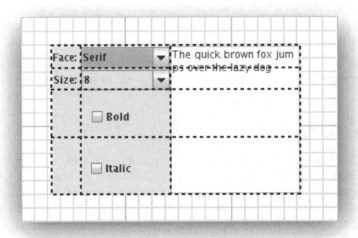

Figure 12.30 Dialog box grid used in design

To describe the layout to the grid bag manager, use the following procedure:

1. Create an object of type GridBagLayout. You don't need to tell it how many rows and columns the underlying grid has. Instead, the layout manager will try to guess it from the information you give it later.

2. Set this GridBagLayout object to be the layout manager for the component.

3. For each component, create an object of type GridBagConstraints. Set field values of the GridBagConstraints object to specify how the components are laid out within the grid bag.

4. Finally, add each component with its constraints by using the call add(component, constraints);

Here's an example of the code needed. (We'll go over the various constraints in more detail in the sections that follow—so don't worry if you don't know what some of the constraints do.)

```
GridBagLayout layout = new GridBagLayout();
panel.setLayout(layout);
GridBagConstraints constraints = new GridBagConstraints();
constraints.weightx = 100;
constraints.weighty = 100;
constraints.gridx = 0;
constraints.gridy = 2;
constraints.gridwidth = 2;
constraints.gridheight = 1;
panel.add(component, constraints);
```

The trick is knowing how to set the state of the GridBagConstraints object. We'll discuss this object in the sections that follow.

12.6.1.1 The gridx, gridy, gridwidth, and gridheight Parameters

The gridx, gridy, gridwidth, and gridheight constraints define where the component is located in the grid. The gridx and gridy values specify the column and row positions of the upper left corner of the component to be added. The gridwidth and gridheight values determine how many columns and rows the component occupies.

The grid coordinates start with 0. In particular, gridx = 0 and gridy = 0 denotes the top left corner. The text area in our example has gridx = 2, gridy = 0 because it starts in column 2 (that is, the third column) of row 0. It has gridwidth = 1 and gridheight = 4 because it spans one column and four rows.

12.6.1.2 Weight Fields

You always need to set the *weight* fields (weightx and weighty) for each area in a grid bag layout. If you set the weight to 0, the area never grows or shrinks beyond its initial size in that direction. In the grid bag layout for Figure 12.29, we set the weightx field of the labels to be 0. This allows the labels to keep constant width when you resize the window. On the other hand, if you set the weights for all areas to 0, the container will huddle in the center of its allotted area instead of stretching to fill it.

Conceptually, the problem with the weight parameters is that weights are properties of rows and columns, not individual cells. But you need to specify them for cells because the grid bag layout does not expose the rows and columns. The row and column weights are computed as the maxima of the cell weights in each row or column. Thus, if you want a row or column to stay at a fixed size, you need to set the weights of all components in it to zero.

Note that the weights don't actually give the relative sizes of the columns. They tell what proportion of the "slack" space should be allocated to each area if the container exceeds its preferred size. This isn't particularly intuitive. We recommend that you set all weights at 100. Then, run the program and see how the layout looks. Resize the dialog to see how the rows and columns adjust. If you find that a particular row or column should not grow, set the weights of all components in it to zero. You can tinker with other weight values, but it is usually not worth the effort.

12.6.1.3 The `fill` and `anchor` Parameters

If you don't want a component to stretch out and fill the entire area, set the `fill` constraint. You have four possibilities for this parameter: the valid values are `GridBagConstraints.NONE`, `GridBagConstraints.HORIZONTAL`, `GridBagConstraints.VERTICAL`, and `GridBagConstraints.BOTH`.

If the component does not fill the entire area, you can specify where in the area you want it by setting the `anchor` field. The valid values are `GridBagConstraints.CENTER` (the default), `GridBagConstraints.NORTH`, `GridBagConstraints.NORTHEAST`, `GridBagConstraints.EAST`, and so on.

12.6.1.4 Padding

You can surround a component with additional blank space by setting the `insets` field of `GridBagConstraints`. Set the `left`, `top`, `right`, and `bottom` values of the `Insets` object to the amount of space that you want to have around the component. This is called the *external padding*.

The `ipadx` and `ipady` values set the *internal padding*. These values are added to the minimum width and height of the component. This ensures that the component does not shrink down to its minimum size.

12.6.1.5 Alternative Method to Specify the `gridx`, `gridy`, `gridwidth`, and `gridheight` Parameters

The AWT documentation recommends that instead of setting the `gridx` and `gridy` values to absolute positions, you set them to the constant `GridBagConstraints.RELATIVE`. Then, add the components to the grid bag layout in a standardized order, going from left to right in the first row, then moving along the next row, and so on.

You would still specify the number of rows and columns spanned, by giving the appropriate `gridheight` and `gridwidth` fields. However, if the component extends to the *last* row or column, you don't need to specify the actual number, but the constant `GridBagConstraints.REMAINDER`. This tells the layout manager that the component is the last one in its row.

This scheme does seem to work. But it sounds really goofy to hide the actual placement information from the layout manager and hope that it will rediscover it.

All this sounds like a lot of trouble and complexity. But in practice, the following recipe makes grid bag layouts relatively trouble free:

1. Sketch out the component layout on a piece of paper.
2. Find a grid such that the small components are each contained in a cell and the larger components span multiple cells.
3. Label the rows and columns of your grid with 0, 1, 2, 3, . . . You can now read off the `gridx`, `gridy`, `gridwidth`, and `gridheight` values.
4. For each component, ask yourself whether it needs to fill its cell horizontally or vertically. If not, how do you want it aligned? This tells you the `fill` and `anchor` parameters.
5. Set all weights to `100`. However, if you want a particular row or column to always stay at its default size, set the `weightx` or `weighty` to `0` in all components that belong to that row or column.
6. Write the code. Carefully double-check your settings for the `GridBagConstraints`. One wrong constraint can ruin your whole layout.
7. Compile, run, and enjoy.

The GUI builder in NetBeans has tools for specifying the constraints visually—see Figure 12.31.

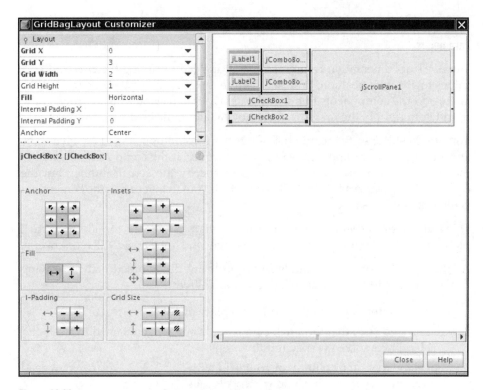

Figure 12.31 Specifying grid bag constraints in NetBeans

12.6.1.6 A Helper Class to Tame the Grid Bag Constraints

The most tedious aspect of the grid bag layout is writing the code that sets the constraints. Most programmers write helper functions or a small helper class for this purpose. We present such a class after the complete code for the font dialog example. This class has the following features:

- Its name is short: GBC instead of GridBagConstraints.

- It extends GridBagConstraints, so you can use shorter names such as GBC.EAST for the constants.

- Use a GBC object when adding a component, such as

    ```
    add(component, new GBC(1, 2));
    ```

- There are two constructors to set the most common parameters: gridx and gridy, or gridx, gridy, gridwidth, and gridheight.

    ```
    add(component, new GBC(1, 2, 1, 4));
    ```

- There are convenient setters for the fields that come in x/y pairs:

```
add(component, new GBC(1, 2).setWeight(100, 100));
```

- The setter methods return this, so you can chain them:

```
add(component, new GBC(1, 2).setAnchor(GBC.EAST).setWeight(100, 100));
```

- The setInsets methods construct the Insets object for you. To get one-pixel insets, simply call

```
add(component, new GBC(1, 2).setAnchor(GBC.EAST).setInsets(1));
```

Listing 12.10 shows the frame class for the font dialog example. The GBC helper class is in Listing 12.12. Here is the code that adds the components to the grid bag:

```
add(faceLabel, new GBC(0, 0).setAnchor(GBC.EAST));
add(face, new GBC(1, 0).setFill(GBC.HORIZONTAL).setWeight(100, 0).setInsets(1));
add(sizeLabel, new GBC(0, 1).setAnchor(GBC.EAST));
add(size, new GBC(1, 1).setFill(GBC.HORIZONTAL).setWeight(100, 0).setInsets(1));
add(bold, new GBC(0, 2, 2, 1).setAnchor(GBC.CENTER).setWeight(100, 100));
add(italic, new GBC(0, 3, 2, 1).setAnchor(GBC.CENTER).setWeight(100, 100));
add(sample, new GBC(2, 0, 1, 4).setFill(GBC.BOTH).setWeight(100, 100));
```

Once you understand the grid bag constraints, this kind of code is fairly easy to read and debug.

 NOTE: The tutorial at http://docs.oracle.com/javase/tutorial/uiswing/layout/gridbag.html suggests that you reuse the same GridBagConstraints object for all components. We find the resulting code hard to read and error-prone. For example, look at the demo at http://docs.oracle.com/javase/tutorial/uiswing/events/containerlistener.html. Was it really intended that the buttons are stretched horizontally, or did the programmer just forget to turn off the fill constraint?

Listing 12.10 gridbag/FontFrame.java

```
1  package gridbag;
2
3  import java.awt.Font;
4  import java.awt.GridBagLayout;
5  import java.awt.event.ActionListener;
6
7  import javax.swing.BorderFactory;
8  import javax.swing.JCheckBox;
9  import javax.swing.JComboBox;
10 import javax.swing.JFrame;
11 import javax.swing.JLabel;
```

(Continues)

Listing 12.10 *(Continued)*

```
12  import javax.swing.JTextArea;
13
14  /**
15   * A frame that uses a grid bag layout to arrange font selection components.
16   */
17  public class FontFrame extends JFrame
18  {
19     public static final int TEXT_ROWS = 10;
20     public static final int TEXT_COLUMNS = 20;
21
22     private JComboBox<String> face;
23     private JComboBox<Integer> size;
24     private JCheckBox bold;
25     private JCheckBox italic;
26     private JTextArea sample;
27
28     public FontFrame()
29     {
30        GridBagLayout layout = new GridBagLayout();
31        setLayout(layout);
32
33        ActionListener listener = event -> updateSample();
34
35        // construct components
36
37        JLabel faceLabel = new JLabel("Face: ");
38
39        face = new JComboBox<>(new String[] { "Serif", "SansSerif", "Monospaced",
40              "Dialog", "DialogInput" });
41
42        face.addActionListener(listener);
43
44        JLabel sizeLabel = new JLabel("Size: ");
45
46        size = new JComboBox<>(new Integer[] { 8, 10, 12, 15, 18, 24, 36, 48 });
47
48        size.addActionListener(listener);
49
50        bold = new JCheckBox("Bold");
51        bold.addActionListener(listener);
52
53        italic = new JCheckBox("Italic");
54        italic.addActionListener(listener);
55
56        sample = new JTextArea(TEXT_ROWS, TEXT_COLUMNS);
57        sample.setText("The quick brown fox jumps over the lazy dog");
58        sample.setEditable(false);
59        sample.setLineWrap(true);
```

```
60      sample.setBorder(BorderFactory.createEtchedBorder());
61
62      // add components to grid, using GBC convenience class
63
64      add(faceLabel, new GBC(0, 0).setAnchor(GBC.EAST));
65      add(face, new GBC(1, 0).setFill(GBC.HORIZONTAL).setWeight(100, 0)
66            .setInsets(1));
67      add(sizeLabel, new GBC(0, 1).setAnchor(GBC.EAST));
68      add(size, new GBC(1, 1).setFill(GBC.HORIZONTAL).setWeight(100, 0)
69            .setInsets(1));
70      add(bold, new GBC(0, 2, 2, 1).setAnchor(GBC.CENTER).setWeight(100, 100));
71      add(italic, new GBC(0, 3, 2, 1).setAnchor(GBC.CENTER).setWeight(100, 100));
72      add(sample, new GBC(2, 0, 1, 4).setFill(GBC.BOTH).setWeight(100, 100));
73      pack();
74      updateSample();
75   }
76
77   public void updateSample()
78   {
79      String fontFace = (String) face.getSelectedItem();
80      int fontStyle = (bold.isSelected() ? Font.BOLD : 0)
81            + (italic.isSelected() ? Font.ITALIC : 0);
82      int fontSize = size.getItemAt(size.getSelectedIndex());
83      Font font = new Font(fontFace, fontStyle, fontSize);
84      sample.setFont(font);
85      sample.repaint();
86   }
87 }
```

Listing 12.11 gridbag/GBC.java

```
1  package gridbag;
2
3  import java.awt.*;
4
5  /**
6   * This class simplifies the use of the GridBagConstraints class.
7   * @version 1.01 2004-05-06
8   * @author Cay Horstmann
9   */
10 public class GBC extends GridBagConstraints
11 {
12    /**
13     * Constructs a GBC with a given gridx and gridy position and all other grid
14     * bag constraint values set to the default.
15     * @param gridx the gridx position
16     * @param gridy the gridy position
17     */
```

(Continues)

Listing 12.11 *(Continued)*

```java
18    public GBC(int gridx, int gridy)
19    {
20       this.gridx = gridx;
21       this.gridy = gridy;
22    }
23
24    /**
25     * Constructs a GBC with given gridx, gridy, gridwidth, gridheight and all
26     * other grid bag constraint values set to the default.
27     * @param gridx the gridx position
28     * @param gridy the gridy position
29     * @param gridwidth the cell span in x-direction
30     * @param gridheight the cell span in y-direction
31     */
32    public GBC(int gridx, int gridy, int gridwidth, int gridheight)
33    {
34       this.gridx = gridx;
35       this.gridy = gridy;
36       this.gridwidth = gridwidth;
37       this.gridheight = gridheight;
38    }
39
40    /**
41     * Sets the anchor.
42     * @param anchor the anchor value
43     * @return this object for further modification
44     */
45    public GBC setAnchor(int anchor)
46    {
47       this.anchor = anchor;
48       return this;
49    }
50
51    /**
52     * Sets the fill direction.
53     * @param fill the fill direction
54     * @return this object for further modification
55     */
56    public GBC setFill(int fill)
57    {
58       this.fill = fill;
59       return this;
60    }
61
62    /**
63     * Sets the cell weights.
```

```
64      * @param weightx the cell weight in x-direction
65      * @param weighty the cell weight in y-direction
66      * @return this object for further modification
67      */
68     public GBC setWeight(double weightx, double weighty)
69     {
70        this.weightx = weightx;
71        this.weighty = weighty;
72        return this;
73     }
74
75     /**
76      * Sets the insets of this cell.
77      * @param distance the spacing to use in all directions
78      * @return this object for further modification
79      */
80     public GBC setInsets(int distance)
81     {
82        this.insets = new Insets(distance, distance, distance, distance);
83        return this;
84     }
85
86     /**
87      * Sets the insets of this cell.
88      * @param top the spacing to use on top
89      * @param left the spacing to use to the left
90      * @param bottom the spacing to use on the bottom
91      * @param right the spacing to use to the right
92      * @return this object for further modification
93      */
94     public GBC setInsets(int top, int left, int bottom, int right)
95     {
96        this.insets = new Insets(top, left, bottom, right);
97        return this;
98     }
99
100     /**
101      * Sets the internal padding
102      * @param ipadx the internal padding in x-direction
103      * @param ipady the internal padding in y-direction
104      * @return this object for further modification
105      */
106     public GBC setIpad(int ipadx, int ipady)
107     {
108        this.ipadx = ipadx;
109        this.ipady = ipady;
110        return this;
111     }
112 }
```

---

java.awt.GridBagConstraints 1.0

- `int gridx, gridy`

  specifies the starting column and row of the cell. The default is 0.

- `int gridwidth, gridheight`

  specifies the column and row extent of the cell. The default is 1.

- `double weightx, weighty`

  specifies the capacity of the cell to grow. The default is 0.

- `int anchor`

  indicates the alignment of the component inside the cell. You can choose between absolute positions:

NORTHWEST	NORTH	NORTHEAST
WEST	CENTER	EAST
SOUTHWEST	SOUTH	SOUTHEAST

  or their orientation-independent counterparts:

FIRST_LINE_START	LINE_START	FIRST_LINE_END
PAGE_START	CENTER	PAGE_END
LAST_LINE_START	LINE_END	LAST_LINE_END

  Use the latter if your application may be localized for right-to-left or top-to-bottom text. The default is CENTER.

- `int fill`

  specifies the fill behavior of the component inside the cell: one of NONE, BOTH, HORIZONTAL, or VERTICAL. The default is NONE.

- `int ipadx, ipady`

  specifies the "internal" padding around the component. The default is 0.

- `Insets insets`

  specifies the "external" padding along the cell boundaries. The default is no padding.

- `GridBagConstraints(int gridx, int gridy, int gridwidth, int gridheight, double weightx, double weighty, int anchor, int fill, Insets insets, int ipadx, int ipady)` 1.2

  constructs a `GridBagConstraints` with all its fields specified in the arguments. This constructor should only be used by automatic code generators because it makes your source code very hard to read.

12.6.2 Group Layout

Before discussing the API of the GroupLayout class, let us have a quick look at the Matisse GUI builder in NetBeans. We won't give you a full Matisse tutorial—see http://netbeans.org/kb/docs/java/quickstart-gui.html for more information.

Here is the workflow for laying out the top of the dialog in Figure 12.13. Start a new project and add a new JFrame form. Drag a label until two guidelines appear that separate it from the container borders:

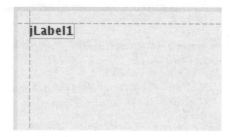

Place another label below the first row:

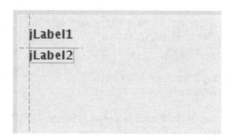

Drag a text field so that its baseline lines up with the baseline of the first label. Again, note the guidelines:

Finally, line up a password field with the label to the left and the text field above.

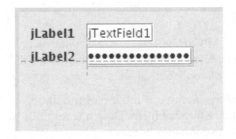

Matisse translates these actions into the following Java code:

```
layout.setHorizontalGroup(
   layout.createParallelGroup(GroupLayout.Alignment.LEADING)
   .addGroup(layout.createSequentialGroup()
      .addContainerGap()
      .addGroup(layout.createParallelGroup(GroupLayout.Alignment.LEADING)
         .addGroup(layout.createSequentialGroup()
            .addComponent(jLabel1)
            .addPreferredGap(LayoutStyle.ComponentPlacement.RELATED)
            .addComponent(jTextField1))
         .addGroup(layout.createSequentialGroup()
            .addComponent(jLabel2)
            .addPreferredGap(LayoutStyle.ComponentPlacement.RELATED)
            .addComponent(jPasswordField1)))
      .addContainerGap(222, Short.MAX_VALUE)));
layout.setVerticalGroup(
   layout.createParallelGroup(GroupLayout.Alignment.LEADING)
   .addGroup(layout.createSequentialGroup()
      .addContainerGap()
      .addGroup(layout.createParallelGroup(GroupLayout.Alignment.BASELINE)
         .addComponent(jLabel1)
         .addComponent(jTextField1))
      .addPreferredGap(LayoutStyle.ComponentPlacement.RELATED)
      .addGroup(layout.createParallelGroup(GroupLayout.Alignment.BASELINE)
         .addComponent(jLabel2)
         .addComponent(jPasswordField1))
      .addContainerGap(244, Short.MAX_VALUE)));
```

That looks a bit scary, but fortunately you don't have to write this code. However, it is helpful to have a basic understanding of the layout actions so that you can spot errors. We will analyze the basic structure of the code. The API notes at the end of this section explain each of the classes and methods in detail.

Components are organized by placing them into objects of type GroupLayout.SequentialGroup or GroupLayout.ParallelGroup. These classes are subclasses of GroupLayout.Group. Groups can contain components, gaps, and nested groups. The various add methods of the group classes return the group object, so that method calls can be chained like this:

```
group.addComponent(. . .).addPreferredGap(. . .).addComponent(. . .);
```

As you can see from the sample code, the group layout separates the horizontal and vertical layout computations.

To visualize the horizontal computations, imagine that the components are flattened so they have zero height, like this:

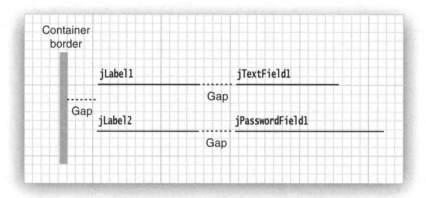

There are two parallel sequences of components, corresponding to the (slightly simplified) code:

```
.addContainerGap()
    .addGroup(layout.createParallelGroup()
        .addGroup(layout.createSequentialGroup()
            .addComponent(jLabel1)
            .addPreferredGap(LayoutStyle.ComponentPlacement.RELATED)
            .addComponent(jTextField1))
        .addGroup(layout.createSequentialGroup()
            .addComponent(jLabel2)
            .addPreferredGap(LayoutStyle.ComponentPlacement.RELATED)
            .addComponent(jPasswordField1)))
```

But wait, that can't be right. If the labels have different lengths, the text field and the password field won't line up.

We have to tell Matisse that we want the fields to line up. Select both fields, right-click, and select Align → Left to Column from the menu. Also line up the labels (see Figure 12.32).

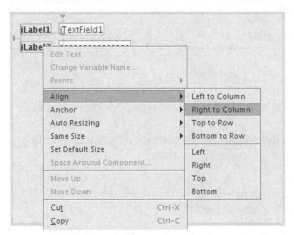

Figure 12.32 Aligning the labels and text fields in Matisse

This dramatically changes the layout code:

```
.addGroup(layout.createSequentialGroup()
  .addContainerGap()
  .addGroup(layout.createParallelGroup(GroupLayout.Alignment.LEADING)
    .addComponent(jLabel1, GroupLayout.Alignment.TRAILING)
    .addComponent(jLabel2, GroupLayout.Alignment.TRAILING))
  .addPreferredGap(LayoutStyle.ComponentPlacement.RELATED)
  .addGroup(layout.createParallelGroup(GroupLayout.Alignment.LEADING)
    .addComponent(jTextField1)
    .addComponent(jPasswordField1))
```

Now the labels and fields are each placed in a parallel group. The first group has an alignment of TRAILING (which means alignment to the right when the text direction is left-to-right):

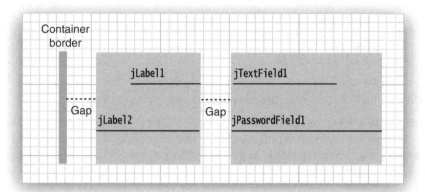

It seems like magic that Matisse can translate the designer's instructions into nested groups—but, as Arthur C. Clarke said, any sufficiently advanced technology is indistinguishable from magic.

For completeness, let's look at the vertical computation. Now you should think of the components as having no width. We have a sequential group that contains two parallel groups, separated by gaps:

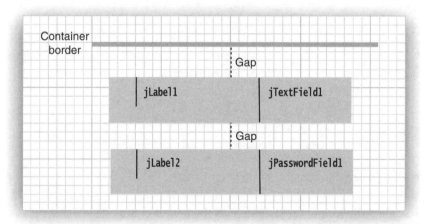

The corresponding code is

```
layout.createSequentialGroup()
  .addContainerGap()
  .addGroup(layout.createParallelGroup(GroupLayout.Alignment.BASELINE)
    .addComponent(jLabel1)
    .addComponent(jTextField1))
  .addPreferredGap(LayoutStyle.ComponentPlacement.RELATED)
  .addGroup(layout.createParallelGroup(GroupLayout.Alignment.BASELINE)
    .addComponent(jLabel2)
    .addComponent(jPasswordField1))
```

As you can see from the code, the components are aligned by their baselines. (The baseline is the line on which the component text is aligned.)

You can force a set of components to have equal size. For example, we may want to make sure that the widths of the text field and the password field match exactly. In Matisse, select both, right-click, and select Same Size → Same Width from the menu (see Figure 12.33).

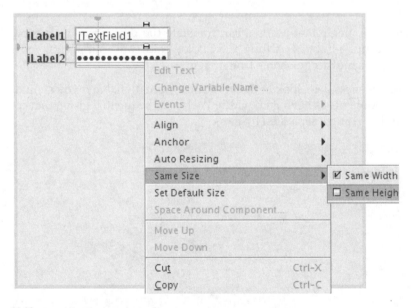

Figure 12.33 Forcing two components to have the same width

Matisse adds the following statement to the layout code:

```
layout.linkSize(SwingConstants.HORIZONTAL, new Component[] {jPasswordField1, jTextField1});
```

The code in Listing 12.12 shows how to lay out the font selector of the preceding section using the `GroupLayout` instead of the `GridBagLayout`. The code may not look any simpler than that of Listing 12.10, but we didn't have to write it. We used Matisse to do the layout and then cleaned up the code a bit.

Listing 12.12   groupLayout/FontFrame.java

```
 1  package groupLayout;
 2
 3  import java.awt.Font;
 4  import java.awt.event.ActionListener;
 5
 6  import javax.swing.BorderFactory;
 7  import javax.swing.GroupLayout;
 8  import javax.swing.JCheckBox;
 9  import javax.swing.JComboBox;
10  import javax.swing.JFrame;
11  import javax.swing.JLabel;
12  import javax.swing.JScrollPane;
13  import javax.swing.JTextArea;
14  import javax.swing.LayoutStyle;
15  import javax.swing.SwingConstants;
16
17  /**
18   * A frame that uses a group layout to arrange font selection components.
19   */
20  public class FontFrame extends JFrame
21  {
22     public static final int TEXT_ROWS = 10;
23     public static final int TEXT_COLUMNS = 20;
24
25     private JComboBox<String> face;
26     private JComboBox<Integer> size;
27     private JCheckBox bold;
28     private JCheckBox italic;
29     private JScrollPane pane;
30     private JTextArea sample;
31
32     public FontFrame()
33     {
34        ActionListener listener = event -> updateSample();
35
36        // construct components
37
38        JLabel faceLabel = new JLabel("Face: ");
39
```

(Continues)

Listing 12.12 *(Continued)*

```
40    face = new JComboBox<>(new String[] { "Serif", "SansSerif", "Monospaced", "Dialog",
41        "DialogInput" });
42
43    face.addActionListener(listener);
44
45    JLabel sizeLabel = new JLabel("Size: ");
46
47    size = new JComboBox<>(new Integer[] { 8, 10, 12, 15, 18, 24, 36, 48 });
48
49    size.addActionListener(listener);
50
51    bold = new JCheckBox("Bold");
52    bold.addActionListener(listener);
53
54    italic = new JCheckBox("Italic");
55    italic.addActionListener(listener);
56
57    sample = new JTextArea(TEXT_ROWS, TEXT_COLUMNS);
58    sample.setText("The quick brown fox jumps over the lazy dog");
59    sample.setEditable(false);
60    sample.setLineWrap(true);
61    sample.setBorder(BorderFactory.createEtchedBorder());
62
63    pane = new JScrollPane(sample);
64
65    GroupLayout layout = new GroupLayout(getContentPane());
66    setLayout(layout);
67    layout.setHorizontalGroup(layout.createParallelGroup(GroupLayout.Alignment.LEADING)
68        .addGroup(
69            layout.createSequentialGroup().addContainerGap().addGroup(
70                layout.createParallelGroup(GroupLayout.Alignment.LEADING).addGroup(
71                    GroupLayout.Alignment.TRAILING,
72                    layout.createSequentialGroup().addGroup(
73                        layout.createParallelGroup(GroupLayout.Alignment.TRAILING)
74                            .addComponent(faceLabel).addComponent(sizeLabel))
75                        .addPreferredGap(LayoutStyle.ComponentPlacement.RELATED)
76                        .addGroup(
77                            layout.createParallelGroup(
78                                GroupLayout.Alignment.LEADING, false)
79                                .addComponent(size).addComponent(face)))
80                    .addComponent(italic).addComponent(bold)).addPreferredGap(
81                LayoutStyle.ComponentPlacement.RELATED).addComponent(pane)
82                .addContainerGap()));
```

```
83
84      layout.linkSize(SwingConstants.HORIZONTAL, new java.awt.Component[] { face, size });
85
86      layout.setVerticalGroup(layout.createParallelGroup(GroupLayout.Alignment.LEADING)
87         .addGroup(
88             layout.createSequentialGroup().addContainerGap().addGroup(
89                 layout.createParallelGroup(GroupLayout.Alignment.LEADING).addComponent(
90                     pane, GroupLayout.Alignment.TRAILING).addGroup(
91                     layout.createSequentialGroup().addGroup(
92                         layout.createParallelGroup(GroupLayout.Alignment.BASELINE)
93                             .addComponent(face).addComponent(faceLabel))
94                         .addPreferredGap(LayoutStyle.ComponentPlacement.RELATED)
95                         .addGroup(
96                             layout.createParallelGroup(
97                                 GroupLayout.Alignment.BASELINE).addComponent(size)
98                                 .addComponent(sizeLabel)).addPreferredGap(
99                             LayoutStyle.ComponentPlacement.RELATED).addComponent(
100                            italic, GroupLayout.DEFAULT_SIZE,
101                            GroupLayout.DEFAULT_SIZE, Short.MAX_VALUE)
102                        .addPreferredGap(LayoutStyle.ComponentPlacement.RELATED)
103                        .addComponent(bold, GroupLayout.DEFAULT_SIZE,
104                            GroupLayout.DEFAULT_SIZE, Short.MAX_VALUE)))
105                    .addContainerGap()));
106     pack();
107  }
108
109  public void updateSample()
110  {
111     String fontFace = (String) face.getSelectedItem();
112     int fontStyle = (bold.isSelected() ? Font.BOLD : 0)
113         + (italic.isSelected() ? Font.ITALIC : 0);
114     int fontSize = size.getItemAt(size.getSelectedIndex());
115     Font font = new Font(fontFace, fontStyle, fontSize);
116     sample.setFont(font);
117     sample.repaint();
118  }
119 }
```

---

javax.swing.GroupLayout 6

- GroupLayout(Container host)

  constructs a GroupLayout for laying out the components in the host container. (Note that you still need to call setLayout on the host object.)

- void setHorizontalGroup(GroupLayout.Group g)
- void setVerticalGroup(GroupLayout.Group g)

  sets the group that controls horizontal or vertical layout.

- void linkSize(Component... components)
- void linkSize(int axis, Component... component)

  forces the given components to have the same size, or the same size along the given axis (one of SwingConstants.HORIZONTAL or SwingConstants.VERTICAL).

- GroupLayout.SequentialGroup createSequentialGroup()

  creates a group that lays out its children sequentially.

- GroupLayout.ParallelGroup createParallelGroup()
- GroupLayout.ParallelGroup createParallelGroup(GroupLayout.Alignment align)
- GroupLayout.ParallelGroup createParallelGroup(GroupLayout.Alignment align, boolean resizable)

  creates a group that lays out its children in parallel.

  Parameters: align   One of BASELINE, LEADING (default), TRAILING, or CENTER

  resizable   true (default) when the group can be resized; false if the preferred size is also the minimum and maximum size

- boolean getHonorsVisibility()
- void setHonorsVisibility(boolean b)

  gets or sets the honorsVisibility property. When true (the default), nonvisible components are not laid out. When false, they are laid out as if they were visible. This is useful when you temporarily hide some components and don't want the layout to change.

- boolean getAutoCreateGaps()
- void setAutoCreateGaps(boolean b)
- boolean getAutoCreateContainerGaps()
- void setAutoCreateContainerGaps(boolean b)

  gets and sets the autoCreateGaps and autoCreateContainerGaps properties. When true, gaps are automatically added between components or at the container boundaries. The default is false. A true value is useful when you manually produce a GroupLayout.

---

javax.swing.GroupLayout.Group

- `GroupLayout.Group addComponent(Component c)`
- `GroupLayout.Group addComponent(Component c, int minimumSize, int preferredSize, int maximumSize)`

  adds a component to this group. The size parameters can be actual (non-negative) values, or the special constants `GroupLayout.DEFAULT_SIZE` or `GroupLayout.PREFERRED_SIZE`. When `DEFAULT_SIZE` is used, the component's `getMinimumSize`, `getPreferredSize`, or `getMaximumSize` is called. When `PREFERRED_SIZE` is used, the component's `getPreferredSize` method is called.

- `GroupLayout.Group addGap(int size)`
- `GroupLayout.Group addGap(int minimumSize, int preferredSize, int maximumSize)`

  adds a gap of the given rigid or flexible size.

- `GroupLayout.Group addGroup(GroupLayout.Group g)`

  adds the given group to this group.

---

javax.swing.GroupLayout.ParallelGroup

- `GroupLayout.ParallelGroup addComponent(Component c, GroupLayout.Alignment align)`
- `GroupLayout.ParallelGroup addComponent(Component c, GroupLayout.Alignment align, int minimumSize, int preferredSize, int maximumSize)`
- `GroupLayout.ParallelGroup addGroup(GroupLayout.Group g, GroupLayout.Alignment align)`

  adds a component or group to this group, using the given alignment (one of `BASELINE`, `LEADING`, `TRAILING`, or `CENTER`).

---

javax.swing.GroupLayout.SequentialGroup

- `GroupLayout.SequentialGroup addContainerGap()`
- `GroupLayout.SequentialGroup addContainerGap(int preferredSize, int maximumSize)`

  adds a gap for separating a component and the edge of the container.

- `GroupLayout.SequentialGroup addPreferredGap(LayoutStyle.ComponentPlacement type)`

  adds a gap for separating components. The type is `LayoutStyle.ComponentPlacement.RELATED` or `LayoutStyle.ComponentPlacement.UNRELATED`.

12.6.3 Using No Layout Manager

There will be times when you don't want to bother with layout managers but just want to drop a component at a fixed location (sometimes called *absolute positioning*).

This is not a great idea for platform-independent applications, but there is nothing wrong with using it for a quick prototype.

Here is what you do to place a component at a fixed location:

1. Set the layout manager to `null`.
2. Add the component you want to the container.
3. Specify the position and size that you want:

```
frame.setLayout(null);
JButton ok = new JButton("OK");
frame.add(ok);
ok.setBounds(10, 10, 30, 15);
```

---

java.awt.Component 1.0

- void setBounds(int x, int y, int width, int height)

  moves and resizes a component.

  Parameters: x, y   The new top left corner of the component

  width, height   The new size of the component

12.6.4 Custom Layout Managers

You can design your own `LayoutManager` class that manages components in a special way. As a fun example, let's arrange all components in a container to form a circle (see Figure 12.34).

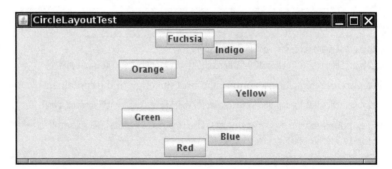

Figure 12.34 Circle layout

Your own layout manager must implement the `LayoutManager` interface. You need to override the following five methods:

```
void addLayoutComponent(String s, Component c);
void removeLayoutComponent(Component c);
Dimension preferredLayoutSize(Container parent);
Dimension minimumLayoutSize(Container parent);
void layoutContainer(Container parent);
```

The first two methods are called when a component is added or removed. If you don't keep any additional information about the components, you can make them do nothing. The next two methods compute the space required for the minimum and the preferred layout of the components. These are usually the same quantity. The fifth method does the actual work and invokes setBounds on all components.

 NOTE: The AWT has a second interface, called LayoutManager2, with ten methods to implement rather than five. The main point of the LayoutManager2 interface is to allow you to use the add method with constraints. For example, the BorderLayout and GridBagLayout implement the LayoutManager2 interface.

Listing 12.13 shows the code for the CircleLayout manager which, uselessly enough, lays out the components along a circle inside the parent. The frame class of the sample program is in Listing 12.14.

Listing 12.13 circleLayout/CircleLayout.java

```
1  package circleLayout;
2
3  import java.awt.*;
4
5  /**
6   * A layout manager that lays out components along a circle.
7   */
8  public class CircleLayout implements LayoutManager
9  {
10     private int minWidth = 0;
11     private int minHeight = 0;
12     private int preferredWidth = 0;
13     private int preferredHeight = 0;
14     private boolean sizesSet = false;
15     private int maxComponentWidth = 0;
16     private int maxComponentHeight = 0;
17
18     public void addLayoutComponent(String name, Component comp)
19     {
20     }
21
```

(Continues)

Listing 12.13 *(Continued)*

```java
22    public void removeLayoutComponent(Component comp)
23    {
24    }
25
26    public void setSizes(Container parent)
27    {
28       if (sizesSet) return;
29       int n = parent.getComponentCount();
30
31       preferredWidth = 0;
32       preferredHeight = 0;
33       minWidth = 0;
34       minHeight = 0;
35       maxComponentWidth = 0;
36       maxComponentHeight = 0;
37
38       // compute the maximum component widths and heights
39       // and set the preferred size to the sum of the component sizes.
40       for (int i = 0; i < n; i++)
41       {
42          Component c = parent.getComponent(i);
43          if (c.isVisible())
44          {
45             Dimension d = c.getPreferredSize();
46             maxComponentWidth = Math.max(maxComponentWidth, d.width);
47             maxComponentHeight = Math.max(maxComponentHeight, d.height);
48             preferredWidth += d.width;
49             preferredHeight += d.height;
50          }
51       }
52       minWidth = preferredWidth / 2;
53       minHeight = preferredHeight / 2;
54       sizesSet = true;
55    }
56
57    public Dimension preferredLayoutSize(Container parent)
58    {
59       setSizes(parent);
60       Insets insets = parent.getInsets();
61       int width = preferredWidth + insets.left + insets.right;
62       int height = preferredHeight + insets.top + insets.bottom;
63       return new Dimension(width, height);
64    }
65
66    public Dimension minimumLayoutSize(Container parent)
67    {
```

```
68          setSizes(parent);
69          Insets insets = parent.getInsets();
70          int width = minWidth + insets.left + insets.right;
71          int height = minHeight + insets.top + insets.bottom;
72          return new Dimension(width, height);
73       }
74
75       public void layoutContainer(Container parent)
76       {
77          setSizes(parent);
78
79          // compute center of the circle
80
81          Insets insets = parent.getInsets();
82          int containerWidth = parent.getSize().width - insets.left - insets.right;
83          int containerHeight = parent.getSize().height - insets.top - insets.bottom;
84
85          int xcenter = insets.left + containerWidth / 2;
86          int ycenter = insets.top + containerHeight / 2;
87
88          // compute radius of the circle
89
90          int xradius = (containerWidth - maxComponentWidth) / 2;
91          int yradius = (containerHeight - maxComponentHeight) / 2;
92          int radius = Math.min(xradius, yradius);
93
94          // lay out components along the circle
95
96          int n = parent.getComponentCount();
97          for (int i = 0; i < n; i++)
98          {
99             Component c = parent.getComponent(i);
100            if (c.isVisible())
101            {
102               double angle = 2 * Math.PI * i / n;
103
104               // center point of component
105               int x = xcenter + (int) (Math.cos(angle) * radius);
106               int y = ycenter + (int) (Math.sin(angle) * radius);
107
108               // move component so that its center is (x, y)
109               // and its size is its preferred size
110               Dimension d = c.getPreferredSize();
111               c.setBounds(x - d.width / 2, y - d.height / 2, d.width, d.height);
112            }
113         }
114      }
115 }
```

Listing 12.14 circleLayout/CircleLayoutFrame.java

```java
1  package circleLayout;
2
3  import javax.swing.*;
4
5  /**
6   * A frame that shows buttons arranged along a circle.
7   */
8  public class CircleLayoutFrame extends JFrame
9  {
10     public CircleLayoutFrame()
11     {
12        setLayout(new CircleLayout());
13        add(new JButton("Yellow"));
14        add(new JButton("Blue"));
15        add(new JButton("Red"));
16        add(new JButton("Green"));
17        add(new JButton("Orange"));
18        add(new JButton("Fuchsia"));
19        add(new JButton("Indigo"));
20        pack();
21     }
22  }
```

---

java.awt.LayoutManager 1.0

- void addLayoutComponent(String name, Component comp)

  adds a component to the layout.

  Parameters: name   An identifier for the component placement

                    comp   The component to be added

- void removeLayoutComponent(Component comp)

  removes a component from the layout.

- Dimension preferredLayoutSize(Container cont)

  returns the preferred size dimensions for the container under this layout.

- Dimension minimumLayoutSize(Container cont)

  returns the minimum size dimensions for the container under this layout.

- void layoutContainer(Container cont)

  lays out the components in a container.

12.6.5 Traversal Order

When you add many components into a window, you need to give some thought to the *traversal order*. When a window is first displayed, the first component in the traversal order has the keyboard focus. Each time the user presses the Tab key, the next component gains focus. (Recall that a component that has the keyboard focus can be manipulated with the keyboard. For example, a button can be "clicked" with the space bar when it has focus.) You may not personally care about using the Tab key to navigate through a set of controls, but plenty of users do. Among them are the mouse haters and those who cannot use a mouse, perhaps because of a handicap or because they are navigating the user interface by voice. For that reason, you need to know how Swing handles traversal order.

The traversal order is straightforward: first, left to right, and then, top to bottom. For example, in the font dialog example, the components are traversed in the following order (see Figure 12.35):

1. Face combo box
2. Sample text area (press Ctrl+Tab to move to the next field; the Tab character is considered text input)
3. Size combo box
4. Bold checkbox
5. Italic checkbox

Figure 12.35 Geometric traversal order

The situation is more complex if your container contains other containers. When the focus is given to another container, it automatically ends up within the top left component in that container and then traverses all other components in that container. Finally, the focus is given to the component following the container.

You can use this to your advantage by grouping related elements in another container such as a panel.

NOTE: Call

```
component.setFocusable(false);
```

to remove a component from the focus traversal. This is useful for painted components that don't take keyboard input.

12.7 Dialog Boxes

So far, all our user interface components have appeared inside a frame window that was created in the application. This is the most common situation if you write *applets* that run inside a web browser. But if you write applications, you usually want separate dialog boxes to pop up to give information to, or get information from, the user.

Just as with most windowing systems, AWT distinguishes between *modal* and *modeless* dialog boxes. A modal dialog box won't let users interact with the remaining windows of the application until he or she deals with it. Use a modal dialog box when you need information from the user before you can proceed with execution. For example, when the user wants to read a file, a modal file dialog box is the one to pop up. The user must specify a file name before the program can begin the read operation. Only when the user closes the modal dialog box can the application proceed.

A modeless dialog box lets the user enter information in both the dialog box and the remainder of the application. One example of a modeless dialog is a toolbar. The toolbar can stay in place as long as needed, and the user can interact with both the application window and the toolbar as needed.

We will start this section with the simplest dialogs—modal dialogs with just a single message. Swing has a convenient JOptionPane class that lets you put up a simple dialog without writing any special dialog box code. Next, you will see how to write more complex dialogs by implementing your own dialog windows. Finally, you will see how to transfer data from your application into a dialog and back.

We'll conclude this section by looking at two standard dialogs: file dialogs and color dialogs. File dialogs are complex, and you definitely want to be familiar with the Swing JFileChooser for this purpose—it would be a real challenge to write your own. The JColorChooser dialog is useful when you want users to pick colors.

12.7.1 Option Dialogs

Swing has a set of ready-made simple dialogs that suffice to ask the user for a single piece of information. The JOptionPane has four static methods to show these simple dialogs:

showMessageDialog	Show a message and wait for the user to click OK
showConfirmDialog	Show a message and get a confirmation (like OK/Cancel)
showOptionDialog	Show a message and get a user option from a set of options
showInputDialog	Show a message and get one line of user input

Figure 12.36 shows a typical dialog. As you can see, the dialog has the following components:

- An icon
- A message
- One or more option buttons

Figure 12.36 An option dialog

The input dialog has an additional component for user input. This can be a text field into which the user can type an arbitrary string, or a combo box from which the user can select one item.

The exact layout of these dialogs and the choice of icons for standard message types depend on the pluggable look-and-feel.

The icon on the left side depends on one of five *message types*:

```
ERROR_MESSAGE
INFORMATION_MESSAGE
WARNING_MESSAGE
QUESTION_MESSAGE
PLAIN_MESSAGE
```

The PLAIN_MESSAGE type has no icon. Each dialog type also has a method that lets you supply your own icon instead.

For each dialog type, you can specify a message. This message can be a string, an icon, a user interface component, or any other object. Here is how the message object is displayed:

String	Draw the string
Icon	Show the icon
Component	Show the component
Object[]	Show all objects in the array, stacked on top of each other
Any other object	Apply toString and show the resulting string

You can see these options by running the program in Listing 12.15.

Of course, supplying a message string is by far the most common case. Supplying a Component gives you ultimate flexibility because you can make the paintComponent method draw anything you want.

The buttons at the bottom depend on the dialog type and the *option type*. When calling showMessageDialog and showInputDialog, you get only a standard set of buttons (OK and OK/Cancel, respectively). When calling showConfirmDialog, you can choose among four option types:

```
DEFAULT_OPTION
YES_NO_OPTION
YES_NO_CANCEL_OPTION
OK_CANCEL_OPTION
```

With the showOptionDialog you can specify an arbitrary set of options. You supply an array of objects for the options. Each array element is rendered as follows:

String	Make a button with the string as label
Icon	Make a button with the icon as label
Component	Show the component
Any other object	Apply toString and make a button with the resulting string as label

The return values of these functions are as follows:

showMessageDialog	None
showConfirmDialog	An integer representing the chosen option
showOptionDialog	An integer representing the chosen option
showInputDialog	The string that the user supplied or selected

The showConfirmDialog and showOptionDialog return integers to indicate which button the user chose. For the option dialog, this is simply the index of the chosen option or the value CLOSED_OPTION if the user closed the dialog instead of choosing an option. For the confirmation dialog, the return value can be one of the following:

```
OK_OPTION
CANCEL_OPTION
YES_OPTION
NO_OPTION
CLOSED_OPTION
```

This all sounds like a bewildering set of choices, but in practice it is simple. Follow these steps:

1. Choose the dialog type (message, confirmation, option, or input).
2. Choose the icon (error, information, warning, question, none, or custom).
3. Choose the message (string, icon, custom component, or a stack of them).
4. For a confirmation dialog, choose the option type (default, Yes/No, Yes/No/Cancel, or OK/Cancel).
5. For an option dialog, choose the options (strings, icons, or custom components) and the default option.
6. For an input dialog, choose between a text field and a combo box.
7. Locate the appropriate method to call in the JOptionPane API.

For example, suppose you want to show the dialog in Figure 12.36. The dialog shows a message and asks the user to confirm or cancel. Thus, it is a confirmation dialog. The icon is a question icon. The message is a string. The option type is OK_CANCEL_OPTION. Here is the call you would make:

```
int selection = JOptionPane.showConfirmDialog(parent,
    "Message", "Title",
    JOptionPane.OK_CANCEL_OPTION,
    JOptionPane.QUESTION_MESSAGE);
if (selection == JOptionPane.OK_OPTION) . . .
```

 TIP: The message string can contain newline ('\n') characters. Such a string is displayed in multiple lines.

The program whose frame class is shown in Listing 12.15 displays six button panels (see Figure 12.37). Listing 12.16 shows the class for the panels. When you click the Show button, the selected dialog is displayed.

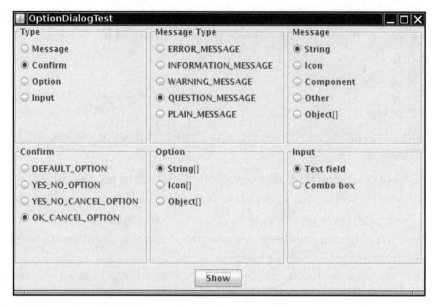

Figure 12.37 The OptionDialogTest program

Listing 12.15 optionDialog/OptionDialogFrame.java

```
1  package optionDialog;
2
3  import java.awt.*;
4  import java.awt.event.*;
5  import java.awt.geom.*;
6  import java.util.*;
7  import javax.swing.*;
8
9  /**
10  * A frame that contains settings for selecting various option dialogs.
11  */
12  public class OptionDialogFrame extends JFrame
13  {
14     private ButtonPanel typePanel;
15     private ButtonPanel messagePanel;
16     private ButtonPanel messageTypePanel;
17     private ButtonPanel optionTypePanel;
18     private ButtonPanel optionsPanel;
19     private ButtonPanel inputPanel;
20     private String messageString = "Message";
21     private Icon messageIcon = new ImageIcon("blue-ball.gif");
22     private Object messageObject = new Date();
```

```
23     private Component messageComponent = new SampleComponent();
24
25     public OptionDialogFrame()
26     {
27        JPanel gridPanel = new JPanel();
28        gridPanel.setLayout(new GridLayout(2, 3));
29
30        typePanel = new ButtonPanel("Type", "Message", "Confirm", "Option", "Input");
31        messageTypePanel = new ButtonPanel("Message Type", "ERROR_MESSAGE", "INFORMATION_MESSAGE",
32              "WARNING_MESSAGE", "QUESTION_MESSAGE", "PLAIN_MESSAGE");
33        messagePanel = new ButtonPanel("Message", "String", "Icon", "Component", "Other",
34              "Object[]");
35        optionTypePanel = new ButtonPanel("Confirm", "DEFAULT_OPTION", "YES_NO_OPTION",
36              "YES_NO_CANCEL_OPTION", "OK_CANCEL_OPTION");
37        optionsPanel = new ButtonPanel("Option", "String[]", "Icon[]", "Object[]");
38        inputPanel = new ButtonPanel("Input", "Text field", "Combo box");
39
40        gridPanel.add(typePanel);
41        gridPanel.add(messageTypePanel);
42        gridPanel.add(messagePanel);
43        gridPanel.add(optionTypePanel);
44        gridPanel.add(optionsPanel);
45        gridPanel.add(inputPanel);
46
47        // add a panel with a Show button
48
49        JPanel showPanel = new JPanel();
50        JButton showButton = new JButton("Show");
51        showButton.addActionListener(new ShowAction());
52        showPanel.add(showButton);
53
54        add(gridPanel, BorderLayout.CENTER);
55        add(showPanel, BorderLayout.SOUTH);
56        pack();
57     }
58
59     /**
60      * Gets the currently selected message.
61      * @return a string, icon, component, or object array, depending on the Message panel selection
62      */
63     public Object getMessage()
64     {
65        String s = messagePanel.getSelection();
66        if (s.equals("String")) return messageString;
67        else if (s.equals("Icon")) return messageIcon;
68        else if (s.equals("Component")) return messageComponent;
69        else if (s.equals("Object[]")) return new Object[] { messageString, messageIcon,
70              messageComponent, messageObject };
```

(Continues)

Listing 12.15 *(Continued)*

```
71       else if (s.equals("Other")) return messageObject;
72       else return null;
73    }
74
75    /**
76     * Gets the currently selected options.
77     * @return an array of strings, icons, or objects, depending on the Option panel selection
78     */
79    public Object[] getOptions()
80    {
81       String s = optionsPanel.getSelection();
82       if (s.equals("String[]")) return new String[] { "Yellow", "Blue", "Red" };
83       else if (s.equals("Icon[]")) return new Icon[] { new ImageIcon("yellow-ball.gif"),
84             new ImageIcon("blue-ball.gif"), new ImageIcon("red-ball.gif") };
85       else if (s.equals("Object[]")) return new Object[] { messageString, messageIcon,
86             messageComponent, messageObject };
87       else return null;
88    }
89
90    /**
91     * Gets the selected message or option type
92     * @param panel the Message Type or Confirm panel
93     * @return the selected XXX_MESSAGE or XXX_OPTION constant from the JOptionPane class
94     */
95    public int getType(ButtonPanel panel)
96    {
97       String s = panel.getSelection();
98       try
99       {
100          return JOptionPane.class.getField(s).getInt(null);
101       }
102       catch (Exception e)
103       {
104          return -1;
105       }
106    }
107
108    /**
109     * The action listener for the Show button shows a Confirm, Input, Message, or Option dialog
110     * depending on the Type panel selection.
111     */
```

```
112    private class ShowAction implements ActionListener
113    {
114       public void actionPerformed(ActionEvent event)
115       {
116          if (typePanel.getSelection().equals("Confirm")) JOptionPane.showConfirmDialog(
117                OptionDialogFrame.this, getMessage(), "Title", getType(optionTypePanel),
118                getType(messageTypePanel));
119          else if (typePanel.getSelection().equals("Input"))
120          {
121             if (inputPanel.getSelection().equals("Text field")) JOptionPane.showInputDialog(
122                   OptionDialogFrame.this, getMessage(), "Title", getType(messageTypePanel));
123             else JOptionPane.showInputDialog(OptionDialogFrame.this, getMessage(), "Title",
124                   getType(messageTypePanel), null, new String[] { "Yellow", "Blue", "Red" },
125                   "Blue");
126          }
127          else if (typePanel.getSelection().equals("Message")) JOptionPane.showMessageDialog(
128                OptionDialogFrame.this, getMessage(), "Title", getType(messageTypePanel));
129          else if (typePanel.getSelection().equals("Option")) JOptionPane.showOptionDialog(
130                OptionDialogFrame.this, getMessage(), "Title", getType(optionTypePanel),
131                getType(messageTypePanel), null, getOptions(), getOptions()[0]);
132       }
133    }
134 }
135
136 /**
137  * A component with a painted surface
138  */
139
140 class SampleComponent extends JComponent
141 {
142    public void paintComponent(Graphics g)
143    {
144       Graphics2D g2 = (Graphics2D) g;
145       Rectangle2D rect = new Rectangle2D.Double(0, 0, getWidth() - 1, getHeight() - 1);
146       g2.setPaint(Color.YELLOW);
147       g2.fill(rect);
148       g2.setPaint(Color.BLUE);
149       g2.draw(rect);
150    }
151
152    public Dimension getPreferredSize()
153    {
154       return new Dimension(10, 10);
155    }
156 }
```

Listing 12.16 optionDialog/ButtonPanel.java

```
1   package optionDialog;
2
3   import javax.swing.*;
4
5   /**
6    * A panel with radio buttons inside a titled border.
7    */
8   public class ButtonPanel extends JPanel
9   {
10     private ButtonGroup group;
11
12     /**
13      * Constructs a button panel.
14      * @param title the title shown in the border
15      * @param options an array of radio button labels
16      */
17     public ButtonPanel(String title, String... options)
18     {
19        setBorder(BorderFactory.createTitledBorder(BorderFactory.createEtchedBorder(), title));
20        setLayout(new BoxLayout(this, BoxLayout.Y_AXIS));
21        group = new ButtonGroup();
22
23        // make one radio button for each option
24        for (String option : options)
25        {
26           JRadioButton b = new JRadioButton(option);
27           b.setActionCommand(option);
28           add(b);
29           group.add(b);
30           b.setSelected(option == options[0]);
31        }
32     }
33
34     /**
35      * Gets the currently selected option.
36      * @return the label of the currently selected radio button.
37      */
38     public String getSelection()
39     {
40        return group.getSelection().getActionCommand();
41     }
42   }
```

---

javax.swing.JOptionPane 1.2

- static void showMessageDialog(Component parent, Object message, String title, int messageType, Icon icon)
- static void showMessageDialog(Component parent, Object message, String title, int messageType)
- static void showMessageDialog(Component parent, Object message)
- static void showInternalMessageDialog(Component parent, Object message, String title, int messageType, Icon icon)
- static void showInternalMessageDialog(Component parent, Object message, String title, int messageType)
- static void showInternalMessageDialog(Component parent, Object message)

shows a message dialog or an internal message dialog. (An internal dialog is rendered entirely within its owner's frame.)

Parameters:	parent	The parent component (can be null)
	message	The message to show on the dialog (can be a string, icon, component, or an array of them)
	title	The string in the title bar of the dialog
	messageType	One of ERROR_MESSAGE, INFORMATION_MESSAGE, WARNING_MESSAGE, QUESTION_MESSAGE, PLAIN_MESSAGE
	icon	An icon to show instead of one of the standard icons

- static int showConfirmDialog(Component parent, Object message, String title, int optionType, int messageType, Icon icon)
- static int showConfirmDialog(Component parent, Object message, String title, int optionType, int messageType)
- static int showConfirmDialog(Component parent, Object message, String title, int optionType)
- static int showConfirmDialog(Component parent, Object message)
- static int showInternalConfirmDialog(Component parent, Object message, String title, int optionType, int messageType, Icon icon)
- static int showInternalConfirmDialog(Component parent, Object message, String title, int optionType, int messageType)
- static int showInternalConfirmDialog(Component parent, Object message, String title, int optionType)
- static int showInternalConfirmDialog(Component parent, Object message)

shows a confirmation dialog or an internal confirmation dialog. (An internal dialog is rendered entirely within its owner's frame.) Returns the option selected by the user (one of OK_OPTION, CANCEL_OPTION, YES_OPTION, NO_OPTION), or CLOSED_OPTION if the user closed the dialog.

(Continues)

---

javax.swing.JOptionPane 1.2 *(Continued)*

Parameters:	parent	The parent component (can be null)
	message	The message to show on the dialog (can be a string, icon, component, or an array of them)
	title	The string in the title bar of the dialog
	messageType	One of ERROR_MESSAGE, INFORMATION_MESSAGE, WARNING_MESSAGE, QUESTION_MESSAGE, PLAIN_MESSAGE
	optionType	One of DEFAULT_OPTION, YES_NO_OPTION, YES_NO_CANCEL_OPTION, OK_CANCEL_OPTION
	icon	An icon to show instead of one of the standard icons

- static int showOptionDialog(Component parent, Object message, String title, int optionType, int messageType, Icon icon, Object[] options, Object default)
- static int showInternalOptionDialog(Component parent, Object message, String title, int optionType, int messageType, Icon icon, Object[] options, Object default)

shows an option dialog or an internal option dialog. (An internal dialog is rendered entirely within its owner's frame.) Returns the index of the option selected by the user, or CLOSED_OPTION if the user canceled the dialog.

Parameters:	parent	The parent component (can be null)
	message	The message to show on the dialog (can be a string, icon, component, or an array of them)
	title	The string in the title bar of the dialog
	messageType	One of ERROR_MESSAGE, INFORMATION_MESSAGE, WARNING_MESSAGE, QUESTION_MESSAGE, PLAIN_MESSAGE
	optionType	One of DEFAULT_OPTION, YES_NO_OPTION, YES_NO_CANCEL_OPTION, OK_CANCEL_OPTION
	icon	An icon to show instead of one of the standard icons
	options	An array of options (can be strings, icons, or components)
	default	The default option to present to the user

- static Object showInputDialog(Component parent, Object message, String title, int messageType, Icon icon, Object[] values, Object default)
- static String showInputDialog(Component parent, Object message, String title, int messageType)
- static String showInputDialog(Component parent, Object message)
- static String showInputDialog(Object message)
- static String showInputDialog(Component parent, Object message, Object default) 1.4
- static String showInputDialog(Object message, Object default) 1.4

(Continues)

---

javax.swing.JOptionPane 1.2 *(Continued)*

- static Object showInternalInputDialog(Component parent, Object message, String title, int messageType, Icon icon, Object[] values, Object default)
- static String showInternalInputDialog(Component parent, Object message, String title, int messageType)
- static String showInternalInputDialog(Component parent, Object message)

shows an input dialog or an internal input dialog. (An internal dialog is rendered entirely within its owner's frame.) Returns the input string typed by the user, or null if the user canceled the dialog.

Parameters:	parent	The parent component (can be null)
	message	The message to show on the dialog (can be a string, icon, component, or an array of them)
	title	The string in the title bar of the dialog
	messageType	One of ERROR_MESSAGE, INFORMATION_MESSAGE, WARNING_MESSAGE, QUESTION_MESSAGE, PLAIN_MESSAGE
	icon	An icon to show instead of one of the standard icons
	values	An array of values to show in a combo box
	default	The default value to present to the user

12.7.2 Creating Dialogs

In the last section, you saw how to use the JOptionPane class to show a simple dialog. In this section, you will see how to create such a dialog by hand.

Figure 12.38 shows a typical modal dialog box—a program information box that is displayed when the user clicks the About button.

Figure 12.38 An About dialog box

To implement a dialog box, you extend the JDialog class. This is essentially the same process as extending JFrame for the main window for an application. More precisely:

1. In the constructor of your dialog box, call the constructor of the superclass JDialog.
2. Add the user interface components of the dialog box.
3. Add the event handlers.
4. Set the size for the dialog box.

When you call the superclass constructor, you will need to supply the *owner frame*, the title of the dialog, and the *modality*.

The owner frame controls where the dialog is displayed. You can supply null as the owner; then, the dialog is owned by a hidden frame.

The modality specifies which other windows of your application are blocked while the dialog is displayed. A modeless dialog does not block other windows. A modal dialog blocks all other windows of the application (except for the children of the dialog). You would use a modeless dialog for a toolbox that the user can always access. On the other hand, you would use a modal dialog if you want to force the user to supply required information before continuing.

 NOTE: As of Java SE 6, there are two additional modality types. A document-modal dialog blocks all windows belonging to the same "document," or more precisely, all windows with the same parentless root window as the dialog. This solves a problem with help systems. In older versions, users were unable to interact with the help windows when a modal dialog was popped up. A toolkit-modal dialog blocks all windows from the same "toolkit." A toolkit is a Java program that launches multiple applications, such as the applet engine in a browser. For more information on these advanced issues, see www.oracle.com/technetwork/articles/javase/modality-137604.html.

Here's the code for a dialog box:

```
public AboutDialog extends JDialog
{
    public AboutDialog(JFrame owner)
    {
        super(owner, "About DialogTest", true);
        add(new JLabel(
            "<html><h1><i>Core Java</i></h1><hr>By Cay Horstmann</html>"),
            BorderLayout.CENTER);

        JPanel panel = new JPanel();
```

```
        JButton ok = new JButton("OK");

        ok.addActionListener(event -> setVisible(false));
        panel.add(ok);
        add(panel, BorderLayout.SOUTH);
        setSize(250, 150);
    }
}
```

As you can see, the constructor adds user interface elements—in this case, labels and a button. It adds a handler to the button and sets the size of the dialog.

To display the dialog box, create a new dialog object and make it visible:

```
JDialog dialog = new AboutDialog(this);
dialog.setVisible(true);
```

Actually, in the sample code below, we create the dialog box only once, and we can reuse it whenever the user clicks the About button.

```
if (dialog == null) // first time
    dialog = new AboutDialog(this);
dialog.setVisible(true);
```

When the user clicks the OK button, the dialog box should close. This is handled in the event handler of the OK button:

```
ok.addActionListener(event -> setVisible(false));
```

When the user closes the dialog by clicking the Close button, the dialog is also hidden. Just as with a JFrame, you can override this behavior with the setDefaultCloseOperation method.

Listing 12.17 is the code for the frame class of the test program. Listing 12.18 shows the dialog class.

Listing 12.17 dialog/DialogFrame.java

```
1  package dialog;
2
3  import javax.swing.JFrame;
4  import javax.swing.JMenu;
5  import javax.swing.JMenuBar;
6  import javax.swing.JMenuItem;
7
8  /**
9   * A frame with a menu whose File->About action shows a dialog.
10  */
```

(Continues)

Listing 12.17 *(Continued)*

```
11  public class DialogFrame extends JFrame
12  {
13     private static final int DEFAULT_WIDTH = 300;
14     private static final int DEFAULT_HEIGHT = 200;
15     private AboutDialog dialog;
16
17     public DialogFrame()
18     {
19        setSize(DEFAULT_WIDTH, DEFAULT_HEIGHT);
20
21        // Construct a File menu.
22
23        JMenuBar menuBar = new JMenuBar();
24        setJMenuBar(menuBar);
25        JMenu fileMenu = new JMenu("File");
26        menuBar.add(fileMenu);
27
28        // Add About and Exit menu items.
29
30        // The About item shows the About dialog.
31
32        JMenuItem aboutItem = new JMenuItem("About");
33        aboutItem.addActionListener(event -> {
34           if (dialog == null) // first time
35              dialog = new AboutDialog(DialogFrame.this);
36           dialog.setVisible(true); // pop up dialog
37        });
38        fileMenu.add(aboutItem);
39
40        // The Exit item exits the program.
41
42        JMenuItem exitItem = new JMenuItem("Exit");
43        exitItem.addActionListener(event -> System.exit(0));
44        fileMenu.add(exitItem);
45     }
46  }
```

Listing 12.18 dialog/AboutDialog.java

```
1  package dialog;
2
3  import java.awt.BorderLayout;
4
5  import javax.swing.JButton;
6  import javax.swing.JDialog;
```

```
 7  import javax.swing.JFrame;
 8  import javax.swing.JLabel;
 9  import javax.swing.JPanel;
10
11  /**
12   * A sample modal dialog that displays a message and waits for the user to click the OK button.
13   */
14  public class AboutDialog extends JDialog
15  {
16     public AboutDialog(JFrame owner)
17     {
18        super(owner, "About DialogTest", true);
19
20        // add HTML label to center
21
22        add(
23           new JLabel(
24              "<html><h1><i>Core Java</i></h1><hr>By Cay Horstmann</html>"),
25           BorderLayout.CENTER);
26
27        // OK button closes the dialog
28
29        JButton ok = new JButton("OK");
30        ok.addActionListener(event -> setVisible(false));
31
32        // add OK button to southern border
33
34        JPanel panel = new JPanel();
35        panel.add(ok);
36        add(panel, BorderLayout.SOUTH);
37
38        pack();
39     }
40  }
```

---

javax.swing.JDialog 1.2

- `public JDialog(Frame parent, String title, boolean modal)`

  constructs a dialog. The dialog is not visible until it is explicitly shown.

Parameters:	parent	The frame that is the owner of the dialog
	title	The title of the dialog
	modal	true for modal dialogs (a modal dialog blocks input to other windows)

12.7.3 Data Exchange

The most common reason to put up a dialog box is to get information from the user. You have already seen how easy it is to make a dialog box object: Give it initial data and call setVisible(true) to display the dialog box on the screen. Now let's see how to transfer data in and out of a dialog box.

Consider the dialog box in Figure 12.39 that could be used to obtain a user name and a password to connect to some online service.

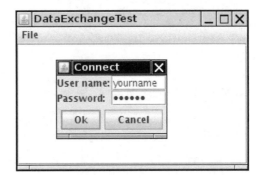

Figure 12.39 Password dialog box

Your dialog box should provide methods to set default data. For example, the PasswordChooser class of the example program has a method, setUser, to place default values into the next fields:

```
public void setUser(User u)
{
    username.setText(u.getName());
}
```

Once you set the defaults (if desired), show the dialog by calling setVisible(true). The dialog is now displayed.

The user then fills in the information and clicks the OK or Cancel button. The event handlers for both buttons call setVisible(false), which terminates the call to setVisible(true). Alternatively, the user may close the dialog. If you did not install a window listener for the dialog, the default window closing operation applies: The dialog becomes invisible, which also terminates the call to setVisible(true).

The important issue is that the call to setVisible(true) blocks until the user has dismissed the dialog. This makes it easy to implement modal dialogs.

You want to know whether the user has accepted or canceled the dialog. Our sample code sets the ok flag to false before showing the dialog. Only the event handler for the OK button sets the ok flag to true; that's how you retrieve the user input from the dialog.

 NOTE: Transferring data out of a modeless dialog is not as simple. When a modeless dialog is displayed, the call to setVisible(true) does not block and the program continues running while the dialog is displayed. If the user selects items on a modeless dialog and then clicks OK, the dialog needs to send an event to some listener in the program.

The example program contains another useful improvement. When you construct a JDialog object, you need to specify the owner frame. However, quite often you want to show the same dialog with different owner frames. It is better to pick the owner frame *when you are ready to show the dialog*, not when you construct the PasswordChooser object.

The trick is to have the PasswordChooser extend JPanel instead of JDialog. Build a JDialog object on the fly in the showDialog method:

```
public boolean showDialog(Frame owner, String title)
{
   ok = false;

   if (dialog == null || dialog.getOwner() != owner)
   {
      dialog = new JDialog(owner, true);
      dialog.add(this);
      dialog.pack();
   }

   dialog.setTitle(title);
   dialog.setVisible(true);
   return ok;
}
```

Note that it is safe to have owner equal to null.

You can do even better. Sometimes, the owner frame isn't readily available. It is easy enough to compute it from any parent component, like this:

```
Frame owner;
if (parent instanceof Frame)
   owner = (Frame) parent;
else
   owner = (Frame) SwingUtilities.getAncestorOfClass(Frame.class, parent);
```

We use this enhancement in our sample program. The JOptionPane class also uses this mechanism.

Many dialogs have a *default button*, which is automatically selected if the user presses a trigger key (Enter in most look-and-feel implementations). The default button is specially marked, often with a thick outline.

Set the default button in the *root pane* of the dialog:

```
dialog.getRootPane().setDefaultButton(okButton);
```

If you follow our suggestion of laying out the dialog in a panel, then you must be careful to set the default button only after you wrapped the panel into a dialog. The panel dialog itself has no root pane.

Listing 12.19 is for the frame class of the program that illustrates the data flow into and out of a dialog box. Listing 12.20 shows the dialog class.

Listing 12.19 dataExchange/DataExchangeFrame.java

```java
1  package dataExchange;
2
3  import java.awt.*;
4  import java.awt.event.*;
5  import javax.swing.*;
6
7  /**
8   * A frame with a menu whose File->Connect action shows a password dialog.
9   */
10 public class DataExchangeFrame extends JFrame
11 {
12    public static final int TEXT_ROWS = 20;
13    public static final int TEXT_COLUMNS = 40;
14    private PasswordChooser dialog = null;
15    private JTextArea textArea;
16
17    public DataExchangeFrame()
18    {
19       // construct a File menu
20
21       JMenuBar mbar = new JMenuBar();
22       setJMenuBar(mbar);
23       JMenu fileMenu = new JMenu("File");
24       mbar.add(fileMenu);
25
26       // add Connect and Exit menu items
27
28       JMenuItem connectItem = new JMenuItem("Connect");
29       connectItem.addActionListener(new ConnectAction());
30       fileMenu.add(connectItem);
31
32       // The Exit item exits the program
```

```
33
34        JMenuItem exitItem = new JMenuItem("Exit");
35        exitItem.addActionListener(event -> System.exit(0));
36        fileMenu.add(exitItem);
37
38        textArea = new JTextArea(TEXT_ROWS, TEXT_COLUMNS);
39        add(new JScrollPane(textArea), BorderLayout.CENTER);
40        pack();
41     }
42
43     /**
44      * The Connect action pops up the password dialog.
45      */
46     private class ConnectAction implements ActionListener
47     {
48        public void actionPerformed(ActionEvent event)
49        {
50           // if first time, construct dialog
51
52           if (dialog == null) dialog = new PasswordChooser();
53
54           // set default values
55           dialog.setUser(new User("yourname", null));
56
57           // pop up dialog
58           if (dialog.showDialog(DataExchangeFrame.this, "Connect"))
59           {
60              // if accepted, retrieve user input
61              User u = dialog.getUser();
62              textArea.append("user name = " + u.getName() + ", password = "
63                 + (new String(u.getPassword())) + "\n");
64           }
65        }
66     }
67 }
```

Listing 12.20 dataExchange/PasswordChooser.java

```
1  package dataExchange;
2
3  import java.awt.BorderLayout;
4  import java.awt.Component;
5  import java.awt.Frame;
6  import java.awt.GridLayout;
7
8  import javax.swing.JButton;
9  import javax.swing.JDialog;
10 import javax.swing.JLabel;
```

(Continues)

Listing 12.20 *(Continued)*

```
11  import javax.swing.JPanel;
12  import javax.swing.JPasswordField;
13  import javax.swing.JTextField;
14  import javax.swing.SwingUtilities;
15
16  /**
17   * A password chooser that is shown inside a dialog
18   */
19  public class PasswordChooser extends JPanel
20  {
21     private JTextField username;
22     private JPasswordField password;
23     private JButton okButton;
24     private boolean ok;
25     private JDialog dialog;
26
27     public PasswordChooser()
28     {
29        setLayout(new BorderLayout());
30
31        // construct a panel with user name and password fields
32
33        JPanel panel = new JPanel();
34        panel.setLayout(new GridLayout(2, 2));
35        panel.add(new JLabel("User name:"));
36        panel.add(username = new JTextField(""));
37        panel.add(new JLabel("Password:"));
38        panel.add(password = new JPasswordField(""));
39        add(panel, BorderLayout.CENTER);
40
41        // create Ok and Cancel buttons that terminate the dialog
42
43        okButton = new JButton("Ok");
44        okButton.addActionListener(event -> {
45           ok = true;
46           dialog.setVisible(false);
47        });
48
49        JButton cancelButton = new JButton("Cancel");
50        cancelButton.addActionListener(event -> dialog.setVisible(false));
51
52        // add buttons to southern border
53
54        JPanel buttonPanel = new JPanel();
55        buttonPanel.add(okButton);
56        buttonPanel.add(cancelButton);
57        add(buttonPanel, BorderLayout.SOUTH);
58     }
```

```
59
60    /**
61     * Sets the dialog defaults.
62     * @param u the default user information
63     */
64    public void setUser(User u)
65    {
66       username.setText(u.getName());
67    }
68
69    /**
70     * Gets the dialog entries.
71     * @return a User object whose state represents the dialog entries
72     */
73    public User getUser()
74    {
75       return new User(username.getText(), password.getPassword());
76    }
77
78    /**
79     * Show the chooser panel in a dialog
80     * @param parent a component in the owner frame or null
81     * @param title the dialog window title
82     */
83    public boolean showDialog(Component parent, String title)
84    {
85       ok = false;
86
87       // locate the owner frame
88
89       Frame owner = null;
90       if (parent instanceof Frame)
91          owner = (Frame) parent;
92       else
93          owner = (Frame) SwingUtilities.getAncestorOfClass(Frame.class, parent);
94
95       // if first time, or if owner has changed, make new dialog
96
97       if (dialog == null || dialog.getOwner() != owner)
98       {
99          dialog = new JDialog(owner, true);
100         dialog.add(this);
101         dialog.getRootPane().setDefaultButton(okButton);
102         dialog.pack();
103      }
104
105      // set title and show dialog
106
```

(Continues)

Listing 12.20 *(Continued)*

```
107        dialog.setTitle(title);
108        dialog.setVisible(true);
109        return ok;
110    }
111 }
```

---

javax.swing.SwingUtilities 1.2

- Container getAncestorOfClass(Class c, Component comp)

  returns the innermost parent container of the given component that belongs to the given class or one of its subclasses.

---

javax.swing.JComponent 1.2

- JRootPane getRootPane()

  gets the root pane enclosing this component, or null if this component does not have an ancestor with a root pane.

---

javax.swing.JRootPane 1.2

- void setDefaultButton(JButton button)

  sets the default button for this root pane. To deactivate the default button, call this method with a null parameter.

---

javax.swing.JButton 1.2

- boolean isDefaultButton()

  returns true if this button is the default button of its root pane.

12.7.4 File Dialogs

In an application, you often want to be able to open and save files. A good file dialog box that shows files and directories and lets the user navigate the file system is hard to write, and you definitely don't want to reinvent that wheel. Fortunately, Swing provides a JFileChooser class that allows you to display a file dialog box similar to the one that most native applications use. JFileChooser dialogs are always modal. Note that the JFileChooser class is not a subclass of JDialog. Instead of calling setVisible(true), call showOpenDialog to display a dialog for opening a file, or call showSaveDialog to display a dialog for saving a file. The button for accepting a file is then automatically labeled Open or Save. You can also supply your own button label with the showDialog method. Figure 12.40 shows an example of the file chooser dialog box.

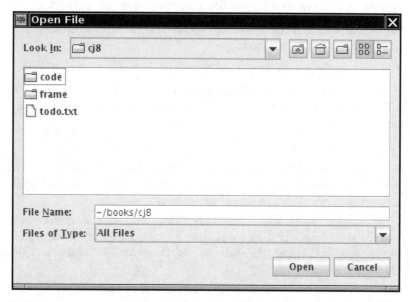

Figure 12.40 File chooser dialog box

Here are the steps to put up a file dialog box and recover what the user chooses from the box:

1. Make a JFileChooser object. Unlike the constructor for the JDialog class, you do not supply the parent component. This allows you to reuse a file chooser dialog with multiple frames.

   For example:

   ```
   JFileChooser chooser = new JFileChooser();
   ```

 TIP: Reusing a file chooser object is a good idea because the JFileChooser constructor can be quite slow, especially on Windows when the user has many mapped network drives.

2. Set the directory by calling the `setCurrentDirectory` method.

   For example, to use the current working directory

   ```
   chooser.setCurrentDirectory(new File("."));
   ```

   you need to supply a `File` object. `File` objects are explained in detail in Chapter 2 of Volume II. All you need to know for now is that the constructor `File(String filename)` turns a file or directory name into a `File` object.

3. If you have a default file name that you expect the user to choose, supply it with the `setSelectedFile` method:

   ```
   chooser.setSelectedFile(new File(filename));
   ```

4. To enable the user to select multiple files in the dialog, call the `setMultiSelectionEnabled` method. This is, of course, entirely optional and not all that common.

   ```
   chooser.setMultiSelectionEnabled(true);
   ```

5. If you want to restrict the display of files in the dialog to those of a particular type (for example, all files with extension .gif), you need to set a *file filter*. We discuss file filters later in this section.

6. By default, a user can select only files with a file chooser. If you want the user to select directories, use the `setFileSelectionMode` method. Call it with `JFileChooser.FILES_ONLY` (the default), `JFileChooser.DIRECTORIES_ONLY`, or `JFileChooser.FILES_AND_DIRECTORIES`.

7. Show the dialog box by calling the `showOpenDialog` or `showSaveDialog` method. You must supply the parent component in these calls:

   ```
   int result = chooser.showOpenDialog(parent);
   ```

   or

   ```
   int result = chooser.showSaveDialog(parent);
   ```

   The only difference between these calls is the label of the "approve button"—the button that the user clicks to finish the file selection. You can also call the `showDialog` method and pass an explicit text for the approve button:

   ```
   int result = chooser.showDialog(parent, "Select");
   ```

   These calls return only when the user has approved, canceled, or dismissed the file dialog. The return value is `JFileChooser.APPROVE_OPTION`, `JFileChooser.CANCEL_OPTION`, or `JFileChooser.ERROR_OPTION`.

8. Get the selected file or files with the `getSelectedFile()` or `getSelectedFiles()` method. These methods return either a single `File` object or an array of `File` objects. If you just need the name of the file object, call its `getPath` method. For example:

```
String filename = chooser.getSelectedFile().getPath();
```

For the most part, these steps are simple. The major difficulty with using a file dialog is to specify a subset of files from which the user should choose. For example, suppose the user should choose a GIF image file. Then, the file chooser should only display files with the extension .gif. It should also give the user some kind of feedback that the displayed files are of a particular category, such as "GIF Images." But the situation can be more complex. If the user should choose a JPEG image file, the extension can be either .jpg or .jpeg. Instead of a way to codify these complexities, the designers of the file chooser povided a more elegant mechanism: to restrict the displayed files, supply an object that extends the abstract class javax.swing.filechooser.FileFilter. The file chooser passes each file to the file filter and displays only those files that the filter accepts.

At the time of this writing, two such subclasses are supplied: the default filter that accepts all files, and a filter that accepts all files with a given extension. However, it is easy to write ad-hoc file filters. You simply implement the two abstract methods of the FileFilter superclass:

```
public boolean accept(File f);
public String getDescription();
```

The first method tests whether a file should be accepted. The second method returns a description of the file type that can be displayed in the file chooser dialog.

 NOTE: An unrelated FileFilter interface in the java.io package has a single method, boolean accept(File f). It is used in the listFiles method of the File class to list files in a directory. We do not know why the designers of Swing didn't extend this interface—perhaps the Java class library has now become so complex that even the programmers at Sun were no longer aware of all the standard classes and interfaces.

You will need to resolve the name conflict between these two identically named types if you import both the java.io and the javax.swing.filechooser packages. The simplest remedy is to import javax.swing.filechooser.FileFilter, not javax.swing.filechooser.*.

Once you have a file filter object, use the setFileFilter method of the JFileChooser class to install it into the file chooser object:

```
chooser.setFileFilter(new FileNameExtensionFilter("Image files", "gif", "jpg"));
```

You can install multiple filters to the file chooser by calling

```
chooser.addChoosableFileFilter(filter1);
chooser.addChoosableFileFilter(filter2);
. . .
```

The user selects a filter from the combo box at the bottom of the file dialog. By default, the "All files" filter is always present in the combo box. This is a good idea—just in case a user of your program needs to select a file with a nonstandard extension. However, if you want to suppress the "All files" filter, call

```
chooser.setAcceptAllFileFilterUsed(false)
```

 CAUTION: If you reuse a single file chooser for loading and saving different file types, call

```
chooser.resetChoosableFilters()
```

to clear any old file filters before adding new ones.

Finally, you can customize the file chooser by providing special icons and file descriptions for each file that the file chooser displays. Do this by supplying an object of a class extending the FileView class in the javax.swing.filechooser package. This is definitely an advanced technique. Normally, you don't need to supply a file view—the pluggable look-and-feel supplies one for you. But if you want to show different icons for special file types, you can install your own file view. You need to extend the FileView class and implement five methods:

```
Icon getIcon(File f);
String getName(File f);
String getDescription(File f);
String getTypeDescription(File f);
Boolean isTraversable(File f);
```

Then, use the setFileView method to install your file view into the file chooser.

The file chooser calls your methods for each file or directory that it wants to display. If your method returns null for the icon, name, or description, the file chooser then consults the default file view of the look-and-feel. That is good, because it means you need to deal only with the file types for which you want to do something different.

The file chooser calls the isTraversable method to decide whether to open a directory when a user clicks on it. Note that this method returns a Boolean object, not a boolean value! This seems weird, but it is actually convenient—if you aren't interested in deviating from the default file view, just return null. The file chooser will then consult the default file view. In other words, the method returns a Boolean to let you choose among three options: true (Boolean.TRUE), false (Boolean.FALSE), or don't care (null).

The example program contains a simple file view class. That class shows a particular icon whenever a file matches a file filter. We use it to display a palette icon for all image files.

```
class FileIconView extends FileView
{
   private FileFilter filter;
   private Icon icon;

   public FileIconView(FileFilter aFilter, Icon anIcon)
   {
      filter = aFilter;
      icon = anIcon;
   }

   public Icon getIcon(File f)
   {
      if (!f.isDirectory() && filter.accept(f))
         return icon;
      else return null;
   }
}
```

Install this file view into your file chooser with the setFileView method:

```
chooser.setFileView(new FileIconView(filter,
   new ImageIcon("palette.gif")));
```

The file chooser will then show the palette icon next to all files that pass the filter and use the default file view to show all other files. Naturally, we use the same filter that we set in the file chooser.

 TIP: You can find a more useful ExampleFileView class in the demo/jfc/FileChooserDemo directory of the JDK. That class lets you associate icons and descriptions with arbitrary extensions.

Finally, you can customize a file dialog by adding an *accessory* component. For example, Figure 12.41 shows a preview accessory next to the file list. This accessory displays a thumbnail view of the currently selected file.

An accessory can be any Swing component. In our case, we extend the JLabel class and set its icon to a scaled copy of the graphics image:

Figure 12.41 A file dialog with a preview accessory

```java
class ImagePreviewer extends JLabel
{
   public ImagePreviewer(JFileChooser chooser)
   {
      setPreferredSize(new Dimension(100, 100));
      setBorder(BorderFactory.createEtchedBorder());
   }

   public void loadImage(File f)
   {
      ImageIcon icon = new ImageIcon(f.getPath());
      if(icon.getIconWidth() > getWidth())
         icon = new ImageIcon(icon.getImage().getScaledInstance(
            getWidth(), -1, Image.SCALE_DEFAULT));
      setIcon(icon);
      repaint();
   }
}
```

There is just one challenge. We want to update the preview image whenever the user selects a different file. The file chooser uses the "JavaBeans" mechanism of notifying interested listeners whenever one of its properties changes. The selected file is a property that you can monitor by installing a PropertyChangeListener. We discuss this mechanism in greater detail in Chapter 11 of Volume II. Here is the code that you need to trap the notifications:

```
chooser.addPropertyChangeListener(event -> {
   if (event.getPropertyName() == JFileChooser.SELECTED_FILE_CHANGED_PROPERTY)
   {
      File newFile = (File) event.getNewValue();
      // update the accessory
      . . .
   }
});
```

In our example program, we add this code to the ImagePreviewer constructor.

Listings 12.21 through 12.23 contain a modification of the ImageViewer program from Chapter 2, in which the file chooser has been enhanced by a custom file view and a preview accessory.

Listing 12.21 fileChooser/ImageViewerFrame.java

```
1   package fileChooser;
2
3   import java.io.*;
4
5   import javax.swing.*;
6   import javax.swing.filechooser.*;
7   import javax.swing.filechooser.FileFilter;
8
9   /**
10   * A frame that has a menu for loading an image and a display area for the
11   * loaded image.
12   */
13  public class ImageViewerFrame extends JFrame
14  {
15     private static final int DEFAULT_WIDTH = 300;
16     private static final int DEFAULT_HEIGHT = 400;
17     private JLabel label;
18     private JFileChooser chooser;
19
20     public ImageViewerFrame()
21     {
22        setSize(DEFAULT_WIDTH, DEFAULT_HEIGHT);
23
24        // set up menu bar
```

(Continues)

Listing 12.21 *(Continued)*

```
25       JMenuBar menuBar = new JMenuBar();
26       setJMenuBar(menuBar);
27
28       JMenu menu = new JMenu("File");
29       menuBar.add(menu);
30
31       JMenuItem openItem = new JMenuItem("Open");
32       menu.add(openItem);
33       openItem.addActionListener(event -> {
34          chooser.setCurrentDirectory(new File("."));
35
36          // show file chooser dialog
37             int result = chooser.showOpenDialog(ImageViewerFrame.this);
38
39             // if image file accepted, set it as icon of the label
40             if (result == JFileChooser.APPROVE_OPTION)
41             {
42                String name = chooser.getSelectedFile().getPath();
43                label.setIcon(new ImageIcon(name));
44                pack();
45             }
46          });
47
48       JMenuItem exitItem = new JMenuItem("Exit");
49       menu.add(exitItem);
50       exitItem.addActionListener(event -> System.exit(0));
51
52       // use a label to display the images
53       label = new JLabel();
54       add(label);
55
56       // set up file chooser
57       chooser = new JFileChooser();
58
59       // accept all image files ending with .jpg, .jpeg, .gif
60       FileFilter filter = new FileNameExtensionFilter(
61             "Image files", "jpg", "jpeg", "gif");
62       chooser.setFileFilter(filter);
63
64       chooser.setAccessory(new ImagePreviewer(chooser));
65
66       chooser.setFileView(new FileIconView(filter, new ImageIcon("palette.gif")));
67    }
68 }
```

Listing 12.22 fileChooser/ImagePreviewer.java

```
1  package fileChooser;
2
3  import java.awt.*;
4  import java.io.*;
5
6  import javax.swing.*;
7
8  /**
9   * A file chooser accessory that previews images.
10  */
11 public class ImagePreviewer extends JLabel
12 {
13    /**
14     * Constructs an ImagePreviewer.
15     * @param chooser the file chooser whose property changes trigger an image
16     *        change in this previewer
17     */
18    public ImagePreviewer(JFileChooser chooser)
19    {
20       setPreferredSize(new Dimension(100, 100));
21       setBorder(BorderFactory.createEtchedBorder());
22
23       chooser.addPropertyChangeListener(event -> {
24          if (event.getPropertyName() == JFileChooser.SELECTED_FILE_CHANGED_PROPERTY)
25          {
26             // the user has selected a new file
27             File f = (File) event.getNewValue();
28             if (f == null)
29             {
30                setIcon(null);
31                return;
32             }
33
34             // read the image into an icon
35             ImageIcon icon = new ImageIcon(f.getPath());
36
37             // if the icon is too large to fit, scale it
38             if (icon.getIconWidth() > getWidth())
39                icon = new ImageIcon(icon.getImage().getScaledInstance(
40                   getWidth(), -1, Image.SCALE_DEFAULT));
41
42             setIcon(icon);
43          }
44       });
45    }
46 }
```

Listing 12.23 fileChooser/FileIconView.java

```
1  package fileChooser;
2
3  import java.io.*;
4  import javax.swing.*;
5  import javax.swing.filechooser.*;
6  import javax.swing.filechooser.FileFilter;
7
8  /**
9   * A file view that displays an icon for all files that match a file filter.
10  */
11 public class FileIconView extends FileView
12 {
13    private FileFilter filter;
14    private Icon icon;
15
16    /**
17     * Constructs a FileIconView.
18     * @param aFilter a file filter--all files that this filter accepts will be shown
19     * with the icon.
20     * @param anIcon--the icon shown with all accepted files.
21     */
22    public FileIconView(FileFilter aFilter, Icon anIcon)
23    {
24       filter = aFilter;
25       icon = anIcon;
26    }
27
28    public Icon getIcon(File f)
29    {
30       if (!f.isDirectory() && filter.accept(f)) return icon;
31       else return null;
32    }
33 }
```

---

javax.swing.JFileChooser 1.2

- JFileChooser()

  creates a file chooser dialog box that can be used for multiple frames.

- void setCurrentDirectory(File dir)

  sets the initial directory for the file dialog box.

(Continues)

---

javax.swing.JFileChooser 1.2 *(Continued)*

- void setSelectedFile(File file)
- void setSelectedFiles(File[] file)

  sets the default file choice for the file dialog box.

- void setMultiSelectionEnabled(boolean b)

  sets or clears the multiple selection mode.

- void setFileSelectionMode(int mode)

  lets the user select files only (the default), directories only, or both files and directories. The mode parameter is one of JFileChooser.FILES_ONLY, JFileChooser.DIRECTORIES_ONLY, and JFileChooser.FILES_AND_DIRECTORIES.

- int showOpenDialog(Component parent)
- int showSaveDialog(Component parent)
- int showDialog(Component parent, String approveButtonText)

  shows a dialog in which the approve button is labeled "Open", "Save", or with the approveButtonText string. Returns APPROVE_OPTION, CANCEL_OPTION (if the user selected the cancel button or dismissed the dialog), or ERROR_OPTION (if an error occurred).

- File getSelectedFile()
- File[] getSelectedFiles()

  gets the file or files that the user selected (or returns null if the user didn't select any file).

- void setFileFilter(FileFilter filter)

  sets the file mask for the file dialog box. All files for which filter.accept returns true will be displayed. Also, adds the filter to the list of choosable filters.

- void addChoosableFileFilter(FileFilter filter)

  adds a file filter to the list of choosable filters.

- void setAcceptAllFileFilterUsed(boolean b)

  includes or suppresses an "All files" filter in the filter combo box.

- void resetChoosableFileFilters()

  clears the list of choosable filters. Only the "All files" filter remains unless it is explicitly suppressed.

- void setFileView(FileView view)

  sets a file view to provide information about the files that the file chooser displays.

- void setAccessory(JComponent component)

  sets an accessory component.

`javax.swing.filechooser.FileFilter` 1.2

- `boolean accept(File f)`

  returns `true` if the file chooser should display this file.

- `String getDescription()`

  returns a description of this file filter, for example, `"Image files (*.gif,*.jpeg)"`.

`javax.swing.filechooser.FileNameExtensionFilter` 6

- `FileNameExtensionFilter(String description, String... extensions)`

  constructs a file filter with the given description that accepts all directories and all files whose names end in a period followed by one of the given extension strings.

`javax.swing.filechooser.FileView` 1.2

- `String getName(File f)`

  returns the name of the file `f`, or `null`. Normally, this method simply returns `f.getName()`.

- `String getDescription(File f)`

  returns a human-readable description of the file `f`, or `null`. For example, if `f` is an HTML document, this method might return its title.

- `String getTypeDescription(File f)`

  returns a human-readable description of the type of the file `f`, or `null`. For example, if `f` is an HTML document, this method might return a string `"Hypertext document"`.

- `Icon getIcon(File f)`

  returns an icon for the file `f`, or `null`. For example, if `f` is a JPEG file, this method might return a thumbnail icon.

- `Boolean isTraversable(File f)`

  returns `Boolean.TRUE` if `f` is a directory that the user can open. This method might return `Boolean.FALSE` if a directory is conceptually a compound document. Like all `FileView` methods, this method can return `null` to signify that the file chooser should consult the default view instead.

12.7.5 Color Choosers

As you saw in the preceding section, a high-quality file chooser is an intricate user interface component that you definitely do not want to implement yourself.

Many user interface toolkits provide other common dialogs: to choose a date/time, currency value, font, color, and so on. The benefit is twofold: Programmers can simply use a high-quality implementation instead of rolling out their own, and users get a consistent experience with these components.

At this point, Swing provides only one additional chooser, the JColorChooser (see Figures 12.42 through 12.44). Use it to let users pick a color value. Like the JFileChooser class, the color chooser is a component, not a dialog, but it has convenience methods to create dialogs that contain a color chooser component.

Here is how you show a modal dialog with a color chooser:

```
Color selectedColor = JColorChooser.showDialog(parent,title, initialColor);
```

Alternatively, you can display a modeless color chooser dialog. Supply the following:

- A parent component
- The title of the dialog
- A flag to select either a modal or a modeless dialog
- A color chooser
- Listeners for the OK and Cancel buttons (or null if you don't want a listener)

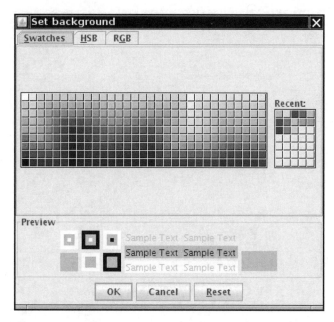

Figure 12.42 The Swatches pane of a color chooser

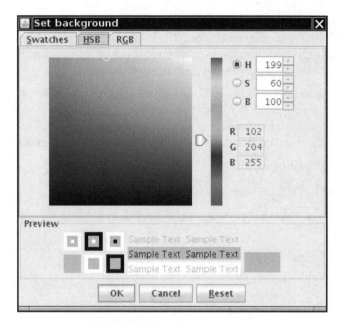

Figure 12.43 The HSB pane of a color chooser

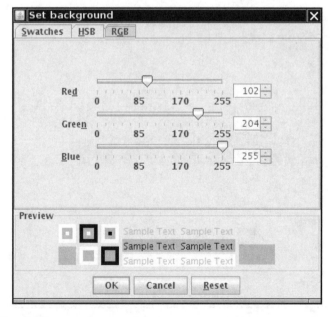

Figure 12.44 The RGB pane of a color chooser

Here is how you make a modeless dialog that sets the background color when the user clicks the OK button:

```
chooser = new JColorChooser();
dialog = JColorChooser.createDialog(
    parent,
    "Background Color",
false /* not modal */,
chooser,
event -> setBackground(chooser.getColor()),
null /* no Cancel button listener */);
```

You can do even better than that and give the user immediate feedback of the color selection. To monitor the color selections, you need to obtain the selection model of the chooser and add a change listener:

```
chooser.getSelectionModel().addChangeListener(event -> {
    do something with chooser.getColor();
});
```

In this case, there is no benefit to the OK and Cancel buttons that the color chooser dialog provides. You can just add the color chooser component directly into a modeless dialog:

```
dialog = new JDialog(parent, false /* not modal */);
dialog.add(chooser);
dialog.pack();
```

The program in Listing 12.24 shows the three types of dialogs. If you click on the Modal button, you must select a color before you can do anything else. If you click on the Modeless button, you get a modeless dialog, but the color change only happens when you click the OK button on the dialog. If you click the Immediate button, you get a modeless dialog without buttons. As soon as you pick a different color in the dialog, the background color of the panel is updated.

Listing 12.24 colorChooser/ColorChooserPanel.java

```
1  package colorChooser;
2
3  import java.awt.Color;
4  import java.awt.Frame;
5  import java.awt.event.ActionEvent;
6  import java.awt.event.ActionListener;
7
8  import javax.swing.JButton;
9  import javax.swing.JColorChooser;
10 import javax.swing.JDialog;
11 import javax.swing.JPanel;
```

(Continues)

Listing 12.24 *(Continued)*

```
12
13  /**
14   * A panel with buttons to pop up three types of color choosers
15   */
16  public class ColorChooserPanel extends JPanel
17  {
18     public ColorChooserPanel()
19     {
20        JButton modalButton = new JButton("Modal");
21        modalButton.addActionListener(new ModalListener());
22        add(modalButton);
23
24        JButton modelessButton = new JButton("Modeless");
25        modelessButton.addActionListener(new ModelessListener());
26        add(modelessButton);
27
28        JButton immediateButton = new JButton("Immediate");
29        immediateButton.addActionListener(new ImmediateListener());
30        add(immediateButton);
31     }
32
33     /**
34      * This listener pops up a modal color chooser
35      */
36     private class ModalListener implements ActionListener
37     {
38        public void actionPerformed(ActionEvent event)
39        {
40           Color defaultColor = getBackground();
41           Color selected = JColorChooser.showDialog(ColorChooserPanel.this, "Set background",
42                 defaultColor);
43           if (selected != null) setBackground(selected);
44        }
45     }
46
47     /**
48      * This listener pops up a modeless color chooser. The panel color is changed when the user
49      * clicks the OK button.
50      */
51     private class ModelessListener implements ActionListener
52     {
53        private JDialog dialog;
54        private JColorChooser chooser;
55
```

```
56      public ModelessListener()
57      {
58         chooser = new JColorChooser();
59         dialog = JColorChooser.createDialog(ColorChooserPanel.this, "Background Color",
60               false /* not modal */, chooser,
61               event -> setBackground(chooser.getColor()),
62               null /* no Cancel button listener */);
63      }
64
65      public void actionPerformed(ActionEvent event)
66      {
67         chooser.setColor(getBackground());
68         dialog.setVisible(true);
69      }
70   }
71
72   /**
73    * This listener pops up a modeless color chooser. The panel color is changed immediately when
74    * the user picks a new color.
75    */
76   private class ImmediateListener implements ActionListener
77   {
78      private JDialog dialog;
79      private JColorChooser chooser;
80
81      public ImmediateListener()
82      {
83         chooser = new JColorChooser();
84         chooser.getSelectionModel().addChangeListener(
85               event -> setBackground(chooser.getColor()));
86
87         dialog = new JDialog((Frame) null, false /* not modal */);
88         dialog.add(chooser);
89         dialog.pack();
90      }
91
92      public void actionPerformed(ActionEvent event)
93      {
94         chooser.setColor(getBackground());
95         dialog.setVisible(true);
96      }
97   }
98 }
```

---

javax.swing.JColorChooser 1.2

- `JColorChooser()`

  constructs a color chooser with an initial color of white.
- `Color getColor()`
- `void setColor(Color c)`

  gets and sets the current color of this color chooser.
- `static Color showDialog(Component parent, String title, Color initialColor)`

  shows a modal dialog that contains a color chooser.

Parameters:	parent	The component over which to pop up the dialog
	title	The title for the dialog box frame
	initialColor	The initial color to show in the color chooser

- `static JDialog createDialog(Component parent, String title, boolean modal, JColorChooser chooser, ActionListener okListener, ActionListener cancelListener)`

  creates a dialog box that contains a color chooser.

Parameters:	parent	The component over which to pop up the dialog
	title	The title for the dialog box frame
	modal	true if this call should block until the dialog is closed
	chooser	The color chooser to add to the dialog
	okListener, cancelListener	The listeners of the OK and Cancel buttons

---

12.8 Troubleshooting GUI Programs

In the next section, we will give a few debugging tips for GUI programming. Then, we will show you how to use the AWT robot to automate GUI testing.

12.8.1 Debugging Tips

If you ever looked at a Swing window and wondered how its designer managed to get all the components to line up so nicely, you can spy on the contents. Press Ctrl+Shift+F1 to get a printout of all components in the hierarchy:

```
FontDialog[frame0,0,0,300x200,layout=java.awt.BorderLayout,...
   javax.swing.JRootPane[,4,23,292x173,layout=javax.swing.JRootPane$RootLayout,...
      javax.swing.JPanel[null.glassPane,0,0,292x173,hidden,layout=java.awt.FlowLayout,...
      javax.swing.JLayeredPane[null.layeredPane,0,0,292x173,...
         javax.swing.JPanel[null.contentPane,0,0,292x173,layout=java.awt.GridBagLayout,...
            javax.swing.JList[,0,0,73x152,alignmentX=null,alignmentY=null,...
```

```
javax.swing.CellRendererPane[,0,0,0x0,hidden]
    javax.swing.DefaultListCellRenderer$UIResource[,-73,-19,0x0,...
javax.swing.JCheckBox[,157,13,50x25,layout=javax.swing.OverlayLayout,...
javax.swing.JCheckBox[,156,65,52x25,layout=javax.swing.OverlayLayout,...
javax.swing.JLabel[,114,119,30x17,alignmentX=0.0,alignmentY=null,...
javax.swing.JTextField[,186,117,105x21,alignmentX=null,alignmentY=null,...
javax.swing.JTextField[,0,152,291x21,alignmentX=null,alignmentY=null,...
```

If you design your own custom Swing component and it doesn't seem to be displayed correctly, you'll really love the *Swing graphics debugger*. Even if you don't write your own component classes, it is instructive and fun to see exactly how the contents of a component are drawn. To turn on debugging for a Swing component, use the `setDebugGraphicsOptions` method of the `JComponent` class. The following options are available:

`DebugGraphics.FLASH_OPTION`	Flashes each line, rectangle, and text in red before drawing it
`DebugGraphics.LOG_OPTION`	Prints a message for each drawing operation
`DebugGraphics.BUFFERED_OPTION`	Displays the operations that are performed on the off-screen buffer
`DebugGraphics.NONE_OPTION`	Turns graphics debugging off

We have found that for the flash option to work, you must disable "double buffering"—the strategy used by Swing to reduce flicker when updating a window. The magic incantation for turning on the flash option is

```
RepaintManager.currentManager(getRootPane()).setDoubleBufferingEnabled(false);
((JComponent) getContentPane()).setDebugGraphicsOptions(DebugGraphics.FLASH_OPTION);
```

Simply place these lines at the end of your frame constructor. When the program runs, you will see the content pane filled in slow motion. Or, for more localized debugging, just call `setDebugGraphicsOptions` for a single component. Control freaks can set the duration, count, and color of the flashes—see the online documentation of the `DebugGraphics` class for details.

If you want to get a record of every AWT event generated in your GUI application, you can install a listener in every component that emits events. This is easily automated, due to the power of reflection. Listing 12.25 shows the `EventTracer` class.

To spy on messages, add the component whose events you want to trace to an event tracer:

```
EventTracer tracer = new EventTracer();
tracer.add(frame);
```

You will then get a textual description of all events, as shown in Figure 12.45.

Listing 12.25 eventTracer/EventTracer.java

```java
1  package eventTracer;
2
3  import java.awt.*;
4  import java.beans.*;
5  import java.lang.reflect.*;
6
7  /**
8   * @version 1.31 2004-05-10
9   * @author Cay Horstmann
10  */
11 public class EventTracer
12 {
13    private InvocationHandler handler;
14
15    public EventTracer()
16    {
17       // the handler for all event proxies
18       handler = new InvocationHandler()
19          {
20             public Object invoke(Object proxy, Method method, Object[] args)
21             {
22                System.out.println(method + ":" + args[0]);
23                return null;
24             }
25          };
26    }
27
28    /**
29     * Adds event tracers for all events to which this component and its children can listen
30     * @param c a component
31     */
32    public void add(Component c)
33    {
34       try
35       {
36          // get all events to which this component can listen
37          BeanInfo info = Introspector.getBeanInfo(c.getClass());
38
39          EventSetDescriptor[] eventSets = info.getEventSetDescriptors();
40          for (EventSetDescriptor eventSet : eventSets)
41             addListener(c, eventSet);
42       }
43       catch (IntrospectionException e)
44       {
45       }
46       // ok not to add listeners if exception is thrown
47
```

```
48    if (c instanceof Container)
49    {
50       // get all children and call add recursively
51       for (Component comp : ((Container) c).getComponents())
52          add(comp);
53    }
54 }
55
56 /**
57  * Add a listener to the given event set
58  * @param c a component
59  * @param eventSet a descriptor of a listener interface
60  */
61 public void addListener(Component c, EventSetDescriptor eventSet)
62 {
63    // make proxy object for this listener type and route all calls to the handler
64    Object proxy = Proxy.newProxyInstance(null, new Class[] { eventSet.getListenerType() },
65       handler);
66
67    // add the proxy as a listener to the component
68    Method addListenerMethod = eventSet.getAddListenerMethod();
69    try
70    {
71       addListenerMethod.invoke(c, proxy);
72    }
73    catch (ReflectiveOperationException e)
74    {
75    }
76    // ok not to add listener if exception is thrown
77 }
78 }
```

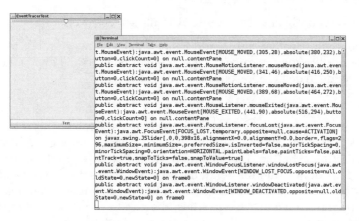

Figure 12.45 The EventTracer class at work

12.8.2 Letting the AWT Robot Do the Work

The Robot class can send keystrokes and mouse clicks to any AWT program. This class is intended for automatic testing of user interfaces.

To get a robot, you need to first get a GraphicsDevice object. You can get the default screen device via this sequence of calls:

```
GraphicsEnvironment environment = GraphicsEnvironment.getLocalGraphicsEnvironment();
GraphicsDevice screen = environment.getDefaultScreenDevice();
```

Then you construct a robot:

```
Robot robot = new Robot(screen);
```

To send a keystroke, tell the robot to simulate a key press and a key release:

```
robot.keyPress(KeyEvent.VK_TAB);
robot.keyRelease(KeyEvent.VK_TAB);
```

For a mouse click, you first need to move the mouse and then press and release a button:

```
robot.mouseMove(x, y); // x and y are absolute screen pixel coordinates.
robot.mousePress(InputEvent.BUTTON1_MASK);
robot.mouseRelease(InputEvent.BUTTON1_MASK);
```

The idea is that you simulate key and mouse input and then take a screenshot to see whether the application did what it was supposed to. To capture the screen, use the createScreenCapture method:

```
Rectangle rect = new Rectangle(x, y, width, height);
BufferedImage image = robot.createScreenCapture(rect);
```

The rectangle coordinates also refer to absolute screen pixels.

Finally, you will usually want to add a small delay between robot instructions so that the application can catch up. Use the delay method and give it the number of milliseconds to delay. For example:

```
robot.delay(1000); // delay by 1000 milliseconds
```

The program in Listing 12.26 shows how you can use a robot. This robot tests the button test program that you saw in Chapter 11. First, pressing the space bar activates the leftmost button. Then the robot waits for two seconds so that you can see what it has done. After the delay, the robot simulates the Tab key and another space bar press to click on the next button. Finally, it simulates a mouse click on the third button. (You may need to adjust the x and y coordinates of the program to actually press the buttons.) The program ends by taking a screen capture and displaying it in another frame (see Figure 12.46).

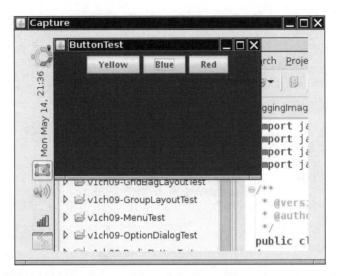

Figure 12.46 Capturing the screen with the AWT robot

 NOTE: You need to run the robot in a separate thread, as shown in the example code. See Chapter 14 for more information about threads.

As you can see from this example, the `Robot` class is not by itself suitable for convenient user interface testing. Instead, it is a basic building block that can be a foundational part of a testing tool. A professional testing tool can capture, store, and replay user interaction scenarios and find out the screen locations of the components so that mouse clicks aren't guesswork.

Listing 12.26 `robot/RobotTest.java`

```
1  package robot;
2
3  import java.awt.*;
4  import java.awt.event.*;
5  import java.awt.image.*;
6  import javax.swing.*;
7
8  /**
9   * @version 1.05 2015-08-20
10  * @author Cay Horstmann
11  */
```

(Continues)

Listing 12.26 *(Continued)*

```java
12  public class RobotTest
13  {
14     public static void main(String[] args)
15     {
16        EventQueue.invokeLater(() ->
17           {
18              // make frame with a button panel
19
20              ButtonFrame frame = new ButtonFrame();
21              frame.setTitle("ButtonTest");
22              frame.setDefaultCloseOperation(JFrame.EXIT_ON_CLOSE);
23              frame.setVisible(true);
24           });
25
26        // attach a robot to the screen device
27
28        GraphicsEnvironment environment = GraphicsEnvironment.getLocalGraphicsEnvironment();
29        GraphicsDevice screen = environment.getDefaultScreenDevice();
30
31        try
32        {
33           final Robot robot = new Robot(screen);
34           robot.waitForIdle();
35           new Thread()
36           {
37              public void run()
38              {
39                 runTest(robot);
40              };
41           }.start();
42        }
43        catch (AWTException e)
44        {
45           e.printStackTrace();
46        }
47     }
48
49     /**
50      * Runs a sample test procedure
51      * @param robot the robot attached to the screen device
52      */
53     public static void runTest(Robot robot)
54     {
```

```
55        // simulate a space bar press
56        robot.keyPress(' ');
57        robot.keyRelease(' ');
58
59        // simulate a tab key followed by a space
60        robot.delay(2000);
61        robot.keyPress(KeyEvent.VK_TAB);
62        robot.keyRelease(KeyEvent.VK_TAB);
63        robot.keyPress(' ');
64        robot.keyRelease(' ');
65
66        // simulate a mouse click over the rightmost button
67        robot.delay(2000);
68        robot.mouseMove(220, 40);
69        robot.mousePress(InputEvent.BUTTON1_MASK);
70        robot.mouseRelease(InputEvent.BUTTON1_MASK);
71
72        // capture the screen and show the resulting image
73        robot.delay(2000);
74        BufferedImage image = robot.createScreenCapture(new Rectangle(0, 0, 400, 300));
75
76        ImageFrame frame = new ImageFrame(image);
77        frame.setVisible(true);
78    }
79 }
80
81 /**
82  * A frame to display a captured image
83  */
84 class ImageFrame extends JFrame
85 {
86    private static final int DEFAULT_WIDTH = 450;
87    private static final int DEFAULT_HEIGHT = 350;
88
89    /**
90     * @param image the image to display
91     */
92    public ImageFrame(Image image)
93    {
94       setTitle("Capture");
95       setSize(DEFAULT_WIDTH, DEFAULT_HEIGHT);
96
97       JLabel label = new JLabel(new ImageIcon(image));
98       add(label);
99    }
100 }
```

---

java.awt.GraphicsEnvironment 1.2

- `static GraphicsEnvironment getLocalGraphicsEnvironment()`

  returns the local graphics environment.

- `GraphicsDevice getDefaultScreenDevice()`

  returns the default screen device. Note that computers with multiple monitors have one graphics device per screen—use the `getScreenDevices` method to obtain an array of all screen devices.

---

java.awt.Robot 1.3

- `Robot(GraphicsDevice device)`

  constructs a robot that can interact with the given device.

- `void keyPress(int key)`
- `void keyRelease(int key)`

  simulates a key press or release.

  Parameters: key   The key code. See the `KeyStroke` class for more information on key codes.

- `void mouseMove(int x, int y)`

  simulates a mouse move.

  Parameters: x, y   The mouse position in absolute pixel coordinates

- `void mousePress(int eventMask)`
- `void mouseRelease(int eventMask)`

  simulates a mouse button press or release.

  Parameters: eventMask   The event mask describing the mouse buttons. See the `InputEvent` class for more information on event masks.

- `void delay(int milliseconds)`

  delays the robot for the given number of milliseconds.

- `BufferedImage createScreenCapture(Rectangle rect)`

  captures a portion of the screen.

  Parameters: rect   The rectangle to be captured, in absolute pixel coordinates

---

This ends our discussion of user interface components. The material in Chapters 10 through 12 showed you how to implement simple GUIs in Swing. Turn to Volume II for more advanced Swing components and sophisticated graphics techniques.

CHAPTER **13**

Deploying Java Applications

In this chapter

At this point, you should be comfortable with using most of the features of the Java programming language, and you've had a pretty thorough introduction to basic graphics programming in Java. Now that you are ready to create applications for your users, you will want to know how to package them for deployment on your users' computers. The traditional deployment choice—which was responsible for the unbelievable hype during the first few years of Java's life—is to use *applets*. An applet is a special kind of Java program that a Java-enabled browser can download from the Internet and run. The hopes were that users would be freed from the hassles of installing software and that they could access their software from any Java-enabled computer or device with an Internet connection.

For a number of reasons, applets never quite lived up to these expectations. Therefore, we will start this chapter with instructions for packaging applications. We then show how your applications can store configuration information and user preferences. You will also learn how to use the ServiceLoader class to load plug-ins into your applications.

Then, we turn to applets and show you what you need to know in case you need to create or maintain them. We also discuss *Java Web Start* mechanism—an alternative approach for Internet-based application delivery which is in many ways similar to applets, but more suitable for programs that do not live in a web page.

13.1 JAR Files

When you package your application, you want to give your users a single file, not a directory structure filled with class files. Java Archive (JAR) files were designed for this purpose. A JAR file can contain both class files and other file types such as image and sound files. Moreover, JAR files are compressed, using the familiar ZIP compression format.

TIP: An alternative to the ZIP format is the "pack200" compression scheme that is specifically tuned to compress class files more efficiently. Oracle claims a compression rate of close to 90% for class files. See http://docs.oracle.com/javase/1.5.0/docs/guide/deployment/deployment-guide/pack200.html for more information.

13.1.1 Creating JAR files

Use the jar tool to make JAR files. (In the default JDK installation, it's in the *jdk*/bin directory.) The most common command to make a new JAR file uses the following syntax:

```
jar cvf JARFileName File1 File2 . . .
```

For example:

```
jar cvf CalculatorClasses.jar *.class icon.gif
```

In general, the jar command has the following format:

```
jar options File1 File2 . . .
```

Table 13.1 lists all the options for the jar program. They are similar to the options of the UNIX tar command.

You can package application programs, program components (sometimes called "beans"—see Chapter 11 of Volume II), and code libraries into JAR files. For example, the runtime library of the JDK is contained in a very large file rt.jar.

Table 13.1 jar Program Options

Option	Description
c	Creates a new or empty archive and adds files to it. If any of the specified file names are directories, the jar program processes them recursively.
C	Temporarily changes the directory. For example, `jar cvf JARFileName.jar -C classes *.class` changes to the classes subdirectory to add class files.
e	Creates an entry point in the manifest (see Section 13.1.3).
f	Specifies the JAR file name as the second command-line argument. If this parameter is missing, jar will write the result to standard output (when creating a JAR file) or read it from standard input (when extracting or tabulating a JAR file).
i	Creates an index file (for speeding up lookups in a large archive).
m	Adds a *manifest* to the JAR file. A manifest is a description of the archive contents and origin. Every archive has a default manifest, but you can supply your own if you want to authenticate the contents of the archive.
M	Does not create a manifest file for the entries.
t	Displays the table of contents.
u	Updates an existing JAR file.
v	Generates verbose output.
x	Extracts files. If you supply one or more file names, only those files are extracted. Otherwise, all files are extracted.
0	Stores without ZIP compression.

13.1.2 The Manifest

In addition to class files, images, and other resources, each JAR file contains a *manifest* file that describes special features of the archive.

The manifest file is called MANIFEST.MF and is located in a special META-INF subdirectory of the JAR file. The minimum legal manifest is quite boring—just

```
Manifest-Version: 1.0
```

Complex manifests can have many more entries. The manifest entries are grouped into sections. The first section in the manifest is called the *main section*. It applies to the whole JAR file. Subsequent entries can specify properties of named entities such as individual files, packages, or URLs. Those entries must begin with a `Name` entry. Sections are separated by blank lines. For example:

```
Manifest-Version: 1.0
lines describing this archive

Name: Woozle.class
lines describing this file
Name: com/mycompany/mypkg/
lines describing this package
```

To edit the manifest, place the lines that you want to add to the manifest into a text file. Then run

```
jar cfm JARFileName ManifestFileName . . .
```

For example, to make a new JAR file with a manifest, run

```
jar cfm MyArchive.jar manifest.mf com/mycompany/mypkg/*.class
```

To update the manifest of an existing JAR file, place the additions into a text file and use a command such as

```
jar ufm MyArchive.jar manifest-additions.mf
```

 NOTE: See `http://docs.oracle.com/javase/8/docs/technotes/guides/jar` for more information on the JAR and manifest file formats.

13.1.3 Executable JAR Files

You can use the `e` option of the `jar` command to specify the *entry point* of your program—the class that you would normally specify when invoking the `java` program launcher:

```
jar cvfe MyProgram.jar com.mycompany.mypkg.MainAppClass files to add
```

Alternatively, you can specify the *main class* of your program in the manifest, including a statement of the form

```
Main-Class: com.mycompany.mypkg.MainAppClass
```

Do not add a `.class` extension to the main class name.

 CAUTION: The last line in the manifest must end with a newline character. Otherwise, the manifest will not be read correctly. It is a common error to produce a text file containing just the `Main-Class` line without a line terminator.

With either method, users can simply start the program as

```
java -jar MyProgram.jar
```

Depending on the operating system configuration, users may even be able to launch the application by double-clicking the JAR file icon. Here are behaviors for various operating systems:

- On Windows, the Java runtime installer creates a file association for the ".jar" extension that launches the file with the javaw -jar command. (Unlike the java command, the javaw command doesn't open a shell window.)
- On Solaris, the operating system recognizes the "magic number" of a JAR file and starts it with the java -jar command.
- On Mac OS X, the operating system recognizes the ".jar" file extension and executes the Java program when you double-click a JAR file.

However, a Java program in a JAR file does not have the same feel as a native application. On Windows, you can use third-party wrapper utilities that turn JAR files into Windows executables. A wrapper is a Windows program with the familiar .exe extension that locates and launches the Java virtual machine (JVM) or tells the user what to do when no JVM is found. There are a number of commercial and open source products, such as Launch4J (http://launch4j.sourceforge.net) and IzPack (http://izpack.org).

On the Macintosh, the situation is a bit easier. The Jar Bundler utility that is a part of XCode lets you turn a JAR file into a first-class Mac application.

13.1.4 Resources

Classes used in both applets and applications often have associated data files, such as:

- Image and sound files
- Text files with message strings and button labels
- Files with binary data—for example, to describe the layout of a map

In Java, such an associated file is called a *resource*.

NOTE: In Windows, the term "resource" has a more specialized meaning. Windows resources also consist of images, button labels, and so on, but they are attached to the executable file and accessed by a standard programming interface. In contrast, Java resources are stored as separate files, not as part of class files. It is up to each program to access and interpret the resource data.

For example, consider a class AboutPanel that displays a message such as the one in Figure 13.1.

Figure 13.1 Displaying a resource from a JAR file

Of course, the book title and copyright year in the panel will change for the next edition of the book. To make it easy to track this change, we will put the text inside a file and not hardcode it as a string.

But where should you put a file such as about.txt? Of course, it would be convenient to simply place it with the rest of the program files inside the JAR file.

The class loader knows how to search for class files until it has located them somewhere on the class path, or in an archive, or on a web server. The resource mechanism gives you the same convenience for files that aren't class files. Here are the necessary steps:

1. Get the Class object of the class that has a resource—for example, AboutPanel.class.
2. If the resource is an image or audio file, call getResource(filename) to get the resource location as a URL. Then read it with the getImage or getAudioClip method.
3. For resources other than images or audio files, use the getResourceAsStream method to read the data in the file.

The point is that the class loader remembers how to locate the class, so it can then search for the associated resource in the same location.

For example, to make an icon with the image file about.gif, do the following:

```
URL url = ResourceTest.class.getResource("about.gif");
Image img = new ImageIcon(url).getImage();
```

That means "locate the about.gif file in the same place where you found the ResourceTest class."

To read in the file about.txt, use these commands:

```
InputStream stream = ResourceTest.class.getResourceAsStream("about.txt");
Scanner in = new Scanner(stream, "UTF-8");
```

Instead of placing a resource file inside the same directory as the class file, you can place it in a subdirectory. You can then use a hierarchical resource name such as

```
data/text/about.txt
```

This resource name is interpreted relative to the package of the class that loads the resource. Note that you must always use the / separator, regardless of the directory separator on the system that actually stores the resource files. For example, on the Windows file system, the resource loader automatically translates / to \ separators.

A resource name starting with a / is called an absolute resource name. It is located in the same way a class inside a package would be located. For example, a resource

```
/corejava/title.txt
```

is located in the corejava directory which may be a subdirectory of the class path, inside a JAR file, or, for applets, on a web server.

Automating the loading of files is all the resource loading feature does. There are no standard methods for interpreting the contents of resource files. Each program must have its own way of interpreting its resource files.

Another common application of resources is the internationalization of programs. Language-dependent strings, such as messages and user interface labels, are stored in resource files, with one file per language. The *internationalization API*, which is discussed in Chapter 5 of Volume II, supports a standard method for organizing and accessing these localization files.

Listing 13.1 is a program that demonstrates resource loading. Compile, build a JAR file, and execute it:

```
javac resource/ResourceTest.java
jar cvfm ResourceTest.jar resource/ResourceTest.mf resource/*.class resource/*.gif resource/*.txt
java -jar ResourceTest.jar
```

Move the JAR file to a different directory and run it again to check that the program reads the resource files from the JAR file, not from the current directory.

Listing 13.1   resource/ResourceTest.java

```
1  package resource;
2
3  import java.awt.*;
4  import java.io.*;
5  import java.net.*;
6  import java.util.*;
7  import javax.swing.*;
8
9  /**
10  * @version 1.41 2015-06-12
11  * @author Cay Horstmann
12  */
13 public class ResourceTest
14 {
15    public static void main(String[] args)
16    {
17       EventQueue.invokeLater(() -> {
18          JFrame frame = new ResourceTestFrame();
19          frame.setTitle("ResourceTest");
20          frame.setDefaultCloseOperation(JFrame.EXIT_ON_CLOSE);
21          frame.setVisible(true);
22       });
23    }
24 }
25
26 /**
27  * A frame that loads image and text resources.
28  */
29 class ResourceTestFrame extends JFrame
30 {
31    private static final int DEFAULT_WIDTH = 300;
32    private static final int DEFAULT_HEIGHT = 300;
33
34    public ResourceTestFrame()
35    {
36       setSize(DEFAULT_WIDTH, DEFAULT_HEIGHT);
37       URL aboutURL = getClass().getResource("about.gif");
38       Image img = new ImageIcon(aboutURL).getImage();
39       setIconImage(img);
40
41       JTextArea textArea = new JTextArea();
42       InputStream stream = getClass().getResourceAsStream("about.txt");
43       try (Scanner in = new Scanner(stream, "UTF-8"))
44       {
45          while (in.hasNext())
46             textArea.append(in.nextLine() + "\n");
47       }
```

```
48        add(textArea);
49      }
50    }
```

---

java.lang.Class 1.0

- URL getResource(String name) 1.1
- InputStream getResourceAsStream(String name) 1.1

  finds the resource in the same place as the class and then returns a URL or input stream that you can use for loading the resource. Returns null if the resource isn't found, so does not throw an exception for an I/O error.

13.1.5 Sealing

We mentioned in Chapter 4 that you can *seal* a Java language package to ensure that no further classes can add themselves to it. You would want to seal a package if you use package-visible classes, methods, and fields in your code. Without sealing, other classes can place themselves into the same package and thereby gain access to its package-visible features.

For example, if you seal the package com.mycompany.util, then no class outside the sealed archive can be defined with the statement

```
package com.mycompany.util;
```

To achieve this, put all classes of the package into a JAR file. By default, packages in a JAR file are not sealed. You can change that global default by placing the line

```
Sealed: true
```

into the main section of the manifest. For each individual package, you can specify whether you want the package sealed or not, by adding another section to the JAR file manifest, like this:

```
Name: com/mycompany/util/
Sealed: true

Name: com/mycompany/misc/
Sealed: false
```

To seal a package, make a text file with the manifest instructions. Then run the jar command in the usual way:

```
jar cvfm MyArchive.jar manifest.mf files to add
```

13.2 Storage of Application Preferences

Users of your applications will usually expect that their preferences and customizations are saved and later restored when the application starts again. First, we will cover the simple approach that Java applications have traditionally taken—storing configuration information in property files. We then turn to the preferences API that provides a more robust solution.

13.2.1 Property Maps

A *property map* is a data structure that stores key/value pairs. Property maps are often used for storing configuration information. Property maps have three particular characteristics:

*   The keys and values are strings.
*   The map can easily be saved to a file and loaded from a file.
*   There is a secondary table for default values.

The Java class that implements a property map is called `Properties`.

Property maps are useful in specifying configuration options for programs. For example:

```
Properties settings = new Properties();
settings.setProperty("width", "200");
settings.setProperty("title", "Hello, World!");
```

Use the `store` method to save map list of properties to a file. Here, we just save the property map in the file `program.properties`. The second argument is a comment that is included in the file.

```
OutputStream out = new FileOutputStream("program.properties");
settings.store(out, "Program Properties");
```

The sample set gives the following output:

```
#Program Properties
#Mon Apr 30 07:22:52  2007
width=200
title=Hello, World!
```

To load the properties from a file, use

```
InputStream in = new FileInputStream("program.properties");
settings.load(in);
```

It is customary to store program properties in a subdirectory of the user's home directory. The directory name is often chosen to start with a dot—on a UNIX system, this convention indicates a system directory which is hidden from the user. Our sample program follows this convention.

To find the user's home directory, you can call the System.getProperties method, which, as it happens, also uses a Properties object to describe the system information. The home directory has the key "user.home". There is also a convenience method to read a single key:

```
String userDir = System.getProperty("user.home");
```

It is a good idea to provide defaults for our program properties, in case a user edits the file by hand. The Properties class has two mechanisms for providing defaults. First, whenever you look up the value of a string, you can specify a default that should be used automatically when the key is not present.

```
String title = settings.getProperty("title", "Default title");
```

If there is a "title" property in the property map, title is set to that string. Otherwise, title is set to "Default title".

If you find it too tedious to specify the default in every call to getProperty, you can pack all the defaults into a secondary property map and supply that map in the constructor of your primary property map.

```
Properties defaultSettings = new Properties();
defaultSettings.setProperty("width", "300");
defaultSettings.setProperty("height", "200");
defaultSettings.setProperty("title", "Default title");
. . .
Properties settings = new Properties(defaultSettings);
```

Yes, you can even specify defaults to defaults if you give another property map parameter to the defaultSettings constructor, but it is not something one would normally do.

Listing 13.2 shows how you can use properties for storing and loading program state. The program remembers the frame position, size, and title. You can also manually edit the file .corejava/program.properties in your home directory to change the program's appearance to the way *you* want.

 CAUTION: For historical reasons, the Properties class implements Map<Object, Object>. Therefore, you can use the get and put methods of the Map interface. But the get method returns the type Object, and the put method allows you to insert any object. It is best to stick with the getProperty and setProperty methods that work with strings, not objects.

NOTE: Properties are simple tables without a hierarchical structure. It is common to introduce a fake hierarchy with key names such as `window.main.color`, `window.main.title`, and so on. But the `Properties` class has no methods that help organize such a hierarchy. If you store complex configuration information, you should use the `Preferences` class instead—see the next section.

Listing 13.2 properties/PropertiesTest.java

```
1  package properties;
2
3  import java.awt.EventQueue;
4  import java.awt.event.*;
5  import java.io.*;
6  import java.util.Properties;
7
8  import javax.swing.*;
9
10 /**
11  * A program to test properties. The program remembers the frame position, size,
12  * and title.
13  * @version 1.01 2015-06-16
14  * @author Cay Horstmann
15  */
16 public class PropertiesTest
17 {
18    public static void main(String[] args)
19    {
20       EventQueue.invokeLater(() -> {
21          PropertiesFrame frame = new PropertiesFrame();
22          frame.setVisible(true);
23       });
24    }
25 }
26
27 /**
28  * A frame that restores position and size from a properties file and updates
29  * the properties upon exit.
30  */
31 class PropertiesFrame extends JFrame
32 {
33    private static final int DEFAULT_WIDTH = 300;
34    private static final int DEFAULT_HEIGHT = 200;
35
36    private File propertiesFile;
37    private Properties settings;
38
39    public PropertiesFrame()
40    {
```

```
41      // get position, size, title from properties
42
43      String userDir = System.getProperty("user.home");
44      File propertiesDir = new File(userDir, ".corejava");
45      if (!propertiesDir.exists()) propertiesDir.mkdir();
46      propertiesFile = new File(propertiesDir, "program.properties");
47
48      Properties defaultSettings = new Properties();
49      defaultSettings.setProperty("left", "0");
50      defaultSettings.setProperty("top", "0");
51      defaultSettings.setProperty("width", "" + DEFAULT_WIDTH);
52      defaultSettings.setProperty("height", "" + DEFAULT_HEIGHT);
53      defaultSettings.setProperty("title", "");
54
55      settings = new Properties(defaultSettings);
56
57      if (propertiesFile.exists())
58         try (InputStream in = new FileInputStream(propertiesFile))
59         {
60            settings.load(in);
61         }
62         catch (IOException ex)
63         {
64            ex.printStackTrace();
65         }
66
67      int left = Integer.parseInt(settings.getProperty("left"));
68      int top = Integer.parseInt(settings.getProperty("top"));
69      int width = Integer.parseInt(settings.getProperty("width"));
70      int height = Integer.parseInt(settings.getProperty("height"));
71      setBounds(left, top, width, height);
72
73      // if no title given, ask user
74
75      String title = settings.getProperty("title");
76      if (title.equals(""))
77         title = JOptionPane.showInputDialog("Please supply a frame title:");
78      if (title == null) title = "";
79      setTitle(title);
80
81      addWindowListener(new WindowAdapter()
82      {
83         public void windowClosing(WindowEvent event)
84         {
85            settings.setProperty("left", "" + getX());
86            settings.setProperty("top", "" + getY());
87            settings.setProperty("width", "" + getWidth());
88            settings.setProperty("height", "" + getHeight());
89            settings.setProperty("title", getTitle());
```

(Continues)

Listing 13.2 *(Continued)*

```
90          try (OutputStream out = new FileOutputStream(propertiesFile))
91          {
92              settings.store(out, "Program Properties");
93          }
94          catch (IOException ex)
95          {
96              ex.printStackTrace();
97          }
98          System.exit(0);
99       }
100    });
101    }
102 }
```

---

java.util.Properties 1.0

- `Properties()`

  creates an empty property map.

- `Properties(Properties defaults)`

  creates an empty property map with a set of defaults.

  Parameters: `defaults`   The defaults to use for lookups

- `String getProperty(String key)`

  gets a property. Returns the string associated with the key, or the string associated with the key in the default table if it wasn't present in the table, or `null` if the key wasn't present in the default table either.

  Parameters: `key`   The key whose associated string to get

- `String getProperty(String key, String defaultValue)`

  gets a property with a default value if the key is not found. Returns the string associated with the key, or the default string if it wasn't present in the table.

  Parameters: `key`   The key whose associated string to get

                    `defaultValue`   The string to return if the key is not present

- `Object setProperty(String key, String value)`

  sets a property. Returns the previously set value of the given key.

  Parameters: `key`   The key whose associated string to set

                    `value`   The value to associate with the key

(Continues)

---

java.util.Properties 1.0 *(Continued)*

- void load(InputStream in) throws IOException

  loads a property map from an input stream.

  Parameters: in   The input stream

- void store(OutputStream out, String header) 1.2

  saves a property map to an output stream.

  Parameters: out   The output stream

                   header   The header in the first line of the stored file

---

java.lang.System 1.0

- Properties getProperties()

  retrieves all system properties. The application must have permission to retrieve all properties, or a security exception is thrown.

- String getProperty(String key)

  retrieves the system property with the given key name. The application must have permission to retrieve the property, or a security exception is thrown. The following properties can always be retrieved:

  ```
  java.version
  java.vendor
  java.vendor.url
  java.class.version
  os.name
  os.version
  os.arch
  file.separator
  path.separator
  line.separator
  java.specification.version
  java.vm.specification.version
  java.vm.specification.vendor
  java.vm.specification.name
  java.vm.version
  java.vm.vendor
  java.vm.name
  ```

 NOTE: You can find the names of the freely accessible system properties in the file security/java.policy in the directory of the Java runtime.

13.2.2 The Preferences API

As you have seen, the Properties class makes it simple to load and save configuration information. However, using property files has these disadvantages:

- Some operating systems have no concept of a home directory, making it difficult to find a uniform location for configuration files.

- There is no standard convention for naming configuration files, increasing the likelihood of name clashes as users install multiple Java applications.

Some operating systems have a central repository for configuration information. The best-known example is the registry in Microsoft Windows. The Preferences class provides such a central repository in a platform-independent manner. In Windows, the Preferences class uses the registry for storage; on Linux, the information is stored in the local file system instead. Of course, the repository implementation is transparent to the programmer using the Preferences class.

The Preferences repository has a tree structure, with node path names such as /com/mycompany/myapp. As with package names, name clashes are avoided as long as programmers start the paths with reversed domain names. In fact, the designers of the API suggest that the configuration node paths match the package names in your program.

Each node in the repository has a separate table of key/value pairs that you can use to store numbers, strings, or byte arrays. No provision is made for storing serializable objects. The API designers felt that the serialization format is too fragile for long-term storage. Of course, if you disagree, you can save serialized objects in byte arrays.

For additional flexibility, there are multiple parallel trees. Each program user has one tree; an additional tree, called the system tree, is available for settings that are common to all users. The Preferences class uses the operating system notion of the "current user" for accessing the appropriate user tree.

To access a node in the tree, start with the user or system root:

```
Preferences root = Preferences.userRoot();
```

or

```
Preferences root = Preferences.systemRoot();
```

Then access the node. You can simply provide a node path name:

```
Preferences node = root.node("/com/mycompany/myapp");
```

A convenient shortcut gets a node whose path name equals the package name of a class. Simply take an object of that class and call

```
Preferences node = Preferences.userNodeForPackage(obj.getClass());
```

or

```
Preferences node = Preferences.systemNodeForPackage(obj.getClass());
```

Typically, `obj` will be the `this` reference.

Once you have a node, you can access the key/value table with methods

```
String get(String key, String defval)
int getInt(String key, int defval)
long getLong(String key, long defval)
float getFloat(String key, float defval)
double getDouble(String key, double defval)
boolean getBoolean(String key, boolean defval)
byte[] getByteArray(String key, byte[] defval)
```

Note that you must specify a default value when reading the information, in case the repository data is not available. Defaults are required for several reasons. The data might be missing because the user never specified a preference. Certain resource-constrained platforms might not have a repository, and mobile devices might be temporarily disconnected from the repository.

Conversely, you can write data to the repository with `put` methods such as

```
put(String key, String value)
putInt(String key, int value)
```

and so on.

You can enumerate all keys stored in a node with the method

```
String[] keys()
```

There is currently no way to find out the type of the value of a particular key.

Central repositories such as the Windows registry traditionally suffer from two problems:

- They turn into a "dumping ground," filled with obsolete information.
- Configuration data gets entangled into the repository, making it difficult to move preferences to a new platform.

The `Preferences` class has a solution for the second problem. You can export the preferences of a subtree (or, less commonly, a single node) by calling the methods

```
void exportSubtree(OutputStream out)
void exportNode(OutputStream out)
```

The data are saved in XML format. You can import them into another repository by calling

```
void importPreferences(InputStream in)
```

Here is a sample file:

```xml
<?xml version="1.0" encoding="UTF-8"?>
<!DOCTYPE preferences SYSTEM "http://java.sun.com/dtd/preferences.dtd">
<preferences EXTERNAL_XML_VERSION="1.0">
    <root type="user">
      <map/>
      <node name="com">
        <map/>
        <node name="horstmann">
          <map/>
          <node name="corejava">
            <map>
              <entry key="left" value="11"/>
              <entry key="top" value="9"/>
              <entry key="width" value="453"/>
              <entry key="height" value="365"/>
              <entry key="title" value="Hello, World!"/>
            </map>
          </node>
        </node>
      </node>
    </root>
</preferences>
```

If your program uses preferences, you should give your users the opportunity of exporting and importing them, so they can easily migrate their settings from one computer to another. The program in Listing 13.3 demonstrates this technique. The program simply saves the position, size, and title of the main window. Try resizing the window, then exit and restart the application. The window will be just like you left it when you exited.

Listing 13.3 preferences/PreferencesTest.java

```java
1  package preferences;
2
3  import java.awt.*;
4  import java.io.*;
5  import java.util.prefs.*;
6
7  import javax.swing.*;
8  import javax.swing.filechooser.*;
9
10 /**
11  * A program to test preference settings. The program remembers the frame
12  * position, size, and title.
```

```
13     * @version 1.03 2015-06-12
14     * @author Cay Horstmann
15     */
16    public class PreferencesTest
17    {
18       public static void main(String[] args)
19       {
20          EventQueue.invokeLater(() -> {
21             PreferencesFrame frame = new PreferencesFrame();
22             frame.setDefaultCloseOperation(JFrame.EXIT_ON_CLOSE);
23             frame.setVisible(true);
24          });
25       }
26    }
27
28    /**
29     * A frame that restores position and size from user preferences and updates the
30     * preferences upon exit.
31     */
32    class PreferencesFrame extends JFrame
33    {
34       private static final int DEFAULT_WIDTH = 300;
35       private static final int DEFAULT_HEIGHT = 200;
36       private Preferences root = Preferences.userRoot();
37       private Preferences node = root.node("/com/horstmann/corejava");
38
39       public PreferencesFrame()
40       {
41          // get position, size, title from preferences
42
43          int left = node.getInt("left", 0);
44          int top = node.getInt("top", 0);
45          int width = node.getInt("width", DEFAULT_WIDTH);
46          int height = node.getInt("height", DEFAULT_HEIGHT);
47          setBounds(left, top, width, height);
48
49          // if no title given, ask user
50
51          String title = node.get("title", "");
52          if (title.equals(""))
53             title = JOptionPane.showInputDialog("Please supply a frame title:");
54          if (title == null) title = "";
55          setTitle(title);
56
57          // set up file chooser that shows XML files
58
59          final JFileChooser chooser = new JFileChooser();
60          chooser.setCurrentDirectory(new File("."));
61          chooser.setFileFilter(new FileNameExtensionFilter("XML files", "xml"));
```

(Continues)

Listing 13.3 *(Continued)*

```java
62
63       // set up menus
64
65       JMenuBar menuBar = new JMenuBar();
66       setJMenuBar(menuBar);
67       JMenu menu = new JMenu("File");
68       menuBar.add(menu);
69
70       JMenuItem exportItem = new JMenuItem("Export preferences");
71       menu.add(exportItem);
72       exportItem
73           .addActionListener(event -> {
74               if (chooser.showSaveDialog(PreferencesFrame.this) == JFileChooser.APPROVE_OPTION)
75               {
76                   try
77                   {
78                       savePreferences();
79                       OutputStream out = new FileOutputStream(chooser
80                           .getSelectedFile());
81                       node.exportSubtree(out);
82                       out.close();
83                   }
84                   catch (Exception e)
85                   {
86                       e.printStackTrace();
87                   }
88               }
89           });
90
91       JMenuItem importItem = new JMenuItem("Import preferences");
92       menu.add(importItem);
93       importItem
94           .addActionListener(event -> {
95               if (chooser.showOpenDialog(PreferencesFrame.this) == JFileChooser.APPROVE_OPTION)
96               {
97                   try
98                   {
99                       InputStream in = new FileInputStream(chooser
100                          .getSelectedFile());
101                      Preferences.importPreferences(in);
102                      in.close();
103                  }
104                  catch (Exception e)
105                  {
106                      e.printStackTrace();
107                  }
108              }
109          });
```

```
110
111      JMenuItem exitItem = new JMenuItem("Exit");
112      menu.add(exitItem);
113      exitItem.addActionListener(event -> {
114         savePreferences();
115         System.exit(0);
116      });
117   }
118
119   public void savePreferences()
120   {
121      node.putInt("left", getX());
122      node.putInt("top", getY());
123      node.putInt("width", getWidth());
124      node.putInt("height", getHeight());
125      node.put("title", getTitle());
126   }
127 }
```

---

java.util.prefs.Preferences 1.4

- `Preferences userRoot()`

  returns the root preferences node of the user of the calling program.

- `Preferences systemRoot()`

  returns the systemwide root preferences node.

- `Preferences node(String path)`

  returns a node that can be reached from the current node by the given path. If `path` is absolute (that is, starts with a /), then the node is located starting from the root of the tree containing this preference node. If there isn't a node with the given path, it is created.

- `Preferences userNodeForPackage(Class cl)`
- `Preferences systemNodeForPackage(Class cl)`

  returns a node in the current user's tree or the system tree whose absolute node path corresponds to the package name of the class `cl`.

- `String[] keys()`

  returns all keys belonging to this node.

(Continues)

`java.util.prefs.Preferences` 1.4 *(Continued)*

- `String get(String key, String defval)`
- `int getInt(String key, int defval)`
- `long getLong(String key, long defval)`
- `float getFloat(String key, float defval)`
- `double getDouble(String key, double defval)`
- `boolean getBoolean(String key, boolean defval)`
- `byte[] getByteArray(String key, byte[] defval)`

    returns the value associated with the given key or the supplied default value if no value is associated with the key, the associated value is not of the correct type, or the preferences store is unavailable.

- `void put(String key, String value)`
- `void putInt(String key, int value)`
- `void putLong(String key, long value)`
- `void putFloat(String key, float value)`
- `void putDouble(String key, double value)`
- `void putBoolean(String key, boolean value)`
- `void putByteArray(String key, byte[] value)`

    stores a key/value pair with this node.

- `void exportSubtree(OutputStream out)`

    writes the preferences of this node and its children to the specified stream.

- `void exportNode(OutputStream out)`

    writes the preferences of this node (but not its children) to the specified stream.

- `void importPreferences(InputStream in)`

    imports the preferences contained in the specified stream.

13.3 Service Loaders

Sometimes, you develop an application with a plug-in architecture. There are platforms that encourage this approach, such as OSGi (http://osgi.org), which are used in development environments, application servers, and other complex applications. Such platforms go well beyond the scope of this book, but the JDK also offers a simple mechanism for loading plug-ins, which we describe here.

Often, when providing a plug-in, a program wants to give the plug-in designer some freedom of how to implement the plug-in's features. It can also be desirable to have multiple implementations to choose from. The ServiceLoader class makes it easy to load plug-ins that conform to a common interface.

Define an interface (or, if you prefer, a superclass) with the methods that each instance of the service should provide. For example, suppose your service provides encryption.

```
package serviceLoader;

public interface Cipher
{
    byte[] encrypt(byte[] source, byte[] key);
    byte[] decrypt(byte[] source, byte[] key);
    int strength();
}
```

The service provider supplies one or more classes that implement this service, for example

```
package serviceLoader.impl;

public class CaesarCipher implements Cipher
{
    public byte[] encrypt(byte[] source, byte[] key)
    {
        byte[] result = new byte[source.length];
        for (int i = 0; i < source.length; i++)
            result[i] = (byte)(source[i] + key[0]);
        return result;
    }

    public byte[] decrypt(byte[] source, byte[] key)
    {
        return encrypt(source, new byte[] { (byte) -key[0] });
    }

    public int strength() { return 1; }
}
```

The implementing classes can be in any package, not necessarily the same package as the service interface. Each of them must have a no-argument constructor.

Now add the names of the classes to a UTF-8 encoded text file in a file in the META-INF/services directory whose name matches the fully qualified class name. In our example, the file META-INF/services/serviceLoader.Cipher would contain the line

```
serviceLoader.impl.CaesarCipher
```

In this example, we provide a single implementing class. You could also provide multiple classes and later pick among them.

With this preparation done, the program initializes a service loader as follows:

```
public static ServiceLoader<Cipher> cipherLoader = ServiceLoader.load(Cipher.class);
```

This should be done just once in the program.

The iterator method of the service loader returns an iterator through all provided implementations of the service. (See Chapter 9 for more information about iterators.) It is easiest to use an enhanced for loop to traverse them. In the loop, pick an appropriate object to carry out the service.

```
public static Cipher getCipher(int minStrength)
{
   for (Cipher cipher : cipherLoader) // Implicitly calls cipherLoader.iterator()
   {
      if (cipher.strength() >= minStrength) return cipher;
   }
   return null;
}
```

---

java.util.ServiceLoader<S> 1.6

- `static <S> ServiceLoader<S> load(Class<S> service)`

  Creates a service loader for loading the classes that implement the given service interface.

- `Iterator<S> iterator()`

  Yields an iterator that lazily loads the service classes. That is, a class is loaded whenever the iterator advances.

13.4 Applets

Applets are Java programs that are included in an HTML page. The HTML page must tell the browser which applets to load and where to put each applet on the web page. As you might expect, the tag needed to use an applet must tell the browser where to get the class files and how the applet is positioned on the web page (size, location, and so on). The browser then retrieves the class files from the Internet (or from a directory on the user's machine) and automatically runs the applet.

When applets were first developed, you had to use Sun's HotJava browser to view web pages that contained applets. Naturally, few users were willing to use a separate browser just to enjoy a new web feature. Java applets became popular when Netscape included a Java virtual machine in its Navigator browser. Microsoft Internet Explorer followed suit. Unfortunately, the Java support in Internet Explorer support soon fell behind and only worked with outdated Java versions, before being dropped altogether.

To solve this problem, Sun Microsystems developed the "Java Plug-in." Using browser extension mechanisms, it plugs in to a variety of browsers and enables them to execute Java applets by using an external Java runtime environment.

For a number of years, this solution was adequate, and applets were commonly used for educational tools, corporate applications, and some games. Unfortunately, Sun Microsystems and, after its demise, Oracle were slow in fixing security vulnerabilities in the Java Virtual Machine that were discovered and exploited from time to time. Since an insecure JVM puts users at real risk, browser manufacturers made it harder to use Java. Some blocked all but the latest versions of the Java Plug-in, and others discontinued support of the plug-in architecture. Oracle's reaction was similarly disappointing. It started requiring that all applets are digitally signed (see Section 13.4.9, "Signed Code," on p. 822).

Nowadays, it is a challenge for developers to deploy Java applets, and for users to run them. Therefore, we believe that the sections that follow will be mostly of interest to readers who need to maintain legacy applets.

NOTE: To run the applets in this chapter in a browser, you need to install the current version of the Java Plug-in and make sure your browser is connected with the plug-in. For testing applets, you also need to configure the plug-in so that it trusts local files. See Section 2.5, "Building and Running Applets," on p. 33 for instructions.

13.4.1 A Simple Applet

For tradition's sake, let's write a NotHelloWorld program as an applet. An applet is simply a Java class that extends the java.applet.Applet class. In this book, we will use Swing to implement applets. All of our applets will extend the JApplet class, the superclass for Swing applets. As you can see in Figure 13.2, JApplet is an immediate subclass of the ordinary Applet class.

NOTE: If your applet contains Swing components, you must extend the JApplet class. Swing components inside a plain Applet don't paint correctly.

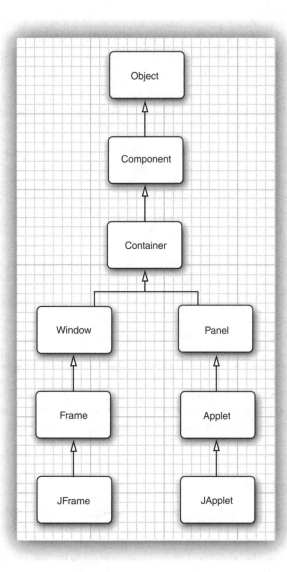

Figure 13.2 Applet inheritance diagram

Listing 13.4 shows the code for an applet version of "Not Hello World."

Notice how similar this is to the corresponding program from Chapter 10. However, since the applet lives inside a web page, there is no need to specify a method for exiting the applet.

Listing 13.4 applet/NotHelloWorld.java

```
1  package applet;
2
3  import java.awt.*;
4  import javax.swing.*;
5
6  /**
7   * @version 1.24 2015-06-12
8   * @author Cay Horstmann
9   */
10 public class NotHelloWorld extends JApplet
11 {
12    public void init()
13    {
14       EventQueue.invokeLater(() -> {
15          JLabel label = new JLabel("Not a Hello, World applet",
16                SwingConstants.CENTER);
17          add(label);
18       });
19    }
20 }
```

To execute the applet, carry out three steps:

1. Compile your Java source files into class files.

2. Package the classes into a JAR file (see Section 13.1.1, "Creating JAR files," on p. 780).

3. Create an HTML file that tells the browser which class file to load first and how to size the applet.

Here are the contents of the file:

```
<applet class="applet/NotHelloWorld.class" archive="NotHelloWorld.jar" width="300" height="300">
</applet>
```

Before you view the applet in a browser, it is a good idea to test it in the *applet viewer* program that is a part of the JDK. To use the applet viewer with our example, enter

```
appletviewer NotHelloWorldApplet.html
```

on the command line. The command-line argument for the applet viewer program is the name of the HTML file, not the class file. Figure 13.3 shows the applet viewer displaying this applet.

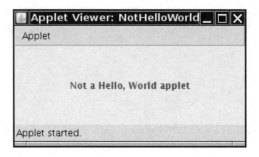

Figure 13.3 Viewing an applet in the applet viewer

The applet viewer is good for the first stage of testing, but at some point you need to run your applets in a real browser to see them as a user might see them. In particular, the applet viewer program shows you only the applet, not the surrounding HTML text. If your HTML file contains multiple `applet` tags, the applet viewer pops up multiple windows.

To properly view the applet, simply load the HTML file into the browser (see Figure 13.4). If the applet doesn't show up, you need to install the Java Plug-in and allow it to load unsigned local applets, as described in Section 2.5, "Building and Running Applets," on p. 33.

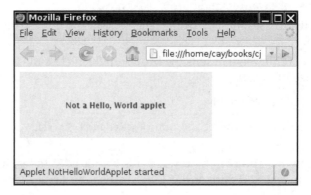

Figure 13.4 Viewing an applet in a browser

TIP: If you make a change to your applet and recompile, you need to restart the browser so that it loads the new class files. Simply refreshing the HTML page will not load the new code. This is a hassle when you are debugging an applet. You can avoid the painful browser restart from the *Java console*. Launch the console and issue the x command, which clears the classloader cache. Then you can reload the HTML page, and the new applet code is used. Under Windows, open the Java Plug-in control in the Windows control panel. Under Linux, run jcontrol and request that the Java console be displayed. The console will pop up whenever an applet is loaded.

It is easy to convert a graphical Java application into an applet that you can embed in a web page. Essentially, all of the user interface code can stay the same. Here are the specific steps:

1. Make an HTML page with the appropriate tag to load the applet code.
2. Supply a subclass of the JApplet class. Make this class public. Otherwise, the applet cannot be loaded.
3. Eliminate the main method in the application. Do not construct a frame window for the application. Your application will be displayed inside the browser.
4. Move any initialization code from the frame window constructor to the init method of the applet. You don't need to explicitly construct the applet object—the browser instantiates it for you and calls the init method.
5. Remove the call to setSize; for applets, sizing is done with the width and height parameters in the HTML file.
6. Remove the call to setDefaultCloseOperation. An applet cannot be closed; it terminates when the browser exits.
7. If the application calls setTitle, eliminate the call to the method. Applets cannot have title bars. (You can, of course, title the web page itself, using the HTML title tag.) /
8. Don't call setVisible(true). The applet is displayed automatically.

---

java.applet.Applet 1.0

- void init()

  is called when the applet is first loaded. Override this method and place all initialization code here.

(Continues)

`java.applet.Applet` 1.0 *(Continued)*

- `void start()`

  override this method for code that needs to be executed *every time* the user visits the browser page containing this applet. A typical action is to reactivate a thread.

- `void stop()`

  override this method for code that needs to be executed *every time* the user leaves the browser page containing this applet. A typical action is to deactivate a thread.

- `void destroy()`

  override this method for code that needs to be executed when the user exits the browser.

- `void resize(int width, int height)`

  requests that the applet be resized. This would be a great method if it worked on web pages; unfortunately, it does not work in current browsers because it interferes with their page layout mechanisms.

13.4.2 The `applet` HTML Tag and Its Attributes

In its most basic form, an example `applet` tag looks like this:

```
<applet code="applet/NotHelloWorld.class" archive="NotHelloWorld.jar"
    width="300" height="100"></applet>
```

You can use the following attributes within the `applet` tag:

- `width, height`

  These attributes are required and give the width and height of the applet, measured in pixels. In the applet viewer, this is the initial size of the applet. You can resize any window that the applet viewer creates. In a browser, you *cannot* resize the applet. You will need to make a good guess about how much space your applet requires to show up well for all users.

- `align`

  This attribute specifies the alignment of the applet. The attribute values are the same as for the `align` attribute of the HTML `img` tag.

- `vspace, hspace`

  These optional attributes specify the number of pixels above and below the applet (`vspace`) and on each side of the applet (`hspace`).

- code

This attribute gives the name of the applet's class file.

The path name must match the package of the applet class. For example, if the applet class is in the package com.mycompany, then the attribute is code="com/mycompany/MyApplet.class". The alternative code="com.mycompany.MyApplet.class" is also permitted.

The code attribute specifies only the name of the class that contains the applet class. Of course, your applet may contain other class files. Once the browser's class loader loads the class containing the applet, it will realize that it needs more class files and will load them.

- archive

This attribute lists the JAR file or files containing classes and other resources for the applet. These files are fetched from the web server before the applet is loaded. JAR files are separated by commas. For example:

```
<applet code="MyApplet.class"
    archive="MyClasses.jar,corejava/CoreJavaClasses.jar"
    width="100" height="150">
```

- codebase

This attribute is the URL from which JAR files (and, in earlier days, class files) are loaded.

- object

This obsolete attribute specifies the name of a file that contains a *serialized* applet object, which was intended for persisting applet state. Since there is no way of signing a serialized file, this feature is no longer useful.

- alt

You can use the alt attribute to display a message when Java is disabled.

If a browser cannot process applets at all, it ignores the unknown applet and param tags. All text between the <applet> and </applet> tags is displayed by the browser. Conversely, Java-aware browsers do not display any text between the <applet> and </applet> tags. You can display messages between these tags for those poor folks. For example:

```
<applet . . . alt="If you activated Java, you would see my applet here">
    If your browser could show Java, you would see my applet here.
</applet>
```

- name

  Scripters can give the applet a `name` attribute that they can use to refer to the applet when scripting. Both Netscape and Internet Explorer let you call methods of an applet on a page through JavaScript.

  To access an applet from JavaScript, you first have to give it a name.

  ```
  <applet ... name="mine"></applet>
  ```

  You can then refer to the object as `document.applets.`*appletname*. For example:

  ```
  var myApplet = document.applets.mine;
  ```

  You can then call applet methods:

  ```
  myApplet.init();
  ```

  The `name` attribute is also essential when you want two applets on the same page to communicate with each other directly. Specify a name for each current applet instance and pass this string to the `getApplet` method of the `AppletContext` interface. We discuss this mechanism, called *inter-applet communication*, later in this chapter.

 NOTE: In `www.javaworld.com/javatips/jw-javatip80.html`, Francis Lu uses JavaScript-to-Java communication to solve an age-old problem: how to resize an applet so that it isn't bound by hardcoded `width` and `height` attributes. This is a good example of the integration between Java and JavaScript.

13.4.3 Use of Parameters to Pass Information to Applets

Just as applications can use command-line information, applets can use parameters that are embedded in the HTML file. This is done by the HTML tag called `param` along with attributes that you define. For example, suppose you want to let the web page determine the style of the font to use in your applet. You could use the following HTML tags:

```
<applet code="FontParamApplet.class" ...>
  <param name="font" value="Helvetica"/>
</applet>
```

You can then pick up the value of the parameter using the `getParameter` method of the `Applet` class:

```
public class FontParamApplet extends JApplet
{
  public void init()
  {
```

```
    String fontName = getParameter("font");
      . . .
  }
  . . .
}
```

NOTE: You can call the `getParameter` method only in the `init` method of the applet, not in the constructor. When the applet constructor is executed, the parameters are not yet prepared. Since the layout of most nontrivial applets is determined by parameters, we recommend that you don't supply constructors to applets. Simply place all initialization code into the `init` method.

Parameters are always returned as strings. You need to convert the string to a numeric type if that is what is called for. You do this in the standard way by using the appropriate method, such as `parseInt` of the `Integer` class.

For example, if we want to add a `size` parameter for the font, the HTML code might look like this:

```
<applet code="FontParamApplet.class" ...>
  <param name="font" value="Helvetica"/>
  <param name="size" value="24"/>
</applet>
```

The following source code shows how to read the integer parameter:

```
public class FontParamApplet extends JApplet
{
  public void init()
  {
    String fontName = getParameter("font");
    int fontSize = Integer.parseInt(getParameter("size"));
      . . .
  }
}
```

NOTE: A case-insensitive comparison is used when matching the `name` attribute value in the `param` tag and the argument of the `getParameter` method.

In addition to ensuring that the parameters match in your code, you should find out whether or not the `size` parameter was left out. You can do this with a simple test for `null`. For example:

```
int fontsize;
String sizeString = getParameter("size");
if (sizeString == null) fontSize = 12;
else fontSize = Integer.parseInt(sizeString);
```

Here is a classic applet that uses parameters to draw a bar chart, shown in Figure 13.5.

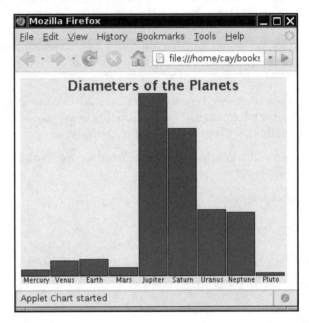

Figure 13.5 A chart applet

This applet takes the labels and the heights of the bars from the `param` values in the HTML file. Here is what the HTML file for Figure 13.5 looks like:

```
<applet code="Chart.class" width="400" height="300">
    <param name="title" value="Diameters of the Planets"/>
    <param name="values" value="9"/>
    <param name="name.1" value="Mercury"/>
    <param name="name.2" value="Venus"/>
    <param name="name.3" value="Earth"/>
    <param name="name.4" value="Mars"/>
    <param name="name.5" value="Jupiter"/>
    <param name="name.6" value="Saturn"/>
    <param name="name.7" value="Uranus"/>
    <param name="name.8" value="Neptune"/>
    <param name="name.9" value="Pluto"/>
    <param name="value.1" value="3100"/>
```

```
<param name="value.2" value="7500"/>
<param name="value.3" value="8000"/>
<param name="value.4" value="4200"/>
<param name="value.5" value="88000"/>
<param name="value.6" value="71000"/>
<param name="value.7" value="32000"/>
<param name="value.8" value="30600"/>
<param name="value.9" value="1430"/>
</applet>
```

You could have set up an array of strings and an array of numbers in the applet, but there are two advantages to using the parameter mechanism instead. You can have multiple copies of the same applet on your web page, showing different graphs: Just put two applet tags with different sets of parameters on the page. And you can change the data that you want to chart. Admittedly, the diameters of the planets will stay the same for quite some time, but suppose your web page contains a chart of weekly sales data. It is easy to update the web page because it is plain text. Editing and recompiling a Java file weekly is more tedious.

In fact, there are commercial JavaBeans components (beans) that make much fancier graphs than the one in our chart applet. If you buy one, you can drop it into your web page and feed it parameters without ever needing to know how the applet renders the graphs.

Listing 13.5 is the source code of our chart applet. Note that the init method reads the parameters, and the paintComponent method draws the chart.

Listing 13.5 chart/Chart.java

```
1  package chart;
2
3  import java.awt.*;
4  import java.awt.font.*;
5  import java.awt.geom.*;
6  import javax.swing.*;
7
8  /**
9   * @version 1.34 2015-06-12
10  * @author Cay Horstmann
11  */
12  public class Chart extends JApplet
13  {
14     public void init()
15     {
16        EventQueue.invokeLater(() -> {
17           String v = getParameter("values");
18           if (v == null) return;
```

(Continues)

Listing 13.5 *(Continued)*

```
19          int n = Integer.parseInt(v);
20          double[] values = new double[n];
21          String[] names = new String[n];
22          for (int i = 0; i < n; i++)
23          {
24             values[i] = Double.parseDouble(getParameter("value." + (i + 1)));
25             names[i] = getParameter("name." + (i + 1));
26          }
27
28          add(new ChartComponent(values, names, getParameter("title")));
29       });
30    }
31 }
32
33 /**
34  * A component that draws a bar chart.
35  */
36 class ChartComponent extends JComponent
37 {
38    private double[] values;
39    private String[] names;
40    private String title;
41
42    /**
43     * Constructs a ChartComponent.
44     * @param v the array of values for the chart
45     * @param n the array of names for the values
46     * @param t the title of the chart
47     */
48    public ChartComponent(double[] v, String[] n, String t)
49    {
50       values = v;
51       names = n;
52       title = t;
53    }
54
55    public void paintComponent(Graphics g)
56    {
57       Graphics2D g2 = (Graphics2D) g;
58
59       // compute the minimum and maximum values
60       if (values == null) return;
61       double minValue = 0;
62       double maxValue = 0;
63       for (double v : values)
64       {
```

```
65      if (minValue > v) minValue = v;
66      if (maxValue < v) maxValue = v;
67   }
68   if (maxValue == minValue) return;
69
70   int panelWidth = getWidth();
71   int panelHeight = getHeight();
72
73   Font titleFont = new Font("SansSerif", Font.BOLD, 20);
74   Font labelFont = new Font("SansSerif", Font.PLAIN, 10);
75
76   // compute the extent of the title
77   FontRenderContext context = g2.getFontRenderContext();
78   Rectangle2D titleBounds = titleFont.getStringBounds(title, context);
79   double titleWidth = titleBounds.getWidth();
80   double top = titleBounds.getHeight();
81
82   // draw the title
83   double y = -titleBounds.getY(); // ascent
84   double x = (panelWidth - titleWidth) / 2;
85   g2.setFont(titleFont);
86   g2.drawString(title, (float) x, (float) y);
87
88   // compute the extent of the bar labels
89   LineMetrics labelMetrics = labelFont.getLineMetrics("", context);
90   double bottom = labelMetrics.getHeight();
91
92   y = panelHeight - labelMetrics.getDescent();
93   g2.setFont(labelFont);
94
95   // get the scale factor and width for the bars
96   double scale = (panelHeight - top - bottom) / (maxValue - minValue);
97   int barWidth = panelWidth / values.length;
98
99   // draw the bars
100  for (int i = 0; i < values.length; i++)
101  {
102     // get the coordinates of the bar rectangle
103     double x1 = i * barWidth + 1;
104     double y1 = top;
105     double height = values[i] * scale;
106     if (values[i] >= 0)
107        y1 += (maxValue - values[i]) * scale;
108     else
109     {
110        y1 += maxValue * scale;
111        height = -height;
112     }
113
```

(Continues)

Listing 13.5 *(Continued)*

```
114        // fill the bar and draw the bar outline
115        Rectangle2D rect = new Rectangle2D.Double(x1, y1, barWidth - 2, height);
116        g2.setPaint(Color.RED);
117        g2.fill(rect);
118        g2.setPaint(Color.BLACK);
119        g2.draw(rect);
120
121        // draw the centered label below the bar
122        Rectangle2D labelBounds = labelFont.getStringBounds(names[i], context);
123
124        double labelWidth = labelBounds.getWidth();
125        x = x1 + (barWidth - labelWidth) / 2;
126        g2.drawString(names[i], (float) x, (float) y);
127     }
128   }
129 }
```

---

java.applet.Applet 1.0

- `public String getParameter(String name)`

  gets the value of a parameter defined with a `param` tag in the web page loading the applet. The string `name` is case sensitive.

- `public String getAppletInfo()`

  is a method that many applet authors override to return a string with information about the author, version, and copyright of the current applet.

- `public String[][] getParameterInfo()`

  is a method that you can override to return an array of `param` tag options that this applet supports. Each row contains three entries: the name, the type, and a description of the parameter. Here is an example:

  ```
  "fps", "1-10", "frames per second"
  "repeat", "boolean", "repeat image loop?"
  "images", "url", "directory containing images"
  ```

13.4.4 Accessing Image and Audio Files

Applets can handle both images and audio. As we write this, images must be in GIF, PNG, or JPEG form, audio files in AU, AIFF, WAV, or MIDI. Animated GIFs are supported, and the animation is displayed.

Specify the locations of image and audio files with relative URLs. The base URL is usually obtained by calling the `getDocumentBase` or `getCodeBase` method. The former gets the URL of the HTML page in which the applet is contained, the latter the URL specified by the applet's codebase attribute.

Give the base URL and the file location to the getImage or getAudioClip method. For example:

```
Image cat = getImage(getDocumentBase(), "images/cat.gif");
AudioClip meow = getAudioClip(getDocumentBase(), "audio/meow.au");
```

You saw in Chapter 10 how to display an image. To play an audio clip, simply invoke its play method. You can also call the play method of the Applet class without first loading the audio clip.

```
play(getDocumentBase(), "audio/meow.au");
```

---

java.applet.Applet 1.0

- URL getDocumentBase()

  gets the URL of the web page containing this applet.

- URL getCodeBase()

  gets the URL of the codebase directory from which this applet is loaded. That is either the absolute URL of the directory referenced by the codebase attribute or the directory of the HTML file if no codebase is specified.

- void play(URL url)
- void play(URL url, String name)

  The first form plays an audio file specified by the URL. The second form uses the string to provide a path relative to the URL in the first parameter. Nothing happens if the audio clip cannot be found.

- AudioClip getAudioClip(URL url)
- AudioClip getAudioClip(URL url, String name)

  The first form gets an audio clip from the given URL. The second form uses the string to provide a path relative to the URL in the first argument. The methods return null if the audio clip cannot be found.

- Image getImage(URL url)
- Image getImage(URL url, String name)

  returns an image object that encapsulates the image specified by the URL. If the image does not exist, it immediately returns null. Otherwise, a separate thread is launched to load the image.

13.4.5 The Applet Context

An applet runs inside a browser or the applet viewer. An applet can ask the browser to do things for it—for example, fetch an audio clip, show a short message in the status line, or display a different web page. The ambient browser can carry out these requests, or it can ignore them. For example, if an applet running inside the applet viewer asks the applet viewer program to display a web page, nothing happens.

To communicate with the browser, an applet calls the getAppletContext method. That method returns an object that implements an interface of type AppletContext. You can think of the concrete implementation of the AppletContext interface as a communication path between the applet and the ambient browser. In addition to getAudioClip and getImage, the AppletContext interface contains several useful methods, which we discuss in the next few sections.

13.4.6 Inter–Applet Communication

A web page can contain more than one applet. If a web page contains multiple applets from the same codebase, they can communicate with each other. Naturally, this is an advanced technique that you probably will not need very often.

If you give name attributes to each applet in the HTML file, you can use the getApplet method of the AppletContext interface to get a reference to the applet. For example, if your HTML file contains the tag

```
<applet code="Chart.class" width="100" height="100" name="Chart1">
```

then the call

```
Applet chart1 = getAppletContext().getApplet("Chart1");
```

gives you a reference to the applet. What can you do with the reference? Provided you give the Chart class a method to accept new data and redraw the chart, you can call this method by making the appropriate cast.

```
((Chart) chart1).setData(3, "Earth", 9000);
```

You can also list all applets on a web page, whether or not they have a name attribute. The getApplets method returns an enumeration object. Here is a loop that prints the class names of all applets on the current page:

```
Enumeration<Applet> e = getAppletContext().getApplets();
while (e.hasMoreElements())
{
```

```
    Applet a = e.nextElement();
    System.out.println(a.getClass().getName());
}
```

An applet cannot communicate with an applet on a different web page.

13.4.7 Displaying Items in the Browser

You have access to two areas of the ambient browser: the status line and the web page display area. Both use methods of the AppletContext interface.

You can display a string in the status line at the bottom of the browser with the showStatus message. For example:

```
showStatus("Loading data . . . please wait");
```

TIP: In our experience, showStatus is of limited use. The browser is also using the status line, and, more often than not, it will overwrite your precious message with chatter like "Applet running." Use the status line for fluff messages like "Loading data . . . please wait," but not for something the user cannot afford to miss.

You can tell the browser to show a different web page with the showDocument method. There are several ways to do this. The simplest is a call to showDocument with one argument, the URL you want to show.

```
URL u = new URL("http://horstmann.com/index.html");
getAppletContext().showDocument(u);
```

The problem with this call is that it opens the new web page in the same window as your current page, thereby displacing your applet. To return to your applet, the user must click the Back button of the browser.

You can tell the browser to show the document in another window by giving a second parameter in the call to showDocument (see Table 13.2). If you supply the special string "_blank", the browser opens a new window with the document, instead of displacing the current document. More importantly, if you take advantage of the frame feature in HTML, you can split a browser window into multiple frames, each having a name. You can put your applet into one frame and have it show documents in other frames. We show you an example of how to do this in the next section.

NOTE: The applet viewer does not show web pages. The showDocument method is ignored in the applet viewer.

Table 13.2 The showDocument Method

Target Parameter	Location
"_self" or none	Show the document in the current frame.
"_parent"	Show the document in the parent frame.
"_top"	Show the document in the topmost frame.
"_blank"	Show in new, unnamed, top-level window.
Any other string	Show in the frame with that name. If no frame with that name exists, open a new window and give it that name.

---

java.applet.Applet 1.2

- public AppletContext getAppletContext()

  gives you a handle to the applet's browser environment. In most browsers, you can use this information to control the browser in which the applet is running.

- void showStatus(String msg)

  shows the specified string in the status line of the browser.

---

java.applet.AppletContext 1.0

- Enumeration<Applet> getApplets()

  returns an enumeration (see Chapter 9) of all the applets in the same context—that is, the same web page.

- Applet getApplet(String name)

  returns the applet in the current context with the given name; returns null if none exists. Only the current web page is searched.

- void showDocument(URL url)
- void showDocument(URL url, String target)

  shows a new web page in a frame in the browser. In the first form, the new page displaces the current page. The second form uses the target parameter to identify the target frame (see Table 13.2).

13.4.8 The Sandbox

Whenever code is loaded from a remote site and then executed locally, security becomes vital. Visiting a web page automatically starts all applets on the page.

Clicking a single link can launch a Java Web Start application. If visiting a web page or clicking a link could execute arbitrary code on the user's computer, criminals would have an easy time stealing confidential information, accessing financial data, or taking over users' machines to send spam.

To ensure that the Java technology cannot be used for nefarious purposes, Java has an elaborate security model that we discuss in detail in Volume II. A *security manager* checks access to all system resources. By default, it only allows those operations that are harmless. To allow additional operations, the user must explicitly approve the applet or application.

What *can* remote code do on all platforms? It is always OK to show images and play sounds, get keystrokes and mouse clicks from the user, and send user input back to the host from which the code was loaded. That is enough functionality to show facts and figures or to interact with an educational program or game. The restricted execution environment is often called the "sandbox." Code that plays in the sandbox cannot alter the user's system or spy on it.

In particular, programs in the sandbox have the following restrictions:

- They can *never* run any local executable program.
- They cannot read from or write to the local computer's file system.
- They cannot find out any information about the local computer, except for the Java version used and a few harmless operating system details. In particular, code in the sandbox cannot find out the user's name, e-mail address, and so on.
- Remotely loaded programs need user consent to communicate with any host other than the server from which they were downloaded; that server is called the *originating host*. This rule is often called "remote code can only phone home." The rule protects users from code that might try to spy on intranet resources.
- All pop-up windows carry a warning message. This message is a security feature to ensure that users do not mistake the window for a local application. The fear is that an unsuspecting user could visit a web page, be tricked into running remote code, and then type in a password or credit card number, which can be sent back to the web server. In early versions of the JDK, that message was very ominous: "Untrusted Java Applet Window." Every successive version watered down the warning a bit: "Unauthenticated Java Applet Window," then "Warning: Java Applet Window." Now it is a minuscule warning triangle that only the most observant users will notice.

The sandbox concept is no longer as meaningful as it used to be. In the past, anyone could deploy sandboxed code, and only code that needed permissions beyond the sandbox needed to be digitally signed. Nowadays all code executed through the Java Plug-in, whether it runs in the sandbox or not, must be digitally signed.

13.4.9 Signed Code

The JAR files of an applet or Java Web Start application must be *digitally signed*. A signed JAR file carries with it a certificate that indicates the identity of the signer. Cryptographic techniques ensure that such a certificate cannot be forged, and that any effort to tamper with the signed file will be detected.

For example, suppose you receive an application that is produced and digitally signed by yWorks GmbH, using a certificate issued by Thawte (see Figure 13.6). When you receive the application, you will be assured of the following:

1. The code is exactly as it was when it was signed; no third party has tampered with it.

2. The signature really is from yWorks.

3. The certificate really was issued by Thawte. (The Java Plug-in knows how to check certificates from Thawte and a number of other certificate vendors, and it is also possible to install alternative "root certificates".)

If you click on the "More Information" link, you are told that the application will run without the security restrictions normally provided by Java. Should you install and run the application? That really depends on your trust in yWorks GmbH.

Getting a certificate from one of the supported vendors costs hundreds of dollars per year, and some certificate issuers require proof of incorporation or a business license. In the past, some Java developers simply generated their own certificates and used them for code signing. Of course, the Java Plug-in has no way of checking the accuracy of these certificates. In the past, the Java Plug-in nevertheless presented the certificate to the user for approval. This was quite worthless since few users understood the difference between secure and insecure certificates. Insecure certificates are no longer supported.

If you want to distribute a Java applet or Web Start application, you no longer have a choice. You must obtain a certificate from a certificate issuer that is supported by the Java Plug-in and use it to sign your JAR files.

If you work for a company, it is likely that your company already has an established relationship with a certificate vendor, and you can simply order a Java code signing certificate. If not, it pays to shop around since prices vary widely, and some vendors are more relaxed about issuing certificates to individuals.

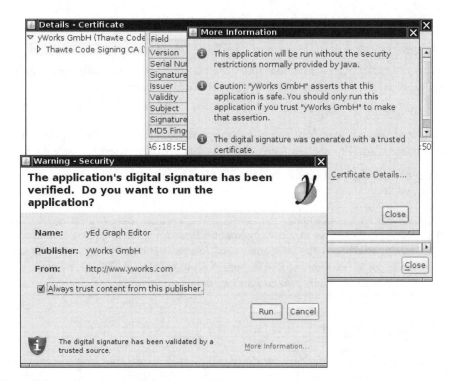

Figure 13.6 A secure certificate

Your certificate will come with instructions to install it into a Java keystore—a password-protected file from where it can be retrieved during the signing process. Keep the keystore file and the password safe.

Next, you need to decide what permissions you want. You have the choice between sandbox permissions and all permissions. Make a manifest file (see Section 13.1.2, "The Manifest," on p. 781).

Include either the line `Permissions: sandbox` or `Permissions: all-permissions`, for example:

```
Manifest-Version: 1.0
Permissions: all-permissions
```

Run the `jar` tool:

```
jar cvfm MyApplet.jar manifest.mf mypackage/*.class
```

The `applet` element of your HTML file should have an attribute `archive="MyApplet.jar"`.

Finally, sign the JAR file. The command looks like this:

```
jarsigner -keystore keystorefile -tsa timestampURL MyApplet.jar keyalias
```

You need to ask your certificate issuer about the URL for time stamping. The key alias was assigned by your certificate issuer. Run the command

```
keytool -keystore keystorefile -list
```

to find out what it was. You can also change it with the `-changealias` option of the `keytool` command. (For more information on `keytool`, turn to Chapter 9 of Volume II.)

Now place the signed JAR file and the HTML file with the `applet` element on your web server.

 NOTE: It is possible to control in great detail which rights to grant a Java application; we discuss this in Chapter 12 of Volume II. However, that system was never put to use in a way that is meaningful to consumers. The Java Plug-in only offers two security levels: sandbox or all permissions.

13.5 Java Web Start

Java Web Start is a technology for delivering applications over the Internet. Java Web Start applications have the following characteristics:

- They are typically delivered through a browser. Once a Java Web Start application has been downloaded, it can be started without using a browser.

- They do not live inside a browser window. The application is displayed in its own frame, outside the browser.

- They do not use the Java implementation of the browser. The browser simply launches an external application whenever it loads a Java Web Start application descriptor. That is the same mechanism used to launch other helper applications such as Adobe Acrobat or RealAudio.

- Digitally signed applications can be given arbitrary access rights on the local machine. Unsigned applications run in a "sandbox" which prohibits potentially dangerous operations.

13.5.1 Delivering a Java Web Start Application

To prepare an application for delivery by Java Web Start, package it in one or more JAR files. Then, prepare a descriptor file in the Java Network Launch Protocol (JNLP) format. Place these files on a web server.

You also need to ensure that your web server reports a MIME type of application/x-java-jnlp-file for files with extension .jnlp. (Browsers use the MIME type to determine which helper application to launch.) Consult your web server documentation for details.

 TIP: To experiment with Java Web Start, install Tomcat from http://jakarta. apache.org/tomcat. Tomcat is a container for servlets and JSP pages, but it also serves web pages. It is preconfigured to serve the correct MIME type for JNLP files. In the following instructions, we assume that you use Tomcat.

Let's try out Java Web Start to deliver the calculator application from Chapter 12. Follow these steps:

1. Compile the program.

   ```
   javac -classpath .:jdk/jre/lib/javaws.jar webstart/*.java
   ```

2. Produce a JAR file with the command

   ```
   jar cvfe Calculator.jar webstart.Calculator  webstart/*.class
   ```

3. Prepare the launch file Calculator.jnlp with the following contents:

   ```
   <?xml version="1.0" encoding="utf-8"?>
   <jnlp spec="1.0+" codebase="http://localhost:8080/calculator/" href="Calculator.jnlp">
       <information>
           <title>Calculator Demo Application</title>
           <vendor>Cay S. Horstmann</vendor>
           <description>A Calculator</description>
           <offline-allowed/>
       </information>
       <resources>
           <java version="1.6.0+"/>
           <jar href="Calculator.jar"/>
       </resources>
       <application-desc/>
   </jnlp>
   ```

   (Note that the version number must be 1.6.0, not 6.0.)

   The launch file format is fairly self-explanatory. For a full specification, see www.oracle.com/technetwork/java/javase/javawebstart.

4. Make a directory *tomcat*/webapps/calculator from which to serve the application. Here *tomcat* is the base directory of your Tomcat installation. Make a subdirectory *tomcat*/webapps/calculator/WEB-INF, and place the following minimal web.xml file inside the WEB-INF subdirectory:

```
<?xml version="1.0" encoding="utf-8"?>
<web-app version="2.5" xmlns="http://java.sun.com/xml/ns/j2ee"
    xmlns:xsi="http://www.w3.org/2001/XMLSchema-instance"
    xsi:schemaLocation="http://java.sun.com/xml/ns/j2ee
        http://java.sun.com/xml/ns/j2ee/web-app_2_5.xsd">
</web-app>
```

5. Place the JAR file and the launch file into the *tomcat*/webapps/calculator directory.

6. Following the process described in Section 2.5, "Building and Running Applets," on p. 33, add the URL http://localhost:8080 to the list of trusted sites in the Java Control Panel. Alternatively, you can sign the JAR file as described in Section 13.4.9, "Signed Code," on p. 822.

7. Start Tomcat by executing the startup script in the *tomcat*/bin directory.

8. Point your browser to the JNLP file. For example, if you use Tomcat, go to http://localhost:8080/calculator/Calculator.jnlp. If your browser has been configured for Java Web Start, you should see the launch window for Java Web Start (see Figure 13.7).

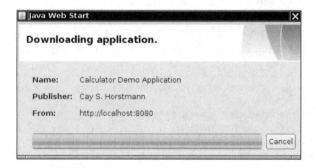

Figure 13.7 Launching Java Web Start

If your browser does not know how to deal with JNLP files, it may offer you the option of associating them with an application. If so, choose *jdk*/bin/javaws. Otherwise, figure out how to associate the MIME type application/x-java-jnlp-file with the javaws application. You can also try reinstalling the JDK which is supposed to do that for you.

9. Soon afterward, the calculator should come up, with a border marking it as a Java application (see Figure 13.8).

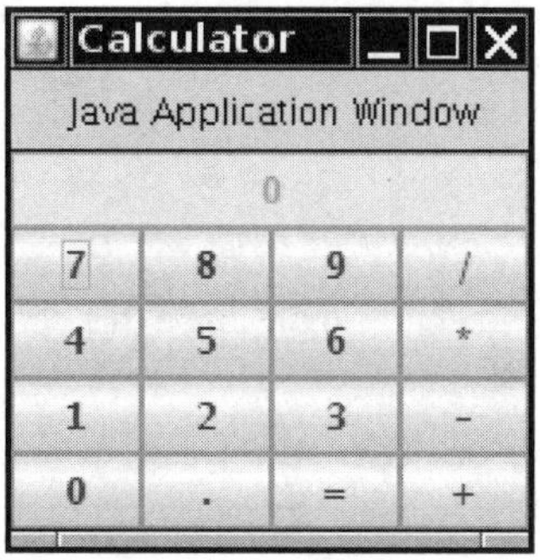

Figure 13.8 The calculator delivered by Java Web Start

10. When you access the JNLP file again, the application is retrieved from the cache. You can review the cache content by using the Java Plug-in control panel (see Figure 13.9). In Windows, look for the Java Plug-in control inside the Windows control panel. Under Linux, run *jdk*/jre/bin/ControlPanel.

Figure 13.9 The application cache

TIP: If you don't want to run a web server while you are testing your JNLP configuration, you can temporarily override the `codebase` URL in the launch file by running

```
javaws -codebase file://programDirectory JNLPfile
```

For example, in UNIX, you can simply issue this command from the directory containing the JNLP file:

```
javaws -codebase file://`pwd` Calculator.jnlp
```

Of course, you don't want to tell your users to launch the cache viewer whenever they want to run your application again. You can have the installer offer to install desktop and menu shortcuts. Add these lines to the JNLP file:

```
<shortcut>
   <desktop/>
   <menu submenu="Accessories"/>
</shortcut>
```

When the user first downloads the application, a "desktop integration warning" is displayed (see Figure 13.10).

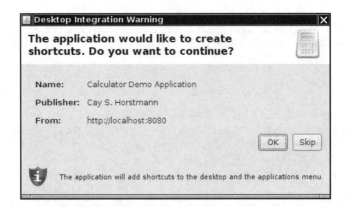

Figure 13.10 The desktop integration warning

You should also supply an icon for the menu shortcut and the launch screen. Oracle recommends that you supply a 32 × 32 and a 64 × 64 icon. Place the icon files on the web server, together with the JNLP and JAR files. Add these lines to the `information` section of the JNLP file:

```
<icon href="calc_icon32.png" width="32" height="32" />
<icon href="calc_icon64.png" width="64" height="64" />
```

Note that these icons are not related to the application icon. If you want the application to have an icon, you need to add a separate icon image into the JAR file and call the setIconImage method on the frame class. (See Listing 13.1 for an example.)

13.5.2 The JNLP API

As an advantage over applets, Java Web Start has an API for sandboxed applications that provides useful services. The JNLP API allows sandboxed applications to access local resources in a secure way. For example, there are services to load and save files. The application can't look at the file system and it can't specify file names. Instead, a file dialog is popped up, and the user selects the file. But before the file dialog is popped up, the user is alerted and must agree to proceed (see Figure 13.11). Furthermore, the API doesn't actually give the program access to a File object. In particular, the application has no way of finding out the file location. Thus, programmers are given the tools to implement "file open" and "file save" actions, but as much system information as possible is hidden from untrusted applications.

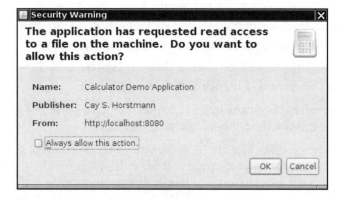

Figure 13.11 A Java Web Start security advisory

The API provides the following services:

- Loading and saving files
- Accessing the clipboard
- Printing
- Downloading a file
- Displaying a document in the default browser
- Storing and retrieving persistent configuration information
- Ensuring that only a single instance of an application executes

To access a service, use the ServiceManager, like this:

```
FileSaveService service = (FileSaveService) ServiceManager.lookup("javax.jnlp.FileSaveService");
```

This call throws an UnavailableServiceException if the service is not available.

 NOTE: You must include the file javaws.jar in the class path if you want to compile programs that use the JNLP API. That file is included in the *jre*/lib subdirectory of the JDK.

We now discuss the most useful JNLP services. To save a file, provide suggestions for the initial path name and file extensions for the file dialog, the data to be saved, and a suggested file name. For example:

```
service.saveFileDialog(".", new String[] { "txt" }, data, "calc.txt");
```

The data must be delivered in an InputStream. That can be somewhat tricky to arrange. The program in Listing 13.6 uses the following strategy:

1. It creates a ByteArrayOutputStream to hold the bytes to be saved.
2. It creates a PrintStream that sends its data to the ByteArrayOutputStream.
3. It prints the information to be saved to the PrintStream.
4. It creates a ByteArrayInputStream to read the saved bytes.
5. It passes that stream to the saveFileDialog method.

You will learn more about streams in Chapter 1 of Volume II. For now, you can just gloss over the details in the sample program.

To read data from a file, use the FileOpenService instead. Its openFileDialog receives suggestions for the initial path name and file extensions for the file dialog and returns a FileContents object. You can then call the getInputStream and getOutputStream methods to read and write the file data. If the user didn't choose a file, the openFileDialog method returns null.

```
FileOpenService service = (FileOpenService) ServiceManager.lookup("javax.jnlp.FileOpenService");
FileContents contents = service.openFileDialog(".", new String[] { "txt" });
if (contents != null)
{
   InputStream in = contents.getInputStream();
   . . .
}
```

Note that your application does not know the name or location of the file. Conversely, if you want to open a specific file, use the ExtendedService:

```
ExtendedService service = (ExtendedService) ServiceManager.lookup("javax.jnlp.ExtendedService");
FileContents contents = service.openFile(new File("c:\\autoexec.bat"));
if (contents != null)
{
   OutputStream out = contents.getOutputStream();
   . . .
}
```

The user of your program must agree to the file access (see Figure 13.12).

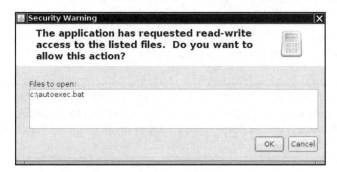

Figure 13.12 File access warning

To display a document in the default browser, use the `BasicService` interface. Note that some systems may not have a default browser.

```
BasicService service = (BasicService) ServiceManager.lookup("javax.jnlp.BasicService");
if (service.isWebBrowserSupported())
   service.showDocument(url);
else . . .
```

A rudimentary `PersistenceService` lets an application store small amounts of configuration information and retrieve it when the application runs again. The mechanism is similar to HTTP cookies. The persistent store uses URLs as keys. The URLs don't have to point to a real web resource. The service simply uses them as a convenient hierarchical naming scheme. For any given URL key, an application can store arbitrary binary data. (The store may restrict the size of the data block.)

For applications to be isolated from each other, each application can only use URL keys that start with its codebase (as specified in the JNLP file). For example, if an application is downloaded from `http://myserver.com/apps`, it can only use keys of the form `http://myserver.com/apps/subkey1/subkey2/...` Attempts to access other keys will fail.

An application can call the `getCodeBase` method of the `BasicService` to find its codebase.

Create a new key with the `create` method of the `PersistenceService`.

```
URL url = new URL(codeBase, "mykey");
service.create(url, maxSize);
```

To access the information associated with a particular key, call the `get` method. That method returns a `FileContents` object through which you can read and write the key data. For example:

```
FileContents contents = service.get(url);
InputStream in = contents.getInputStream();
OutputStream out = contents.getOutputStream(true); // true = overwrite
```

Unfortunately, there is no convenient way to find out whether a key already exists or whether you need to create it. You can hope that the key exists and call `get`. If the call throws a `FileNotFoundException`, you need to create the key.

 NOTE: Both Java Web Start applications and applets can print, using the normal printing API. A security dialog pops up, asking the user for permission to access the printer. For more information on the printing API, turn to Chapter 7 of Volume II.

The program in Listing 13.6 is a simple enhancement of the calculator application. This calculator has a virtual paper tape that keeps track of all calculations. You can save and load the calculation history. To demonstrate the persistent store, the application lets you set the frame title. If you run the application again, it retrieves your title choice from the persistent store (see Figure 13.13).

Listing 13.6 webstart/CalculatorFrame.java

```
 1  package webstart;
 2
 3  import java.io.BufferedReader;
 4  import java.io.ByteArrayInputStream;
 5  import java.io.ByteArrayOutputStream;
 6  import java.io.FileNotFoundException;
 7  import java.io.IOException;
 8  import java.io.InputStream;
 9  import java.io.InputStreamReader;
10  import java.io.OutputStream;
11  import java.io.PrintStream;
12  import java.net.MalformedURLException;
13  import java.net.URL;
14
15  import javax.jnlp.BasicService;
16  import javax.jnlp.FileContents;
17  import javax.jnlp.FileOpenService;
```

```
18  import javax.jnlp.FileSaveService;
19  import javax.jnlp.PersistenceService;
20  import javax.jnlp.ServiceManager;
21  import javax.jnlp.UnavailableServiceException;
22  import javax.swing.JFrame;
23  import javax.swing.JMenu;
24  import javax.swing.JMenuBar;
25  import javax.swing.JMenuItem;
26  import javax.swing.JOptionPane;
27
28  /**
29   * A frame with a calculator panel and a menu to load and save the calculator history.
30   */
31  public class CalculatorFrame extends JFrame
32  {
33     private CalculatorPanel panel;
34
35     public CalculatorFrame()
36     {
37        setTitle();
38        panel = new CalculatorPanel();
39        add(panel);
40
41        JMenu fileMenu = new JMenu("File");
42        JMenuBar menuBar = new JMenuBar();
43        menuBar.add(fileMenu);
44        setJMenuBar(menuBar);
45
46        JMenuItem openItem = fileMenu.add("Open");
47        openItem.addActionListener(event -> open());
48        JMenuItem saveItem = fileMenu.add("Save");
49        saveItem.addActionListener(event -> save());
50
51        pack();
52     }
53
54     /**
55      * Gets the title from the persistent store or asks the user for the title if there is no prior
56      * entry.
57      */
58     public void setTitle()
59     {
60        try
61        {
62           String title = null;
63
64           BasicService basic = (BasicService) ServiceManager.lookup("javax.jnlp.BasicService");
65           URL codeBase = basic.getCodeBase();
66
```

(Continues)

Listing 13.6 *(Continued)*

```
67         PersistenceService service = (PersistenceService) ServiceManager
68              .lookup("javax.jnlp.PersistenceService");
69         URL key = new URL(codeBase, "title");
70
71         try
72         {
73            FileContents contents = service.get(key);
74            InputStream in = contents.getInputStream();
75            BufferedReader reader = new BufferedReader(new InputStreamReader(in));
76            title = reader.readLine();
77         }
78         catch (FileNotFoundException e)
79         {
80            title = JOptionPane.showInputDialog("Please supply a frame title:");
81            if (title == null) return;
82
83            service.create(key, 100);
84            FileContents contents = service.get(key);
85            OutputStream out = contents.getOutputStream(true);
86            PrintStream printOut = new PrintStream(out);
87            printOut.print(title);
88         }
89         setTitle(title);
90      }
91      catch (UnavailableServiceException | IOException e)
92      {
93         JOptionPane.showMessageDialog(this, e);
94      }
95   }
96
97   /**
98    * Opens a history file and updates the display.
99    */
100  public void open()
101  {
102     try
103     {
104        FileOpenService service = (FileOpenService) ServiceManager
105             .lookup("javax.jnlp.FileOpenService");
106        FileContents contents = service.openFileDialog(".", new String[] { "txt" });
107
108        JOptionPane.showMessageDialog(this, contents.getName());
109        if (contents != null)
110        {
```

```
111            InputStream in = contents.getInputStream();
112            BufferedReader reader = new BufferedReader(new InputStreamReader(in));
113            String line;
114            while ((line = reader.readLine()) != null)
115            {
116                panel.append(line);
117                panel.append("\n");
118            }
119         }
120      }
121      catch (UnavailableServiceException e)
122      {
123         JOptionPane.showMessageDialog(this, e);
124      }
125      catch (IOException e)
126      {
127         JOptionPane.showMessageDialog(this, e);
128      }
129   }
130
131   /**
132    * Saves the calculator history to a file.
133    */
134   public void save()
135   {
136      try
137      {
138         ByteArrayOutputStream out = new ByteArrayOutputStream();
139         PrintStream printOut = new PrintStream(out);
140         printOut.print(panel.getText());
141         InputStream data = new ByteArrayInputStream(out.toByteArray());
142         FileSaveService service = (FileSaveService) ServiceManager
143               .lookup("javax.jnlp.FileSaveService");
144         service.saveFileDialog(".", new String[] { "txt" }, data, "calc.txt");
145      }
146      catch (UnavailableServiceException e)
147      {
148         JOptionPane.showMessageDialog(this, e);
149      }
150      catch (IOException e)
151      {
152         JOptionPane.showMessageDialog(this, e);
153      }
154   }
155 }
```

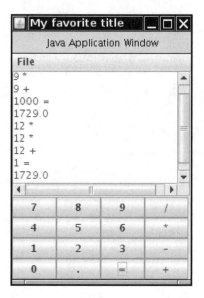

Figure 13.13 The WebStartCalculator application

`javax.jnlp.ServiceManager`

- `static String[] getServiceNames()`

  returns the names of all available services.

- `static Object lookup(String name)`

  returns a service with a given name.

`javax.jnlp.BasicService`

- `URL getCodeBase()`

  returns the codebase of this application.

- `boolean isWebBrowserSupported()`

  returns `true` if the Web Start environment can launch a web browser.

- `boolean showDocument(URL url)`

  attempts to show the given URL in a browser. Returns `true` if the request succeeded.

---

javax.jnlp.FileContents

- `InputStream getInputStream()`

  returns an input stream to read the contents of the file.

- `OutputStream getOutputStream(boolean overwrite)`

  returns an output stream to write to the file. If `overwrite` is `true`, then the existing contents of the file are overwritten.

- `String getName()`

  returns the file name (but not the full directory path).

- `boolean canRead()`
- `boolean canWrite()`

  returns `true` if the underlying file is readable or writable.

---

javax.jnlp.FileOpenService

- `FileContents openFileDialog(String pathHint, String[] extensions)`
- `FileContents[] openMultiFileDialog(String pathHint, String[] extensions)`

  displays a user warning and a file chooser. Returns content descriptors of the file or files that the user selected, or `null` if the user didn't choose a file.

---

javax.jnlp.FileSaveService

- `FileContents saveFileDialog(String pathHint, String[] extensions, InputStream data, String nameHint)`
- `FileContents saveAsFileDialog(String pathHint, String[] extensions, FileContents data)`

  displays a user warning and a file chooser. Writes the data and returns content descriptors of the file or files that the user selected, or `null` if the user didn't choose a file.

---

javax.jnlp.PersistenceService

- `long create(URL key, long maxsize)`

  creates a persistent store entry for the given key. Returns the maximum size granted by the persistent store.

(Continues)

---

javax.jnlp.PersistenceService *(Continued)*

- `void delete(URL key)`

  deletes the entry for the given key.

- `String[] getNames(URL url)`

  returns the relative key names of all keys that start with the given URL.

- `FileContents get(URL key)`

  gets a content descriptor through which you can modify the data associated with the given key. If no entry exists for the key, a `FileNotFoundException` is thrown.

This concludes our discussion of Java software deployment. In the final chapter of this volume, we will cover the important topic of concurrent programming.

Concurrency

In this chapter

You are probably familiar with *multitasking*—your operating system's ability to have more than one program working at what seems like the same time. For example, you can print while editing or downloading your email. Nowadays, you are likely to have a computer with more than one CPU, but the number of concurrently executing processes is not limited by the number of CPUs. The operating system assigns CPU time slices to each process, giving the impression of parallel activity.

Multithreaded programs extend the idea of multitasking by taking it one level lower: Individual programs will appear to do multiple tasks at the same time. Each task is usually called a *thread*, which is short for thread of control. Programs that can run more than one thread at once are said to be *multithreaded*.

So, what is the difference between multiple *processes* and multiple *threads*? The essential difference is that while each process has a complete set of its own variables, threads share the same data. This sounds somewhat risky, and indeed it can be, as you will see later in this chapter. However, shared variables make communication between threads more efficient and easier to program than interprocess communication. Moreover, on some operating systems, threads are more "lightweight" than processes—it takes less overhead to create and destroy individual threads than it does to launch new processes.

Multithreading is extremely useful in practice. For example, a browser should be able to simultaneously download multiple images. A web server needs to be able to serve concurrent requests. Graphical user interface (GUI) programs have a separate thread for gathering user interface events from the host operating environment. This chapter shows you how to add multithreading capability to your Java applications.

Fair warning: Concurrent programming can get very complex. In this chapter, we cover all the tools that an application programmer is likely to need. However, for more intricate system-level programming, we suggest that you turn to a more advanced reference, such as *Java Concurrency in Practice* by Brian Goetz et al. (Addison-Wesley Professional, 2006).

14.1 What Are Threads?

Let us start by looking at a program that does not use multiple threads and that, as a consequence, makes it difficult for the user to perform several tasks with that program. After we dissect it, we will show you how easy it is to have this program run separate threads. This program animates a bouncing ball by continually moving the ball, finding out if it bounces against a wall, and then redrawing it. (See Figure 14.1.)

As soon as you click the Start button, the program launches a ball from the upper left corner of the screen and the ball begins bouncing. The handler of the Start button calls the `addBall` method. That method contains a loop running through 1,000 moves. Each call to `move` moves the ball by a small amount, adjusts the direction if it bounces against a wall, and redraws the panel.

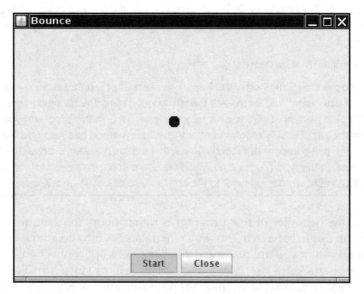

Figure 14.1 Using a thread to animate a bouncing ball

```
Ball ball = new Ball();
panel.add(ball);
for (int i = 1; i <= STEPS; i++)
{
   ball.move(panel.getBounds());
   panel.paint(panel.getGraphics());
   Thread.sleep(DELAY);
}
```

The call to Thread.sleep does not create a new thread—sleep is a static method of the Thread class that temporarily stops the activity of the current thread for the given number of milliseconds.

The sleep method can throw an InterruptedException. We discuss this exception and its proper handling later. For now, we simply terminate the bouncing if this exception occurs.

If you run the program, the ball bounces around nicely, but it completely takes over the application. If you become tired of the bouncing ball before it has finished its 1,000 moves and click the Close button, the ball continues bouncing anyway. You cannot interact with the program until the ball has finished bouncing.

NOTE: If you carefully look over the code at the end of this section, you will notice the call

```
comp.paint(comp.getGraphics())
```

inside the addBall method of the BounceFrame class. That is pretty strange—normally, you'd call repaint and let the AWT worry about getting the graphics context and doing the painting. But if you try to call comp.repaint() in this program, you'll find that the panel is only repainted after the addBall method has returned. Also note that the ball component extends JPanel; this makes it easier to erase the background. In the next program, in which we use a separate thread to compute the ball position, we can go back to the familiar use of repaint and JComponent.

Obviously, the behavior of this program is rather poor. You would not want a program you use to behave in this way when you ask it to do a time-consuming job. After all, when you are reading data over a network connection, it is all too common to be stuck in a task that you would *really* like to interrupt. For example, suppose you download a large image and decide, after seeing a piece of it, that you do not need or want to see the rest; you certainly would like to be able to click a Stop or Back button to interrupt the loading process. In the next section, we will show you how to keep the user in control by running crucial parts of the code in a separate *thread*.

Listings 14.1 through 14.3 show the code for the program.

Listing 14.1 bounce/Bounce.java

```
1  package bounce;
2
3  import java.awt.*;
4  import java.awt.event.*;
5  import javax.swing.*;
6
7  /**
8   * Shows an animated bouncing ball.
9   * @version 1.34 2015-06-21
10  * @author Cay Horstmann
11  */
12 public class Bounce
13 {
14    public static void main(String[] args)
15    {
16       EventQueue.invokeLater(() -> {
17          JFrame frame = new BounceFrame();
18          frame.setDefaultCloseOperation(JFrame.EXIT_ON_CLOSE);
```

```
19          frame.setVisible(true);
20       });
21    }
22 }
23
24 /**
25  * The frame with ball component and buttons.
26  */
27 class BounceFrame extends JFrame
28 {
29    private BallComponent comp;
30    public static final int STEPS = 1000;
31    public static final int DELAY = 3;
32
33    /**
34     * Constructs the frame with the component for showing the bouncing ball and
35     * Start and Close buttons
36     */
37    public BounceFrame()
38    {
39       setTitle("Bounce");
40       comp = new BallComponent();
41       add(comp, BorderLayout.CENTER);
42       JPanel buttonPanel = new JPanel();
43       addButton(buttonPanel, "Start", event -> addBall());
44       addButton(buttonPanel, "Close", event -> System.exit(0));
45       add(buttonPanel, BorderLayout.SOUTH);
46       pack();
47    }
48
49    /**
50     * Adds a button to a container.
51     * @param c the container
52     * @param title the button title
53     * @param listener the action listener for the button
54     */
55    public void addButton(Container c, String title, ActionListener listener)
56    {
57       JButton button = new JButton(title);
58       c.add(button);
59       button.addActionListener(listener);
60    }
61
62    /**
63     * Adds a bouncing ball to the panel and makes it bounce 1,000 times.
64     */
65    public void addBall()
66    {
```

(Continues)

Listing 14.1   *(Continued)*

```
67      try
68      {
69         Ball ball = new Ball();
70         comp.add(ball);
71
72         for (int i = 1; i <= STEPS; i++)
73         {
74            ball.move(comp.getBounds());
75            comp.paint(comp.getGraphics());
76            Thread.sleep(DELAY);
77         }
78      }
79      catch (InterruptedException e)
80      {
81      }
82   }
83 }
```

Listing 14.2   bounce/Ball.java

```
1  package bounce;
2
3  import java.awt.geom.*;
4
5  /**
6   * A ball that moves and bounces off the edges of a rectangle
7   * @version 1.33 2007-05-17
8   * @author Cay Horstmann
9   */
10 public class Ball
11 {
12    private static final int XSIZE = 15;
13    private static final int YSIZE = 15;
14    private double x = 0;
15    private double y = 0;
16    private double dx = 1;
17    private double dy = 1;
18
19    /**
20     * Moves the ball to the next position, reversing direction if it hits one of the edges
21     */
22    public void move(Rectangle2D bounds)
23    {
24       x += dx;
25       y += dy;
```

```
26        if (x < bounds.getMinX())
27        {
28           x = bounds.getMinX();
29           dx = -dx;
30        }
31        if (x + XSIZE >= bounds.getMaxX())
32        {
33           x = bounds.getMaxX() - XSIZE;
34           dx = -dx;
35        }
36        if (y < bounds.getMinY())
37        {
38           y = bounds.getMinY();
39           dy = -dy;
40        }
41        if (y + YSIZE >= bounds.getMaxY())
42        {
43           y = bounds.getMaxY() - YSIZE;
44           dy = -dy;
45        }
46     }
47
48     /**
49      * Gets the shape of the ball at its current position.
50      */
51     public Ellipse2D getShape()
52     {
53        return new Ellipse2D.Double(x, y, XSIZE, YSIZE);
54     }
55 }
```

Listing 14.3 bounce/BallComponent.java

```
1  package bounce;
2
3  import java.awt.*;
4  import java.util.*;
5  import javax.swing.*;
6
7  /**
8   * The component that draws the balls.
9   * @version 1.34 2012-01-26
10   * @author Cay Horstmann
11   */
12 public class BallComponent extends JPanel
13 {
14    private static final int DEFAULT_WIDTH = 450;
15    private static final int DEFAULT_HEIGHT = 350;
```

(Continues)

Listing 14.3 *(Continued)*

```
16
17     private java.util.List<Ball> balls = new ArrayList<>();
18
19     /**
20      * Add a ball to the component.
21      * @param b the ball to add
22      */
23     public void add(Ball b)
24     {
25        balls.add(b);
26     }
27
28     public void paintComponent(Graphics g)
29     {
30        super.paintComponent(g); // erase background
31        Graphics2D g2 = (Graphics2D) g;
32        for (Ball b : balls)
33        {
34           g2.fill(b.getShape());
35        }
36     }
37
38     public Dimension getPreferredSize() { return new Dimension(DEFAULT_WIDTH, DEFAULT_HEIGHT); }
39  }
```

---

java.lang.Thread 1.0

- static void sleep(long millis)

  sleeps for the given number of milliseconds.

  Parameters: millis   The number of milliseconds to sleep

14.1.1 Using Threads to Give Other Tasks a Chance

We will make our bouncing ball program more responsive by running the code that moves the ball in a separate thread. In fact, you will be able to launch multiple balls, each moved by its own thread. In addition, the AWT *event dispatch thread* will continue running in parallel, taking care of user interface events. Since each thread gets a chance to run, the event dispatch thread has the opportunity to notice that the user clicks the Close button while the balls are bouncing. The thread can then process the "close" action.

We use ball-bouncing code as an example to give you a visual impression of the need for concurrency. In general, you need to be wary of any long-running computation. Your computation is likely to be a part of some bigger framework, such as a GUI or web framework. Whenever the framework calls one of your methods, there is usually an expectation of a quick return. If you need to do any task that takes a long time, your task should run concurrently.

Here is a simple procedure for running a task in a separate thread:

1. Place the code for the task into the `run` method of a class that implements the `Runnable` interface. That interface is very simple, with a single method:

```
public interface Runnable
{
    void run();
}
```

Since `Runnable` is a functional interface, you can make an instance with a lambda expression:

```
Runnable r = () -> { task code };
```

2. Construct a `Thread` object from the `Runnable`:

```
Thread t = new Thread(r);
```

3. Start the thread:

```
t.start();
```

To make our bouncing ball program into a separate thread, we need only place the code for the animation inside the `run` method of a `Runnable`, and then start a thread:

```
Runnable r = () -> {
    try
    {
        for (int i = 1; i <= STEPS; i++)
        {
            ball.move(comp.getBounds());
            comp.repaint();
            Thread.sleep(DELAY);
        }
    }
    catch (InterruptedException e)
    {
    }
};
Thread t = new Thread(r);
t.start();
```

Again, we need to catch an `InterruptedException` that the `sleep` method threatens to throw. We will discuss this exception in the next section. Typically, interruption is used to request that a thread terminates. Accordingly, our run method exits when an InterruptedException occurs.

Whenever the Start button is clicked, the ball is moved in a new thread (see Figure 14.2).

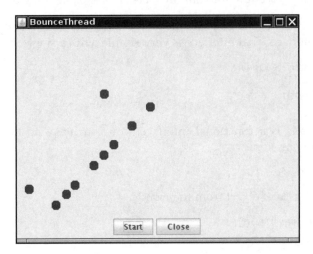

Figure 14.2 Running multiple threads

That's all there is to it! You now know how to run tasks in parallel. The remainder of this chapter tells you how to control the interaction between threads.

The complete code is shown in Listing 14.4.

NOTE: You can also define a thread by forming a subclass of the Thread class, like this:

```
class MyThread extends Thread
{
   public void run()
   {
      task code
   }
}
```

Then you construct an object of the subclass and call its start method. However, this approach is no longer recommended. You should decouple the *task* that is to be run in parallel from the *mechanism* of running it. If you have many tasks, it is too expensive to create a separate thread for each of them. Instead, you can use a thread pool—see Section 14.9, "Executors," on p. 920.

CAUTION: Do *not* call the `run` method of the `Thread` class or the `Runnable` object. Calling the `run` method directly merely executes the task in the *same* thread—no new thread is started. Instead, call the `Thread.start` method. It creates a new thread that executes the `run` method.

Listing 14.4 bounceThread/BounceThread.java

```java
1  package bounceThread;
2
3  import java.awt.*;
4  import java.awt.event.*;
5
6  import javax.swing.*;
7
8  /**
9   * Shows animated bouncing balls.
10  * @version 1.34 2015-06-21
11  * @author Cay Horstmann
12  */
13 public class BounceThread
14 {
15    public static void main(String[] args)
16    {
17       EventQueue.invokeLater(() -> {
18          JFrame frame = new BounceFrame();
19          frame.setTitle("BounceThread");
20          frame.setDefaultCloseOperation(JFrame.EXIT_ON_CLOSE);
21          frame.setVisible(true);
22       });
23    }
24 }
25
26 /**
27  * The frame with panel and buttons.
28  */
29 class BounceFrame extends JFrame
30 {
31    private BallComponent comp;
32    public static final int STEPS = 1000;
33    public static final int DELAY = 5;
34
35    /**
36     * Constructs the frame with the component for showing the bouncing ball and
37     * Start and Close buttons
38     */
```

(Continues)

Listing 14.4 *(Continued)*

```java
39    public BounceFrame()
40    {
41       comp = new BallComponent();
42       add(comp, BorderLayout.CENTER);
43       JPanel buttonPanel = new JPanel();
44       addButton(buttonPanel, "Start", event -> addBall());
45       addButton(buttonPanel, "Close", event -> System.exit(0));
46       add(buttonPanel, BorderLayout.SOUTH);
47       pack();
48    }
49
50    /**
51     * Adds a button to a container.
52     * @param c the container
53     * @param title the button title
54     * @param listener the action listener for the button
55     */
56    public void addButton(Container c, String title, ActionListener listener)
57    {
58       JButton button = new JButton(title);
59       c.add(button);
60       button.addActionListener(listener);
61    }
62
63    /**
64     * Adds a bouncing ball to the canvas and starts a thread to make it bounce
65     */
66    public void addBall()
67    {
68       Ball ball = new Ball();
69       comp.add(ball);
70       Runnable r = () -> {
71          try
72          {
73             for (int i = 1; i <= STEPS; i++)
74             {
75                ball.move(comp.getBounds());
76                comp.repaint();
77                Thread.sleep(DELAY);
78             }
79          }
80          catch (InterruptedException e)
81          {
82          }
83       };
```

```
84        Thread t = new Thread(r);
85        t.start();
86     }
87  }
```

---

java.lang.Thread 1.0

- Thread(Runnable target)

  constructs a new thread that calls the run() method of the specified target.

- void start()

  starts this thread, causing the run() method to be called. This method will return immediately. The new thread runs concurrently.

- void run()

  calls the run method of the associated Runnable.

---

java.lang.Runnable 1.0

- void run()

  must be overridden and supplied with instructions for the task that you want to have executed.

14.2 Interrupting Threads

A thread terminates when its run method returns—by executing a return statement, after executing the last statement in the method body, or if an exception occurs that is not caught in the method. In the initial release of Java, there also was a stop method that another thread could call to terminate a thread. However, that method is now deprecated. We discuss the reason in Section 14.5.15, "Why the stop and suspend Methods Are Deprecated," on p. 896.

Other than with the deprecated stop method, there is no way to *force* a thread to terminate. However, the interrupt method can be used to *request* termination of a thread.

When the interrupt method is called on a thread, the *interrupted status* of the thread is set. This is a boolean flag that is present in every thread. Each thread should occasionally check whether it has been interrupted.

To find out whether the interrupted status was set, first call the static Thread.currentThread method to get the current thread, and then call the isInterrupted method:

```
while (!Thread.currentThread().isInterrupted() && more work to do)
{
    do more work
}
```

However, if a thread is blocked, it cannot check the interrupted status. This is where the InterruptedException comes in. When the interrupt method is called on a thread that blocks on a call such as sleep or wait, the blocking call is terminated by an InterruptedException. (There are blocking I/O calls that cannot be interrupted; you should consider interruptible alternatives. See Chapters 1 and 3 of Volume II for details.)

There is no language requirement that a thread which is interrupted should terminate. Interrupting a thread simply grabs its attention. The interrupted thread can decide how to react to the interruption. Some threads are so important that they should handle the exception and continue. But quite commonly, a thread will simply want to interpret an interruption as a request for termination. The run method of such a thread has the following form:

```
Runnable r = () -> {
    try
    {
        . . .
        while (!Thread.currentThread().isInterrupted() && more work to do)
        {
            do more work
        }
    }
    catch(InterruptedException e)
    {
        // thread was interrupted during sleep or wait
    }
    finally
    {
        cleanup, if required
    }
    // exiting the run method terminates the thread
};
```

The isInterrupted check is neither necessary nor useful if you call the sleep method (or another interruptible method) after every work iteration. If you call the sleep method when the interrupted status is set, it doesn't sleep. Instead, it clears the status (!) and throws an InterruptedException. Therefore, if your loop calls sleep, don't check the interrupted status. Instead, catch the InterruptedException, like this:

```
Runnable r = () -> {
   try
   {
      . . .
      while (more work to do)
      {
         do more work
         Thread.sleep(delay);
      }
   }
   catch(InterruptedException e)
   {
      // thread was interrupted during sleep
   }
   finally
   {
      cleanup, if required
   }
   // exiting the run method terminates the thread
};
```

 NOTE: There are two very similar methods, `interrupted` and `isInterrupted`. The `interrupted` method is a static method that checks whether the *current* thread has been interrupted. Furthermore, calling the `interrupted` method *clears* the interrupted status of the thread. On the other hand, the `isInterrupted` method is an instance method that you can use to check whether any thread has been interrupted. Calling it does not change the interrupted status.

You'll find lots of published code in which the `InterruptedException` is squelched at a low level, like this:

```
void mySubTask()
{
   . . .
   try { sleep(delay); }
   catch (InterruptedException e) {} // Don't ignore!
   . . .
}
```

Don't do that! If you can't think of anything good to do in the `catch` clause, you still have two reasonable choices:

- In the catch clause, call `Thread.currentThread().interrupt()` to set the interrupted status. Then the caller can test it.

```
void mySubTask()
{
   . . .
   try { sleep(delay); }
   catch (InterruptedException e) { Thread.currentThread().interrupt(); }
   . . .
}
```

- Or, even better, tag your method with `throws InterruptedException` and drop the `try` block. Then the caller (or, ultimately, the `run` method) can catch it.

```
void mySubTask() throws InterruptedException
{
   . . .
   sleep(delay);
   . . .
}
```

---

java.lang.Thread 1.0

- `void interrupt()`

  sends an interrupt request to a thread. The interrupted status of the thread is set to true. If the thread is currently blocked by a call to `sleep`, then an `InterruptedException` is thrown.

- `static boolean interrupted()`

  tests whether the *current* thread (that is, the thread that is executing this instruction) has been interrupted. Note that this is a static method. The call has a side effect—it resets the interrupted status of the current thread to `false`.

- `boolean isInterrupted()`

  tests whether a thread has been interrupted. Unlike the `static interrupted` method, this call does not change the interrupted status of the thread.

- `static Thread currentThread()`

  returns the `Thread` object representing the currently executing thread.

14.3 Thread States

Threads can be in one of six states:

- New
- Runnable
- Blocked
- Waiting
- Timed waiting
- Terminated

Each of these states is explained in the sections that follow.

To determine the current state of a thread, simply call the getState method.

14.3.1 New Threads

When you create a thread with the new operator—for example, new Thread(r)—the thread is not yet running. This means that it is in the *new* state. When a thread is in the new state, the program has not started executing code inside of it. A certain amount of bookkeeping needs to be done before a thread can run.

14.3.2 Runnable Threads

Once you invoke the start method, the thread is in the *runnable* state. A runnable thread may or may not actually be running. It is up to the operating system to give the thread time to run. (The Java specification does not call this a separate state, though. A running thread is still in the runnable state.)

Once a thread is running, it doesn't necessarily keep running. In fact, it is desirable that running threads occasionally pause so that other threads have a chance to run. The details of thread scheduling depend on the services that the operating system provides. Preemptive scheduling systems give each runnable thread a slice of time to perform its task. When that slice of time is exhausted, the operating system *preempts* the thread and gives another thread an opportunity to work (see Figure 14.4). When selecting the next thread, the operating system takes into account the thread *priorities*—see Section 14.4.1, "Thread Priorities," on p. 858 for more information.

All modern desktop and server operating systems use preemptive scheduling. However, small devices such as cell phones may use cooperative scheduling. In such a device, a thread loses control only when it calls the `yield` method, or when it is blocked or waiting.

On a machine with multiple processors, each processor can run a thread, and you can have multiple threads run in parallel. Of course, if there are more threads than processors, the scheduler still has to do time slicing.

Always keep in mind that a runnable thread may or may not be running at any given time. (This is why the state is called "runnable" and not "running.")

14.3.3 Blocked and Waiting Threads

When a thread is blocked or waiting, it is temporarily inactive. It doesn't execute any code and consumes minimal resources. It is up to the thread scheduler to reactivate it. The details depend on how the inactive state was reached.

- When the thread tries to acquire an intrinsic object lock (but not a `Lock` in the `java.util.concurrent` library) that is currently held by another thread, it becomes *blocked*. (We discuss `java.util.concurrent` locks in Section 14.5.3, "Lock Objects," on p. 868 and intrinsic object locks in Section 14.5.5, "The `synchronized` Keyword," on p. 878.) The thread becomes unblocked when all other threads have relinquished the lock and the thread scheduler has allowed this thread to hold it.

- When the thread waits for another thread to notify the scheduler of a condition, it enters the *waiting* state. We discuss conditions in Section 14.5.4, "Condition Objects," on p. 872. This happens by calling the `Object.wait` or `Thread.join` method, or by waiting for a `Lock` or `Condition` in the `java.util.concurrent` library. In practice, the difference between the blocked and waiting state is not significant.

- Several methods have a timeout parameter. Calling them causes the thread to enter the *timed waiting* state. This state persists either until the timeout expires or the appropriate notification has been received. Methods with timeout include `Thread.sleep` and the timed versions of `Object.wait`, `Thread.join`, `Lock.tryLock`, and `Condition.await`.

Figure 14.3 shows the states that a thread can have and the possible transitions from one state to another. When a thread is blocked or waiting (or, of course, when it terminates), another thread will be scheduled to run. When a thread is reactivated (for example, because its timeout has expired or it has succeeded in acquiring a lock), the scheduler checks to see if it has a higher priority than the currently running threads. If so, it preempts one of the current threads and picks a new thread to run.

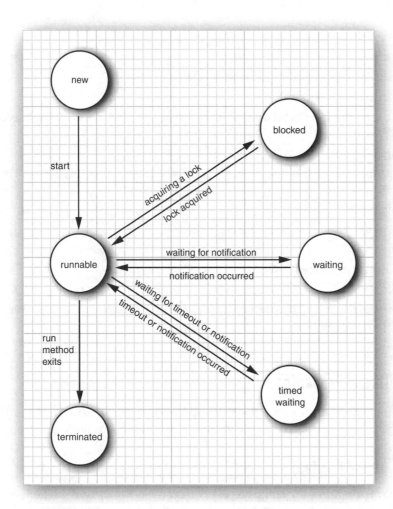

Figure 14.3 Thread states

14.3.4 Terminated Threads

A thread is terminated for one of two reasons:

- It dies a natural death because the run method exits normally.
- It dies abruptly because an uncaught exception terminates the run method.

In particular, you can kill a thread by invoking its stop method. That method throws a ThreadDeath error object that kills the thread. However, the stop method is deprecated, and you should never call it in your own code.

`java.lang.Thread` 1.0

- `void join()`

  waits for the specified thread to terminate.

- `void join(long millis)`

  waits for the specified thread to die or for the specified number of milliseconds to pass.

- `Thread.State getState()` 5.0

  gets the state of this thread: one of NEW, RUNNABLE, BLOCKED, WAITING, TIMED_WAITING, or TERMINATED.

- `void stop()`

  stops the thread. This method is deprecated.

- `void suspend()`

  suspends this thread's execution. This method is deprecated.

- `void resume()`

  resumes this thread. This method is only valid after `suspend()` has been invoked. This method is deprecated.

14.4 Thread Properties

In the following sections, we discuss miscellaneous properties of threads: thread priorities, daemon threads, thread groups, and handlers for uncaught exceptions.

14.4.1 Thread Priorities

In the Java programming language, every thread has a *priority*. By default, a thread inherits the priority of the thread that constructed it. You can increase or decrease the priority of any thread with the `setPriority` method. You can set the priority to any value between MIN_PRIORITY (defined as 1 in the `Thread` class) and MAX_PRIORITY (defined as 10). NORM_PRIORITY is defined as 5.

Whenever the thread scheduler has a chance to pick a new thread, it prefers threads with higher priority. However, thread priorities are *highly system dependent*. When the virtual machine relies on the thread implementation of the host platform, the Java thread priorities are mapped to the priority levels of the host platform, which may have more or fewer thread priority levels.

For example, Windows has seven priority levels. Some of the Java priorities will map to the same operating system level. In the Oracle JVM for Linux, thread priorities are ignored altogether—all threads have the same priority.

Beginning programmers sometimes overuse thread priorities. There are few reasons ever to tweak priorities. You should certainly never structure your programs so that their correct functioning depends on priority levels.

 CAUTION: If you do use priorities, you should be aware of a common beginner's error. If you have several threads with a high priority that don't become inactive, the lower-priority threads may *never* execute. Whenever the scheduler decides to run a new thread, it will choose among the highest-priority threads first, even though that may starve the lower-priority threads completely.

`java.lang.Thread` 1.0

- `void setPriority(int newPriority)`

  sets the priority of this thread. The priority must be between `Thread.MIN_PRIORITY` and `Thread.MAX_PRIORITY`. Use `Thread.NORM_PRIORITY` for normal priority.

- `static int MIN_PRIORITY`

  is the minimum priority that a `Thread` can have. The minimum priority value is 1.

- `static int NORM_PRIORITY`

  is the default priority of a `Thread`. The default priority is 5.

- `static int MAX_PRIORITY`

  is the maximum priority that a `Thread` can have. The maximum priority value is 10.

- `static void yield()`

  causes the currently executing thread to yield. If there are other runnable threads with a priority at least as high as the priority of this thread, they will be scheduled next. Note that this is a static method.

14.4.2 Daemon Threads

You can turn a thread into a *daemon thread* by calling

```
t.setDaemon(true);
```

There is nothing demonic about such a thread. A daemon is simply a thread that has no other role in life than to serve others. Examples are timer threads that send regular "timer ticks" to other threads or threads that clean up stale cache entries.

When only daemon threads remain, the virtual machine exits. There is no point in keeping the program running if all remaining threads are daemons.

Daemon threads are sometimes mistakenly used by beginners who don't want to think about shutdown actions. However, this can be dangerous. A daemon thread should never access a persistent resource such as a file or database since it can terminate at any time, even in the middle of an operation.

`java.lang.Thread` 1.0

- `void setDaemon(boolean isDaemon)`

  marks this thread as a daemon thread or a user thread. This method must be called before the thread is started.

14.4.3 Handlers for Uncaught Exceptions

The `run` method of a thread cannot throw any checked exceptions, but it can be terminated by an unchecked exception. In that case, the thread dies.

However, there is no `catch` clause to which the exception can be propagated. Instead, just before the thread dies, the exception is passed to a handler for uncaught exceptions.

The handler must belong to a class that implements the `Thread.UncaughtExceptionHandler` interface. That interface has a single method,

```
void uncaughtException(Thread t, Throwable e)
```

You can install a handler into any thread with the `setUncaughtExceptionHandler` method. You can also install a default handler for all threads with the static method `setDefaultUncaughtExceptionHandler` of the `Thread` class. A replacement handler might use the logging API to send reports of uncaught exceptions into a log file.

If you don't install a default handler, the default handler is `null`. However, if you don't install a handler for an individual thread, the handler is the thread's `ThreadGroup` object.

 NOTE: A thread group is a collection of threads that can be managed together. By default, all threads that you create belong to the same thread group, but it is possible to establish other groupings. Since there are now better features for operating on collections of threads, we recommend that you do not use thread groups in your programs.

The `ThreadGroup` class implements the `Thread.UncaughtExceptionHandler` interface. Its `uncaughtException` method takes the following action:

1. If the thread group has a parent, then the `uncaughtException` method of the parent group is called.
2. Otherwise, if the `Thread.getDefaultUncaughtExceptionHandler` method returns a non-`null` handler, it is called.
3. Otherwise, if the `Throwable` is an instance of `ThreadDeath`, nothing happens.
4. Otherwise, the name of the thread and the stack trace of the `Throwable` are printed on `System.err`.

That is the stack trace that you have undoubtedly seen many times in your programs.

---

java.lang.Thread 1.0

- `static void setDefaultUncaughtExceptionHandler(Thread.UncaughtExceptionHandler handler)` 5.0
- `static Thread.UncaughtExceptionHandler getDefaultUncaughtExceptionHandler()` 5.0

  sets or gets the default handler for uncaught exceptions.

- `void setUncaughtExceptionHandler(Thread.UncaughtExceptionHandler handler)` 5.0
- `Thread.UncaughtExceptionHandler getUncaughtExceptionHandler()` 5.0

  sets or gets the handler for uncaught exceptions. If no handler is installed, the thread group object is the handler.

---

java.lang.Thread.UncaughtExceptionHandler 5.0

- `void uncaughtException(Thread t, Throwable e)`

  defined to log a custom report when a thread is terminated with an uncaught exception.

  Parameters: t   The thread that was terminated due to an uncaught exception

                e   The uncaught exception object

---

java.lang.ThreadGroup 1.0

- void uncaughtException(Thread t, Throwable e)

    calls this method of the parent thread group if there is a parent, or calls the default handler of the Thread class if there is a default handler, or otherwise prints a stack trace to the standard error stream. (However, if e is a ThreadDeath object, the stack trace is suppressed. ThreadDeath objects are generated by the deprecated stop method.)

14.5 Synchronization

In most practical multithreaded applications, two or more threads need to share access to the same data. What happens if two threads have access to the same object and each calls a method that modifies the state of the object? As you might imagine, the threads can step on each other's toes. Depending on the order in which the data were accessed, corrupted objects can result. Such a situation is often called a *race condition*.

14.5.1 An Example of a Race Condition

To avoid corruption of shared data by multiple threads, you must learn how to *synchronize the access*. In this section, you'll see what happens if you do not use synchronization. In the next section, you'll see how to synchronize data access.

In the next test program, we simulate a bank with a number of accounts. We randomly generate transactions that move money between these accounts. Each account has one thread. Each transaction moves a random amount of money from the account serviced by the thread to another random account.

The simulation code is straightforward. We have the class Bank with the method transfer. This method transfers some amount of money from one account to another. (We don't yet worry about negative account balances.) Here is the code for the transfer method of the Bank class.

```
public void transfer(int from, int to, double amount)
   // CAUTION: unsafe when called from multiple threads
{
   System.out.print(Thread.currentThread());
   accounts[from] -= amount;
   System.out.printf(" %10.2f from %d to %d", amount, from, to);
   accounts[to] += amount;
   System.out.printf(" Total Balance: %10.2f%n", getTotalBalance());
}
```

Here is the code for the Runnable instances. The run method keeps moving money out of a given bank account. In each iteration, the run method picks a random target account and a random amount, calls transfer on the bank object, and then sleeps.

```
Runnable r = () -> {
   try
   {
      while (true)
      {
         int toAccount = (int) (bank.size() * Math.random());
         double amount = MAX_AMOUNT * Math.random();
         bank.transfer(fromAccount, toAccount, amount);
         Thread.sleep((int) (DELAY * Math.random()));
      }
   }
   catch (InterruptedException e)
   {
   }
};
```

When this simulation runs, we do not know how much money is in any one bank account at any time. But we do know that the total amount of money in all the accounts should remain unchanged because all we do is move money from one account to another.

At the end of each transaction, the transfer method recomputes the total and prints it.

This program never finishes. Just press Ctrl+C to kill the program.

Here is a typical printout:

```
. . .
Thread[Thread-11,5,main]   588.48 from 11 to 44 Total Balance: 100000.00
Thread[Thread-12,5,main]   976.11 from 12 to 22 Total Balance: 100000.00
Thread[Thread-14,5,main]   521.51 from 14 to 22 Total Balance: 100000.00
Thread[Thread-13,5,main]   359.89 from 13 to 81 Total Balance: 100000.00

. . .
Thread[Thread-36,5,main]   401.71 from 36 to 73 Total Balance:  99291.06
Thread[Thread-35,5,main]   691.46 from 35 to 77 Total Balance:  99291.06
Thread[Thread-37,5,main]    78.64 from 37 to 3 Total Balance:  99291.06
Thread[Thread-34,5,main]   197.11 from 34 to 69 Total Balance:  99291.06
Thread[Thread-36,5,main]    85.96 from 36 to 4 Total Balance:  99291.06

. . .
Thread[Thread-4,5,main]Thread[Thread-33,5,main]        7.31 from 31 to 32 Total Balance:
99979.24
      627.50 from 4 to 5 Total Balance:  99979.24
. . .
```

As you can see, something is very wrong. For a few transactions, the bank balance remains at $100,000, which is the correct total for 100 accounts of $1,000 each. But after some time, the balance changes slightly. When you run this program, errors may happen quickly, or it may take a very long time for the balance to become corrupted. This situation does not inspire confidence, and you would probably not want to deposit your hard-earned money in such a bank.

The program in Listings 14.5 and 14.6 provides the complete source code. See if you can spot the problems with the code. We will unravel the mystery in the next section.

Listing 14.5   unsynch/UnsynchBankTest.java

```java
1  package unsynch;
2
3  /**
4   * This program shows data corruption when multiple threads access a data structure.
5   * @version 1.31 2015-06-21
6   * @author Cay Horstmann
7   */
8  public class UnsynchBankTest
9  {
10     public static final int NACCOUNTS = 100;
11     public static final double INITIAL_BALANCE = 1000;
12     public static final double MAX_AMOUNT = 1000;
13     public static final int DELAY = 10;
14
15     public static void main(String[] args)
16     {
17        Bank bank = new Bank(NACCOUNTS, INITIAL_BALANCE);
18        for (int i = 0; i < NACCOUNTS; i++)
19        {
20           int fromAccount = i;
21           Runnable r = () -> {
22              try
23              {
24                 while (true)
25                 {
26                    int toAccount = (int) (bank.size() * Math.random());
27                    double amount = MAX_AMOUNT * Math.random();
28                    bank.transfer(fromAccount, toAccount, amount);
29                    Thread.sleep((int) (DELAY * Math.random()));
30                 }
31              }
32              catch (InterruptedException e)
33              {
34              }
35           };
```

```
36            Thread t = new Thread(r);
37            t.start();
38        }
39     }
40  }
```

Listing 14.6 unsynch/Bank.java

```
1  package unsynch;
2
3  import java.util.*;
4
5  /**
6   * A bank with a number of bank accounts.
7   * @version 1.30 2004-08-01
8   * @author Cay Horstmann
9   */
10  public class Bank
11  {
12     private final double[] accounts;
13
14     /**
15      * Constructs the bank.
16      * @param n the number of accounts
17      * @param initialBalance the initial balance for each account
18      */
19     public Bank(int n, double initialBalance)
20     {
21        accounts = new double[n];
22        Arrays.fill(accounts, initialBalance);
23     }
24
25     /**
26      * Transfers money from one account to another.
27      * @param from the account to transfer from
28      * @param to the account to transfer to
29      * @param amount the amount to transfer
30      */
31     public void transfer(int from, int to, double amount)
32     {
33        if (accounts[from] < amount) return;
34        System.out.print(Thread.currentThread());
35        accounts[from] -= amount;
36        System.out.printf(" %10.2f from %d to %d", amount, from, to);
37        accounts[to] += amount;
38        System.out.printf(" Total Balance: %10.2f%n", getTotalBalance());
39     }
40
```

(Continues)

Listing 14.6   *(Continued)*

```
41    /**
42     * Gets the sum of all account balances.
43     * @return the total balance
44     */
45    public double getTotalBalance()
46    {
47       double sum = 0;
48
49       for (double a : accounts)
50          sum += a;
51
52       return sum;
53    }
54
55    /**
56     * Gets the number of accounts in the bank.
57     * @return the number of accounts
58     */
59    public int size()
60    {
61       return accounts.length;
62    }
63 }
```

14.5.2 The Race Condition Explained

In the previous section, we ran a program in which several threads updated bank account balances. After a while, errors crept in and some amount of money was either lost or spontaneously created. This problem occurs when two threads are simultaneously trying to update an account. Suppose two threads simultaneously carry out the instruction

```
accounts[to] += amount;
```

The problem is that these are not *atomic* operations. The instruction might be processed as follows:

1. Load `accounts[to]` into a register.
2. Add `amount`.
3. Move the result back to `accounts[to]`.

Now, suppose the first thread executes Steps 1 and 2, and then it is preempted. Suppose the second thread awakens and updates the same entry in the account array. Then, the first thread awakens and completes its Step 3.

That action wipes out the modification of the other thread. As a result, the total is no longer correct (see Figure 14.4).

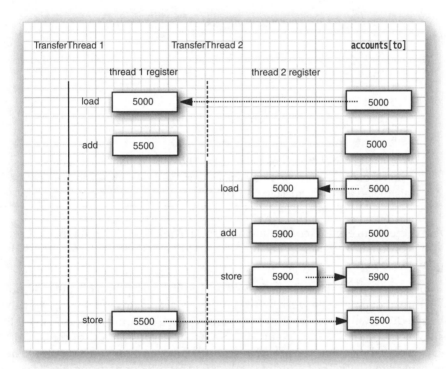

Figure 14.4 Simultaneous access by two threads

Our test program detects this corruption. (Of course, there is a slight chance of false alarms if the thread is interrupted as it is performing the tests!)

NOTE: You can actually peek at the virtual machine bytecodes that execute each statement in our class. Run the command

```
javap -c -v Bank
```

to decompile the `Bank.class` file. For example, the line

```
accounts[to] += amount;
```

is translated into the following bytecodes:

```
aload_0
getfield        #2; //Field accounts:[D
iload_2
dup2
daload
dload_3
dadd
dastore
```

What these codes mean does not matter. The point is that the increment command is made up of several instructions, and the thread executing them can be interrupted at any instruction.

What is the chance of this corruption occurring? We boosted the chance of observing the problem by interleaving the print statements with the statements that update the balance.

If you omit the print statements, the risk of corruption is quite a bit lower because each thread does so little work before going to sleep again, and it is unlikely that the scheduler will preempt it in the middle of the computation. However, the risk of corruption does not go away completely. If you run lots of threads on a heavily loaded machine, the program will still fail even after you have eliminated the print statements. The failure may take a few minutes or hours or days to occur. Frankly, there are few things worse in the life of a programmer than an error that only manifests itself once every few days.

The real problem is that the work of the `transfer` method can be interrupted in the middle. If we could ensure that the method runs to completion before the thread loses control, the state of the bank account object would never be corrupted.

14.5.3 Lock Objects

There are two mechanisms for protecting a code block from concurrent access. The Java language provides a `synchronized` keyword for this purpose, and Java SE 5.0 introduced the `ReentrantLock` class. The `synchronized` keyword automatically provides a lock as well as an associated "condition," which makes it powerful and convenient for most cases that require explicit locking. However, we believe that it is easier to understand the synchronized keyword after you have seen locks and conditions in isolation. The java.util.concurrent framework provides separate classes for these fundamental mechanisms, which we explain here and in Section 14.5.4, "Condition Objects," on p. 872. Once you have understood these building blocks, we present the synchronized keyword in Section 14.5.5, "The synchronized Keyword," on p. 878.

The basic outline for protecting a code block with a ReentrantLock is:

```
myLock.lock(); // a ReentrantLock object
try
{
    critical section
}
finally
{
    myLock.unlock(); // make sure the lock is unlocked even if an exception is thrown
}
```

This construct guarantees that only one thread at a time can enter the critical section. As soon as one thread locks the lock object, no other thread can get past the lock statement. When other threads call lock, they are deactivated until the first thread unlocks the lock object.

 CAUTION: It is critically important that the unlock operation is enclosed in a finally clause. If the code in the critical section throws an exception, the lock must be unlocked. Otherwise, the other threads will be blocked forever.

 NOTE: When you use locks, you cannot use the try-with-resources statement. First off, the unlock method isn't called close. But even if it was renamed, the try-with-resources statement wouldn't work. Its header expects the declaration of a new variable. But when you use a lock, you want to keep using the same variable that is shared among threads.

Let us use a lock to protect the transfer method of the Bank class.

```
public class Bank
{
    private Lock bankLock = new ReentrantLock(); // ReentrantLock implements the Lock interface
    . . .
    public void transfer(int from, int to, int amount)
    {
        bankLock.lock();
```

```
try
{
   System.out.print(Thread.currentThread());
   accounts[from] -= amount;
   System.out.printf(" %10.2f from %d to %d", amount, from, to);
   accounts[to] += amount;
   System.out.printf(" Total Balance: %10.2f%n", getTotalBalance());
}

finally
{
   bankLock.unlock();
}
   }
}
```

Suppose one thread calls transfer and gets preempted before it is done. Suppose a second thread also calls transfer. The second thread cannot acquire the lock and is blocked in the call to the lock method. It is deactivated and must wait for the first thread to finish executing the transfer method. When the first thread unlocks the lock, then the second thread can proceed (see Figure 14.5).

Try it out. Add the locking code to the transfer method and run the program again. You can run it forever, and the bank balance will not become corrupted.

Note that each Bank object has its own ReentrantLock object. If two threads try to access the same Bank object, then the lock serves to serialize the access. However, if two threads access different Bank objects, each thread acquires a different lock and neither thread is blocked. This is as it should be, because the threads cannot interfere with one another when they manipulate different Bank instances.

The lock is called *reentrant* because a thread can repeatedly acquire a lock that it already owns. The lock has a *hold count* that keeps track of the nested calls to the lock method. The thread has to call unlock for every call to lock in order to relinquish the lock. Because of this feature, code protected by a lock can call another method that uses the same locks.

For example, the transfer method calls the getTotalBalance method, which also locks the bankLock object, which now has a hold count of 2. When the getTotalBalance method exits, the hold count is back to 1. When the transfer method exits, the hold count is 0, and the thread relinquishes the lock.

In general, you will want to protect blocks of code that update or inspect a shared object, so you can be assured that these operations run to completion before another thread can use the same object.

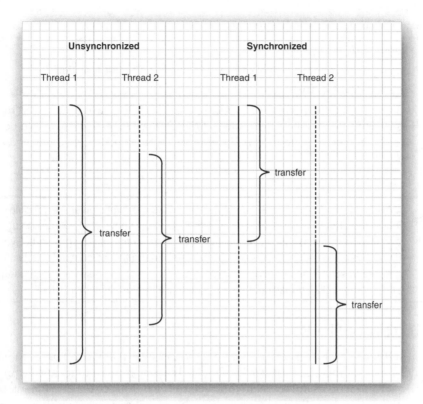

Figure 14.5 Comparison of unsynchronized and synchronized threads

 CAUTION: Be careful to ensure that the code in a critical section is not bypassed by throwing an exception. If an exception is thrown before the end of the section, the `finally` clause will relinquish the lock, but the object may be in a damaged state.

`java.util.concurrent.locks.Lock` 5.0

- `void lock()`

  acquires this lock; blocks if the lock is currently owned by another thread.

- `void unlock()`

  releases this lock.

---

java.util.concurrent.locks.ReentrantLock 5.0

- ReentrantLock()

  constructs a reentrant lock that can be used to protect a critical section.

- ReentrantLock(boolean fair)

  constructs a lock with the given fairness policy. A fair lock favors the thread that has been waiting for the longest time. However, this fairness guarantee can be a significant drag on performance. Therefore, by default, locks are not required to be fair.

 CAUTION: It sounds nice to be fair, but fair locks are *a lot slower* than regular locks. You should only enable fair locking if you truly know what you are doing and have a specific reason to consider fairness essential for your program. Even if you use a fair lock, you have no guarantee that the thread scheduler is fair. If the thread scheduler chooses to neglect a thread that has been waiting a long time for the lock, it doesn't get the chance to be treated fairly by the lock.

14.5.4 Condition Objects

Often, a thread enters a critical section only to discover that it can't proceed until a condition is fulfilled. Use a *condition object* to manage threads that have acquired a lock but cannot do useful work. In this section, we introduce the implementation of condition objects in the Java library. (For historical reasons, condition objects are often called *condition variables*.)

Let us refine our simulation of the bank. We do not want to transfer money out of an account that does not have the funds to cover the transfer. Note that we cannot use code like

```
if (bank.getBalance(from) >= amount)
    bank.transfer(from, to, amount);
```

It is entirely possible that the current thread will be deactivated between the successful outcome of the test and the call to transfer.

```
if (bank.getBalance(from) >= amount)
    // thread might be deactivated at this point
    bank.transfer(from, to, amount);
```

By the time the thread is running again, the account balance may have fallen below the withdrawal amount. You must make sure that no other thread can modify the balance between the test and the transfer action. You do so by protecting both the test and the transfer action with a lock:

```
public void transfer(int from, int to, int amount)
{
   bankLock.lock();
   try
   {
      while (accounts[from] < amount)
      {
         // wait
         . . .
      }
      // transfer funds
      . . .
   }
   finally
   {
      bankLock.unlock();
   }
}
```

Now, what do we do when there is not enough money in the account? We wait until some other thread has added funds. But this thread has just gained exclusive access to the bankLock, so no other thread has a chance to make a deposit. This is where condition objects come in.

A lock object can have one or more associated condition objects. You obtain a condition object with the newCondition method. It is customary to give each condition object a name that evokes the condition that it represents. For example, here we set up a condition object to represent the "sufficient funds" condition.

```
class Bank
{
   private Condition sufficientFunds;
   . . .
   public Bank()
   {
      . . .
      sufficientFunds = bankLock.newCondition();
   }
}
```

If the transfer method finds that sufficient funds are not available, it calls

```
sufficientFunds.await();
```

The current thread is now deactivated and gives up the lock. This lets in another thread that can, we hope, increase the account balance.

There is an essential difference between a thread that is waiting to acquire a lock and a thread that has called await. Once a thread calls the await method, it enters a *wait set* for that condition. The thread is *not* made runnable when the lock is available. Instead, it stays deactivated until another thread has called the `signalAll` method on the same condition.

When another thread has transferred money, it should call

```
sufficientFunds.signalAll();
```

This call reactivates all threads waiting for the condition. When the threads are removed from the wait set, they are again runnable and the scheduler will eventually activate them again. At that time, they will attempt to reenter the object. As soon as the lock is available, one of them will acquire the lock *and continue where it left off*, returning from the call to `await`.

At this time, the thread should test the condition again. There is no guarantee that the condition is now fulfilled—the `signalAll` method merely signals to the waiting threads that it *may be* fulfilled at this time and that it is worth checking for the condition again.

 NOTE: In general, a call to `await` should be inside a loop of the form

```
while (!(ok to proceed))
   condition.await();
```

It is crucially important that *some* other thread calls the `signalAll` method eventually. When a thread calls `await`, it has no way of reactivating itself. It puts its faith in the other threads. If none of them bother to reactivate the waiting thread, it will never run again. This can lead to unpleasant *deadlock* situations. If all other threads are blocked and the last active thread calls `await` without unblocking one of the others, it also blocks. No thread is left to unblock the others, and the program hangs.

When should you call `signalAll`? The rule of thumb is to call `signalAll` whenever the state of an object changes in a way that might be advantageous to waiting threads. For example, whenever an account balance changes, the waiting threads should be given another chance to inspect the balance. In our example, we call `signalAll` when we have finished the funds transfer.

```
public void transfer(int from, int to, int amount)
{
   bankLock.lock();
   try
   {
      while (accounts[from] < amount)
         sufficientFunds.await();
      // transfer funds
      . . .
```

```
      sufficientFunds.signalAll();
   }
   finally
   {
      bankLock.unlock();
   }
}
```

Note that the call to `signalAll` does not immediately activate a waiting thread. It only unblocks the waiting threads so that they can compete for entry into the object after the current thread has relinquished the lock.

Another method, `signal`, unblocks only a single thread from the wait set, chosen at random. That is more efficient than unblocking all threads, but there is a danger. If the randomly chosen thread finds that it still cannot proceed, it becomes blocked again. If no other thread calls `signal` again, then the system deadlocks.

 CAUTION: A thread can only call `await`, `signalAll`, or `signal` on a condition if it owns the lock of the condition.

If you run the sample program in Listing 14.7, you will notice that nothing ever goes wrong. The total balance stays at $100,000 forever. No account ever has a negative balance. (Again, press Ctrl+C to terminate the program.) You may also notice that the program runs a bit slower—this is the price you pay for the added bookkeeping involved in the synchronization mechanism.

In practice, using conditions correctly can be quite challenging. Before you start implementing your own condition objects, you should consider using one of the constructs described in Section 14.10, "Synchronizers," on p. 934.

Listing 14.7 synch/Bank.java

```
 1 package synch;
 2
 3 import java.util.*;
 4 import java.util.concurrent.locks.*;
 5
 6 /**
 7  * A bank with a number of bank accounts that uses locks for serializing access.
 8  * @version 1.30 2004-08-01
 9  * @author Cay Horstmann
10  */
11 public class Bank
12 {
```

(Continues)

Listing 14.7 *(Continued)*

```
13    private final double[] accounts;
14    private Lock bankLock;
15    private Condition sufficientFunds;
16
17    /**
18     * Constructs the bank.
19     * @param n the number of accounts
20     * @param initialBalance the initial balance for each account
21     */
22    public Bank(int n, double initialBalance)
23    {
24       accounts = new double[n];
25       Arrays.fill(accounts, initialBalance);
26       bankLock = new ReentrantLock();
27       sufficientFunds = bankLock.newCondition();
28    }
29
30    /**
31     * Transfers money from one account to another.
32     * @param from the account to transfer from
33     * @param to the account to transfer to
34     * @param amount the amount to transfer
35     */
36    public void transfer(int from, int to, double amount) throws InterruptedException
37    {
38       bankLock.lock();
39       try
40       {
41          while (accounts[from] < amount)
42             sufficientFunds.await();
43          System.out.print(Thread.currentThread());
44          accounts[from] -= amount;
45          System.out.printf(" %10.2f from %d to %d", amount, from, to);
46          accounts[to] += amount;
47          System.out.printf(" Total Balance: %10.2f%n", getTotalBalance());
48          sufficientFunds.signalAll();
49       }
50       finally
51       {
52          bankLock.unlock();
53       }
54    }
55
56    /**
57     * Gets the sum of all account balances.
58     * @return the total balance
59     */
```

```
60    public double getTotalBalance()
61    {
62       bankLock.lock();
63       try
64       {
65          double sum = 0;
66
67          for (double a : accounts)
68             sum += a;
69
70          return sum;
71       }
72       finally
73       {
74          bankLock.unlock();
75       }
76    }
77
78    /**
79     * Gets the number of accounts in the bank.
80     * @return the number of accounts
81     */
82    public int size()
83    {
84       return accounts.length;
85    }
86 }
```

---

java.util.concurrent.locks.Lock 5.0

- Condition newCondition()

  returns a condition object associated with this lock.

---

java.util.concurrent.locks.Condition 5.0

- void await()

  puts this thread on the wait set for this condition.

- void signalAll()

  unblocks all threads in the wait set for this condition.

- void signal()

  unblocks one randomly selected thread in the wait set for this condition.

14.5.5 The synchronized Keyword

In the preceding sections, you saw how to use Lock and Condition objects. Before going any further, let us summarize the key points about locks and conditions:

- A lock protects sections of code, allowing only one thread to execute the code at a time.
- A lock manages threads that are trying to enter a protected code segment.
- A lock can have one or more associated condition objects.
- Each condition object manages threads that have entered a protected code section but that cannot proceed.

The Lock and Condition interfaces give programmers a high degree of control over locking. However, in most situations, you don't need that control—you can use a mechanism that is built into the Java language. Ever since version 1.0, *every object in Java has an intrinsic lock*. If a method is declared with the synchronized keyword, the object's lock protects the entire method. That is, to call the method, a thread must acquire the intrinsic object lock.

In other words,

```
public synchronized void method()
{
   method body
}
```

is the equivalent of

```
public void method()
{
   this.intrinsicLock.lock();
   try
   {
      method body
   }
   finally { this.intrinsicLock.unlock(); }
}
```

For example, instead of using an explicit lock, we can simply declare the transfer method of the Bank class as synchronized.

The intrinsic object lock has a single associated condition. The wait method adds a thread to the wait set, and the notifyAll / notify methods unblock waiting threads. In other words, calling wait or notifyAll is the equivalent of

```
intrinsicCondition.await();
intrinsicCondition.signalAll();
```

NOTE: The wait, notifyAll, and notify methods are final methods of the Object class. The Condition methods had to be named await, signalAll, and signal so that they don't conflict with those methods.

For example, you can implement the Bank class in Java like this:

```
class Bank
{
    private double[] accounts;

    public synchronized void transfer(int from, int to, int amount) throws InterruptedException
    {
        while (accounts[from] < amount)
            wait(); // wait on intrinsic object lock's single condition
        accounts[from] -= amount;
        accounts[to] += amount;
        notifyAll(); // notify all threads waiting on the condition
    }

    public synchronized double getTotalBalance() { . . . }
}
```

As you can see, using the synchronized keyword yields code that is much more concise. Of course, to understand this code, you have to know that each object has an intrinsic lock, and that the lock has an intrinsic condition. The lock manages the threads that try to enter a synchronized method. The condition manages the threads that have called wait.

 TIP: Synchronized methods are relatively straightforward. However, beginners often struggle with conditions. Before you use wait/notifyAll, you should consider using one of the constructs described in Section 14.10, "Synchronizers," on p. 934.

It is also legal to declare static methods as synchronized. If such a method is called, it acquires the intrinsic lock of the associated class object. For example, if the Bank class has a static synchronized method, then the lock of the Bank.class object is locked when it is called. As a result, no other thread can call this or any other synchronized static method of the same class.

The intrinsic locks and conditions have some limitations. Among them:

- You cannot interrupt a thread that is trying to acquire a lock.
- You cannot specify a timeout when trying to acquire a lock.
- Having a single condition per lock can be inefficient.

What should you use in your code—Lock and Condition objects or synchronized methods? Here is our recommendation:

- It is best to use neither Lock / Condition nor the synchronized keyword. In many situations, you can use one of the mechanisms of the java.util.concurrent package that do all the locking for you. For example, in Section 14.6, "Blocking Queues," on p. 898, you will see how to use a blocking queue to synchronize threads that work on a common task. You should also explore parallel streams—see Volume II, Chapter 1.

- If the synchronized keyword works for your situation, by all means, use it. You'll write less code and have less room for error. Listing 14.8 shows the bank example, implemented with synchronized methods.

- Use Lock / Condition if you really need the additional power that these constructs give you.

Listing 14.8 synch2/Bank.java

```java
 1  package synch2;
 2
 3  import java.util.*;
 4
 5  /**
 6   * A bank with a number of bank accounts that uses synchronization primitives.
 7   * @version 1.30 2004-08-01
 8   * @author Cay Horstmann
 9   */
10  public class Bank
11  {
12     private final double[] accounts;
13
14     /**
15      * Constructs the bank.
16      * @param n the number of accounts
17      * @param initialBalance the initial balance for each account
18      */
19     public Bank(int n, double initialBalance)
20     {
21        accounts = new double[n];
22        Arrays.fill(accounts, initialBalance);
23     }
24
25     /**
26      * Transfers money from one account to another.
27      * @param from the account to transfer from
28      * @param to the account to transfer to
29      * @param amount the amount to transfer
30      */
```

```
31   public synchronized void transfer(int from, int to, double amount) throws InterruptedException
32   {
33      while (accounts[from] < amount)
34         wait();
35      System.out.print(Thread.currentThread());
36      accounts[from] -= amount;
37      System.out.printf(" %10.2f from %d to %d", amount, from, to);
38      accounts[to] += amount;
39      System.out.printf(" Total Balance: %10.2f%n", getTotalBalance());
40      notifyAll();
41   }
42
43   /**
44    * Gets the sum of all account balances.
45    * @return the total balance
46    */
47   public synchronized double getTotalBalance()
48   {
49      double sum = 0;
50
51      for (double a : accounts)
52         sum += a;
53
54      return sum;
55   }
56
57   /**
58    * Gets the number of accounts in the bank.
59    * @return the number of accounts
60    */
61   public int size()
62   {
63      return accounts.length;
64   }
65 }
```

---

java.lang.Object 1.0

- void notifyAll()

  unblocks the threads that called wait on this object. This method can only be
  called from within a synchronized method or block. The method throws an
  IllegalMonitorStateException if the current thread is not the owner of the object's lock.

(Continues)

`java.lang.Object` 1.0 *(Continued)*

- void notify()

  unblocks one randomly selected thread among the threads that called `wait` on this object. This method can only be called from within a synchronized method or block. The method throws an `IllegalMonitorStateException` if the current thread is not the owner of the object's lock.

- void wait()

  causes a thread to wait until it is notified. This method can only be called from within a synchronized method or block. It throws an `IllegalMonitorStateException` if the current thread is not the owner of the object's lock.

- void wait(long millis)
- void wait(long millis, int nanos)

  causes a thread to wait until it is notified or until the specified amount of time has passed. These methods can only be called from within a synchronized method or block. They throw an `IllegalMonitorStateException` if the current thread is not the owner of the object's lock.

  | *Parameters:* | millis | The number of milliseconds |
  | | nanos | The number of nanoseconds, not exceeding 1,000,000 |

14.5.6 Synchronized Blocks

As we just discussed, every Java object has a lock. A thread can acquire the lock by calling a synchronized method. There is a second mechanism for acquiring the lock: by entering a *synchronized block*. When a thread enters a block of the form

```
synchronized (obj) // this is the syntax for a synchronized block
{
    critical section
}
```

then it acquires the lock for `obj`.

You will sometimes find "ad hoc" locks, such as

```
public class Bank
{
    private double[] accounts;
    private Object lock = new Object();
    . . .
```

```
public void transfer(int from, int to, int amount)
{
   synchronized (lock) // an ad-hoc lock
   {
      accounts[from] -= amount;
      accounts[to] += amount;
   }
   System.out.println(. . .);

}
}
```

Here, the lock object is created only to use the lock that every Java object possesses.

Sometimes, programmers use the lock of an object to implement additional atomic operations—a practice known as *client-side locking*. Consider, for example, the Vector class, which is a list whose methods are synchronized. Now suppose we stored our bank balances in a Vector<Double>. Here is a naive implementation of a transfer method:

```
public void transfer(Vector<Double> accounts, int from, int to, int amount) // Error
{
   accounts.set(from, accounts.get(from) - amount);
   accounts.set(to, accounts.get(to) + amount);
   System.out.println(. . .);
}
```

The get and set methods of the Vector class are synchronized, but that doesn't help us. It is entirely possible for a thread to be preempted in the transfer method after the first call to get has been completed. Another thread may then store a different value into the same position. However, we can hijack the lock:

```
public void transfer(Vector<Double> accounts, int from, int to, int amount)
{
   synchronized (accounts)
   {
      accounts.set(from, accounts.get(from) - amount);
      accounts.set(to, accounts.get(to) + amount);
   }
   System.out.println(. . .);
}
```

This approach works, but it is entirely dependent on the fact that the Vector class uses the intrinsic lock for all of its mutator methods. However, is this really a fact? The documentation of the Vector class makes no such promise. You have to carefully study the source code and hope that future versions do not introduce unsynchronized mutators. As you can see, client-side locking is very fragile and not generally recommended.

14.5.7 The Monitor Concept

Locks and conditions are powerful tools for thread synchronization, but they are not very object oriented. For many years, researchers have looked for ways to make multithreading safe without forcing programmers to think about explicit locks. One of the most successful solutions is the *monitor* concept that was pioneered by Per Brinch Hansen and Tony Hoare in the 1970s. In the terminology of Java, a monitor has these properties:

- A monitor is a class with only private fields.
- Each object of that class has an associated lock.
- All methods are locked by that lock. In other words, if a client calls `obj.method()`, then the lock for `obj` is automatically acquired at the beginning of the method call and relinquished when the method returns. Since all fields are private, this arrangement ensures that no thread can access the fields while another thread manipulates them.
- The lock can have any number of associated conditions.

Earlier versions of monitors had a single condition, with a rather elegant syntax. You can simply call `await accounts[from] >= amount` without using an explicit condition variable. However, research showed that indiscriminate retesting of conditions can be inefficient. This problem is solved with explicit condition variables, each managing a separate set of threads.

The Java designers loosely adapted the monitor concept. *Every object* in Java has an intrinsic lock and an intrinsic condition. If a method is declared with the `synchronized` keyword, it acts like a monitor method. The condition variable is accessed by calling `wait` / `notifyAll` / `notify`.

However, a Java object differs from a monitor in three important ways, compromising thread safety:

- Fields are not required to be `private`.
- Methods are not required to be `synchronized`.
- The intrinsic lock is available to clients.

This disrespect for security enraged Per Brinch Hansen. In a scathing review of the multithreading primitives in Java, he wrote: "It is astounding to me that Java's insecure parallelism is taken seriously by the programming community, a quarter of a century after the invention of monitors and Concurrent Pascal. It has no merit" [Java's Insecure Parallelism, *ACM SIGPLAN Notices* 34:38–45, April 1999].

14.5.8 Volatile Fields

Sometimes, it seems excessive to pay the cost of synchronization just to read or write an instance field or two. After all, what can go wrong? Unfortunately, with modern processors and compilers, there is plenty of room for error.

- Computers with multiple processors can temporarily hold memory values in registers or local memory caches. As a consequence, threads running in different processors may see different values for the same memory location!

- Compilers can reorder instructions for maximum throughput. Compilers won't choose an ordering that changes the meaning of the code, but they make the assumption that memory values are only changed when there are explicit instructions in the code. However, a memory value can be changed by another thread!

If you use locks to protect code that can be accessed by multiple threads, you won't have these problems. Compilers are required to respect locks by flushing local caches as necessary and not inappropriately reordering instructions. The details are explained in the Java Memory Model and Thread Specification developed by JSR 133 (see www.jcp.org/en/jsr/detail?id=133). Much of the specification is highly complex and technical, but the document also contains a number of clearly explained examples. A more accessible overview article by Brian Goetz is available at www.ibm.com/developerworks/library/j-jtp02244.

 NOTE: Brian Goetz coined the following "synchronization motto": "If you write a variable which may next be read by another thread, or you read a variable which may have last been written by another thread, you must use synchronization."

The volatile keyword offers a lock-free mechanism for synchronizing access to an instance field. If you declare a field as volatile, then the compiler and the virtual machine take into account that the field may be concurrently updated by another thread.

For example, suppose an object has a boolean flag done that is set by one thread and queried by another thread. As we already discussed, you can use a lock:

```
private boolean done;
public synchronized boolean isDone() { return done; }
public synchronized void setDone() { done = true; }
```

Perhaps it is not a good idea to use the intrinsic object lock. The isDone and setDone methods can block if another thread has locked the object. If that is a concern, one can use a separate lock just for this variable. But this is getting to be a lot of trouble.

In this case, it is reasonable to declare the field as `volatile`:

```
private volatile boolean done;
public boolean isDone() { return done; }
public void setDone() { done = true; }
```

The compiler will insert the appropriate code to ensure that a change to the `done` variable in one thread is visible from any other thread that reads the variable.

 CAUTION: Volatile variables do not provide any atomicity. For example, the method

```
public void flipDone() { done = !done; } // not atomic
```

is not guaranteed to flip the value of the field. There is no guarantee that the reading, flipping, and writing is uninterrupted.

14.5.9 Final Variables

As you saw in the preceding section, you cannot safely read a field from multiple threads unless you use locks or the `volatile` modifier.

There is one other situation in which it is safe to access a shared field—when it is declared `final`. Consider

```
final Map<String, Double> accounts = new HashMap<>();
```

Other threads get to see the `accounts` variable after the constructor has finished.

Without using `final`, there would be no guarantee that other threads would see the updated value of `accounts`—they might all see `null`, not the constructed `HashMap`.

Of course, the operations on the map are not thread safe. If multiple threads mutate and read the map, you still need synchronization.

14.5.10 Atomics

You can declare shared variables as `volatile` provided you perform no operations other than assignment.

There are a number of classes in the `java.util.concurrent.atomic` package that use efficient machine-level instructions to guarantee atomicity of other operations without using locks. For example, the `AtomicInteger` class has methods `incrementAndGet` and `decrementAndGet` that atomically increment or decrement an integer. For example, you can safely generate a sequence of numbers like this:

```
public static AtomicLong nextNumber = new AtomicLong();
// In some thread...
long id = nextNumber.incrementAndGet();
```

The incrementAndGet method atomically increments the AtomicLong and returns the post-increment value. That is, the operations of getting the value, adding 1, setting it, and producing the new value cannot be interrupted. It is guaranteed that the correct value is computed and returned, even if multiple threads access the same instance concurrently.

There are methods for atomically setting, adding, and subtracting values, but if you want to make a more complex update, you have to use the compareAndSet method. For example, suppose you want to keep track of the largest value that is observed by different threads. The following won't work:

```
public static AtomicLong largest = new AtomicLong();
// In some thread...
largest.set(Math.max(largest.get(), observed)); // Error--race condition!
```

This update is not atomic. Instead, compute the new value and use compareAndSet in a loop:

```
do {
   oldValue = largest.get();
   newValue = Math.max(oldValue, observed);
} while (!largest.compareAndSet(oldValue, newValue));
```

If another thread is also updating largest, it is possible that it has beat this thread to it. Then compareAndSet will return false without setting the new value. In that case, the loop tries again, reading the updated value and trying to change it. Eventually, it will succeed replacing the existing value with the new one. This sounds tedious, but the compareAndSet method maps to a processor operation that is faster than using a lock.

In Java SE 8, you don't have to write the loop boilerplate any more. Instead, you provide a lambda expression for updating the variable, and the update is done for you. In our example, we can call

```
largest.updateAndGet(x -> Math.max(x, observed));
```

or

```
largest.accumulateAndGet(observed, Math::max);
```

The accumulateAndGet method takes a binary operator that is used to combine the atomic value and the supplied argument.

There are also methods getAndUpdate and getAndAccumulate that return the old value.

NOTE: These methods are also provided for the classes `AtomicInteger`, `AtomicIntegerArray`, `AtomicIntegerFieldUpdater`, `AtomicLongArray`, `AtomicLongFieldUpdater`, `AtomicReference`, `AtomicReferenceArray,` and `AtomicReferenceFieldUpdater`.

When you have a very large number of threads accessing the same atomic values, performance suffers because the optimistic updates require too many retries. Java SE 8 provides classes `LongAdder` and `LongAccumulator` to solve this problem. A `LongAdder` is composed of multiple variables whose collective sum is the current value. Multiple threads can update different summands, and new summands are automatically provided when the number of threads increases. This is efficient in the common situation where the value of the sum is not needed until after all work has been done. The performance improvement can be substantial.

If you anticipate high contention, you should simply use a `LongAdder` instead of an `AtomicLong`. The method names are slightly different. Call `increment` to increment a counter or `add` to add a quantity, and `sum` to retrieve the total.

```
final LongAdder adder = new LongAdder();
for (. . .)
   pool.submit(() -> {
      while (. . .) {
         . . .
         if (. . .) adder.increment();
      }
   });
. . .
long total = adder.sum());
```

 NOTE: Of course, the `increment` method does *not* return the old value. Doing that would undo the efficiency gain of splitting the sum into multiple summands.

The `LongAccumulator` generalizes this idea to an arbitrary accumulation operation. In the constructor, you provide the operation, as well as its neutral element. To incorporate new values, call `accumulate`. Call `get` to obtain the current value. The following has the same effect as a `LongAdder`:

```
LongAccumulator adder = new LongAccumulator(Long::sum, 0);
// In some thread...
adder.accumulate(value);
```

Internally, the accumulator has variables $a_1, a_2, \ldots, a_n$. Each variable is initialized with the neutral element (0 in our example).

When accumulate is called with value v, then one of them is atomically updated as $a_i = a_i$ op v, where op is the accumulation operation written in infix form. In our example, a call to accumulate computes $a_i = a_i + v$ for some i.

The result of get is a_1 op a_2 op . . . op a_n. In our example, that is the sum of the accumulators, $a_1 + a_2 + \ldots + a_n$.

If you choose a different operation, you can compute maximum or minimum. In general, the operation must be associative and commutative. That means that the final result must be independent of the order in which the intermediate values were combined.

There are also DoubleAdder and DoubleAccumulator that work in the same way, except with double values.

14.5.11 Deadlocks

Locks and conditions cannot solve all problems that might arise in multithreading. Consider the following situation:

1. Account 1: $200
2. Account 2: $300
3. Thread 1: Transfer $300 from Account 1 to Account 2
4. Thread 2: Transfer $400 from Account 2 to Account 1

As Figure 14.6 indicates, Threads 1 and 2 are clearly blocked. Neither can proceed because the balances in Accounts 1 and 2 are insufficient.

It is possible that all threads get blocked because each is waiting for more money. Such a situation is called a *deadlock*.

In our program, a deadlock cannot occur for a simple reason. Each transfer amount is for, at most, $1,000. Since there are 100 accounts and a total of $100,000 in them, at least one of the accounts must have must have at least $1,000 at any time. The thread moving money out of that account can therefore proceed.

But if you change the run method of the threads to remove the $1,000 transaction limit, deadlocks can occur quickly. Try it out. Set NACCOUNTS to 10. Construct each transfer runnable with a max value of 2 * INITIAL_BALANCE and run the program. The program will run for a while and then hang.

 TIP: When the program hangs, press Ctrl+\. You will get a thread dump that lists all threads. Each thread has a stack trace, telling you where it is currently blocked. Alternatively, run jconsole, as described in Chapter 7, and consult the Threads panel (see Figure 14.7).

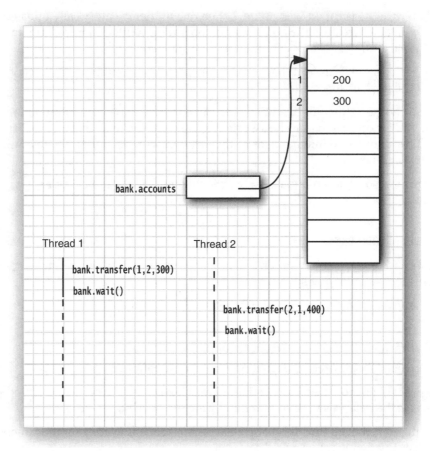

Figure 14.6 A deadlock situation

Another way to create a deadlock is to make the *i*th thread responsible for putting money into the *i*th account, rather than for taking it out of the *i*th account. In this case, there is a chance that all threads will gang up on one account, each trying to remove more money from it than it contains. Try it out. In the SynchBankTest program, turn to the run method of the TransferRunnable class. In the call to transfer, flip fromAccount and toAccount. Run the program and see how it deadlocks almost immediately.

Here is another situation in which a deadlock can occur easily: Change the signalAll method to signal in the SynchBankTest program. You will find that the program eventually hangs. (Again, it is best to set NACCOUNTS to 10 to observe the effect more quickly.) Unlike signalAll, which notifies all threads that are waiting for added funds, the signal method unblocks only one thread. If that thread can't proceed,

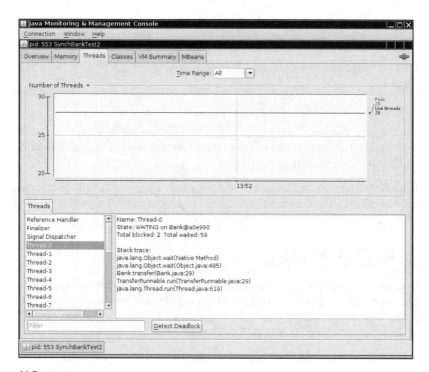

Figure 14.7 The Threads panel in jconsole

all threads can be blocked. Consider the following sample scenario of a developing deadlock:

1. Account 1: $1,990
2. All other accounts: $990 each
3. Thread 1: Transfer $995 from Account 1 to Account 2
4. All other threads: Transfer $995 from their account to another account

Clearly, all threads but Thread 1 are blocked, because there isn't enough money in their accounts.

Thread 1 proceeds. Afterward, we have the following situation:

1. Account 1: $995
2. Account 2: $1,985
3. All other accounts: $990 each

Then, Thread 1 calls signal. The signal method picks a thread at random to unblock. Suppose it picks Thread 3. That thread is awakened, finds that there isn't enough money in its account, and calls `await` again. But Thread 1 is still running. A new random transaction is generated, say,

1. Thread 1: Transfer $997 from Account 1 to Account 2

Now, Thread 1 also calls `await`, and *all* threads are blocked. The system has deadlocked.

The culprit here is the call to `signal`. It only unblocks one thread, and it may not pick the thread that is essential to make progress. (In our scenario, Thread 2 must proceed to take money out of Account 2.)

Unfortunately, there is nothing in the Java programming language to avoid or break these deadlocks. You must design your program to ensure that a deadlock situation cannot occur.

14.5.12 Thread–Local Variables

In the preceding sections, we discussed the risks of sharing variables between threads. Sometimes, you can avoid sharing by giving each thread its own instance, using the `ThreadLocal` helper class. For example, the `SimpleDateFormat` class is not thread safe. Suppose we have a static variable

```
public static final SimpleDateFormat dateFormat = new SimpleDateFormat("yyyy-MM-dd");
```

If two threads execute an operation such as

```
String dateStamp = dateFormat.format(new Date());
```

then the result can be garbage since the internal data structures used by the `dateFormat` can be corrupted by concurrent access. You could use synchronization, which is expensive, or you could construct a local `SimpleDateFormat` object whenever you need it, but that is also wasteful.

To construct one instance per thread, use the following code:

```
public static final ThreadLocal<SimpleDateFormat> dateFormat =
    ThreadLocal.withInitial(() -> new SimpleDateFormat("yyyy-MM-dd"));
```

To access the actual formatter, call

```
String dateStamp = dateFormat.get().format(new Date());
```

The first time you call `get` in a given thread, the lambda in the constructor is called. From then on, the `get` method returns the instance belonging to the current thread.

A similar problem is the generation of random numbers in multiple threads. The `java.util.Random` class is thread safe. But it is still inefficient if multiple threads need to wait for a single shared generator.

You could use the ThreadLocal helper to give each thread a separate generator, but Java SE 7 provides a convenience class for you. Simply make a call such as

```
int random = ThreadLocalRandom.current().nextInt(upperBound);
```

The call ThreadLocalRandom.current() returns an instance of the Random class that is unique to the current thread.

---

java.lang.ThreadLocal<T> 1.2

- T get()

  Gets the current value of this thread. If get is called for the first time, the value is obtained by calling initialize.

- protected initialize()

  Override this method to supply an initial value. By default, this method returns null.

- void set(T t)

  Sets a new value for this thread.

- void remove()

  Removes the value for this thread.

- static <S> ThreadLocal<S> withInitial(Supplier<? extends S> supplier) 8

  Creates a thread local variable whose initial value is produced by invoking the given supplier.

---

java.util.concurrent.ThreadLocalRandom 7

- static ThreadLocalRandom current()

  returns an instance of the Random class that is unique to the current thread.

14.5.13 Lock Testing and Timeouts

A thread blocks indefinitely when it calls the lock method to acquire a lock that is owned by another thread. You can be more cautious about acquiring a lock. The tryLock method tries to acquire a lock and returns true if it was successful. Otherwise, it immediately returns false, and the thread can go off and do something else.

```
if (myLock.tryLock())
{
    // now the thread owns the lock
```

```
        try { . . . }
        finally { myLock.unlock(); }
    }
    else
        // do something else
```

You can call `tryLock` with a timeout parameter, like this:

```
    if (myLock.tryLock(100, TimeUnit.MILLISECONDS)) . . .
```

`TimeUnit` is an enumeration with values `SECONDS`, `MILLISECONDS`, `MICROSECONDS`, and `NANOSECONDS`.

The `lock` method cannot be interrupted. If a thread is interrupted while it is waiting to acquire a lock, the interrupted thread continues to be blocked until the lock is available. If a deadlock occurs, then the `lock` method can never terminate.

However, if you call `tryLock` with a timeout, an `InterruptedException` is thrown if the thread is interrupted while it is waiting. This is clearly a useful feature because it allows a program to break up deadlocks.

You can also call the `lockInterruptibly` method. It has the same meaning as `tryLock` with an infinite timeout.

When you wait on a condition, you can also supply a timeout:

```
    myCondition.await(100, TimeUnit.MILLISECONDS))
```

The `await` method returns if another thread has activated this thread by calling `signalAll` or `signal`, or if the timeout has elapsed, or if the thread was interrupted.

The `await` methods throw an `InterruptedException` if the waiting thread is interrupted. In the (perhaps unlikely) case that you'd rather continue waiting, use the `awaitUninterruptibly` method instead.

---

java.util.concurrent.locks.Lock 5.0

- `boolean tryLock()`

  tries to acquire the lock without blocking; returns `true` if it was successful. This method grabs the lock if it is available even if it has a fair locking policy and other threads have been waiting.

- `boolean tryLock(long time, TimeUnit unit)`

  tries to acquire the lock, blocking no longer than the given time; returns `true` if it was successful.

- `void lockInterruptibly()`

  acquires the lock, blocking indefinitely. If the thread is interrupted, throws an `InterruptedException`.

---

java.util.concurrent.locks.Condition 5.0

- boolean await(long time, TimeUnit unit)

  enters the wait set for this condition, blocking until the thread is removed from the wait set or the given time has elapsed. Returns false if the method returned because the time elapsed, true otherwise.

- void awaitUninterruptibly()

  enters the wait set for this condition, blocking until the thread is removed from the wait set. If the thread is interrupted, this method does not throw an InterruptedException.

14.5.14 Read/Write Locks

The java.util.concurrent.locks package defines two lock classes, the ReentrantLock that we already discussed and the ReentrantReadWriteLock. The latter is useful when there are many threads that read from a data structure and fewer threads that modify it. In that situation, it makes sense to allow shared access for the readers. Of course, a writer must still have exclusive access.

Here are the steps that are necessary to use a read/write lock:

1. Construct a ReentrantReadWriteLock object:

   ```
   private ReentrantReadWriteLock rwl = new ReentrantReadWriteLock();
   ```

2. Extract the read and write locks:

   ```
   private Lock readLock = rwl.readLock();
   private Lock writeLock = rwl.writeLock();
   ```

3. Use the read lock in all accessors:

   ```
   public double getTotalBalance()
   {
      readLock.lock();
      try { . . . }
      finally { readLock.unlock(); }
   }
   ```

4. Use the write lock in all mutators:

   ```
   public void transfer(. . .)
   {
      writeLock.lock();
      try { . . . }
      finally { writeLock.unlock(); }
   }
   ```

`java.util.concurrent.locks.ReentrantReadWriteLock` 5.0

- `Lock readLock()`

  gets a read lock that can be acquired by multiple readers, excluding all writers.

- `Lock writeLock()`

  gets a write lock that excludes all other readers and writers.

14.5.15 Why the stop and suspend Methods Are Deprecated

The initial release of Java defined a `stop` method that simply terminates a thread, and a `suspend` method that blocks a thread until another thread calls `resume`. The `stop` and `suspend` methods have something in common: Both attempt to control the behavior of a given thread without the thread's cooperation.

The `stop`, `suspend`, and `resume` methods have been deprecated. The `stop` method is inherently unsafe, and experience has shown that the `suspend` method frequently leads to deadlocks. In this section, you will see why these methods are problematic and what you can do to avoid problems.

Let us turn to the `stop` method first. This method terminates all pending methods, including the `run` method. When a thread is stopped, it immediately gives up the locks on all objects that it has locked. This can leave objects in an inconsistent state. For example, suppose a `TransferRunnable` is stopped in the middle of moving money from one account to another, after the withdrawal and before the deposit. Now the bank object is *damaged*. Since the lock has been relinquished, the damage is observable from the other threads that have not been stopped.

When a thread wants to stop another thread, it has no way of knowing when the `stop` method is safe and when it leads to damaged objects. Therefore, the method has been deprecated. You should interrupt a thread when you want it to stop. The interrupted thread can then stop when it is safe to do so.

 NOTE: Some authors claim that the `stop` method has been deprecated because it can cause objects to be permanently locked by a stopped thread. However, that claim is not valid. A stopped thread exits all synchronized methods it has called—technically, by throwing a `ThreadDeath` exception. As a consequence, the thread relinquishes the intrinsic object locks that it holds.

Next, let us see what is wrong with the `suspend` method. Unlike `stop`, `suspend` won't damage objects. However, if you suspend a thread that owns a lock, then the lock is unavailable until the thread is resumed. If the thread that calls the suspend method tries to acquire the same lock, the program deadlocks: The suspended thread waits to be resumed, and the suspending thread waits for the lock.

This situation occurs frequently in graphical user interfaces. Suppose we have a graphical simulation of our bank. A button labeled Pause suspends the transfer threads, and a button labeled Resume resumes them.

```
pauseButton.addActionListener(event -> {
    for (int i = 0; i < threads.length; i++)
        threads[i].suspend(); // Don't do this
});
resumeButton.addActionListener(event -> {
    for (int i = 0; i < threads.length; i++)
        threads[i].resume();
});
```

Suppose a paintComponent method paints a chart of each account, calling a getBalances method to get an array of balances.

As you will see in Section 14.11, "Threads and Swing," on p. 937, both the button actions and the repainting occur in the same thread, the *event dispatch thread*. Consider the following scenario:

1. One of the transfer threads acquires the lock of the bank object.
2. The user clicks the Pause button.
3. All transfer threads are suspended; one of them still holds the lock on the bank object.
4. For some reason, the account chart needs to be repainted.
5. The paintComponent method calls the getBalances method.
6. That method tries to acquire the lock of the bank object.

Now the program is frozen.

The event dispatch thread can't proceed because the lock is owned by one of the suspended threads. Thus, the user can't click the Resume button, and the threads won't ever resume.

If you want to safely suspend a thread, introduce a variable suspendRequested and test it in a safe place of your run method—in a place where your thread doesn't lock objects that other threads need. When your thread finds that the suspendRequested variable has been set, it should keep waiting until it becomes available again.

14.6 Blocking Queues

You have now seen the low-level building blocks that form the foundations of concurrent programming in Java. However, for practical programming, you want to stay away from the low-level constructs whenever possible. It is much easier and safer to use higher-level structures that have been implemented by concurrency experts.

Many threading problems can be formulated elegantly and safely by using one or more queues. Producer threads insert items into the queue, and consumer threads retrieve them. The queue lets you safely hand over data from one thread to another. For example, consider our bank transfer program. Instead of accessing the bank object directly, the transfer threads insert transfer instruction objects into a queue. Another thread removes the instructions from the queue and carries out the transfers. Only that thread has access to the internals of the bank object. No synchronization is necessary. (Of course, the implementors of the thread-safe queue classes had to worry about locks and conditions, but that was their problem, not yours.)

A *blocking queue* causes a thread to block when you try to add an element when the queue is currently full or to remove an element when the queue is empty. Blocking queues are a useful tool for coordinating the work of multiple threads. Worker threads can periodically deposit intermediate results into a blocking queue. Other worker threads remove the intermediate results and modify them further. The queue automatically balances the workload. If the first set of threads runs slower than the second, the second set blocks while waiting for the results. If the first set of threads runs faster, the queue fills up until the second set catches up. Table 14.1 shows the methods for blocking queues.

The blocking queue methods fall into three categories that differ by the action they perform when the queue is full or empty. If you use the queue as a thread management tool, use the put and take methods. The add, remove, and element operations throw an exception when you try to add to a full queue or get the head of an empty queue. Of course, in a multithreaded program, the queue might become full or empty at any time, so you will instead want to use the offer, poll, and peek methods. These methods simply return with a failure indicator instead of throwing an exception if they cannot carry out their tasks.

 NOTE: The poll and peek methods return null to indicate failure. Therefore, it is illegal to insert null values into these queues.

Table 14.1 Blocking Queue Methods

Method	Normal Action	Action in Special Circumstances
add	Adds an element	Throws an IllegalStateException if the queue is full
element	Returns the head element	Throws a NoSuchElementException if the queue is empty
offer	Adds an element and returns true	Returns false if the queue is full
peek	Returns the head element	Returns null if the queue is empty
poll	Removes and returns the head element	Returns null if the queue is empty
put	Adds an element	Blocks if the queue is full
remove	Removes and returns the head element	Throws a NoSuchElementException if the queue is empty
take	Removes and returns the head element	Blocks if the queue is empty

There are also variants of the offer and poll methods with a timeout. For example, the call

```
boolean success = q.offer(x, 100, TimeUnit.MILLISECONDS);
```

tries for 100 milliseconds to insert an element to the tail of the queue. If it succeeds, it returns true; otherwise, it returns false when it times out. Similarly, the call

```
Object head = q.poll(100, TimeUnit.MILLISECONDS)
```

tries for 100 milliseconds to remove the head of the queue. If it succeeds, it returns the head; otherwise, it returns null when it times out.

The put method blocks if the queue is full, and the take method blocks if the queue is empty. These are the equivalents of offer and poll with no timeout.

The java.util.concurrent package supplies several variations of blocking queues. By default, the LinkedBlockingQueue has no upper bound on its capacity, but a maximum capacity can be optionally specified. The LinkedBlockingDeque is a double-ended version. The ArrayBlockingQueue is constructed with a given capacity and an optional parameter to require fairness. If fairness is specified, then the longest-waiting threads are given preferential treatment. As always, fairness exacts a significant performance penalty, and you should only use it if your problem specifically requires it.

The PriorityBlockingQueue is a priority queue, not a first-in/first-out queue. Elements are removed in order of their priority. The queue has unbounded capacity, but retrieval will block if the queue is empty. (See Chapter 9 for more information on priority queues.)

A `DelayQueue` contains objects that implement the `Delayed` interface:

```
interface Delayed extends Comparable<Delayed>
{
    long getDelay(TimeUnit unit);
}
```

The `getDelay` method returns the remaining delay of the object. A negative value indicates that the delay has elapsed. Elements can only be removed from a `DelayQueue` if their delay has elapsed. You also need to implement the `compareTo` method. The `DelayQueue` uses that method to sort the entries.

Java SE 7 adds a `TransferQueue` interface that allows a producer thread to wait until a consumer is ready to take on an item. When a producer calls

```
q.transfer(item);
```

the call blocks until another thread removes it. The `LinkedTransferQueue` class implements this interface.

The program in Listing 14.9 shows how to use a blocking queue to control a set of threads. The program searches through all files in a directory and its subdirectories, printing lines that contain a given keyword.

A producer thread enumerates all files in all subdirectories and places them in a blocking queue. This operation is fast, and the queue would quickly fill up with all files in the file system if it was not bounded.

We also start a large number of search threads. Each search thread takes a file from the queue, opens it, prints all lines containing the keyword, and then takes the next file. We use a trick to terminate the application when no further work is required. In order to signal completion, the enumeration thread places a dummy object into the queue. (This is similar to a dummy suitcase with a label "last bag" in a baggage claim belt.) When a search thread takes the dummy, it puts it back and terminates.

Note that no explicit thread synchronization is required. In this application, we use the queue data structure as a synchronization mechanism.

Listing 14.9 blockingQueue/BlockingQueueTest.java

```
1  package blockingQueue;
2
3  import java.io.*;
4  import java.util.*;
5  import java.util.concurrent.*;
```

```
6
7  /**
8   * @version 1.02 2015-06-21
9   * @author Cay Horstmann
10  */
11 public class BlockingQueueTest
12 {
13    private static final int FILE_QUEUE_SIZE = 10;
14    private static final int SEARCH_THREADS = 100;
15    private static final File DUMMY = new File("");
16    private static BlockingQueue<File> queue = new ArrayBlockingQueue<>(FILE_QUEUE_SIZE);
17
18    public static void main(String[] args)
19    {
20       try (Scanner in = new Scanner(System.in))
21       {
22          System.out.print("Enter base directory (e.g. /opt/jdk1.8.0/src): ");
23          String directory = in.nextLine();
24          System.out.print("Enter keyword (e.g. volatile): ");
25          String keyword = in.nextLine();
26
27          Runnable enumerator = () -> {
28             try
29             {
30                enumerate(new File(directory));
31                queue.put(DUMMY);
32             }
33             catch (InterruptedException e)
34             {
35             }
36          };
37
38          new Thread(enumerator).start();
39          for (int i = 1; i <= SEARCH_THREADS; i++) {
40             Runnable searcher = () -> {
41                try
42                {
43                   boolean done = false;
44                   while (!done)
45                   {
46                      File file = queue.take();
47                      if (file == DUMMY)
48                      {
49                         queue.put(file);
50                         done = true;
51                      }
52                      else search(file, keyword);
53                   }
54                }
```

(Continues)

Listing 14.9 *(Continued)*

```
55              catch (IOException e)
56              {
57                  e.printStackTrace();
58              }
59              catch (InterruptedException e)
60              {
61              }
62          };
63          new Thread(searcher).start();
64      }
65   }
66   }
67
68   /**
69    * Recursively enumerates all files in a given directory and its subdirectories.
70    * @param directory the directory in which to start
71    */
72   public static void enumerate(File directory) throws InterruptedException
73   {
74      File[] files = directory.listFiles();
75      for (File file : files)
76      {
77         if (file.isDirectory()) enumerate(file);
78         else queue.put(file);
79      }
80   }
81
82   /**
83    * Searches a file for a given keyword and prints all matching lines.
84    * @param file the file to search
85    * @param keyword the keyword to search for
86    */
87   public static void search(File file, String keyword) throws IOException
88   {
89      try (Scanner in = new Scanner(file, "UTF-8"))
90      {
91         int lineNumber = 0;
92         while (in.hasNextLine())
93         {
94            lineNumber++;
95            String line = in.nextLine();
96            if (line.contains(keyword))
97               System.out.printf("%s:%d:%s%n", file.getPath(), lineNumber, line);
98         }
99      }
100  }
101 }
```

---

java.util.concurrent.ArrayBlockingQueue<E> 5.0

- ArrayBlockingQueue(int capacity)
- ArrayBlockingQueue(int capacity, boolean fair)

  constructs a blocking queue with the given capacity and fairness settings. The queue is implemented as a circular array.

---

java.util.concurrent.LinkedBlockingQueue<E> 5.0
java.util.concurrent.LinkedBlockingDeque<E> 6

- LinkedBlockingQueue()
- LinkedBlockingDeque()

  constructs an unbounded blocking queue or deque, implemented as a linked list.

- LinkedBlockingQueue(int capacity)
- LinkedBlockingDeque(int capacity)

  constructs a bounded blocking queue or deque with the given capacity, implemented as a linked list.

---

java.util.concurrent.DelayQueue<E extends Delayed> 5.0

- DelayQueue()

  constructs an unbounded blocking queue of Delayed elements. Only elements whose delay has expired can be removed from the queue.

---

java.util.concurrent.Delayed 5.0

- long getDelay(TimeUnit unit)

  gets the delay for this object, measured in the given time unit.

`java.util.concurrent.PriorityBlockingQueue<E>` 5.0

- `PriorityBlockingQueue()`
- `PriorityBlockingQueue(int initialCapacity)`
- `PriorityBlockingQueue(int initialCapacity, Comparator<? super E> comparator)`

  constructs an unbounded blocking priority queue implemented as a heap.

  | *Parameters* | `initialCapacity` | The initial capacity of the priority queue. Default is 11. |
  | | `comparator` | The comparator used to compare elements. If not specified, the elements must implement the `Comparable` interface. |

`java.util.concurrent.BlockingQueue<E>` 5.0

- `void put(E element)`

  adds the element, blocking if necessary.

- `E take()`

  removes and returns the head element, blocking if necessary.

- `boolean offer(E element, long time, TimeUnit unit)`

  adds the given element and returns `true` if successful, blocking if necessary until the element has been added or the time has elapsed.

- `E poll(long time, TimeUnit unit)`

  removes and returns the head element, blocking if necessary until an element is available or the time has elapsed. Returns `null` upon failure.

`java.util.concurrent.BlockingDeque<E>` 6

- `void putFirst(E element)`
- `void putLast(E element)`

  adds the element, blocking if necessary.

- `E takeFirst()`
- `E takeLast()`

  removes and returns the head or tail element, blocking if necessary.

(Continues)

---

java.util.concurrent.BlockingDeque<E> 6 *(Continued)*

- `boolean offerFirst(E element, long time, TimeUnit unit)`
- `boolean offerLast(E element, long time, TimeUnit unit)`

  adds the given element and returns true if successful, blocking if necessary until the element has been added or the time has elapsed.

- `E pollFirst(long time, TimeUnit unit)`
- `E pollLast(long time, TimeUnit unit)`

  removes and returns the head or tail element, blocking if necessary until an element is available or the time has elapsed. Returns `null` upon failure.

---

java.util.concurrent.TransferQueue<E> 7

- `void transfer(E element)`
- `boolean tryTransfer(E element, long time, TimeUnit unit)`

  transfers a value, or tries transferring it with a given timeout, blocking until another thread has removed the item. The second method returns `true` if successful.

14.7 Thread-Safe Collections

If multiple threads concurrently modify a data structure, such as a hash table, it is easy to damage that data structure. (See Chapter 9 for more information on hash tables.) For example, one thread may begin to insert a new element. Suppose it is preempted in the middle of rerouting the links between the hash table's buckets. If another thread starts traversing the same list, it may follow invalid links and create havoc, perhaps throwing exceptions or being trapped in an infinite loop.

You can protect a shared data structure by supplying a lock, but it is usually easier to choose a thread-safe implementation instead. The blocking queues that we discussed in the preceding section are, of course, thread-safe collections. In the following sections, we discuss the other thread-safe collections that the Java library provides.

14.7.1 Efficient Maps, Sets, and Queues

The `java.util.concurrent` package supplies efficient implementations for maps, sorted sets, and queues: `ConcurrentHashMap`, `ConcurrentSkipListMap`, `ConcurrentSkipListSet`, and `ConcurrentLinkedQueue`.

These collections use sophisticated algorithms that minimize contention by allowing concurrent access to different parts of the data structure.

Unlike most collections, the size method of these classes does not necessarily operate in constant time. Determining the current size of one of these collections usually requires traversal.

 NOTE: Some applications use humongous concurrent hash maps, so large that the size method is insufficient because it returns an int. What is one to do with a map that has over two billion entries? Java SE 8 introduces a mappingCount method that returns the size as a long.

The collections return *weakly consistent* iterators. That means that the iterators may or may not reflect all modifications that are made after they were constructed, but they will not return a value twice and they will not throw a ConcurrentModificationException.

 NOTE: In contrast, an iterator of a collection in the java.util package throws a ConcurrentModificationException when the collection has been modified after construction of the iterator.

The concurrent hash map can efficiently support a large number of readers and a fixed number of writers. By default, it is assumed that there are up to 16 *simultaneous* writer threads. There can be many more writer threads, but if more than 16 write at the same time, the others are temporarily blocked. You can specify a higher number in the constructor, but it is unlikely that you will need to.

 NOTE: A hash map keeps all entries with the same hash code in the same "bucket." Some applications use poor hash functions, and as a result all entries end up in a small number of buckets, severely degrading performance. Even generally reasonable hash functions, such as that of the String class, can be problematic. For example, an attacker can slow down a program by crafting a large number of strings that hash to the same value. As of Java SE 8, the concurrent hash map organizes the buckets as trees, not lists, when the key type implements Comparable, guaranteeing $O(\log(n))$ performance.

`java.util.concurrent.ConcurrentLinkedQueue<E>` 5.0

- `ConcurrentLinkedQueue<E>()`

  constructs an unbounded, nonblocking queue that can be safely accessed by multiple threads.

`java.util.concurrent.ConcurrentSkipListSet<E>` 6

- `ConcurrentSkipListSet<E>()`
- `ConcurrentSkipListSet<E>(Comparator<? super E> comp)`

  constructs a sorted set that can be safely accessed by multiple threads. The first constructor requires that the elements implement the `Comparable` interface.

`java.util.concurrent.ConcurrentHashMap<K, V>` 5.0
`java.util.concurrent.ConcurrentSkipListMap<K, V>` 6

- `ConcurrentHashMap<K, V>()`
- `ConcurrentHashMap<K, V>(int initialCapacity)`
- `ConcurrentHashMap<K, V>(int initialCapacity, float loadFactor, int concurrencyLevel)`

  constructs a hash map that can be safely accessed by multiple threads.

Parameters	`initialCapacity`	The initial capacity for this collection. Default is `16`.
	`loadFactor`	Controls resizing: If the average load per bucket exceeds this factor, the table is resized. Default is `0.75`.
	`concurrencyLevel`	The estimated number of concurrent writer threads.

- `ConcurrentSkipListMap<K, V>()`
- `ConcurrentSkipListSet<K, V>(Comparator<? super K> comp)`

  constructs a sorted map that can be safely accessed by multiple threads. The first constructor requires that the keys implement the `Comparable` interface.

14.7.2 Atomic Update of Map Entries

The original version of `ConcurrentHashMap` only had a few methods for atomic updates, which made for somewhat awkward programming. Suppose we want to count how often certain features are observed. As a simple example, suppose multiple threads encounter words, and we want to count their frequencies.

Can we use a `ConcurrentHashMap<String, Long>`? Consider the code for incrementing a count. Obviously, the following is not thread safe:

```
Long oldValue = map.get(word);
Long newValue = oldValue == null ? 1 : oldValue + 1;
map.put(word, newValue); // Error--might not replace oldValue
```

Another thread might be updating the exact same count at the same time.

 NOTE: Some programmers are surprised that a supposedly thread-safe data structure permits operations that are not thread safe. But there are two entirely different considerations. If multiple threads modify a plain `HashMap`, they can destroy the internal structure (an array of linked lists). Some of the links may go missing, or even go in circles, rendering the data structure unusable. That will never happen with a `ConcurrentHashMap`. In the example above, the code for `get` and `put` will never corrupt the data structure. But, since the sequence of operations is not atomic, the result is not predictable.

A classic trick is to use the `replace` operation, which atomically replaces an old value with a new one, provided that no other thread has come before and replaced the old value with something else. You have to keep doing it until `replace` succeeds:

```
do
{
   oldValue = map.get(word);
   newValue = oldValue == null ? 1 : oldValue + 1;
} while (!map.replace(word, oldValue, newValue));
```

Alternatively, you can use a `ConcurrentHashMap<String, AtomicLong>` or, with Java SE 8, a `ConcurrentHashMap<String, LongAdder>`. Then the update code is:

```
map.putIfAbsent(word, new LongAdder());
map.get(word).increment();
```

The first statement ensures that there is a `LongAdder` present that we can increment atomically. Since `putIfAbsent` returns the mapped value (either the existing one or the newly put one), you can combine the two statements:

```
map.putIfAbsent(word, new LongAdder()).increment();
```

Java SE 8 provides methods that make atomic updates more convenient. The `compute` method is called with a key and a function to compute the new value. That function receives the key and the associated value, or `null` if there is none, and it computes the new value. For example, here is how we can update a map of integer counters:

```
map.compute(word, (k, v) -> v == null ? 1 : v + 1);
```

NOTE: You cannot have `null` values in a `ConcurrentHashMap`. There are many methods that use a `null` value as an indication that a given key is not present in the map.

There are also variants `computeIfPresent` and `computeIfAbsent` that only compute a new value when there is already an old one, or when there isn't yet one. A map of `LongAdder` counters can be updated with

```
map.computeIfAbsent(word, k -> new LongAdder()).increment();
```

That is almost like the call to `putIfAbsent` that you saw before, but the `LongAdder` constructor is only called when a new counter is actually needed.

You often need to do something special when a key is added for the first time. The `merge` method makes this particularly convenient. It has a parameter for the initial value that is used when the key is not yet present. Otherwise, the function that you supplied is called, combining the existing value and the initial value. (Unlike `compute`, the function does *not* process the key.)

```
map.merge(word, 1L, (existingValue, newValue) -> existingValue + newValue);
```

or, more simply,

```
map.merge(word, 1L, Long::sum);
```

It doesn't get more concise than that.

 NOTE: If the function that is passed to `compute` or `merge` returns `null`, the existing entry is removed from the map.

 CAUTION: When you use `compute` or `merge`, keep in mind that the function that you supply should not do a lot of work. While that function runs, some other updates to the map may be blocked. Of course, that function should also not update other parts of the map.

14.7.3 Bulk Operations on Concurrent Hash Maps

Java SE 8 provides bulk operations on concurrent hash maps that can safely execute even while other threads operate on the map. The bulk operations traverse the map and operate on the elements they find as they go along. No effort is made to freeze a snapshot of the map in time. Unless you happen to know that the map is not being modified while a bulk operation runs, you should treat its result as an approximation of the map's state.

There are three kinds of operations:

- search applies a function to each key and/or value, until the function yields a non-null result. Then the search terminates and the function's result is returned.

- reduce combines all keys and/or values, using a provided accumulation function.

- forEach applies a function to all keys and/or values.

Each operation has four versions:

- *operation*Keys: operates on keys.

- *operation*Values: operates on values.

- *operation*: operates on keys and values.

- *operation*Entries: operates on Map.Entry objects.

With each of the operations, you need to specify a *parallelism threshold*. If the map contains more elements than the threshold, the bulk operation is parallelized. If you want the bulk operation to run in a single thread, use a threshold of Long.MAX_VALUE. If you want the maximum number of threads to be made available for the bulk operation, use a threshold of 1.

Let's look at the search methods first. Here are the versions:

```
U searchKeys(long threshold, BiFunction<? super K, ? extends U> f)
U searchValues(long threshold, BiFunction<? super V, ? extends U> f)
U search(long threshold, BiFunction<? super K, ? super V,? extends U> f)
U searchEntries(long threshold, BiFunction<Map.Entry<K, V>, ? extends U> f)
```

For example, suppose we want to find the first word that occurs more than 1,000 times. We need to search keys and values:

```
String result = map.search(threshold, (k, v) -> v > 1000 ? k : null);
```

Then result is set to the first match, or to null if the search function returns null for all inputs.

The forEach methods have two variants. The first one simply applies a *consumer* function for each map entry, for example

```
map.forEach(threshold,
    (k, v) -> System.out.println(k + " -> " + v));
```

The second variant takes an additional *transformer* function, which is applied first, and its result is passed to the consumer:

```
map.forEach(threshold,
    (k, v) -> k + " -> " + v, // Transformer
    System.out::println); // Consumer
```

The transformer can be used as a filter. Whenever the transformer returns null, the value is silently skipped. For example, here we only print the entries with large values:

```
map.forEach(threshold,
    (k, v) -> v > 1000 ? k + " -> " + v : null, // Filter and transformer
    System.out::println); // The nulls are not passed to the consumer
```

The reduce operations combine their inputs with an accumulation function. For example, here is how you can compute the sum of all values:

```
Long sum = map.reduceValues(threshold, Long::sum);
```

As with forEach, you can also supply a transformer function. Here we compute the length of the longest key:

```
Integer maxlength = map.reduceKeys(threshold,
    String::length, // Transformer
    Integer::max); // Accumulator
```

The transformer can act as a filter, by returning null to exclude unwanted inputs. Here, we count how many entries have value > 1000:

```
Long count = map.reduceValues(threshold,
    v -> v > 1000 ? 1L : null,
    Long::sum);
```

 NOTE: If the map is empty, or all entries have been filtered out, the reduce operation returns null. If there is only one element, its transformation is returned, and the accumulator is not applied.

There are specializations for int, long, and double outputs with suffixes ToInt, ToLong, and ToDouble. You need to transform the input to a primitive value and specify a default value and an accumulator function. The default value is returned when the map is empty.

```
long sum = map.reduceValuesToLong(threshold,
    Long::longValue, // Transformer to primitive type
    0, // Default value for empty map
    Long::sum); // Primitive type accumulator
```

 CAUTION: These specializations act differently from the object versions where there is only one element to be considered. Instead of returning the transformed element, it is accumulated with the default. Therefore, the default must be the neutral element of the accumulator.

14.7.4 Concurrent Set Views

Suppose you want a large, thread-safe set instead of a map. There is no ConcurrentHashSet class, and you know better than trying to create your own. Of course, you can use a ConcurrentHashMap with bogus values, but then you get a map, not a set, and you can't apply operations of the Set interface.

The static newKeySet method yields a Set<K> that is actually a wrapper around a ConcurrentHashMap<K, Boolean>. (All map values are Boolean.TRUE, but you don't actually care since you just use it as a set.)

```
Set<String> words = ConcurrentHashMap.<String>newKeySet();
```

Of course, if you have an existing map, the keySet method yields the set of keys. That set is mutable. If you remove the set's elements, the keys (and their values) are removed from the map. But it doesn't make sense to add elements to the key set, because there would be no corresponding values to add. Java SE 8 adds a second keySet method to ConcurrentHashMap, with a default value, to be used when adding elements to the set:

```
Set<String> words = map.keySet(1L);
words.add("Java");
```

If "Java" wasn't already present in words, it now has a value of one.

14.7.5 Copy on Write Arrays

The CopyOnWriteArrayList and CopyOnWriteArraySet are thread-safe collections in which all mutators make a copy of the underlying array. This arrangement is useful if the threads that iterate over the collection greatly outnumber the threads that mutate it. When you construct an iterator, it contains a reference to the current array. If the array is later mutated, the iterator still has the old array, but the collection's array is replaced. As a consequence, the older iterator has a consistent (but potentially outdated) view that it can access without any synchronization expense.

14.7.6 Parallel Array Algorithms

As of Java SE 8, the Arrays class has a number of parallelized operations. The static Arrays.parallelSort method can sort an array of primitive values or objects. For example,

```
String contents = new String(Files.readAllBytes(
    Paths.get("alice.txt")), StandardCharsets.UTF_8); // Read file into string
String[] words = contents.split("[\\P{L}]+"); // Split along nonletters
Arrays.parallelSort(words);
```

When you sort objects, you can supply a Comparator.

```
Arrays.parallelSort(words, Comparator.comparing(String::length));
```

With all methods, you can supply the bounds of a range, such as

```
values.parallelSort(values.length / 2, values.length); // Sort the upper half
```

 NOTE: At first glance, it seems a bit odd that these methods have parallel in their name, since the user shouldn't care how the sorting happens. However, the API designers wanted to make it clear that the sorting is parallelized. That way, users are on notice to avoid comparators with side effects.

The parallelSetAll method fills an array with values that are computed from a function. The function receives the element index and computes the value at that location.

```
Arrays.parallelSetAll(values, i -> i % 10);
// Fills values with 0 1 2 3 4 5 6 7 8 9 0 1 2 . . .
```

Clearly, this operation benefits from being parallelized. There are versions for all primitive type arrays and for object arrays.

Finally, there is a parallelPrefix method that replaces each array element with the accumulation of the prefix for a given associative operation. Huh? Here is an example. Consider the array [1, 2, 3, 4, . . .] and the × operation. After executing Arrays.parallelPrefix(values, (x, y) -> x * y), the array contains

$$[1, 1 \times 2, 1 \times 2 \times 3, 1 \times 2 \times 3 \times 4, . . .]$$

Perhaps surprisingly, this computation can be parallelized. First, join neighboring elements, as indicated here:

$$[1, 1 \times 2, 3, 3 \times 4, 5, 5 \times 6, 7, 7 \times 8]$$

The gray values are left alone. Clearly, one can make this computation in parallel in separate regions of the array. In the next step, update the indicated elements by multiplying them with elements that are one or two positions below:

$$[1, 1 \times 2, 1 \times 2 \times 3, 1 \times 2 \times 3 \times 4, 5, 5 \times 6, 5 \times 6 \times 7, 5 \times 6 \times 7 \times 8]$$

This can again be done in parallel. After $\log(n)$ steps, the process is complete. This is a win over the straightforward linear computation if sufficient processors are available. On special-purpose hardware, this algorithm is commonly used, and users of such hardware are quite ingenious in adapting it to a variety of problems.

14.7.7 Older Thread-Safe Collections

Ever since the initial release of Java, the Vector and Hashtable classes provided thread-safe implementations of a dynamic array and a hash table. These classes are now considered obsolete, having been replaced by the ArrayList and HashMap classes. Those classes are not thread safe. Instead, a different mechanism is supplied in the collections library. Any collection class can be made thread safe by means of a *synchronization wrapper*:

```
List<E> synchArrayList = Collections.synchronizedList(new ArrayList<E>());
Map<K, V> synchHashMap = Collections.synchronizedMap(new HashMap<K, V>());
```

The methods of the resulting collections are protected by a lock, providing thread safe access.

You should make sure that no thread accesses the data structure through the original unsynchronized methods. The easiest way to ensure this is not to save any reference to the original object. Simply construct a collection and immediately pass it to the wrapper, as we did in our examples.

You still need to use "client-side" locking if you want to *iterate* over the collection while another thread has the opportunity to mutate it:

```
synchronized (synchHashMap)
{
   Iterator<K> iter = synchHashMap.keySet().iterator();
   while (iter.hasNext()) . . .;
}
```

You must use the same code if you use a "for each" loop because the loop uses an iterator. Note that the iterator actually fails with a ConcurrentModificationException if another thread mutates the collection while the iteration is in progress. The synchronization is still required so that the concurrent modification can be reliably detected.

You are usually better off using the collections defined in the java.util.concurrent package instead of the synchronization wrappers. In particular, the ConcurrentHashMap map has been carefully implemented so that multiple threads can access it without blocking each other, provided they access different buckets. One exception is an array list that is frequently mutated. In that case, a synchronized ArrayList can outperform a CopyOnWriteArrayList.

---

java.util.Collections 1.2

- static <E> Collection<E> synchronizedCollection(Collection<E> c)
- static <E> List synchronizedList(List<E> c)
- static <E> Set synchronizedSet(Set<E> c)
- static <E> SortedSet synchronizedSortedSet(SortedSet<E> c)
- static <K, V> Map<K, V> synchronizedMap(Map<K, V> c)
- static <K, V> SortedMap<K, V> synchronizedSortedMap(SortedMap<K, V> c)

  constructs a view of the collection whose methods are synchronized.

14.8 Callables and Futures

A Runnable encapsulates a task that runs asynchronously; you can think of it as an asynchronous method with no parameters and no return value. A Callable is similar to a Runnable, but it returns a value. The Callable interface is a parameterized type, with a single method call.

```
public interface Callable<V>
{
   V call() throws Exception;
}
```

The type parameter is the type of the returned value. For example, a Callable<Integer> represents an asynchronous computation that eventually returns an Integer object.

A Future holds the *result* of an asynchronous computation. You can start a computation, give someone the Future object, and forget about it. The owner of the Future object can obtain the result when it is ready.

The Future interface has the following methods:

```
public interface Future<V>
{
   V get() throws . . .;
   V get(long timeout, TimeUnit unit) throws . . .;
   void cancel(boolean mayInterrupt);
   boolean isCancelled();
   boolean isDone();
}
```

A call to the first get method blocks until the computation is finished. The second method throws a TimeoutException if the call timed out before the computation finished. If the thread running the computation is interrupted, both methods throw an InterruptedException. If the computation has already finished, get returns immediately.

The isDone method returns false if the computation is still in progress, true if it is finished.

You can cancel the computation with the cancel method. If the computation has not yet started, it is canceled and will never start. If the computation is currently in progress, it is interrupted if the mayInterrupt parameter is true.

The FutureTask wrapper is a convenient mechanism for turning a Callable into both a Future and a Runnable—it implements both interfaces. For example:

```
Callable<Integer> myComputation = . . .;
FutureTask<Integer> task = new FutureTask<Integer>(myComputation);
Thread t = new Thread(task); // it's a Runnable
t.start();
. . .
Integer result = task.get(); // it's a Future
```

The program in Listing 14.10 puts these concepts to work. This program is similar to the preceding example that found files containing a given keyword. However, now we will merely count the number of matching files. Thus, we have a long-running task that yields an integer value—an example of a Callable<Integer>.

```
class MatchCounter implements Callable<Integer>
{
    public MatchCounter(File directory, String keyword) { . . . }
    public Integer call() { . . . } // returns the number of matching files
}
```

Then we construct a FutureTask object from the MatchCounter and use it to start a thread.

```
FutureTask<Integer> task = new FutureTask<Integer>(counter);
Thread t = new Thread(task);
t.start();
```

Finally, we print the result.

```
System.out.println(task.get() + " matching files.");
```

Of course, the call to get blocks until the result is actually available.

Inside the call method, we use the same mechanism recursively. For each subdirectory, we produce a new MatchCounter and launch a thread for it. We also stash the FutureTask objects away in an ArrayList<Future<Integer>>. At the end, we add up all results:

```
for (Future<Integer> result : results)
    count += result.get();
```

Each call to get blocks until the result is available. Of course, the threads run in parallel, so there is a good chance that the results will all be available at about the same time.

Listing 14.10 future/FutureTest.java

```java
1  package future;
2
3  import java.io.*;
4  import java.util.*;
5  import java.util.concurrent.*;
6
7  /**
8   * @version 1.01 2012-01-26
9   * @author Cay Horstmann
10  */
11 public class FutureTest
12 {
13    public static void main(String[] args)
14    {
15       try (Scanner in = new Scanner(System.in))
16       {
17          System.out.print("Enter base directory (e.g. /usr/local/jdk5.0/src): ");
18          String directory = in.nextLine();
19          System.out.print("Enter keyword (e.g. volatile): ");
20          String keyword = in.nextLine();
21
22          MatchCounter counter = new MatchCounter(new File(directory), keyword);
23          FutureTask<Integer> task = new FutureTask<>(counter);
24          Thread t = new Thread(task);
25          t.start();
26          try
27          {
28             System.out.println(task.get() + " matching files.");
29          }
30          catch (ExecutionException e)
31          {
32             e.printStackTrace();
33          }
34          catch (InterruptedException e)
35          {
36          }
37       }
38    }
39 }
40
41 /**
42  * This task counts the files in a directory and its subdirectories that contain a given keyword.
43  */
44 class MatchCounter implements Callable<Integer>
45 {
```

(Continues)

Listing 14.10 *(Continued)*

```
46    private File directory;
47    private String keyword;
48
49    /**
50     * Constructs a MatchCounter.
51     * @param directory the directory in which to start the search
52     * @param keyword the keyword to look for
53     */
54    public MatchCounter(File directory, String keyword)
55    {
56       this.directory = directory;
57       this.keyword = keyword;
58    }
59
60    public Integer call()
61    {
62       int count = 0;
63       try
64       {
65          File[] files = directory.listFiles();
66          List<Future<Integer>> results = new ArrayList<>();
67
68          for (File file : files)
69             if (file.isDirectory())
70             {
71                MatchCounter counter = new MatchCounter(file, keyword);
72                FutureTask<Integer> task = new FutureTask<>(counter);
73                results.add(task);
74                Thread t = new Thread(task);
75                t.start();
76             }
77             else
78             {
79                if (search(file)) count++;
80             }
81
82          for (Future<Integer> result : results)
83             try
84             {
85                count += result.get();
86             }
87             catch (ExecutionException e)
88             {
89                e.printStackTrace();
90             }
91       }
```

```
92        catch (InterruptedException e)
93        {
94        }
95        return count;
96   }
97
98   /**
99    * Searches a file for a given keyword.
100   * @param file the file to search
101   * @return true if the keyword is contained in the file
102   */
103  public boolean search(File file)
104  {
105     try
106     {
107        try (Scanner in = new Scanner(file, "UTF-8"))
108        {
109           boolean found = false;
110           while (!found && in.hasNextLine())
111           {
112              String line = in.nextLine();
113              if (line.contains(keyword)) found = true;
114           }
115           return found;
116        }
117     }
118     catch (IOException e)
119     {
120        return false;
121     }
122  }
123 }
```

---

java.util.concurrent.Callable<V> 5.0

- V call()

  runs a task that yields a result.

---

java.util.concurrent.Future<V> 5.0

- V get()
- V get(long time, TimeUnit unit)

  gets the result, blocking until it is available or the given time has elapsed. The second method throws a TimeoutException if it was unsuccessful.

(Continues)

---

java.util.concurrent.Future<V> 5.0 *(Continued)*

- boolean cancel(boolean mayInterrupt)

  attempts to cancel the execution of this task. If the task has already started and the mayInterrupt parameter is true, it is interrupted. Returns true if the cancellation was successful.

- boolean isCancelled()

  returns true if the task was canceled before it completed.

- boolean isDone()

  returns true if the task completed, through normal completion, cancellation, or an exception.

---

java.util.concurrent.FutureTask<V> 5.0

- FutureTask(Callable<V> task)
- FutureTask(Runnable task, V result)

  constructs an object that is both a Future<V> and a Runnable.

14.9 Executors

Constructing a new thread is somewhat expensive because it involves interaction with the operating system. If your program creates a large number of short-lived threads, it should use a *thread pool* instead. A thread pool contains a number of idle threads that are ready to run. You give a Runnable to the pool, and one of the threads calls the run method. When the run method exits, the thread doesn't die but stays around to serve the next request.

Another reason to use a thread pool is to throttle the number of concurrent threads. Creating a huge number of threads can greatly degrade performance and even crash the virtual machine. If you have an algorithm that creates lots of threads, you should use a "fixed" thread pool that bounds the total number of concurrent threads.

The Executors class has a number of static factory methods for constructing thread pools; see Table 14.2 for a summary.

Table 14.2 Executors Factory Methods

Method	Description
newCachedThreadPool	New threads are created as needed; idle threads are kept for 60 seconds.
newFixedThreadPool	The pool contains a fixed set of threads; idle threads are kept indefinitely.
newSingleThreadExecutor	A "pool" with a single thread that executes the submitted tasks sequentially (similar to the Swing event dispatch thread).
newScheduledThreadPool	A fixed-thread pool for scheduled execution; a replacement for java.util.Timer.
newSingleThreadScheduledExecutor	A single-thread "pool" for scheduled execution.

14.9.1 Thread Pools

Let us look at the first three methods in Table 14.2 (we will discuss the remaining methods in Section 14.9.2, "Scheduled Execution," on p. 926). The newCachedThreadPool method constructs a thread pool that executes each task immediately, using an existing idle thread when available and creating a new thread otherwise. The newFixedThreadPool method constructs a thread pool with a fixed size. If more tasks are submitted than there are idle threads, the unserved tasks are placed on a queue. They are run when other tasks have completed. The newSingleThreadExecutor is a degenerate pool of size 1 where a single thread executes the submitted tasks, one after another. These three methods return an object of the ThreadPoolExecutor class that implements the ExecutorService interface.

You can submit a Runnable or Callable to an ExecutorService with one of the following methods:

```
Future<?> submit(Runnable task)
Future<T> submit(Runnable task, T result)
Future<T> submit(Callable<T> task)
```

The pool will run the submitted task at its earliest convenience. When you call submit, you get back a Future object that you can use to query the state of the task.

The first submit method returns an odd-looking Future<?>. You can use such an object to call isDone, cancel, or isCancelled, but the get method simply returns null upon completion.

The second version of submit also submits a Runnable, and the get method of the Future returns the given result object upon completion.

The third version submits a Callable, and the returned Future gets the result of the computation when it is ready.

When you are done with a thread pool, call shutdown. This method initiates the shutdown sequence for the pool. An executor that is shut down accepts no new tasks. When all tasks are finished, the threads in the pool die. Alternatively, you can call shutdownNow. The pool then cancels all tasks that have not yet begun and attempts to interrupt the running threads.

Here, in summary, is what you do to use a thread pool:

1. Call the static newCachedThreadPool or newFixedThreadPool method of the Executors class.

2. Call submit to submit Runnable or Callable objects.

3. If you want to be able to cancel a task, or if you submit Callable objects, hang on to the returned Future objects.

4. Call shutdown when you no longer want to submit any tasks.

For example, the preceding example program produced a large number of short-lived threads, one per directory. The program in Listing 14.11 uses a thread pool to launch the tasks instead.

For informational purposes, this program prints out the largest pool size during execution. This information is not available through the ExecutorService interface. For that reason, we had to cast the pool object to the ThreadPoolExecutor class.

Listing 14.11   threadPool/ThreadPoolTest.java

```
1  package threadPool;
2
3  import java.io.*;
4  import java.util.*;
5  import java.util.concurrent.*;
6
7  /**
8   * @version 1.02 2015-06-21
9   * @author Cay Horstmann
10  */
11 public class ThreadPoolTest
12 {
13    public static void main(String[] args) throws Exception
14    {
15       try (Scanner in = new Scanner(System.in))
16       {
17          System.out.print("Enter base directory (e.g. /usr/local/jdk5.0/src): ");
18          String directory = in.nextLine();
19          System.out.print("Enter keyword (e.g. volatile): ");
```

```
20          String keyword = in.nextLine();
21
22          ExecutorService pool = Executors.newCachedThreadPool();
23
24          MatchCounter counter = new MatchCounter(new File(directory), keyword, pool);
25          Future<Integer> result = pool.submit(counter);
26
27          try
28          {
29             System.out.println(result.get() + " matching files.");
30          }
31          catch (ExecutionException e)
32          {
33             e.printStackTrace();
34          }
35          catch (InterruptedException e)
36          {
37          }
38          pool.shutdown();
39
40          int largestPoolSize = ((ThreadPoolExecutor) pool).getLargestPoolSize();
41          System.out.println("largest pool size=" + largestPoolSize);
42       }
43    }
44 }
45
46 /**
47  * This task counts the files in a directory and its subdirectories that contain a given keyword.
48  */
49 class MatchCounter implements Callable<Integer>
50 {
51    private File directory;
52    private String keyword;
53    private ExecutorService pool;
54    private int count;
55
56    /**
57     * Constructs a MatchCounter.
58     * @param directory the directory in which to start the search
59     * @param keyword the keyword to look for
60     * @param pool the thread pool for submitting subtasks
61     */
62    public MatchCounter(File directory, String keyword, ExecutorService pool)
63    {
64       this.directory = directory;
65       this.keyword = keyword;
66       this.pool = pool;
67    }
68
```

(Continues)

Listing 14.11 *(Continued)*

```
69    public Integer call()
70    {
71       count = 0;
72       try
73       {
74          File[] files = directory.listFiles();
75          List<Future<Integer>> results = new ArrayList<>();
76
77          for (File file : files)
78             if (file.isDirectory())
79             {
80                MatchCounter counter = new MatchCounter(file, keyword, pool);
81                Future<Integer> result = pool.submit(counter);
82                results.add(result);
83             }
84             else
85             {
86                if (search(file)) count++;
87             }
88
89          for (Future<Integer> result : results)
90             try
91             {
92                count += result.get();
93             }
94             catch (ExecutionException e)
95             {
96                e.printStackTrace();
97             }
98       }
99       catch (InterruptedException e)
100      {
101      }
102      return count;
103   }
104
105   /**
106    * Searches a file for a given keyword.
107    * @param file the file to search
108    * @return true if the keyword is contained in the file
109    */
110   public boolean search(File file)
111   {
112      try
113      {
```

```
114        try (Scanner in = new Scanner(file, "UTF-8"))
115        {
116           boolean found = false;
117           while (!found && in.hasNextLine())
118           {
119              String line = in.nextLine();
120              if (line.contains(keyword)) found = true;
121           }
122           return found;
123        }
124     }
125     catch (IOException e)
126     {
127        return false;
128     }
129  }
130 }
```

---

java.util.concurrent.Executors 5.0

- `ExecutorService newCachedThreadPool()`

  returns a cached thread pool that creates threads as needed and terminates threads that have been idle for 60 seconds.

- `ExecutorService newFixedThreadPool(int threads)`

  returns a thread pool that uses the given number of threads to execute tasks.

- `ExecutorService newSingleThreadExecutor()`

  returns an executor that executes tasks sequentially in a single thread.

---

java.util.concurrent.ExecutorService 5.0

- `Future<T> submit(Callable<T> task)`
- `Future<T> submit(Runnable task, T result)`
- `Future<?> submit(Runnable task)`

  submits the given task for execution.

- `void shutdown()`

  shuts down the service, completing the already submitted tasks but not accepting new submissions.

---

java.util.concurrent.ThreadPoolExecutor 5.0

- `int getLargestPoolSize()`

  returns the largest size of the thread pool during the life of this executor.

14.9.2 Scheduled Execution

The `ScheduledExecutorService` interface has methods for scheduled or repeated execution of tasks. It is a generalization of `java.util.Timer` that allows for thread pooling. The `newScheduledThreadPool` and `newSingleThreadScheduledExecutor` methods of the `Executors` class return objects that implement the `ScheduledExecutorService` interface.

You can schedule a `Runnable` or `Callable` to run once, after an initial delay. You can also schedule a `Runnable` to run periodically. See the API notes for details.

---

java.util.concurrent.Executors 5.0

- `ScheduledExecutorService newScheduledThreadPool(int threads)`

  returns a thread pool that uses the given number of threads to schedule tasks.

- `ScheduledExecutorService newSingleThreadScheduledExecutor()`

  returns an executor that schedules tasks in a single thread.

---

java.util.concurrent.ScheduledExecutorService 5.0

- `ScheduledFuture<V> schedule(Callable<V> task, long time, TimeUnit unit)`
- `ScheduledFuture<?> schedule(Runnable task, long time, TimeUnit unit)`

  schedules the given task after the given time has elapsed.

- `ScheduledFuture<?> scheduleAtFixedRate(Runnable task, long initialDelay, long period, TimeUnit unit)`

  schedules the given task to run periodically, every `period` units, after the initial delay has elapsed.

- `ScheduledFuture<?> scheduleWithFixedDelay(Runnable task, long initialDelay, long delay, TimeUnit unit)`

  schedules the given task to run periodically, with `delay` units between completion of one invocation and the start of the next, after the initial delay has elapsed.

14.9.3 Controlling Groups of Tasks

You have seen how to use an executor service as a thread pool to increase the efficiency of task execution. Sometimes, an executor is used for a more tactical reason, simply to control a group of related tasks. For example, you can cancel all tasks in an executor with the shutdownNow method.

The invokeAny method submits all objects in a collection of Callable objects and returns the result of a completed task. You don't know which task that is—presumably, it is the one that finished most quickly. Use this method for a search problem in which you are willing to accept any solution. For example, suppose that you need to factor a large integer—a computation that is required for breaking the RSA cipher. You could submit a number of tasks, each attempting a factorization with numbers in a different range. As soon as one of these tasks has an answer, your computation can stop.

The invokeAll method submits all objects in a collection of Callable objects, blocks until all of them complete, and returns a list of Future objects that represent the solutions to all tasks. You can process the results of the computation when they are available, like this:

```
List<Callable<T>> tasks = . . .;
List<Future<T>> results = executor.invokeAll(tasks);
for (Future<T> result : results)
   processFurther(result.get());
```

A disadvantage of this approach is that you may wait needlessly if the first task happens to take a long time. It would make more sense to obtain the results in the order in which they are available. This can be arranged with the ExecutorCompletionService.

Start with an executor, obtained in the usual way. Then construct an ExecutorCompletionService. Submit tasks to the completion service. The service manages a blocking queue of Future objects, containing the results of the submitted tasks as they become available. Thus, a more efficient organization for the preceding computation is the following:

```
ExecutorCompletionService<T> service = new ExecutorCompletionService<>(executor);
for (Callable<T> task : tasks) service.submit(task);
for (int i = 0; i < tasks.size(); i++)
   processFurther(service.take().get());
```

---

java.util.concurrent.ExecutorService 5.0

- T invokeAny(Collection<Callable<T>> tasks)
- T invokeAny(Collection<Callable<T>> tasks, long timeout, TimeUnit unit)

    executes the given tasks and returns the result of one of them. The second method throws a TimeoutException if a timeout occurs.

- List<Future<T>> invokeAll(Collection<Callable<T>> tasks)
- List<Future<T>> invokeAll(Collection<Callable<T>> tasks, long timeout, TimeUnit unit)

    executes the given tasks and returns the results of all of them. The second method throws a TimeoutException if a timeout occurs.

---

java.util.concurrent.ExecutorCompletionService<V> 5.0

- ExecutorCompletionService(Executor e)

    constructs an executor completion service that collects the results of the given executor.

- Future<V> submit(Callable<V> task)
- Future<V> submit(Runnable task, V result)

    submits a task to the underlying executor.

- Future<V> take()

    removes the next completed result, blocking if no completed results are available.

- Future<V> poll()
- Future<V> poll(long time, TimeUnit unit)

    removes and returns the next completed result, or return null if no completed results are available. The second method waits for the given time.

14.9.4 The Fork–Join Framework

Some applications use a large number of threads that are mostly idle. An example would be a web server that uses one thread per connection. Other applications use one thread per processor core, in order to carry out computationally intensive tasks, such as image or video processing. The fork-join framework, which appeared in Java SE 7, is designed to support the latter. Suppose you have a processing task that naturally decomposes into subtasks, like this:

```
if (problemSize < threshold)
    solve problem directly
else
{
```

> *break problem into subproblems*
> *recursively solve each subproblem*
> *combine the results*
> }

One example is image processing. To enhance an image, you can transform the top half and the bottom half. If you have enough idle processors, those operations can run in parallel. (You will need to do a bit of extra work along the strip that separates the two halves, but that's a technical detail.)

Here, we will discuss a simpler example. Suppose we want to count how many elements of an array fulfill a particular property. We cut the array in half, compute the counts of each half, and add them up.

To put the recursive computation in a form that is usable by the framework, supply a class that extends RecursiveTask<T> (if the computation produces a result of type T) or RecursiveAction (if it doesn't produce a result). Override the compute method to generate and invoke subtasks, and to combine their results.

```
class Counter extends RecursiveTask<Integer>
{
    . . .
    protected Integer compute()
    {
        if (to - from < THRESHOLD)
        {
            solve problem directly
        }
        else
        {
            int mid = (from + to) / 2;
            Counter first = new Counter(values, from, mid, filter);
            Counter second = new Counter(values, mid, to, filter);
            invokeAll(first, second);
            return first.join() + second.join();
        }
    }
}
```

Here, the invokeAll method receives a number of tasks and blocks until all of them have completed. The join method yields the result. Here, we apply join to each subtask and return the sum.

 NOTE: There is also a get method for getting the current result, but it is less attractive since it can throw checked exceptions that we are not allowed to throw in the compute method.

Listing 14.12 shows the complete example.

Behind the scenes, the fork-join framework uses an effective heuristic for balancing the workload among available threads, called *work stealing*. Each worker thread has a deque (double-ended queue) for tasks. A worker thread pushes subtasks onto the head of its own deque. (Only one thread accesses the head, so no locking is required.) When a worker thread is idle, it "steals" a task from the tail of another deque. Since large subtasks are at the tail, such stealing is rare.

Listing 14.12 `forkJoin/ForkJoinTest.java`

```java
1  package forkJoin;
2
3  import java.util.concurrent.*;
4  import java.util.function.*;
5
6  /**
7   * This program demonstrates the fork-join framework.
8   * @version 1.01 2015-06-21
9   * @author Cay Horstmann
10  */
11 public class ForkJoinTest
12 {
13    public static void main(String[] args)
14    {
15       final int SIZE = 10000000;
16       double[] numbers = new double[SIZE];
17       for (int i = 0; i < SIZE; i++) numbers[i] = Math.random();
18       Counter counter = new Counter(numbers, 0, numbers.length, x -> x > 0.5);
19       ForkJoinPool pool = new ForkJoinPool();
20       pool.invoke(counter);
21       System.out.println(counter.join());
22    }
23 }
24
25 class Counter extends RecursiveTask<Integer>
26 {
27    public static final int THRESHOLD = 1000;
28    private double[] values;
29    private int from;
30    private int to;
31    private DoublePredicate filter;
32
33    public Counter(double[] values, int from, int to, DoublePredicate filter)
34    {
35       this.values = values;
36       this.from = from;
```

```
37       this.to = to;
38       this.filter = filter;
39    }
40
41    protected Integer compute()
42    {
43       if (to - from < THRESHOLD)
44       {
45          int count = 0;
46          for (int i = from; i < to; i++)
47          {
48             if (filter.test(values[i])) count++;
49          }
50          return count;
51       }
52       else
53       {
54          int mid = (from + to) / 2;
55          Counter first = new Counter(values, from, mid, filter);
56          Counter second = new Counter(values, mid, to, filter);
57          invokeAll(first, second);
58          return first.join() + second.join();
59       }
60    }
61 }
```

14.9.5 Completable Futures

The traditional approach for dealing with nonblocking calls is to use event handlers, where the programmer registers a handler for the action that should occur after a task completes. Of course, if the next action is also asynchronous, the next action after that is in a different event handler. Even though the programmer thinks in terms of "first do step 1, then step 2, then step 3," the program logic becomes dispersed in different handlers. It gets worse when one has to add error handling. Suppose step 2 is "the user logs in." You may need to repeat that step since the user can mistype the credentials. Trying to implement such a control flow in a set of event handlers, or to understand it once it has been implemented, is challenging.

The CompletableFuture class of Java SE 8 provides an alternative approach. Unlike event handlers, completable futures can be *composed*.

For example, suppose we want to extract all links from a web page in order to build a web crawler. Let's say we have a method

```
public void CompletableFuture<String> readPage(URL url)
```

that yields the text of a web page when it becomes available. If the method

```
public static List<URL> getLinks(String page)
```

yields the URLs in an HTML page, you can schedule it to be called when the page is available:

```
CompletableFuture<String> contents = readPage(url);
CompletableFuture<List<URL>> links = contents.thenApply(Parser::getLinks);
```

The thenApply method doesn't block either. It returns another future. When the first future has completed, its result is fed to the getLinks method, and the return value of that method becomes the final result.

With completable futures, you just specify what you want to have done and in which order. It won't all happen right away, of course, but what is important is that all the code is in one place.

Conceptually, CompletableFuture is a simple API, but there are many variants of methods for composing completable futures. Let us first look at those that deal with a single future (see Table 14.3). (For each method shown, there are also two Async variants that I don't show. One of them uses a shared ForkJoinPool, and the other has an Executor parameter.) In the table, I use a shorthand notation for the ponderous functional interfaces, writing T -> U instead of Function<? super T, U>. These aren't actual Java types, of course.

You have already seen the thenApply method. The calls

```
CompletableFuture<U> future.thenApply(f);
CompletableFuture<U> future.thenApplyAsync(f);
```

return a future that applies f to the result of future when it is available. The second call runs f in yet another thread.

The thenCompose method, instead of taking a function T -> U, takes a function T -> CompletableFuture<U>. That sounds rather abstract, but it can be quite natural. Consider the action of reading a web page from a given URL. Instead of supplying a method

```
public String blockingReadPage(URL url)
```

it is more elegant to have that method return a future:

```
public CompletableFuture<String> readPage(URL url)
```

Now, suppose we have another method that gets the URL from user input, perhaps from a dialog that won't reveal the answer until the user has clicked the OK button. That, too, is an event in the future:

```
public CompletableFuture<URL> getURLInput(String prompt)
```

Here we have two functions `T -> CompletableFuture<U>` and `U -> CompletableFuture<V>`. Clearly, they compose to a function `T -> CompletableFuture<V>` if the second function is called when the first one has completed. That is exactly what `thenCompose` does.

The third method in Table 14.3 focuses on a different aspect that I have ignored so far: failure. When an exception is thrown in a `CompletableFuture`, it is captured and wrapped in an unchecked `ExecutionException` when the `get` method is called. But perhaps `get` is never called. In order to handle an exception, use the `handle` method. The supplied function is called with the result (or `null` if none) and the exception (or `null` if none), and it gets to make sense of the situation.

The remaining methods have `void` result and are normally used at the end of a processing pipeline.

Table 14.3 Adding an Action to a `CompletableFuture<T>` Object

Method	Parameter	Description
thenApply	T -> U	Apply a function to the result.
thenCompose	T -> CompletableFuture<U>	Invoke the function on the result and execute the returned future.
handle	(T, Throwable) -> U	Process the result or error.
thenAccept	T -> void	Like `thenApply`, but with `void` result.
whenComplete	(T, Throwable) -> void	Like `handle`, but with `void` result.
thenRun	Runnable	Execute the `Runnable` with `void` result.

Now let us turn to methods that combine multiple futures (see Table 14.4).

The first three methods run a `CompletableFuture<T>` and a `CompletableFuture<U>` action in parallel and combine the results.

The next three methods run two `CompletableFuture<T>` actions in parallel. As soon as one of them finishes, its result is passed on, and the other result is ignored.

Finally, the static `allOf` and `anyOf` methods take a variable number of completable futures and yield a `CompletableFuture<Void>` that completes when all of them, or any one of them, completes. No results are propagated.

Table 14.4 Combining Multiple Composition Objects

Method	Parameter	Description
thenCombine	CompletableFuture<U>, (T, U) -> V	Execute both and combine the results with the given function.
thenAcceptBoth	CompletableFuture<U>, (T, U) -> void	Like thenCombine, but with void result.
runAfterBoth	CompletableFuture<?>, Runnable	Execute the runnable after both complete.
applyToEither	CompletableFuture<T>, T -> V	When a result is available from one or the other, pass it to the given function.
acceptEither	CompletableFuture<T>, T -> void	Like applyToEither, but with void result.
runAfterEither	CompletableFuture<?>, Runnable	Execute the runnable after one or the other completes.
static allOf	CompletableFuture<?>...	Complete with void result after all given futures complete.
static anyOf	CompletableFuture<?>...	Complete with void result after any of the given futures completes.

NOTE: Technically speaking, the methods in this section accept parameters of type CompletionStage, not CompletableFuture. That is an interface with almost forty abstract methods, implemented only by CompletableFuture. The interface is provided so that third-party frameworks can implement it.

14.10 Synchronizers

The java.util.concurrent package contains several classes that help manage a set of collaborating threads—see Table 14.5. These mechanisms have "canned functionality" for common rendezvous patterns between threads. If you have a set of collaborating threads that follow one of these behavior patterns, you should simply reuse the appropriate library class instead of trying to come up with a handcrafted collection of locks and conditions.

Table 14.5 Synchronizers

Class	What It Does	Notes
CyclicBarrier	Allows a set of threads to wait until a predefined count of them has reached a common barrier, and then optionally executes a barrier action.	Use when a number of threads need to complete before their results can be used. The barrier can be reused after the waiting threads have been released.
Phaser	Like a cyclic barrier, but with a mutable party count.	Introduced in Java SE 7.
CountDownLatch	Allows a set of threads to wait until a count has been decremented to 0.	Use when one or more threads need to wait until a specified number of events have occurred.
Exchanger	Allows two threads to exchange objects when both are ready for the exchange.	Use when two threads work on two instances of the same data structure, with the first thread filling one instance and the second thread emptying the other.
Semaphore	Allows a set of threads to wait until permits are available for proceeding.	Use to restrict the total number of threads that can access a resource. If the permit count is one, use to block threads until another thread gives permission.
SynchronousQueue	Allows a thread to hand off an object to another thread.	Use to send an object from one thread to another when both are ready, without explicit synchronization.

14.10.1 Semaphores

Conceptually, a semaphore manages a number of *permits*. The number is supplied in the constructor. To proceed past the semaphore, a thread requests a permit by calling acquire. (There are no actual permit objects. The semaphore simply keeps a count.) Since only a fixed number of permits is available, a semaphore limits the number of threads that are allowed to pass. Other threads may issue permits by calling release. Moreover, a permit doesn't have to be released by the thread that acquires it. Any thread can release any number of permits, potentially increasing the number of permits beyond the initial count.

Semaphores were invented by Edsger Dijkstra in 1968, for use as a *synchronization primitive*. Dijkstra showed that semaphores can be efficiently implemented and that they are powerful enough to solve many common thread synchronization problems. In just about any operating systems textbook, you will find implementations of bounded queues using semaphores.

Of course, application programmers shouldn't reinvent bounded queues. Usually, semaphores do not map directly to common application situations.

14.10.2 Countdown Latches

A CountDownLatch lets a set of threads wait until a count has reached zero. The countdown latch is one-time only. Once the count has reached 0, you cannot increment it again.

A useful special case is a latch with a count of 1. This implements a one-time gate. Threads are held at the gate until another thread sets the count to 0.

Imagine, for example, a set of threads that need some initial data to do their work. The worker threads are started and wait at the gate. Another thread prepares the data. When it is ready, it calls countDown, and all worker threads proceed.

You can then use a second latch to check when all worker threads are done. Initialize the latch with the number of threads. Each worker thread counts down that latch just before it terminates. Another thread that harvests the work results waits on the latch, and proceeds as soon as all workers have terminated.

14.10.3 Barriers

The CyclicBarrier class implements a rendezvous called a *barrier*. Consider a number of threads that are working on parts of a computation. When all parts are ready, the results need to be combined. When a thread is done with its part, we let it run against the barrier. Once all threads have reached the barrier, the barrier gives way and the threads can proceed.

Here are the details. First, construct a barrier, giving the number of participating threads:

```
CyclicBarrier barrier = new CyclicBarrier(nthreads);
```

Each thread does some work and calls await on the barrier upon completion:

```
public void run()
{
   doWork();
   barrier.await();
   . . .
}
```

The `await` method takes an optional timeout parameter:

```
barrier.await(100, TimeUnit.MILLISECONDS);
```

If any of the threads waiting for the barrier leaves the barrier, then the barrier *breaks*. (A thread can leave because it called `await` with a timeout or because it was interrupted.) In that case, the `await` method for all other threads throws a `BrokenBarrierException`. Threads that are already waiting have their `await` call terminated immediately.

You can supply an optional *barrier action* that is executed when all threads have reached the barrier:

```
Runnable barrierAction = . . .;
CyclicBarrier barrier = new CyclicBarrier(nthreads, barrierAction);
```

The action can harvest the results of the individual threads.

The barrier is called *cyclic* because it can be reused after all waiting threads have been released. In this regard, it differs from a `CountDownLatch` which can only be used once.

The `Phaser` class adds more flexibility, allowing you to vary the number of participating threads between phases.

14.10.4 Exchangers

An `Exchanger` is used when two threads are working on two instances of the same data buffer. Typically, one thread fills the buffer, and the other consumes its contents. When both are done, they exchange their buffers.

14.10.5 Synchronous Queues

A synchronous queue is a mechanism that pairs up producer and consumer threads. When a thread calls `put` on a `SynchronousQueue`, it blocks until another thread calls `take`, and vice versa. Unlike the case with an `Exchanger`, data are only transferred in one direction, from the producer to the consumer.

Even though the `SynchronousQueue` class implements the `BlockingQueue` interface, it is not conceptually a queue. It does not contain any elements—its `size` method always returns `0`.

14.11 Threads and Swing

As we mentioned in the introduction to this chapter, one of the reasons to use threads in your programs is to make your programs more responsive. When your program needs to do something time consuming, you should fire up another worker thread instead of blocking the user interface.

However, you have to be careful what you do in a worker thread because, perhaps surprisingly, Swing is *not thread safe*. If you try to manipulate user interface elements from multiple threads, your user interface can become corrupted.

To see the problem, run the upcoming test program in Listing 14.13. When you click the Bad button, a new thread is started whose run method tortures a combo box, randomly adding and removing values.

```
public void run()
{
   try
   {
      while (true)
      {
         int i = Math.abs(generator.nextInt());
         if (i % 2 == 0)
            combo.insertItemAt(new Integer(i), 0);
         else if (combo.getItemCount() > 0)
            combo.removeItemAt(i % combo.getItemCount());
         sleep(1);
      }
      catch (InterruptedException e) {}
   }
}
```

Try it out. Click the Bad button. Click the combo box a few times. Move the scrollbar. Move the window. Click the Bad button again. Keep clicking the combo box. Eventually, you should see an exception report (Figure 14.8).

What is going on? When an element is inserted into the combo box, the combo box fires an event to update the display. Then, the display code springs into action, reading the current size of the combo box and preparing to display the values. But the worker thread keeps going—occasionally resulting in a reduction of the count of the values in the combo box. The display code then thinks that there are more values in the model than there actually are, asks for a nonexistent value, and triggers an ArrayIndexOutOfBounds exception.

This situation could have been avoided if programmers could lock the combo box object while displaying it. However, the designers of Swing decided not to expend any effort to make Swing thread safe, for two reasons. First, synchronization takes time, and nobody wanted to slow down Swing any further. More importantly, the Swing team checked out the experience other teams had with thread-safe user interface toolkits. What they found was not encouraging. Programmers using thread-safe toolkits turned out to be confused by the demands for synchronization and often created deadlock-prone programs.

```
Terminal                                                                    _□X
File  Edit  View  Terminal  Tabs  Help
559)
        at javax.swing.JComponent.getPreferredSize(JComponent.java:1627)
        at javax.swing.ScrollPaneLayout.layoutContainer(ScrollPaneLayout.java:76
9)
        at java.awt.Container.layout(Container.java:1432)
        at java.awt.Cont┌SwingThreadTest ___□X┐r.java:1421)
        at java.awt.Cont│ Good    Bad  1710247468 ▾│iner.java:1519)
        at java.awt.Cont└──────────────────────────┘r.java:1491)
        at javax.swing.RepaintManager.validateInvalidComponents(RepaintManager.j
ava:635)
        at javax.swing.SystemEventQueueUtilities$ComponentWorkRequest.run(System
EventQueueUtilities.java:127)
        at java.awt.event.InvocationEvent.dispatch(InvocationEvent.java:209)
        at java.awt.EventQueue.dispatchEvent(EventQueue.java:597)
        at java.awt.EventDispatchThread.pumpOneEventForFilters(EventDispatchThre
ad.java:273)
        at java.awt.EventDispatchThread.pumpEventsForFilter(EventDispatchThread.
java:183)
        at java.awt.EventDispatchThread.pumpEventsForHierarchy(EventDispatchThre
ad.java:173)
        at java.awt.EventDispatchThread.pumpEvents(EventDispatchThread.java:168)
        at java.awt.EventDispatchThread.pumpEvents(EventDispatchThread.java:160)
        at java.awt.EventDispatchThread.run(EventDispatchThread.java:121)
█ ▌
```

Figure 14.8 Exception reports in the console

14.11.1 Running Time-Consuming Tasks

When you use threads together with Swing, you have to follow two simple rules.

1. If an action takes a long time, do it in a separate worker thread and never in the event dispatch thread.

2. Do not touch Swing components in any thread other than the event dispatch thread.

The reason for the first rule is easy to understand. If you take a long time in the event dispatch thread, the application seems "dead" because it cannot respond to any events. In particular, the event dispatch thread should never make input/output calls, which might block indefinitely, and it should never call sleep. (If you need to wait for a specific amount of time, use timer events.)

The second rule is often called the *single-thread rule* for Swing programming. We discuss it further on page 951.

These two rules seem to be in conflict with each other. Suppose you fire up a separate thread to run a time-consuming task. You would usually want to update the user interface to indicate progress while your thread is working. When your task is finished, you'd want to update the GUI again. But you can't touch Swing components from your thread. For example, if you want to update a progress bar or a label text, you can't simply set its value from your thread.

To solve this problem, you can use, in any thread, two utility methods to add arbitrary actions to the event queue. For example, suppose you want to periodically update a label in a thread to indicate progress. You can't call `label.setText` from your thread.

Instead, use the `invokeLater` and `invokeAndWait` methods of the `EventQueue` class to have that call executed in the event dispatching thread.

Here is what you do. Place the Swing code into the `run` method of a class that implements the `Runnable` interface. Then, create an object of that class and pass it to the static `invokeLater` or `invokeAndWait` method. For example, here is how to update a label text:

```
EventQueue.invokeLater(() -> {
    label.setText(percentage + "% complete");
});
```

The `invokeLater` method returns immediately when the event is posted to the event queue. The `run` method of the `Runnable` is executed asynchronously. The `invokeAndWait` method waits until the `run` method has actually been executed.

For updating a progress label, the `invokeLater` method is more appropriate. Users would rather have the worker thread make more progress than have the most precise progress indicator.

Both methods execute the `run` method in the event dispatch thread. No new thread is created.

Listing 14.13 demonstrates how to use the `invokeLater` method to safely modify the contents of a combo box. If you click the Good button, a thread inserts and removes numbers. However, the actual modification takes place in the event dispatching thread.

Listing 14.13 swing/SwingThreadTest.java

```
1  package swing;
2
3  import java.awt.*;
4  import java.util.*;
5
6  import javax.swing.*;
7
8  /**
```

```
 9    * This program demonstrates that a thread that runs in parallel with the event
10    * dispatch thread can cause errors in Swing components.
11    * @version 1.24 2015-06-21
12    * @author Cay Horstmann
13    */
14   public class SwingThreadTest
15   {
16      public static void main(String[] args)
17      {
18         EventQueue.invokeLater(() -> {
19            JFrame frame = new SwingThreadFrame();
20            frame.setTitle("SwingThreadTest");
21            frame.setDefaultCloseOperation(JFrame.EXIT_ON_CLOSE);
22            frame.setVisible(true);
23         });
24      }
25   }
26
27   /**
28    * This frame has two buttons to fill a combo box from a separate thread. The
29    * "Good" button uses the event queue, the "Bad" button modifies the combo box
30    * directly.
31    */
32   class SwingThreadFrame extends JFrame
33   {
34      public SwingThreadFrame()
35      {
36         final JComboBox<Integer> combo = new JComboBox<>();
37         combo.insertItemAt(Integer.MAX_VALUE, 0);
38         combo.setPrototypeDisplayValue(combo.getItemAt(0));
39         combo.setSelectedIndex(0);
40
41         JPanel panel = new JPanel();
42
43         JButton goodButton = new JButton("Good");
44         goodButton.addActionListener(event ->
45            new Thread(new GoodWorkerRunnable(combo)).start());
46         panel.add(goodButton);
47         JButton badButton = new JButton("Bad");
48         badButton.addActionListener(event ->
49            new Thread(new BadWorkerRunnable(combo)).start());
50         panel.add(badButton);
51
52         panel.add(combo);
53         add(panel);
54         pack();
55      }
56   }
57
```

(Continues)

Listing 14.13 *(Continued)*

```
58  /**
59   * This runnable modifies a combo box by randomly adding and removing numbers.
60   * This can result in errors because the combo box methods are not synchronized
61   * and both the worker thread and the event dispatch thread access the combo
62   * box.
63   */
64  class BadWorkerRunnable implements Runnable
65  {
66     private JComboBox<Integer> combo;
67     private Random generator;
68
69     public BadWorkerRunnable(JComboBox<Integer> aCombo)
70     {
71        combo = aCombo;
72        generator = new Random();
73     }
74
75     public void run()
76     {
77        try
78        {
79           while (true)
80           {
81              int i = Math.abs(generator.nextInt());
82              if (i % 2 == 0)
83                 combo.insertItemAt(i, 0);
84              else if (combo.getItemCount() > 0)
85                 combo.removeItemAt(i % combo.getItemCount());
86              Thread.sleep(1);
87           }
88        }
89        catch (InterruptedException e)
90        {
91        }
92     }
93  }
94
95  /**
96   * This runnable modifies a combo box by randomly adding and removing numbers.
97   * In order to ensure that the combo box is not corrupted, the editing
98   * operations are forwarded to the event dispatch thread.
99   */
100 class GoodWorkerRunnable implements Runnable
101 {
102    private JComboBox<Integer> combo;
103    private Random generator;
104
```

```
105    public GoodWorkerRunnable(JComboBox<Integer> aCombo)
106    {
107       combo = aCombo;
108       generator = new Random();
109    }
110
111    public void run()
112    {
113       try
114       {
115          while (true)
116          {
117             EventQueue.invokeLater(() ->
118                {
119                   int i = Math.abs(generator.nextInt());
120                   if (i % 2 == 0)
121                      combo.insertItemAt(i, 0);
122                   else if (combo.getItemCount() > 0)
123                      combo.removeItemAt(i % combo.getItemCount());
124                });
125             Thread.sleep(1);
126          }
127       }
128       catch (InterruptedException e)
129       {
130       }
131    }
132 }
```

---

java.awt.EventQueue 1.1

- `static void invokeLater(Runnable runnable)` 1.2

  causes the run method of the runnable object to be executed in the event dispatch thread after pending events have been processed.

- `static void invokeAndWait(Runnable runnable)` 1.2

  causes the run method of the runnable object to be executed in the event dispatch thread after pending events have been processed. This call blocks until the run method has terminated.

- `static boolean isDispatchThread()` 1.2

  returns true if the thread executing this method is the event dispatch thread.

14.11.2 Using the Swing Worker

When a user issues a command for which processing takes a long time, you will want to fire up a new thread to do the work. As you saw in the preceding section, that thread should use the EventQueue.invokeLater method to update the user interface. The SwingWorker class reduces the tedium of implementing background tasks.

The program in Listing 14.14 has commands for loading a text file and for canceling the file loading process. You should try the program with a long file, such as the full text of *The Count of Monte Cristo*, supplied in the gutenberg directory of the book's companion code. The file is loaded in a separate thread. While the file is being read, the Open menu item is disabled and the Cancel item is enabled (see Figure 14.9). After each line is read, a line counter in the status bar is updated. After the reading process is complete, the Open menu item is reenabled, the Cancel item is disabled, and the status line text is set to Done.

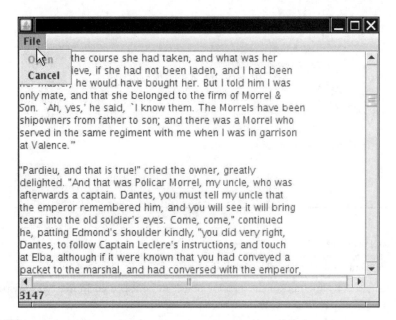

Figure 14.9 Loading a file in a separate thread

This example shows the typical UI activities of a background task:

- After each work unit, update the UI to show progress.
- After the work is finished, make a final change to the UI.

The SwingWorker class makes it easy to implement such a task. Override the doInBackground method to do the time-consuming work and occasionally call publish to communicate work progress. This method is executed in a worker thread. The publish method causes a process method to execute in the event dispatch thread to deal with the progress data. When the work is complete, the done method is called in the event dispatch thread so that you can finish updating the UI.

Whenever you want to do some work in the worker thread, construct a new worker. (Each worker object is meant to be used only once.) Then call the execute method. You will typically call execute on the event dispatch thread, but that is not a requirement.

It is assumed that a worker produces a result of some kind; therefore, SwingWorker<T, V> implements Future<T>. This result can be obtained by the get method of the Future interface. Since the get method blocks until the result is available, you don't want to call it immediately after calling execute. It is a good idea to call it only when you know that the work has been completed. Typically, you call get from the done method. (There is no requirement to call get. Sometimes, processing the progress data is all you need.)

Both the intermediate progress data and the final result can have arbitrary types. The SwingWorker class has these types as type parameters. A SwingWorker<T, V> produces a result of type T and progress data of type V.

To cancel the work in progress, use the cancel method of the Future interface. When the work is canceled, the get method throws a CancellationException.

As already mentioned, the worker thread's call to publish will cause calls to process on the event dispatch thread. For efficiency, the results of several calls to publish may be batched up in a single call to process. The process method receives a List<V> containing all intermediate results.

Let us put this mechanism to work for reading in a text file. As it turns out, a JTextArea is quite slow. Appending lines from a long text file (such as all lines in *The Count of Monte Cristo*) takes considerable time.

To show the user that progress is being made, we want to display the number of lines read in a status line. Thus, the progress data consist of the current line number and the current line of text. We package these into a trivial inner class:

```
private class ProgressData
{
    public int number;
    public String line;
}
```

The final result is the text that has been read into a StringBuilder. Thus, we need a SwingWorker<StringBuilder, ProgressData>.

In the doInBackground method, we read a file, a line at a time. After each line, we call publish to publish the line number and the text of the current line.

```
@Override public StringBuilder doInBackground() throws IOException, InterruptedException
{
    int lineNumber = 0;
    Scanner in = new Scanner(new FileInputStream(file), "UTF-8");
    while (in.hasNextLine())
    {
        String line = in.nextLine();
        lineNumber++;
        text.append(line).append("\n");
        ProgressData data = new ProgressData();
        data.number = lineNumber;
        data.line = line;
        publish(data);
        Thread.sleep(1); // to test cancellation; no need to do this in your programs
    }
    return text;
}
```

We also sleep for a millisecond after every line so that you can test cancellation without getting stressed out, but you wouldn't want to slow down your own programs by sleeping. If you comment out this line, you will find that *The Count of Monte Cristo* loads quite quickly, with only a few batched user interface updates.

 NOTE: You can make this program behave quite smoothly by updating the text area from the worker thread, but this is not possible for most Swing components. We show you the general approach in which all component updates occur in the event dispatch thread.

In the process method, we ignore all line numbers but the last one, and we concatenate all lines for a single update of the text area.

```
@Override public void process(List<ProgressData> data)
{
    if (isCancelled()) return;
    StringBuilder b = new StringBuilder();
    statusLine.setText("" + data.get(data.size() - 1).number);
    for (ProgressData d : data) b.append(d.line).append("\n");
    textArea.append(b.toString());
}
```

In the done method, the text area is updated with the complete text, and the Cancel menu item is disabled.

Note how the worker is started in the event listener for the Open menu item.

This simple technique allows you to execute time-consuming tasks while keeping the user interface responsive.

Listing 14.14 swingWorker/SwingWorkerTest.java

```java
1  package swingWorker;
2
3  import java.awt.*;
4  import java.io.*;
5  import java.util.*;
6  import java.util.List;
7  import java.util.concurrent.*;
8
9  import javax.swing.*;
10
11 /**
12  * This program demonstrates a worker thread that runs a potentially time-consuming task.
13  * @version 1.11 2015-06-21
14  * @author Cay Horstmann
15  */
16 public class SwingWorkerTest
17 {
18    public static void main(String[] args) throws Exception
19    {
20       EventQueue.invokeLater(() -> {
21          JFrame frame = new SwingWorkerFrame();
22          frame.setDefaultCloseOperation(JFrame.EXIT_ON_CLOSE);
23          frame.setVisible(true);
24       });
25    }
26 }
27
28 /**
29  * This frame has a text area to show the contents of a text file, a menu to open a file and
30  * cancel the opening process, and a status line to show the file loading progress.
31  */
32 class SwingWorkerFrame extends JFrame
33 {
34    private JFileChooser chooser;
35    private JTextArea textArea;
36    private JLabel statusLine;
37    private JMenuItem openItem;
38    private JMenuItem cancelItem;
39    private SwingWorker<StringBuilder, ProgressData> textReader;
40    public static final int TEXT_ROWS = 20;
41    public static final int TEXT_COLUMNS = 60;
42
```

(Continues)

Listing 14.14 *(Continued)*

```java
43    public SwingWorkerFrame()
44    {
45       chooser = new JFileChooser();
46       chooser.setCurrentDirectory(new File("."));
47
48       textArea = new JTextArea(TEXT_ROWS, TEXT_COLUMNS);
49       add(new JScrollPane(textArea));
50
51       statusLine = new JLabel(" ");
52       add(statusLine, BorderLayout.SOUTH);
53
54       JMenuBar menuBar = new JMenuBar();
55       setJMenuBar(menuBar);
56
57       JMenu menu = new JMenu("File");
58       menuBar.add(menu);
59
60       openItem = new JMenuItem("Open");
61       menu.add(openItem);
62       openItem.addActionListener(event -> {
63             // show file chooser dialog
64             int result = chooser.showOpenDialog(null);
65
66             // if file selected, set it as icon of the label
67             if (result == JFileChooser.APPROVE_OPTION)
68             {
69                textArea.setText("");
70                openItem.setEnabled(false);
71                textReader = new TextReader(chooser.getSelectedFile());
72                textReader.execute();
73                cancelItem.setEnabled(true);
74             }
75          });
76
77       cancelItem = new JMenuItem("Cancel");
78       menu.add(cancelItem);
79       cancelItem.setEnabled(false);
80       cancelItem.addActionListener(event -> textReader.cancel(true));
81       pack();
82    }
83
84    private class ProgressData
85    {
86       public int number;
87       public String line;
88    }
89
```

```
90    private class TextReader extends SwingWorker<StringBuilder, ProgressData>
91    {
92       private File file;
93       private StringBuilder text = new StringBuilder();
94
95       public TextReader(File file)
96       {
97          this.file = file;
98       }
99
100      // The following method executes in the worker thread; it doesn't touch Swing components.
101
102      @Override
103      public StringBuilder doInBackground() throws IOException, InterruptedException
104      {
105         int lineNumber = 0;
106         try (Scanner in = new Scanner(new FileInputStream(file), "UTF-8"))
107         {
108            while (in.hasNextLine())
109            {
110               String line = in.nextLine();
111               lineNumber++;
112               text.append(line).append("\n");
113               ProgressData data = new ProgressData();
114               data.number = lineNumber;
115               data.line = line;
116               publish(data);
117               Thread.sleep(1); // to test cancellation; no need to do this in your programs
118            }
119         }
120         return text;
121      }
122
123      // The following methods execute in the event dispatch thread.
124
125      @Override
126      public void process(List<ProgressData> data)
127      {
128         if (isCancelled()) return;
129         StringBuilder b = new StringBuilder();
130         statusLine.setText("" + data.get(data.size() - 1).number);
131         for (ProgressData d : data) b.append(d.line).append("\n");
132         textArea.append(b.toString());
133      }
134
135      @Override
136      public void done()
137      {
```

(Continues)

Listing 14.14 *(Continued)*

```
138            try
139            {
140                StringBuilder result = get();
141                textArea.setText(result.toString());
142                statusLine.setText("Done");
143            }
144            catch (InterruptedException ex)
145            {
146            }
147            catch (CancellationException ex)
148            {
149                textArea.setText("");
150                statusLine.setText("Cancelled");
151            }
152            catch (ExecutionException ex)
153            {
154                statusLine.setText("" + ex.getCause());
155            }
156
157            cancelItem.setEnabled(false);
158            openItem.setEnabled(true);
159        }
160    };
161 }
```

---

javax.swing.SwingWorker<T, V> 6

- abstract T doInBackground()

  is the method to override to carry out the background task and to return the result of the work.

- void process(List<V> data)

  is the method to override to process intermediate progress data in the event dispatch thread.

- void publish(V... data)

  forwards intermediate progress data to the event dispatch thread. Call this method from doInBackground.

- void execute()

  schedules this worker for execution on a worker thread.

- SwingWorker.StateValue getState()

  gets the state of this worker, one of PENDING, STARTED, or DONE.

14.11.3 The Single-Thread Rule

Every Java application starts with a `main` method that runs in the main thread. In a Swing program, the main thread is short lived. It schedules the construction of the user interface in the event dispatch thread and then exits. After the user interface construction, the event dispatch thread processes event notifications, such as calls to `actionPerformed` or `paintComponent`. Other threads, such as the thread that posts events into the event queue, are running behind the scenes, but those threads are invisible to the application programmer.

Earlier in the chapter, we introduced the single-thread rule: "Do not touch Swing components in any thread other than the event dispatch thread." In this section, we investigate that rule further.

There are a few exceptions to the single-thread rule.

- You can safely add and remove event listeners in any thread. Of course, the listener methods will be invoked in the event dispatch thread.

- A small number of Swing methods are thread safe. They are specially marked in the API documentation with the sentence *This method is thread safe, although most Swing methods are not.* The most useful among these thread-safe methods are:

  ```
  JTextComponent.setText
  JTextArea.insert
  JTextArea.append
  JTextArea.replaceRange
  JComponent.repaint
  JComponent.revalidate
  ```

 NOTE: We used the `repaint` method many times in this book, but the `revalidate` method is less common. Its purpose is to force a layout of a component after the contents have changed. The traditional AWT has a `validate` method to force the layout of a component. For Swing components, you should simply call `revalidate` instead. (However, to force the layout of a `JFrame`, you still need to call `validate`—a `JFrame` is a `Component` but not a `JComponent`.)

Historically, the single-thread rule was more permissive. Any thread was allowed to construct components, set their properties, and add them into containers, as long as none of these components had been *realized*. A component is realized if it can receive paint or validation events. This is the case after the `setVisible(true)` or `pack` (!) methods have been invoked on the component, or after the component has been added to a container that has been realized.

That version of the single-thread rule was convenient. It allowed you to create the GUI in the `main` method and then call `setVisible(true)` on the top-level frame of the application. There was no bothersome scheduling of a `Runnable` on the event dispatch thread.

Unfortunately, some component implementors did not pay attention to the subtleties of the original single-thread rule. They launched activities on the event dispatch thread without ever bothering to check whether the component was realized. For example, if you call `setSelectionStart` or `setSelectionEnd` on a `JTextComponent`, a caret movement is scheduled in the event dispatch thread, even if the component is not visible.

It might well have been possible to detect and fix these problems, but the Swing designers took the easy way out. They decreed that it is never safe to access components from any thread other than the event dispatch thread. Therefore, you need to construct the user interface in the event dispatch thread, using the calls to `EventQueue.invokeLater` that you have seen in all our sample programs.

Of course, there are plenty of programs that are not so careful and live by the old version of the single-thread rule, initializing the user interface on the main thread. Those programs incur the slight risk that some of the user interface initialization may cause actions on the event dispatch thread that conflict with actions on the main thread. As we said in Chapter 10, you don't want to be one of the unlucky few who run into trouble and waste time debugging an intermittent threading bug. Therefore, you should simply follow the strict single-thread rule.

You have now reached the end of Volume I of *Core Java*. This volume covered the fundamentals of the Java programming language and the parts of the standard library that you need for most programming projects. We hope that you enjoyed your tour through the Java fundamentals and that you found useful information along the way. For advanced topics, such as networking, advanced AWT/Swing, security, and internationalization, please turn to Volume II.

Java Keywords

Keyword	Meaning	See Chapter
abstract	An abstract class or method	5
assert	Used to locate internal program error	7
boolean	The Boolean type	3
break	Breaks out of a switch or loop	3
byte	The 8-bit integer type	3
case	A case of a switch	3
catch	The clause of a try block catching an exception	7
char	The Unicode character type	3
class	Defines a class type	4
const	Not used	
continue	Continues at the end of a loop	3
default	The default clause of a switch, or a default method in an interface	3, 6
do	The top of a do/while loop	3
double	The double-precision floating-number type	3
else	The else clause of an if statement	3
enum	An enumerated type	3

Keyword	Meaning	See Chapter
extends	Defines the parent class of a class, or an upper bound of a wildcard	4
final	A constant, or a class or method that cannot be overridden	5
finally	The part of a try block that is always executed	7
float	The single-precision floating-point type	3
for	A loop type	3
goto	Not used	
if	A conditional statement	3
implements	Defines the interface(s) that a class implements	6
import	Imports a package	4
instanceof	Tests if an object is an instance of a class	5
int	The 32-bit integer type	3
interface	An abstract type with methods that a class can implement	6
long	The 64-bit long integer type	3
native	A method implemented by the host system	12 (Vol. II)
new	Allocates a new object or array	3
null	A null reference (note that null is technically a literal, not a keyword)	3
package	A package of classes	4
private	A feature that is accessible only by methods of this class	4
protected	A feature that is accessible only by methods of this class, its children, and other classes in the same package	5
public	A feature that is accessible by methods of all classes	4
return	Returns from a method	3
short	The 16-bit integer type	3
static	A feature that is unique to a class or interface, not to instances of a class	3, 6

Keyword	Meaning	See Chapter
strictfp	Use strict rules for floating-point computations	2
super	The superclass object or constructor, or a lower bound in a wildcard	5
switch	A selection statement	3
synchronized	A method or code block that is atomic to a thread	14
this	The implicit argument of a method, or a constructor of this class	4
throw	Throws an exception	7
throws	The exceptions that a method can throw	11
transient	Marks data that should not be persistent	2 (Vol. II)
try	A block of code that traps exceptions	7
void	Denotes a method that returns no value	3
volatile	Ensures that a field is coherently accessed by multiple threads	14
while	A loop	3

Index